History of Asia

From Early Times to the Present

HISTORY
OF
ASIA

From Early Times to the Present

B.V. Rao

NEW DAWN PRESS, INC.
UK • USA • INDIA

NEW DAWN PRESS GROUP

Published by New Dawn Press Group
New Dawn Press, Inc., 244 South Randall Rd # 90, Elgin, IL 60123
e-mail: sales@newdawnpress.com

New Dawn Press, 2 Tintern Close, Slough, Berkshire, SL1-2TB, UK
e-mail: salesuk@newdawnpress.org

New Dawn Press (An Imprint of Sterling Publishers (P) Ltd)
A-59, Okhla Industrial Area, Phase-II, New Delhi-110020, India
e-mail: info@sterlingpublishers.com
www.sterlingpublishers.com

History of Asia: From Early Times to the Present
©2005, B.V. Rao
ISBN 1 932705 36 8 (PB)
1 932705 47 3 (HB)

PRINTED IN INDIA

CONTENTS

PART I
EAST ASIA

PART II
SOUTH-EAST ASIA

PART III

SOUTH ASIA

PART IV
CENTRAL ASIA

PART V
WEST ASIA

PREFACE TO THE SECOND EDITION

The first edition had to be revised and updated in view of interesting events and developments which have taken place in Asiatic countries during the last five years. Thus there is need to apprise the students studying in colleges and universities, and, also candidates appearing for competitive examinations about the current history of Asia.

World events have cast a shadow on Asia. The September 11 terrorist attack on the US in 2001, and the consequent 'war on terror' have had great impact on Asiatic countries. It has been emphasised that religious fundamentalism has no place in democratic societies. Some countries have not tolerated political dissidence, most notably in countries reeling under dictatorship. Movements for gaining independence are gaining importance in some countries – particularly in Indonesia and Sri Lanka.

The Asian financial crisis left a trail of woes for some South-East-Asian countries. Recently the incurable SARS virus in China spread to neighbouring countries. The bird flu have affected a few countries. Environmental pollution caused by forest fires, floods and famines, have caused serious problems for some countries.

The Tsunami (giant tidal waves) his the (coastal regions of the Indian Ocean on Dec 26, 2004 particularly Indonesia, Thailand, the Andaman Nicobar islands and the Tamil Nadu (India), and Sri Lanka. It has taken a heavy toll of lives (more than 2,25,000) besides causing great destruction. It may take more than a decade to rehabilitate the families of the victims whose lives have become miserable now.

In this gloomy picture, we see a ray of hope in the success of ASEAN and SAARC meetings which promote regional co-operation.

22.01.2005
Bangalore

B.V. Rao

PREFACE TO THE FIRST EDITION

Although there are many textbooks available on Asian history, most of them have been written by foreigners and are, as such meant to be used by foreign students. Of those written by Indian authors, many are good, while others are unsatisfactory. The subject has been included in the syllabi of many universities, and students and teachers would, I am sure, welcome the publication of new books. Therefore, I have ventured to present this new book with the hope that the academic community would find it useful.

What are the features of this new book? I have presented the matter in a user-friendly manner, and added maps to enable students and teachers to easily locate countries, towns, and boundaries. In the study of Asia, the study of maps becomes very important. Again, chronology is an important matter, and therefore, I have given it wherever necessary. I have covered the history of many countries of Asia up to 1970, but in some cases it is extended up to 2000.

The book is divided into five parts, the first deals with East Asia (China, Japan, and Korea), the second, South-East Asia, covers the history of eight countries, the third is directed towards the study of South Asia (India, Pakistan, Bangladesh, Nepal, Bhutan and Sri Lanka), the fourth includes three countries (Afghanistan, Iran and Iraq), and the fifth, West Asia.

Some countries are bound to play an increasing role in world affairs as they have turned into economic giants (Japan, China, Taiwan, Korea and of course, Singapore). As India enters the next millennium in a period of political uncertainty, she has to learn many lessons from the success stories of some of the countries which are experiencing an economic boom. I am sure the secret of their success may lie hidden in their history, and our students should be able to search it.

I am grateful to Mr. Venkatesh for typing the matter, and Shyam Sunder for making maps.

26.2.2001   B.V. Rao
Bangalore

PART I

EAST ASIA

1

EARLY AND MEDIEVAL CHINA

INTRODUCTION

Among all the countries of the Asian continent, China is the largest, and most populous. It is situated in the central-eastern part of the Asian continent. The Westerners regarded China and Japan as countries of the Far East. Due to her long isolation, China developed a culture of its own which was unique in many respects. Currently she has twenty-one provinces (in contrast to eighteen during ancient times), five autonomous regions and three municipalities—Beijing, Shanghai and Tientsin.

Her culture and civilization developed on the plain region which is situated in-between the rivers Huang-Ho (also called 'Ch'ing's Sorrow') and Yangtze-Kiang. These rivers flow from the west to the east for thousands of miles thereby making the plains fertile. The other rivers like the Amur also had an impact on the livelihood of the people and evolution of history. The physical features and agro-climatic conditions of China permit us to divide her into two geographical divisions, i.e., the north and the south. As mentioned earlier, the north is drained by the Huango-Ho and the plains enable farmers sometimes to produce three crops in a year. Beijing, the Chinese capital, is situated on the eastern coast. The south is separated from the north by the Ch'inling mountains. The Yangtze (3430 miles long) drains an area of 7,50,000 square miles, and it is navigable and overflows the banks during heavy monsoon. Rice, cotton and silk are chiefly produced. Some of the big cities of this region include Shanghai, Hangchow, Wuchang and Hanyang. It is the south-eastern coast of China which witnessed the advent of Westerners in the fifteenth century and their main activities were centred at Canton, Macao and Hong Kong.

Traditionally China had been known as the Middle Kingdom and divided into eighteen provinces with four dependencies, namely, Manchuria, Inner Mongolia, Sinkiang and Tibet. Let us examine briefly the history and culture of ancient China before stepping into the modern period, which begins with the Western encroachments on Chinese sovereignty in the nineteenth century.

DYNASTIC AND CULTURAL HISTORY

Prior to the history of Shang rule (1766-1122 BC), we know a little but this knowledge is in the form of mythology, tradition and legends. The Shang dynasty began its rule from Ching-Chan initially, but moved over to An-Yang in the north. Their life was largely sustained by agriculture and trade. They knew bronze casting and used cowrie shells as money. They offered sacrifices on important occasions and their culture spread as far as Yangtze (400 miles to the south). Their kingdom came to be known as "Chung-Kuo". Unable to tolerate the tyrannical rule of the last ruler Chou-Hsin the slaves revolted. Subsequently several tribesmen of the Wei Valley in western China led an invasion and brought about the downfall of the Shang dynasty. It was after a century, China witnessed the long regime of the Chou emperors (1030-221 BC). Their empire was too vast to be centrally administered and therefore they hit upon the idea of decentralization of authority, with the vassals (relatives of the Emperor) of different grades and ranks enjoying autonomy over their respective districts or provinces. The Emperor could count upon their loyalty, and the sovereignty and territorial integrity could be maintained. Wu Wang built a large empire after undertaking several military expeditions, and the southern border of his empire touched the river Yangtze. He held firm control over the feudal lords. The central authority declined by the middle of the eighth century BC and China witnessed the rule of the feudal lords, with the Emperor remaining a mere figurehead. The last two centuries of Chou rule witnessed total chaos, what with feudal lords asserting their independence and attacking others. It was during this period of political turmoil, that China came under the influence of several great philosophers with Confucius leading the trail. His moral sayings had the greatest effect upon all, i.e., the rulers and the ruled, parents and children, teachers and students, husbands and wives, and on brothers and friends. He encouraged ancestor worship, filial piety, and respect to authority. The writings of Lao Tze (604-517 BC), a mystic thinker, urged his followers to lead a simple life in harmony with nature and give up selfishness, greed and wickedness. He insisted upon moral virtues and good conduct to govern individual life. Like Confucianism, the teachings of Lao-Tze became a religion called Taoism. Meng Tzu (Mencius, 372-289 BC) was a follower of Confucius who prevailed upon the rulers and administrators to end corruption, forced labour and forced taxes.

Shi-Huang Ti ("The First Emperor")

A powerful lord of the Ch'in overthrew the Chou dynasty around 256 BC, and this new dynasty produced its greatest warrior and statesman in 221 bc, namely, Shi-Huang Ti ("The First Emperor"). He ended feudalism, China's greatest curse, and subdued all the rebellious feudal lords. He built the largest empire after extensive conquests and commenced the construction of the Great Wall for protecting it from foreign invaders. His empire was well-knit with a centralised bureaucratic system of administration. His empire consisting of thirty-six provinces was ably and efficiently governed and the erstwhile feudal lords were compelled to stay in the capital city. He introduced uniform weights and measures, standardised the Chinese coinage, simplified the Chinese script, and built a "radiating system of roads." Shi-Huang Ti ordered the destruction of the then existing Chinese literature ("Burning of the Books") by condemning it as "feudal" but spared some books on subjects like medicine, agriculture, pharmacy and divination. Confucian scholars and writers were driven out of the country. He encouraged new writings and new thoughts. The Ch'in empire which included southern China and northern Vietnam fell soon after the death of Shi-Huang Ti and the Hans conquered it.

The Han Emperor Wu Ti (Martial Emperor)

The Han age in Chinese history spanned over the next four centuries and it is described as the "Golden Age". Among the Han emperors, Wu Ti (141-87 BC) may be regarded the greatest for it was he who extended the boundaries of the Chinese empire to include outlying states like Korea, Manchuria in the north, and Pamirs and Khokand in Central Asia and northern Vietnam in the south. He conquered Central Asia so that Chinese merchants could have profitable trade with West Asian countries. Besides being known as "Martial Emperor", Wu Ti undertook a project of canal construction to link the Chinese capital with the Yellow River. These canals provided transport facilities to the merchants. China gained access to information about countries in Central Asia due to Chang Ch'ien's two expeditions carried out at the behest of Emperor Wu Ti.

Life for the peasants became difficult and China witnessed great population growth. When conditions became unbearable the peasants revolted in 22 BC. It was then that Wang Mang (of the Hsin dynasty), who replaced the Han rule and introduced several reforms—all aiming at bringing about socialism. Therefore he was called "China's first socialist". His great reforms included nationalising the land and freeing the slaves. But famines and droughts forced peasants to revolt in Shantung, and eventually the nomads of the border region killed Wang Mang (AD 23). The Han rule once again emerged, this time the popular emperor being Kuang Wu Ti. He and his successor reconquered southern China, northern Vietnam and Central Asia (AD 73).

During the two Han dynasties, China registered great cultural growth. Confucian literature and thoughts revived. There was a great deal of search which went on for collecting Confucian literature by scholars, and in this effort, the sincere attempt of Wang Mang cannot be ignored. For example, Emperor Wu Ti championed the cause of Confucianism, and set up a State university where a band of fifty scholars tried to revive Confucian studies. It became a practice to select good scholars after holding an examination to join the civil service. Materials for writing, such as paper (made from rags), camel-brush and ink were invented which facilitated the development of learning. The imperial library received manuscripts, and scholars pursued their studies in the imperial university (124 BC). Buddhism entered China during the Han age. The age witnessed the writings of Ssu-ma Chien, the great historian.

Han culture has to its credit amazing inventions such as lunar calendar, a seismograph, paper, ink and brush, porcelain. The textile techniques of the age were far ahead of any country in Asia or Europe. Among other inventions were the water-powered mill and the method of iron-casting.

Silk Route

China broke off her self-imposed isolation, and her merchants carried embroidered silk, glazed pottery and bronze vessels which were in great demand to the Roman Empire. Chinese merchants went to these countries through the route known as the Silk Route—the route used by the Chinese army earlier. China established diplomatic relations with countries with which her merchants traded, and brought home glass, amber and precious stones.

THE TANG DYNASTY

The Han empire declined and fell due to certain economic policies and the internal rivalry of the ruling class. It was after four centuries of political chaos that the country was reunited by the Tang dynasty. Its founder was T'ai Tsung ("Grand Ancestor," AD 626-49). He inaugurated the second golden age by conquest, administrative reorganization, cultural regeneration, and diplomatic contacts with the civilised world. T'ai Tsung defeated the Turks and conquered the Tarim basin in Central Asia. The Chinese suzerainty was established over unified Tibet. Korea remained unsubdued till it was conquered by his successor, Kao Tsung. It is said of T'ai Tsung that he gave up wars like Emperor Ashoka and devoted his attention to improving the conditions of his subjects. He cut down court expenses, appointed sincere and honest officials, reduced taxes and made Chinese capital look very attractive.

Enlightened Emperor

The Tang power was felt beyond the traditional boundaries of China, namely, Tibet, southern Siberia, Central Asia and Southeast Asia during the time of Kao Tsung. After a short period of rule of the puppet emperors and Empress Wu, there came Emperor Ming Huang ("Enlightened Emperor") whose long reign witnessed a golden age in Chinese literature and fine arts. The most celebrated poet of the age was undoubtedly Lin Po who produced thirty volumes of great lyrical poetry. The Chinese paintings breathed a new spirit since earlier ones had perished. The Chinese produced beautiful jade objects and artistic bronze vessels which were in great demand since the days of Shang rule. Glazed pottery continued to hold the attention of foreigners. Some of the interesting things which were produced during the age of the Tangs were encyclopedias and block printing. The Tangs continued the school and examination system. Empress Wu patronised Buddhism and subsequently, it adapted itself to Chinese ideas and institutions.

Under the Tangs, China came into contact with her great neighbour, India, and the countries of Southeast Asia. Tea was introduced. This was the same Chinese tea which has become the most popular drink in the world today. Gun powder was discovered and it was used for making firecrackers. The wheel barrow became popular as a mode of transportation on the narrow footpaths.

THE SUNG DYNASTY

After the rule of the "Five Dynasties" came the Sung dynasty which ruled China for three centuries (AD 960-1279). The dynasty was founded by T'ai Tsu ("Grand Progenitor"). He and his brother T'ai Tsung extended control over the entire Chinese empire except for the far-flung provinces of Annam (North Vietnam), Central Asia and north-east and north-western parts. Kaifeng became their capital from where the power of the Sung emperors was wielded. Their administration was highly centralised and run by bureaucrats who were selected after an elaborate examination system. The Sung period saw the civil service at its best, and the government's stability depended upon it. Civil servants (mandarins) enjoyed great prestige and authority irrespective of who governed the empire.

As the population increased and poor peasants were unable to bear the burden of heavy taxes, Emperor Shen Tsung appointed Wang An-Shih to tackle the financial crisis the empire was facing. Wang introduced several reforms which restored the financial soundness of the Government, stabilized prices, and at the same time helped the poor peasants. He was hailed as China's second great socialist. But his reforms were opposed by the big landowning bureaucrats, influential merchants and big moneylenders. After the Emperor's death, the reforms were set aside.

The Sung period witnessed a brisk maritime trade. Sea-going junks carried silk, porcelain and tea to far-off destinations such as India, the East Indies and the east coast of Africa. This was possible due to the invention of mariner's compass (AD 1021).

NEO-CONFUCIANISM

Other inventions of the time included the abacus (a calculating board) used by merchants, and gun powder, which was used for making firecrackers during the Tang period, was now used for making bombs grenades and rockets. It is likely that trade with the Arabs brought the knowledge of Algebra, and some more progress was achieved in block printing. While the Tang period enriched Chinese poetry, the Sung contributed substantially to prose writing. Han Yu and Ou-Yang Hsiu were great writers of the ninth and eleventh centuries respectively. The latter was a historian, and standard scholarship included historical writings and compilation of encyclopedias. Another great product of Sung's intellectual thinking was the Neo-Confucianism—a quest for reorganizing society in changing times but on the basis of "Confucian vision. Han Yu of the ninth and Chu Hsi of the twelfth century were great exponents of Neo-Confucianism. Thus Chinese thinking remained in the traditional mould of Chu Hsi for several centuries. As a result, Chinese society remained stable but rigid.

RAPID GROWTH OF MONEY ECONOMY

One of the most interesting features of Chinese economy during this period was the rapid growth in the use of money so much so that merchants preferred paper currency and paper credit. Private banker businesses thrived and they started issuing certificates of deposit which could be encashed at a later date at some discount, the discount being treated as a service charge. The Chinese Government printed a large number of currency notes that it could redeem during times of financial trouble thereby giving stimulus to trade and commerce.

MONGOL CONQUEST OF CHINA (AD 1211-1348)

The Mongol conquest of China began under its greatest leader, Genghis Khan with the occupation of north-west China around 1217. By 1279, his grandson Kublai established Peking (Beijing) as his winter capital after defeating the Sung forces. He chose the Chinese dynastic name 'Yuan' to distinguish his period. Although Kublai was known for his despotic rule he tried to minimise the hostility of the Chinese by protecting Confucian temples and exempting Confucian scholars from paying taxes. However, all the top positions were given to foreigners, and not to Confucian scholars. The Venetian merchant, Marco Polo, has left the record (*Description of the World*) of his long stay (1275-92) in China under the patronage of Kublai. Mongol rule in China did not last for more than a century. But during this period China came into contact with West Asia, and her Arab trade prospered. Arab merchants reached Peking by land establishing caravan routes from Baghdad to Peking and sea routes along Hormuz to southern Chinese ports including Zayton.

It was during the Mongol period that Islam made deep inroads into China. The Mongol dynasty was overthrown by the Chinese peasants who, a few years earlier, had faced severe hardships due to famine and floods. The hero who organised a peasant rebellion was a Buddhist monk named Chu-Yuan-chang. He and his followers seized Nanking in 1356 and Peking in 1368 after defeating the country commanders. Chu declared himself the First Emperor of the Ming dynasty (Ming meaning "Brilliant"). He ruled China as Hung Wu.

THE MING DYNASTY

Being a native dynasty, the Ming Emperor was able to restore order and peace throughout the empire with considerable ease. It was during this period that seventeen noteworthy emperors brought about considerable expansion of the empire. The most remarkable feature of this period was the seven great maritime expeditions undertaken by a Muslim court-eunuch named Yung-Lo (1405-33). These expeditions were carried out so as to bring many parts of South and Southeast Asia under the hegemony of the Chinese emperor. Again, China desired to establish commercial contact with the countries under her domination. However, the desired goals were not fulfilled because she failed to convert her maritime supremacy to her commercial advantage. Thus her isolation from the rest of the world continued till the European adventurers forced her to compromise to their advantage. The Chinese Government had to encounter Japanese pirates on her seas indicating her vulnerability to foreign pressures.

The Mongols continued their raids on her border territories. War with Japan (1592-97) over the domination of the Korean peninsula forced her to compromise. It cost her a good deal in terms of men, money and materials. On the domestic front the Government underlined the importance of the 'examination system' and individual scholarship as the criteria for the selection of civil service personnel. The Ming Government repaired the Great Wall of China, fortified many strategic towns and protected Nanking by constructing a moat. The Portuguese arrived in the south and settled in Macao. The Ming emperors built palaces and tombs, most notably the imperial palace of Peking. During the Ming period China registered rapid economic growth along with an increase in population. Foochow and Shanghai became great centres of inland and foreign trade. Their silk industry as well as banking attracted the attention of foreign merchants. Canton exported iron pans to other countries.

Eventually in the middle of the seventeenth century (1644) the Chinese rebels succeeded in weakening the empire by fomenting frequent rebellions. The end came when the Manchus (barbarian invaders) expelled the Ming ruler and started their reign. The Manchus, also known as Ch'ings, migrated from the south-eastern parts of Manchuria. Their great leader was Nurhachi (1559-1626) who united the four main Jurchen tribes in the north and with the help of the native Chinese rebels brought about the collapse of the Ming empire. His posthumous title was T'ai Tsu ("the Grand Progenitor"). He set up his headquarters at Mukden and reorganised the system of administration with the cooperation of the native Chinese. He and his successors conquered the whole of China, including the neighbouring kingdoms which were brought under the 'tribute system'. Korea became a vassal state and Inner Mongolia, a dependent state. The Chinese Government extended its sway over several other states such as the Dzungarias, the Tarim Basin, the Ili region and Tibet. However, all these were not incorporated into the Chinese empire, but to control them a few Chinese garrisons were stationed. In the name of the Chinese Emperor many military expeditions were launched against Siam, Burma and Nepal as a ploy to ward off the danger from the Western nations. But these expeditions failed to achieve their objectives. In the course of time, the Manchu emperors found it difficult to control many parts of the far-flung empire, although there appeared some semblance of unity.

The decline has been attributed to many factors such as the corrupt bureaucracy, over-burdened population, rebellious groups such as the 'White Lotus', famines, and the uprisings by tributary chieftains. Economic conditions deteriorated as a consequence of costly military expeditions to such an extent that the collapse became inevitable by the middle of the nineteenth century, though the phantom empire continued till 1911. By far the foremost factor that brought about the fall of the empire was the advent of the European merchants into China bringing with them their military and technological superiority.

POLITICAL IDEAS AND INSTITUTIONS IN CHINA

In old China, monarchy became the most popular form of government. It became hereditary and the King became a sacred person. When empires were built the notion of a monarch being the Emperor and 'Son of Heaven' gained ground. He was to enjoy unlimited authority in theory and practice. However, there were certain restraints on the despotic tendencies of emperors. These censors acted as a check on an erring court or faulty imperial edicts and the popular belief among the Chinese that the outbreak of natural calamities occurred as a consequence of the Emperor's misrule. Besides these, there were certain conventions, usage and customs which the Emperor could not ignore. The Emperor's court consisting of ministers, councillors and noblemen wielded the desired influence on the Emperor and prevented him from taking any rash step.

The central government was composed of six boards, such as administration, ceremonies, public works, revenue, war and punishments, each headed by a minister. There were two other branches of the government, namely, the censorate and the military. Officers working in the government offices were trained in the Hanlin Academy and conducted themselves on the lines of Confucian formulae. They preserved the honour of the Emperor and shared his sovereign powers whenever opportunities arose either at the Centre or in the provinces.

Chinese Laws

The laws of China were evolved so as to govern human conduct based on a harmony with nature. The moral laws of the country bound both the citizens and the Emperor together. The Emperor was to set an example for others through 'his own virtual conduct'. Morality stood above the law and the virtuous reigned supreme. As the 'Son of Heaven' the Emperor issued edicts and passed laws and the courts, legislature and the bureaucracy had to enforce them without any opposition. Our modern concept of the rule of law did not operate in China. In fact, some of the laws of China in those days were the ones which came from the bureaucrats in the name of the Emperor. Hence there was an old saying: 'Avoid litigation; going to law is going to trouble.'

General Administration

Traditionally China had been divided into eighteen provinces and four dependent states, namely, Manchuria, Inner Mongolia, Sinkiang and Tibet. The latter enjoyed autonomous status but was subjected to some supervision. Each province was divided into Tao and Shies (circuits and districts respectively) and various cadres of officials were in charge of these administrative units. The provincial government obeyed the orders of the central government and remitted revenue as and when necessary, still retaining some discretion to follow its own path. The imperial court had the power to recruit, appoint, promote and transfer officials. Most of these officials served a term of three years before being transferred to other administrative units. The provincial governors not only looked after their respective provinces, but supervised examinations, commanded local garrisons, settled important disputes as judges and controlled the manufacture and sale of grains and salt.

The local administration of a district or town was in the hands of magistrates who performed many functions, the main functions being the collection of revenues, trying civil and criminal cases and maintaining law and order. The local gentry carried out certain duties which were ignored by state officials. The commoners looked upon the gentry with respect since they represented the common man. The local gentry were looked upon by commoners as leaders of the community as a whole because they could secure justice and relief in times of distress. It is said that 'the gentry were the eyes and the ears of local government and public opinion'.

As for the villages and towns in each district the officials concerned were nominated either by the village elders or the local community and confirmed by the magistrates. The Governments existing in these places were run by elders on the basis of prevailing custom, usage and conventions. By and large the people of these regions considered Peking as the forbidden city since it was far away, and the emperor inaccessible or unapproachable.

The Civil Service

In old China, scholarship was highly respected and the government conducted Civil Service examinations for three days, each day consisting of three sessions. Thousands of candidates appeared in the examination hoping to get through at the county and prefecture levels. After a process of filtration a few hundred successful candidates went to Peking for the pre-final test. The final test took place in the presence of the Emperor himself! The examination system tested the knowledge of the candidate in Confucian thoughts and wisdom. As one historian puts it, the test did not lay stress on the individual's free thought and reasoning or expression. Hence when they were appointed as officials, they were hardly in a position to grapple with problems created by the foreigners.

2

THE ADVENT OF EUROPEANS

After considerable geographical exploration Europeans set foot on the soil of China. Among the first to arrive were the Portuguese in 1517 who, in the course of time, established their settlement in Macao in 1557 but under Chinese supervision. The mission of Jesuit pioneer, Matteo Ricci was successful in that he was able to convert about two hundred Chinese into Christians. Subsequently, he converted a few members of the Chinese royal family. The Portuguese spread the knowledge of Western sciences among Chinese scholars. They entered the Chinese court and served as interpreters, astronomers, cartographers, painters, engravers, architects and engineers. However, the success of the Jesuit mission did not last long. The Confucian scholars began to oppose the spread of Christianity, and the action of the Pope in challenging the order of the Chinese Emperor in 1715 over the ancient rites was persecuted. But the trade with the foreigners continued, though the Chinese Government reiterated that the foreign barbarians had nothing to offer that China did not possess.

Other European powers like Spain (1575), Holland (1604), Britain (1637) and the USA (1784) tried to establish commercial contacts with China foreseeing the profits that would accrue. Out of these European powers, the one which was quite successful in establishing a rapport with the Chinese Government was Russia.

Sino-Russian Relations

Russia's relations with China were marked by border conflicts, boundary disputes and illegal immigration. To come to an amicable settlement, China signed the Treaty of Nertchinsk with Russia by which the latter extended her control over the Amur Valley. It paved the way for closer relations between the two, including the setting up of the Russian Embassy in the Chinese capital. The Russian Orthodox Church was opened in Peking by 1727. Chinese ports were opened for Russian trade in the same year the two countries concluded a boundary settlement by which China gained control over the Mongols while Russia secured commercial concessions at Kiakhta and Nertchinsk. Russia got the right to establish educational institutions and religious missions in

Peking. What is significant is that China treated Russia as an equal partner, which is quite in contrast to how she treated other European powers which were knocking at the gates of Canton. These foreign merchants were treated as 'barbarians' who left their homeland for the sake of money. They were treated as petitioners begging China for trade concessions.

The Canton Trade

The next to arrive on the Chinese coast were the Spaniards. They were allowed to trade at Canton. The Dutch settled in Taiwan in the 1660s which was not until then occupied by the Chinese but served as their forward base for trade with the Japanese. However, they were ousted by the local officials of the Ming Emperor. In the course of time, the Dutch improved their relations with the Manchu Government which came to power subsequently. The English team arrived under the leadership of Captain Waddel to make an attempt to trade with the Chinese at Canton but the mission failed. In 1685 the Chinese opened the port of Canton for trade and issued the necessary licence to the European trading missions and the British East India Company. Subsequently another port, Ningpo, was also opened for trade for the Britishers. The Chinese Imperial Commissioner at Canton (Hoppo) allowed the British to set up a permanent factory at Canton and the ships of the British East India Company started arriving there quite regularly each year and trade was carried through the media of Hong merchants (selected group of Chinese merchants by the Government).

What caused the disenchantment with the Hong merchants and the Chinese Government?

At Canton the Western merchants met with several restrictions and hardships. The restrictions were as follows:

a)   Representation of grievances should be submitted to the Hong merchants.

b)   Chinese merchants were forbidden to teach the Chinese language to Western merchants and almost all of them did not know English.

c)   If Hong merchants refused to consider the grievances, only then should they be submitted to the Hoppo (Chinese Government official). He could not be contacted directly. The petition regarding grievances should be addressed to him and handed over to his guards standing outside his office compound.

d)   Foreigners were forbidden to use sedan-chairs and had to walk.

e)   Foreigners could not employ Chinese men or women as their servants.

f)   All Westerners accused of crime had to stand trial according to Chinese laws, to be tried by Chinese judges and undergo punishment, if sentenced. They were not to claim any immunity.

g) But by far, the most humiliating condition was that Western merchants were called "barbarians" who had deserted their homeland and ancestors in order to earn money in a foreign land and hence were treated in a most despicable manner. China tried to have contact with Western merchants on her own terms and in a contemptuous manner according to the Western merchants.

The Hong merchants with the connivance of the officials at the Hoppo aimed at creating conditions of uncertainty and there was no way to approach the imperial court or the Emperor himself.

Thus Western merchants who were eager to have trade with China had to counter innumerable obstacles. This situation changed with the advent of the "opium wars".

The Opium Wars in China

The bulk of China's trade with the outside world through Canton was silk, tea and porcelain products for which she received silver in exchange. China's attitude towards the Western world was that she had everything and did not accept anything from the Western merchants. She treated Western merchants as "barbarians" living at her mercy. She viewed Western merchants with great suspicion. It was unfortunate that neither the Chinese policy-makers at the imperial court nor the local bureaucrats trained in Confucian ways knew how to handle difficult situations posed by Western merchants. Peking, the imperial capital, was far from the main port city of Canton where all the commercial activities were taking place. The mandarins underestimated the strength of the Western world and her superiority in science and technology. The Imperial Commissioner at Canton, named Lin Tse-hsu, was a typical mandarin who arrived at Canton in March 1839. He was sent to deal with the deteriorating economic situation, vide, the unfavourable balance of trade resulting in the depletion of the inflow of silver. This was mainly caused by the illegal import of opium by Chinese merchants with the connivance of Western merchants, particularly the British. He addressed an appeal to Queen Victoria to impress upon her traders the ill-effects of opium consumption. The Chinese were addicted to opium as a result of its encouragement by her merchants. He wanted the Queen to realise that the import of opium had been banned in China much earlier through an imperial decree.

Commissioner Lin went hammer and tongs when Western merchants did not mend their ways but colluded with corrupt Chinese officials to continue the contraband trade. Cantonese merchants, both Chinese and foreign, were ordered to surrender all their stocks at opium and assure the government that they would stop trading in this banned item. He took another step by ordering his men to surround foreign settlements with the intention of stopping all supplies to them: food, water and labour. It was this drastic step that forced British Captain Elliot to surrender 20,000 chests of opium, which Lin dumped into the sea "with great fanfare". Although he pleased his Emperor with this precipitated action he realised he was in trouble. As the British had not given a pledge that they would desist from this nefarious trade, he apprehended British retaliatory action. Hence he closed the river approach to Canton and strengthened the fortifications.

Lin gave the Emperor the impression that he knew how to deal with the situation. Urged by British merchants, a British fleet approached Canton in June 1840 and demanded from the Chinese Government compensation for loss of opium and the necessary cost of the expedition. Expecting no response, the British fleet blockaded Canton, and subsequently a force of 2,000 troops sent from India occupied it. The said fleet moved along the Chinese coast and blockaded strategic points lying between Canton and Shanghai. In the meantime, Lin had been transferred and the new successor was trying his best to salvage the situation. However, he failed and was punished. His successor, a cousin of the Emperor, also failed to put up the desired resistance. The British were successful in forcing their terms on the unwilling Chinese Government in May 1841. However, the British Government was not satisfied. The war continued with the British fleet attacking the Chinese ports of Amoy, Ningpo and Tinghai. The British forces entered Shanghai and proceeded towards Nanking. The Chinese troops were helpless both on land and the sea and were unable to resist the inroads on her territories. It all ended in the government coming to terms with the British on board the British ship *Cornwallis*—by signing the Treaty of Nanking (August 29, 1842).

The Terms of the Treaty of Nanking:

a)   Protection of the British subjects in China.

b)   British to trade in four important ports, namely, Amoy, Foochow, Ningpo and Shanghai which was to be supervised by consular authorities and superintendents of trade.

c)   Cession of the island of Hong Kong in perpetuity.

d)   Compensation of twenty-one million dollars to be paid in four instalments (six million for the loss of opium, twelve million for the cost of the war and three million for the debts owed by the Chinese authorities).

e)   The Cohong stood to be abolished.

f)   Easy communications through diplomatic channels.

g)   Tariff regulation regulating foreign trade.

In 1843, the supplementary treaty of the Bogue granted the most favoured nation treatment which included:

a) Limited right to travel for the British in and around the ports,

b) the extra-territoriality.

Naturally the other Western nations too clamoured for such a treaty and they got it. It must be remembered that the British shook the tree, the others came quickly to help pick up fruit. Thus France and the USA became beneficiaries, thanks to the early lead given by the British. The treaty entered with the latter (Caleb Cushing signed it on behalf of the USA) for a period of twelve years, was called Wanghsia, and was subject to renewal. It provided for extra-territorial jurisdiction, i.e., US citizens accused of crime would be tried by American judges according to American laws. The Treaty with France (Whampoa, October 1844) granted Catholic missionaries the permission to build churches at the treaty ports. Subsequently, the Portuguese, the Belgians, the Norwegians and the Swedes also signed treaties with China with many concessions. Canton and other treaty ports along the Chinese coast became the hub of commercial activity.

The significance of the Nanking Treaty need not be overstressed at this point since it did not mention anything about the opium trade (except for compensation). The Western powers left control of this illicit trade. It was now under Chinese statutes. It was a pity that this trade did not stop. In fact, it increased, and Canton alone accounted for nearly six hundred shops for the sale of this dangerous commodity. The export of opium rose from seventeen million pounds in 1843 to hundred and thirty million pounds by 1857, indicating that the Chinese were helpless victims of the circumstances. Naturally the demand for opium increased resulting in an adverse balance of trade for China. In the meantime, British goods such as cotton and steel found a ready market in China.

The Second Opium War

Unfortunately for China, as she had agreed to revise the treaties, the British and the Americans pressed for it in 1856. The Chinese Commissioner considered their demands with great indifference for he did not want to compromise with Western nations further, and a show of strength became necessary. Why did the Western nations insist on browbeating China? Firstly, China had signed all the treaties under duress, and therefore had no intention of compromising her position further by agreeing for renewal. Secondly, the Western powers were eager to have the treaties renewed at any cost, suspecting that if there was delay, they may not achieve their goal. Thirdly, the official policy of China appeared to deny and delay to a maximum extent, causing great anxiety to Western merchants about the bona fides of the government. It was in these circumstances, the Western nations, specially Britain and France, found excuses to go to war with China. The USA gave moral support but was not belligerent herself.

War was forced on China when a Chinese vessel named *Lorcha Arrow* flying a British flag was seized by a Chinese police patrol at Canton on charges of smuggling and piracy. The British Captain of the vessel protested and the vessel was returned, though not the crew, by Commissioner Yeh. It must be remembered that the registration of the ship had expired and the Chinese had every right to seize it. Since the return of the crew was not followed by an apology, the British gun boats went into action against Canton. The people there were provoked with the result that foreign settlements outside Canton were razed to the ground. A full scale war was in the offing. The French had their reasons too for joining the British in a joint expedition. A French missionary, Abbe Chapdelaine, had strayed into the restricted area for carrying out his missionary work. He was found guilty by a magistrate and sentenced to death. His death was considered by the French a "judicial murder", and Emperor Napoleon III of France took advantage of the opportunity by declaring war on China so as to retrieve his sagging popularity at home.

Anglo-French Joint Expedition

While Russian and American ministers were interested in the revision of the treaty, they agreed not to participate in the joint expedition launched by Britain and France. The Anglo-French naval force blockaded Canton for a while, moved over to Shanghai and forced the Chinese officials to agree for the revision. When the expedition was asked to go back to Canton for negotiations, the force moved further and surrounded Tientsin. The gravity of the situation was realised, and the Chinese Government signed the Treaty of Tientsin on June 26, 1858, which contained the following provisions:

a) Diplomatic relations on the footing of equality were to be established between Britain and China with the former's minister residing at Peking.

b) China agreed to open ten more ports for British trade.

c) The British were to enjoy the freedom of travel and conduct missionary activity.

d) The idea of extra-territoriality was clearly defined.

e) British vessels were to have access to all treaty ports.

f) An indemnity of four million silver dollars was to be paid to the British Lord Elgin who successfully carried out the expedition as well as secured this treaty. He was definitely elated at his achievement. Unfortunately the treaty was made effective for only one year, and was subject to ratification. The Chinese Government was not happy with the clause which included foreign residents residing in Peking. It must be noted that China had signed similar treaties with the USA and Russia after the conclusion of the Tientsin Treaty. When the British found that the Chinese Government was wavering to ratify the treaty the following year, the continuation of the war became inevitable.

The expedition was led by Lord Elgin's brother, Bruce. The British expedition suffered heavy losses near Taku forts (expedition mounted by 200 warships, 10,000 British and 6,000 French troops), and Lord Elgin who returned to take command finally succeeded in destroying the forts and captured Tientsin. In the meantime, the summer palace of the Chinese Emperor was razed to the ground by the British to show their indignation at having suffered heavy losses in the previous engagement. Also their delegates who had gone to meet the Chinese counterparts for negotiations had been taken captive near Tientsin. The Chinese Imperial Government got scared at the presence of belligerent foreigners in its own capital and agreed to approve the Treaty of Tientsin and Peking conventions.

As the Emperor and his court had fled to Sianfu before the arrival of the British, it was Prince Kung, the Emperor's brother, who approved the newly imposed conditions in the Peking Treaty (October 1860). They included heavier war indemnity (sixteen million dollars), opening of Tientsin for foreign trade, allowing Chinese labour to work abroad and permitting missionaries to move about freely in China and build churches, and ceding Kowloon peninsula (situated opposite to Hong Kong) to the British in perpetuity. China's earlier treaties with Russia at Aigun and Tientsin were now ratified in November 1860, ceding the trans-Ussuri territory. Thus Western nations inflicted the most humiliating conditions on China whose Emperor was living in a fool's paradise. The outbreak of the T'aiping rebellion at home had sapped all her energies and China could not meet the challenge posed by foreign nations. It was Russia which had taken maximum advantage of China's weakness as evidenced by the expansion of her territories at the cost of the latter. Russia's diplomatic triumph resulting in the acquisition of vast Chinese territories surpassed the victory of Western nations, thanks to the services of her diplomats—Muraviev and General Nikolai Ignatiev. In the course of time Russia extended her empire to the Pacific coastline which enabled her to build the naval base and city, Vladivostok.

It is time to know what had happened in the imperial palace during the first half of the nineteenth century, because the decline of the Manchus had begun and the future appeared bleak in the wake of rebellions, costly wars, palace intrigues and the doubling of population. The early Manchu emperors, though foreigners, were men of integrity and ability and the Ching power reached its zenith of glory under Emperor Ch'ien-lung. His conquests included Dzungaria, Burma, Vietnam and Nepal but during his last years the administration had become intolerably corrupt. During his successors' time the White Lotus Rebellion took place.

Why Were Rebellions So Common in China?

It must be remembered that the Manchus were foreigners and constituted only two per cent of the Chinese population. Conscious of their drawback they adopted the culture of the Chinese, and recruited a large number of the Chinese into the administration. They were friendly and obliging in the eyes of the northern Chinese and what was interesting was that these foreigners adopted Confucian traditions and customs. However, the southerners treated them with contempt. They were not given representation in the civil service, nor treated with respect. What was galling to the southerners was that they were paying most of the taxes even in times of distress while the northerners were let off. The Manchu administration was corrupt to the core in the south. Therefore, the south became a breeding ground for all rebellions and revolutions.

It was in 1821 that Emperor Tao Kuang succeeded to the Dragon Throne and his regime witnessed widespread drought which wrought great havoc on central and northern China, and also had the first opium war with its disastrous consequences as mentioned earlier. To make matters worse, droughts and floods (1847 and 1849) ravaged the country followed by the death of the Emperor (1850). His successor, Hsien Feng (1851-61), chose a debauched career, and the actual power was wielded by his concubine who later became the Empress Dowager Tzu Hsi (also known as Yehonala and the Old Buddha) in 1861. It was during this time of great agrarian distress that rich landlords were let off with light taxes and the crushing tax burden fell on the poor peasants. The need of the hour was relief and reforms, but neither the Emperor nor the administration was able to do anything since they were busy dealing with the foreigners who were becoming a nuisance.

In the meantime, the Chinese army had lost its valour and morale after being defeated in the first opium war. Their salaries were not paid and the prices of the essential commodities began to rise alarmingly. Corruption among the senior officers of the army was rampant. It appeared as though "Heaven had withdrawn its Mandate from the Manchus".

3

THE T'AIPING REBELLION (1850-64)

During this period China was deeply convulsed by a serious rebellion of such great magnitude that left nearly twenty-five million dead. This rebellion was called T'aiping, meaning paradoxically 'great peace', but characterised by great violence and recurrent tragedies on account of the struggle carried on against the continuance of the weak and corrupt Manchu (Ching) dynasty. Rural misery in China had many tales to narrate all going to prove how corrupt and inefficient the alien dynasty had been and how impervious it was to the plight of millions of Chinese living in thousands of villages in the south. During the period the rebels controlled half of China and mainly in the valley of the Yangtze. It was with great difficulty and with the assistance of foreigners that this rebellion could be suppressed. The leader of the rebels was a Christian fanatic named Hung Hsiu-Chuan (1814-64) whose movement was to bring about the collapse of the ruthless, inefficient and corrupt Manchu Government and establish "a society based on justice, in which the strong shall not oppress the weak, the wise exploit the ignorant, the brave impose upon the timid."

Hung belonged to a peasant community called Hakka which migrated from northern China long time ago. He was born near Canton in a prosperous family and decided to be a scholar and a bureaucrat. Unfortunately he failed frequently to pass the higher examinations and suffered from mental depression. After a couple of years Hung began to experience some visions where God appeared to have assigned him the mission to destroy Manchu rule and reconstruct Chinese society based on social and economic justice. It was in 1843 that he came to be influenced by Christianity, and became a convert and set up a secret society, called the 'Society of God'. Joined by his friend, Feng Yun-shan, he spread his new religion to the people of Kwangsi, a province which the Manchus found difficult to govern.

The movement of Hung first began with the breaking of the Buddhist and Taoist idols and it got a fresh momentum with the joining of Yang Hsies-chang, a charcoal burner. The movement called 'Shang Ti Hui', got the support of the members of the White Lotus Society (a secret society founded in AD 380 by a Buddhist monk named Hua Yiu). Internally the movement was well-organised to launch an attack against the Manchu imperial army after the appointment of princes governing north, south, east and west with the Lord of the Princes being Hung himself. A new dynasty was ushered in called T'aiping T'ien-kuo, with Hung becoming the 'Heavenly Prince', after the seizure of a hilly town called Yuganchow. The idea of universal brotherhood was spread, and the movement became quite popular with millions of poor peasants who were against the continuance of Manchu rule.

Who were the main pillars of support to the T'aiping rebellion? It was the poor peasants and artisans who were oppressed by the corrupt Manchu officials. These peasants lent liberal support to the movement. Increased population and mismanagement of the economy, especially on the food front, had made the regime of the Manchus unbearable. Cottage industry had suffered badly due to the import of foreign goods, including the banned opium. Tax was calculated in terms of silver but paid in copper.

What was the immediate cause which led to the outbreak of the rebellion? The Chinese troops forced the charcoal workers belonging to the Society of God to give some contributions which they refused. This led to a serious quarrel and rioting took place. The Emperor sent two commissioners to quell the riots. Hung became very annoyed and declared his revolt with the slogan, "Exterminate the Manchus".

Hung built a powerful military force commanded by great generals to defend the movement against the Chinese imperial army which had been ordered to go into action. The highly disciplined T'aiping army controlled some parts of China, mainly the Yangtze Valley and others, and in 1853 captured Nanking itself. The dazzling victories of the T'aiping unnerved the Manchus and paved the way for other rebellions in China. For example, the Nieu rebellion broke out in 1853 in the area west of the Grand Canal. Protestant missionaries who came into contact with the T'aiping welcomed the inauguration of the new dynasty. However, the situation suddenly changed from one of warmth to hostility, thanks to the opposition of the Catholic missionaries and Western merchants. The Westerners saw through Hung's pretensions of being the Son of God or Brother of Jesus Christ and raised a hue and cry against him. In the midst of the victories of Hung, the West concluded the treaties of T'ientsin and Peking with the Manchus setting at rest the rumour of likely Western support to the T'aiping rebels.

Modern Reforms of Hung

During the course of the rebellion Hung tried to introduce some modern reforms in the region temporarily controlled by him. They included:

a) His followers were forbidden from consuming opium, alcoholic drinks and committing adultery. Slavery, witchcraft, gambling, tobacco smoking and chewing were also banned.

b) They were to obey the Ten Commandments.

c) Women were to enjoy equal rights and their foot-binding was abolished. They were recruited into the army and their labour was properly organised.

d) A programme of land reforms was chalked out which envisaged distribution of the land to the landless. Land-holdings were divided into nine grades according to productivity. Every landless family was given a piece of land commensurate with the size of the family. The new society's basic unit was fixed at twenty-five families, and one officer was appointed to look after this community, with special emphasis on education, social welfare and religion.

Every peasant who had joined his movement had to become a soldier and Hung's government assumed civil and military character. The new political, social and economic order which he envisaged was tried at Nanking during the formative period. However, it did not spread to the countryside he controlled. Hung's control over his assistants who commanded different regions as princes ran into trouble and many assassinations of leaders followed. Only Li Hsi-Ch'eng survived his purge and continued to command T'aiping forces till the last years. The mediocres remained in charge and they quarrelled among themselves making Hung's control over his region weak. Hung's loosely knit organisation began to crack as the scholar-class was disgusted and stopped intellectual and moral support. In fact, great scholars felt that Manchu rule was better. In the midst of campaigns, Hung had no time to give a concrete shape to many of his new ideas and failed to stem the rot in time. His decline became imminent when the Emperor assigned the task of crushing the rebellion to Tseng Kuo-Fan, a famous Confucian scholar and soldier of Hunan, stationed at Peking.

Hung's shortcomings were many. After his dazzling victories against the Manchus he should have marched to Peking instead of capturing the opulent Nanking. He and his soldiers wasted too much time indulging in all kinds of pleasures and gave up all the principles which forged them into a united front. Hung's pleasure-loving life set a bad example to the others. He soon forgot about the land reforms he had promised to the peasants. Hung's failings made the task of Tseng easy. His newly created imperial army crushed the strongholds of the T'aipings, drove them out of central Yangtze Valley and finally captured Nanking. Hung committed suicide by drinking poison and his followers were defeated one by one. By July 1864, this great rebellion (modern communists and even Sun Yat Sen believed so) was crushed. A few rebellions of the Muslim minorities living in the north-west and south-western parts of China petered out mainly because they had no local support like the T'aipings. However, they underlined the fact that in those regions the Manchus had failed to assert their authority.

The suppression of the rebellion owes its success to three great Chinese statesmen, namely, Tse Kua-Fan, Tso Tsung-Tang and Li-Hung-Chang. In fact, during the next few decades these three figures along with the Empress Dowager, Tsu-Li, play a predominant role. A little known story about the suppression includes the role of an American adventurer and a Britisher, namely Ward and Major Charles Gordon. It must be remembered that Tseng took Li-Hung-Chang into confidence, and the latter took the assistance of the American adventurer, Ward, to create a small force of 4,000 Chinese soldiers, trained in Western methods of warfare.

This force gained resounding victories. After Ward's death, Major Charles Gordon, helped the Chinese army to capture Soochow from the hands of the rebels. With French assistance, another Chinese contingent captured Hangchow before Nanking fell.

Significance of the Rebellion

The underlying significance of the rebellion was that the ideals cherished by Hung endeared him to a large populace which had undergone untold sufferings due to the misrule and oppression of the Manchus. Reforms was the need of the hour and the Manchus had not learnt any lessons at all. Therefore, the future for the Manchus was bleak as long as they opposed reforms.

The superiority of Western methods of warfare and weaponry manifested itself during the course of the suppression of this rebellion. Ward and Gordon did their bit to help Tseng and Li-Hung-Chang to suppress this rebellion without much difficulty during the last stages of the war. But what became evident was that the claim of the Emperor that he was the "Son of Heaven" was no longer valid. The imperial government became vulnerable to the inroads of the West. That the ancient wisdom of China was sufficient to counteract the superiority of Western science and technology fooled no one. China learnt these bitter lessons the hard way (unlike the Japanese) during the next few decades.

Modern communists regard the T'aiping rebellion as the forerunner of the Chinese Revolution of 1949. Sun Yat Sen considered it a great event and Communists like Mao considered it an event of great significance. This was because Hung prepared a blueprint for a new Chinese society based on social and economic justice. His plan to introduce land reforms in an elaborate manner, to bring about a just rural society and usher in peace was hailed by modern communists.

4

DISMEMBERMENT OF CHINA

The Tung Chih Restoration

The Chinese term Tung Chih means "Union for Order". In Chinese history, a restoration of the dynastic leadership of the Ching occurred at the time of the T'aiping rebellion. In fact, it was the revival of the Ching (Manchu) dynasty with effective leadership in the 1860s and to some it indicated that the empire need not fear internal rebellions and foreign interference any more.

Fortunately, the revived imperial government got the assistance of great leaders who were votaries of the Confucian traditions. They were great scholars who could visualise what changes China must undergo in order to survive in the new situation. The greatest among them was Tseng Kuo-Fan, the scholar-general who came to the rescue of the imperial government when the T'aipings had conquered a part of China. Tseng's followers were all Chinese scholar-soldiers like him and with a mission to help restore order. Tseng advocated the spread of Western education as a panacea for the ills facing China. His follower, Li-Hung-Chang, also stressed the same kind of education. In 1861 the Emperor died, and in a coup organised by his brother, Prince Kung, and Empress Dowager, Tzu-Hsi, a boy Emperor was nominated. Prince Kung played an important role in not only saving the empire but also reviving it.

The period 1860-1900 marked the beginning of a new era in Chinese history in the sense that the Ching dynasty set itself the task of self-strengthening exercises so as to meet the challenges posed by internal and external threats. China had already been humiliated enough by the foreigners including the Japanese. China's great thinkers, moulded on Confucian traditions, believed that she should adopt Western languages and science. Feng Kuei-Fen was one such votary who wished a harmonious combination of Confucian and Western learning. He believed that if China adopted western technology, many of her problems could be overcome.

Wang-T'ao also thought of desirable changes which China should undergo in view of the changed situation. He was impressed by the Japanese achievements after she adopted Western science and technology to help modernise herself.

Being a journalist known as the 'father of Chinese journalism', his writings reflected the necessity of reforms. The old examination system and certain laws had to be given up. He called for a new mindset to be developed among Confucian scholars.

Another great writer was Yen Fu. He was widely travelled and a scholar of repute. He urged the Chinese to give up their old sense of superiority while dealing with Westerners, since the latter was in no way 'inferior'. He translated several English books, spread Western ideas, and underlined the need for a democratic system of government to replace an authoritarian one. Some of his books were banned by an imperial edict since many young men were influenced by his writings and translations (translations included the books of Montesquieu, John Stuart Mill, Herbert Spencer, and Adam Smith).

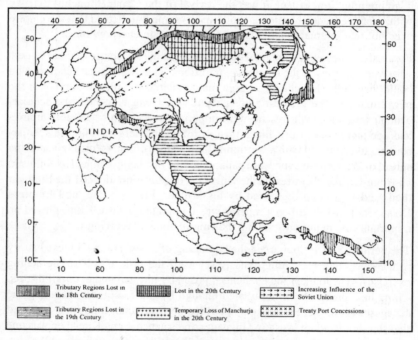

Partition of Chinese Empire

Among those who were strongly influenced by Yen's writings was reformer, named K'ang Yu-wei, who was to play a leading role in bringing about what is known as the Hundred Days Reforms. Being a highly educated landlord, he devoted all energies to the service of society. He was highly impressed by the orderliness and prosperity of Hong Kong, then under British control, and began studying many translations in Shanghai. He subsequently published two good books, titled, *The Grand Unity*, and *Confucius as Reformer*.

His reinterpretation of Confucius impressed many because he said Confucius envisaged the unity of mankind and the commonwealth of nations as the last stage of progress. According to K'ang Yu-wei that stage had arrived. He addressed a few letters to the Emperor and to the court about the need for reforms to save China from humiliation at the hands of Western nations and Japan. But his advice went unheeded. This led to terrible consequences and K'ang advocated a constitutional monarchy similar to that of Japan.

K'ang's fervent appeals for reform struck a chord of sympathy with Emperor Kuang who appointed him as his chief adviser to carry out the necessary reforms, called the Hundred Days Reforms (1898). The object of K'ang reforms was to transform China from a feudal set-up into a modern industrial state, with a modern bureaucracy and a modern system of education. But before we study about these reforms, let us examine the foreign policy pursued by China after the treaties of Tientsin and Peking.

China's Foreign Relations

In keeping with its philosophy of self-strengthening it became necessary that China's relations with Western nations undergo a change for the better. So it changed its policy from one of hostile indifference to a policy of cooperation. China gave up her traditional stance of superiority and allowed the Western nations to participate in the maintenance of the treaty system. The new British minister, Rutherford Alcock, realised that in view of the changed situation, British merchants in the treaty ports should not make aggressive demands on China. She had the potential and inclination to modernise herself and the minister no doubt anticipated "a revolution as has been never seen since the world began". The new foreign policy of China was working towards achieving that objective.

Cooperation with foreigners could not be achieved until China took them into confidence. Therefore, Chinese diplomats sought foreign help in training themselves in the art of modern diplomacy. It was in these circumstances that a new organisation called "Tsungli Yamen", the embryonic form of Foreign Office, was set up in 1861 in Peking with Prince Kung playing an important role. The new organisation was a Grand Council with the Emperor presiding over it in order to arrive at foreign policy decisions. The trained Chinese diplomats of this office handled many important matters in foreign relations. There were two other commissioners working in this field based at Nanking and Tientsin who were directly responsible to the Chinese Emperor. The T'aiping rebellion accelerated the decentralisation process in the foreign policy decision-making. As the Chinese diplomats did not know Western languages they had to join an Interpreter's College, known as Tung Wen Kuan, in Peking for learning not only Western languages but also the techniques of conducting diplomacy. Schools of Western culture were set up in Tientsin and Shanghai for the young Chinese officials to absorb Western ideals and culture.

The Maritime Customs Service

A modernised Maritime Customs Service organisation came into being thanks to the efforts of a British diplomat, Horatio Nelson Lay. He had worked as a foreign inspector in charge of assessment of duties at Shanghai since 1855 and his salary was paid from the imperial treasury. Knowing the Chinese language and culture he was able to organise things to suit the provisions of the Tientsin Treaty. It was he who expanded the Customs Service for the Chinese and his services were very much appreciated by the government. Subsequently he was promoted as the Inspector General of the Customs Service. He was also nominated as member of the Tsungli Yamen. However, he fell into disrepute when he purchased a fleet of eight British ships with British crewmen and desired to retain his control over them as against the wishes of the Chinese Government.

Lay was succeeded by Robert Hart. During his time many foreigners were recruited into the organisation. They all worked under Chinese superintendents. By 1875 the foreign staff included 252 British employees and another 156 drawn from sixteen other Western nations. The modern customs service served as an important organisation which helped in maintaining friendly relations with foreign merchants. Hart was also instrumental in setting up the Interpreter's College (Tung Wen Kuan) in Peking, as mentioned earlier.

Arsenals and Shipyards

Tseng Kuo-Fan and Li-Hung-Chang advocated scientific and technological base for Chinese industries. In the course of time, arsenals and shipyards were set up on most modern lines. Their efforts bore fruit when the Kiagnan arsenal at Shanghai was established. In due course the Chinese built their first steamship with a foreign engine in 1866. Foochow also had another arsenal and shipyard. Railroads and telegraph made a beginning and Hankow could boast of a modern steel factory. There was an increasing demand by Chinese scholars for access to scientific treatises and manuals produced by the West. Around 1870 the activities of the Christian missions, both Catholic and Protestant, began to increase.

Chinese Response to the Christian Missions

The increased activities of the Christian missionaries, both Catholic and Protestant, had a highly disturbing effect upon the local Chinese masses who were wedded to Confucianism. They treated the Chinese as heathens and their society as perverted with its odd customs and habits. By 1870 there were 250 European Jesuits and also many Chinese Christian priests carrying on missionary propaganda and proselytising activity. The convention of 1860 allowed the French to buy land, construct churches and buildings, and rent out their property. There were more than 350 Protestant missionaries with their families who were all sent by an English man named Hudson Taylor in 1866. Those sent by Taylor wore Chinese dress and propagated Christianity, sometimes deriding Chinese religion and culture. Native Chinese who got converted to Christianity got special protection from their church, a thing envied by the non-Christian Chinese. This was bound to create communal disharmony by sowing seeds of discontent. Petty quarrels between Christians and Chinese sometimes assumed serious proportions requiring the intervention of Chinese officials. During the period 1860-99 riots broke out against the Christian missionaries but the government took steps to defuse the tension. Christianity began to make steady progress as if to challenge those who chose "Confucian scholarship as a path of advancement". Propaganda literature specially appealing to the poor Chinese was being distributed. The Chinese lost their fortitude and their indignation against the missionaries culminated in the massacre at Tientsin in 1870. Let us examine the events which led to this upsurge.

The Tientsin Massacre

The common Chinese began to treat the spread of Christianity as a great threat, next only to that of the T'aiping rebellion. The protection and privileges enjoyed by the foreign missionaries and converted Chinese created jealousy and hatred, and a feeling spread that their religion and society was no longer safe. The Catholic Sisters of Charity started its activity by founding an orphanage for the poor Chinese children. Since it could not attract many people the society began to accept even sick children and this was viewed by the Chinese with great suspicion. Many rumours were afloat about this organisation and it was believed that the children were enticed to the orphanage for heinous purposes. A furious Chinese mob attacked the orphanage church and the French Consulate. The Consul asked the mob to disperse, but when it did not, shot was fired to disperse it. Fortunately it missed the Chinese magistrate who had come there to make enquiries. The unruly mob was enraged by this act and killed twenty foreigners, which included ten nuns. Furthermore, a number of Chinese Christians were killed and the French Consulate was burnt. This incident soured the relations between the Chinese Government and the French and therefore the situation had to be defused. It was Tseng who dealt with the situation which culminated in the punishment of the culprits, and substantial compensation and an apology from the Chinese Government to the French

Government. Were it not for Tseng Kuo-Fan's deft diplomacy during the negotiations, the image of the Chinese Government would have suffered immensely.

Further Inroads into Chinese Sovereignty

It may be remembered that the British representative, Rutherford Alcock, forced the Chinese Government to agree to the British terms in 1869 and a convention was signed which provided for a "limited right of a most favoured treatment for the British in China..." Other foreign nations—after the Tientsin Massacre —also demanded similar treatment. They pressed for these demands. By 1870, foreigners were enjoying security and comforts in all the fifteen port towns where they had their own settlements. They collected taxes within their jurisdiction and looked after the Customs Services on behalf of the imperial government of China. They did not adapt themselves to the ways of the Chinese but always exhibited an air of superiority and a nonchalant attitude. The foreign merchants put pressure on their governments to exert pressure on China for more trade concessions, facilities and privileges. They hardly bothered whether this would encroach on the sovereignty of China. Incidentally, the Western nations too competed with each other in exerting their pressure on China directly and sometimes indirectly, that is through China's vassal states, namely, Li Ch'iu islands, Korea, Annam, Laos, Siam and so on. Though all of them acknowledged Chinese sovereignty, they enjoyed full autonomy. How did the Western nations establish their spheres of influence over China's autonomous or tributary states?

The Chinese Turkestan

This north-western province of China provides a classic example of Russian interference. Being a Muslim-populated region and prone to frequent revolts, China was fast losing control. Of particular importance in this region was Kashgaria, where all the trade routes of Central Asia meet. Unfortunately, due to difficult terrain, the Chinese army had no control over the local Muslims called Khojas. When they revolted, they were driven out from the area. All of them settled in Khokand. The Chinese governors eventually allowed the Muslim chieftains to control Kashgaria but their loyalty was always suspect. Again this region was in trouble when Yakub, a Khokandian general, seized it and started independent rule. The Russians did not like the British support to Yakub and feared their interference in the Russia-China border region. The Russians responded to this situation by moving their troops into the Ili River Valley region and occupied the commercial centre of Kuddja. The Russians promised the Chinese Government (the Sino-Russian agreement of 1851) that they would vacate when the situation became normal.

Thus the Central Asian region of China was susceptible to local revolts and foreign interference. Finally, China decided to regain its authority. What caused this swift response was the revolt of the Muslims in the 1870s. Tso Tsung-tang, an able Chinese general, led an attack and mercilessly slaughtered the Muslim rebels in Urumchi (1876-78). His troops marched further to the Tarim basin and crushed Yakub's revolt resulting in his death in 1877. Thus the entire region of Turkestan, except the Ili region where Russians were camping, was regained by the Chinese Government. The Chinese Government decided to recover the Ili region too and hence opened negotiations. Chung Ho, the leader of the Chinese team, signed the Treaty of Livadia with the Russians which, however, highly compromised Chinese interests. When he returned to the capital, he was tried and faced punishment. He was saved because Queen Victoria intervened on his behalf. Subsequently, the Russians signed the Treaty of St. Petersburg in 1881 resulting in the evacuation of their troops. The Chinese Government converted their north-western region of Turkestan into the province of Sikiang (meaning "The New Dominion"). The Russians were permitted to open their consulate, buy land, set up factories, and trade with the local people right up to the Great Wall of China. China's political and military strategists were satisfied with the results brought about by this treaty.

The French Conquer Indo-China

France which could not get many advantages from China like the British, planned to make spiritual and political conquests over China's vassal state like Vietnam (known as Annam to the Chinese). Hundreds of French Catholic missionaries started arriving there to carry on their activities since the people were divided over social and religious adherence because of peculiar geographical incongruity (for example, the Hanoi and Mekong deltas looked apart.) The Nguyen rulers, specially Minh Mang (1820-41), Thieu-Tri (1841-47), and Tu-Duc (1848-83) struggled hard to bring unity between the peoples of these two regions but with limited success. This was because they were faced with formidable problems like natural disasters, inflation, rebel movements and so on. (This is elaborated upon in another chapter). These rulers desired to establish a Chinese model of bureaucracy. The eastern coastline of Vietnam became vulnerable to foreign influence, more so from the French Catholic missionaries during the previous two centuries. By the middle of the nineteenth century the French Catholic Church became a force to be reckoned with in Vietnam. However, during the period 1848-60, a violent reaction to foreign influence set in resulting in the death of thousands of converted Vietnamese including some European missionaries. This violent outburst against foreigners gave an opportunity to the French Emperor, Napoleon III (whose penchant for publicity about his foreign exploits is well known), to intervene.

In 1859, the French army captured Saigon and subsequently conquered three provinces surrounding it. Unfortunately, for Vietnam a rebellion had broken out in Tonking at that time which demanded utmost attention and effective response. Under these compelling circumstances the helpless Vietnamese monarch, Tu Duc, signed a treaty with France in 1862 ceding the three provinces. By this treaty, the monarch promised to open his country for French trade, grant liberties to Catholic missionaries, and allow a "vague control over Vietnam's foreign relations."

The troubles were not over for this unfortunate monarch, as yet another rebellion broke out, this time against the French. Unable to suppress this rebellion, he sought help from the French forces. The French not only succeeded in suppressing this rebellion but also established their control over what was then known as Cochin-China. More surprisingly, this situation enabled the French to establish a protectorate over nearby Cambodia (1863-64). King Norodom (1860-1904) of Cambodia accepted the French offer of assistance to suppress a rebellion in his country and this led to the development of a French colony in Cambodia. Nearby Siam became another target for the French to extend its control and this was achieved by a treaty with that country's monarch in 1867. Cambodia's dependence on Siam ended. The French ambition of establishing its colony, known as Indo-China, had almost succeeded but the goal of opening up trade links with China from the south, through the Mekong and Red Rivers, had not yet been achieved. The French continued to explore the Mekong River region further and one of their expeditions resulted in the discovery of Ankorvat. Subsequently, they shifted attention to the Red River region hoping to discover a new route to south-west China through Tonking.

The Sino-French War

The French conquest of Indo-China was bound to provoke China into a full-scale war with France as China's sovereignty over her vassal states was endangered. It must be remembered that China had claimed her sovereignty over these states since 1664. The Vietnamese ruler, obviously harassed by the French, appealed to the Chinese Government to come to his rescue. The Sino-French war began, resulting in the French capture of Hanoi. It was converted into a French protectorate. Hostilities continued since the French ably defended their strategic posts. In 1884, the French forces got resounding victories against the Chinese which led to the dismissal of Prince Kung. After a tiresome vacillation China agreed to the Li-Fournier convention in 1885, after the mediation of Robert Hart. China lost control over the vassal states after this war. France converted Cochin-China into her colony and continued indirect rule over Cambodia, Annam and Tonking. France called her empire Indo-China in 1887. In 1893 France added Laos which Siam ceded. Only Siam remained independent thanks to the Anglo-French rivalry during this time. The French Government followed the policy of assimilation by imposing its culture on the local population. It introduced the Western system of administration and built roads and bridges. Explorations into the history and culture of the conquered territories were carried out successfully.

China learnt some bitter lessons. It was probably the first modern war waged against a foreign power which she lost. She discovered that the use of modern weapons alone would not suffice to win a war. The need of the hour was "modern organisation and leadership", which she lacked. The French victories demoralised her forces and exposed her to further exploitation by the Western nations and Japan.

The most significant outcome of this war was the rise of nationalism, at least in the southern parts of China. Besides their obvious frustration at losing the war, the Chinese realised the necessity of rectifying several things in the country. Their hatred towards foreigners and foreign missionaries provided a breeding ground for new recruits to the upcoming Boxer Movement. Although this was a patriotic movement it was dubbed xenophobic by the Westerners.

With the gradual Westernisation of China, hundreds of poor Chinese began to emigrate to other countries during the second half of the nineteenth century. The *coolie* trade became a common phenomenon, i.e., Chinese workers (coolies) began to emigrate to the coasts of California (US), Cuba and Peru to earn their daily bread. This large scale emigration was of two types, namely, free emigration and contract labour. Contract labourers suffered immensely due to the miserable conditions meted out to them by their employers. The coolie trade pursued by the Portuguese from their Chinese settlement at Macao was by far the most reprehensible act of perfidy.

While Japan had become a modern nation during the last decade of the nineteenth century, thanks to the period of Meiji Restoration, China was still in a stage of transition. She was yet to come to terms with the modernised Western nations who were carving out the spheres of influence—euphemistically known as the "cutting of the Chinese melon". She was without a dynamic leader who could liberate her from the shackles of the Western nations—remember the unequal treaties imposed on her by them. In Napoleon's words she was still a sleeping dragon. This makes us turn our attention to her small, but dynamic neighbour, Japan. Japan's experience with the West was different. We shall examine her story in another chapter.

Spheres of Influence; Cutting of the Chinese Melon

China's defeat at the hands of Japan had ominous portent. It let loose the greed of the Western powers to grab as much Chinese territory as possible by methods most unfair. Unequal treaties were imposed upon this hapless nation, and the first to take advantage was Russia. She put up a false show of friendship with China and persuaded France to give loans to China so as to enable the latter to pay compensation to Japan. Russia too gave some amount to help China for this purpose. In return China gave permission to Russia to build the Chinese Eastern Railway across Manchuria connecting Vladivostok. The Chinese statesman, Li-Hung-Chang, visited Russia and concluded a secret treaty directed against Japan. In furtherance of this friendship Russia stationed her naval squadron at Port Arthur. In addition, Russia got a twenty-five-year lease of the Liaotung peninsula (southern tip of Manchuria) with Port Arthur and Yalienwan, and also some railway concessions from China in 1898. Russia's acquisitions in China made other European powers and Japan jealous. Therefore, these powers realised the weakness of China and put up their own demands for territorial and commercial concessions knowing full well that they were compromising her territorial integrity and sovereignty.

An intense competition for dismembering China started due to the rivalry among European powers following large concessions Russia got from China as cited above. Finally, a subtle understanding among these powers was reached on how they should 'cut the Chinese melon' (partition of China) and share it. For example, France and Russia, Russia and Germany, and Germany and Britain decided to carve out spheres of influence in the mainland of China with their bullying tactics, i.e., by forcing China to accept their illegal demands and seizures, and thereafter getting them legalised through what is known as unequal treaties. In 1897, a German fleet forcibly occupied the Tsing tao in the Kiachow bay (Shantung). The Russian fleet seized Port Arthur (Liaotung peninsula). The French fleet took the Kwangchow harbour near Canton. Britain got leases opposite Hong Kong, and a naval base at Weihaiwai.

Still not satisfied, the Western powers forcibly got mining, railway and tariff concessions from China. France acquired mining concessions in south-western China, and extended her railways from Tonqking. The French railway constructions penetrated the Yunnan province in the early decade of the twentieth century. Britain carried out her projects deep in the valley of Yangtze. She was engaged in the construction of a railway line to Burma. She forced China to open a greater number of treaty ports for her trade and enjoyed a concession to extend the railway line an additional 2,800 miles.

So at the end of the nineteenth century the Western powers brought about the disintegration of China into spheres of influence. In fact they would have brought about her actual partition, had it not been for the timely intervention of the United States which came forward with her 'open door' policy. To conclude, in the words of Clyde and Beers, "... her great Confucian society had suffered successive military defeats; she had been subjected to unequal treaty system; her influence and control over the tributary states had been destroyed; and as the century drew to a close her strategic harbours had become foreign naval bases." At last the Manchu empire, which had survived for centuries, was tottering.

5

BOXER REBELLION (1900)

After the end of the Hundred Days Reforms (June-September 1898) in China, Chinese Emperor Kuang Hsu was deposed by Empress Dowager who was assisted by Yuan Shi Kai. She was not happy with the reforms introduced by the Chinese scholar-cum-administrator, Kang Yu Wei, because they threatened the "twin pillars of her regime", namely, "Classical learning and organised corruption". Her third regency in China began when the Emperor went into "forced seclusion". She believed that reforms should come from below, even if it were through violence. However, she introduced a very moderate dose of reforms which did not take China the way the Meiji reforms took Japan to its final goal. Since her slow pace of reforms did not satisfy the masses, it had to be achieved through a great deal of violence. China witnessed one of the worst rebellions in her history—the Boxer Rebellion.

The Boxer Movement (Xenophobic)

Since the revolution could not be achieved through radical reforms from above, there was no alternative other than violent protests from the masses. What attracted the attention of those who desired the overthrow of the Manchu Government was that it had compromised China's sovereignty and territorial integrity by signing agreements with Western barbarians. The Boxer Movement was started by a secret society called I-ho Chuan (which when translated becomes "Righteous and Harmonious fists"). The members of this secret society observed Taoist sorcery and rituals and also went through some exercises similar to the present day boxing. All this was necessary, as it would harmonise the mind and the body in preparation for a combat. It was believed that even bullets fired at them would have no effect. The Boxers adored some Chinese fictional heroes, and had a slogan like "overthrow the Ch'ing, destroy the foreigner."

The movement attracted all those who had developed contempt for foreign missionaries, foreigners, and Chinese-Christians. The hatred was intensified after some years because foreign missionaries enjoyed a number of privileges in China, which included proselytisation and free movement. The members of the secret society were made to believe that their culture was far superior to the foreigner, and the latter was responsible for all the ills facing their country. They believed that their country's problems began after the defeat following the opium wars, and finally ended with the great humiliation at the hands of Japan (viz, Sino-Japanese war—1895). China's defeat at the hands of culturally inferior Japan caused deep humiliation—more than what was caused by the exploitation of Western nations.

Western critics have described the Boxer Movement as extremely xenophobic, since it aimed at destroying Christianity and Christian missionaries in China. However, this was not totally true, since the Boxers were intensely patriotic. For them the Christian missionaries and converts were obstacles in the way of achieving their objectives. What made the Boxer Movement gain further momentum was the compelling economic conditions. China had gone through a harrowing experience during the nineteenth century, mostly because of rebellions and droughts. In 1898, floods ravaged the provinces of Shantung, Kiangsi, Anhwei, and Kiangsu. In the midst of these sufferings, people were subjected to the payment of heavy taxes. Banditry and lawlessness prevailed in many parts of the country.

It was in these circumstances, that the Western nations exploited pitiable conditions in China by wrenching trade concessions, leaseholds, and permission to build railways. Permitting foreign missionaries to carry on their work of conversion caused great bitterness. The Chinese felt disgusted when they saw the converted Chinese becoming more aggressive and receiving protection from the Western nations. In these circumstances the Boxers felt outraged and encouraged the people to revolt against the Manchu Government.

Government's Clandestine Support to Boxer Movement

The Manchu Government headed by Empress Dowager handled carefully a politically volatile situation by diverting the attention of the Boxers to the atrocities caused by Christian missionaries. Chinese officials secretly supported the cause of the Boxer Movement with the intention of expelling the foreigners. The Boxers naturally expected the government to help them in achieving their final objective, i.e., to expel the foreigners. The hatred against the Manchu Government was conveniently forgotten by the Boxers and they carried out their attacks against the Christian missionaries and churches in 1889-90.

The Course of Boxer Movement

The leaders of the Boxer Movement were secretly assisted by the Chinese officials who responded to the slogan "support the Ch'ing, destroy the foreigners". The Boxer's violent activities against the Christian missionaries began in the coastal province of Shantung in 1899. The governor of that province openly supported the Boxer Movement. Subsequently, the Boxers carried out their marauding activities against the foreigners in many northern provinces of China. Many governors of these provinces encouraged the Boxers to carry out nefarious activities such as attacking and destroying churches, hospitals and schools, and murdering the Christian converts.

The Western embassies in Peking appealed to the Manchu Government to curb the activities of the Boxers. However, their appeal fell on deaf ears. The Boxers killed hundreds of Chinese converts in many parts of northern China. In June 1900, the Boxers laid siege to the foreign consulates in Peking and Tientsin with the support of government officials. It should be remembered that the Boxer Movement directed against foreigners was confined to the northern provinces of China. The south was not affected much and the provincial governments there did not show any sympathy to the Boxer Movement.

Foreign Interference

When foreign embassies were under siege, foreign powers acted in unison and sent a task force—a naval fleet for the purpose of threatening the Manchu Government with dire consequences if it did not go to the rescue of foreigners. The combined forces would also directly go to control the siege. It was under these circumstances that Empress Dowager declared war. This was probably China's fourth encounter with the Western nations during a period of sixty years. About 250 foreigners were killed during the course of action, some of the most notable casualties during this episode were the murders of the German and Japanese ministers. In the meantime, the governors of the southern provinces had promised western powers that they would maintain law and order. They would take action against the Boxers if they did not send their warships to the Yangtze Valley. It must be remembered that many governors of the south including the Chinese commander-in-chief, Yuan Shi Kai, ignored the Manchu Government's call for a war against the Western nations.

When the task force reached Peking and Tientsin, the Boxers fled. Even the Manchu Government was forced to flee. Thus the Western nations successfully carried out their attacks against the Boxers. The Boxer Movement collapsed and the Chinese officials in the south started their negotiations with the Western nations for concluding a peace agreement. They expected a milder punishment from the Western nations because the Boxer Movement was only an uprising against foreigners in China and not against foreign nations. The international force consisting of 40,000 troops occupied northern parts of China, including the capital, Peking. A Russian force occupied large parts of Manchuria.

The Boxer Protocol

The Boxer Protocol came as a result of protracted negotiations between the Manchu Prince Li-Hung-Chang, and the participating Western nations. It was signed on September 7, 1901 by China. Eleven representatives of the Western nations concluded this agreement. The terms of the protocol have been described as "severe and humiliating for China". The terms are as follows:

(1) China had to apologise to Germany and Japan for the murder of a minister and a chancellor respectively and agree to construct a memorial for the former.

(2) Punish Chinese officials for supporting the Boxer Movement.

(3) Suspend official examinations in forty-five Chinese cities where violent outbreaks had taken place (half of them were in Shensi province).

(4) Agree to expand, fortify and garrison the foreign legations in Peking.

(5) Destroy Taku forts and allow the occupation of foreigners at thirteen places to ensure free access to Peking.

(6) Raise import duties to five per cent and pay $333 million as war indemnity. China was prohibited from importing arms and ammunition from foreign countries.

Finally, the Chinese Government had to publish edicts in order to prevent such violent outbreaks in future after agreeing for further revision of commercial treaties with foreign powers.

Many critics doubted the wisdom of the Western nations in imposing many humiliating conditions on the Chinese Government at a time when it was hardly in a position to bear it. They also felt that the terms of the Boxer protocol would further enrage the masses. In the words of Clyde and Beers, "the Boxer Movement was an unmistakable symptom of China's growing unrest, of her resentment against foreign intrusion and exploitation, and of her will to resist" And Fairbank, Reischauer and Craig mention that "the Boxer rising and the protocol marked the nadir of the Ch'ing dynasty's foreign relations and left little hope for its long continuance".

The Open Door Policy

China became extremely vulnerable to foreign influence and control after signing the Boxer protocol. In fact, the Western powers were very ambitious about the partitioning of China into several colonies. However, this could not take place because of two reasons, namely, rivalry among the European powers themselves on the one side and the United States Government advocating the Open Door policy towards China on the other. At the end of the nineteenth century the United States entertained imperial ambitions and began to seriously think of extending her commercial interest over many countries in the Pacific Ocean. For US foreign policy-makers, China attracted a great deal of attention. The US Government proposed what is called the Open Door policy with regard to China with the intention of not only promoting her commercial interests in that country but also preventing foreign powers from partitioning China.

In fact, the 'Open Door policy' was originally initiated by Britain but unfortunately did not meet with adequate response from other European powers. However, when this was promoted by the United States Government, it became a great success. Why was the Open Door policy advocated by the USA? To answer this question we have to understand the political situation prevailing in China in 1897-98 when Russia and Germany began to establish their spheres of influence. They acquired naval and other leaseholds hoping that Britain would follow suit. However, Britain became wary of this move because she was not interested in power rivalry although she was eager to secure her commercial hold on China. She was also nervous about Russia and Germany making common cause over China and tilting the balance of power in their favour. In these circumstances Britain urged the United States Government for joint action to compel other foreign powers to accept the Open Door policy.

The Shaping of the Open Door Policy

American President McKinley and Secretary of State John Sherman were at a loss to understand why the European powers were establishing their spheres of influence at the cost of China and Japan. Even Britain went ahead by establishing her sphere of influence in the Yangtze Valley and established the leaseholds in the Kowloon province and the Wei Hai Wei. The American Ambassador in Britain, John Hay, was trying to make the US State Department understand that leaseholds and spheres of influence established by the European powers in China were compromising the business interests of the Americans, and at the same time endangering the territorial integrity and sovereignty of China. When John Hay became the Secretary of State, he told his adviser, Rock Hill, to prepare notes on the Open Door policy with regard to China. They were finally approved by the US President. These notes were sent to Britain, Russia and Germany in September 1899.

The notes condemned the establishment of spheres of influence by European powers, and in its place advocated the Open Door policy. The Open Door policy included: (a) keeping the administration of the treaty ports free, (b) not to interfere in the administration of the customs authorities in China and (c) not to adopt discriminatory practices in the matters of railroad rates and harbour dues. With the exception of Britain, the response of other Western powers was one of indifference and the reply sent to the notes was evasive. John Hay claimed subsequently that the British response was indeed satisfactory and that his policy had been accepted by other powers.

Hay's second note in July 1900, at a time when the foreign embassies in Peking Tientsin were under siege by the Boxers, reiterated America's intention of bringing permanent peace and security to China, and preserving Chinese territorial integrity and administrative entity. The second note assured China of the protection of her rights guaranteed by friendly powers by treaty and international law. The US intended to "safeguard" for the world principle of equal and impartial trade with all parts of the Chinese empire. All the powers agreed to maintain this status in China, and thus China was saved from the loss of territorial integrity and independence. Her sovereignty was maintained, thanks to the US Open Door policy. Subsequently, Secretary of State John Hay took too much credit for stopping the "melon cutting' in China. It must be remembered that at the same time what prevented the partition of China was the ongoing mutual rivalries and jealousies among the Western powers in Japan. American interests in the Far East were sought to be promoted by the Open Door policy, since the USA had been looking for new areas of commercial exploitation. It must be remembered that the United States had already acquired a number of islands such as Cuba, Hawaii, Guam and the Philippines.

Reforms of Empress Dowager

The Empress returned to the Chinese capital and inaugurated a new phase of reforms similar to the one introduced during the Hundred Days Reforms. These reforms related to administration, education, the army and the navy, opium traffic and other social problems. Unfortunately, the new reforms did not go a long way towards mitigating the sufferings of the masses, the reforms failed mainly because of the lack of conviction on the part of the Empress. She was an unscrupulous and shrewd politician who tried to keep her control over the administration without bothering too much about improving the conditions in China. The "old Buddha", as she was known, died on November 15, 1908. A day prior to her death, the ailing and secluded Emperor, Kuanghsu, had passed away. China became leaderless for a short period. Before her death, the Empress had nominated her three-year-old grand nephew Pu Yi as her successor. He ruled China from 1909-12 with his father, Prince Chun, acting as his regent.

The experience gained from the Boxer tragedy had made a few things clear to the Manchu courtiers. These were (a) that the very existence of the government depended upon protecting national interests, (b) the Confucian ideas and traditions alone could not be depended upon as a political guide for the future, (c) that the political system in China needed to undergo changes, and these could be brought about by emulating the Japanese model and (d) that the Chinese society should shed some age-old inhibitions so as to readily respond to further challenges. In the short run, "it was reformers, not revolutionaries, who mainly prepared the ground for revolution".

We shall examine briefly the reforms introduced by Empress Dowager. They were introduced in response to the three memorials presented to her by the Yangtze Viceroys who maintained peace with the foreigners during the Boxer Rebellion, and at the same time remained loyal to the Manchu dynasty. They outlined the broad reforms that the Chinese system needed at that time. The educational system received top priority and focus of attention. China had an educational system which was Confucian in mould and tradition. This system proved to be useful for the conduct of the civil service examination. The old Chinese bureaucrats (mandarins) did not like the idea of introducing reforms into this system. But a few progressive scholars like Kang Yu Wei insisted that the age-old Confucian system was not desirable since it failed to deliver results at critical times in Chinese history. During the Hundred Days Reforms, progressive scholars also urged the abolition of the traditional Civil Service examination. In 1903, the Viceroys of Yangtze including Yuan Shi Kai also suggested gradual abolition of this examination system. It was in 1905, that the old civil service examination was abolished. They ceased to be conducted at places where Boxers had revolted (*see* Boxer Protocol), and naturally the Chinese-converts gained advantage because of this outcome.

A national policy on education was ushered in by an imperial edict which helped in the evolution of national school system. This school system would combine the study of Confucian classics with learning of such subjects by students as history of the western nations, modern political systems and the progress in science and technology. In 1904, the reformers recommended Japan's model of education system which included schools from the kindergarten level to the university.

The Chinese students welcomed new changes in their education system although the local mandarins were opposed to change. However, by 1910, China could boast of 57,267 schools, 89,362 teachers and 16,26,529 enrolled students. These students and teachers were exposed to the influence of Western culture and civilisation. They constituted a class, the educated bourgeoisie, whose members finally took up jobs in the government service. However, there were some who turned into revolutionaries. Some of the meritorious students were encouraged by the government to go abroad for higher studies.

Military Reforms

It took nearly seven decades, for the Chinese rulers to realise that their defence system was extremely weak and vulnerable. The need of the hour was a national army without a regional bias. In the earlier decades, the Chinese army was divided into three groups, the police constabulary, the regional armies, and the guards maintained by the imperial court. During the T'aiping rebellion, Tseng Kuo-Fan and his colleagues tried to modernise the military organisation to some extent. However, they could not achieve substantial progress. It was only in the 1880s and the 1890s that the Chinese Government could think of hastening the process of modernisation of the army.

This was accomplished by Yuan Shi Kai, the Governor of Hopei, with the assistance of German instructors in 1895. Yuan Shi Kai became the commander-in-chief of the imperial army, and always assisted the Empress Dowager to realise her ambition. It was Yuan who was responsible for organising the six divisions of the Peiyang army. One of those who received military training in Paoting was Chiang Kai-Shek who was to play an important role in the post-revolution period. The cadets in these military academies went to Japan to receive advanced military training. The graduates coming out of these academies were imbued with a great sense of patriotism. In the course of time, the Japanese instructors replaced the Germans in military academies. Lack of central direction, inadequate financing and absence of the industrial revolution continued to bedevil the modernisation process in China. Yuan Shi Kai was not very popular in the court as well as with the Peiyang army which was controlled by the Ministry of War. Therefore, he was dismissed after the death of Empress Dowager.

Administrative Reforms

Since long, China had inherited a loosely-knit administration with no vigorous control over a large number of provinces. The latter always enjoyed semi-autonomous status. Provincial governors and provincial interests played an important role, thereby encouraging centrifugal forces to operate. The Centre's duty had all along been to serve the interests of the provinces, without developing any of its own mechanisms to perform new functions with tact and speed. The T'aiping and Boxer uprisings exposed the cracks that had developed in the Centre-province relations, besides drawing attention to the weaknesses of the Manchu Emperor.

By the early twentieth century, the process of modernising the central machinery of administration began as a response to the many challenges facing the nation. Some of the terms of the Boxer Protocol signed by China necessitated modernisation of administration. To give an example, the Tsungli Yamen was converted into a full-fledged "modern ministry of foreign affairs", which in turn paved the way for the establishment of the Ministry of War. Other ministries which were set up were those of education, police, internal affairs, commerce and so on. However, the modernisation of financial control and administration could not be undertaken since the collection of revenue by the Imperial

Maritime Customs Service was carried out by the concerned governments of foreign nations.

This was because China had to give war-indemnity to those foreign powers which defeated her, according to the Boxer Protocol. However, attempts were made to estimate the national income of the country. But these efforts did not bear fruit because the provinces were not prepared to compromise on the issue of so-called autonomy. Similar was the fate of legal reforms, because Chinese society was wedded to Confucian tradition. The drafting of the criminal code was completed in 1807 but was not approved because it was found to be radical. The law-makers, however, tried to revise the Ching code in 1910 which provided for mitigating the harshness of the corporal punishments, and laid stress on individual responsibility. The Ministry of Commerce was further enlarged to include subjects like agriculture, industry and commerce, and looked after various economic activities such as the construction of railroads, holding of industrial exhibitions, mining and so on. The Ministry of Finance was reorganised in 1906, but it could not achieve central control over various economic activities. This was due to lack of dynamic leadership on the one hand, and the continuation of traditional structure of government on the other.

Constitutional Reforms

China, like Japan, tried to combine administrative modernisation and constitutionalism from 1906 to 1911 without much success. China tried to imitate Japan's successful experiment in establishing constitutional monarchy. However, this did not succeed. The Chinese exhibited the symptoms of nationalism in the early twentieth century when the Chinese coolies were ill-treated by the United States Government. There were waves of protest, and agitation was carried on by students, merchants and the press, all advocating the boycott of American goods.

Empress Dowager's shrewd move in 1908 to bring about a gradual constitutional government over a period of nine years was unfortunately fraught with disastrous consequences. She allowed seventeen provinces of China to have their elected assemblies, but did not provide for the election of representatives to the national Parliament. In other words, she did not like any opposition to the continuation of her regime. The revolutionaries in China did not like her attitude, and after her death established a Republic in the south (1911-12). The demand for a government to be controlled by a national Parliament with a cabinet type of government became vociferous in 1910. After the death of the Empress, the regent was under pressure, and he promised to establish the same in 1913. On popular demand, he appointed a cabinet consisting of eight Manchu ministers, one Mongol, and four other Chinese ministers in 1911.

6

THE OUTBREAK OF CHINESE
REVOLUTION (1911)

A quarter of a century preceding the Chinese Revolution of 1911 witnessed tremendous growth of population, coupled with increasing recurrence of natural calamities such as droughts, famines and floods. This increase in the population was to the tune of fifty million, and during this period many Chinese began to migrate to Manchuria, Indo-China and Malay states. A few years before the outbreak of the 1911 revolution, China suffered from the ravages of droughts which took a heavy toll of lives, besides forcing millions to starve. To add to their sufferings, the Chinese government was compelled by circumstances (mainly due to the Boxer Protocol) to impose a heavy burden of taxes upon her subjects. Besides, the government had to meet the cost of modernisation.

Comparative Lack of Industrialisation

Unlike Japan, China was yet to make its mark in modern industrialisation. It was not until the turn of the century, a small beginning was made. The treaty ports attracted the attention of a few Chinese industrialists for starting factories, especially textiles. However, a few British came in a big way to start the textile industry in the port-city of Shanghai. A few woollen mills, flour mills, tobacco and paper industries were also started. A chemical plant came up. Foreign capital played a dominant role. Steel mills came up much later. The Chinese industrialists and merchants living in the treaty-ports sent their children to English-medium schools run by missionaries, and some of them migrated to countries of Southeast Asia. Some of the Chinese industries experienced a boom period during the World War I. Japan needed raw materials and markets for her industrial progress, and hence desired to conquer China.

Agitation over Railroad Construction

The reform programme undertaken by the Manchu Government steadily encroached on the autonomy of the provinces. It became evident that the Manchu dynasty was bent upon carrying out the reform programme in order to save itself from impending disaster. The issue was whether the provinces would forsake their zealously guarded autonomy. This issue came to the forefront with the proposed construction of railways by the Central government. It was strongly felt by the people in the provinces that the railway construction should be undertaken by the provincial governments rather than by the Central government. It was also felt that the funds needed for the construction should be raised by the local authorities rather than from foreign banks.

The issue of financing railway construction became complicated when many provinces could not raise enough resources. Raising of large funds became necessary because huge bribes had to be given to please bureaucrats. Therefore, the people felt doubtful of the cost-benefit involved in the railway construction. Hence the Centre, early in 1911, brought about centralization of control with regard to railway construction. Loans from foreign banks were sought for the construction of Hanskow-Szechuan, and Hankow-Canton railway routes. The Centre tried to secure the approval of the provincial governments for the programme of rail construction, but the people, particularly in Szechuan lodged serious protests.

The provincial bureaucrats became angry at the Centre's encroachment on provincial autonomy. They felt enraged when they came to know that the Central government had mortgaged many of its assets to a joint consortium of American, French, British and German bankers for the purpose of securing a loan amounting to six million pounds. The patriotic Chinese felt that this measure was adopted to curb the activities of the provincial governors. The Chinese business tycoon who advocated centralisation of rail construction was Sheng Hsuan-Huai, who had been patronised by Li-Hung-Chang and Cheng Chi Pheng, his other enterprises included steamship companies and steel industries.

Sun Yat Sen and the Chinese Revolution of 1911

The reforms ushered in by the Manchu dynasty were put to severe test in the case of railway construction. The provinces insisted first on non-interference in their internal matters, and secondly, resisted attempts at the centralisation of railroad constructions. It was this issue or controversy which sparked off a revolution in the southern parts of China. Among the leaders who spearheaded the movement, the most prominent was Sun Yat Sen. It must be remembered that Japan had been a great source of inspiration to all the Chinese revolutionaries in 1911 because many Chinese reformers had taken shelter there. It was during the early twentieth century that Okuma, the leader of the Japanese Progressive Party, expressed his desire that Japan "should repay her cultural debt to China" by guaranteeing her sovereignty and freedom. He urged his country to assist her in the programme of modernisation. Unfortunately, at this time both Kang Yu Wei and Sun Yat Sen, did not see eye to eye on many points relating to reforms. The former remained loyal to the Manchu dynasty, while the latter to the cause of the revolution.

Life of Sun Yat Sen (1866-1925)

Sun Yat Sen was born in 1866 in Hsiang-Shang village near Canton. He was born in a peasant family and his father owned large tracts of land. In the course of time, Sun joined a Church-of-England school at Honolulu where he had gone to meet his brother. He returned to his village as a Christian convert. Subsequently, he tried to put up his practice in the Portuguese colony of Macao. He was jailed by the Portuguese because they insisted that he should have learnt Portuguese before setting up his practice. In the course of time, he joined a secret society. After the outbreak of the Sino-Japanese war, he started a secret society—Hsing-Chung Hui (Revive China). The avowed purpose was to revive Chinese society by tending to improve the quality of life through the media of education, press and modern methods of agriculture. Along with some of his followers, he attempted to capture Canton, but failed. He quickly left for Japan fearing the wrath of the government. He spent most of his time in Japan with the Chinese students as well as the members of the Chinese secret societies (under Japanese names).

He went to London in 1896 to carry on the propaganda for Chinese liberation. The members of the Chinese legation came to know of his activity and brought about his arrest and imprisonment. However the Chinese legation had to release him at the instance of the British Government which was influenced by Sir James Cantlie, a former teacher of Sun Yat Sen.

The suppression of the Boxer Rebellion proved to be a serious setback to all the revolutionaries in China, who were unfortunately not united in action. It was during this period of deep humiliation, and lack of ideological vacuum, that Sun Yat Sen enunciated his doctrine and plan of action. He advocated the adoption of the three principles meant for guiding the nation and the people. These three principles were, *San Min Chu-i, Min-Tsu-Chu-i* and *Min-Sheng-Chu-i*. The first principle related to nationalism identifying the term with people and race. To Sun Yat Sen, it meant the end of the rule of the alien race, the Manchus, and also the end of the semi-colonial conditions imposed on China by the Westerners. The second principle included the concepts of Western democracies, such as representative governments based on elections, initiative, referendum and the existence of the three branches of government (in the case of China it was five, including those of supervision and examination). The Min-Sheng-Chu-i meant people's livelihood denoting socialism, probably in response to the challenges posed by the evils of the industrial revolution in the west. In other words, socialism, should act as a shield to protect the interests of the poor, from the wealthier classes. Sun's brand of socialism was not Marxist in character but derived from the inspiration of writings of Henry George who advocated single tax theory. Sun Yat Sen advocated his plan of action in three stages—(1) three years of military government, (2) six years under provisional government and (3) constitutional government with elected representatives.

Sun's party received patronage from many revolutionary groups and affluent Chinese communities based in Honolulu and few other cities in the USA and Japan. He formed the Chinese United League (CUL) at Tokyo in 1905 which included many like-minded revolutionary groups. Branches of the CUL worked secretly in many provinces of China and also in San Francisco, Honolulu, Brussels and Singapore. The mouthpiece of the League was the *Minpao*, a journal published with a strong appeal to the students to establish a republic in China after the overthrow of the Manchu dynasty. The writers contributing for this journal included Sun Yat Sen, Wang Ching Wei and Hu-Han-Min. The revolutionary movements in China led by the followers of Sun Yat Sen suffered setbacks in 1907-8 in Kwangung, Kwangsi and Yunnan. In 1909, many revolutionaries suffered persecution and executions. Even the financial support from the overseas patrons stopped—all this happened due to the pressures exerted by the Manchu Government. Wang Ching Wei attempted to kill Prince Regent in Peking but failed, he was arrested and imprisoned.

In February 1910, the new imperial army revolted, but it was crushed. During the same year, there was a civilian revolt which was also suppressed. All these abortive attempts proved that there was no coordination among the various groups of revolutionaries and Huang Hsing concluded that only a charismatic person could spearhead the revolution successfully. The revolts made it clear to the Manchu dynasty that the mandate of heaven had ceased.

The railway protection movement in Szechwan province in 1911, forced the Manchu Emperor to seriously think of abdication. The students and soldiers joined hands with the members of the secret societies in Hopei, and the spark of the revolution was ignited by the newly created army in Wuchang on October 10, 1911. The local Governor General as well as the commanders of the army fled.

The foreign powers were afraid of facing the wrath of the Chinese at this critical juncture and remained neutral. The neutrality in a way helped the downfall of the Manchu dynasty. The anti-Manchu rebellions spread to many towns in southern parts of China and it evoked an enthusiastic response from the people in general. Some south-central and north-western provinces declared their independence. China was heading towards civil war since the northern regions remained under Central control whereas the southern provinces had declared their independence. The Manchu court invited Yuan Shi Kai (who had been dismissed from his post as commander-in-chief) in a last bid to retrieve its position. This cunning and unscrupulous officer accepted the offer of the

Manchu court to lead the army in order to save the Manchu dynasty from disaster. However, his acceptance was not without conditions.

In the meanwhile, the revolutionaries in the southern provinces seized control of more than two dozen centres, and elected Sun Yat Sen as provisional President of the Chinese Republic. Nanking became the headquarters of the new capital. Sun Yat Sen returned from the United States and assumed office as the President of the Republic on January 1, 1912. It must be remembered that the northern provinces had remained loyal to the Manchu court, and Yuan Shi Kai had taken the lead to contain the spread of the revolution in the south. Sun Yat Sen and the southern Republic started negotiations with Yuan Shi Kai so that the Manchu Emperor could be deposed and a republic permanently established. Sun Yat Sen was prepared to surrender his authority as President of the Provisional Republic to Yuan Shi Kai if he helped in the overthrow of the Manchu dynasty. Both of them desired to avert a civil war.

Yuan Shi Kai played his trump card with the Manchu court by promising pension to the last Emperor Pu Yi, if he abdicated. The last Chinese Emperor abdicated bowing to end the mandate of the heaven on February 12, 1912, thus bringing down the curtain on the last imperial dynasty in China. Yuan Shi Kai was not prepared to accept Nanking as the capital of the New Republic, as it was far away from the north. In the meantime, the Imperial Army had mutinied in Peking soon after his resumption of office as President of the New Republic on March 10, 1912. President Yuan Shi Kai promised the people of China an elected parliament and a constitutional government.

Yuan's Phantom Republic

Yuan Shi Kai had no desire to respect the popular will of the Chinese expressed through the elected representatives of Parliament. He had no respect even for the new constitution which was republican in character. In fact, he did not like any restraints on his authority. In other words, he wanted to remain a dictator. Some of his actions provoked the revolutionists. They were soon disappointed to know that he had been defying the mandate of the people. They found him to be extremely cunning and unscrupulous. Yuan's betrayal came much sooner than the people expected. During the next four years, China witnessed a struggle for power between Yuan Shi Kai who was employing all means at his command, i.e., military force, assassination, blackmail and corruption and the revolutionaries who desired a parliamentary form of government. Unfortunately, Yuan Shi Kai had been influencing the Western diplomats, and with their support he remained a dictator. However the revolutionary leaders were equally eager to bring about his downfall.

The election of 1913 ended in the victory of Kuomintang or Nationalist Party (an amalgamation of all the revolutionary groups led by Sun Yat Sen). This party obtained a majority of seats in the national Parliament and posed a great threat to the continuation of Yuan as President of the Republic. Yuan took steps to eliminate all the opposition leaders by employing force. The main opposition leader, Sung Chiao-jen, was assassinated. When the plot of his assassination came to light, revolt broke out in many parts of China. But the President crushed these revolts mercilessly by employing military force. The situation became so volatile that Sun Yat Sen with his followers fled to Japan. Yuan banned the opposition Kuomintang Party and replaced the Parliament in 1915 with a constitutional council consisting of handpicked members. This council introduced a new constitution providing for presidential government in the form of Yuan's dictatorship.

In the course of time, Yuan tried to follow the advice of his American mentor, Dr Frank Goodnow who had suggested that constitutional monarchy was best suited to the Chinese type of political situation. Therefore, a constitutional monarchy was set up in December 1915. In other words, Yuan became a constitutional monarch although many Western countries stoutly opposed this move. In the meantime, revolts had occurred in far-off provinces like Tibet and Mongolia. Yuan's political moves provoked violent protests everywhere in China. Then the situation went out of his control. Yuan abdicated his throne in March 1916. He died in June of the same year.

Separatist Movements

The national unity of China was in danger during the period of Yuan's regime because many separatist movements were spreading in the provinces. For e.g., the Tibetans rose in rebellion and declared their independence after expelling the Chinese troops. They concluded an agreement with the new Mongolian Government in 1930 to protect themselves from Chinese domination. Yuan's attempt to restore Chinese rule in Tibet succeeded only partially because he encountered British opposition. The British diplomacy worked out a solution so that China could control the eastern part of Tibet while the West remained autonomous (of course subject to Chinese sovereignty (China appointed a Resident at) Lhasa and kept a small contingent of forces.

During the Chinese Revolution of 1911, the Mongols grew restless, because the Chinese started migrating towards inner Mongolia. China desired to control this region but the Mongols would not tolerate this. This situation led to Russia supporting the Mongol rebellion. In 1911, the Mongols established an independent government at Urga, which was soon recognised by Russia. Eventually, Russia and China agreed on conferring a status of autonomy on Outer Mongolia, of course under Chinese suzerainty. In 1924, the Mongolians established an independent republic and came under Russian control. Inner Mongolia was divided into four provinces in 1912. Sinkiang, a Chinese dependency up to 1878, became the nineteenth province of China subsequently.

Dollar Diplomacy

The Dollar Diplomacy of the United States was on a high pitch when Yuan established his dictatorship in China. It was believed in Western circles that he alone had the capacity to hold all the parts of China together, and they decided to support him in this endeavour. Frank Goodnow's idea of reviving constitutional monarchy in the person of Yuan Shi Kai gave further credence to this conviction. A consortium of Western bankers, namely, British, French and German offered loans to China, and subsequently the United States Government also joined this group. Russia and Japan also did not lag behind. However, with the advent of President Wilson's administration, the United States withdrew her support to the consortium. In spite of this factor, the Western nations arrived at an agreement to offer a loan to China in April 1930.

The Era of Warlords

China witnessed a period of 'Warlordism', from 1916-28. This was a period of chaos in Chinese history. The warlordism in China was the outcome of the political set-up which was introduced by Yuan Shi Kai. He allowed military governors to share power with him in running the provincial governments as long as they remained loyal to him. After his death, these warlords challenged the Centre with local support and established independent governments.

Therefore, there was a conspicuous absence of central authority. The warlords set at nought the fruits of the 1911 revolution. China was receding from a constitutional government to an unparalleled situation of chaos with every warlord trying to expand his political base and support. These warlords were not interested in establishing a constitutional government. Many warlords were afraid of a functioning democracy because it would bring conflicting loyalties between the rulers and the ruled, and between the Centre and the provinces.

In the midst of this chaos, there were few exceptions. For example, the warlord and Governor of Shensei province, Yen Hsi-Shan, introduced some reforms in his administration, especially land reforms. He encouraged students to study science and technology and established good educational institutions. He desired the economic modernisation of his province. Unlike others, he supported the Kuomintang forces in 1927, which were winning battles against the other warlords. For rendering great service to the country, the Kuomintang Government (which came to power in 1927) appointed him as a minister.

Social Change

During the period of warlordism, Chinese society experienced a gradual social transformation. The urban centres in China attracted the educated and converted Christians. There was a migration of population from the villages to the cities many villagers became wage-earners in industrial cities. Their new status promoted a kind of individuality. The Confucian values of family life gradually got eroded. The joint family system in China began to decline. Unfortunately, the period of Warlordism beset the country with numerous problems, which resulted in the lowering of the quality of life in China. Warlords engendered problems such as landlessness, growth of multiplicity of tenancies, banditry, coolie labour and so on. In urban centres, scholars and philosophers yearned for the coming of a new era which would usher in democracy on constitutional government. They welcomed "Western values, such as materialism, and pragmatism". Among the scholars, Li Ta Chao and Chen founded Marxist study groups to attract the young minds.

After the death of Yuan Shi Kai, Sun Yat Sen made an abortive attempt to establish a parallel government in China with its headquarters at Canton. His efforts succeeded to some extent because of the support rendered by the warlords controlling the provinces of Yuan and Kwangsi. However, the other warlords proved to be extremely selfish and ambitious and therefore did not see eye to eye with his democratic idealism. Therefore, he was forced to leave Canton in 1920. However, his chief supporter, Chen Chiun-Ming continued his struggle to establish a democratic government at Canton. Sun Yat Sen discovered that the Western nations always focused their attention on the warlords who successively controlled Peking. They began to recognise only the government of the warlord who controlled Peking as the legitimate government of China. Naturally, Sun Yat Sen was very disappointed at this attitude. Unfortunately, he was not given any support by the Western nations in establishing a democratic and republican government in China. Under these circumstances, he sought the support of the Soviet Union.

The May Fourth Movement (1919)

Hu Shih, a Chinese student of philosophy (returning from the US) tried to replace the then existing Chinese language (based on Confucian tradition), with the new literary language. He was assisted in his effort by another student, Chen Tu Hsiu, studying at the Peking University. Thus China witnessed a literary renaissance with the patronage of the Western educated students. Newspapers and journals started publishing articles in the reformed language written by the Western educated scholars.

In the aftermath of this literary movement, Peking witnessed the return of the Chinese delegates from the Versailles Conference (1919) without getting any assurance from the peacemakers about Japan vacating the occupied provinces. Amidst the upsurge of national feelings, thousands of Chinese students protested against the weakness of the government on 4 May. But the Peking Government crushed this organised student protest. Hundreds of students were arrested and jailed. Merchants closed their shops and workers went on strike supporting this students' movement.

The May Fourth Movement was an intellectual movement of considerable significance in modern Chinese history. During the dark period of warlordism, this movement became a beacon of hope. Sun Yat Sen took advantage of the disgruntled educated middle class to build his political party and tried to shape the future destiny of China.

The Support of the Soviet Union

When Lenin came to power in Russia after the Revolution, he made a unilateral declaration that the USSR on its own, was giving up all its extraterritorial rights and privileges in China. This was quite in contrast to the earlier policies followed by Russia. However, this was in consistence with his policy of correcting the wrongs of the Western imperialists. Sun Yat Sen was overwhelmed at this friendly gesture and looked forward to increasing cooperation from the new Soviet Government under the leadership of Lenin. Unfortunately, Sun Yat Sen died in 1925 without realising this dream. In fact, he accepted the offer of friendship of the Soviet Government before his death.

The Soviet Government sent its emissary, Joffe, to Canton and Peking for the purpose of providing aid to the Nationalist Party and the Nationalist Government. It must be mentioned here that the so-called Peking Government under a warlord had lost its credibility due to internal rivalries. When Sun Yat Sen was alive, he sent Chiang Kai Shek, his closest colleague, to Moscow for training in the art of reorganising the Kuomintang Party and the Kuomintang army. In the meantime, the Soviet Union sent Michael Borodin as its adviser to the Canton Government for the purpose of reviving the Nationalist Party with the inclusion of a number of Chinese communists. Chiang played a very important role as the President of the Whampoa military academy after returning from Russia.

The Soviet Union asked all the communists in China to join the Kuomintang Party (Nationalist Party) so as to put a united front to challenge the regime of warlords in China. With the passing away of Sun Yat Sen, there was a deep void in the Kuomintang Party. Cracks began to appear in the party because of the rift between the rightists and the leftists (communists). This rift resulted in the expulsion of some rightists. At the same time more communists began to replace them. The Kuomintang Party decided that it should wage a war against the warlords and establish a nationalist government. It was also decided that the party should undertake a "northern expedition" to defeat the warlords and unite the country. The responsibility of carrying out this important task fell on the shoulders of Chiang Kai Shek, President of the Whampao Military Academy. The plan for carrying out the expedition was prepared by the Russian military adviser, General Blucher.

Chiang Kai Shek

The rift between the rightists and the leftists continued. Chiang was a rightist and he began to hate the communists who had joined the Kuomintang Party in large numbers. He discovered that the communist members were working against his interests. Therefore, the task that was entrusted to him was beset with a large number of difficulties. However, Chiang succeeded in securing the support of the Chinese merchants, and the members of the breakaway group who had earlier opposed the entry of communists into the Kuomintang Party. Chiang also secured the support of the moderates of the Hankow Government, and the non-communist leaders of the left wing, especially Wang Ching-Wei. It was no easy task for Chiang to carry on his fight against the communist members who were dominating the Kuomintang Party. He also did not like the interference of the Soviet Union. In the course of time, Chiang was successful in making Nanking the seat of his capital. The communists had theirs at Hankow. By 1927, Chiang's fortune changed for the better with the assistance of Christian General Feng-Yu-Hsiang.

During the period 1928-31, Chiang successfully overcame the resistance of many warlords who had challenged him earlier. In 1928, Chang Tso Lin, the leader of the Peking Government, withdrew to Manchuria on the advance of Chiang's forces. He later died in a train accident. By 1931, the Japanese delivered a serious blow to Manchuria which was a part of China. The Japanese invasion of Manchuria led to the unity of all the nationalist forces in China and the cessation of the rivalry of the warlords. Chiang became a great leader of China at that time.

Chiang and His Nationalist Government

Born at Chikow (Cheking province) on October 31, 1887, Chiang was the son of a poor peasant. He lost his father when he was nine, and came under the control of his mother. As a boy, he grew sensitive to his country's troubles and tribulations. He realised the deep humiliation his country had suffered due to the vagaries of Western imperial powers. The Boxer Rebellion and its aftermath deeply influenced Chiang. He realised that without superior arms and technology, China had no chance of containing the influence of the imperial West. With his mother's encouragement, he became a soldier and hoped to liberate his country from the clutches of Western nationals.

After the initial military training, he left for Japan in 1906 to pursue further military studies. Unfortunately, he could not gain admission there. It was in Japan that he met Chen Chi-Mai, a Chinese revolutionary, who influenced his future career. Chiang returned to China and joined the Paoting military academy, where he distinguished himself as the best cadet. He went to Tokyo for advanced military studies. He joined the Tung Meng Hai which was founded by Sun Yat Sen. Chiang became a follower of Sun Yat Sen. The latter regarded Chiang as his disciple. Together, they worked to end the regime of warlords and establish the democratic republic in China.

Relations with Foreign Powers

While the Soviet Union showed her sympathy and support for the establishment of a nationalist government by giving up her extraterritorial rights and privileges in China, the other Western powers remained unaffected. However, these powers which refused to recognise the regime of the Kuomintang Party when Sun Yat Sen was alive, were forced to do so by logic of circumstances. The mass upsurge in 1926-27 characterised by industrial strike in Wuhan, and the anti-British demonstration had their impact. Anticipating further violence, the British gave up their concessions in Hankow, and the Kiuking agreements were signed.

Negotiations for New Treaties

After ousting the old regime at Peking, the Kuomintang Nationalist Government called upon all foreign powers to negotiate new treaties replacing the old, which would be in consistence with the maintenance of the territorial integrity and sovereignty of China. This notice given to Western powers was an indication of the new mood of defiance on the part of the Nationalist Government. In other words, Chiang's Government desired to put an end to the unequal treaties imposed upon China in the nineteenth century. Chiang had expelled the Soviet communists and broken off diplomatic relations with the Soviet Union. The year 1928 witnessed new agreements between China and the foreign powers. The only exception was Japan. The United States was the first power to concede tariff autonomy under the broad-based and most favoured nation treatment. Thus, Chiang succeeded in ending the unequal treaties and thereby restoring China's territorial integrity and sovereignty. Many of the warlords were defeated and expelled from their regions with the advance of the Nationalist army.

Consolidation of the Nationalist Government

Let us examine how the military and political authority of the Nationalist Government was established in China. Britain was the first nation to appreciate China's grievance and therefore, granted tariff autonomy, but subjected it to a few conditions. The most important condition was that China should introduce an effective tariff law and as this was being done, there occurred the tragedy of March 1927 wherein, some rebellious Chinese soldiers belonging to the Nationalist army attacked foreign residences, killed foreigners, and looted their properties at Nanking. This incident caused a serious setback to the efforts that Chiang's Government had made to introduce a new tariff law. Chiang Kai Shek owned responsibility for this outrage and promptly agreed to pay compensation, and offer an apology to the concerned foreign powers. Thereupon, the United States Government signed a treaty in July 1928, which granted customs autonomy. Britain, Belgium, Italy, Germany and France all signed similar treaties. China became free from foreign control in 1929. However, the issue of extra-territorial rights continued. The Nationalist Government, encouraged by Russia and Germany, requested other powers to concede to this demand. It must be noted that foreign powers, enjoying extra-territorial rights in China, exercised their authority over the local Chinese citizens. They finally agreed to accept this demand on condition that China modernise her political and judicial systems by introducing the necessary reforms. China agreed to do this, despite the delay in implementing the desired reforms.

In 1931, the Kuomintang Nationalist Government hastened the process of doing away with the privileges enjoyed by the foreign powers. For e.g., China began to assert her authority over the Shanghai Municipal Council and the mixed courts, which were exclusively manned by foreign powers. Foreign nationals in Nanking were placed under Chinese jurisdiction, and new courts of law were created in Nanking to give effect to this. The Chinese Government also established its control over the maritime customs administration, the salt revenue administration, and the post offices. The government was successful in its efforts to reduce the number of foreign concession areas from thirty-three to thirteen. The Kuomintang Nationalist Government was undoubtedly on its way towards achieving full independence from foreign control, but the Japanese attack of Manchuria came as a bolt from the blue.

Chinese Economy Under the Nationalist Government

China, under Chiang's control, followed the growth model of totalitarian regimes such as Nazi Germany, Japan and the Soviet Union. Unfortunately, the government hardly controlled its finances on the pattern of democratic countries so as to bring about rapid economic development. Nearly thirty foreign banks began to function at the treaty ports—the most important being Hong Kong and Shanghai Banking Corporations. Besides these two major banking corporations, there were other minor Chinese banks, which functioned in order to offer credit facilities to the people. T V Soong, the Finance Minister, tried to bring about "fiscal revolution", i.e., recovery of tariff autonomy and increase in the customs revenue. In addition to the above, the government suppressed likin taxes and abolished the tael system. The government exercised greater control over the credit system in the country, and in 1935 introduced monetary reforms. China introduced the paper currency, to link its monetary system with foreign monetary systems, and also to establish a sound banking system along modern lines.

In 1937, the Agricultural Credit Corporation offered short term credits to the farming population. To some extent, this measure enabled small peasants to obtain loans easily and be free from the clutches of the moneylenders. Unfortunately, many programmes which were on the anvil could not be carried out by the Nationalist Government due to its inefficiency and corruption. The Chiang period witnessed ever-increasing influence of the Americans in the educational and cultural life of China.

Chiang and the Communists

Although Chiang had achieved the unification of China after defeating the warlords and liberated her from the shackles of unequal treaties, which the Western powers had imposed, he was unable to grapple with various domestic problems. He could also not counter the threat posed by Japan. The most crucial problem faced by the government was dealing with the communists. Two years after the death of Sun Yat Sen, the communists, who were in a minority in the Kuomintang Party, found an opportunity to strengthen their position. It must be remembered that the Chinese Communist Party exploited every opportunity when China launched anti-imperialist movements by means of student's strikes and demonstrations. The British trade in Hong Kong came to a standstill in 1925 because of student demonstrations. A large number of youths who joined the Youth Corps in cities were supported by the Chinese Communist Party (CCP). The CCP began to initiate labour movements in the cities and also organise peasant movements in rural areas. In the meantime, the year 1927 witnessed the two wings of the Kuomintang Party—the left and the right—coming together. This resulted in the isolation of the communists. These communists developed great faith in the class struggle and social revolution. The rejuvenated Kuomintang supported anti-communist elements and brought about the expulsion of communists in July 1927. In the course of time, the communists treated Chiang's Government as the primary enemy because the latter launched a series of persecutions. Chiang became the undisputed leader of a strong and united China by July 1927.

7

THE RISE OF COMMUNIST CHINA

When there was no correct guidance from Moscow, the Chinese Communist Party (CCP) was left on its own. The persecution and execution of thousands of communists by the Nationalist Government in China seriously affected the very existence of the Chinese Communist Party. During this critical moment, one member rose to meet the challenge. He was Mao Tse-tung. He displayed commendable qualities of leadership. He organised revolts within the Nationalist army on the one hand, and mobilised peasants against the government on the other (August-September 1927). Unfortunately, both these attempts failed, resulting in the execution of all the rebels. Even at this critical juncture in his career, Mao did not lose hope and courage in spite of having lost many young leaders.

It was during this time that Madam Sun Yat Sen gave a shot in the arm to the communist cause by criticising Chiang's Government for getting support from the capitalist class consisting of merchants, traders, landlords, bankers and warlords. She also criticised Chiang's Government for not improving the lot of the masses.

The persecution as well as execution of the communists compelled Mao and his followers to take refuge in the mountainous Ching-Kang-Shan region which eventually became his rebel base. From the time Mao submitted a report in 1927 on the peasant-movement, he was of the opinion that the poor Chinese peasants, and not the proletariat, could effectively act as vanguards for achieving the communist revolution. He proclaimed the emergence of the Chinese Soviet Republic at Juichin in the Kiangsi province in November 1931. He hoped to further consolidate and expand his revolutionary base so as to pose a serious threat to the Nationalist Government. In order to establish a Soviet Republic in China and train the Red Guards to carry out this task, he needed a trustworthy military commander. He found Chu Teh suited for this purpose. Both Mao and Chu Teh began to secretly organise and lead the peasants revolt against the Nationalist Government. The peasants of the Kiangsi region provided the necessary force to Mao and Chu Teh to carry out the great struggle. The Red Army led by them became a serious threat to Chiang's Nationalist China.

Mao and Chu Teh declared their personal and ideological differences from the Moscow-led Chinese Communist Central Committee. They desired to carry on the struggle without any guidance from Moscow. The poor peasants of the China region came under the strong influence of Mao, and volunteered to join the Red Army. Furthermore, they provided necessary material support, and arranged secret hideouts for the communist guerillas when the enemy approached. More importantly, the peasants gathered necessary information about the enemy movements and conveyed the same to Mao's Red Army. The Red Army became the main bastion for peasant protection from the exploitation of the ruthless landlords and moneylenders. Land holdings of the big landlords were confiscated by the Red Army and redistributed among the poor peasants.

The Red Army conquered extensive territories in the Kiangsi province and the surroundings of Hupeh, and foiled the attempts of the Nationalist Army to conquer this region. In addition, the Secretary General of the Communist Party, namely Li Lisan, ordered the Red Army to attack the cities where the Nationalist forces had strongly entrenched themselves. Mao, who had differences with Li Lisan, compelled the Communist Party's central committee to shift its headquarters from Shanghai to the Kiangsi region which was controlled by him. It may be said that about this time (1932) power shifted from the Moscow-inspired Central Committee to Mao himself.

Life-sketch of Mao

Mao was born in a village called Shao-Shan in Hsiang-Tan district of Hunan province on December 26, 1893. He was born in a poor peasant family and his father was in the grain business. Mao's schooling began when he was eight years old. At the age of thirteen, he joined his father's business. He had an academic bent of mind. He started reading a large number of novels and political works. The book which stimulated his interest in knowing about the conditions of China was Cheng Kuan-Ying's *Words of Warning to an Affluent Age*. He was compelled to leave his home at the age of fifteen because of his scholastic interest. He joined a new school at Hsiang-Hsiang where he received Western education. In the course of time, he grew fond of the writings of the Chinese reformers like Kang Ku Wei and Liang Chi-Chao. Mao's favourite personalities in history included General Washington, Napoleon, Peter the Great, Abraham Lincoln and Chinese emperors Shi Want Ti and Wu Ti.

He developed a dislike for his fellow students because they did not like his rustic manners and dress. These students belonged to the rich landlord families and suffered from a superiority complex. He got admission in Tungshan school at Changsha where he made in-depth studies on politics and economics. It was in Changsha that he came to know of the political developments in China after reading the newspapers. Subsequently, he joined the revolution started by Sun

Yat Sen's *Tung Meng Hui*. Mao became a great scholar and "developed new ideas and techniques". He was a pragmatist and tried to apply his new ideas and techniques to the changing political situation. He met Li Lisan who eventually became the Secretary General of the Chinese Communist Party. However, Li Lisan did not make any deep impression on him. Mao married the daughter of his professor Yang Chang-Chi. This professor later joined Peking University. Mao got a job in the library of Peking University. He organised a union of Hunan's students in June 1919 and gave a call for a strike to protest against the handing over of the Shantung Peninsula to Japan following the Versailles settlement. Mao joined the Marxist study group founded by Li Ta-Chao in 1919. Subsequently, he started a branch of the Young Corps in Changsha. Eventually, Mao became one of the founders of the Chinese Communist Party which held its first session in Shanghai in July 1921.

Nationalist Army Fails to Conquer Rebel Bases

The Nationalist army made several attempts to destroy the communist bases in Kiangsi. The early attempts took place in 1932 and the rest in 1933, but all of them failed, thanks to the Red Army adopting the tactics of guerilla warfare under Mao's dynamic leadership. It must be remembered that Mao wrote profusely on guerilla warfare after gaining considerable experience prior to and after the famous Long March.

The Long March (1934-35)

In 1933, Chiang Kai Shek launched a large-scale attack on the Kiangsi region in general and the Soviet Republic at Jui Chin in particular to compel the Red Army to surrender. The Nationalist army under the command of Chiang scored spectacular victories against the communists and forced 100,000 communists to flee or surrender. Thousands of them were executed after being taken captive. It appeared that communism would be wiped out in China. At this critical juncture, Mao rose to the occasion. His great leadership was put to severe test. Leading his followers, Mao began the historic "Long March" (October 1934 to October 1935) to break the circle of the Kuomintang army by swift night movements. He was quite successful in delivering heavy blows on the enemy by adopting guerilla warfare. It took almost a year for his followers to cover a distance of 6,000 miles. They followed a circuitous route, and fought continuous battles, to reach the northern province of Shensi. A few divisions consisting of 20,000 communist troops finally reached the destination after passing through "sun dried dusty region of loess soil." Yenan became the headquarters of the communists in 1936. Mao's leadership remained unchallenged and Moscow's guidance became unnecessary. Relations with Moscow came under severe strain.

The Work of the Communists During the Yenan Period

During the Yenan period (1936-45), Mao forced the Moscow-oriented Chinese communists to accept his leadership. He discarded the Stalinist theory of bringing about a communist revolution backed by the proletariat (urban workers) and favoured rural-based peasant movements. During the next decade, Mao's followers chalked out programmes for seeking peasant support to bring about a communist revolution. Free from the threats of the Kuomintang army, Mao's followers inaugurated many programmes for rural uplift. The reforms included reduction of rents payable by tenants to the landlords (instead of confiscation of lands) and introducing universal franchise for electing representatives to the local councils on the basis of two-thirds majority system. The people in general voted the communists to power. As for economic plans, the Communist Party laid emphasis on the increase in food production, land reclamation, labour exchange among farmers, and running of small-scale industrial cooperatives. The Red Army guards helped farmers to grow more food. Mao conducted political training camps for the farmers to impart ideological orientation, i.e., converting the free-thinking farmers into communists. He prepared the rural people to fight the Japanese aggressors by taking the assistance of the Red Army. The strength of the Chinese Communist Party rose from 40,000 members to 12,00,000 within eight years (1937-45). On July 7, 1937 there occurred an incident near the Marco Polo bridge, which culminated in the Japanese invasion of northern China. This and other factors forced Chiang Kai Shek to seek the cooperation of the Chinese communists.

Japanese Invasion of Manchuria

Chiang Kai Shek was under pressure to seek communist cooperation when the Japanese invaded Manchuria (1931). Chiang's Nationalist Government felt despondent and helpless. It appealed to the League of Nations to do the needful. Unfortunately, the League was not strong enough to check the Japanese aggression. When the League's Council accused Japan of being the aggressor, the Japanese delegate expressed his defiance by walking out. Being helpless, Chiang followed a policy of appeasement—that is "neither obstructing Japanese completely nor conceding all they asked". The Nationalist Government under Chiang planned to destroy the communists at home first before repulsing the aggression of the Japanese.

In this predicament, the Kuomintang Party was unable to evolve a positive response to the Japanese threat. In fact, the party itself was facing dissension within its own rank and file. There was one section in the party which demanded that the Japanese aggression should be checked under any circumstances. They attacked Chiang's policy of appeasement towards the Japanese aggressors. When Chiang was on a visit to Sian he was kidnapped and taken captive by the commander-in-chief, Chang Hsuesh Liang. Chang objected to Chiang's policy of fighting the communists at home when the Japanese were occupying Chinese territories. He advocated the importance of putting up a joint front consisting of communist and nationalist forces to meet the threat of the aggressor. Chiang was released from his captivity only when he agreed to take the help of the communists to face the Japanese menace.

United Front against Japan

The communists also expressed their eagerness to join the proposed United Front and agreed on September 22, 1937 to work with the Nationalist Party. In a resolution the communists agreed to implement the three principles of Sun Yat Sen, stop their enmity towards the Kuomintang Government, and cease their propaganda war. They agreed to place the Red Army at the disposal of the Nationalist Government, disband the Chinese Soviet Republics, stop confiscation of lands from the landlords and so on. The Nationalist Government accepted all these terms and reached what is described as an "uneasy arms truce" with the communists. This was no genuine political settlement for the simple reason that both the parties viewed each other with mistrust.

The Course of the Sino-Japanese War

Under Japanese pressure, the army of the Nationalist Government had to flee from its strong base in the east. It shifted its headquarters to the west where it had no roots. It was in these circumstances that the communists gained considerable advantages because the west and the north-west had come under their influence. They had established strong bases in this region from where they could launch repeated attacks to dislodge the Japanese forces. They were quite successful in this mission. They established what is called "liberated areas".

The Nationalist army could boast of no such achievement in spite of its best efforts. This situation proved that the communists had gained several advantages in rural areas with popular support. In fact, the communists were quite justified in taking credit for liberating the country from Japanese occupation. The Japanese were unable to make any headway with their conquest in north-western China, particularly in the Shensi region, since their attacks were blunted by the communists who adopted guerilla warfare.

In December 1931, the Japanese captured Nanking and the local Chinese population was butchered. The Japanese opened two more fronts in their war against China, namely the central and the southern. While they gained initial advantages, they suffered a series of setbacks due to stiff Chinese resistance during the period 1938-41. The Nationalist Government, which had gone on the defensive, as mentioned earlier, shifted its headquarters to the west by making Chungking, the seat of their capital. Japan's conquest included the Yangtze Valley in the south, and Peiping and Chahar regions in the north.

Having failed to conquer the rest of China, and not having made progress in peace and diplomatic initiatives, the Japanese resorted to establishing puppet regimes as a propaganda ploy. For e.g., they established the State of Manchukuo in Manchuria, and crowned the last Manchu emperor, Pu Yi, to be its king. In the central part of China, Japan installed another puppet government with Nanking as its capital.

When Canton and Hangkow fell into the hands of the Japanese in 1938, the Japanese Prime Minister, Konoe, declared the establishment of the New Order in East Asia and offered its leadership to Chiang Kai Shek. But, this was to be under Japanese control and supervision. When there was no response, the Japanese tried to placate Chiang's rival, Wang Ching-Wei (a close associate of Sun Yat Sen) by offering the leadership of the reorganised Nationalists Government with Nanking as the capital. The purpose of the new order in East Asia was to ensure Japan's domination over China. Japan decided to establish her business monopoly and prevent foreign assistance from reaching China. Japan used her propaganda machine to tell the Chinese people that she was the one who liberated her from Western domination.

Rivalry Between CCP and the Nationalist Government

Deeply jealous of the growing success of the Communist Party, the Nationalist Government prevented the movements of the members of the Chinese Communist Party in its north-western base. The Nationalist Government made an attempt to organise and control the areas, which were not under Japanese occupation through its new administrative machinery. But it did not evoke any positive response from the people. However, this was not so in "liberated areas" which came under communist control. Chiang tried to evoke popular sympathy for his Government by publishing a book, *China's Destiny*, in which he expressed his new ideas. However, the book did not evoke any positive reaction from the people since Chiang's government was incompetent to change the volatile political situation in China. Moreover, Chiang's failure may be attributed to the inefficiency of the Government manned by corrupt officials. It was quite disappointing to note that Chiang's reforms did not ameliorate the conditions of the poor people in China because of corrupt administration. In fact, these reforms were calculated to buttress his authority.

Mao's Objectives

The situation was in total contrast to Mao's practical approach to China's problems, particularly on the issue of rural poverty. The CCP organised and controlled peasant associations under its leadership. It encouraged self-sufficiency in food production by letting its soldiers work with the farmers in all the areas under its control. The CCP founded many small-scale industrial cooperatives for the purpose of employing the rural poor. One of Mao's many goals was to keep the members of the CCP highly disciplined and motivated. They underwent training with the necessary ideological orientation. Mao attempted to raise a million-man army probably to match the strength of the army under the Nationalist Government. He also proposed to drive out the Japanese aggressors by using this new force. The common peasants who joined his party were called "rural proletarians". Indeed, Mao may be credited with having created "a party, an army, and mass support in rural territorial base". Mao used the Chinese Communist Party (CCP) to accomplish many of his projected tasks during the period of "united front" directed against Japan. For Mao, the period of the United Front was to act as a transition towards achieving the long-term goals of the CCP.

The Kuomintang-CCP rivalry entered a new phase when Japan conquered the Hainan island. The strategies evolved by both for defeating Japan differed. The CCP believed in launching guerilla warfare as its main strategy to drive out the aggressors, whereas the Nationalist Government evolved a different strategy. Therefore, these two rivals could not see eye to eye about defeating the enemy although they kept up the pretence of being united. The incidents which occurred in 1941 and also at Anwei made cooperation between the two impossible. Some political moves were initiated to bring about settlement between the two but these moves failed. There were suggestions that the two parties should form a coalition government but Chiang was not ready to accept this. He was afraid of provoking the right wing elements of his party.

Renewed efforts were made by the United States Government through the mediation of US Ambassador George C Marshall after the Second World War for the establishment of a coalition government (Nationalists and Communists) in China. But this effort also failed. Civil war became inevitable in China after the Japanese surrendered to the Allied forces in 1945 bringing the Second World War to an end. Russia accepted Japan's surrender of Manchuria, and it was taken over by the Nationalists Government. Large quantities of Japanese arms and equipment fell into the hands of the CCP.

The Civil War (1946-49)

The Chinese Civil War from 1946-49 was one of the big struggles of modern times" (Fairbank et al, *East Asia Tradition and Transformation*). Throwing away all the pretence of unity against the common enemy, the Nationalist and communist forces scrambled to gain control over the erstwhile Japanese-occupied areas. Mao's ideological reform movement called *Cheng feng* enabled the CCP to attain a vantage position in spite of its inferiority compared to the strength of the Nationalist force. The Nationalist Government undoubtedly enjoyed superior military advantage i.e., three million men carrying American arms and equipment compared to a million men under the command of the CCP. Unfortunately, it had lost its revolutionary fervour or popular appeal due to "widespread corruption, spiralling inflation, and deteriorating morale among the military" (Clyde and Beers, *The Far East*).

On the other hand, the peasants stood solidly behind the CCP in its military manoeuvres such as cutting the rail and road communications in the country and so on which left the army of the Nationalist Government isolated and surrounded. In the course of time, the army under the CCP grew in size and power, and Mao (who incidentally wrote a book on guerila warfare after his "Long March") recommended guerila tactics to attain political and military objectives. The army of the Nationalist Government suffered a series of defeats at the hands of the communists and left behind large quantities of arms and equipment. The CCP mounted several offensives with great vigour and confidence.

Many small battles were fought which spread over thousands of square miles. The Nationalist Government ultimately lost Manchuria to the communists. It could not get adequate support from the US. It was forced to surrender northern China including Peking to the communists. Furthermore, the communists launched fresh offensives against the Nationalist army in the central and eastern Chinese regions which yielded positive results. Even in urban centres, the Nationalist army was unable to make any headway. The people lost sympathy for the government. This led to inflation and widespread corruption.

Chiang's Nationalist Government became highly demoralised. US assistance was of no use to him because it came too late. It was in these circumstances (1949) that Peking fell into the hands of the communists. Subsequently, the other cities like Tientsin, Nanking, Shanghai, Canton and Chunking were also taken over by the communists. Chiang's army lost its morale and began to retreat from various places. In these circumstances Chiang was left with no alternative but to negotiate. Subsequently, he resigned his Presidency and made good his escape with his forces to Taiwan (Formosa) in March 1950. In the meantime, the CCP declared the establishment of the People's Republic of China at Peking on 1 October 1949.

Causes of Communist Victory

A thorough examination of the causes which led to the victory of the communists in the Civil War would reveal many failures of the US-supported Chiang Government. While his Government continued to survive with the support of the urban middle class in China, he could not secure substantial support from the rural areas. The Nationalist Government under Chiang was more interested in pleasing the urban middle class than implementing a concrete programme of action to alleviate the sufferings of the rural masses. There were hardly any reforms introduced to improve their conditions.

Millions of peasants, who had suffered untold misery due to droughts and misrule, had no sympathy for Chiang's Government. The economic depression of 1929 aggravated their conditions further. The government lost its main base of support when the rank and file of the rural areas joined the communists. Furthermore, the administration of the Kuomintang was beset with corruption.

Thirdly, the Japanese invasion of Manchuria laid bare the utter incompetence and inefficiency of the government. To add insult to injury, Chiang was unwilling to seek the support of the communists in dealing with the Japanese menace. It became apparent that the communists proved more patriotic than the Nationalist Party in view of their offer of support in most adverse circumstances. Chiang Kai Shek had to pay a heavy price for many of his follies.

On the communist side, Mao proved to be a great and charismatic leader of the masses. His great leadership and popularity prevailed even after the "Long March". He symbolised the advent of New China, able and self-confident, to meet many challenges in the future. By sheer faith, ideology and will power, and with massive support from rural areas, Mao was able to dislodge Chiang's Government in China. Compelled by circumstances, the Kuomintang army under Chiang had to flee the country.

8

COMMUNIST CHINA

The triumph of communism as an ideology despite its conflict with brute force was nowhere more manifest than in the victory of Mao Tse-tung in 1949. On October 1, 1949, Mao proclaimed from the Tiananmen tower (the Gateway of Heavenly Peace) in Peking (now called Beijing) the birth of the People's Republic of China. In a colourful ceremony attended by six hundred delegates on October 10, 1949, the People's Republic began to function with Mao Tse-tung as the elected Chairman. A plan on how the new government would function was drawn up in September 1949 by the Chinese People's Political Conference in Peking. It drafted three important constitutional documents. The first one related to the common programme of general principles, the second to the organisation law of the Central People's Government, and the third referred to the organisation law of the Chinese People's Consultative Conference. The first created an interim constitution, the second established a provisional government and the third gave legal credibility to the new civilian set-up to replace military dominance.

Details of Administrative Set-up

The highest policy making body in the People's Republic was the Central People's Government Council. It established the highest executive organisation called the State Administrative Council (SAC). The next organisation to be established was the Revolutionary Military Council. In addition, the said council established the highest judicial organisation called the Supreme People's Court, and also the People's Procurator General (supervisory body). The State Administrative Council acted as a Cabinet Government. It was composed of twenty members headed by Chou En-lai, a close colleague of Mao Tse-tung. In other words, Chou became the Premier with four Vice-Premiers assisting him in carrying out many of his minor duties.

The other members of the SAC included the Secretary General who controlled several government departments through specific committees appointed for the purpose. All the local governments right from the village to the city level were linked to the Central People's Government through the SAC. The Communist Party workers were appointed to key posts. It must be remembered that the People's Republic of China was a democratic coalition government with the members of few other political parties joining them (after the fall of the Kuomintang Government under Chiang). These political parties included the National Salvation Association, National Democratic Reconstruction, and China Chih Kung Tang. However, this coalition government was undoubtedly dominated by the communists and sought to eliminate the reactionary classes in China. The Chinese Government under Mao attracted a large number of liberal intellectuals into its fold who had given up their hopes on the survival of the Nationalist Government earlier. The communists set up "a tripod of power-party, government, and army, each forming a separate echelon but tied together by the communist leadership." (Fairbank, et al)

The strength of the Communist Party grew enormously from 1947 to 1961 (from 2.7 to 17 million members) with the Central Committee assuming great importance. However, the power was exercised by its political bureau consisting of nineteen members—seven out of them being most powerful. The party structure consisted of eight layers descending from six regional bureaus to branch committees functioning in villages, factories, schools and the army.

Similar to the party structure, was that of the government. Members of these two wings were transferred frequently from one wing to the other. The People's Representative Congress (PRC) emerged right from the villages to the top level national organisation at Peking. The National People's Congress assembled for the first time in 1954. It provided a platform for the representatives to voice the grievances of their constituencies but exercised little power.

The New Constitution (1954)

After the new Constitution came into force, in 1954, the structure of the government was reorganised with the Premier (Chou En-lai) enjoying unlimited powers and heading a state council composed of sixteen Vice-Premiers and heads of seventy ministries. An office of the State Council and the Party Central Committee supervised the work of the major departments of the government. The Communist Party evolved the policy framework and the government carried it out. It is to be repeated that the party members occupied all the key posts in the administration, and hence there was no delay in implementing the party policies at all levels.

Party Propaganda

Public organisations and associations which played an important role before the outbreak of the communist revolution also supported the policies and programmes of the CCP. These organisations and associations included the trade unions, the Democratic Youth, the Democratic Women, peasant cooperatives and student's associations. Party workers played an important role in arranging the training programmes for these organisations. They motivated the members of all these organisations and associations to toe the party line. Mao's speeches and writings moulded the thinking of the members of these associations. The party propaganda machine was vigorously mobilised by the party workers to achieve the objectives of many of their plans and schemes. In fact, public organisations and associations tried to bridge the gap between the public at large and the officialdom.

Communist Indoctrination

The People's Revolutionary Army which was well paid supported the changes sought by the leaders of the CCP. The People's courts also contributed substantially towards helping the party workers to carry out their work of bringing all the dissidents to trial. The dissidents were accused of anti-national activities in the people's courts and punished severely. Unfortunately, they did not get the benefit of a fair trial. At every level free thinking in China was stifled through the instruments of 'indoctrination' and 'social pressure'. Social pressure was mounted against the dissidents and anti-national elements through a well-organised propaganda machine.

Elimination of Feudal Elements

Mao not only believed in peasant-supported political revolution as witnessed in 1949 but also in the economic transformation of the nation supplemented through ideological campaign. Peasants were mobilised by the government to start pogroms against landlords. His strategy resulted in the massacre of tens of thousands of landlords in China during the period 1951-53. Mao eliminated feudal lords, capitalists and imperialist elements in many other ways. He applied the Marxist-Leninist doctrines. With his own technique he tried to eliminate class struggle. He desired to build a strong and socialist China.

Economic Reconstruction

The Civil War wrought great havoc on the Chinese economy so much so that it required a Herculean effort to restore it to the pre-war level. The economy had to be reorganised on a new model to achieve the goals of communism. The main drawback of the Chinese economy was the lack of modern industrialisation. Except for those industries that had been left behind by the Japanese after the conclusion of the Second World War, the rest were small and local. Therefore, Mao declared that China should follow the Soviet example of building modern industries, with an emphasis on heavy industry. Therefore a "shift to the cities" became necessary.

Industrial Progress

Mao's China needed not only substantial capital outlay but also technical assistance in order to bring about the material transformation of China. In 1950, China and the Soviet Union concluded some agreements of economic assistance which provided three hundred million dollars loan, bilateral trade, and technical assistance. Tens of thousands of Soviet technical experts came to China for helping her in the task of building modern industries. It is estimated that the financial assistance provided by the Soviet Union reached around two billion dollars for the economic development of China by 1956, and an extra one billion dollars for modernising the Chinese defence. Mao selected only those projects which he considered essential for building the economy with the available resources in China. The First Five Year Plan was inaugurated in 1953.

Infrastructure Development

A network of railroads was built and expanded (from 10,000 to 15,000 miles); and highways extended to a length of 75,000 miles by 1952. The banking system in the country was centralised, and a uniform currency was introduced. Private enterprises were allowed to function but subjected to gradual State control. The State extended its control over many sectors of the economy which included import-export trade, commerce and banking, heavy industries and railways. To a large extent inflation was controlled by balancing the budget. The government controlled the prices of foodgrains and major commodities by State trading. Payment of taxes was strictly enforced.

In rural development, the main feature of the government's policy was to redistribute land to the landless by means of implementing radical land reform programmes during the period 1950-53. The twin objectives of implementing land reforms was to increase food production and promote wider distribution of agrarian prosperity. It must be remembered that 10 per cent of the rural population owned 70-75 per cent of the cultivable lands in China. This inequity had to be overcome. The Agrarian Reform Act of 1950 was passed.

Land reform legislations were implemented successfully so as to achieve the alleviation of rural poverty. At the same time, it served as an effective instrument of social change. The government carried out the land reform policy phase by phase. During the first phase, lands of the rich landlords was confiscated during the revolution of 1949 and distributed to the poor and the landless. However, the poor and the landless were unable to reap the benefits due to lack of credit facilities. So in the second phase, the "mutual aid teams" were formed with groups of poor peasants. Even this measure was not found to be satisfactory. Therefore, in the third phase (1955-56), the poor farmers joined the agricultural producers' cooperatives to avail themselves of many commercial benefits.

These advanced cooperatives began to function over land of sizes varying from hundred to five hundred hectares. These cooperatives raised the agricultural yield through the pooling of resources. Even this was found to be inadequate from the point of view of the objectives of agrarian reforms. Hence, the fourth and the last phase in 1958 began. There was a regrouping of agricultural cooperatives into People's Agricultural Communes.

The Commune System

This implied that individual ownership of land was abolished, and the land-owning peasants now worked in the communes. By 1970, there were about 26,000 communes. Each commune was divided into a production-brigade and each brigade into a number of work teams (consisting of 25 to 35 families). Communes could be big with a strength of about 50,000 people working in an area of 12,000 hectares, or small with 9,000 people working in an area of 3,000 hectares. Whatever the defects in the implementation of land reform measures in China, food production increased substantially from 108 million tonnes in 1949 to 246 million by the early 1970s. The rural population was better off compared to most of the developing countries. In the end it was believed that people's communes producing more food would pave the way for growth of industrialisation with concomitant benefits accruing in the form of full employment and so on. The communes took up vast projects such as reforestation, dam construction and so on.

Social Change

The Chinese Revolution of 1949 brought about far-reaching social changes. It struck at the ties of the old family system and values, with women enjoying equal rights. They enjoyed not only the property rights, but also the right to divorce by the Marriage Law of 1950. A large number of women started to work in the communes, factories, and offices, departing from the old tradition of sticking to home life. Communism encouraged atheism, and therefore, Confucianism and Taoism came under severe attack. However, the other religions did not receive bad treatment from the communists. Superstitions and traditional science and technology did not find place in the new social set-up. Foreign missionaries were jailed or expelled since they were considered spies. The communes in rural areas broke up family values. All the adults were asked to work on projects for months without having any time to meet the obligations of family life. The old and the infants spent time in hostels and messes. The Chinese communes turned peasants into agricultural workers with proletarian attitudes.

The Chinese Educational System

The Chinese communists used education as an important tool to refashion society to their line of thinking. One of their important reforms in this field included the simplification of the Chinese script by eliminating hundreds of complicated characters. The Communist Party launched a vigorous campaign for the spread of literacy. As a consequence of this propaganda, the strength in schools and colleges increased greatly by 1956. Nearly 62 million children attended primary schools, five million middle schools, and 3,80,000 students colleges and higher technical schools. The thinking of students was oriented towards showing loyalty towards the CCP party and its leaders. Mao launched the "Hundred Flowers Movement" in 1957, which tried to change the bourgeoise attitude of his people. This was accomplished through the media of lectures, mass communication, radio and TV, controlled press and censored literature.

Great Leap Forward (1957-59)

This movement implied the adoption of radical strategy by Mao for rapid economic development of the country by launching Five Year Plans. Mao scored a victory over the moderate faction led by Lin-Shao-Chi, particularly over the adoption of a strategy to increase agricultural output. Lin opposed collectivisation and stood for orderly progress. The leaders at Moscow favoured Lin's strategy of development and gave their moral support. But Mao defeated the Soviet line of thinking in the party by scoring a victory. The second Five Year Plan finally adopted Mao's strategy of economic development – the Great Leap Forward – instead of the Soviet strategy advocated by Lin. Mao tried to speed up the process of socialisation through his directives. Year after year, the government published statistics showing spectacular economic growth mainly achieved through substantial progress in agriculture, industries and trade. The people of China were made to believe that their country was going to become very prosperous within a period of ten years.

However, by 1959, it was discovered that Mao had committed blunders. His economic and foreign policies came under fire. He was severely criticised for his failure to achieve the Great Leap Forward and forced to step down from the chairmanship. It is estimated that 27 million people might have lost their lives during this time. During the next three years (1959-61) China witnessed an economic collapse. The moderate sections in the Chinese Communist Party received much attention and they adopted an economic policy of "readjustment, consolidation, falling out and rising standards". By 1964, China was on her way to achieving quick economic recovery.

Cultural Revolution (1966-69)

One of Mao's famous quotations includes: "Power comes out of the barrel of the gun". Mao tried to consolidate his hold over the army during the period of readjustment. He knew of the inevitable struggle for power in the party and government between himself and Lin. His differences with Lin over the strategy to be adopted for bringing prosperity again became the focus of attention. While Lin was betting on "scientific and organisational expertise" which was adopted by all Western countries, Mao believed in releasing the "mass energy" (both inventive and creative) through his profound thoughts. He thought it would be a better substitute for the so-called scientific and organisational expertise advocated by Lin. He considered Lin "revisionist", and his approach counterproductive. He detested foreign aid for achieving economic progress as it came with strings attached. He impressed the Chinese to depend upon the virtue of self-reliance.

Although Mao resigned the chairmanship due to the failure of his schemes such as the "Great Leap Forward" and the "Communes", he manoeuvred to get his close colleague, Lin Piao, appointed as Defence Minister and head of the People's Liberation Army (PLA). Mao felt that Lin Piao would be greatly obliged, and support him in any future power struggle with the opponents. Mao used non-party elements to wage a war against the conservative members of the CCP. He was quite successful in maintaining supreme status over the other party leaders. He used the Red Guards and the PLA to achieve his objective. Between 1959 and 1966, the struggle for power began with Lin Piao supporting him. It was during this time, that the Chinese army was subjected to a rectification campaign. The soldiers who opposed Mao were eliminated, and the rest were indoctrinated with Mao's infallible thoughts. Subsequently, Lin Piao was appointed Vice-Premier.

Mao launched the Cultural Revolution on April 18, 1966 by appealing to the people to follow his thoughts and participate in the great revolution. A group was formed under Mao's control for spreading the Cultural Revolution in China. This group took over the *Peking Daily*, and other newspapers as well as Radio Peking, and started propagating Mao's thoughts. Mao's Cultural Revolution included plans for economic development. In 1964, China exploded the first atom bomb, and in 1967 the first hydrogen bomb. Mao died on September 9, 1976 at the age of 82. He is considered by many as one of the world's greatest leaders and statesmen.

China's Foreign Policy under Mao

After the 1948 revolution, Mao's China denounced western countries as imperialists and reactionaries. The major portion of the blame was attributed to the United States which rendered active assistance to Chiang Kai Shek to fight the communists. Communist China adopted the policy of maintaining friendly relations with all neighbouring countries of Asia. The Soviet Union remained a friend and an "elder brother" till Khrushchev came to power. China recommended her model of 'liberation' for emulation to all the ex-colonies and less developed countries of Asia and Africa. The United States supported

Chiang's Taiwan (Formosa) by recognising his government and kept Communist China out of the United Nations.

Communist China adopted peaceful coexistence as one of the important facets of her foreign policy and established close links with neutral countries of Asia and Africa. She ratified the Panchasheel Policy indicating her willingness to maintain peace with neighbouring countries. However, her peaceful intentions were belied, when she invaded India in 1962. Mao believed in establishing China's hegemony over all the Asiatic countries. In fact, Mao aspired for China's status as a superpower.

Sino-American Relations

During the pre-revolutionary days the United States government remained very friendly with China and even advocated the Open Door policy so as to see that China was not colonised by European powers. In fact, the US assisted China during the regime of Chiang with economic and military aid. During the Second World War, the US was quite sympathetic towards China because Japan had conquered a major portion of the former's territory. The US government made some mistakes during the time of the rift which developed between the Communists and the Nationalists. It underestimated the strength of the Communists during the Civil War. Instead of remaining neutral, the US assisted Chiang with economic and military aid. Though she was not actively involved in the Civil War, the communists hated US interference. When Chiang failed to rout the communists and fled to Taiwan (Formosa), the US continued its support to Chiang. The US Government refused to recognise the establishment of the People's Republic of China under Mao's leadership. The US opposed the admission of Mao's China to the United Nations. Since then, the Sino-American relationship took a bad turn.

It was unfortunate that relations between the two great countries remained bad till the advent of President Nixon. Some of the main reasons were:

(1) anti-communist lobby in the US, (2) China's support to North Korea during the Korean War (1950-1952), (3) the US Government's continued support to Taiwan, and (4) the steps taken by the US government to contain communist China by setting up military alliances with her neighbours. During the time of President Eisenhower, his Secretary of State, John Foster Dulles, concluded a mutual security pact with Taiwan and Japan. This was directed against the People's Republic of China. In the course of time, Dulles was responsible for concluding another military alliance with some of the Asian neighbours of China called South-East Asia Treaty Organisation (SEATO). In addition to military alliances, the United States government appealed to the Allies to impose economic embargo. The US Government had earlier repeatedly vetoed

the admission of the People's Republic of China into the United Nations. Thus, the United States made all efforts to see that China remained isolated. However, China's response was equally hostile towards the US. She maintained friendship with many of the Asiatic countries which had not joined the military alliances formed by the United States. During the Korean war, relations between the United States and Communist China touched a new low. There was a time when the anti-communist lobby in the United States advocated atom-bombing mainland China to avoid further escalation of the Korean war. Communist China supported North Korea in the latter's effort to cross the 38th parallel and take over South Korea.

China's Relations with Asiatic Countries

China maintained friendly relations with Asiatic countries, especially after the Bandung Conference (1955) which adopted Nehru's policy of Panchasheel as the basis of relationship among member countries. During the time of the Indo-China war, the United States Government extended full support to France and this was opposed by communist China. Peking supported Ho Chi Minh of North Vietnam in his efforts to bring about the unification of Vietnam. The United States Government mistook the efforts of Ho Chi Minh as another instance of Communist expansionism in South-East Asia. The long war in Vietnam finally brought about the defeat of the United States which ultimately agreed for peace. In the Geneva Conference which followed, the parties to the dispute agreed for an election. It was unfortunate that after the elections, South Vietnam could not agree to a referendum. The war continued with disastrous consequences.

China fully supported Ho Chi Minh which resulted in his victory over South Vietnam. It paved the way for the Paris peace treaty. It was a great defeat for the US Government. When Nixon got elected to the US Presidency, he started talking about peace in Vietnam. He made sincere efforts to extend goodwill towards Communist China. The Ping-Pong diplomacy continued resulting in Nixon's visit to China in February 1972. Nixon's visit was welcomed by the people of China, and normal diplomatic relations were restored. These eventually led to the admission of Communist China to the United Nations. Taiwan was expelled, though the United States maintained good relations with her also.

Sino-Soviet Relations

In foreign policy, China under Mao began to take an independent line which was in tune with the policy of the Soviet Union. In the early years the Soviet Union looked upon China as her protege, and therefore, maintained extremely good relations. In fact, the Soviet Union extended liberal economic and technical assistance to Communist China for building her economy. The friendly relations got further strengthened following the denunciation of Stalin at the 20th conference of the Communist Party of the Soviet Union (CPSU). However, with the advent of Khrushchev as a leader of Soviet Union, China's relations came under severe strain. China supported the autonomy of the Soviet-controlled East European countries. Khrushchev's friendly gestures to President Tito of Yugoslavia roused suspicions among the Chinese communist leaders. But the Soviet Union continued to maintain friendly relations and even promised China to share nuclear secrets after her launch of the Inter-Continental Ballistic Missiles (ICBM). However, the supposed sharing of the nuclear secrets between the two did not take place, which caused great indignation among the Chinese communist leaders. Mao was very angry with the Soviet Union, for the latter did not help China in acquiring Taiwan.

The differences between these two communist giants continued to crop up every now and then. Mao, for example, did not like Khrushchev's friendly gestures to US diplomats and Senators. Khrushchev went to the extent of adopting a policy of co-existence as the main facet of the Soviet Union's foreign policy, which was in total contrast to the earlier stand. China began to look upon the policy of co-existence as a giveaway to the capitalist and imperialist countries. The policy of co-existence came under severe test, when Communist China criticised India, a strong ally of the Soviet Union, for giving shelter to Dalai Lama following the Chinese invasion of Tibet. The border incidents between China and India continued, with China claiming large tracts of Indian territory along the MacMahon line. China also claimed a part of NEFA territories in India. Violating the principles of the Panchasheel agreement, China invaded India on October 20, 1962.

China was angry when Khrushchev ordered the removal of Soviet missiles from Cuba in order to avert a likely nuclear war. President Kennedy had earlier threatened a nuclear war if the Soviet Union did not remove her missiles from Cuba. China did not like the Soviet Union to buckle under American threat.

During the period of Khrushchev, China took full advantage of the discomfiture of the Soviet Union and increased its influence over her neighbouring countries such as Burma, Thailand, Malaya and North Vietnam. However, she lost her prestige among many Asiatic countries because of her invasion of India, and also due to the violent anti-Communist riots in Indonesia. The riots had been secretly sponsored by the Chinese communists. With the fall of President Sukarno, the Chinese influence in Indonesia began to decline. The tensions between the Soviet Union and Mao's China escalated in 1969 because of their border disputes. Both China and the Soviet Union quarreled over the acquisition of a number of islands near the confluence of the rivers Amur and Ussuri.

These quarrels led to border clashes with serious consequences. China attacked the Soviet-German agreement in 1970 as yet another example of collusion between the US and the Soviet Union to carve out spheres of influence in Europe. The Soviet Union began to amass her troops on the Sino-Soviet border so as to threaten Peking.

In the meantime, Mao began to befriend the United States so as to use her against the Soviet Union. Unfortunately, he did not live long. Before his death, Mao purged his party of great leaders such as Lin Piao describing him as a Russian stooge. He did not like any other colleague to surpass him. Under his control, China regarded the Soviet Union as a revisionist country practising social-imperialism. A personality cult developed in China about Mao who was regarded as the greatest leader of the world. Nevertheless, there is no doubt that China under Mao made rapid strides of progress.

Mao's Legacy

Although Mao's Great Leap Forward and the Cultural Revolution failed to yield dividends and caused great hardships, it must be said that he laid the foundation for a strong and stable state. In fact, his successors found it easy to build a superstructure. What were the tangible achievements of Mao? Well, it was he who enabled China to discover and exploit the oil resources, kept his nation debt-free, completed land reforms, and made the country recover from agricultural failures. Besides, he launched a grand nuclear programme which enabled his nation to ward off threats of the western powers. China achieved the status of a superpower after securing a seat in the Security Council of the UN (1971). The West's Open Door policy enabled China to exploit "the technology and markets of the developed world."

Deng Xiaoping (1976-97)

This short-statured and stout man was not the designated successor of Mao, but he came to the forefront due to the efforts of Chou En-lai. Following the deaths of Mao and Chou there was a power struggle. Madam Mao (known as Jiang Qing) and her "Gang of Four" challenged Deng's succession, but they were soon punished. Deng rejected Mao's idea of building socialism by means of class struggle and realised the great havoc caused by Great Leap Forward and the Cultural Revolution. Deng persuaded the party's Third Plenum to reject the postulates of the Cultural Revolution *in toto* and approve the importance of economic construction. He appealed to all that 'economic construction' should replace Mao's idea of class struggle for achieving economic development of the country. In simple words, it means that economics and not politics should play a meaningful role in bringing about socio-political stability of the country, particularly after the ravages caused by the Cultural Revolution.

Deng advocated building socialism through the medium of "socialist market economy", that is "socialism with Chinese characteristics". The 15th Congress approved it in September 1997, and China's progress thus assumed a new ideological banner. Deng's blueprint of reforms came to be known as the "four modernizations", namely, modernization of agriculture, industry, science and technology and defence. The government created Special Economic Zones, mostly situated in the coastal region to give concrete shape to Deng's theory.

His Contribution

Before his death Deng Xiaoping left behind him seasoned leaders like Jiang Zemin, Li Peng, Zhu Rongji and Vice President Hu Jintao, to build the nation with great commitment. Deng gave the Chinese People's Republic a new constitution as early as 1982. Under his leadership, China encouraged small scale enterprises in rural and urban areas, and significantly dismantled the rural communes (set up during the Great Leap Forward movement). The lands were returned to individual peasants under long term leases. As mentioned earlier, the government set up Special Economic Zones where market forces would have a free reign. In the early years of his leadership, he brought order and good governance to the nation, particularly following the chaos caused by the Cultural Revolution. He also represented the continuity of the revolution, in spite of his deviation from Mao's line of thinking. He made economics take a front seat. The most difficult task he faced was the introduction of a western system of democracy into his reforms. He failed to accomplish this task with the result there occurred the Tiananmen tragedy (1989). This tragedy was responsible for the slowdown of the economic reforms.

The Tiananmen Square Tragedy

Thousands of Chinese students gathered outside 'the Great Hall of the People' known as Tiananmen Square in 1989 to demand political reforms and liberalisation. This demonstration was crushed by the government, leaving behind an estimated 5,000 dead and 10,000 injured. All the student leaders were arrested. It sent shock-waves throughout the world, with the US Government adopting a hostile attitude towards China. Premier Zhao Ziyang lost his job for his inept handling of the situation and Li Peng was given the job to repair the damage. The dissident student leader, Wang Dan, was released in April 1998. The nation's image was sullied by international criticism and sanctions. China's human rights record, child population policy, prison-labour conditions, and media censorship came under severe criticism. China got isolated from the rest of the world once again. Nevertheless, she eventually emerged as a great power to be reckoned with.

Besides being a nuclear power, China has made rapid advance in space technology. In April 1970, the country's first earth satellite was launched. In

July 1996, China conducted its last nuclear test — the 45th. There is absolutely no doubt that China's armed forces, coupled with nuclear superiority would deter any enemy—including the US—from undertaking any adventure. China increased its defence expenditure on account of modernization of weapons system and the manufacture of nuclear missiles. China signed the Nuclear Non-proliferation Treaty, and adopted a no-first use policy with regard to nuclear strike against enemies.

China's Economic Growth

The man who has hogged all attention in recent years in China is Premier Zhu Rongji, Jiang's trusted colleague from Shanghai. He took control of the Chinese economy through periods of crisis and boom. Known as the 'top cop' he has made sincere efforts to root out corruption. Nearly 1,58,000 people, most of them party officials, have been sentenced on charges of corruption, embezzlement and other economic offences since 1993. He has succeeded in convincing the seniors on the importance of reducing the number of ministries from 40 to 29, and reduced the size of Chinese bureaucracy by 50 per cent. He has brought down the rate of inflation from 24 per cent (in 1993) to one per cent in 1999. He has steered China clear from the maelstrom of the 'economic crisis' which affected many South-East Asian countries since 1997. The exchange rate of Yuan was maintained, and no attempt was made to devalue the currency. Nearly 500 state-controlled companies have remained healthy and contributed their mite to the Exchequer. Zhu Rongji has endeared himself to his compatriots as a charming and intelligent minister, and has impressed the international media.

After a long wait, the US waived its objection to the entry of China into the World Trade Organization (WTO). One must remember that China's economy today is the second largest and it has a GDP growth rate between 8 to 10 per cent. Its exports to the US, Japan, India and the EU countries have risen phenomenally. The Chinese government encouraged thousands of entrepreneurs to open businesses along the eastern coast, and the Communist Party welcomed them to join into its fold. Property right was there in the Statute Book long ago but it had no meaning. There were no guarantees that it would be respected. There was the ever-widening gap between the urban rich and the rural poor after the market reforms were introduced. The media reported the existence of the extremely rich moving about in the cities in luxury cars – some of them imported, and enjoying Western way of life, a thing unheard of during the era of Mao. The rural poor remained in squalor, and this is what the reforms did. Social unrest and discontent are bound to spread.

In March 2003, the Jiang Zemin's mantle of leadership was passed on without any hitch to the newly elected President Hu Jintao. The old team gracefully retired except for Jiang Zemin who continued. He was appointed to head the defence committee, which is the most powerful organ of the Communist Party. In October 2003, China successfully launched a manned space mission after spending nearly $ 2.2 billion. China is now depending on high-tech weapons system and hopes to reduce its military strength from 3 million to 2.5 million. If the present GDP growth continues for another decade the Chinese economy may replace the US, as the front runner. China is at present leading in manufactures and hardware technology.

The Chinese constitution has been recently amended (March 2004) so as to provide protection to private property. Strangely, a mention of 'human rights' appears in the document. In fact, China had granted many rights in the past, such as religious rights, consumer rights, right to travel abroad and also the right to freedom of speech. Political analysts point out that these rights exist only in 'theory' but the state is the one which decides how these rights are to be protected. Many say that the state is the biggest violator of these rights. Courts and tribunals hardly look into people's grievances. The recent amendment is approved so as to stem social unrest and discontent. Religious minorities in Xinjiang and Tibet are not happy. A few years ago, Falun Gong, a quasi-religious sect witnessed its members being prosecuted by the government. The Chinese government hardly tolerates political dissidence. The pro-democracy movement in Hong Kong is under scrutiny by the Chinese government. The people of Hong Kong are not allowed to choose their leader (the present incumbent is the government nominee) even though Hong Kong enjoys special status.

Foreign Relations

China's relation with the US goes back to the days of the Chinese Communist revolution of 1949. The US held China as a renegade or pariah and blocked its entry into the UN. However, after US President Nixon's visit to China in 1972, US cooled down its hostility thus enabling China to replace Taiwan in the UN. The 'ping pong' diplomacy followed by President Nixon continued till Communist China was granted most favoured nation status with regard to its trade with the US. The US also agreed, to follow 'One China Policy', thus indicating that it considered Taiwan to be an integral part of the mainland. American businessmen were happy at the prospect of China opening up for American trade and business.

However, this normalisation of relations received a setback after the Tiananmen Square Tragedy, 1989. China's crackdown on political dissidents sent alarm signals to the US administration, and President Bush (Sr) imposed economic sanctions. When the Cold War ended in 1989, the US began its campaign on 'human rights', an ideology through which it tried to dominate the world with the support of the European Union and the UN.

China's poor track-record on human rights, its support to Communist North Korea, and the supply of missiles and missiles-technology to Pakistan, Iran and Saudi Arabia caused great concern to the US. A few years ago, the US accused China of having stolen nuclear blueprints from the US through espionage.

On the other side, China viewed the US actions such as, supply of high tech weapons to Taiwan, encouraging pan-Mongolia movement, giving moral support to dissidents in Tibet, assuring military support to Taiwan if attacked, with great concern.

The above ups and downs in Sino-US relations seems to have come to an end after the terrorist attack on the US on 9 September 2001. This incident has changed the situation altogether since the US administration under George W Bush declared 'global war on terrorism'. China assumes an important role in the US scheme of things. China supported the US war against Taliban-controlled Afghanistan but denied the same over the US led war on Iraq. China disapproved US action in Iraq because it had no UN mandate. China's independent foreign policy has caused concern in the US. The US is heavily dependent on the Chinese support in diffusing the situation created by North Korea. The US considers North Korea as one of the 'axes of evil'. North Korea's nuclear ambitions, and its potential to create another war, have caused great anxiety in the US administration. The US-sponsored 'six nations meet' in Beijing took place recently to urge China to rein in North Korea's ambition to go nuclear (North Korea appears to have produced a few atom-bombs already) in return for aid.

Britain transferred its power over Hong Kong to Communist China in 1997 as per agreement and thus established good relations. Deng Xiaoping's foreign policy included 'the reunification of the motherland' and Hong Kong was given special status in tune with 'one country, two systems'.

China and Russia came closer after establishing 'special relationship' and this is after resolving border disputes. China established friendly relations with countries in Central Asia and Vietnam after resolving border disputes.

China's pro-Pakistan policy irked India, but after the visits of Indian leaders (Rajiv Gandhi, Vajpayee and Natwar Singh) in the recent past, things are becoming normal. China and India have decided to adopt 'Panchasheel' and resolve the border dispute amicably through peaceful negotiations. India welcomed China's negotiations of Sikkim's merger. China and India have welcomed China's negotiations of Sikkim's merger. China and India have decided to raise their bilateral trade to $ 10 billion by 2005.

China had long standing suspicion with regard to Japan's strategic relations with the US and therefore their relations remained unfriendly. An attempt to normalise relations began with the visit to China by the Japanese emperor a few years ago. The emperor refused to apologise to the Chinese about the war crimes committed by the Japanese soldiers in China during their occupation (World War II). But Japan may improve its relations with China in the near future, because China may be helpful in resolving the North Korean problem.

Macao

Macao, which had remained a Portuguese colony for nearly 443 years, was transferred to China on the midnight of December 19, 1999. China has agreed to guarantee its separate identity and treat it as a special zone like Hong Kong. President Jiang Zemin hopes that the transfer of Macao may be considered as a precursor to the integration of yet another rebel province, Taiwan (Formosa) headed by Lee Ten-hiu, with the Chinese People's Republic.

Situated on the mouth of the Pearl River at China's Southeast Coast, the port of Chinese Macao assumed importance with the arrival of the Portuguese in 1518. Portuguese merchants and sailors took shelter in 1557 and engaged themselves in trade with the mainland Chinese, the Japanese and the people of some countries in Southeast Asia. When the Japanese Shogun closed the port of Nagasaki to the Westerners for fear that these Christians would spread Christianity if they come there, Macao became the most important Portuguese enclave commanding the sea-route towards mainland China, Japan and ports of Southeast Asia. In 1557 the Portuguese leased the land from the Chinese government, and since then Macao became an important trading centre and supply station.

However, during the middle of the nineteenth century, the British developed Hong Kong (situated near Macao), and this led to the decline of the Portuguese-Macao. After a treaty with the Chinese government in 1887 Portuguese declared it as their colony. Macao was called a Portuguese province in 1961, and subsequently as Chinese territory under Portuguese administration in 1974. In 1987 Portugal decided to hand over the territory to Communist China by December 20, 1999.

Today this port attracts large number of tourists and gamblers, in fact it is called 'Monte Carlo of the East' (or perhaps Las Vegas).

9

THE OPENING OF JAPAN

Like ancient China, ancient Japan too remained secluded from the rest of the world. Japan consists of four main islands, Hokkaido, Honshu, Shikoku and Kyushu. All of them are spread in the north-south direction and situated off the coast of Korea. The Sea of Japan separates these islands from the rest of the Asiatic countries. The early history of Japan is full of myths and legends. The Japanese believe that their land was born out of the union of God Izanagi and Goddess Izanami. They also believe that Jimmu, the grandson of the Sun Goddess, became the first emperor of their country. It was the association of the Sun Goddess with the birth of their country that brought the nickname, "the land of the Rising Sun".

During the early centuries of the Christian era, Japan was ruled by several clans, the most important being the ruling clan of the Japanese emperor. Each clan worshipped a common ancestor and its chieftain recognised the Japanese emperor as his leader. By the eighth century AD, a feudal type of government existed, and characteristically Japanese society too became feudal.

The Chinese influence over Japan had been considerable during the Han dynasty. Chinese travellers and traders established contacts with Japan and the Japanese learnt the art of writing from the Chinese. The Chinese works of Confucius inspired Japanese writers, poets and philosophers. The Buddhist monks of China came to Japan and established Buddhist monasteries. Shotoku Taishi, a Japanese emperor of the Nara period, took personal interest in the spread of Buddhism in his country for which he is described as "Ashoka of Japan".

The Heian Period (AD 794-1185)

This period of Japanese history saw the shifting of the seal of the capital from Nara to Heian-Kyo or Kyoto. The new capital was associated with Heian culture which was a mixture of Chinese and Japanese cultures. The Japanese court came to be known for its splendour and glory. The Japanese rulers patronised fine arts, calligraphy, poetry, literature, the construction of Buddhist monasteries, and the laying of beautiful gardens. A highly cultured and aristocratic society existed like the one during the period of French King Louis XIV. Among the most powerful clans, the most noteworthy was the Fujiwara. From humble beginnings in the tenth century, this clan reached great heights of popularity and prestige by the eleventh century. It gave the country able administrators and diplomats. The Japanese emperors thought it appropriate to marry their daughters to the powerful male members of this clan. After the fall of the Fujiwaras, Japan came to be dominated by the two powerful military clans, namely, Taira and Minamoto. These two struggled for supremacy and finally Yoritomo of the latter became the shogun (military commander).

Yoritomo ruled a major part of Japan from 1192 as a dictator and the Japanese Emperor recognised this fact. The Emperor showered gifts of money and land on Yoritomo and his followers. The government of the shogun, known by the name Bakufu (Tent government), practically replaced the Emperor's authority and set up its headquarters at Kamakura. The country developed a military culture and tradition from this period.

Hojo's Administration

After Yoritomo's death, his successors were superseded by his wife's family, the Hojos. They gave Japan a clean and efficient administration. It was a period known for spiritual fervour. Hojo's rule was deeply disturbed by the invasions of the army of Kublai Khan in 1274 and 1281 but the Japanese were successful in driving them out. However, these invasions marked the beginning of the unpopularity of the Hojos, and Ashikaga Takauji, member of one of the ruling clans, took advantage of the opportunity.

Ashikaga Shogunate

Supported by the Japanese Emperor, he overthrew the Hojo and declared himself as the shogun. He was able to replace the Emperor by putting his puppet on the throne in AD 1338. It was after nearly two centuries (1573) that the Ashikaga rule became unpopular and faced stiff opposition from the provincial overlords of Japan. This situation was followed by a civil war, with feudal lords supporting the rebellious and independent Sastuma on the one side, and the Mikado (the Emperor) supported by the shogun on the other. Thus the Ashikaga shogunate could not exercise effective control from its capital, Kyoto.

It was during the period of Ashikaga shogunate that we see the rise of the military caste of Japan, known as the *samurai*. Another important thing to remember was the spread of Zen Buddhism (austere form of Buddhism). China's influence over Japan's learning and art was conspicuous. The Japanese trade and industry had grown considerably. The feudal society of the provinces merged with the new civilian society of the imperial capital. It was during this period of deep crisis that the Europeans began to knock at the doors of Japan.

The first to set foot on the soil of Japan was the Portuguese governor of Malacca, named Antonio Galvano (1542). He was subsequently followed by the Christian missionaries. The most famous among them were the Jesuits led by Francis Xavier (he became a saint later) who came to spread Christianity. They were followed by Portuguese traders who entered into trade relations with the feudal lords. It was the Portuguese who introduced musket which impressed the Japanese feudal lords-cum-bureaucrats (Daimios). Then the Dutch followed suit. In the meantime, the political crisis in Japan ended in 1573 after Oda Nobunaga destroyed the power of the Ashikaga shogunate. He kept firm control over the rebellious feudal lords, and in the course of time Japan witnessed peace and prosperity. He permitted the Christian missionaries to propagate their faith and many Japanese were converted to Christianity. The Japanese Government maintained good relations with the foreigners. In 1582, Nobunaga was assassinated and the task of strengthening the country fell on the shoulders of his commander, Toyotomi Hideyoshi.

Hideyoshi proved to be a great patriot and statesman. He was alarmed when he heard that the Europeans were arming their camps and bringing gunships without his permission. Furthermore, the Christian missionaries were bringing about mass conversions and provoking the local population. He decided to halt all this by taking drastic steps. First, he banned all missionary activity in 1587. This was followed by their expulsion in 1591. During this time more than 20,000 Japanese Christians lost their lives. The government issued two decrees by which all foreigners were forbidden from entering Japan and no Japanese would be permitted to go out of the country. Those who violated these two decrees were to be executed. However, to keep a small window open for the West, some Dutch traders were allowed to trade under severe conditions, ie, through the island of Deshima near the harbour of Nagasaki. What was surprising was that Japan shut the doors for the Westerners for the next centuries — she was totally isolated from the rest of the world — till Commodore Perry with his American naval squadron started knocking at her doors once again in July 1853.

The anti-foreign feeling which ran high was taken advantage of by Hideyoshi to turn himself into a dictator. He waged a war against Korea, which had acknowledged the suzerainty of China. After his death, Tokugawa Leyasu of the Tokugawa family succeeded him as the shogun in 1603. During the next 265 years Japan came to be ruled by the Tokugawa shogunate, and the Japanese Emperor (Mikado) retired from active political life. But the people and the shogunate always treated the Japanese emperors with greatest respect, for they were considered divine. Many ruling clans in the provinces paid their homage to him. Under the Tokugawa shogunate Japan turned into a highly centralised feudal state.

The Japanese Feudal Society

The Tokugawa shoguns over a period of time exercised enormous power as civil and military authority rested in their hands. The powerful feudal lords were kept under strict control and therefore, Japan remained united and peaceful. Bureaucrats among them were called Daimyos who constituted a class, next only to the shogun in the power structure. The shogun kept a strict vigil over this class through an espionage system. Next in importance was the *samurai*, the warrior class (or caste), whose bravery and loyalty could be depended upon by the ruling elite to serve their purpose. The merchants, artisans and the peasants formed the lowest class. The Tokugawa shoguns encouraged Confucian values among the members of all classes for the purpose of pre-empting any uprisings or revolts. The Tokugawa shoguns ruled from their headquarters in Yedo, strategically situated when viewed from military, political and economic angles. This class system took deep roots in Japanese society until the advent of the Meiji revolution (1868).

Commodore Perry's Visit

The United States Government was deeply influenced by the pervading spirit in its country known as the 'Manifest Destiny'. The Americans believed that their country was ordained by God or destiny to rule or influence the whole world. In tune with the prevailing mood of the country, the US Government deputed Commodore Perry of the naval squadron to explore ways and means to establish diplomatic contacts with the countries in the Far East. The underlying purpose was to open up these countries for trade, and Perry focussed his attention on Japan. It must be remembered that the earlier two visits of American officials to the Japanese coast had failed to achieve the same purpose. Commodore Mathew C Perry was chosen by US President Fillimore to forcefully represent the US interests in Japan. Carrying a message to the Japanese Government from his President he arrived at the Yedo bay with a small fleet consisting of four ships (July 1853). He impressed the Japanese officials about the purpose of his mission. He desired to see the Emperor to hand over the President's message and wait for his response. He was hardly aware that it was the shogun who was ruling the country. The Japanese officials satisfied him by promising to do the needful. They, however, told him that it would take time. Perry impressed the Japanese officials with his no nonsense attitude and assured them he would return next spring to receive the reply from the Japanese Government.

Perry's refusal to route his request to the Japanese through the Dutch and also his demand for treatment as a representative of a great power had a telling effect. It made the shogun government nervous because it was conscious of the might of the technologically and scientifically advanced countries. Perry's show of strength, the seriousness of his purpose, and his veiled threat, compelled the shogun to consult the assembly of elders for the first time. The opinion among them was divided, some were for opening the country for western trade while others were against it. The shogun was confused, but some wise men prevailed upon him to agree to the terms of the government of the United States.

As promised, Perry's second visit to Japan, this time leading a much bigger fleet was undertaken to show the might of the United States. After landing, he was received with honour and courtesy, and his presents (miniature models of railways and telegraph), books and liquor were gratefully accepted. Amidst rejoicing, Japan signed the treaty of Kanagawa on March 31, 1854. The treaty provided for the opening of the ports of Shimoda and Hakodate for some naval facilities. The US Government was given permission to appoint its consul at Shimoda and avail itself of certain facilities like going to the rescue of some ship-wrecked US sailors. Although the treaty by itself did not offer much, it led to momentous consequences. For the first time, after a gap of two and half centuries, Japan had come out of self-imposed isolation. Thus Perry's visit became historic. It had far- reaching consequences for Japan and the shogunate as following events were to prove. What is interesting is that Japan's response to the West was totally different from that of China. Japan's willingness to come out of her seclusion and accept the proposals of the West on her terms was in total contrast to the Chinese policy of vacillation and drift.

Treaties with Other Powers

The other Western powers did not lose time in securing treaties. Sir James Stirling, a British Admiral, cajoled the Japanese to sign the treaty at Nagasaki in October 1854. The Russians did not lag behind. Count Putiativ secured a treaty from the Japanese at Shimoda in February 1855. The Dutch got theirs in January 1856 which permitted them to extend their activities beyond Nagasaki. The treaties permitted Western governments to station their consuls at Shimoda and Hakodate and enjoy limited extraterritorial rights in keeping with their status.

The Harris Treaty

A New York merchant named Townshend Harris was appointed the first consul at Shimoda by the US Government. Although his stay there was lonely and made inhospitable by the Japanese, his tremendous patience paved the way for establishing a rapport with the Japanese Government. It was after this success that he impressed upon the Japanese Government the desirability of having a full-fledged commercial treaty with his government. The Japanese signed a treaty, named after him, in June 1857. This treaty practically conceded most favourable terms to the US Government, which among others, included, the opening of new ports for trade, diplomatic representation, appointment of new consuls in the treaty-ports, extraterritorial rights and freedom of religious practice. Other European powers, namely, Britain, Russia and Holland also clamoured for the same concessions, and Japan accorded the same. These western powers were successful in totally ending her self-imposed isolation.

Fall of the Shogunate

It was the decision to open the doors of the country to the West which brought the ignominious end of the shogunate. It must be remembered that this decision was taken at a time when anti-foreign feelings were running high in Japan. The enemies of the shogun decided to strike when the imperial court itself was in a restless condition. To everyone in Japan it looked like a great betrayal. The ten ruling clans of Japan decided to save the country from the ignominious shogun by raising the cry "Exterminate the barbarians and bring the emperor". From 1859 to 1868 the anti-foreign feelings ran very high. An American interpreter, Hensken, was murdered by a Japanese chauvinist. Richardson, a British visitor from Hong Kong, was killed by a *samurai* belonging to the Sastuma lord. The British and American legations became special targets of attack. The western powers demanded compensation and apology in the beginning but it did not bring any relief. Violence against foreigners continued unabated.

It was under these circumstances that the British bombarded the town of Kagasuma in 1863 followed by an attack in the next year by the combined naval forces of the US, Britain, France and the Dutch on Shimonoseki. The attack had the desired effect on the Sastuma and Choshu clans which had earlier organised the attack of western ships. The shogun had become most unpopular and the cry to the Emperor to take charge of running the government directly had its impact. The Emperor issued two edicts rescinding the earlier orders of the shogun compelling the Daimyos to stay at the court in Yedo every other year, and holding members of their families hostage.

Many ruling clans began to defy the authority of the shogun and he was not willing to surrender his power to 'evil' advisers of the Emperor. He later announced his intention to resign. The issue was forced upon him by the leaders of the Western clan by rising in rebellion. This enraged the shogun who decided to crush it. A civil war appeared imminent. The Emperor realised that he should intervene. His court issued the "Restoration Rescript" announcing the abolition of the shogunate. Thus the last shogun, Keiki, was stripped off his rank and his followers were ordered to go out of Yedo. The shogun's palace was seized and he was ordered to retire. Some of his hot-tempered followers went berserk but their revolt was crushed. In 1868, the Meiji Emperor declared the Charter of Oath containing five articles to the nobles, the Daimyos and other officials present at the imperial palace in Kyoto. Japan was destined to become a power to be reckoned with after the Emperor took over charge as Head of the State and Government.

10

THE MEIJI REVOLUTION

The abolition of the shogunate and the resumption of power by the Japanese Emperor may be considered epoch-making in Japanese history. It had momentous consequences as mentioned earlier. A new era began with the Emperor declaring a Charter of Oath, a document similar in some respects to that of the Declaration of the Rights of Man of the days of the French Revolution. It was followed by an inspiring speech from the Emperor to those present at his imperial palace. In this speech, the Emperor declared that the winds of change had already started blowing from the West, and the nation would commit itself "to bring welfare and happiness to our one billion subjects and expand over the unlimited span of ocean and waves to bring forth our national influence, and put our nation on a foundation solid as a rock".

The new era was to be characterised by the harmonious mixture of the old and new, the old denoting all the best elements of the ancient Japanese culture, and the new suggesting the absorption of all that was good in Western civilisation. In this respect Japan differed widely from her neighbour, China, who looked upon Western civilisation with contempt and suspicion. Japan seized the opportunity provided by the West to modernise herself, although it was a hard choice to make in view of the anti-foreign feelings. Fortunately, the new Emperor, Mutsuhito (although very young, 16 years) was nevertheless bold and dynamic. Under his able leadership Japan was to chart a new course in order to become a mighty Asiatic nation during the next three decades.

The New Political System

The end of the shogunate with its attendant evils, a legacy of feudalism, marked the beginning of a new era. As for the feudalism which had permeated Japanese society for more than a thousand years, it had no place in the new set-up. The new political system, which was to replace the old, was democracy dominated by a centralised oligarchy. The process of change from the old to the new system was made easy by the voluntary surrender of power to the Emperor by the four most powerful western clans in 1869 — namely, the Satsuma, Chosu, Hizen and Tosu. It must be remembered that they were the ones who were instrumental in bringing about the Meiji restoration. This was followed by all the retainers, daimyos and *samurais*. The Emperor was highly impressed and provided compensation through a revenue settlement so that they could retain their respect and dignity. The members of the four great clans were permitted to stay at Tokyo (earlier called Yedo), the new capital of Japan.

Abolition of Feudalism

The compensation package for the *daimyos* (feudal lords) was in the form of a pension amounting to one-tenth of the revenue they would have derived from their fiefs. In some cases, it included the debts incurred by them. In any case the one-tenth compensation was indeed higher than the nominal income they were deriving earlier. It was the *samurai* class which was affected badly. It faced near-extinction since the old feudal army retained by the lords and the Emperor no longer continued. In their place the Emperor raised a national army to which the *samurai* offered their services. However, not all of them got recruited since the new army was not based on any class or caste. Hence those who changed their occupation from being soldier to being business class proved to be lucky. The members of the erstwhile feudal class turned to business as their new vocation. Some others joined the new administrative service.

So far as the peasants were concerned, the government replaced the old masters (feudal lords). It received its revenue not on the basis of production of crops but on the value of the land. They had to suffer since the government gave them the option to pay a high land tax or sell their lands. Rigorous collection of land tax by the new government put many poor and marginal peasants to great hardships. The new revenue policy thus caused great discontent which resulted in what is called 'rice riots'. Along with the disaffected *samurais*, the poor peasants fought pitched battles against the government officials who had come for collection of revenue.

Educational Reforms

The superiority of the West mainly rested upon its scientific and technological know-how. This was the product of the advanced educational system. Hence, the Emperor laid stress upon introducing a new educational system based on the Western system of education. This implied the revamping of the existing educational system. Ever since Perry's visit, Japanese scholars were encouraged to go abroad (the old restriction was lifted secretly) with a view to learning about the progress made by the West so as to enable the country's policy makers to prepare a new blueprint. What the Japanese realised was that they were at least a century behind in the educational field compared to the West. The necessity to catch up with the West became an important item on their agenda. The Japanese Government was determined to bring about the changes and hence followed a series of reforms.

All travel restrictions to go abroad for higher education were removed. Students were encouraged to go abroad to acquire knowledge of science and technology which would be useful to the country after their return. Imparting of education which was restricted only to the children of the elite in Japanese society was extended to all. Education became compulsory for all children by 1871. Every boy and girl from the age of six had to go to school by an imperial decree which in effect said that "all people, high or low, and of both sexes should receive education so that there should not be found one family in the whole empire, nor one member of family, ignorant and illiterate". The government provided liberal grants to secondary and university education. Women's education at the advanced level was recognised by 1902. Women's role in the household as a housewife and mother was laid stress on at the level of secondary education.

Being exposed to the influence of Western classics, the younger generation in Japan espoused the cause of Western education and values. Among the advocates of this cause was Fukuzawa Yukichi, the founder of Keio University. The prestigious University of Tokyo was founded in 1877. While the French influence in university education became conspicuous, the German influence was found more in vocational education. Again meritorious students were encouraged to go abroad for higher education so that on their return they could help the country in its modernisation programme. The business schools sent their good students to the United States for study at advanced centres like Harvard and Cambridge. Other good students who chose political science, law and scientific study went to France. Those interested in maritime studies went to Britain while those opting for science, medicine and military affairs went to Germany. The foreign-educated scholars prepared their country to reach its goal of modernisation by the fag end of the nineteenth century. Thus the educational system acted as a powerful catalyst of change and Japan emerged out of the cocoon of medievalism and entered a modern era.

Economic Development

The economic roots of the country lay deep in the feudal structure of society and this had to change. Therefore, the Meiji leaders desired to bring about this change and their goal was similar to that of Western nations – to build a strong economic base. Fortunately, Japan enjoyed peace and stability after the Meiji restoration which enabled the policy-makers to introduce a Western model of economy. However, this dream was made difficult on account of the meagre revenues derived from the customs, the domestic borrowings and other sources. But the Japanese overcame these bottlenecks through ingenious methods. The Iwakura mission which had gone abroad to learn the secrets of the dynamism of Western industrial societies returned. It gave a new thrust in the direction of

Japan's rapid economic development. Japan sought the help of foreign economic advisors, notably British, German and American, to make her task easy. But they remained employed for a short period, and were thereafter succeeded by the Japanese themselves.

Industrial Progress

Some of the main industries like ship-building, ammunition and textiles had flourished during the Tokugawa regime, but to bring about rapid economic growth on modern lines, the government took over these industries. In the next few decades, they witnessed rapid expansion through government subsidies. The Japanese government paid great attention to her infrastructure, particularly transport and communications. The first railroad appeared in 1872 connecting the imperial capital, Tokyo, with Yokohama, and in 1874 from Osaka to Kobe. The introduction of the modern postal system followed. Telegraph lines were laid connecting all important cities by 1894. Lighthouses, dockyards and piers came up. The government undertook construction of roads, bridges and public buildings. Small businessmen set up shops, bicycle and textile factories, printing, foundry and cigarette factories.

Japan's shipping lines played a remarkable role in the growth of trade and commerce. Yusen Karha and Osaka Shosen Kaisha did yeoman service for this cause. Japan established a stock exchange and a chamber of commerce for stimulating trade and commerce. But what was more important was the development of a sound banking system for the country's overall economic development. National Credit Banks were set up on the American model in 1882 to meet the growth in needs and currency. The Central Bank of Japan was established with the full backing of the government. In order to finance foreign trade, the Yokohama Specie Bank was founded. In the meantime, the Central Bank introduced a uniform currency thereby replacing the paper currencies issued by the feudal lords earlier. A decimal system of currency named the yen became the national currency. The Postal Savings Banks were opened for the purpose of introducing public savings. Therefore, the Meiji restoration could look forward to a bright future for the country and the people. But what came as a great and pleasant surprise was the constitutional reforms.

The New Constitution (1889)

It may be noted that Japan's great response to the onslaught of Western civilisation came in the form of a new constitution. It was indeed the greatest gift the Emperor conferred on his subjects. The new constitution combined the best elements of Japanese tradition and western modernity. The divine origin of kingship continued but was based on a democratic framework. The new constitution was the product of intensive study of the working of Western democracies with particular reference to the Prussian monarchy. The burden of framing a new constitution fell on the shoulders of the Meiji leaders. These Meiji leaders decided on two important points. Firstly, they decided to legitimise their own power on the basis of popular consent. Secondly, they formulated into the new constitution ideals of western liberalism and philosophy in tune with the Japanese way of life.

The Emperor's Charter of Oath broke new ground. This oath proclaimed by the Emperor included an assembly for the debate of the people and a pledge to respect the rights of the people. Therefore, there was no place for rebellion or revolt, and hence the suppression of the Sastuma rebellion in 1877. The Meiji leaders who strengthened the monarchy also created strong and stable political institutions. Most of them were either from the Sastuma or Choshu clans and their monopoly over offices of the government irked Itagaki Taisuki of Tosa and the councillors of Hizen. They formed a political party to expose political corruption. The result was the exposure of the Hokkaido scandal. A cabinet minister named Okuma Shigenobu had to resign. The most prominent Meiji thereafter submitted a memorial to the Emperor to grant a constitutional government. These and other events culminated in the issue of an imperial edict which ushered in a parliamentary form of government within constitutional framework but most of the powers were vested in the hands of the Emperor. In other words the rights of the people would be restricted.

Political Parties

In the 1890s Japan witnessed the emergence of three political parties, namely, Jiyuto (Liberal Party), Kaishinto (Progressive Party) and Rikken Teiseioto (Imperialist Party), the leaders being Itagaki, Okuma and the government respectively. Regarding their policies and programmes, there was nothing clear-cut except that they advocated constitutional and other reforms. What overshadowed the policies and programmes was the charisma of the leaders and loyalty to them. The leaders supported the demand for some kind of responsible government which the Genro (Emperor's Council of Elders) was not willing to concede. Hence many politicians succumbed to the temptations of offices offered by the Genro.

The first national election to the Japanese Diet (Parliament) took place in July 1890. The Diet was hardly in a position to make a mark as a debating forum, leave alone influence or formulate policies for the government. The formulation of polices, and the influence to bear on them were carried out by the ruling oligarchy and the Privy Council. It was the Genro which called the shots. Although a political party may win a majority of seats in the Diet, it still did not enjoy the authority of choosing the prime minister. The prime minister and his cabinet colleagues were appointed by the Emperor and therefore, remained responsible to him and not the parliament.

The elite in the Japanese government was constituted by the imperial family, the Genro (elder statesmen) and the Peers of the Upper House of Legislature. This House included important members of the Kuge, the daimyo and select professional classes. It was most unfortunate that the successive Japanese governments experienced political uncertainty and instability, proving the point that the transition was going to be difficult.

Ito became Prime Minister and his cabinet was made up of his close colleagues of the party known as the Seiyukai and ex-bureaucrats. His contribution was that he made the constitutional government work without any hitch. His government did not survive for long. He resigned, paving the way for the government of Katsura Taro – a Choshu general – who continued up to 1906. Unfortunately, his government came to an end in 1906 over the issue of victory over Russia in the Russo-Japanese war. His opponents attacked his government for failing to take diplomatic advantage and secure better terms while signing the treaty of Portsmouth with defeated Russia.

Riots broke out which Katsura Taro's government was unable to control and it took a toll of nearly a thousand men. During the next six years there were changes of government with leadership passing between Saionji and Katsura. The oligarchy of the party was maintained through its leaders till the end of the First World War. The Japanese Emperor Mutsihito died in 1912 and his successor Taisho Tenno (1912-26) was sick and mentally ill. Although Japan had constitutional government, still she continued to be a "paternalistic and authoritarian state".

Further Economic Growth

In the early twentieth century Japan witnessed remarkable growth, particularly in agriculture and industry. There was a sudden increase in labour, probably preceding development in agriculture. Unfortunately, the rice riots had no substantial impact and the land reforms failed. The cultivating tenants had to bear a huge burden (ranging from 45 per cent to 60 per cent) of land tax.

Japan embraced the gold standard in 1897 and started to borrow capital heavily from Western countries. But what gave a fillip to her industrial growth was the outbreak of the First World War. Surprisingly, several Asiatic countries including India asked Japan to supply many consumer goods and arms since the European markets were not accessible due to war. At the end of the war, Japan turned from a debtor-country to a creditor! It should be remembered that Japan's new found prosperity did not reach the masses because of the entrenched bureaucracy and politicians. It was in these circumstances that a new political party was born, namely the Social Democratic Party in 1901 founded by Katayama Sen and Kotoku Denjiro. But the Japanese government continued the policy of repression when workers and miners demanded an increase in wages and better living conditions.

11

CONFLICTS IN EAST ASIA

In the nineteenth century both China and Japan faced the threat of foreign domination due to their own weaknesses. But what set them at each other's throat was Korea, which became a bone of contention. Let us examine why this small country had become a focus of attention, and the underlying causes which culminated in the war. But first a brief historical background about this small country.

Korean mythology informs us that the state was founded around 2333 BC (or some say 1122 BC) The latter date was associated with a Chinese prince of the Shang dynasty who fled his country for some reason and settled in southern Manchuria. It was he who founded Choson, also known as Korea. The direct rule of China over Korea began in 109 BC following the conquest of the Han Emperor. Since then there was a strong cultural influence of the Chinese over Korea. However, the Chinese rule over Korea declined from the late fourth century AD to the early seventh with the emergence of three native kingdoms, namely, Koguryo in the north, Paekche in the south-west and Silla in the south-east. In the early seventh century the Sui emperors of China sent three military expeditions for the reconquest of Korea but all of them failed miserably. The Tang emperors also made some attempts in this direction but met with very limited success. The kingdom of Silla, a part of Korea, agreed to pay tribute to China. It was around 1231 that Korea was invaded by the Mongols who established their control and spread their cultural influence through matrimonial alliances with the Korean rulers and aristocracy. But for the common man the Mongol occupation inflicted great hardships since their rulers had to pay tributes to the Mongol emperor.

Mongol power in China declined in the middle of the fourteenth century with the result that its influence waned in the court. Subsequently, the Ming Emperor decided to re-establish his control over Korea. A Korean general by the name Yi Song-gye took advantage of the internal situation and put an end to the Koryo dynasty. During the next five centuries (1392-1910), Korea was ruled by a new dynasty, the Yi dynasty. Its end came when Japan annexed Korea in 1910. The Yi rulers of Korea used to send regular tribute – missions to the ruling Chinese emperors. The Chinese influence on Korea was such that in the sixteenth century the Korean Government expelled a few undesirable Japanese at the instance of the Chinese Government.

Korea's Contact with the West

In 1593, the Japanese Christian soldiers were punished by the Korean Government, and at this time a Spanish Jesuit named Gregario de Cespedes looked after them. The Dutch were also unsuccessful in establishing their commercial contacts with the Korean Government. Similar attempts by other European traders also failed at the end of the eighteenth and the beginning of the nineteenth centuries. Christianity eventually spread to Korea due to the efforts of the Spanish and French Jesuits.

Whenever British, Russian, and French missions arrived at the Korean capital for establishing trade relations, the Korean Government pretended that she was a 'dependent' state of China. In other words Korea was denying herself the status of autonomy. Therefore, the question of Korea's status was not settled even when the French force sought China's permission to attack Korea for the genocide of Christian converts in 1866. To the French it looked as though the Chinese Government had no *locus standi* in Korea. Foreign pressure to open the doors of Korea became persistent from 1866. The American merchants too showed interest but the Korean government spurned their offer. It was not until 1875-76 that the Japanese broke the impasse with their gun-boat diplomacy. A Japanese gun-boat (engaged in marine-surveys) near the Korean coast was fired upon by the Korean coast guards. The Japanese Government ordered naval retaliation. Scared at the prospect of a full invasion, Korea signed a treaty with Japan, known as the Treaty of Kangwa (February 27, 1876).

The Treaty of Kangwa provided for the opening of three Korean ports for foreign commerce. Japan recognised the independence of Korea (in effect it meant that Korea was no more a dependant state of China). Diplomatic relations were established between the two countries. But there was some confusion in the sense that Japan treated Korea as an independent and sovereign state while Korea continued to believe that it did not disrupt her ancient ties with China. China was led to believe that Korea enjoyed equal status with Japan while continuing her autonomous status within the Chinese empire. These misconceived perceptions were bound to be cleared in the course of time, particularly before and after the Sino-Japanese war.

After two decades, China felt that she was fast losing her grip (Confucian dominance) over Korea and hence took steps to check the drift. These included better diplomatic ties, increased military strength for Korea, and an appeal to her to have relations with the United States. In 1882, the United States signed a treaty with Korea establishing diplomatic and commercial ties. Britain, Russia, Germany and France established diplomatic relations with Korea believing the latter was a sovereign power. Korea was still under the impression that she was a dependent state of China.

Prelude to Sino-Japanese War

The Korean court consisted of two groups of politicians, one which favoured relations with foreign powers, and the other which was totally averse to it. In these circumstances, a plot was hatched to expel the Queen, but it failed. The Korean mobs attacked the Japanese consular office, and its officials fled to the coast hoping to reach their country. A British ship rescued them from the wrath of the Koreans. This incident provoked the Japanese government to send her troops to Korea; and China, not to be left behind, also sent her troops there. The Chinese troops arrested the father of the Korean King and forcibly took him to Tientsin for the purpose of punishing him. In the meantime, Japan succeeded in extracting a government apology, indemnity, and "right to legation guard at Seoul." China pretended she was Korea's Lord-Protector but Japan would have none of it. China tightened her control over Korea by signing a commercial treaty in 1882 converting the latter to the status of a "boundary state of China."

Tientsin Convention

The situation became critical since Japan was not prepared to lose her control over Korea. She criticised the conduct of China and hoped to see Korea as an independent state. In 1884, a clash between the Chinese soldiers and the Japanese legation guards brought the two statesmen of China and Japan, namely Li Hung-Chang and Ito, to the negotiating table at Tientsin. The two agreed to withdraw their troops from Korea. Again if any one sent troops, the other would be notified.

Causes of Sino-Japanese War (1894-95)

While Korea attracted the attention of many foreign powers with trade prospects, there was considerable rivalry between Britain and Russia over gaining control over the situation. However, it was Japan which was to reap maximum benefits. She enjoyed the initial advantage of having a favourable trade with Korea, a situation not palatable to the Chinese statesman, Li Hung-Chang. He became extremely nervous about the growing influence of Japan, and therefore, took necessary steps which included the establishment of a naval base at Port Arthur. He also planned to have a rail connection between Shanhaikwan and Vladivostok. Russia was also planning to build the Trans-Siberian railways hoping to expand her sphere of influence in this area. The news of Russia's ambition caused great resenment in Japan. The latter did not want a competitor who would thwart her ambitions, specially over Korea. She was prepared to fight.

There were other reasons too for Japan's ruling politicians welcoming a war to acquire control over Korea. The constitutional government in Japan was not running smoothly since the cabinet was responsible to the Emperor and not to Parliament (Diet). Then there was the deadlock over the sanction of enlarged defence budget and the Diet was not budging from its rigid stand. The Emperor's intervention appeared imminent. It was in this kind of situation that the Japanese militarists and bureaucrats welcomed a conflict over Korea as this would divert the attention of the public and unite all the political parties at home.

Immediate Cause

The revolt of Tong Hak in Korea finally culminated in a military conflict. Tong Hak was originally a religious sect in Korea which, in the course of time, gathered all politically oppressed Koreans under its umbrella. It chalked out a radical programme which was not acceptable to the Korean Government. Tong Hak leaders were anti-foreign, anti-Christian and anti-Japanese. When Tong Hak staged a revolt in the southern provinces, the government sent troops to crush it. The government troops suffered a defeat and the Chinese ruler, Yuan Shi Kai, urged Li Hung-Chang to send Chinese troops to assist the Korean Government (June 1894). China, in accordance with the Tientsin convention, notified Japan of her intention to send troops to Korea. But what caused Japanese to be angry was that China mentioned Korea as her tributary State.

By the time, the Japanese troops reached Korea, the Tong Hak rebellion had been suppressed, thanks to the assistance of the Chinese troops. It was then that the Japanese Government played its trump card, ie, to provoke China to a war. Japan proposed to the Chinese Government that a joint front constituting both should bring about the much needed reforms in Korea. The Chinese Government refused to accept the Japanese proposal giving the reason that this would tantamount to interfering in Korea's internal matters. It also questioned the Japanese right to interfere in Korea's internal matters at the same time. It was then that Japan asked Korea whether she was a tributary State of China. When she received a vague reply, the Japanese troops marched into the Korean capital and took its king captive. She then went about reorganising the administration of Korea to suit her convenience. Japan ordered the new Government of Korea to expel the Chinese troops from her soil assuring the Koreans that her assistance would be available. The Sino-Japanese war broke out on August 1, 1894.

Course of the War

As Japan seemed to be the aggressor, she met with hostile attitude from Britain and Russia. Japan tried to assuage their feelings by declaring that she had no intention of annexing Korea but only to see that the much needed reforms in Korea were carried out. Both the countries were satisfied with this explanation and hoped that things would be all right when China defeated Japan. However, the course of events took an altogether new turn, in the sense that the Japanese scored spectacular victory over her adversary. The Chinese army was no match to the numerically inferior but technologically superior Japanese army. Li Hung-Chang's Peiyang fleet, which he assiduously built as the main fighting machine (25 vessels including nine modern ships) failed to defend the nation. China's naval fleet could not be further strengthened due to paucity of funds. No doubt the Dowager Queen was more interested in rebuilding the Summer Palace. The attack of the Peiyang fleet was repulsed successfully by the Japanese off the Yalu River in September 1894. It became quite clear to both Russia and Britain that China would be defeated, and the latter took measures to see that China was not further humiliated by Japan. Britain was prepared to intervene to stop the war. But the British intention to save China met with a cold response, specially from Germany and the United States. The winter months of 1895 witnessed further humiliation of the Chinese army at the hands of Japan. The Japanese troops took Wei Hai Wai, crossed Manchuria, and captured New Chewing and Yung Kow. Thereafter they got ready to march upon the Chinese capital itself! China's cup of humiliation reached its brim and she begged for peace in the absence of any support from Britain and her allies. Li Hung-Chang conducted the negotiations with the Japanese, and the result was the conclusion of the treaty of Shimonoseki. With the signing of the treaty the state of war between the two countries came to an end.

Terms of the Treaty (17 April 1895)

Japan was in a position to get several of her demands fulfilled. According to the treaty, (a) China recognised the independence of Korea, (b) gave away Taiwan, the Pescodores and the Liaotung peninsula, (c) paid 300 million taels as war indemnity and (d) conducted a new commercial treaty with Japan on the basis of most favoured nation treatment including the opening of seven new ports for trade. In 1896, China signed another commercial treaty with Japan giving further concessions relating to "industry and manufacturers" in the treaty ports.

The Aftermath

As anticipated by the Japanese politicians, war followed by the victory had benevolent effects. The nation became strong and the quarrels between the government and the Diet ceased. The defence budgets were passed without much opposition. In her euphoria, Japan pushed forward vigorously her policy of expansionism in Asia. Her new acquisitions like Port Arthur and Liaotung peninsula enabled her, to some extent, to influence the policy of the Chinese Government.

For China, the defeat and the signing of the humiliating treaty, heralded the impending downfall of the Manchu dynasty. The age-old Confucian values incorporated into her foreign policy had to be given up in the new circumstances. For the so-called Middle Kingdom, there were no tributary states over which she could exercise her authority. The Chinese intellectuals had to give up Confucian ideals and adopt a Western political ideology to survive. The Confucian scholar-bureaucrats stood discredited. The new commercial treaty of 1896 signed with Japan elevated the latter's status equal to that of Western powers. The Western powers considered Japan a 'power to be reckoned with' and the latter got the nickname 'yellow peril' (by Kaiser's cartoon). China's defeat also heralded the end of the tribute system.

Japan's victory came as a rude shock to Russia for she hardly expected a small country to defeat a big one. She wished to acquire some regions of the Far East at the expense of China and Japan. For this purpose the Russian Emperor launched the Trans-Siberian railway in 1891. With the support of her allies Russia forced Japan to give up the acquisition of the Liaotung peninsula, which the latter got from her treaty with China. Japan was hardly in a position to resist Russia's pressure for that would have forced her to wage another war. Further, she was hardly in a position to fight and, therefore, unwillingly yielded.

12

THE RISE OF JAPANESE IMPERIALISM

As noted earlier, the Sino-Japanese war may be said to be the starting point of Japan's growing ambition to become a big power. Unfortunately, she was unable to reap the benefits of the Treaty of Shimonoseki which she signed with China. This was mainly due to the intervention of the three European powers — Russia, France and Germany. The notes presented by these powers to Japan declared that "... the possession of the peninsula of Liaotung claimed by Japan, would be a constant menace to the capital of China, would at the same time render illusory the independence of Korea..." Japan was left with no choice but to fight these three European powers, for which she was totally unprepared.

Therefore, she was compelled to accept the new terms offered by the three powers. It mainly included monetary compensation. Japan returned the Liaotung peninsula to China by the Chefoo convention in exchange for 30 million Kuping-taels. The Japanese military and naval staff felt terribly humiliated because they were the ones who insisted on the possession of Liaotung peninsula as a means to dominate China. Similarly, the Japanese public felt bitter at the irony of events, ie, victory without benefits. Their indignation was sought to be tempered by an imperial rescript. What should be revealed here is "that the excessive demands of the militarists had turned military victory into diplomatic defeat". What was more galling to the Japanese was the fact that the three European powers, which carved out spheres of influence over China, were not permitting Japan to follow in their footsteps. By this they were setting a double standard which deeply hurt the Japanese national pride. Therefore, Japan waited patiently for another opportunity to settle scores — particularly with Russia, who was considered the chief villain.

Russia wanted to check Japan's imperial ambition. Otherwise, her own interest in China would be in jeopardy. Pretending to be China's saviour, she cast her eyes on the ice-free-port, prospects of undertaking Trans-Siberian railway construction unto Vladivostok, and further acquisition from China. France too entered the fray, not because Japan would gain, but because Russia would tilt the balance of power in her favour. Germany was equally interested in some more acquisitions in China, thanks to Russia's pre-occupation in the

Middle East. France knew that Russia should not get away with a lion's share, if partition of China took place.

Russia took the initiative in helping China to secure a loan from France in July 1895. This was to enable China to give compensation to Japan after the former's defeat in the Sino-Japanese war. In fact, Russia wanted China to depend on her. The Russian diplomat, Count Witte had manoeuvred to bring about this kind of situation. Some banks of Britain and Germany also lent money to China amounting to 16 million pounds.

Sino-Russian Agreements

The Sino-Russian agreements had an impact upon relations with Japan. When Li Hung-Chang went to the coronation ceremony of the Russian Tsar, he met the Russian prince. There was a proposal to establish cultural ties between the two countries. It was to be followed by an agreement for the construction of railroads across Manchuria which was to be financed by Russia. This was to enable Russia to provide adequate protection to China from surprise military attacks by any adversary. The outcome of this proposal led to the Li-Lebonov secret treaty concluded on June 3, 1896 which was aimed against Japan. This secret treaty permitted Russia to use certain treaty ports of China. Furthermore, it was to allow the construction of Trans-Siberian railway by Russia across Manchuria.

After a few years, the terms of the secret-treaty came to light. Subsequently, the Chinese Eastern Railway Company gave Russia many territorial and tariff concessions, including military control over the area of operation. The result was that railway construction over a distance of 1,000 miles was completed in 1904. This gave Russia easy access to the Pacific coast. This railway construction was part of Russia's plan to build a political and commercial empire. In other words, the Russian policy of 'peaceful penetration' was successful. Russia acquired the lease of Port Arthur, which became one of the causes for the Russo-Japanese war. The Russians in Manchuria made Port Arthur their strongest base and looked forward to grabbing a lion's share in the likely partition of China. To the Japanese, the peaceful penetration of Russia over Manchuria appeared like a dagger thrust into her heart. To sum up, China became totally dependent on Russia for her protection.

The Anglo-Japanese Alliance (1902)

In these circumstances, Japan looked forward to having a strong ally to promote her cause. It was at this time Britain came to her rescue by not only giving moral support but by lending military assistance to contain Russia's expansionism. Why was Britain interested in making Japan, a pigmy among Asiatic countries, her ally? This was because Russia had been following what is called a "forward policy" in the Middle East. The British Government in India was afraid of Russia's expansionism. It appeared as though Russia had decided to invade India.

There developed what is called "Russo-phobia" among the British administrators governing India. Russia had been expanding her influence even in the Far-East, thanks to the weakness of Chinese administration. There was a feeling among British statesmen at that time that Britain's "splendid isolationism" should end. She should reorient her foreign policy to the changing situation in the Far-East. It was during this time that the balance of power theory came to play a significant role. At any rate, Britain desired to stop Russia from expanding at the expense of China.

The change in the Japanese leadership, namely the replacement of Ito Hirobumi — who believed firmly in reaching an agreement with Russia rather than Britain — by General Katsura Taro (a follower of General Yamagata Aritomo and his philosophy) brought about inevitable conflict with Russia. Negotiations between Japan and Britain succeeded because both countries had common interests, and Russia happened to be their common enemy. The Anglo-Japanese alliance was concluded on January 10, 1902.

The provisions of the treaty included mutual support to China's territorial sovereignty and integrity, support for the open door policy, and "recognition of their special interests" in China. Britain recognised Japan's special interests in Korea. The most important clause of the treaty was directed against Russia. In other words, Britain and Japan agreed to remain neutral if anyone was attacked, but would come to the rescue if the attacker was helped by any other power.

Significance of the Anglo-Japanese Treaty

Japan's alliance with England marked a distinct advantage in the sense that Britain treated Japan on an equal footing. Japan was given the status of a big power. The treaty encouraged Japan to extend her sphere of influence over China. Furthermore, Britain gave a green signal to Japan so that she could launch military expeditions against her enemies. The alliance gave Japan an imperial status. This alliance forced Russia to give assurance to China that she would retreat from Manchuria gradually, in three phases. The Anglo-Japanese alliance implied that "Japanese and English diplomacy would work hand-in-hand at Peking to check Russia, failing which Japan would oppose her in the field while England prevented Russia from securing active support from any other power." (Vinacke).

Russia's non-compliance of troop withdrawal from Manchuria precipitated the outbreak of the Russo-Japanese war. Japan did not like the Russian presence in Manchuria. But the war actually broke out for another important reason. Russia ignored Japanese special interests in Korea. Japan was annoyed because she had more or less accepted Russia's special interest in Manchuria, whereas the latter was not prepared to do so in the case of Korea. Russia did not satisfy Japan's demand that she be granted special rights in Korea.

The Russo-Japanese War (1904-05)

It was most unfortunate that the war took place between Russia and Japan in Manchuria which belonged to China. The war began with a large body of Russian troops occupying the Trans-Siberian region which threatened the security of Korea. Japan broke off her relations with Russia on February 6, 1904. On February 8, the Russian fleet in Port Arthur came under Japanese torpedo attack. This conflict turned into a large scale war by February 10, 1904.

After crossing the Yellow River, Japan's army entered Manchuria while her Navy went into action. The Japanese Navy captured Port Arthur and Darien. The Russians were pushed back from Manchuria. The Japanese scored brilliant victories against the Russians and captured Mukden, the capital of Manchuria. The Russians who were humiliated began to appeal to their Baltic fleet to come to their rescue. Unfortunately, their Baltic fleet could not move fast enough to reach the Far East due to the naval blockade by the British Navy near the Suez Canal zone. However, on reaching the Far-Eastern waters, the Baltic fleet suffered a crushing defeat at the hands of the Japanese at the Straits of Tsushima. The hero of this naval victory was Admiral Tojo. Both the countries were totally exhausted by September 1905, and eagerly responded to President Theodore Roosevelt's appeal for burying the hatchet. It was due to his efforts that Japan and Russia concluded a peace treaty — the Treaty of Portsmouth (September 5, 1905).

Terms of the Treaty of Portsmouth

Russia was represented by Count Witte and Rosen, and Japan by Kamura and Takahura. Russia acknowledged Japan's permanent interests in Korea. Japan acquired the lease on the Liaotung peninsula from Russia with the consent of China. Japan also acquired the southern section of the eastern railroad from Chang Chun to Port Arthur. Japan was also equally interested in collecting the war indemnity from Russia because of popular domestic demand. It must be remembered that the war proved to be very expensive for Japan and she looked forward to compensate herself at the expense of Russia. However, she failed to receive due compensation from Russia on account of blundering diplomats. Japan also gained fishing rights in the Siberian waters.

The Japanese diplomats who concluded the treaty faced noisy demonstrations when they returned home. The demonstrators were angry because Japan's military victory was not followed by any monetary gain. What the militarists gained, the diplomats lost. The noisy demonstration ended in great violence and took a heavy toll of lives. The only consolation that Japan got was the acquisition of the Southern half of Sakhalin in place of war indemnity. During the next few years Japan turned Korea into a protectorate. Subsequently, she annexed Korea in 1910. Unfortunately, the annexation of Korea was not liked by the Koreans. The Japanese Resident-General in Korea was assassinated by a Korean patriot.

Significance of the Treaty

After the Russo-Japanese war, Japan turned into a typical modern nation and inherited the traits of Western imperialism. She became the first imperialist power in the history of modern Asia. She achieved this status by vying with many other Western nations on an equal footing. To the Asian countries, the defeat of Russia, a European power, at the hands of Japan, had far-reaching consequences. These Asiatic countries were inspired by Japan's victory over Russia, and their on-going national movements received a great fillip. They looked upon Japan as a leader, and followed her example.

Japan and Manchuria

It must be remembered that during the course of the Russo-Japanese war, the Japanese forces occupied Seoul in February 1904. After the conclusion of the war, Korea was turned into a protectorate by the Japanese Government. Japan was empowered to regulate Korea's financial and external affairs. Japanese governors and police officials were appointed to ensure law and order in Korea. The US President, Mr W H Taft, gave his consent to the new set-up of the Japanese in Korea. Japan turned her attention to the newly acquired state of southern Manchuria. These events caused anxiety to US businessmen as they felt that they would not be welcomed in the region. China had to give her consent to Japan's new acquisition from Russia, and hence the Sino-Japanese treaty.

Sino-Japanese Treaty (December 22, 1905)

By this treaty, Japan received substantial concession from China in the form of trade, licence for railway construction and exploitation of forest wealth. It was followed by secret protocols. The most important clause in these protocols was that the Chinese Government undertook a pledge not to construct railway lines parallel to the Japanese Southern Manchurian Railway. In the meantime, the Yokohama Special Bank served to promote the interests of Japan for exploiting the newly acquired Manchuria. Manchuria was divided between

Russia and Japan, and the nation most affected so far as the Open Door policy was concerned was the US. In the wake of Sino-Japanese agreement, came the Franco-Japanese and Russo-Japanese agreements. All these agreements established "the doctrine of spheres of influence." This doctrine which was in force for a couple of decades affected China's territorial integrity and "the principle of equal opportunity".

Annexation of Korea (1910)

Let us examine the events culminating in the annexation of Korea by Japan. As mentioned earlier, Korea became a protectorate in the first instance. However, Japan was not satisfied with regard to the status of Korea. In fact, Japan desired to further integrate Korea under Japanese control. In other words Japan wanted Korea to become a Japanese colony. However, this move was stoutly opposed by some sections in Korea, notably the royal family which was in disgrace. Unfortunately, the opposition was overruled and the Korean Emperor was made to abdicate his throne in favour of his son. Japan appointed a Resident-General to directly supervise the administration of Korea. After the secret Russo-Japanese treaty of 1907, Japan's Foreign Minister Komura took steps to bring Korea under Japanese control. This move unfortunately resulted in the assassination of the Resident-General, Prince Ito, at Harbin in October 1909.

The Japanese were outraged and demanded outright annexation of Korea. The Japanese Emperor was compelled to yield to this public demand. The young Korean prince, who happened to be the nominal head of the state, was allowed to escape, and Japan declared the annexation of Korea in August 1910. Britain, because of her alliance with Japan, had to recognise this *fait accompli*. The Anglo-Japanese alliance was, however, renewed in 1911, but this time it was directed against Germany. In 1912 Meiji Emperor Mutsihito died and his son Taisho (who was a permanent invalid) ascended the Japanese throne. Since the new Emperor was physically and mentally weak, the Japanese generals and militarists took advantage of this situation.

Japan's Entry into the Great War

The outbreak of the First World War in 1914 provided a wonderful opportunity to Japan to establish her hegemony over China. While the Western powers were preoccupied with war against Germany, they hardly took any interest in the political developments taking place in the Far East. Japan remained virtually free to carry out her imperial ambitions. The renewal of the Anglo-Japanese alliance in 1911 gave further encouragement to Japan to establish her control over many regions in the Far East. Britain expected that Japan would check Germany's aggressive activities in the Far East. Japanese Prime Minister Okuma made clear his intention to join the Great War on the side of Britain and France. Japan served an ultimatum to Germany demanding withdrawal of all his ships from the Far East. The ultimatum asked Germany to give up the Shantung leasehold. When the ultimatum got no response from Germany, Japan declared war in August 1914.

The Japanese forces occupied German's possessions in the Far East, particularly a large number of islands such as Marshall, Mariana and Caroline islands. Furthermore, they landed in China, and overran the German Shantung peninsula including the port of Tsingtao (November 1914). Japan's intrusion into Chinese territory outside the German leasehold evoked strong resentment from the Chinese Government. The Chinese Government led by Yuan Shi Kai demanded Japanese withdrawal from this region. But Japan rejected the Chinese demand. China was too weak to carry out any deterrent action. In fact, Britain, Russia and France desired to have some share in the Japanese conquests. The Japanese considered China a prospective colony.

The Twenty-one Demands (May 1915)

Japan sprang a sudden surprise on China with her notorious and secret twenty-one demands in May 1915. These demands aimed at converting China into a Japanese colony. Japan also hoped to turn Manchuria into a full-fledged colony. What were the reasons for Japan's bullying tactics? Firstly, Japan felt that compared with the status of other European powers in China, she was inferior. In fact, she felt that she enjoyed fewer number of concessions in China than others. Secondly, Japan was a debtor-nation which could not match her position with other Western nations, unless China fully came under her control. Thirdly, Japan realised that the Yuan Shi Kai Government had no solid base of support either from the European powers or from the Chinese masses. Therefore, she felt that it was an opportune time to fully exploit China's weakness by making twenty-one demands. The twenty-one demands fall conveniently into five groups.

The demands in the first group wholly cancelled Germany's sphere of influence in the Shantung peninsula, and accorded the same to Japan. The second group of demands contained Japan's "paramount interests" in South Manchuria and Eastern Inner Mongolia. It required China to recognise Japan's permanent interest in these regions. The third group contained demands which called upon China to give consent to Japan's sole monopoly over mining operations in the Yangtze Valley. The fourth group of demands asked China to promise that she would not transfer the coastal territories to other foreign powers. The fifth group of demands (couched as "requests") included several political, economic, religious, railway and territorial concessions from China. These demands revealed Japan's ulterior motives with regard to her relations with China.

These demands were notified to China secretly on May 7, 1915, with an ultimatum that their non-compliance within twenty-four hours would result in immediate retaliation. The Chinese Government under Yuan Shi Kai was scared, and accepted many of these demands except those affecting China's sovereignty. Unfortunately, Britain and France were too preoccupied with the Great War, and were therefore, unable to render any help to China at this juncture. Surprisingly, Japan played her cards well and secured support for her unjust demands from the European partners. It may be noted that even the United States more or less agreed to give full freedom to Japan to exploit China. This understanding was arrived at by the Lansing-Ishii agreement in 1917 concluded between the US and Japan. The US Government was afraid of a possible Japanese withdrawal from the war if this agreement was not reached. Thus, Chinese interests were totally scarified by these great powers.

While the allied powers were engaged in defeating Germany during the war, Russian forces withdrew due to the outbreak of the revolution (1917). The Russian withdrawal left a deep void, and the European allies felt that only Japan could fill it in the Far East. Hence, Japan took full advantage of this situation and, got the approval of the Allies regarding the twenty-one demands. At the conclusion of the Great War, Japan surpassed other big powers in achieving her goal. Her economic status also improved considerably.

13

JAPAN AND THE WASHINGTON CONFERENCE

The Great War wrought several changes in the international scene. Germany, France and Russia lost their pre-eminence in international affairs. But, Britain, the USA and Japan continued to dominate the scene. The signing of the Paris peace treaty did not resolve many problems. Other problems relating to all the interested powers, especially the US, Japan and Britain, had to be discussed and issues resolved. Japan's imperialistic ambitions during the course of the war had attracted the attention of Britain and the United States. The other European powers were also equally concerned about Japan's hegemonistic role in the Far East.

The United States was seriously concerned about Japanese expansionist ideas in the Far East, especially with regard to China. This was because her Pacific interests were dangerously clashing with those of the Japanese. One must remember that the United States had been able to establish her control over a number of islands in the Pacific Ocean, and also over the Philippines. To promote her business interests in China, she advocated the Open Door policy with regard to China. Unfortunately, during the war, Japan insisted on China accepting her 21 secret demands, and this affected the Open Door policy. In fact, the United States Government did not like secret diplomacy and blackmail. Britain felt outraged because she was not consulted by Japan when she put forward her 21 demands.

Therefore, Britain and the United States, who had become close allies after the war felt that Japan should be somehow restrained from harassing China. This was particularly so when US-Japanese relations had soured. In addition to this, it was felt by all the powers concerned that there should be some limitation on the armament race which was still continuing. It was at the instance of President Wilson of the United States, that the Washington Conference was convened.

In the meantime, Japan had come forward with her demand for the doctrine of racial equality to be accepted by the Western powers, particularly by the United States Government. It must be remembered that the United States Government followed a policy of discrimination with regard to the immigration of Japanese and Chinese labourers to the USA. The new immigration laws in the United States aimed at preventing large-scale immigration of skilled labourers from Japan and China. All arrangements were made for the convening of the conference in Washington DC by the US Secretary of State, Hughes, and the invitees were Britain, France, Italy, Belgium, China, the Netherlands and Portugal.

The ostensible purpose for convening this conference was to discuss the limitation of armaments and also the Far Eastern question. Russia was excluded mainly because she was going through the Bolshevik Revolution. The conference was convened at a time when there was too much anti-Japanese feeling among the Chinese. In fact, the Chinese were boycotting Japanese goods. It appeared that if the conference failed to arrive at an agreement, there would be a war between the United States and Japan. Britain was caught in a compromising position because she was tied to Japan by the Anglo-Japanese alliance of 1902 (which was renewed in 1905 and 1915). She eagerly desired to terminate her alliance with Japan because the United States Government did not recognise the "special interests" of Britain and Japan with regard to Far Eastern affairs. There was a question of China's territorial integrity and sovereignty, which had been violated by Japan as mentioned earlier. The noisy demonstrations against the Japanese inroads into China indicated the rise of the latter's nationalism. China was asserting her rights to abrogate the extra territorial rights of foreign powers.

In the meantime, pressure was building up both within and outside the United States which had a bearing upon the convening of this conference. For example, the US Congress, at the instance of Senator Borah of Idaho, passed a resolution asking the government to take steps to halt the arms race. The US Congress desired the implementation of the Wilsonian programme of peace. Lord Li of the British Government also proposed a meeting of the concerned powers for concluding a naval agreement.

The Washington Conference began with the US President warmly welcoming all the delegates at the venue of the Washington Memorial Constitutional Hall on November 11,1921. Secretary Hughes outlined the necessity of halting arms race as there was no war. The conference hoped to achieve an end to the existing mutual rivalries among nations, and establish a climate for international peace through peaceful negotiations of international disputes. The address of the Secretary of State was forthright and frank. He impressed upon the audience that nations had assembled there "not for general resolutions — but for action". During the course of this famous post-war international conference resolutions were passed and six treaties were concluded. Among the treaties, the most important were the Four Power Pacific Treaty, the Five Power Naval Agreement and the Nine Power Treaty. Let us examine the terms and objectives of these agreements.

The Four Power Pacific Treaty

The Four Power Treaty which was signed by Britain, the United States, France and Japan, was to remain in force for ten years (1921-31). The terms included were a) the right of each member to be respected concerning their insular possessions and insular dominions in the Far East, b) to settle their disputes or differences over regions in the Pacific, if any, in a joint conference provided they could not be settled at the diplomatic level, c) to be in touch with one another, if their rights were threatened by any other power's aggressive action. What this treaty tried to achieve was to replace the Anglo-Japanese alliance with the alliance of the four. In other words, the USA was assured of her possessions in the Philippines and other nearby islands. It served as a restraint on the growing imperial ambitions of Japan.

The Five Power Treaty (Naval Armament Limitation)

The Four Power Treaty had certain limitations which did not include a check on the race for naval armaments. Japan was to be persuaded to sign the Naval Armament Limitation Treaty only with little concessions. Japan wanted clear assurance from Britain and the USA that they would not pose a serious threat to her interests or possessions in the Far East. In other words, she was trying to restrain the US and Britain who desired to build naval bases at Hong Kong, Manila, Guam and other Pacific islands. Britain, France and the United States reached an agreement to give this assurance to Japan by including the principle of non-fortification (mentioned in Article 19 of the Five-Power Treaty). France put pressure on others to confine it to only capital ships. When concluded on February 6, 1922, the Five Power Treaty (Britain, France, the United States, Japan and Italy) provided for a ten year holiday in capital ship construction, and the scrapping of hundreds of thousands of tonnes of capital ships. Furthermore, it limited the capital ship tonnage ratio to 5,25,000; 5,25,000; 3,15,000; 1,75,000; 1,75,000 for Britain, the USA, France, Italy and Japan respectively. The treaty was to remain in force for 10 years, and thereafter to be renewed if found necessary. Japan was satisfied. She was one of the beneficiaries under this naval agreement. Her position in the Pacific was not at all threatened. In addition, she was saved from a mad race regarding naval construction. Britain also gained because the treaty excluded the fortification of Australia and New Zealand. The United States neither gained nor lost anything in view of the Nine Power Treaty which was concluded soon after this treaty.

The Nine Power Treaty

All the participating nations of this conference signed this treaty on February 6, 1922. This treaty was mainly concerned with the sovereignty and territorial integrity of the Republic of China. They agreed 1) not to take advantage of the chaotic situation prevailing in China, 2) to uphold principles of Open Door policy, 3) respect China's neutrality if she chose to remain neutral and 4) not sign any other treaty violating the sanctity of this treaty. But the language of some of the provisions of this treaty unfortunately happened to be ambiguous, providing ample scope for future complications. But the signatories conveniently ignored what the US had achieved, that the Open Door policy was binding on all contracting parties to the agreement. The contracting parties were now subjected to a code of conduct which governed their mutual relations. It was like the following of international law by modern nations today.

China's Demands

The Chinese demanded the restoration of tariff autonomy and the revocation of extra-territoriality enjoyed by all foreign powers in China. These demands were not conceded, but China was permitted to increase her tariff rates. A commission was to be appointed to examine the issue of terminating the extra-territorial rights enjoyed by foreign powers in China, and bring about some modifications. Similarly, the powers cared little to fulfil China's demands for the abrogation of the clause concerning "special rights" of Japan and Russia over Manchuria, which she unfortunately agreed to under duress in May 1915. Secretary of State Hughes and British Minister Arthur Balford tried to pacify China by agreeing to arrange a meeting with Japan.

This was to break the deadlock existing on this issue between the two. Their efforts met with success in the sense that Japan and China began to have negotiations on outstanding issues which remained outside the scope of the Washington Conference. The Sino-Japanese meeting resulted in an agreement by which Japan agreed to restore to China the Shantung peninsula, if China provided monetary compensation. The Japanese softened their attitude after 36 meetings and signed this treaty on February 4, 1922. The treaty included the return of Kioachou to China by Japan but provided for Japanese control over Tsinan-Tsingtao railways for 15 years. Despite signing this treaty, Japan continued to exercise its economic and political control over this region.

The other issues discussed related to the United States and Japanese governments. They concentrated on the withdrawal of the latter's forces from Siberia and North Sakhalin, and the claims of the US over the Yap island. Both these issues were settled amicably with Japan agreeing to withdraw from Siberia. Regarding the US claims over the Yap island, Japan signed a treaty conceding residential and communication rights to American citizens residing at Yap in return for the US recognition to the Japanese mandate over former German islands in the North Pacific. It was obvious from the above factors that the US Secretary of State had scored diplomatic victories on all fronts.

The key question to be asked was whether China, whose sovereignty and territorial integrity had been a subject of discussion, received any benefit at all from this conference. The answer is yes and no. The Nine Power Treaty was an affirmation of international principles adopted with regard to China, but it all depended upon the great powers for its enforcement. Britain and the US were parties to this treaty, and therefore, it was expected that the said treaty would stand the test of time.

But other foreign powers, were not prepared to give up the gains derived from unequal treaties so easily. Although they promised to give up their leaseholds, they had no intention of doing so. Japan was the only exception. But they gave up minor concessions, like the withdrawal of foreign post offices, and radio stations set up in China. Foreign troops were to be withdrawn from the non-leaseholds in China. China was not granted total tariff autonomy, but with some modifications in its working, allowed to increase her revenue. To conclude in the words of Vinacke, "China may be considered to have gained from the conference because she did not lose more than what has already been lost ..." The Shantung question having been settled amicably between China and Japan, it was expected that they would remain friendly. More so when Japan was not to lose her sphere of influence developed during the Great War.

14

RISE AND FALL OF PARTY GOVERNMENTS IN JAPAN

The Great War hastened the process of modern industrialization of Japan to a great extent. The Japanese conquests and subsequent colonization may be said to be the most important factor in the rapid economic growth of Japan. Pre-occupation of the European powers during the course of the war in the European theatre, indirectly provided inputs to Japanese imperialism and overseas trade. Many Asian countries began to import Japanese goods since the war prevented any imports from the European countries. It was this factor which accelerated the industrialisation of Japan further. Moreover, the Japanese began to produce goods of very high quality.

The Japanese textile business grew by leaps and bounds. In addition, Japan showed great promise of becoming a fully democratic country, unlike the authoritarian regimes set up by Genro in the early days. One of the important signs of this promising future was the rise and growth of party government in Japan. In other words, the Genro lost its hold, and the last of the Genro, Saionji, was in sympathy with the development of party government. In the meantime, Japan experienced liberal intellectual currents sweeping across many parts of Asia. The cause of the liberal movement was championed by Professor Yashino Sakuzo. The universal suffrage movement was in full progress with labour unions supporting it.

The most vehement opposition towards the establishment came from the militarists. It must be remembered that the militarists, since the Meiji era, were mainly responsible for the emergence of Japan as a major power in the world. However, after the Great War, there was a marked decline in their popularity. Incidentally, public opinion in Japan was against any further overseas expansion of Japanese territories. The Japanese military expedition to Siberia proved highly expensive besides being unnecessary. In 1924, many soldiers were retrenched, and the expenditure of the army was considerably reduced – from 42 per cent of the budget to 29 per cent in 1925. Another important factor which promoted the cause of party government in Japan was the rule of liberal businessmen. They sought to influence the government through their lobbies. They were afraid of losing potential markets in China, if the party governments adopted a stiff attitude. However, many Japanese believed that their nation should retain her rights in Manchuria and support the programme on disarmament.

The party government made commendable progress during the period 1918-1931, though it was checked later by the Defence Ministry and the bureaucracy. The Defence Ministry was in favour of enjoying an autonomous status which was not in consistence with the ideology of party governments. The political parties were making hectic efforts to gain credibility by providing a responsible government. This was during the period of transition, from the oligarchic type (traditional in style and led by Genro) of government to a government led by party cabinets. Japan enjoyed a period of liberal democracy after the universal franchise was adopted.

Cabinet Governments

There were no less than 12 successive cabinet governments during the period 1918-32. These cabinet governments tried to introduce reforms even though the average tenure of each cabinet government was not more than two years. One of the popular cabinet governments was led by Hara Takashi who was a protege of Ito. He worked in the foreign office for sometime, and subsequently became the editor of *Osaka Mainichi*.

He joined the Saionji cabinet and evinced keen interest in several liberal movements. He called himself a "commoner" despite his noble birth. As prime minister, he was able to reconcile the differences existing among the various factions. His cabinet consisted mainly of bureaucrats which included General Tanaka Giichi, who was acting as Minister of War. Hara Takashi introduced reforms relating to the extension of franchise and further expansion of the educational system. But he could go no farther in so far as introducing these reforms were concerned. These reforms aimed at promoting the interests of businessmen and landowners. Though he failed to promote representative and responsible government, he was credited with having "built the most powerful party Japan had ever known". Hara met a tragic end when he was stabbed to death by a misguided patriot in November 1921.

After the end of Hara's cabinet, the next important party cabinet was set up by Kato Takaaki in 1924. It was a coalition party cabinet which included leaders from other political parties such as Keneseikai, Seiyukai and Kakushin club. Kato with a "long and distinguished political career" was president of the first named. He had been included in the second Okuma Cabinet as foreign minister. Kato's greatest achievement lay in establishing a responsible government. Among the reforms he introduced, the most important were the measures to curb wasteful expenditure of the government. He introduced budgetary-reductions for the overgrown Japanese army and navy. Similarly, the Japanese bureaucracy was cut to size through retrenchment. By 1925, Kato introduced manhood suffrage. Despite Kato's reforms, the Japanese economy did not make substantial progress. His second ministry also failed to usher in necessary reforms for improving the conditions in Japan. This was because the peers and the bureaucracy came in its way. Political observers in those days were of the opinion that political and constitutional reforms were coming to an end. Unfortunately, Kato's ministry got the Peace-Preservation Bill passed into a law which aimed at gagging the press, and banning the activities of communists and anarchists.

After Kato's death in 1926, his close colleague Wakatsuki Reijiro succeeded. He faced a lot of difficulties in carrying out reforms because of the obstacles created by the army and the Privy Council. They attacked his government for adopting a soft policy towards China. The Privy Council declared the emergency measures introduced by the cabinet to avert the banking crisis in 1927, as unconstitutional. It brought about the fall of the Wakatsuki Cabinet. The Seiyukai took advantage of this opportunity, and having no leader of its own, asked General Tanaka Giichi to be its president (1927). As a minister in the Hara Cabinet, Tanaka had become unpopular with the militarists. But, as prime minister in 1927, Tanaka aimed at encouraging economic nationalism which suited the temperament of bureaucrats and the militarists. Tanaka adopted what is known as "positive foreign policy" in international relations. This was to enable Japan to claim her legitimate place as a big power in the comity of nations. He gave up the conciliatory policy of his predecessor in foreign affairs, especially with regard to China. He wanted Japan to dominate the Asiatic countries, if not the whole world.

He prepared the plan known as the "Tanaka Memorial" for implementation. This memorial envisaged the subservience of China as a first step towards the establishment of Japan's hegemony over Asia. He would not brook any opposition, and therefore, suppressed all radical movements. Japan's foreign trade assumed great importance because the Zaibatsu (syndicate of corporate heads) was interested in it. Tanaka faced many difficulties before he could carry out his plan. His government was attacked by the opposition party, the Minseito. This opposition party condemned the phrases used in Japan's renunciation of war. This declaration of renunciation pointed to the Japanese withdrawal from the Chinese province of Shantung.

Tanaka's eventual resignation took place due to two reasons: Firstly, his forward policy with regard to China "backfired" owing to the strong resentment of the Chinese. The Chinese started boycotting Japanese goods to express their strong resentment. In the meantime, the Zaibatsu advocated the formula of peaceful economic penetration of China. Secondly, Tanaka clashed with the militarists with regard to the involvement of the Japanese division of the Kwantung army in the assassination of the Chinese warlord, Chang Tso Lin. Tanaka's resignation incidentally proved that the militarists were quite capable of unseating a civilian government with great ease.

The Minseito Cabinet (1929-31)

Hamaguchi Yako became the president of the Minseito, a political party which emerged as an alternative to the Seiyukai party. Shidehara played an important role in Hamaguchi's Government in so far as foreign relations were concerned. The Japanese foreign policy was based on friendship with the US and Britain. Hamaguchi and Shidehara decided that their country should not enter into an arms race. For accomplishing this objective, Japan participated in the London Naval Conference in 1930, and accepted the decisions taken by the earlier Washington Conference with regard to maintenance and construction of capital ships. Hamaguchi persuaded a few Japanese admirals of moderate temperament to override the majority opinion which rejected this foreign law. Subsequently, Hamaguchi's Cabinet came under attack by the army, the Privy Council and the Seiyukai for extending concessions to the Western powers at the London Conference. Hamaguchi stoutly defended his foreign policy. Unfortunately, his career was cut short by an assassin's bullet in November 1930. Subsequently, the Minseito Cabinet was led by Wakatsuki, but by this time the militarists had gained an upper hand in policy making. The attack on Manchuria carried out by the Kwantung division of the Japanese army may be cited as evidence.

Japanese Militarism

The failure of the party government in Japan gave rise to militarism. The Japanese army had, since the Siberian expedition in the 1920s, showed its capacity for independent action. Although, the general staff of the army was a part of the cabinet, it was independent of it. It came directly under the control of the Emperor. The army strategists desired the conquest of Manchuria as quite essential to serve as a "buffer" against Russian expansion in Northern China. The Japanese Government under party cabinet supported the militarists describing the "Mukden incident" as defensive. It ordered the army to retreat to the railway zone.

However, the Kwantung division of the Japanese army disobeyed and occupied the whole of Manchuria in China. Several ministers in the Wakatsuki Cabinet supported the army action with the result that the cabinet resigned in December 1932. The next cabinet was led by Inukai belonging to the Seiyukai party. He tried to stem the growing power of the army but to no avail. In the meantime, the Japanese army made further advances into China without the support of the party cabinet. An angry Inukai was left with no alternative but to compromise his position. He attempted to forestall the further advance of the Japanese army by opening direct negotiations with the Chinese Government. Unfortunately, his life was also cut short by an assassin's bullet in May 1932.

The next two prime ministers, Saito (1932-34) and Admiral Okada (1934-36), were docile and approved the actions of the Japanese army. However, the political parties in the Japanese Diet criticised the aggressive postures of the Japanese army. But these criticisms fell on deaf ears and indicated that the political parties had lost their power and influence on the army.

Failure of the Party Government

One does not have to seek far to trace the causes for the failure of the party government in Japan during the period 1924-1932. Political parties appeared to be artificial creations in a country where oligarchy had taken deep roots. Since most of the Genro had faded except Saijonji, political parties desired to replace it. Unfortunately, the Meiji constitution appeared to favour the rule of oligarchy instead of party governments. Hence the party governments served as an antithesis to the spirit of the constitution. Secondly, the absence of the middle class in Japan acted as a hindrance to the emergence of stable party governments. Thirdly, members of the political parties remained loyal to the party leaders and not to the principles of the party. Fourthly, Zaibatsu (a group of corporate heads) which had become powerful, opposed the evolution of the political parties based on democratic principles. This was because it was afraid of losing its power and influence. It must be remembered, that in the public mind the party leaders were always in touch with the Zaibatsu, and therefore, the depression of 1929, was caused by them. Fifthly, the labour movements in the country also hindered the growth of party governments in general. Sixthly, the political parties themselves did not contribute much to strengthen their hold over the government vis-a-vis the other branches of the government like the army, the Privy Council and the Emperor. It was not uncommon for serious quarrels to break out among the political parties. Finally, the militarists who desired independent action hardly showed any subservience to party government, and to alienate public sympathy for it, espoused ultra nationalistic tendencies among the people. Therefore, political assassinations became the order of the day. What sealed the fate of political parties in Japan was the National Mobilisation Law, which was passed in 1938. The said legislation favoured a military dictatorship to replace parliamentary democracy in Japan. Political parties in Japan were abolished by a law in 1940.

Fascist Dictatorship

The economic depression of 1929-31 precipitated matters both at home and abroad eventually giving scope to the Japanese militarists to foist a dictatorship in their country. The rise of nationalism in China following the northward march of the Kuomintang troops threatened Japan's precarious position in Manchuria. Furthermore, the emergence of dictators in Italy, Germany and Spain influenced the course of events. Japan's entry into the Second World War became inevitable. She desired to establish her hegemony over Asiatic countries. Unwittingly, the Mikado (Japanese Emperor) became a "symbol of national unity" for the purpose of carrying out the ambitions of the militarists. The Japanese soldiers laid down their lives very bravely during the Second World War with the strong conviction that their Emperor was invincible.

15

JAPANESE IMPERIALISM AND THE SECOND WORLD WAR

After the conclusion of the Washington Conference, each participant felt satisfied that there would not be conflicts in future in the Far East. They were convinced that China and Japan would settle their disputes amicably. It was this situation which created an air of complacency. After the Washington Conference, the Western powers were too pre-occupied with the domestic problems created by the worldwide economic depression of 1929. They did not suspect that Japan would continue to covet Chinese territories. It must be remembered that Japan agreed to hand over the Shantung leasehold to China and she did. But she continued to remain adamant regarding the ending of unequal treaties. In other words, Japan desired to dominate China as future course of events began to prove.

Japan coveted Manchuria, the northern part of China, on the ground that she had won it after the 1895 war. She saved it from Russia in 1905 by the Russo-Japanese war. Her argument was that it belonged to her because she had developed it. She insisted that China should recognise the treaties connected with the Manchurian possession indicating the Japanese "special position". But the Chinese continued to waver and built parallel lines to the Southern Manchurian railway (which was owned and maintained by Japan).

In 1928, the Nationalist Government in China thought of divesting the Japanese Government of their administrative and political functions in Manchuria. This factor caused great irritation. China was alarmed at seeing Japanese guards outside the railway zone, and the Japanese Government permitting the Koreans to settle in Manchuria after 1910. Japan viewed the rising tide of Chinese nationalism with great concern. In the meantime, her economy began to sag due to economic depression. The militarists under the leadership of Tanaka tried to divert the attention of the public from domestic failures by undertaking some overseas adventures. What upset Japan was that the son of Chang Tso Lin, after the murder of his father, finally decided to acknowledge his subordinate status to the Chinese Government. There were other factors also which heightened tension and hostility between Japan and China. The murder of the Japanese intelligence officer, Captain Nakamura, by Chinese troops in inner Mongolia was one such.

Japanese and Chinese policies in the Far East clashed over the control of Manchuria. Manchuria had great potential for providing the much-needed food and natural resources for the Japanese. The Zaibatsu (conglomeration of business houses) encouraged the militarists to undertake foreign adventure, especially the conquest of Manchuria. It may be remembered that Japan, after the treaty of Portsmouth with Russia, virtually dominated the southern parts of Manchuria. Her investments were locked up in many industrial projects in Manchuria such as railway construction. The threat of being dislodged from this vantage position gave a good opportunity to the Japanese militarists to launch a war against China. Therefore, Sino-Japanese relations almost reached a flash point, and the Mukden incident became the immediate cause of the conflict. This war could have been averted if Japanese statesmen had been taken into confidence by the militarists.

The Mukden Incident

The Japanese stage-managed to bring about this incident on the night of September 18, 1931. A bomb exploded on the tracks of South Manchurian railways, which resulted in the death of the Chinese warlord, Chang Tso Lin. The Japanese commanders accused China of attempting to blow up the railway tracks. It gave a good opportunity to the Japanese army to conduct military operations and capture Chang Chun and Kirin. The Japanese attack continued for the next three months resulting in the conquest of the whole of South Manchuria, and some regions in the North. By early 1932, the conquest of Manchuria became a *fait-accompli*.

The Chinese Protest

While the Japanese advance was underway, China appealed to the League of Nations to come to her rescue by invoking Article 11. The League of Nations acknowledged her protest as valid and asked member countries to apply economic sanctions against Japan. However, the League's demand for Japanese withdrawal from Manchuria fell on deaf ears. The Western powers were not interested in this issue, and the United States was afraid of getting too involved in this imbroglio. She kept aloof but agreed to consult the members of the League of Nations regarding application of the Kellogg-Briand Pact. The US Secretary of State, Stimson, gave a hint to Japan about her responsibility to the League, and compliance to the terms laid down in the Kellogg-Briand Pact and the Nine Power Treaty. Britain was very concerned about the situation but could do nothing due to her pre-occupation with the problems caused by the economic depression.

The Manchuko State

On February 18, 1932, Japan declared the establishment of an independent Manchuko state comprising the territories conquered by her in Manchuria. The Japanese appointed the last Emperor of China, Henry Pu-Yi, as the Regent of this state on March 9, 1932. As a logical sequence, Japan was the first country to accord formal recognition to the new state in September 1932. The League of Nations did not take kindly to the Japanese pre-emptive actions and branded Japan as the aggressor. Japan felt humiliated and the Japanese delegate walked out showing Japan's defiance to this world body (1933). Japan continued to flout the laws of the League and went ahead with the conquest of Jehol. The Japanese army advanced further to the south and captured Peking. The Chinese Government was forced to conclude the Tangku truce by which it accepted the Manchuko State as a buffer.

The Results of the Conquest of Manchuria

Thus, Japan's plan to establish a buffer state in north-western China was carried out by the Japanese army. This conquest enabled Japan to smuggle goods into Nationalist China on the one hand, and prevent Russia from going to the assistance of China on the other. Secondly, the sagging economy of Japan – a result of her economic slump and great depression (1926 and 1929 respectively) – received a shot in the arm after the creation of the puppet state in Manchuria. Japan considered her conquest not as a hostile action against China, but as a necessary step towards her survival as a great power in Asia. But, the Japanese aggression roused national feelings in China, and their response was quick. The Chinese adopted a national boycott of Japanese goods. The Japanese aggression compelled the nationalists and the communists in China to bury the hatchet and respond effectively. They made common cause to fight Japan. Russia and other Western nationals felt outraged at the naked aggression of Japan. Unfortunately, the League of Nations remained helpless. It, however, appointed the Lytton Commission to investigate whether Japan had committed aggression or not.

The Establishment of Parallel Nationalist Government

While the Kuomintang forces retreated after their failure to stem the Japanese offensive, the Japanese established a puppet Nationalist Government (as in Manchuria) at Nanking headed by Wang-Ching-Wei, a former member of the Kuomintang Nationalist party, and a rival of Chiang Kai Shek. This puppet Nationalist Government ruled over the Japanese-held area. It concluded a treaty of friendship with Japan. Wang announced his plans to liberate China from Chiang's dictatorship. He also announced plans to bring about rapid economic progress in his state. He concluded another treaty with Japan for the purpose of ending communism in Northern China and Inner Mongolia.

Diplomatic and Military Offensives by Japan

After conquering half of mainland China, Japan joined Italy and Germany in signing the anti-Comintern pact in 1937 for the purpose of developing closer relations. But 1940, it turned into a military alliance. It provided for the prevention of military attacks from any third party against them and also included a financial package to boost their defence preparedness. This alliance was directed against Britain, France and the United States. However, Japan tried to pacify Russia in 1941 by signing a neutrality pact, which provided for territorial integrity, and adoption of neutrality in case of a military attack by any third party. Thus, Japan felt secure in Northern China after averting a likely war with Russia. She went on with further conquests of countries lying in South-East Asia. In the course of time, the Sino-Japanese war merged itself into the Second World War.

The United States Government was alarmed at the Japanese conquest of South-East Asian countries, which violated the rules and spirit of the treaties signed at the Washington Conference. Unfortunately, Britain also remained a silent spectator till Japan concluded an alliance with her enemies, namely, Germany and Italy.

During the course of the Second World War, France surrendered to Germany. Japan persuaded Germany to let French Indo-China come under her control. She also desired the Dutch East Indies for the purpose of augmenting her resources in furtherance of her future conquests in South-East Asia. The United States remained neutral during the early stages of the Second World War, but watched with great concern the defeat of many democratic countries in Europe including France. It was Britain which offered stiff resistance to the invading German forces. It was most unfortunate that Russia under Stalin concluded a No-War Pact with Germany. The long wait of the Americans was over when the Congress passed the Lend-lease Act to help Britain in her conflict with Germany. It hinted at the possibility of the US joining the allies to save democracy from the brutal aggression of Germany under the Nazi leader, Adolf Hitler. But, what clinched the issue of her joining the war was Japan's extensive conquests in South-East Asia in 1941.

Pearl Harbour Attack

Japan was of the opinion that her acts of aggression in South-East Asia had alienated the sympathies of the United States, which had emerged as the greatest power in the world. Therefore, she took necessary steps to overcome the likely US embargo, particularly on oil. It became necessary for her to conquer countries in South-East Asia to overcome this problem. In the meantime, the Japanese militarists under Admiral Tojo, the War Minister were preparing for a war with the US, if the embargo was not lifted by October 1941. The Japanese

Emperor approved the secret plan of launching a war against the US, if that would serve Japan's ambition to conquer the whole of Asia. Japan expected Germany to win the Second World War in Europe, and end resistance to her conquest in China. Japan launched diplomatic and military offensives in order to achieve her objective. There may have been a secret understanding among the three Axis powers, Germany, Italy and Japan, to divide the world into three zones — Europe, Africa and Asia — for the purpose of establishing their hegemony. Japan depended upon diplomacy with the US so as to avoid open confrontation. The United States proved to be a great stumbling block to Japanese ambitions of world conquest. Cordell Hull, the US Secretary of State, who shaped the US policy in the Far East, was totally opposed to the Japanese acts of aggression. Japan's proposal to withdraw from Indo-China so as to keep her conquest of China was rejected by Hull. Hull proposed a ten-point programme asking Japan to withdraw from Indo-China as well as Mainland China. The Japanese militarists led by Admiral Tojo then decided to launch a surprise attack on the US forces at Pearl Harbour.

Trade between the US and Japan came to a halt with President Roosevelt rejecting the proposal for a meeting with Prime Minister Konoe of Japan somewhere in the Pacific region. In the meantime, the Japanese high command led by the War Minister, Admiral Tojo, gained an upper hand in Japan's domestic politics. Prime Minister Konoe resigned and he was succeeded by Admiral Tojo. A special envoy was sent to the United States to continue the talks, and at the same time the Japanese fleet received orders to move towards Pearl Harbour, where the US Pacific fleet and Air Force were stationed.

The Japanese Air Force launched a surprise attack on the US Pacific fleet at Pearl Harbour in the early hours of December 7, 1941. It resulted in large-scale destruction of the US fleet at Pearl Harbour leaving 2,343 dead, 1,272 wounded and 960 missing. The dramatic suddenness of this premeditated and heinous act perpetrated by Japan while the negotiations were still on, forced the United States to enter the Second World War on the side of the Allies. Japan declared war on the US, and the latter along with Britain declared war on Japan. Italy and Germany declared war on the US on December 11, 1941. It must be remembered that the US Ambassador to Japan had forewarned the US Government about an impending Japanese surprise attack on the US forces earlier. A few hours after the Pearl Harbour attack, the Japanese forces attacked US bases in the Philippines.

The Conquest of South-East Asia

Since the US fleet at Pearl Harbour was almost destroyed, and its Air Force totally crippled, Japan easily conquered the Philippines, Borneo and Celebes. Japanese forces moved from Indo-China and conquered all the territories lying between Thailand and Burma. Hong Kong, Singapore and Rangoon fell one by one into the hands of the Japanese. The Japanese achieved spectacular victories both on sea and on land in 1942. The Burma-road situated in North Burma was closed, cutting off all supplies to China. Even some ports on the east coast of South India were under threat from the Japanese fleet. From December 1941 to mid-1944 Japan had conquered East and South-East Asia with the exception of Australia.

The Japanese invasion was followed by Japan's cultural war. The Japanese language became the official language of communication in all the conquered countries. Japan started the work of consolidation in the conquered territories. The most direct impact of Japanese aggression in Southeast Asia was the rise of nationalism among the subject people. For example, North Vietnam may be cited as a classic example. When did Japan's success come to an end?

The Allied Preparations for War and Peace

The year 1943 may be said to have "marked the end of Japan's march to conquest and the beginning of ultimate defeat". Unless the free countries got united, there was no hope of scoring victories against the dictators of Germany, Italy and Japan. A move to stand united was reached on January 1, 1942, when 26 nations agreed to support the "United Action" against the aggressors (Atlantic Charter). Roosevelt, Churchill and T V. Soong met at Quebec (Canada) and prepared a detailed plan for the purpose of defeating the aggressors. Thereafter, came the Moscow Conference where the US, Britain and Russia proclaimed the principles of maintaining peace. Since Asia was left out of the agenda, it was dealt with in yet another meeting attended by Roosevelt, Churchill and Chiang Kai Shek at Cairo (November 1943). In the Teheran Conference (December 1943), Joseph Stalin, Roosevelt and Churchill gave finishing touches to the plan of action for defeating Germany. The Dumbarton Oaks Conference attended by the big powers except France discussed the plans for replacing the League of Nations, (which had become defunct) with another world body, the United Nations for maintaining peace. In the Yalta Conference (1945), Stalin, Churchill and Roosevelt jointly announced the holding of the San Francisco Conference for drafting a charter to herald the birth of the United Nations.

The Allies Offensives in the Asia-Pacific

The Allies devoted much attention during the early years of the war to plan for the defeat of Germany. At the same time, they provided Chiang Kai Shek of China with money and materials under the Lend-lease Act, and appointed General Stilwell to carry out the task. Germany suffered a series of defeats in early 1943 at the hands of the Allies and this enabled the Allies to focus their attention on the Asia-Pacific region which had been overrun by Japan. The

Allied counter-offensive against the Japanese forces began in May 1942. The engagement took place at the Coral Sea. Though the battle was a drawn affair, it paved the way for success in the next engagement, ie, at the Midway island. The Japanese fleet was intercepted by the American planes with the result that Japan lost four of her important aircraft carriers. The Allied forces under General MacArthur adopted the strategy of destroying the Japanese Merchant-Marine, the Navy and the Naval Air power on the one hand, and carrying out aerial bombardment of Japanese cities on the other. This strategy worked well to weaken Japan's hold over its far-flung empire.

In the meantime, the amphibious forces of the Allies reconquered several islands which were under Japanese control. One of the biggest expeditions launched by the Allies was for the conquest of the Philippines. General Douglas MacArthur carried out this task in October 1944. During the summer of 1944, the fleet of the allies sunk about 700 Japanese vessels thereby halting the progress of a war industry, The American B-29 bombers were used from the soil of liberated China to invade the Japanese cities and the Japanese-controlled Manchuria. In the meantime, the Allied forces liberated Burma from Japanese control in May 1944 and thereafter marched towards Imphal. This same force liberated Rangoon on May 3, 1946.

End of Unequal Treaties

The United States and Britain tried to bolster China's morale by giving up the extra-territorial and special rights by signing necessary treaties to this effect. The other Western powers also followed suit. China became a free and sovereign country and prepared to fight the aggressor. Madam Chiang Kai-Shek paid a visit to the United States to secure US support for Chiang's Government. The United States made serious efforts to unite the communists and the nationalists in China for the purpose of facing the common enemy, ie, Japan. The US sent Vice-President Henry Wallace to carry out this task. Unfortunately, US efforts in this direction failed and from then on, China received much less attention. It, however, got financial support.

After the fall of Iowa Gime, the next target of Allied attack was Okinawa which fell in June 1945 and resulted in heavy casualties on both sides. The US B-29 bombers flew many sorties and dropped incendiary bombs on many Japanese cities including Tokyo in March 1945. These raids caused heavy destruction and loss of many lives — 6,68,000 civilian lives. The Japanese arsenal lost 2.3 million tonnes of bombs, Japan faced defeat but continued to fight. This was because the government was led by the militarists under the leadership of Admiral Tojo who did not believe in surrender. The Allies received some confusing messages from Japan regarding surrender after some negotiations. But the Allies led by the United States demanded unconditional surrender. The Potsdam Conference in Germany where the Allies met in July 1945 told Japan to choose peace, security and justice if she surrendered, or "utter destruction" if she refused. The American generals led by United States' President Truman (in his capacity as supreme commander-in-chief) decided to use the atom bomb to ensure Japan's immediate surrender. Leaflets were dropped from the Allied planes on Japanese towns and cities urging the people to impress upon their government the danger of a nuclear war. However, the Japanese response was negative. Therefore, on August 6, 1945, a US plane dropped an atom bomb on Hiroshima causing horrendous destruction.

Russia moved her troops from Europe to Asia after agreeing to help the Allies in their war efforts. She declared war on Japan on August 8, and invaded the Japanese-held Manchuria. The following day, the Japanese city of Nagasaki was destroyed by another atom bomb. The dropping of nuclear bombs on Japan had the desired effect. The Japanese people and government suffered immensely.

But, the Japanese army command remained adamant although the Cabinet and the Supreme Council desired surrender. The imperial conference was convened for this purpose on August 14, which witnessed a tie, three voting for and three voting against unconditional surrender to the Allies. It was the Japanese Emperor himself who clinched this issue by favouring unconditional surrender. Thus, Japan, which was proud and sensitive sent a message to the Allies agreeing to surrender. General Douglas MacArthur, the Supreme Commander of the Allied Forces in the Asia-Pacific region , accepted the formal Japanese surrender on board the US ship *Missouri* in the Tokyo bay on September 2, 1945. The Japanese Emperor delivered the surrender speech which was broadcast to the whole nation. He asked all the Japanese forces everywhere to lay down their arms. Thus the Second World War came to an end amidst a nuclear holocaust in which the Japanese suffered terribly. For the Japanese who always considered their Emperor "divine" and their nation " invincible", it was a great humiliation. The Allied forces took all the Japanese commanders captive and punished them for committing war crimes.

16

THE POST-WAR JAPAN

The post-war occupation of the Allies brought about significant changes—more revolutionary in character than the period witnessed after the Meiji restoration. The most significant changes occurred in political, economic, educational and social fields which culminated in the modernisation and westernization of Japan. Eventually, Japan became one of the leading industrial giants of modern times. Significantly, the post-war occupation did not lead to the usual and undesirable passion for revenge like the one which took place after the First World War in Germany. In fact, Japan did not nurture any hatred towards those who punished her. Japan established a new ethical code of conduct which was to make her one of the most highly advanced countries in the world. Let us examine the post-war history of Japan, which gives an insight into the remarkable recovery of a country which had suffered the worst holocaust in modern times. This "New Japan" was in the making (1945-52) thanks to the Allied occupation.

The Role of the United States

The position of Japan after the surrender was that of an occupied country. The United States Government appointed General Douglas MacArthur (one of the great heroes of the Second World War) as the Supreme Commander of Allied Powers (SCAP) with full authority to establish an administration in Japan which was to be manned mainly by the American and British troops. The occupation forces led by General MacArthur had the following objectives to achieve.

1. To destroy the vestiges of Japanese imperialism by ensuring that Japan henceforth should not pose a threat to world peace and security.

2. To bring about a transformation in her political system so as to make future Japanese governments more accountable to the people.

    These main objectives were to be achieved by means of the following measures:

1. By restricting her sovereign authority to the jurisdiction of four main islands and a few others.

2. By destroying her military and industrial complex.

3. By punishing those who were found guilty of war crimes and the rest by barring them from holding offices in future.

4. By introducing necessary reforms in the educational system and other major segments of the economy.

More than 80 million Japanese came to be looked after by the American and British military and civilian officials. While the Japanese felt that they were being administered by their own officials, in actual fact these officials were taking orders from the staff of General MacArthur. The staff was experienced, and many of them had specialised knowledge of Japanese culture. With "crusading zeal", they worked hard to turn Japan from the perilous path of dictatorship to a peaceful, prosperous and democratic country.

In accordance with the agreements signed at Cairo, Potsdam and Yalta conferences, the Japanese sovereignty was confirmed only to the four main islands and other minor adjacent islands as mentioned above. The rest of the territories were divided between the United States and Russia. Russia took charge of Kurile islands and Southern Sakhalin. The US forces took possession of the Caroline, Mariana and Marshall Islands. In addition, the US occupied Bonin and Ryuku islands. Korea was declared an independent country, but the US took charge of the South, and Russia the North, with 38° parallel as the dividing line. In the meantime, the Nationalist army of China occupied Formosa (Taiwan), a part of Manchuria and the Pescadores

Demilitarisation of Japan and War Trials

In accordance with the treaty signed by Japan, the Allies disbanded her army, Navy and Air Force. In addition to this, she surrendered all her military hardware, naval and air bases, defence laboratories and so on to the Allies. Many scientists working in the defence laboratories and workers of munition factories were retrenched. Even the workers employed in the steel, chemical and machine tool industries were retrenched. After this came the trial of the Japanese leaders who were mainly responsible for Japan's entry into the war.

The trial began according to the principles of the Charter of the International Military Tribunal. Seven leading war criminals, including Admiral Tojo, were hanged in 1948 and the rest (with the exception of two) were awarded life imprisonment. After this, many organisations and societies which clamoured for war were dissolved and nearly 200,000 Japanese soldiers were dismissed. Many politicians were barred from holding public offices in future. The war trials demonstrated to the Japanese the intention of the Allies to make Japan a peaceful country. The Japanese military leaders who were taken as prisoners of war by the Allied forces in the Philippines, and in China, were put on trial and sentenced to life imprisonment.

The New Constitution

The Japanese Emperor proclaimed a new constitution in 1947 with the approval of the Commander of the Allied Forces. This new constitution included a preamble, which was in total contrast to the Meiji constitution. In the Meiji constitution, the emphasis was on the dictatorial powers of the monarch. In the new constitution, the preamble put an emphasis on the sovereignty of the Japanese people. The new constitution gave Japan a true parliamentary democracy based on universal franchise. The Japanese cabinet was henceforth made accountable to Parliament and not to the Emperor. The Japanese Parliament became supreme (unlike in the pre-war period) after the abolition of the Privy Council, the services, and the Emperor's private secretariat.

Under the new constitution, the cabinet was required to consist of only the members of the majority party, with both Houses having fully elected representatives. The members of the Japanese Diet (Parliament) were elected for a period of four years in the case of the Lower House (House of Representatives) and for a period of six years in the case of the Council (Senate). The Judiciary was made independent of the executive branch with the Supreme Court having the power to decide whether laws passed by the legislature were constitutional or otherwise.

The Japanese Supreme Court was established on the model of the Supreme Court of the United States. The local governments in the towns and cities enjoyed autonomy, and the most important officials were chosen by the local citizens. Finally, the constitution provided guarantees regarding fundamental rights to be enjoyed by the citizens. The Emperor was stripped off his divine status, and there was a definite break with the Shinto tradition. The constitution provided for the renunciation of the war in tune with the spirit of the Kellogg-Briand Treaty of 1928. Furthermore, the constitution imposed a ban on the Japanese army going abroad.

The new constitution which replaced the old one in Japan was likely to meet with many difficulties when put into practice. It was for the new generation of Japanese to accept the principles which it adopted. Everything depended upon how the new constitution would adapt to the changing times. Would the new government accept the changes? It was in this area that the Allies, who were governing Japan, succeeded. The new generation of Japanese luckily did not like the principles and practices of the old Japanese tradition. They were prepared to welcome changes. Therefore, the administration of Japan, which was subsequently run by the Japanese officials became very efficient. The civilian authority over the military was fully established after the end of the occupation period.

Educational Reforms

It was realised by the Allied occupation forces that if reforms introduced in Japan had to last, it would be necessary to remould the educational system to the changing time and environment. The new educational system had to infuse "democratic values" and "democratic ways" among students and teachers. The revamping of the educational system came at an appropriate time, since the Japanese were going through a trauma of defeat. They were fast losing their faith in the old educational system. Unlike in the other Asiatic colonies, the Japanese were not illiterate. Since education was made compulsory up to six years, the Japanese children were able to read and write. The new educational system tried to cater to the needs of society by improving the quality of teachers. In the early stages, the Japanese teachers were afraid of importing printed matter from the West for they believed that it contained "dangerous thoughts".

Among the important reforms, the most noteworthy was the extension of compulsory education for children from six to nine years of age. Subsequently, many students continued their studies up to the high school level, and some went up to the college level. The college level course was extended for a further period of four years. The new educational system was not rigid and the students were allowed to change their course of study in favour of the desired course. Great emphasis was laid on the qualitative change.

The new educational system afforded opportunities to students to harness their talents. The school texts and classroom projects laid emphasis on awareness of individual rights and promoted values of democracy. While the pre-war educational system was considered "elitist", the new system opened the doors of all the schools to all the students irrespective of their class and wealth. Higher education was given importance so that Japan would rise to the status of any advanced country in the West. As regards Japanese teachers, the American influence pervaded with emphasis on "modern methods of instruction". During the period of occupation multi-faculty universities on the model of American universities were founded. There was no gender discrimination while admitting students into the schools, colleges and universities. It must be remembered that the new constitution gave equal rights to women.

Social Change

The Allied occupation made a lasting impact on the conservative society in Japan. The emphasis on granting equal rights to women, particularly in avenues like education and politics, struck at the very roots of traditional Japanese society. The conservative character of this society underwent further changes, particularly in family life due to the spread of modern education. The authority of the old parents over grown-up children weakened. Grown-up boys and girls moved about more freely than before, and the modern educational system gave them a sense of confidence and equal status to face new challenges in life. The Japanese women were aware of their legal rights. The elders watched the emerging aspects of modern life with great anxiety, because they considered it immoral. They began to criticise the new educational system as the main source for degrading moral standards, particularly when a boy chose the girl he loved as his life-partner.

Growing Urbanisation

In rural areas, children started attending schools. Some of them went to cities either for continuing higher education or for seeking jobs. This migration from rural areas to towns and cities began to increase during the second half of the twentieth century. The towns and cities provided job opportunities to the Japanese youth because of rapid industrialisation. In the course of time, small towns turned into big cities with numerous factories coming up everywhere. The labourers from rural areas also started migrating to the cities in search of jobs.

The Destruction of the Zaibatsu

The Allied occupation destroyed the *Zaibatsu* at one stroke. By Zaibatsu we mean a combination of giant industrial enterprises run by highly aristocratic families who became highly influential in Japanese politics. It was this highly aristocratic class which enjoyed so much political clout with the militarists during the pre-war period. This interesting phenomenon attracted the attention of the allied occupation forces. Necessary steps had to be taken to break its stranglehold on Japanese policies and business. The leaders of the Zaibatsu were forbidden from entering business and politics and their wealth was taken away after imposing heavy taxes. Their assets were transferred to the new government. Their monopoly over trade and business practices were highly restricted.

The Allied occupation of Japan encouraged the growth of labour unions and their movements so as to keep a check on the concentration of wealth among the few. The labour unions which came into existence registered seven million workers as their members. In the early stages of the occupation period, the labour unions behaved in a most irresponsible manner, sometimes resorting to strikes at the instigation of the communists. However, this unhealthy trend was checked in due course of time. The new government lost its sympathy for them and helped the employers to put down the strikes without mercy.

Economic Scene

Among the reforms introduced to develop the Japanese economy, the most outstanding were the land reforms. During the pre-war period, Japan witnessed the concentration of agricultural lands in the hands of absentee landlords, whose treatment of the tenants was anything but kind. With the new government coming into existence, the lands owned by the absentee landlords, in excess of ten acres, were purchased. They were sold to the tenants on easy terms of credit. Even the owner of ten acres of land had to rent out two-and-a-half acres to tenants. The redistribution of agricultural lands to the cultivating tenants and landless agricultural labourers went a long way towards ensuring rural prosperity. In the course of time, the Japanese farmers grew rich and invested their capital on the lands they owned to increase productivity. The most extraordinary success story of Japan during the post-war period related to widespread modern industrialisation. By 1972, Japan was ranked as the third most industrialised country in the world.

Japanese Coalition Politics

The political life of Japan is dominated by the three main political parties, namely, the Liberal Democratic Party, the Socialist, and the Democratic Socialist. The first two are important since they hold ideologies which are poles apart. The Liberal Democrats stand for the free enterprise system, faith in private party and favour continuing ties with the Western nations. They advocate social legislation and establishment of a rapport with the common people. Naturally the rich farmers and businessmen extend their patronage to this party. The Liberal Democrats enjoyed a majority in the Lower House, and its government ruled the country for nearly three decades, from 1955 to 1994.

The opposition Socialists receive around one-third of the votes on an average, mostly from workers. It stands for the nationalisation of basic industries and advocates legislation to help the downtrodden. The Democratic Socialists are in a minority and help the government to carry out important reforms to develop the country without harming the interest of the poor.

Political scandals have rocked the country during the past ten years and invariably the Liberal Democrats have been found to be involved. Tsutomu Hat was the last prime minister of the Liberal Democratic Party. He ruled for two months, and was replaced by the Socialist Chairman, Tomiichi Murayama. Murayama led a coalition government which included Liberal Democrats in

June 1994. Murayama's Government was the 66th government in Japan in a period of five decades. Political instability has become a bane at a time when the Japanese voters are very much concerned about their sluggish economy. However, in October 1996, the Liberal Democrats staged a comeback winning 239 seats in the Lower House – 12 short of majority – and Ryutaro Hashimoto became the PM heading a coalition government. The Socialists and Sakigake parties lost many seats in the Lower House, while the newly formed political party, Japan Democratic Party, made its mark by securing 60 seats. The LDP seems to have rejuvenated itself, and its success may be attributed to the disarray prevailing in the opposition parties.

A month prior to Hashimoto's election as prime minister, the residents of Okinawa island, where the US military bases are situated, protested against the proposal of their government to accord sanction for its continuation. A plebiscite held there clearly confirmed it. But Hashimoto persuaded the Mayor and other local officials to approve the proposal by offering financial aid to develop Okinawa. The influence of the US Government over Japan could be discerned in the incident.

In July 1998, Hashimoto had to make his graceful exit because of the ruling LDP's defeat in the election to the Upper House of Parliament. Hashimoto's fall may also be traced to the anger shown by the voters against his apathy in tackling serious economic problems facing the country. The economic recession which hit this nation in 1991 has intensified further. During the three previous years, the value of the yen fell by 40 per cent. Going back further, the Japanese equity and property markets had a gloomy period. During the period 1996-98, a series of bank failures eroded the confidence of the people. The number of unemployed reached 2.46 million. Many companies have downed their shutters. The Japanese government finally admitted that their "economy had sunk into recession" in June 1998. It is estimated that Japan's bad debts amount to one trillion US dollars.

Keizo Obuchi, the New PM

Keizo Obuchi is 62 years old and had worked earlier as Foreign Minister under Hashimoto. He replaced Hashimoto as the Prime Minister on July 29, 1998. The people of Japan have high hopes that he would save Japan from economic recession, the worst since World War II. With mild manners and no enemies he is known for taking bold decisions. He was elected the PM by the LDP after holding a secret ballot.

The people of Japan placed great faith in his ability to steer the country clear of deep recession, the worst since the World War II. Unfortunately, he belied their hopes as the recession posed a formidable challenge. Failing banks, rising unemployment and host of other associated problems raised their ugly heads. In the general election held in 2000 the LDP coalition won 233 seats in a 480 member house, and Yoshiro More was elected the PM. He proved incompetent for the task that lay ahead, and therefore had to resign. The LDP chose Junichiro Koizumi, a charismatic leader as the prime minister. After assuming his office, Koizumi has taken several steps to save the country from the recession. Today, Japan is witnessing a new era of economic revival. Many failed banks and companies have shown signs of recovery and it is hoped that the high rate of unemployment would soon come down.

Foreign Relations (1952-2004)

The Allied occupation of Japan ended in 1952, but before the American troops left, the US and Japan signed a Mutual Security Pact. Since Japan has agreed to remain as a peaceful country and would not send its troops to fight abroad (the Japanese Constitution makes a mention of it), the US government undertook the role of defending Japan against foreign aggression. The Pact provided for stationing American troops and fighter jets in few Japanese cities. Yoshida Shigeru, whose reign in Japan witnessed economic revival, resisted the US attempts to rearm Japan. The US then wanted Japan to support its fight against the spread of communism. Shigeru desired that Japan should play a subordinate role in the US security system.

After the Second World War Japan's relations with Russia remained hostile. During the Cold War era, Russia and Japan did not remain on friendly terms. The dispute over the possession of the Kuerile Islands embittered their relations, but with the cessation of the Cold War in the eighties, relations improved. Japan's relation with China improved after signing a treaty of 'Friendship and Cooperation' in 1978. In 1972, Japan recognised 'One China' policy which in fact derecognised Taiwan's move towards independence. In the same year, the UN expelled Taiwan, and Communist China took its place. In November 1998 the Chinese leader, Jiang Zemin visited Japan and expected Japan to tender apology for its war crimes during the Second World War. Japan expressed only 'remorse' not apology. Japan extended 390 billion Yen as loans to China. Japan's relations with the Stalinist regime of North Korea has not been friendly. Like the US, Japan was worried about the secret supply of missiles by North Korea to Pakistan, Iran and Libya. When North Korea admitted that it is having a nuclear programme, in violation of the non-proliferation treaty, Japan suffered a jolt. Japan has been taking steps to improve its relations with North Korea. It has offered financial assistance on condition that North Korea give up its nuclear programme. Japan would like to see that kidnapped Japanese prisoners held by North Korean government be released. In fact the Japanese PM is putting pressure on North Korea along with other interested countries to give up making nuclear bombs. Japan under PM Koizumi is improving its defence capabilities, by launching its ballistic missile projects, despite the US-Japanese mutual security pact. Japan sent spy satellites into space in March 2003. Koizumi's government has decided to send Japanese troops to Iraq at the request of the US government. Political analysts believe that Japan has given up its policy of 'pacifism' in spite of constitutional restraint.

17

SOUTH AND NORTH KOREA, HONG KONG AND TAIWAN

The world had taken little notice of Korea until Korean war broke out in 1950. This small country, situated on the east coast of China is also known by other names "Chosen" and "Land of the Morning Calm". Being a mountainous country, she has a few plains mostly located in the south. China, Japan and Russia are in close proximity. Most of the Koreans living in the north took to fishing while their southern counterparts took to agriculture. Eventually, the north developed into an industrial region.

Early History

The people belonged to the Mongoloid race, and the early settlers might have come from Mongolia or Manchuria or China. While their written language looks like Chinese characters, the spoken language is akin to the Japanese. Early in their history, the Koreans embraced Buddhism, and some Confucianism and Taoism, despite the fact the they had their own ancient religion called *Chondokyo*. It was much later that Christianity spread to South Korea.

Among the earliest to rule Korea were the Chinese. During the Chou dynasty in China, a ruling family member of the Chinese ancestry ruled Manchuria and the northern part of Korea. In the course of time, the north was divided into small kingdoms, and separate families started ruling them. Foremost among the well-known groups was the Silla group which ruled over the entire Korean peninsula. They ousted the Japanese from the far south. The Chinese influence on Korea was substantial during the period of Tangs.

It was in the tenth century that Korya, a royal house, began to rule Korea. Their rule continued for nearly four centuries. The Chinese influence became much more predominant in spheres like art, religion, philosophy and so on. After the Mongol conquest of China, Korea was ruled by the royal House of Yi. This House fell a few years before the Manchus took over China. Korea came to be known for its beautiful pottery, court music and an old phonetic alphabet. The Koreans invented printing (moveable type) and produced warships and hot air through ducts to heat food in the kitchen.

Like Japan, Korea also remained in self-imposed isolation for quite some time. She had frequent contacts with China and some trade with Japan. People in those days used to call her "The Hermit Kingdom". It was in the middle of the nineteenth century that the Westerners sailed into the harbours of this Hermit Kingdom for trade (the same time Japan was forced to open her doors to the Westerners.) While most foreigners were turned away, the Japanese were persistent.

Modern History

The Sino-Japanese war of 1895 ended in China's defeat, and the latter's influence over Korea ended. A decade later, the Japanese defeated the Russians (Russo-Japanese War) and put an end to their rivalry over the possession of Korea. In another five years, the Japanese conquest of Korea was complete. The Japanese assuaged the feelings of the conquered Koreans by promising them independence. During the period of Japanese occupation, the Japanese exploited Korea. The Japanese bought rice cheaply and got many jobs for their countrymen in Korea. Landless farmer went to the cities in search of jobs but the jobs they secured fetched them low wages. The Japanese had scant regard for the appalling conditions prevailing in the conquered country.

Rise of Nationalism

In the course of time, the Koreans found that the Japanese had no intention of developing their country but wanted to govern it for promoting their self-interest. They demanded at least a self-rule. When it was denied, they prepared themselves for a long struggle. World War I was over in 1919, and the people in the colonised countries had enough courage to demand self-rule from their masters and Korea was no exception. While in most cases, it was conceded to subject nations, it was denied to the Koreans. The Japanese brutally suppressed the great Korean Uprising resulting in the death of over 2000 Koreans, besides injuries to nearly 20,000. Due to ruthless repression, some of the nationalists went abroad but carried on their work to achieve their goal. Among the nationalists-in-exile was Syngman Rhee who was to become the first president of South Korea after independence. He carried on the work like his contemporary, Sun Yat Sen of China, from his headquarters in Hawaii. In the Cairo Conference of 1943, the Allied powers discussed the issue of granting independence to Taiwan after the war, while Korea remained neglected.

During the last days of the war, North Korea was taken over by the Soviet troops after the Japanese surrender. A month later the American troops arrived in South Korea. The 38th Parallel became the line dividing north-south Korea and the Soviets did not agree to a plan to unite Korea or for UN supervised elections. The Soviets turned North Korea into a Communist State, while the

South came under American influence. In 1948, a republic was set up in South Korea with Syngman Rhee as the President.

The Korean War (1950 – 53)

The Korean War began when the Communist troops of North Korea crossed the 38th Parallel (supposed to be the border) and attacked South Korea. The war which began between the two Koreas on June 25, 1950 ended after three long years (July 25, 1953). When the United Nations demanded that North Korea withdraw her troops from South Korea in 1950, the latter refused. Therefore, a UN army (consisting of troops drawn from 15 nations) led by the US Commander, General Douglas MacArthur (man who compelled Japan to surrender in 1945), went into action. After suffering initial setbacks, the UN army reached the Yalu River near Manchuria. It was then that Communist China rushed her troops to help North Korea. When MacArthur suggested bombing of China, he was dismissed by President Truman of the US.

SOUTH KOREA

Rhee and His Successors

The first president was a controversial leader, and his rule is best described as autocratic. His presidency (1948-60) witnessed rampant corruption and misrule. He turned the state into a police state in order to keep himself in power. Elections were rigged to ensure victory for his party. People found his governance intolerable, and there were student riots in the capital Seoul. Rhee had to go and he was succeeded by General Chung Hee Park. General elections were finally held. General Park's party won. South Korea went through a bad patch marked by political instability. General Park was assassinated in 1979. Chung Doo Hwan, an army General, came to power in a military backed coup. Along with his protégé, Roh Tae Woo (another army General) he set up a military Junta which ruled the country by martial law for nearly 13 years (1980-93). Hundreds of opponents were arrested and sent to jail, the most prominent being the opposition leader Kim Dae Jung. There was a nation-wide protest.

There were three candidates in the 1987 general elections running for the post of the president, namely Roh Tae Woo (representing the ruling Democratic Justice Party), Kim Young Sam, and Kim Dae Jung. Roh won by a clear majority of 36.30 per cent of the votes, while the others secured 26.60 and 25.60 per cent, respectively. As it was a direct presidential election taking place for the first time since 1971, the opponents charged Roh (candidate of the ruling party) with rigging the election. However, the people of South Korea, who were fed up with army generals turning into presidents, elected a civilian president, Kim Young Sam, in 1993. President Kim appointed a three-judge panel to try the two former presidents, Chung Doo-Hwan and Roh Tae Woo for their involvement in the 1979 military coup, for the imposition of martial law, and for the imprisoning of thousands of opponents during their periods of governance. The panel convicted Chung for treason and sentenced him to death. The same panel convicted Roh on charges of staging the coup of 1979 and sentenced him to 22 ½ years of imprisonment. The judgements were pronounced on August 26, 1996 in the presence of the two accused former presidents. These two former presidents had allegedly taken $ 600 million as bribes during their tenure. In the December 1997 presidential elections, the much persecuted and jailed Kim Dae Jung won.

An Asian Tiger

Despite the political instability since achieving independence, South Korea has been able to achieve the near impossible—an economic miracle and she completed land reforms and achieved 98 per cent literacy. She registered an economic growth rate of 8.6 per cent per annum since the 1960s. The per capita income rose from $ 94 in 1960 to $195 in 1969, and then to $ 10,160 by 1998! No doubt that people have described her as one of the Asian Tigers (besides, Taiwan, Hong Kong and Singapore). A part of her spectacular success should be attributed to the huge investment made by the United States and Japan. The rest should go to the intelligent and hard working people. Unlike other countries, South Korea took an early lead in the export-led growth – exports of electronic goods, textiles, steel, chemicals, automobiles and ships. South Korea leads the rest of the world in ship-building (second in rank) and construction business. By 1994 her exports crossed the $ 100 billion mark. This economic boom took a nose-drive in 1998 due to the East Asian financial crisis. The IMF came out with a bail-out package of $ 57 billion for the economic recovery. Several of Korea's biggest business conglomerates (known as Chaebol) are today struggling to survive. In the midst of this economic crisis, former President Kim Young Sam's son was involved in a scam in 1997. The new president will have to take bold decisions to overcome some of the problems facing his nation. One of the earliest decisions taken by the president was to declare general amnesty for the prisoners (including 400 political prisoners).

Kim Dae Jung followed the 'Sun Shine' policy of engagement with the Stalinist regime of North Korea under Kim II Jong. For the first time the two countries opened their common border for exchange visits of families living on both sides. The heavily guarded border witnessed the opening of railway line construction linking both countries. As President Kim could not make headway in tackling corruption – considered as a great curse – and growing opposition from students – a majority of them anti-American – he became unpopular. It must be remembered that 37,000 American soldiers remained (after the end of the Korean War) in South Korea to bolster its defence against North Korea's military threat.

On December 19, 2002, Roh Moo Hyun was elected the new president following the defeat of his political rival, the leader of the Grand National Party. Roh had been a popular human-rights lawyer and law-maker. He won the election by promising 'to clean up dirty-money' politics and prevent a possible war between the US and North Korea. He promised to follow the sun shine policy of his predecessor by continuing negotiations with North Korea for the unification of North and South Koreas. He wants better relations with his northern neighbour who has shocked the world by pursuing a nuclear programme. It is rumoured that North Korea already has five or six atom bomb. This manufacture of nuclear weapons is in clear violation of the non-proliferation treaty it had signed in 1994.

During the Iraq war, he promised the US administration that South Korea would support the US led coalition by sending troops – a promise that has not gone well with the common people. Furthermore, the South Korean economy has been hit by a recession during this year. After returning from his trip to the US the press and the public have been criticising him for his inept handling of several domestic and international issues. His closest aides are facing corruption charges. After he became the executive-president of South Korea he patronised the Uri Party even before the parliamentary elections. Naturally his political opponents made it an issue for his impeachment. The National Assembly proceeded with the impeachment in March 2004 but the country's Constitution Bench cleared him from charges of corruption and "economic mismanagement". The president, today, is still facing many challenges, and those that hurt his popularity include the controversial despatch of South Korean troops to Iraq and his inability to resolve the "North Korean nuclear crisis".

NORTH KOREA

The Democratic People's Republic of Korea was established on September 9, 1948 with Kim II Sung as the President. With the patronage of the Soviet Union and the People's Republic of China, she acquired the traits of a totalitarian state. The president became all powerful despite the trappings of democracy. The Korean war sapped her energies and she had to depend on the financial and technical assistance of the Communist neighbours. The early years witnessed collectivisation of agriculture and nationalization of industries. As arable lands are limited, she suffered from frequent food shortages.

"With significant natural resources, North Korea has sought to build a nationalistic economy based on its *juche* ideology of self-reliance, with priority on developing heavy industry … In the early years the planners strategy succeeded, but in the long run the economy began to decline. This was due to the depletion of natural resources, sharp cuts in aid from China and the Soviet Union, and the fall of East European markets. Heavy investments in unproductive defence industry created problems and the economy began to decline. It was in these circumstances that North Korea began to manufacture and export missiles to other countries. In fact, the missile exports earned her the much needed foreign currency.

Notwithstanding the havoc caused by the Korean war, North Korea considers South Korea as enemy number one. Despite the US support to South Korea, North Korea planned to invade the South in April 1960. But she was dissuaded from undertaking this adventure by her allies, Communist China and the former Soviet Union. The *Pueblo* incident of January 1968 highlights the aggressive posture of the Pyongyang regime to the outside world. In this case, the North Korean Navy seized the US ship *Pueblo*, claiming that it was on an espionage mission in her territorial water. The US Government was furious but did not think of attacking North Korea fearing for the safety of the captive crew.

In 1992 Kim II Jong consolidated his power in North Korea so as to replace the ageing Kim II Sung. In 1985, North Korea signed the Nuclear Non-Proliferation Treaty at the request of the then Soviet Union, but reversed its stand in March 1993. It again reversed its stand possibly to extract concessions from the US Government. North Korea today is capable of producing nuclear weapons, and with its advanced missiles system could threaten South Korea and Japan. A lot of tension developed when the US called on North Korea for an overall nuclear inspection. In 1994, Kim II Jong succeeded Kim II Sung after the latter's death.

North Korea had signed nuclear non-proliferation treaty, and also an agreement with the US about not making nuclear weapons in 1994. Violating all these agreements, she continued to remain hostile towards South Korea and the US President Bush once declared North Korea as member of axes of evil. The US maintained a strong contingent of 37,000 US soldiers to defend South Korea. In October 2002, North Korea informed the US that it has nuclear weapon programme since the latter has not fulfilled its obligation of supplying fuel oil and nuclear power reactors (1994 agreement). This announcement of the Stalinist regime of North Korea has sent shock waves affecting neighbouring Japan and South Korea.

The US is now taking the help of China to diffuse the situation. Recently Japan tried to normalise its relations with North Korea and expressed regrets for having ill-treated her subjects during the Second World War. Japan has assured North Korea that it would give aid and requested the return of Japanese hostages (taken by North Korea) during the Second World War.

The six nation meeting held in China recently tried to persuade North Korea to give up its nuclear ambition in return for aid, but there was no satisfactory response. North Korea says that nuclear weapons are needed to defend itself from American attacks. North Korea has raised an armed force of million men.

North-South Unification

Since 1994 attempts are being made to bring about peace between the two Koreas, and if possible to bring about their unification. Restrictions on the flow of visitors to each other's country were liberalized. From the day of his taking over the presidency Kim Dae Jung (South Korea) has been following what is known as 'sunshine policy' of North-South reconciliation. He is determined to establish cordial relations with the North. Let us wait and watch how the two Koreas are going to be united in the new millennium.

HONG KONG

The defeat in the Opium War of China at the hands of the British led to the cession of Hong Kong island and a few surrounding rocks in 1841. In 1860, Britain received the Kowloon section of the peninsula from the Chinese. The city of Kowloon, ie, Hong Kong's busiest section, grew at the tip of the peninsula. In 1898, Britain got another opportunity to expand this small colony. She acquired about 370 square miles of land north of Kowloon called the New Territories on a lease basis – leased for 99 years.

Economic Development

The crown colony of Hong Kong lying on the South east coast of China (also near the mouth of the river Canton) grew into a financial power house in East Asia during the 20th century. A majority of the people speak Cantonese (Chinese) and English. Wealthy businessmen all over the world used to visit Hong Kong to explore business opportunities and financial services. They set up their companies there because it was a free port. Its big warehouses stored goods which were destined for many parts of the world – not excluding Communist China. Hong Kong became a conduit for many foreign investments. After the Communist Revolution in 1949, China could have easily seized Hong Kong, but she did not do so for obvious reasons. Hong Kong provided a great source of income for Communist China – through banks, store houses, business ventures and remittances of Hong Kong-Chinese to their families on the mainland. China received foreign direct investment of $ 100 billion over a period of 15 years (1981-96) through Hong Kong.

Hong Kong's Transfer

Britain signed an agreement with Communist China in 1984 for the transfer of Hong Kong on July 1, 1997. It must be remembered that the lease period expired in 1997. China also agreed to treat Hong Kong as a special administrative region and allow the market economy to continue for another 50 years (2047). On July 1,1997, Communist China assumed sovereignty over Hong Kong at a glittering ceremony held in the presence of Prince Charles and the last British Governor, Chris Paten.

The Chinese communist government has been making serious attempts to clamp its iron·rule over Hong Kong despite granting a special status, that of Special Administered Territory by which the latter has retained its past political and economic individuality. In other words China adopted the principle of "one country, two systems" towards Hong Kong.

The pro-democracy activists in Hong Kong are showing resentment whenever Beijing makes attempts to foist its rule. In fact, they resented the appointment of Chief Executive (now Tung Chee Hwa) by the Chinese government, who is keen in carrying out the wishes of his master. Political activists desire that the Chief Executive should be elected by them. Tung Chee Hwa, the Beijing nominee is at present trying to get a new security bill passed, which is being totally opposed by the freedom-loving people of Hong Kong.

The pro-democracy activists recently held a rally on the 'New Year Day' (2004) in Hong Kong in memory of those killed at the Tiananmen Square in 1989 and denounced Beijing's oppressive policy.

TAIWAN

During the course of Manchu invasion in the early 17th century, many Chinese fled the country and occupied the islands known today as Taiwan. The Portuguese who had settled there earlier had named these as Formosa. The Dutch drove the Portuguese out of these islands before occupying it, later the new Chinese settlers pushed them out. The aborigines of these islands lived in the mountains and spoke a Malay dialect. In the 19th century Japan gained control over these islands but after continuous migrations of the Chinese from the mainland during the 18th and 19th centuries, she was losing control. After the Second World War, Taiwan was transferred to Chinese control, as agreed upon at the Cairo Conference in 1943 (Chiang Kai Shek was a participant). However the restoration did not improve the situation in Taiwan, since the Chinese governor behaved in an autocratic manner. Chiang no doubt replaced the governor, but could not pay much attention to the problems of the Taiwanese due to his preoccupation with the Civil War. When his army was finally defeated on the mainland by the Communist guerillas under Mao in 1949, Chiang escaped with his followers and settled in Taiwan. Thus the Nationalist army under the leadership of Chiang gained control over Taiwan, and also nearby islands, namely Pescadores, Matsu and Quemoy. With the support of the United

States, Chiang used to say that there would be one China, and he would regain control over the mainland after driving out the Communists. Mao agreed with his proposition and declared that Taiwan belonged to the mainland. Taiwan came under martial law under Chiang, and its government was recognised by the West. She was given representation in the United Nations (also in the Security Council) as the sole legal government. This farce went on until 1971 when the People's Republic of China took its legitimate seat in the UN by replacing Taiwan (also called Nationalist China). Taiwan lost her seat in the UN. President Nixon's visit to Communist China in February 1972 ended the long enmity, but the US continued to follow the two-China policy. The US did it for strategic reasons, since she continues to consider Communist China as a potential threat to her interests in the Pacific region. Martial law was lifted in 1987 in Taiwan but the period of emergency continued till 1991 (considered the longest period for any country).

Fastest Growing Economy

Taiwan is described as one of the four Asian Tigers for its fastest growing economy. She made rapid strides of progress in areas like agriculture and industry. She completed land reforms and secured a decent standard of living for her subjects. The quality of life improved enormously with universal education and health facilities enjoyed by her citizens. The nation's capital, Taipei, is buzzing with commercial activity. Her products like textiles, automobiles and so on have reached the world markets. She has foreign exchange reserves of $ 98 billion and is now ranked among the 10 leading capital exporters in the world.

Taiwan Today

Today Taiwan's separate identity and existence remains totally at the mercy of the US administration, since the latter has adopted 'one China' policy. This policy was evolved over a period of time, probably to appease the communist government in the mainland China. But time and again the US administration has been pointing out to the mainland Chinese government about its 'human rights' violations. In other words, the US administration is postponing the issue of Taiwan's merger with the mainland China.

After the cessation of long emergency, the Taiwanese established a democratic system of administration under a president. After four years of rule by the KMT president, the power passed on to the new President Chen-Shui-ben of the Democratic Progressive Party, whose proposal for a referendum on Taiwan's independence and sovereignty did not evoke much response. One must remember that the Taiwanese Constitution makes a reference to Taiwan being a part of China. The KMT party opposed the referendum.

President Chen's re-election in March 2004 remained controversial. Chen's followers are enthusiastic about Taiwan's independence on the basis 'Taiwan is not China' like Hong Kong and Macao.

Communist China is furious at Chen's attempts to declare independence. The communist government was about to attack Taiwan a few years ago, but was restrained by the US administration. Recently, the new Chinese Prime Minister Wen Jiabao said that China will pay any price to prevent the independence of Taiwan.

It must be remembered that nearly 4,50,000 Taiwanese businessmen are in China to carry on their business. It is said they have invested one hundred million dollars. It is too early to predict whether Taiwanese move for independence would succeed in the face of China's aggressive attitude on the one side, and America's decision to follow 'one China' policy on the other.

PART II

SOUTHEAST ASIA

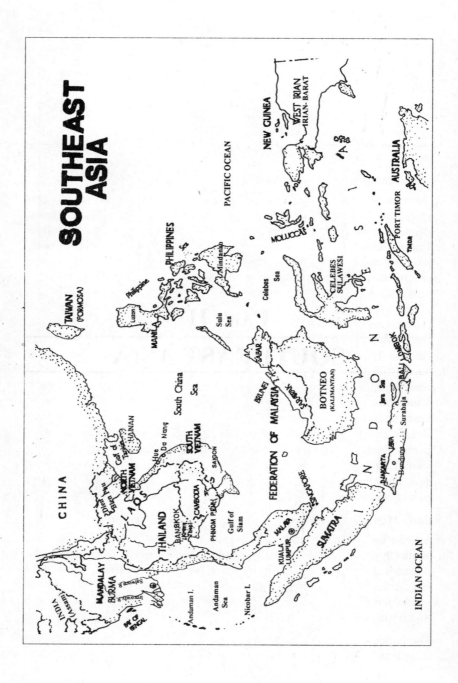

18

BURMA (MYANMAR)

Introduction (Geographical Setting)

The term South-East Asia refers to countries, south of China bound by two oceans, the Indian and the Pacific. In other words it includes two geographical regions, namely the mainland nations such as Burma, Thailand, Laos, Cambodia (Kampuchea) and Vietnam, and the insular nations such as Malaysia, Singapore, Indonesia and the Philippines. The factors that are common to most of these nations are the tropical monsoons (south-west and north-east) and rice production through irrigation agriculture. The rivers which flow in the mainland are the Irrawaddy, the Chindwin and the Salween in Burma; Chao Praya in Thailand, the Red River (Song Koi) and Black River (Song Bo) in Vietnam. The Mekong River passes through Laos, Thailand, Kampuchea and South Vietnam. These rivers bring alluvial soil and form deltas. These deltas in Lower Burma, Central Thailand, Kampuchea and Central Vietnam attracted immigrants in search of food and shelter from northern parts since centuries. A long time ago, people migrated from southern China and eastern Tibet to these regions, and these migrations had been continuous. For example, the Malays came from the southern part of China during the earliest phase of history. Racially the mainland countries belong to the Mongoloid groups. The South-East Asian countries had come under Sino-Indian influence since a long time. Their national cultures became more apparent from the sixteenth century AD with the advent of Islam and the Europeans.

Early Migrations to Burma

At least six ethnic groups entered Burma at different times from Tibet and South China. They were known as Mons, Shans, Karens, Chins, Kachins and Burmans. The last name is in majority in today's Myanmar (ie Burma) and the rest are the Chinese. Being closest to India, Burma was probably the first to imbibe the elements of Indian culture, particularly religions (Hinduism and Buddhism) and Sanskrit literature.

The Indian traders were the first to enter the land of Suvamabhumi (lower Burma and Malay Peninsula) and transplanted Indian culture to the Mons before the advent of the Christian era. Emperor Ashoka sent Dharmamahamatras to spread Buddhism and the Mons learnt Sanskrit and Pali. They evolved their script similar to the South-Indian languages.

Around the third century AD, the Pyus migrated from south-west China to Burma and built their capital at Sri Kshetra. They became adherents of Hinduism and Buddhism and the Monks of the latter established schools for children. They were found to be the most peace-loving people in the world and very few crimes were recorded during this time. They left a rich legacy in the form of Buddhist Stupas, cylindrical with pointed dome much like Orissan architecture found in Bhubaneswar. It was during this time that Buddha Ghosha visited Thaton. All these are seen in and around their capital city Prome, a few miles from their capital Sri Kshetra. Again the Pyus introduced the Vikrama Era, named after their Vikrama dynasty beginning in AD 638. This Vikrama Samvat legacy spread to nearby countries of Thailand and Kampuchea. Pyus civilisation declined after the invasions of the Thais in AD 832.

The Burmans probably migrated from China via Tibet around the 2nd century of the Christian era and conquered the Pyus kingdom. They embraced Mahayana Buddhism and built their capital Pagan around AD 849. However after sometime Hinayana Buddhism was adopted as the official religion.

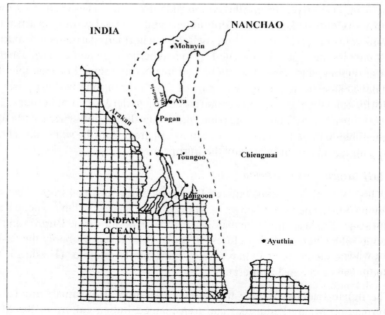

Pagon Kingdom of Burma AD 1044-1287

Among the Burman kings, the greatest was King Anawratha or Aniruddha (AD 1044-77). He may be regarded as the founder of the State of Burma. Incidentally, the boundaries of his large empire, which he built after several conquests fit with the present boundaries of the State of Burma (renamed as Myanmar in 1988) Among the non-Burman kingdoms which he conquered, the most important was the culturally advanced Kingdom of the Mons in the South. This conquest of Anawratha had great impact on the political and cultural history of his country. It was after his contact with the famous Mon-Monk Shin Avanhan, that King Anawratha changed his religious leanings towards Hinayana Buddhism. His interest in spreading Hinayana Buddhism compelled him to plunder the kingdom of another Mon king of Thaton from where he snatched away 30 seats of Buddhist canons, and thousands of priests and artisans. He took a large number of the subjects of Thaton as prisoners including the king. The subjects of King Anawratha got converted from Mahayana Buddhism to Hinayana Buddhism. In fact, Hinayana Buddhism had been flourishing in South India and Ceylon in those times, from where it spread to the Mon kingdoms in Burma. Like Emperor Ashoka in the olden days, King Anawratha spread the Hinayana faith to the mainland of South-East Asia. Only Vietnam remained an exception. He maintained good relations with Ceylon and got a replica of Buddhist tooth which was consecrated in the newly built Pagoda in Pagan.

The culturally advanced Mons dominated the Pagan court. The Mons never forgave the Burmans for conquering their kingdom, and all attempts to pacify them by the descendants of King Anawratha did not meet with success. In the meantime, the Burman kings adopted the Indian political traditions and practices in their Imperial court. The Pagan kingdom of Burmans was attacked and broken up by the Mongols in 1287, which subsequently paved the way for the rise of Thai power in the mainland of South-East Asia. The Mons of Pegu declared themselves independent of Burman control.

The Toungoo Dynasty (AD 1531 – 1732)

The Burmans were successful in uniting their country with the establishment of the Toungoo dynasty. The Toungoo king named Tabinshweti (1531-50) and thereafter his brother-in-law Bayinnaung (1550-81) reunited and expanded the country after a series of battles with Ayudhya. The main reason for the outbreak of the war between the two kingdoms was the Burmese King's request for white elephants which was turned down by the King of Ayudhya. Secondly, there was a dispute between these two kingdoms over the possession of a small kingdom named Chiengmai. But Tabinshweti's failure to capture Ayudhya (Thailand) resulted in the revolt of the Mon minority against him. Subsequently, Tabinshweti was assassinated by the Mons in 1551. His brother-in-law

Bayinnaung continued the imperial policy and finally conquered Chiengmai. The Laotion King Settatirat who opposed the claim of Bayinnaung over Chiengmai sent his forces to resist the Burman army, but it failed. The Burman King then turned his forces against Ayudhya and its king Chakrapath surrendered. Chakrapath and his family members were taken as hostages to Burma. Prince Mahin, son of Chakrapath succeeded to the throne and pledged his loyalty to the Burmese King.

A second war became inevitable when Chakrapath (who turned into a Monk) joined his son in Ayudhya and revolted against the Burmese suzerainty. The Burmese forces defeated and killed Chakrapath, and Chakrapath's son was taken captive. Ayudhya was occupied for the next fifteen years. It was not long before the people of Ayudhya came under the dynamic leadership of "The Black Prince", Pra Naret who not only liberated Ayudhya but also invaded Burma five times. He was successful in conquering the southern parts of Moulmein and Tavoy. The Burmese empire was shaken up by the Mon and Shan rebellions. It was not until the seventeenth century that the war between Burma and Ayudhya came to an end, with the result that the Burmese capital was shifted to Ava in the North. Both these kingdoms were highly engrossed in checking the influence of foreigners, ie, Burma in conflict with China, and Ayudhya in trouble with the Dutch and the French. The Chinese army invaded Burma in 1658 to capture the last Ming Emperor, Yung Li, who had taken refuge there. It was during this time that the Mons raised the banner of revolt against Burma and declared their independence in 1740. In 1752 the Mons captured the Burmese capital Ava which led to the fall of the Toungoo dynasty.

The Konbaung Dynasty (1752 – 1885)

The next dynasty to rule over Burma was that of the Konbaung whose leader Alaungapaya was responsible for the liberation of his kingdom and also the capital Ava from the tutelage of the Mons. With the assistance of the other Burmese chiefs, he drove the Mons to the South. Subsequently, central Burma and Pegu were liberated right up to the point Dagoon, which was renamed as Rangoon. The forces of Alaungapaya laid a siege to Ayudhya which was met with stout resistance from the Thais. In the long run, this war resulted in his defeat and death. His forces retreated. The Burmese-Thai conflict continued during the time of Hsinbyushin (second son of Alaungapaya). After a long siege, Ayudhya was captured. It was plundered and devastated, and its inhabitants were taken to Burma as slaves.

In the meantime, China under the Manchu emperors attacked Burma four times during the period 1766-69, but all of them were repulsed. Subsequently, Hsinbyushin continued his attack on Ayudhya (Thailand) and the imperial policy continued even during the time of his brother. However, the Thais under the new Chakri dynasty of Bangkok were successful in defending their country. The Burmese thereafter moved their forces beyond their borders along the western side for the conquest of Manipur, Assam and Kachar which precipitated a conflict with the British East India Company.

THE BRITISH CONQUEST OF BURMA

First Burmese War (1824 – 26)

The Burmese put forward their demand that the British East India Company cede Chittagong, Murshidabad, Kasim Bazaar, etc, but could not pursue the matter due to pre-occupation with the war with Siam (Thailand). After Siam's defeat the Burmese renewed the demand on the British and followed it up by an attack on Shahpuri, an island near Chittagong. The British East India Company under the Governor-General, Lord Amherst, declared war on Burma. Unfortunately, the military expeditions could not achieve their objective since the British company was unable to take effective steps. Hence the war dragged on for nearly two years but in the end the Burmese forces surrendered. The Burmese Government signed the treaty of Yandaboo. According to this treaty, the Burmese king agreed to cede Arakan and Tenasserim. He agreed to pay the war indemnity of one million pounds to the British company in four instalments and also signed a commercial treaty. He agreed to receive a British resident in his court. For the British East India Company, the war proved to be very expensive in terms of money and casualties. As the treaty contained loopholes it led to misunderstanding and bad faith between the two parties. The Burmese began to hate the British because the latter's resident in their court acted like a spy. The British did not return Arakan and Tenasserim, but converted them into British colonies. The King's brother, Therawaddy who headed a nationalist party, succeeded to the throne after a coup.

In the meantime, the British were preparing an estimate of the Burmese natural resources with a view to promoting trade not only with Burma but also China (through Burma). They were also looking forward to the construction of a road leading to China via Burma. The British textile manufacturers were very excited at the prospect of a thriving trade with the Burmese and the Chinese after the completion of this road. The new king was not happy with the machinations of the British officials in Burma and put a stop to all foreign explorations in 1897. He was prepared to risk a war. In 1840, the British Resident, Major Burney, became disappointed at the unfriendly attitude, of the Burmese Government and returned to India. Thus relations between Burma and the British East India Company turned sour.

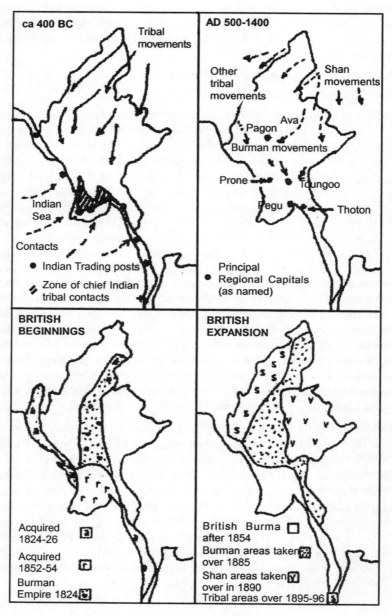

Historical Development in Burma

Second Burmese War (1852)

The Burmese Government took drastic steps to check the goods coming from India to the British firms in Rangoon, particularly the bullion. It considered the bullion trade with foreigners as contraband. The British merchants trading in teak, complained to the Indian Governor-General about a new order of the Burmese Government which included the teak trade as a royal monopoly. The complaints of the British traders of Burma lodged with the commissioner became frequent and sometimes misrepresented as the Burmese Government's policy of repression. The merchants in Rangoon also wrote to the Calcutta Chamber of Commerce to pursue the matter with the British East India Company for redressing their grievances. When Lord Dalhousie heard these complaints from the two British captains who were fined by the Burmese Government for their indiscretions, he ordered Commodore Lambert to go to Rangoon to investigate. Lambert's battleships reached the Burmese coast and captured a Burmese royal ship which was patrolling the area. Naturally the Burmese Government was provoked. Dalhousie and Lambert needed an excuse to provoke the Burmese into declaring a war.

The second Burmese war was fought and the Burmese forces were defeated for the second time resulting in the British forces occupying Rangoon and Lower Burma (up to Toungoo). Burma sued for peace and offered all concessions. The war resulted in annexation of lower Burma (Pegu) to the Company territories. There was trouble in the Burmese court which made the British extend their border to another fifty miles to include the most coveted teak forests of Toungoo. The leader who opposed the Burmese King was Mindon-Min who finally replaced the Burmese King. He started fresh negotiations with Lord Dalhousie without giving up hope of receiving the lost territories. King Mindon tried to check the growing ambitions of the British company by denying a full-fledged treaty which the British demanded. Ultimately, it was Phayre, the British envoy, who succeeded in securing a treaty from Mindon in 1862 regarding trade with China via Burma. This treaty expired in 1866.

Third Burmese War

In 1866-67 King Mindon faced rebellions in Upper Burma, which were followed by personal tragedies, ie, the murders of many of his relatives and friends committed by his rebellious sons. He needed British help badly. The British took advantage of this situation and demanded several concessions that would have affected the sovereign status of Burma. In spite of this, the Burmese King signed the treaty in 1867 with the British. When he found in due course of time that the British created problems for him, he cultivated the friendship of France, by offering a commercial treaty on highly favourable terms. The British were jealous and felt cheated. They were also furious. When a consul named Augustus Margary was killed on the Burma-Chinese border, the British accused the Burmese government of complicity. In the meantime King Mindon died and Anglo-Burmese relations reached their lowest ebb. Prince Theebaw succeeded King Mindon and signed the treaty with the French, which the British considered as having compromised their position in Burma. Eventually France received preferential treatment which provoked the British.

The main reason for the war with Burma was that a British trading company, namely, the Bombay-Burma Trading Corporation was found guilty by the Burmese council and had to lose its prized possession-the royal teak forests to the French syndicate. The French Syndicate was very eager to take over the royal teak forests from British control in Burma. The British Government was provoked and sent an ultimatum to the Burmese government to rescind the order passed on the Bombay-Burma Trading Corporation or face war. The Burmese reply did not satisfy the British Government. Therefore, the latter declared war. The Burmese were defeated, with the result that Upper Burma was annexed to the British-Indian Dominions in 1885. The King and his family were taken prisoners and sent to western India. The treatment given by the British Government to the Burmese monarch provoked the Burmese to revolt and it took nearly five years for the British to totally suppress the revolt.

ORIGINS OF THE BURMESE NATIONAL MOVEMENT

The nationalist movement in Burma began in the early part of the twentieth century. It was a direct consequence of the British political and economic policies which aimed at exploiting the country and the people. Large tracts of cultivated lands were taken possessions of by Indian money lenders known as Chettiars. These *nattu-kotti* Chettiars from South India charged as much as 50 per cent interest on money borrowed by poor peasants who pledged their lands and crops as security. Any failure to repay the amount resulted in the land being transferred to the money lender, quite in contrast to the Burmese tradition where lands of the peasants were inalienable. By 1939, twenty-five per cent of the cultivated lands were in the hands of money lenders.

The British revenue laws in Burma caused tremendous insecurity among the poor peasants for they were afraid of losing their only source of sustenance, their lands, to the foreigners. The British exploited the natural resources of Burma, such as the teak forests and mines by employing cheap foreign labour, mostly the low paid Indian labourers. The railways and shipping companies in Burma were engaged in further exploitation of the rich natural resources without bringing about benefits to the country and the people. Foreign businessmen, mostly British and Indian, never entertained the idea of sharing their profits with the people of Burma. The Indians were hated by the Burmese for they were considered foreigners who supported British exploitation. Most professional jobs in Burma were given by the British to the Indians.

The British administration included changes in the indigenous political system of Burma thereby denying local autonomy to the village. The *myothugyi* system (village government headed by the village headmen) was replaced by the salaried class of village headmen whose jobs were at the mercy of the conquerors. The destruction of this old system caused communication gap between the rulers and the ruled resulting in suspicion and distrust among the Burmese villagers.

The activities of European Christian missionaries in Burmese villages caused grave apprehensions among the generally orthodox Buddhists in Burma. The Christian missionaries opened schools to attract large number of Burmese children and competed with the Buddhist-run schools. The British Government supported the Christian missionaries in all possible manner which proved to be prejudicial to the interests of the Buddhist schools. Therefore, the Buddhist monasteries in Burma became centres of resistance to alien rule during the time of the national movement.

Another reason which made the Burmese resentful of British rule was the employment of Indians and the Karen tribe to government jobs in preference to the Burmese subjects. It went to show that the British had no trust in the Burmese. Finally, the Burmese never reconciled themselves to the fact that their country had become an Indian province. They desired to maintain their separate identity as an ancient kingdom enjoying rich and glorious traditions.

Burmese National Movement

The rise of nationalism in Asia was the direct outcome of European colonial rule and exploitation. It manifested itself in India in 1885 with the establishment of the Indian National Congress, and also in China with the outbreak of the Boxer rebellion in 1899. Furthermore, the defeat of Russia (regarded as a European country) at the hands of Japan (a tiny Asiatic country) in 1904-05 exploded the myth about the invincibility of the Europeans. The fall of the mighty Manchu dynasty and the birth of the Chinese Republic under Sun Yat Sen were events of far-reaching significance and left a deep impression on the Burmese who were suffering under alien rule. Furthermore, the influence of Karl Marx and Nikolai Lenin spread all over Asia because they denounced capitalist countries for causing untold miseries by their exploitation. The latter tried to prove it in his book, *Imperialism, the Highest Stage of Capitalism.* Gandhiji's entry into the freedom movement in India in 1919 also strongly influenced the Burmese masses.

The Young Men's Buddhist Association (YMBA) which was founded on the pattern of YMCA in 1906 became the main motivating factor in the upsurge of Burmese nationalism. It opened native schools for children and imparted education with a bias towards native culture and pride on the one hand, and promoted national awareness on the other. In a relatively short time the YMBA entered the political arena and provided able leaders to fight for freedom.

During the great war (1914-18), the British promised to introduce political reforms in India, and naturally the Burmese too hoped for a bright future. However, while reforms were ushered in India in 1919, the Burmese were denied the same. The British passed the Rangoon University Act which denied autonomous status to Rangoon University in contrast to Indian universities which generally enjoyed autonomous status. Therefore, the General Council of the Buddhist Association (the renamed YMBA) on the one side and the Rangoon University students on the other began to agitate against British discrimination. Its General Council put forward many extra demands which the British categorically rejected.

These protests eventually compelled the British to grant "dyarchy" in 1921. However, the Burmese nationalists refused to have anything from the British till all the demands such as control over land ownership rights and immigration were met. The Simon Commission recommended that Burma be separated from India in response to the popular Burmese demand. But now the Burmese looked upon this recommendation with suspicion fearing that Burma would be permanently colonised.

The worldwide economic depression in 1929 had disastrous effects upon the Burmese economy, especially in the sectors of agriculture and industries. There was large-scale unemployment in Burma and the prices of foodstuffs dipped very low. The wrath of Burmese peasants towards the rapacious moneylenders and landlords, who began to exploit their helplessness, knew no bounds. Riots broke out in Burma in 1930-31 against the Indian and Chinese which resulted in large-scale looting, arson and killings. The peasant rebellion grew under the leadership of a Buddhist monk, Saya San leader of General Council of Buddhist Association (GCBA), who in the meantime proclaimed himself the King of Burma. The political situation in Burma began to worsen and therefore, the British rulers were left with no alternative but to crush the rebellion mercilessly. After a prolonged trial, the Buddhist monk who proclaimed himself the King of Burma was executed in 1937.

Of the political parties, which emerged during the national movement, the most important was Sinyetha Party (poor man's party) which demanded a check on Indian emigration, introduction of lands reforms, protection of peasants from money lenders, and reduction in taxes. It was founded by Dr Ba Maw, who earlier had become famous as an advocate and pleaded the case of Saya San. Dr Ba Maw subsequently organised the "Forward Block" after joining another political party called the Thakin. This merger of the Forward Block and the Thakin Party encouraged the Burmese to revolt against British rule.

Yet another political party which attached the Burmese extremists was the Thakin Party which was a product of Rangoon University students' organizations called *Dohbama Asiayone*. The Thakin Party stood for revival of Burmese – Buddhist cultural traditions and encouraged students to go on strike against the British educational system on numerous occasions. Some of the prominent future leaders of the nation, namely U Nu and Thankin-Aung San, had been active participants. Their activities were not liked by the British Government which urged Rangoon University to rusticate them. The Thakin Party was an out and out leftist oriented organisation which followed the principle of Marxism and Leninism. Although it did not like the foreigners including the members of the Indian community in Burma, it had high regard for the Indian National Congress and its leaders.

The Japanese Occupation of Burma

In 1940, ie, during the middle of the Second World War, Japan contacted the Burmese Thakin Party through its agent, namely, Colonel Suzuki, offering military assistance to Burma to overthrow British rule on condition that it supported its cause. The offer was rejected since Aung San was getting ready to go to Shanghai to seek the help of the Chinese Communist Party. He was arrested by the Japanese but subsequently released after he declared that he had come to seek the help of the Japanese. The Japanese agreed to train Aung San and the "thirty Heroes" to enable them to organise a small army of liberation which would drive the British out of Burma.

During the war, Burma witnessed a united front of many political parties, namely, the Thakins, the Sinyetha, and Buddhist organizations. All these political parties worked in unison to force the British out of Burma. The moderate Myochit party led by U Saw formed a government at the instance of the British. At the round-table conference U Saw demanded dominion status for Burma which was rejected. On his return, he was accused of being in secret contact with the Japanese and arrested by the British. At the time of Japanese occupation of Burma, all the nationalist leaders except Ba Maw were jailed. The Burmese hoped that with the Japanese victory over the British, Burma would achieve independence. But their high hopes were dashed to the ground since the Japanese never entertained the idea of Burma remaining independent. This Japanese attitude earned undying hatred of the Burmese.

During the occupation, the Japanese desecrated many Buddhist pagodas. It was in these circumstances that the Burmese nationalists began an underground resistance movement in August 1944. This underground movement was called Anti-Fascist People's Freedom League (AFPFL) which was led by a famous communist leader named Than Tun. Aung San, the leader of the thirty Heroes, became the League's president. All the political parties including the Communist Party, the Burmese National army and the People's Revolutionary Party made common cause against Japanese rule in Burma.

The revolt against the Japanese was initiated by the AFPFL in March 1945. A major part of Northern Burma was affected. The resistance to Japanese rule in Burma incidentally helped the British force to reoccupy Burma during the last years of the war. The Japanese forces withdrew from Rangoon because of local resistance and the invading British forces. The victorious British forces which occupied Burma after driving out the Japanese agreed to remain there till the political situation in Burma returned to normalcy. In the meantime, the British Government declared amnesty to all the members of AFPFL who had earlier supported the Japanese occupation of Burma. It must be remembered that during the last year of the war many Indian traders and businessmen quit Burma.

Burmese Independence

Events in India in 1947 had its impact on the Burmese too for the British had decided to give independence to Burma. The British formed an interim government in Burma with Aung San as Prime Minister in October 1946. At the general election held in April 1947, the AFPFL secured absolute majority. Elections were held for choosing members of the Constituent Assembly which would draft the Constitution for independent Burma. However, U Saw, a defector from the AFPFL, who desired a more revolutionary programme for the country brought about the assassination of Aung San and six other leaders. He hoped to take advantage of the chaotic situation by organising a revolt against the British by blaming them for the assassinations. Unfortunately, his plan failed and the AFPFL government was set up by Nu. He brought U Saw to trial, found him guilty and executed him. Burma became free on January 4, 1948 and the government was headed by U Nu.

POST-INDEPENDENCE ERA

The new constitution, promulgated in January 1948, declared Burma as a sovereign democratic republic. Burma did not become a member of Commonwealth. The new constitution provided a British parliamentary model with the prime minister as the head of the government and an elected president as a titular sovereign. Burma was to be a federal union, with a parliament consisting of two houses. U Nu's Government ran its course for the next fourteen years. During the last years it faced internal troubles from the communists and other insurgents. A military coup led by General Ne Win brought about the fall of U Nu's government. General Ne Win ruled Burma with an iron fist. He was not prepared to allow civil liberties to be enjoyed by his subjects. He crushed the revolts of insurgents mercilessly. The Burmese were fed up with his military rule and rose in rebellion in mid-1988. The chaotic situation in Burma was brought to an end by the Burmese armed forces which established the State Law and Order Restoration Council (SLORC). It was to pave the way for a government to be elected by the people. Two years later, the first free elections (after a gap of nearly thirty years) were held and the National League for Democracy (NLD) won a clear majority. But the Burmese army dominating the SLORC was reluctant to transfer power to the NLD. It is unfortunate that Burma today has not achieved substantial economic development mainly due to military rule. The main opposition to military rule continues, particularly by a group led by the opposition leader, Aung San Suu Kyi (who won the Nobel Peace Prize for championing democratic rule in Burma). The Burmese military rulers kept her in prison for a long time, even to the extent of defying world public opinion. After achieving independence, Burma followed a strictly neutral policy with regard to her foreign relations.

Repression Continues

In Myanmar, the conflict between Aung San Suu Kyi and the ruling military Junta continues to attract world attention. Showing scant regard for world opinion, the Burmese military rulers are putting enormous pressure on the free movement of the leader of the pro-democracy movement, Aung San Suu Kyi. On July 24, 1998, she was prevented from visiting her party cadres spread around the countryside. Her white car was stopped by the Burmese security guards from proceeding at a bridge in Anyarsu village. Observing non-violent protest against her oppressors, she sat in the white car for six days without taking food and water. The military government forcibly took her back to Yangon (Rangoon). It must be remembered that on August 8, 1988, thousands of people led by students held a protest march in all major cities in Myanmar against the long-time ruler, General Ne Win. A Commission of the International Labour Organisation (ILO) in August 1998 stated that the military regime was engaging in forced labour on a massive scale. Women and children are abused and made to work freely, and that too in dangerous places.

The human rights abuse in the case of Myanmar has gone too far, and the United States Government has imposed economic sanctions. In recent years Myanmar's economy has turned from bad to worse, and the World Bank has refused to sanction new loans since the old ones have not been repaid. The increasing isolation of Myanmar under the military leaders is causing great concern to the world community. How long can the world tolerate human rights abuses? The non-violent movement of the National League for Democracy (NLD) led by its valiant leader, Aung San Suu Kyi, leaves a ray of hope for the oppressed.

After yielding to the pressure of the international community, the ruling junta secretly met the NLD leader, Aung San Suu Kyi in December 2000 to negotiate for ushering in democracy. The UN's Special Envoy, Razali Ismail tried to facilitate the talks between these two parties. The NLD leader was released from house arrest after much persuasion by the UN in May 2002. The international community was disappointed when the talks between the two failed and the NLD leader was taken into 'Safe Custody' by the ruling military junta in May 2003.

The people of Myanmar have been suffering great hardships under the rule of the military junta. Today this country suffers from the lowest per capita income (\$ 300) and human rights abuses. The spread of AIDS has become an alarming issue. The NLD leader has remained as the beacon of hope for the common people. The international community has high expectation that the military junta would release Aung San Suu Kyi and her followers soon and usher in democracy, not later than 2006 when Myanmar would chair the ASEAN conference.

19
THAILAND (SIAM)

The original name of Thailand was Siam. The word *Thai* (meaning free) is an ethnic term assigned to peoples inhabiting mainly Thailand today. The Thais have been residing in several parts of South-East Asia also. The Thais came to Thailand from southern parts of China between the eighth and the thirteenth centuries. In the course of time, they settled in the North-Eastern parts of Burma, Northern Thailand and Northern Laos. Traces of rice cultivation have been found as early as 6000 BC. They developed Neolithic culture with special bias towards the evolution of Bronze metallurgy, during the second and third century AD, Central and Southern Siam (Thailand) was having trade with India. In other words, it paved the way for the Hindu colonization of Thailand, which must have taken place around the third century AD.

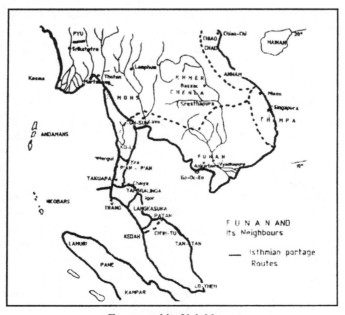

Funan and its Neighbours

Funanese Kingdom

Even before the beginning of Hindu colonization, there appeared the Funanese kingdom which was founded by an Indian Brahmin named Kaundinya (1st century AD). The greatest ruler of the early Funanese kingdom was Fan Shi-Man. Under his leadership the Funanese kingdom extended its control over the neighbouring regions including Central Thailand (3rd century AD). Sino-Indian trade began to flourish during this time mainly because the Funanese kingdom was acting as the main intermediary between India and China. The court of the Funanese kingdom adopted Sanskrit as the court language and the Funanese kings adopted Hindu customs and ceremonies. After the fall of the Funanese kingdom, we see the rise of the Khmer empire built by the Khmers who were related to the Mons of Lower Burma. Thus Central Thailand along with the neighbouring regions passed into the hands of the Khmers.

The Kingdom of Nanchao

During the eighth century AD the Thais became free and established the kingdom of Nanchao (Yunnan). This kingdom attacked the Pyus of Burma in the ninth century, and its expansion was made easy by the weakness of the Khmer empire from the tenth century to the thirteenth century. When the Mongols conquered the kingdom of Nanchao in 1253 the Thais migrated in thousands towards the south and occupied the northern parts of the Khmer empire. Their capital was shifted to Ayudhya. From the thirteenth to the fifteenth century the Thai kingdom witnessed the rule of three great kings, namely, Rama Khamheng, Ramadhipati and Trailok. Thai culture took definite shape and turn with the contributions of these three monarchs.

Rama Khamheng (1283-1317)

His main contribution was to enable his citizens to live in peace and prosperity by organising an able and efficient government. With his humble beginning as the Chief of a small state called Sukhotai or Cukhodaya (meaning "Dawn of Happiness"), he came to an understanding with another Thai Chief Mangrai, for the expansion of his kingdom into an empire. It was only after this understanding that the Sukhotai Kingdom became an empire following the conquest of Upper Menam, Upper Mekong and the Lower Salween Valley. The Sukhotai empire came to be known as the cradle of Siamese civilization. Although the Thais maintained a distinct identity of their own with their culture different from Mon-Khmer civilization yet, they still borrowed political, administrative and artistic traditions from the latter. The Hinayana form of Buddhism became the official religion and the Thai language received its alphabet in due course of time. Although the Thais retained some of the traditions of their ancient homeland (Nanchao), they copied liberally from

India, her script, religion and art form. The Thais borrowed a few things from the Mongols also, particularly the organization of their military-command structure. Their society was fashioned along the lines of the Mongols such as the two-tier system, namely, the ruling aristocracy, and the rest consisting mainly of the serfs and the slaves.

Ramadhipati (1350–69)

The next great ruler of Thailand was Ramadhipati who made Central Thailand the base of his military operations. Ayudhya became the seat of his capital like Sri Rama (of the *Ramayana*) who ruled from Ayodhya in India. In the course of time, Ayudhya became the main centre of Thai power and culture.

Ramadhipati built an empire which included parts of the Mon country, the entire Menam Valley, and a large part of Malay peninsula. It was during his time, that the common law replaced the customary laws of the Nanchao period which had by then become obsolete and inadequate. The common law continued to secure the complex society of the Thais' individual liberty and other freedoms. Unfortunately, these freedoms were denied to the serfs and slaves because they happened to be non-Thais. This common law was replaced by the laws of the Western nations during the second half of the nineteenth century.

Trailok (1448–88)

The third great monarch of Thailand was Trailok, whose lasting contribution may said to be of giving a final shape to the "country's administrative and social structure". It must be remembered that just 17 years before Trailok ascended the throne, the Thais conquered the Angkor kingdom of the Khmers thereby adding large chunks of territory and alien populations to their empire. The immigrant Khmers, well-versed in the art of administration, helped Trailok to introduce several new principles and methods of administration. What followed was a series of administrative reforms which aimed at centralization of administration after the separation of civil and military functions. The social and judicial systems came to be reformed. The reforms also included a code of convention to settle disputes mainly concerning the succession to the throne.

Centralisation of Government and Administration

The process began when the centre, in the place of weltering small and independent states, established big provinces, each coming under a Chayo Praya (governor) who owed allegiance to the king. Secondly, the Thai armies, which were stationed in the provinces, came under the control of the Central Government. Furthermore, the Central Government introduced many changes which not only established political stability, but increased sources of revenue. The separation of military and civilian administration followed the pattern of the Khmers, that is, having five departments each. The civilian administration had:

1.   The interior department led by the chief minister
2.   Department of local self-government
3.   Finance department
4.   Agriculture department
5.   Royal households

The military administration was also divided into five departments each coming under a Kalahom, ie, a minister.

King Trailok reorganised the social system on the basis of Saktina grades, and linked it to the judicial system. In modern sense, it meant that all his subjects were *not* equal according to law and the law recognised the superior status of persons based on landholdings. Different classes of people existed in his kingdom and the King decided how much land each class should own, although it was obvious that all lands in the country belonged to him. In the matter of succession to the throne, Trailok set up the office of heir-apparent, *braha maha uparaja,* so as to avoid disputed successions in future.

Early Contacts with the West

The Portuguese were the first to develop contact with the Thais in 1511, followed by the Dutch. The Dutch set up a factory at Ayudhya in 1613. The French missionaries came in 1662 to convert the people. They were successful in converting the chief minister of Thailand (Constantine Phaulkan) to Christianity. This chief minister was subsequently murdered by the Thais mainly because he was championing the cause of Christianity. The British established commercial relations with the Thais in the 1670s during the reign of King Narai.

Thailand got into trouble because of the wars with the Burmese from the 16th to 18th centuries. With the frequent invasion of the Burmese, Ayudhya disintegrated into five sections each led by a prince. The only hope of reviving the glory of former Ayudhya lay in the leadership of Phya Taksin. But his failure resulted in a rebellion which finally turned into a civil war. It was at this critical juncture that Ayudhya witnessed the emergence of the Chakri dynasty with its first ruler, Chaophya Chakri. It was he who restored law and order. He made Bangkok the seat of his capital. Thus the era of Thai-Ayudhya ended. The Chakri dynasty began to rule Thailand with its headquarters at Bangkok from 1782. The present King of Thailand 'Bhumibol Adhulyadej Abuldet' belongs to the Chakri dynasty. It must be remembered that all the kings of the Chakri dynasty from 1782 bore the title of Rama, after the famous King of Ayodhya (India).

Rama I (1782-1809)

The reign of Rama I witnessed peace and prosperity, and also the restoration of moral standards among the civil servants and Buddhist monks. The King summoned a council of the Buddhist monks to redraft the Buddhist scripture *Tripitaka* (the three baskets), which had perished during the destruction of Ayudhya. Theravada Buddhism was elevated to the status of the official religion, and the King took an oath to protect the observance of this faith.

Revision of the Code of Laws

The next important step taken by Rama I was to revise the ancient code of laws which had come into force during the days of King Ramadhipati in the fifteenth century. What he desired was that the new code should suit the needs of the changing times. For the purpose of revising this code, he appointed eleven jurists and several scholars to complete this task. The code of 1805 was the product of their strenuous efforts. Thus Rama I brought to bear on Thailand his great work of consolidation and reconstruction. Another important feature of his reign was the efflorescence of Thai literature, particularly prose. The King himself composed a part of *Phra Rajanibondh* (royal writings), and the most noteworthy was the *Ramakien* or *Rakiti*, a plagiarised *Ramayana*. Many Thais today consider this literary piece as a great contribution of the King, and its drama version is frequently enacted on the stage during the celebration of national festivals.

The Javanese tales of Panji and the story of Aniruddha (grandson of Lord Krishna) have been adopted by the Thais for the dance and drama performances. Similarly, many important literary works of Persia and China were translated during this time. Thailand extended its control over the Sultans of Kedah, Kelantan, Perlis and Trengannu (Malay states).

The good work of Rama I was continued by his son Rama II who ruled from 1809 to 1824. During the time of Rama III, Britain, the US and other European powers exerted pressure on Thailand to sign treaties granting free trade. It was because of the heavy pressure exerted by the US that Thailand concluded a limited agreement with the US.

KING MANGKHUT

The credit for keeping Thailand free from western colonization in the 19th century goes to two most remarkable Thai kings, namely Rama IV (also known as Mangkhut) and Rama V (also known Chulalongkorn). Both these kings scored diplomatic triumphs over the British and the French by playing upon each other's sentiments (depending upon circumstances) in order to keep their country free from external control. Although through these diplomatic moves they might have ceded some parts of their territory, but by and large, they saved the country from colonization. Incidentally, both France and Britain wanted a buffer state to exist in South-East Asia so as to avoid conflicts, and Thailand served this purpose.

Just as Japan could not avert the threat of western countries in the 19th century, similarly King Mangkhut of Thailand decided not to keep the Westerners out of his country. He desired to modernize his country on the model of Japan which was reaping the benefits of the knowhow of western science and technology. King Mangkhut was not prepared to disturb what was good in the age-old traditions and customs, but desired that certain things had to change. Striking a balance between tradition and modernity, King Mangkhut introduced necessary social and economic changes through reforms. His reforms came in the form of "advice". He hoped that his nobles would extend full support.

Foreign Relations

The western nations had no difficulty in establishing a rapport with his government and signed treaties of trade and friendship. In the meantime, reforms were introduced in banking, currency, communication and transport systems and so on, as a prelude to a treaty with the British, namely the Anglo-Siamese Treaty of 1855. This Anglo-Siamese Treaty provided for extra-territoriality and tariff control. Thus Britain enjoyed a status of most favored nation. Other western nations also demanded similar treatment from the Government of Thailand. Therefore, the King had to offer similar concessions to many, including the United States. In the meantime, the US sent Townsend Harris as an emissary to Thailand and he received a warm reception on his arrival. Other western nations, which received liberal commercial concessions, were France, Denmark, Portugal, Holland, Prussia, Belgium, Italy, Norway, and Sweden, during the period 1856-68. King Mangkhut sought guarantees from these western powers to assist Thailand in preserving her independence. The treaty with France provided for the acceptance of Christian missionaries and their work of conversion in Thailand.

Modernisation

The process of modernisation of Thailand was facilitated by King Mangkhut. During his time a network of road and communication systems helped to knit several parts of Thailand into one nation. A printing press was established for the publication of books, both native and western. The educational system in Thailand was revamped. Several programmes concerning health and public works were undertaken by the government. The banking system was modernised along with foreign trade, and several British firms were permitted to be established in Bangkok. The British influence, rather than the French, predominated the modernisation of the country. Before Mangkhut died, he signed the treaty with the French whereby the latter recognized Thailand's control over two of the former Cambodian provinces, Siam Reap and Battambong.

KING CHULALONGKORN (1868-1910)

The process of modernisation was further accelerated by the British-educated Mangkhut's son, Chulalongkorn (Rama V). Although the British and the French applied pressure on him to offer more and more concessions, it was this King who tactfully avoided conflicts with them. He tried his best to maintain the integrity and sovereignty of his country. He gained rich experience from his foreign travels (Java and India) and introduced several reforms. These reforms tried to bring about changes in the judicial system, revenue administration, taxation and trade (including Opium trade). He abolished the age-old practice of prostration before the royal presence at the time of his coronation ceremony (1873). He introduced measures which aimed at abolishing slavery in gradual phases. He discontinued the practice of compelling members of certain classes from joining the army and police forces. The railways and telegraphs made their appearance in Thailand in 1875 and 1893 respectively. English medium schools and colleges were set up in the country and the government did not neglect elementary education of children.

The rest of his reforms pertained to the administrative system which was to be based on the model of Western nations. Several experts helped the King to restructure the administrative system. As regards the political system, Thailand maintained a benevolent monarchy with a Privy Council which was to act in advisory capacity. Besides this, there was a small Council of State. The King being the head of the state became the Chief-Executive, and also acted as chairman of the Council of State. The government was not accountable to the people, but to the monarch who enjoyed absolute powers until the outbreak of the revolution of 1932.

Foreign Relations

During the 1880s, Britain and France extended their control over South-East Asia in general. France was eager to extend her control over Indo-China including control over Laos. The French felt that Vietnam had a better claim over Laos than Thailand. It was this ambition of the French that caused anxiety to King Chulalongkorn and he decided to see that the volatile situation in Indo-China did not go out of control. He did not want his country to become a colony of the French or the English. He initiated the desired diplomatic moves in this respect. Fortunately, it resulted in an understanding with the British on the French possessions in Indo-China. It was at his instance, that Britain rejected the French proposal to serve the ends of both (Britain and France). But his negotiations with Britain and France brought about a marginal loss of Thai territories. France succeeded in snatching away Laos from Thailand (1893).

Britain signed a treaty with France by which Thailand was to remain a buffer zone between the two. Britain signed a convention in 1909 with Thailand by which the latter agreed not to offer concessions or rights south of the 11th Parallel to any power. Britain in return agreed to protect the rights of Thailand. She further agreed to help Thailand to construct its railways by offering a soft loan. Thailand agreed to cede some of her territories in the Malay States, namely, Kelantan, Trengannu, Kedah and Perlis in reciprocity. To sum up the King gave peripheral areas as a bargaining point, in order to protect the core of his kingdom.

The two sons of Chulalongkorn, namely, Maha Vajiravudh (1910-25) and Prajadhipok (1925-35) succeeded one after the other as Rama VI and Rama VII respectively. Both had been highly westernized and therefore, tried to introduce radical reforms in the economic and social spheres. Rama VI introduced compulsory education and established a university named after his father in 1917. He also introduced public schools and encouraged the scout movement. He encouraged the Thai women to imitate western women in their dress, customs and manners. His bodyguards wore colourful uniforms. Thailand could boast of a club and a rugby football team which were started by the king. His eagerness to Westernise the Thai traditional society provoked the orthodox elements to rebel. Two attempts were made by these sections to assassinate him and both failed.

During the Great War, Thailand declared her hostility towards Germany in order to please the Allies. Her government was eager to acquire German shipping and railway interests during the course of the war. It was at this time that the Western powers, led by the United States, voluntarily gave up their extra-territorial rights over Thailand. Thailand was made a member of the League of Nations. The Government of Thailand brought about a legislation by which slavery was abolished. Many Thai students started going abroad for higher studies.

Rama VII (Prajadhipok)

He continued to carry forward the democratic reform process with a liberal outlook. Unfortunately, the conservative-minded Thai aristocracy and also the members of the princely families were not happy. They resisted his attempts to democratise the Privy Council and the Supreme Council of the state by converting them into a bicameral legislature. In this struggle, the Thai aristocrats succeeded in securing some rights and privileges for themselves in Parliament and also in the civil service. The reforms of Prajadhipok could not satisfy the demands of the educated middle class, because they did not go far enough. In the meantime, Thailand witnessed several modern features of public utilities such as the airport, hospitals, banking system, the opening of libraries and museums, and the establishment of royal institutes for literature and architecture.

The Bloodless Revolution of 1932

The worldwide economic depression hit Thailand hard. In 1932, the Thai Government was compelled to introduce heavy cuts in the budget resulting in reduction of the salaries of civil servants with no prospect of further promotions. Thailand's economic problem began to increase because of her determination to stick to the gold standard at a time when several countries had abandoned it. As a result, the exports of Thailand, particularly those of rice and teak, began to decline sharply. With government revenues falling, there were further cuts in the budget. As a results the educated unemployed and the disgruntled army officials hatched a plot and overthrew the government on June 24, 1932 (when the King was away in New York). This revolution was known as the Bloodless Revolution because the coup leaders did not want any outside interference in the internal affairs of their country.

After the revolution, the army played an important role in Thai politics. For a few years, Thailand witnessed a struggle for power between two parties, namely the middle class led by Pridi Phanomyong (a leftist and university professor) and Phibun Songkhram, an ultra-nationalist army colonel with military support. The latter had the support of the rightists. While these factions fought for power, there were others such as Prince Baroradej and Sri Sitthi Songkhram (a royalist general) who also staged a counter coup. After fierce fighting, Phibun Songkhram of the people's army smashed the counter coup. The struggle ultimately resulted in the abdication of King Prajadhipok in 1935 in favour of his ten-year-old son, Ananda. A constitutional monarchy of the British model was established.

The architect of the first post-revolutionary constitution was Pridi of the People's Party who became the country's first prime minister. The assembly was composed of the nominated members by the king on the recommendation of the ruling party and also by an indirect election from the local bodies. The king being the head of the executive branch of the government was made responsible to the Assembly. The princely members of the royal family were not eligible to serve the government in any capacity, but some of them were employed in diplomatic service. The new constitution remained in force till 1946.

After Pridi's fall came the Government of Phraya Phahom 1933-38 which outlawed the Communist Party and invalidated Pridi's economic plan. There were no drastic changes introduced in the political and economic spheres. Only the members of the ruling family were excluded from high posts in the administrative set-up which had been enlarged with the inclusion of the members

Only the members of the ruling family were excluded from high posts in the administrative set-up which had been enlarged with the inclusion of the members of the educated elite. While the peasants remained contented with their lot, the common people were alarmed at the dominance of the Chinese community over their economy.

Militant Nationalism

During the second half of the 1930s, Thailand witnessed the upsurge of ultra-nationalism, religious revivalism and militarism. These trends become evident when we see the successive governments attempting to check the Chinese domination over its economy, restrictions imposed on Chinese immigration, the deporting of the aliens, and the closing of Chinese schools and the Press in Thailand. The Thai Government passed strictures on the Christians and urged them to the reconvert themselves to Buddhism. In foreign relations, Thailand demanded the return of her Cambodian provinces of Siam Reap and Battambong from the French. Another example that could be cited for the upsurge of Thai nationalism was the renaming of their country from Siam to Thailand (the land of the free) in 1939. Even the British who were influential felt the pinch of Thai's economic nationalism when their contractors had to accept new conditions while getting their leases of teak forests renewed. The direct rule of the army began in December 1938 and it was undoubtedly the outcome of militant nationalism. Luang Phibun Songkhram became the prime minister of the country.

Alliance between Thailand and Japan (1940)

Militant nationalism in Thailand manifested itself with the slogan "Asia for Asians" followed by the condemnation of Western imperialism. This emotional outburst paved the way for an alliance with Japan in 1940. The Thais admired Japanese for their patriotism and success over the western imperialists. When the Second World War broke out, Thailand declared her hostility towards France and demanded the return of her Cambodian provinces. During the war, Japan intervened on behalf of Thailand and secured these two regions from France. Unfortunately, these two regions were soon occupied by the Japanese forces. The latter started demanding various concessions such as transit, the supply of food and raw materials during the war. Thailand was forced to oblige. Japan rewarded Thailand's help with territories acquired during the war in the neighboring states of Burma, Malaya and Laos. In 1942, the Thai Government declared war on Britain and the USA at the instance of Japan, which alienated the sympathies of the common people. Pridi organised a resistance movement against the Thai Government over this issue, and this movement was called "Free Thai Movement" which was supported by the Americans and the British. Inside Thailand, this movement received support from the general public which did not like martial law, the short supply of goods, and inflation, all caused by the government which had the support of the Japanese forces. Even the Chinese community in Thailand supported the Free Thai movement since the government had seized their assets. Furthermore, it became quite clear to the Thais that their country was being exploited by the Japanese Government.

The Fall of Phibun's Government

During the closing years of the war (1944), the fortunes turned in favour of the Western Allies, and in Thailand, the National Assembly forced Phibun Songkhram to resign. In the meantime, the Anglo-US forces started bombing the Japanese military installations in Thailand. It was then that the new government headed by Khuang Aphaiwong, with the support of Pridi, started secret negotiations with the western Allies for saving Thailand from a possible Allied occupation. Britain proposed to convert Thailand into her protectorate but the US disapproved of it. The pro-Japanese Prime Minister Phibun was arrested and sent to Japan as war criminal in 1945. The Japanese forces in Thailand were disarmed and expelled.

Peace Settlement

In the peace settlement with Britain, Thailand agreed to cede territories she got after December 7, 1941. She agreed to compensate Britain for the losses caused to her citizens in Thailand during the war. Similarly, France was compensated with territories taken from her during the war. Thailand was admitted as a member of the United Nations in 1946. The Thai Government established friendly relations with the Kuomintang Government in China, agreed to grant the most favoured nation status to the United States, and permitted the communist party to function in her country in order to please the Soviet Union.

The Post-war Period

After the war, the militant nationalism had run its course. The anti-western stand taken by the Thai Government during the war weakened. Thailand remained free from colonial rule at a time when other South-East Asian countries had come under Western imperialism. Post-war Thailand witnessed the inclusion of an amendment to the constitution of 1932 by which the powers of the king were restricted. The unicameral legislature was abolished, and in its place came a bicameral legislature, which was composed of elected representatives.

The politics of Thailand centred on three important political groups, the first consisted of Phibun, Sarit Thanarat, Thanom KittiKachorn and Paraphat Charusathien all supported by the army. The second group consisted of Pridi Phanamyong who led the middle class intellectual group, and the third by the royalist Khuang Aphaiwong and Seni Pramoj.

Political Instability

Seni Pramoj who had been an Ambassador to the United States became the prime minister with Pridi as his advisor. The restoration of parliamentary democracy in Thailand unfortunately did not have smooth sailing, since it produced nine administrations in rapid succession. Pridi himself became the prime minister, but with King Mahidol's assassination, his government fell. Political instability followed the fall of Pridi's government, what with politicians throwing morals to the wind and corrupt administrators ruling the roost. The Thai army became restive and Pridi had to flee the country because he was falsely accused of bringing about the king's assassination. Even the coup leaders, particularly the army General (Sarit Thanarat) and police chief General Phao Sriyanan, failed to reach an agreement on the issue of establishing a stable government.

This volatile political situation provided an excellent opportunity to Phibun to stage a successful coup on April 6, 1948. He enjoyed the support of the king and the army when he became the prime minister of the country. In fact, parliamentary democracy came to an end, and the military rule led by the king and the prime minister began for the next twenty-five years. The Thai monarchy, supported by the army, became the symbol of political unity in the country. The king wielded far more influence in the country than what was envisaged in the constitution. The king's great concern for the welfare of the common people was reflected in the effective implementation of the socio-economic programmes. He rarely interfered in the day-to-day administration of the country. This was carried out by Phibun Songkhram who imposed restrictions on the Chinese immigrations. His government supervised and controlled the Chinese language schools and newspapers. The Thai Government became quite alarmed at the success of the communists in China in 1949. It feared an upsurge of communist activity in its own territory and therefore, took steps to prevent such an occurrence. The steps included enforcing of strict naturalisation laws and the imposition of heavy fees for alien registration. In the fifties, the government banned the functioning of the Communist Party in the country.

However, it was in the foreign policy that Thailand took a decisive step. It must be remembered that Thailand was surrounded by China on the one side, Communist Pathet Laos on the other and North Vietnam on yet another. The Chinese and the North Vietnamese had been continuously encouraging insurgency in Thailand and therefore, the government had to seek the help of the United States. It was in these circumstances that Thailand was forced to join the US-led SEATO (South East Asia Treaty Organisation).

The Coup of 1957

Phibun's domination of the Thai military government ended in 1957 after Sarit Tanarat condemned the prevailing widespread corruption, irregularities and also the intimidation of voters by Phibun in the general election. Sarit was supported by university professors and college students who staged a bloodless coup on September 16, 1957. Phibun was forced to flee the country. It must be remembered that he played a prominent role in the 1932 revolution . In 1957, he was disliked for his corrupt practices, and it was learnt that he kept ill-gotten wealth in Swiss banks. Sarit governed the country for the next six years, a period in which the Thai Government received substantial American military and economic aid.

Thailand Involved in Vietnam War

Sarit nominated Marshal Thanom Kittikachorn to succeed him. It was during his time that the Vietnam war was in full swing and the American government used Thailand as a base of military operations against North Vietnam. Both China and North Vietnam resented this and China in retaliation encouraged the Thai Patriotic Front in Thailand in 1965 for carrying out subversive activities against the Thai Government and for its eventual overthrow. North Vietnam provided training to Thai tribal groups on the north-eastern borders of Thailand for the purpose of insurgency.

From 1969-1971, there were some changes in the government policy and this was reflected in the drafting of a new constitution and holding of general elections. Parliamentary debates on many issues, critical reviews of government policies by opposition leaders and so on became the marked features. Prospects for the ushering in of democracy in Thailand brightened with the freedom of the Press. However, when Kittikachorn found out that his government was being severely criticised he scrapped the constitution and dissolved the National Assembly. The freedom of the Press was curbed and individual rights were denied in 1971. In respect of foreign policy, Thailand continued to remain a faithful ally of the US in spite of perceptible changes in US foreign policy under President Nixon. Thailand expected better economic relations with the United States and provided many facilities for the stationing of American troops in spite of criticism at home. The cessation of the Vietnam, war following the Paris peace accord, disappointed Thailand because the accord did not provide for the withdrawal of North Vietnamese troops stationed on her borders with Laos and Cambodia. Thailand perceived that a united Vietnam under the leadership of Ho Chi Minh posed a serious threat to her security.

Students' Revolt (1973)

The wrath of the people over the scrapping of the constitution and denial of their freedom took the form of a revolt organised by students against the Kittikachorn Government. The government did its best to suppress this revolt and arrested 12 student leaders for violating the ban imposed on political activity. The revolt took a very violent form and hundreds were killed and several hundreds injured on October 14, 1973. The Thai king intervened at this juncture and restored civilian rule. Thus Thailand became free from military rule after a gap of 25 years. The king appointed Sanya Thamassat, a former Chief Justice of the Supreme Court as prime minister, after forcing Kittikachorn and his deputy to go into exile.

Military Coups

In the aftermath of the students' revolt, the civilian administration was unable to maintain law and order. Therefore, in 1974, the military toppled the government after a bloody coup and assumed power. In fact, Thailand experienced at least 15 coups, or attempted military coups, during the period 1935-85. The attempted coup of September 1985 did not succeed and thus democracy was saved. The civilian government which survived for the longest period was that of General Prem Tinsulanonda. Ever since he assumed power in 1981, the Thai Government showed its stability because the people had developed respect for civilian rule. The prime minister has kept the Thai Government free from scandals.

It should be noted that in the recent history of Thailand, the army has played a crucial role. Unfortunately, the civilian rule of General Prem experienced moments of crisis. One such was when General Arhit, the Army Chief, challenged the government's economic reforms which included a 17 per cent devaluation of Thai currency. However, the government did not yield, and Arhit did not make things worse after realizing that the prime minister enjoyed overwhelming support of the people. General Prem also maintained formal contacts with the army, and allowed it to play a meaningful role in the civilian government. This approach was in tune with 'special clauses' included in the 1979 Constitution. General Prem's civilian government extended the service tenure of General Arhit by one year thereby avoiding a potential threat of a military takeover.

Monarchy Respected

Elections were held in 1988, and the civilian rule continued. But this democratically elected government was toppled by a military coup led by General Suchinda Kraprayoon in 1991. His military rule was replaced by another in September 1992. General elections were held in July 1995, and a new government assumed the reins of administration. King Bhumibol of Thailand became the longest reigning monarch on June 9, 1996 since he completed his fiftieth year on the throne. Like in Japan, the person of the king symbolises national unity and integrity in Thailand. All the powers ultimately reside in the monarchy, and hence Thailand's constitutional monarchy is highly respected by one and all. Thailand was about to join the club of the 'Four Tigers' of Asia as the fastest growing economy until the recession hit her badly. Thai is the official language, and baht the currency. Bangkok serves as the capital of Thailand. Buddhism is the official religion. Thailand is the biggest exporter of rice, and agriculture sustains 60 per cent of her population.

Recession (1997-2001)

The Thai economy was badly battered by a recession in 1997 which spread to other parts of South-East Asia. In fact, the recession began in Thailand when its currency baht lost much of its value. The fall of baht compelled Thai companies to pay billions of dollars in repayment of short-term loans. This precipitated the stock and real estate markets to crash. It is said that the Thai economy shrank by nearly 80 per cent in 1998. Thailand was compelled to borrow $ 3.4 billion from the IMF since there was the flight of foreign capital. Nearly two million people remained unemployed.

It was at this critical juncture that Thailand witnessed the rise of Thanksin Sinawatra as the new leader. He is described as the 'iron-fisted' reformer. He believes in state control. After he was elected the prime minister of the country in 2001, Thailand has shown great signs of economic recovery. This billionaire prime minister introduced several economic reforms for reviving the otherwise stagnant economy. Ironically this PM never believes in capitalism and adopts policy of state control (ie command economy).

In recent times, Thailand, a Buddhist country, has been witnessing Muslim militants from the southern part of the country attacking police posts in Yala, Pattani and Songkhla provinces along the border with Malaysia. Southern Thailand is dominated by Muslims, and has been witnessing Islamic revolts in recent years. Thanksin says that this is supported by corrupt politicians, drug-peddlers and Muslim militants. The recent Tsunami (December 26, 2004) battered the Thai sea-coast destroying many tourist spots, and the government is doing its best to mitigate the sufferings of those who survived.

20

LAOS (LANG CHANG)

Laos is a land-locked country in South-East Asia with its boundaries touching several of her neighbours such as China, Cambodia, Myanmar, Thailand and Vietnam. In her early history, she was deeply influenced by Indian culture, although ethnically Laotians are divided into four major groups, namely Lao Lum (C Valley Lao), Lao Tai (Tribal Thai), Lao Theng (Lao of Mountain sides) and Lao Sung (Lao of Mountain tops). Indian culture spread to Laos through the Chinese, Khmers and Thais, and probably from the time of Emperor Ashoka. Originally, Laotians lived in small principalities along the border of South China from the first century AD, and one of the kings, Luang Limao was influenced by Mahayana Buddhism in the first century AD. In the course of time, the Laotians migrated to Nanchao in Yunnan due to Chinese incursions and built a powerful kingdom under the leadership of King Sinhanara. His successors governed this kingdom till the middle of the seventh century AD. Thereafter the Khmer kings of Chenla ruled Laos.

It was not until the middle of the fourteenth century that Laos emerged as a unified state. The credit for this goes to King Fa Ngum who founded the *Lang Chang* (meaning million elephants) which included Luang Prabang and Vientiane in 1353. After marrying the daughter of the King of Ayudhya, Fa Ngum's control and influence extended to the upper Mekong region. He was very ambitious and fought many battles with the neighbouring kingdoms in order to expand his small kingdom into an empire. The seat of his capital was Luang Prabang. His successors maintained good relations with the powerful kingdoms of Thailand and Annam. Another Laotian King, Photisarath (1520-47) became famous after he built Wat Visoun. He converted himself into a Buddhist monk in AD 1525. His son Setathirath shifted the capital from Luang Prabang to Vian-Chang (Vientiane) in order to improve the commercial relations with the kingdoms of Thailand and Annam. Laos was fortunate enough to be free from the incursions of the Europeans in South-East Asia for a long time. Probably this was due to its peculiar geographical position. Laos came to be profoundly influenced by Hindu culture as reflected in her literature, religion and art.

French Colonial Rule

French Premier Jules Ferry advocated aggressive imperialism in the Far East as well as in South-East Asia. He enunciated this forward policy for the main reason that it would improve French trade with South-East Asian countries. France continued to extend her colonial rule in the Tongking delta. It was soon followed by Annam after signing a treaty with France in 1873 thereby accepting the French protectorate. By 1885, the French empire included Cochin-China and Kampuchea. Thailand was feeling the thrust of French imperialism on the one side and British pressure on the other. Her fate as an independent country hung in balance. To save herself from French subjugation, she had to cede control over Laos, which was her province at that time. France put forward her claim as overlord of Annam, since the latter had better claim over Laos than Thailand. In 1889, the French Ambassador to Britain, Wadington suggested to the British Government the division of Thailand along with Mekong River and the ceding of Laos to France. The proposal was rejected, but because of certain geo-political implications it was agreed in 1893 that Thailand would remain a buffer state. France put pressure on Thailand by a show of force and the latter had to cede Laos which became a French protectorate from 1893.

Indirect Rule of the French

The French Government was of the opinion that French culture "was of universal value and superiority". Therefore, they forced all high level Laotian officials to imbibe French culture. The native officials continued to function under the king with the headquarters at Luang Prabang. The native courts, councils and assemblies also continued to function in a routine manner but with a difference. The difference was that the French official known as Resident-Superieur was at the helm directing, superintending and controlling the levers of administration through the native officials. In other words, the native people, bureaucrats and even the king had little influence over many policy matters. The French officials enjoyed all key positions in the administrative hierarchy and remained proud of the fact that they had brought about political modernisation of the country based on French culture. Unfortunately, the French policies led to harmful effects on the "rice-farming economy" leading to poverty with attendant social evils. The age-old political and social institutions in Laos began to decline. Only the landlords, moneylenders and corrupt bureaucrats began to derive benefits from French rule. In the course of time, the educated middle class became assertive and took up the cause of liberating the country from the shackles of colonial rule.

National Movement in Laos

As was the case elsewhere in South-East Asia, the national movement in Laos was also more or less the direct outcome of the policies of the French which proved to be exploitative and harmful. But the movement made substantial progress in the wake of Japanese occupation of different parts of China and South-East Asia during the Second World War. Since the Japanese required raw materials and markets in Indo-China they needed the cooperation of the natives. Japan, therefore, established what is called "Greater East Asia Co-Prosperity Sphere" in which all countries occupied by her were to derive mutual benefits. Japan was doing this at a time, when she had begun to suffer from the harmful effects of economic depression and the politics of the thirties.

Anti-colonial Movements in Laos

Japan took pride in considering herself as the liberator of countries which she had occupied from western imperial powers. The Japanese government in occupation allowed the natives of the countries to have their own internal administration. In the case of Laos, the French officials, unfortunately, began to act under Japanese control and supervision till March 1945. However, in the end, the Japanese deposed the Vichy French Government, jailed French officials, and permitted the Laotians to declare their independence from France.

When the Japanese found that the prime minister of Laos, Savong Vatthana who also happened to be the Crown Prince, was not inclined to cancel the treaty of protectorate signed with the French some 50 years ago, they asked Prince Phetsarath to replace him. Prince Phetsarath refused to give permission to the French senior Resident to return to Laos, since Laos had become independent. In this melodrama, King Sesasavan Vong intervened to declare Laos as a French Protectorate and asked Prince Phetsarath to resign. The action of the Laotian monarch thus paved the way for the launching of a national movement called Lao Issarak (Free Laos) by the common people but headed by the western-educated elite belonging to the royal family. The most prominent among them were Prince Suvanna Phouma and Souphannou Vong (brothers of Prince Phetsarath). In the provisional government elected by the provisional people's assembly all under a provisional constitution, the two brothers occupied ministerial posts. In the course of time, the provisional government deposed the monarch when he refused to invalidate the French protectorate.

It was during the last few months of 1945, that the French Government sent troops to re-establish its authority in Laos. The troops were successful in defeating the forces of Lao Issarak and capturing Vientiane in 1946. A month later, the French troops captured the royal capital, Luang Prabang. The French government restored monarchy and the members of the Lao Issarak were forced to flee the country. These members set up their government in exile and operated from the borders of Thailand with prince Phetsarath as their leader. This government also included Suvanna Phouma and Souphannou Vong as Deputy Prime Minister and Defence Minister respectively. It must be remembered that the Lao Issarak government in exile had not come under the influence of communism.

The moderate elements in Lao Issarak led by Suvanna Phouma made a bold attempt to negotiate the terms of liberation of Laos with the French authorities, but the latter refused to grant total independence. The attitude of the French brought about a split in Lao Issarak in 1949 with moderates led by Suvanna Phouma, and the extremists by Souphannou Vong. The latter met the leaders of Vietminh in North Vietnam and declared the formation of a guerilla outfit called Pathet Lao (land of the Lao) in 1950.

Constitutional Concessions to Laos

France came under severe pressure and finally granted autonomy to Laos along with the other two states in Indo-China and enabled them to become members of the United Nations. Further political concessions to the Laotian Government came in October 1949, which permitted the exiled members of Lao Issarak to return to Laos except Prince Phetsarath. It was this concession by the French that enabled Suvanna Phouma to head the Laotian Government in 1951. However, he was still controlled by the French government. In October 1953, Laos became an independent member of the French Union.

In the meantime, Pathet Lao started operating from the borders of Laos-Vietnam with its political wing, the Lao Communist Party, which was formed in 1952. The Communist Party members and militia were trained by the Vietminh forces of North Vietnam. The Lao Communist Party gradually extended its control over the two north-eastern provinces, namely, Phong Saly and Sam Neua, in 1954.

Geneva Conference 1954

After the fall of Dien Bien Phu, France found it difficult to hold on to the Indo-China states. The Geneva Conference of 1954 was convened to establish peace in Indo-China. This conference was able to bring about the grant of total independence to Laos. At the same time, it recognised the hold of Pathet Lao over the two north-eastern provinces. The peace makers of the Geneva Conference hoped to see that the liberation movements would ultimately lead to the unification of the country. They also hoped that different factions in Cambodia and Vietnam would overcome their differences and work in harmony according to the terms of the agreement.

Thus there was no reason for Pathet Lao to continue its struggle when it could reach an amicable agreement with the existing Laotian Government. Prince Suvanna Phouma expected his half-brother to bury the hatchet, liquidate the communist Pathet Lao forces, and ultimately join the mainstream of Laos' national life.

Between 1955 and 1957 prospects looked bright in Laos with Souphannou Vong and a few members of Pathet Lao joining the National Union Government led by Suvanna Phouma and it was also expected that the two battalions of Pathet Lao would integrate themselves with the Royal Laotian army. General elections would be held with NLHX (the Communist Party of Pathet Lao) taking part. Laos' foreign policy was to be based on neutrality and non-alignment.

The Vietnam war was at its height at this point and the Vietminh and the US forces were locked in combat. It must be remembered that US foreign policy in those days was principally based on containing the spread of communism. Therefore, the US Government was helping South Vietnam to check the infiltration of the forces of Vietnam in the south. It was this Vietnam war with US involvement that deeply disturbed the political atmosphere in Laos. The United States wanted a government in Laos which would help her to contain communism and at the same time not allow its soil to be used as a base (incidentally the Ho Chi Minh trail passed through Laos) by the enemies of South Vietnam.

Therefore, in the Laotian elections of 1958 , the leftists (Communists) won a victory which upset the rightists as well as the neutrals. These two defeated parties demanded the expulsion of Pathet Lao members of the cabinet and demanded a pro-western attitude. The Laotian Government was forced to arrest the leaders of Pathet Lao and put them in prison. All these events took place after the CDNI (Committee for the Defence of National Interest) was formed by the rightists who came to power.

The new government sent the neutralist, Suvanna Phouma, as ambassador to France. Subsequently, two of the three Pathet Lao battalions were forced to integrate with the national army. Prince Souphannou Vong and his followers were jailed in 1958, but they escaped from prison two years later. These jailed members settled in the north-eastern part of Laos to create trouble for the newly formed government in Laos. Laos remained as a country without peace, thanks to the rivalry of the superpowers in South-East Asia. After the Geneva agreement, foreign forces, especially the Vietminh, withdrew.

Economic Conditions

It was on December 2, 1975 that Laos was proclaimed as Laos-Lao People's Republic. In the 1980, Laos depended heavily on the military and financial assistance from Vietnam. Since 1988, Thailand and the US have been helpful to this country by way of their investments. The Laotian regime is dominated by its 75-year-old President, Khamtai Siphandon. He is described as the "last of the revolutionary leaders who led the Pathet Lao guerillas to victory in 1975..." By and large, the present regime in Laos is under the influence of Vietnam. The recent recession has slowed down the pace of economic reforms, and the old President has been accused of inept leadership. The currency (kip) has fallen by nearly 80 per cent to an American dollar since June 1997. The economic situation worsened further with the currency losing some more value, and Laotian banks going broke. The talks with the IMF for loans have failed. The World Bank turned down a request for a $ 20 million credit. Even a trade agreement with the US Government has fallen through. Vientiane is the country's capital, and the per capita income is $ 360.

21

THE PHILIPPINES

The modern Philippines, with its capital seat at Manila, has an area of 2,99,404 sq kms, comprising more than 7,107 islands and a population of 72.7 million. Philippines has no regular history to boast of until the arrival of Spaniards in 1570. The principal religions are Christianity and Islam and the people speak Filipino and English. Situated at a distance of 600 miles across the South-China Sea from the coast of Vietnam, the Philippines, in prehistoric times, was inhabited by a race of Aetas. Archaeologists have traced Neolithic, Bronze age settlements (Bato caves) in Samar and early iron age and urn burial sites in Masbate. We also observe cultural influence of Hinduism in the Philippines since people in the early ages had come into contact with the Sri Vijaya kingdom. About ten per cent of the Negrito population of the present day Philippines claimed their ancestry to Indonesia. In other words, Indonesian emigrants must have settled in the south coast of the Philippines before the advent of the Christian era. A big group of Malay immigrants arrived in the 15th century bringing Islam with them. It must be remembered that the Malays of Mindanao and South Palawan had embraced Islam earlier. At the time of the Spanish conquest of Philippines, Islam had spread to many parts of the southern Philippines.

During the thirteenth century, people living in Luzon island worshipped idols. The chiefs used white umbrellas. In the course of time, the people of Luzon received merchandise from Chinese and Japanese traders. Their influence was also felt on the Filipinos because many of them began to worship the spirits of the ancestors represented by figures of animals.

The Spanish Conquest

Following the decision of the Council of Trent (European Reformation period) it was decided by the Catholic Church to refurbish its image all over the world. King Philip II of Spain acted as the Champion-agent of the spread of Catholicism all over Europe and the rest of the world. This missionary zeal motivated the Spanish explorers to spread the Catholic faith among the heathens of Asia. After Ferdinand Magellan's voyage (1521-22), Spain put forward her claim to the spice islands, but after the treaty of Sargossa in 1529, the Portuguese

Government permitted Spain to conquer the Philippines. It was not until 1565, that the Spaniards established their first settlement in Cebu which was followed by the conquest of Luzon in 1566. In 1567, the Spaniards occupied a small town called Manila. In the beginning, the Spanish conquest of the Philippines was opposed by the Chinese of Taiwan, the Dutch, the British and also the Muslim inhabitants of the southern islands of Mindanao and Sulu (whom the Spaniards called Moros). They were all afraid that the Spaniards may create political and economic problems for them. However, it was in the first half of the nineteenth century, that their resistance to the Spanish rule was overcome by the Spanish Government.

The Catholic Church in the Philippines

The Church propagated the Christian faith among the Filipinos and brought about large-scale conversions, but the converted Filipinos continued to practise their ancient rituals and also believed in animistic spirits. The Catholic Church somehow had to tolerate these practices. Every village in the Philippines had a church where a priest met the people regularly, learnt their language (Tagalog), and spread Christian faith. The Spaniards granted lands to individuals on certain conditions, particularly to those who got converted to Christianity, and these lands came to be known as Encomiendas. After a long time, the descendants of these landowners came to be known as Encomenderos and they became virtual landed proprietors. There were estates of the Frias which were given on lease to Filipino-Mestizos on a fifty-fifty basis. Then there were Pueblos, that is, lands owned by the common residents.

Spanish Trade

The Spanish trade from Manila to their colony in Mexico continued with the export of items like silk, porcelain, spices and jewellery. These were all received from the Chinese merchants. The Chinese merchants of Manila had brisk trade with the natives of the Philippines. Since, the Philippines had nothing to import or export, the Spanish directed the trade of Manila-based Chinese merchants to other Spanish colonies. Thus the Mexican dollar reigned in South-East Asia for nearly three centuries. Attempts of the Spaniards to gain a foothold in mainland China and Japan failed in the sixteenth and seventeenth centuries. In spite of the attacks of the locals like Moros, the Chinese and the Dutch, the Spaniards were able to establish their administration on the model of Spanish-ruled Mexico. The Spaniards were able to establish their authority over many islands and brought about their integration in the administrative set-up. Forced labour of the non-Christians was permitted in the Philippines. The attacks of the Dutch ceased after 1648 when Spain recognised the independence of the Netherlands. The Bishop of Manila exercised great influence and power over the people, since he was next in rank to the Spanish

Governor-General. Then, there was the *audience,* the court of Governor General, under the treasury office all situated at Manila.

Early Rebellions Against Spanish Rule

In the course of time, Spanish rule became very oppressive, due to forced labour, loss of lands, and tribute payments. All these atrocities resulted in a number of rebellions during the seventeenth and eighteenth centuries. In the beginning, it was easy to rebel since Spain had not fully succeeded in establishing her control over hundreds of islands scattered everywhere. Leaders of non-Christian subjects often found it easy to organise revolts against Spanish rule in the name of religion. In 1621, there were revolts in Bohol and Leyte which were easily crushed by the Spanish Government because they were not properly co-ordinated. Then there was the serious revolt at Luzon in 1649, by the Visayan labourers in the Manila shipyard. But this was also crushed. Another revolt in the Pampanga section of Luzon in 1660-61 also did not succeed, although it spread widely.

British Occupation of Manila

The revolts against Spanish rule became frequent in the 18th century, since the Filipinos no longer tolerated the Spanish atrocities. However, the third in the series of revolts which occurred in the 18th century coincided with the British-Indian occupation of Manila, which lasted twenty months. This occupation ended after signing the Paris Treaty (1763) between Britain and Spain.

Secularisation Programme

It was then that Spanish King Charles III, seriously considered introducing reforms in the much distressed colony of the Philippines. The first of these reforms was introduced by Governor de La Torre which aimed at eliminating the hold of the dominant clergy over the subjects. The Jesuit Society was expelled from the Philippines in 1768 and further denunciation of the role of the friars by the government continued. Then the Spanish Government in the Philippines, began to blame the Church for interfering in state matters and causing great suffering to the Filipinos. The government began recruiting secular minded priests for the church-posts. But this secularisation programme did not achieve its objective.

Economic Reforms

The Spanish Governor attempted to introduce economic reforms so as to make the Philippines self-sufficient. The government encouraged the natives to cultivate cotton, sugarcane, mulberry trees, tobacco, indigo and hemp. At the same time, the government encouraged the growth of industries and commerce. The Spanish Governor founded the "Economic Society of the Friends of the Country" for the purpose of encouraging industry and commerce. A new commercial code in 1769 provided for the establishment of the Chamber of Commerce. But in the middle of the 19th century, Manila's foreign trade and business showed sharp decline, and this was due to the opening of Chinese ports, including the port of Hong Kong, to British trade. However, the opening of the Suez Canal in 1869 gave stimulus to Filipino trade.

Rise of Filipino Nationalism

The educated middle class, developed regular contacts with many Europeans who came to the Philippines for the purpose of business. The books they got with them and the new thoughts they spread brought changes in the outlook of the otherwise conservative Filipinos. Some Filipino students went abroad for higher studies, and returned home with new ideas. Colleges, libraries, clubs, newspapers and periodicals awakened sentiments of nationalism and political consciousness.

Jose Rizal

The torch of freedom among the Filipino youth was lighted by Jose Rizal, a multifaceted and highly talented personality in Filipino history. Born to Catholic parents, he hailed from Calamba, a farming town, which was dominated by the land-owning Dominican friars. He became sensitive to all kinds of oppression during his younger days, and on his trip abroad, he decided to work for reviving the dignity and freedom of Filipinos. He decided to expose the omissions and commissions of "friarocracy" to the world. Rizal's writings attacked the friarocracy and therefore, they were banned by the colonial government headed by Governor-General Terrero. In the meantime, Rizal had set up a civic association named Liga Eilipina whose aim was to unite the Filipinos everywhere for the purpose of opposing Spanish cruelty and injustice. The Spanish authorities arrested him and subsequently jailed him. The moderate phase of nationalism in Philippines ended with the imprisonment of Jose Rizal.

Katipunan

After the dissolution of Liga Filipina, there arose a militant organisation named Katipunan which was founded by Andrews Bonifacio. The objective of this organisation was to secure freedom for Filipinos by bringing about a violent overthrow of Spanish rule. In a bid to make this organisation popular, Bonifacio declared Rizal (who had been deported to Depitan by the Spanish authorities) the honorary president. This was done without the consent of Rizal and subsequent events resulted in the persecution of Rizal as a traitor. The execution of Rizal in 1896 by the Spanish authorities greatly strengthened the cause of the national movement. Rizal's emotional poem titled *Ultimo Adios*, became a great source of inspiration for all the patriots and is cherished even today. The Katipunan could not achieve its objective because there arose two factions within it, the first led by Bonifacio, and the other by Aguinaldo (a young school teacher). Aguinaldo and his followers proclaimed the Philippines a republic in March 1897 and carried on the struggle against the Spanish authorities. In the end, Aguinaldo agreed for peace, and the Spanish Government promised to usher in political and administrative reforms. But these promises were not kept and Aguinaldo left for Hong Kong on exile.

Aguinaldo Seeks American Help

Pretending to be on exile in Hong Kong, Aguinaldo secretly started purchasing weapons with whatever money was paid to him by the Spanish Government. In the meantime, he sought foreign assistance for the overthrow of the Spanish Government in the Philippines. He came into contact with the American Consul, Pratt, and subsequently, with Commodore Dewey of the American Asiatic Squadron. Both these American officers had by then received instructions to destroy the Spanish Fleet at the Manila Bay (*refer* Spanish-American War). The destruction of the Spanish Fleet was considered essential to the ultimate victory of the Americans in the Spanish-American war. Unaware of the desire of the Americans to fulfil their aspiration of "Manifest destiny", Aguinaldo agreed to assist the Americans in the destruction of the Spanish fleet. With his support the American troops ultimately captured Manila after destroying the Spanish fleet in May 1899. Unfortunately for Aguinaldo, the United States Government, concluded a secret treaty with Spain in December 1898, which provided a sum of twenty million dollars as compensation to Spain for the loss of the Philippines. The secret deal between the two countries took Aguinaldo and his followers by surprise because the Philippines was to come under the rule of the United States. Tens of thousands of patriotic Filipinos had died during the military rule established by the US Government. The American colonial regime became very oppressive and Aguinaldo was captured in 1901. To the Americans it cost nearly $200,000,000 to suppress the revolt of the Filipinos, more than what they had paid to Spain for gaining control over the Philippines! In the end, America realized that she would have been better off if she had not taken control of the Philippines, but the United States army had different ideas.

After the conquest of the Philippines, the United States Government realized the intensity of the patriotic struggle of the Filipinos. However, the American Government was doubtful whether the Filipinos had developed the capacity and ability to govern themselves. It was, therefore, decided that the American Administration should gain the confidence of the Filipinos. It was in this direction that the first step was taken by the American Government. It replaced the American military regime with a civilian administration under the leadership of William H. Taft. The next step was taken towards eliminating all the ugly features of Spanish rule, particularly in the sphere of landholdings. The Organisations Act of 1902 provided for the separation of the State from the Church. The act declared that all the lands owned by friars as public property were available for sale to the public. The new laws tried to protect the interests of small Filipino farmers, and in 1916 the unsold lands of the Friars were kept at the disposal of the Philippines legislature. In the meantime, the American Government established the Supreme Court, introduced the *Habeas Corpus* and provided for registration of civil marriages.

Further Democratisation

The American Government introduced political reforms in 1907, which allowed Filipinos to elect representatives to a general assembly, which was authorised to pass necessary legislation on domestic matters, particularly in the areas of finance and land reforms. Two Filipino leaders, namely, Sergio Osmena and Manuel Quezon, figured prominently on the political scene. In the early decades of the twentieth century, the latter was considered by the Filipinos as the "Father of Philippines Independence". The American Governor-General, his cabinet and the Upper House still retained the power to reject some of the popular demands of the Filipinos. It was during this time two political parties emerged on the political scene, namely, the Conservative Federal Party (which desired the merger of the Philippines with the United States) and the not-so-well-organised *Nacionalistas* (seeking total independence).

Economic Depression (1929-34)

American farm and business interests anxious to combat the effects of economic depression, influenced American policy makers to grant the Philippines her independence. The first step in this direction was taken by the American Congress in passing the Tydings-Mc Duffie Act (1934) providing for not only the creation of Commonwealth of the Philippines, but also setting the date for total independence, ie July 4, 1946. The Act envisaged a constitutional convention for the purpose of drafting a new constitution wherein the United States would have control over foreign relations, tariff and coinage during the transitional period. The US Supreme Court would also have the powers to review some cases already settled in the local courts in the Philippines.

Japanese Occupation

The Japanese began to control several mine-owning companies and other business enterprises in the Philippines. In the early stages of the Second World War Japan had absolutely no intention of conquering the Philippines. But the tough stand taken by the United States Government towards Japan provoked the Japanese to plan the conquest of the Philippines. The US' vested interests in the Philippines were contrary to Japanese interests. After the Pearl Harbour attack and the conquest of Indo-China, Japan conquered the Philippines. Japan destroyed air-bases at the Clark Field and naval bases at Cante. The Philippine Government was forced to go into exile and the Japanese established a puppet government in its place. However, the Japanese began to face stiff resistance from the Filipino guerillas. The efforts of the Japanese to persuade the Filipinos to follow their way of thinking failed miserably. In October 1943, Japan promised to grant independence. But in 1944, the forces led by American General MacArthur succeeded in capturing many of the islands of the Philippines. In the meantime, the president of the Philippines, the Queen, died and Omen occupied this post. After the liberation of the Philippines by General MacArthur, the American Government handed over power to the Filipinos on July 4, 1946.

The Huk Rebellion

The independence of the Philippines was soon threatened by the outbreak of Huk rebellion. Agrarian discontent of the early twentieth century had not been crushed totally, and the members of the Hukbalahap (Huk) considered themselves as the legitimate successors of those leaders who took part in the anti-Spanish colonial revolution. Their objective was to drive the feudal landlords out, thereby liberating the oppressed peasants. Their struggle continued during the second and the third decade of the twentieth century, and also during the post-independence period. It was encouraged by the Communist Party in the country.

The Huk rebellions became frequent after the occupation of the Philippines by the Japanese. The Japanese Government aggravated the conditions of the poor peasants by demanding a greater share of foodgrains for feeding its army. In the meantime, the Communist Party secretly organized a liberation force from among the discontented peasants which carried on its struggle against the Japanese, and also against the native feudal elements by adopting guerilla tactics. In the course of time, this violent movement attracted other disgruntled elements such as the unemployed youth, the bandits and so on into its fold. The Hukbalahap seized large estates, killed oppressive landlords, and redistributed the lands to the poor peasants in the province of Luzon. The movement continued even after the surrender of Japan because the United States Forces encouraged the anti-guerilla movement among the civilized Filipino gentry .

Post-war Decades

The post-war government of the Philippines under President Manuel Roxas and his successors offered no solution to the rebellious Huks due to increase in pressure from the US Government. These post-war governments acted like American stooges and therefore, the Huks changed its name into People's army of Liberation, after being inspired by the success of the Chinese revolution of 1949.

The main objective of the People's Army of Liberation (PAL) was to overthrow the American-backed government of Quirino. The American advisers had to be liquidated. But the Huk movement suffered a great setback after the appointment of Ramon Magsaysay as the nation's defence minister. He tackled the problem of Huk rebellion on two fronts; firstly, he organized a counter-insurgency movement to contain the PAL and secondly, he tried to wean away many guerillas from the path of violence by introducing necessary land reforms for their betterment. This was followed by granting general amnesty to those who surrendered to the government. As a result of these measures, the PAL lost much of its strength, and a few of its hard-core elements hid in the mountains of Luzon.

Ramon Magsaysay of the Nacionalistas was elected president of the Philippines in 1953. His new government introduced several populist reforms, the most important being the land reforms. The new Agricultural Tenancy Act broke up the strangle-hold of feudal landlords on the poor peasants . He also took steps to redress the grievances of the common people and took his country on the path of industrialization. He became the most beloved leader of the Filipinos. He died in an air crash in March 1957.

During the next five years, the Philippines witnessed political chaos, Gracia who succeeded Magsaysay promised to continue the liberal policy of his predecessors but failed to keep his word. His feud with his Vice-President Macapagal turned the government into a hotbed of corruption and nepotism. In 1961, Macapagal of the Liberal Party got elected president, and his misdoings surpassed those of his predecessors. His Land Reform Act failed miserably due to lack of effective implementation. However, the two other measures, namely, the abolition of vexatious foreign exchange regulation, and the delinking of Filipino currency from the American dollar, helped to some extent in eliminating corruption. It also made the Filipino products more competitive in the world market.

Ferdinand Marcos (1965)

In the 1965 general election, Ferdinand Marcos, the most handsome person of the Nacionalista Party, was elected president. During the election time, he had promised a number of populist measures which included economic reforms, particularly the land reforms. His first term of office witnessed the affluence of the big landlords mainly due to the Rice Revolution, and the impoverishment of small and marginal farmers. As a result, the Huk movement received a much-needed shot in the arm. But President Marcos cleverly manoeuvred to much-needed shot in the arm. But President Marcos cleverly manoeuvred to get himself elected for a second term, thanks to the services rendered by corrupt officials. He exploited the volatile political situation in his country (caused by repeated outbreaks of riots by students, communists and farmers) to advance his personal interests.

Foreign Policy

In foreign policy, the Philippines developed a "Special Relationship" with the United States on account of her continuing economic dependence on the latter. With the passage of the Philippines Trade Act by the US Congress which provided for free trade between the two, the US was in a favourable position. The US took full advantage of Philippine tutelage, and gained the right to exploit her natural resources. However, this advantage was set at naught by the Laurel-Langley reforms.

In respect of the defence of the Philippines, the United States signed a military agreement in 1957, which provided leases for American military bases for 99 years. As a result, the Americans were able to expand their air-force base at Clark Field and the Naval base at the Subic Bay. Although this military agreement guaranteed the much-needed security for the country, the common Filipinos became irritated by the awesome military presence of the United States army on their native soil. Ferdinand Marcos got the treaty revised by the United States (leases terminated in 1991) in order to please his compatriots.

Marcos' Dictatorship

Marcos ruled the Philippines like a dictator from 1965 to 1986. He was re-elected President for the second term in 1969. In 1970, the students held public demonstrations to protest against the election for constituting the Constitutional Convention. The continuing unrest in the country forced President Marcos to declare martial law. A constitutional amendment passed in October 1972 enabled the President to enjoy the powers of the prime minister also. Those who opposed his dictatorship were imprisoned. It was about this time (1973) that Benigno Aquino (a Senator) returned from the United States with his family. He was to be nominated as Vice-President, but Marcos sent him to prison. Marcos remained in power through corrupt means even though the Constitution allowed him to remain in office for only two terms. The martial law was lifted in 1981 coinciding with the arrival of the Pope. A new amendment to the Constitution, passed in 1981, permitted him to assume the combined powers of the President as well as those of the prime minister. The tenure of the Presidency was extended – from four years to six years. In the 1981 elections, Marcos was re-elected, but amidst vehement opposition. The country was in chaos, and the popular Opposition leader, Benigno Aquino (popularly known to his compatriots as Nimoy) was shot dead in August 1983 soon after he landed from the plane. Everybody in the Philippines knew who was responsible for Aquino's assassination.

Aquino's assassination eventually brought down the curtain on Marcos' dictatorship in 1985. Capitalizing on the disarray in the opposition, Marcos cleverly announced a "snap" presidential election in late 1985. Rising to the occasion, Corazon Aquino, the widow of Benigno, brought about the unity of anti-Marcos forces to fight the election. Marcos was too clever. He got himself re-elected for the next term by rigging the elections. The streets of Manila were barricaded and the army moved in to quell the revolt. Corazon led the non-violent protest, and a section of the army led by General Fidel Ramos and the defence minister joined the revolt against Marcos. The Catholic Church led by Bishop Jaimie Cardinal Sin appealed to the people to invoke people's power to protect these two military officials from danger. President Marcos realized that his chips were down, and he quit the country in a helicopter graciously provided by the US. The people elected Corazon Aquino as the new president of the Philippines.

Corazon Aquino

During the next few years Corazon Aquino had to face many problems such as the insurgency of Muslim separatists and economic-slowdown. Marcos and his profligate wife, Imelda, had impoverished the country by misrule, nepotism and corruption. The Communists posed a serious threat to the integrity of the country. A new constitution was ratified by the people through a referendum in 1987. Many attempts were made to topple Aquino's government, but all of them failed. The 1987 Constitution provided for a bicameral legislature. Corazon was given the 1998 Ramon Magsaysay Award for international understanding.

In May 1992 the country held its first free presidential elections and General Fidel Ramos became the president. The United States Government vacated the Subic Bay Naval base at the end of the year. Vice-President Joseph Estrada succeeded Fidel Ramos on May 29, 1998 as the 13th president of the Philippines.

Joseph Estrada

He was a college drop out and a big star of the movies. This swashbuckling hero of the Filipino movies plunged into politics of the country and eventually became the Vice-President. He may have had a smooth sailing in his acting career, but in the real world he was facing a number of problems. The Muslim rebels of Mindanao are giving the President sleepless nights. Their organisation known as the MILF (Mindanao Islamic Liberation Force) has been carrying on the secessionist movement for the last 22 years, and it is virtually ruling the island. This movement is receiving funds from various fundamentalist organisations in the world (not excluding the exiled Arab multi-millionaire, Osama bin-Laden). His predecessor, General Fidel Ramos, deemed it necessary and wise to hold talks with this group in 1997, and subsequently signed a cease-fire agreement. This cease-fire did not last long when Estrada's government continued its crack-down policy. On the eve of further peace talks, the actor-turned-President said : "If they want war, we will give them war." With the resumption of fighting between the government and the secessionists, 80,000 civilians fled their homes in Mindanao.

In a similar mood, the new President has stopped peace talks with the Communist New People's Army (CNPA) and the National Democratic Front. The NPA has been active in the countryside since the late 1960s, and since Marcos' time has controlled large areas. Joseph Estrada said that his government would focus its attention on eradicating poverty and improving agriculture.

Within a short period of time, the Filipinos realised that their so called swash-buckling hero has turned into a villain, by dragging the country into a cesspool of "corruption and cronyism". He betrayed the trust reposed in him by the people as proved by scandals concerning him and his cronies. Scandal concerning the stock exchange destroyed investors' confidence. Joseph Estrada started ruling the country by decree, and decisions were taken by the midnight cabinet amidst wining and dining in his palace. Estrada's close friends were involved in a number of scandals, and there were a series of silent protests by the public in the beginning. To assuage the feelings of the public Joseph Estrada made some attempts to carry out reforms including appointment of Anticorruption Commission. With many scandals exposed, his popularity plunged from 65 per cent in June 1999 to 20 per cent in May 2000. By the year end the opposition parties decided to impeach the president for his corruption and other misdemeanors. In January 2001, rallies were held in support of and against the president. After a mass uprising, Estrada knew that his days were numbered and therefore retired. His Vice-President, Gloria Macapagal Arroyo was swept to power amidst great rejoicings on January 20th. The Filipino army remained neutral.

Gloria Macapagal Arroyo

During her three years stint in presidential office, Gloria Macapagal Arroyo has not been able to steer the country from economic collapse (the fall out of Asian financial crisis in 1997). Economic analysts point out that "Chronic unemployment, yawning deficit and uncollected taxes are sinking Philippines". It is said that nearly 40 per cent of the people in the country live on $ 2 a day when most of the well-to-do avoid paying taxes or resorts to cheating. Corruption is rampant and cronyism has become the order of the day. It is ironic to see that as a 'trained economist' and a veteran politician (daughter of former president), Gloria Macapagal Arroyo is unable to control the situation and frequently seeks the support of the US government. Her carrying forward the reform process has not been encouraging.

The territorial sovereignty and integrity was threatened by the Moro Islamic Liberation Front which has established its base in the South. Its aim is to gain independence. Then there is the danger posed by the extreme Islamic militant group called Abu Sayyaf.

Philippines joined the US led coalition forces in the Iraqi war recently by sending its troops. However, the troops had to be ordered to return to the country when the Iraqi resistance forces took a Filipino truck driver as hostage. The Iraqi kidnappers released the truck driver, Angelo dela cruz, after seeing that Filipino troops were leaving their country.

22

MALAYSIA (SUVARNADVIPA)

Today's Malaysia in South-East Asia occupies an area of 330,434 sq kms with a population of about 21.5 million. A majority of Malaysians speak Bahasa-Malaysia. Kuala Lumpur is the capital of the country. Malaysia's ethnic population includes Malays, Chinese and Indians and they are spread all over her thirteen states. Malaysia produces the largest quantities of rubber and tin in the world today.

The ancestors of the people of Malaysia may have migrated from southern parts of China around 2500 BC. Today's ethnic element in South-East Asia in general and Malaysia in particular is composed of brown-skinned Malays. The proto-Malays, who came from China earlier, brought with them the Neolithic culture. The Bueteor-Malays who came to Malaysia in 300 BC introduced the bronze culture and spread a common language.

Hindu Kingdoms and Buddhist Elements

In the early centuries of the Christian era, India and China were having brisk maritime trade with the result that a few Hindu colonies took birth in Malaysia. The Sanskrit inscriptions of the fourth century AD suggest the existence of the Hindu colonies of Kankasuka and Tamralinga, among several others, which played an important role in the spread of Hindu culture. In the kingdom of Ch'ih-tu, the king became a Saivite and his court was graced by several hundred Brahmins. The small kingdom of Tun Sun came to be known for its trade and was inhabited by a large Brahmin population according to the Chinese sources. Another Hindu kingdom known as Pan Pan sent its ambassadors to China in AD 527, 530 and 536 and one of them carried the supposed tooth of the Buddha as a gift to the Chinese emperor. Another important settlement was Nakhon Sri Dhammarat which was situated on the bay of Bandon which turned into a Buddhist colony. This colony contained a stupa surrounded by a number of temples. Similar was the case of another settlement, Caiya, originally Brahminical but turning into a Buddhist one. It must not be forgotten that Sri Vijaya and Sailendra empires included large parts of Malay peninsula. Sailendras called Malaysia Kalinga thereby suggesting that people there might have been the emigrant of the kingdom of Kalinga (India). The Hindu and Buddhist influence on the Malay population continued till the advent of Islam.

The Spread of Islam

The spread of Islam was the work of the newly converted Muslims who came to trade in this region during the late 13th century. During 11th and 12th centuries Islam spread to South-East Asia in a peaceful manner unlike India. Malacca became a great centre for the propagation of Islam and surprisingly it permitted the new converts to follow the age-old Hindu customs and traditions and also the *Keramat* (an object inherited by spirits) Parameshwara, the exiled prince of Palembang of the 15th century, decided to make Malacca a great port city. He established a close relationship with the Muslim kingdoms of Sumatra. His son Magadh, who came to power, got himself converted to Islam in order to oblige his Muslim father-in-law, the Sultan of Pasai. Subsequently, mass conversions of merchants, soldiers, and slaves took place in the neighbouring islands emulating the example of Malacca. It must be remembered that Islamisation had nothing to do with day-to-day business of the merchants, and Malacca soon became a great centre of learning. The kingdom of Malacca turned into an empire with a number of tin-producing states (Klang, Selangor and Bemam) paying annual tributes. Tun Perak brought further glory by conquering Pahang, Johore, Benkalin, the Carimon islands, Bintang and several small Sumatran kingdoms in the second half of the fifteenth century.

The Portuguese Rule

After Tun Perak's death, a rival dynasty led by Tun Mutahir came to power in Malacca. His whimsical rule turned very arbitrary and corrupt with the result that he was executed in 1510, and the next year witnessed the capture of Malacca by the Portuguese. The Portuguese ruled Malacca for nearly 130 years (1511-1641). They lost control of Malacca to the Dutch due to the hostilities of the Muslim kingdoms of Johore, Achin and Java.

A century and a half of Dutch rule over the East Indies came to an end due to revolutionary and Napoleonic wars in Europe. The British took over the Dutch interests in the Indian Archipelago at the specific request of King William V. Even after the defeat of Napoleon, the Dutch interests continued due to the loss of Ceylon (1815) and subsequently the Malay peninsula (1824). A European agreement of 1824 carved out spheres of influence, leaving the Malay peninsula to the British, and Indonesian islands to the Dutch.

British Acquisition in the Straits

The acquisition of the straits of Malacca and nearby islands was under consideration in the face of Franco-Dutch rivalry. And in 1786, a British officer, Francis Light, negotiated with the Sultan of Kedah for the acquisition of the

Penang island for the British. Subsequently, a coastal strip on the mainland of Malaya called Province Wellesley was acquired. By a peculiar logic of circumstances, Thomas Stamford Raffles, the British Governor of Java (which was restored to the Dutch in 1818) prepared the necessary plan for the acquisition of the island of Singapore by outright purchase. The British had no use of Malacca, since it had lost its fort and harbour to the others. Raffles looked upon Singapore as a suitable alternative and cajoled the local chief and his overload Rian Sultan to lease the present site of Singapore in 1823-24

By 1824-26, the British had acquired Penang, Wellesley, Malacca (received from the Dutch after ceding Benkulen) and Singapore, with the last serving as the main trading and administrative headquarters in the Straits. Britain's trade with China flourished and Singapore served as a free port. Singapore attracted many big businessmen and traders from China, the United States, Britain and the nearby countries of South-East Asia. The European powers using the straits of Malacca suppressed piracy in this region. In the course of time, the British acquired Labuan island at the instance of the British adventurer, James Brooke, who enabled them to suppress piracy. The Sultan of Brunei felt very happy and subsequently the British acquired North Borneo by helping Dent Brother's enterprise.

Forward Policy of the British

The British Government was not ready to accept full responsibility for the administration of the states acquired in the Malay peninsula till 1871 because of the continuous rivalry of the European powers on the one hand and the troubles created by the influx of Chinese immigrants into this region on the other. However, the situation changed after 1871, when the British got wind of the rumour that France or Germany might occupy Malaya.

Frequent British Intervention

Political turmoil in Malaya compelled the British merchants to appeal to their government to intervene and restore order. The outgoing ministry of Gladstone appointed Sir Andrew Clarke to deal with the volatile political situation in Malaya. With his arrival, British intervention in the internal matters of the different sultanates of Malaya became the order of the day. Timely British intervention resulted in the ending of the disputed succession in Perak and also a likely civil war in Selangor. The British established what is known as the Resident systems in Perak, Selangor, Negri Sembilan and Pahang. Johore was turned into a British protectorate in 1895.

Birth of Malay Federation

The British created the Federation of the Malay States by uniting four states, namely, Perak, Selangor and Negri Sembilan which was composed of nine

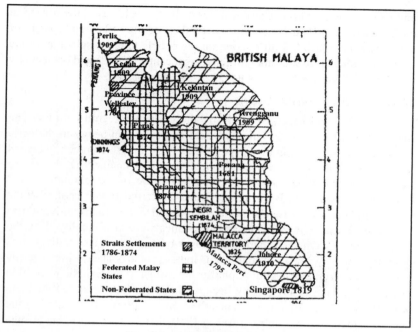

Development of British Malaya
1786-1910

Murangkaban states including Surjei Ujoing under the control of a British Resident-General whose headquarters were situated in Kuala Lumpur. The British Residents working in these states received necessary instructions from the Resident-General, Swettenbam, from time to time. The rulers and the Residents of these states gathered periodically to discuss and solve individual and mutual problems facing their states. The British thus carried on this type of indirect rule through Resident system without disturbing the local institutions in Malaya. In 1909, Thailand ceded four states to the British, namely, Kedah, Perlis, Kelantan and Trengannu as a part of their bargain by signing the Anglo-Thai convention. On the whole, the Malay peninsula came under British control, some administered as crown colonies, some others as protected states, and the rest as unfederated states with British Residents.

Impact of British Rule

Decades of British rule over Malaya eventually led to the rise of political consciousness among the people. The reasons for this may be the unity of the country through administration and other features of modernization, such as introduction of Postal and Telegraph systems, the Railroad system, application of scientific methods of cultivation of rubber, sugar cane, coconuts and coffee, and intense mining of tin. These features of British rule paved the way for a class system. The British also introduced their courts of law and system of administration which left little scope for the people to enjoy self-rule. In the meantime, Singapore was emerging as a great centre of trade and business by the middle of the twentieth century.

Malaya – A Multi-racial Society

Malaya had a multi-racial society by the early nineteenth century. The immigration of Chinese in large numbers to this region began in the early nineteenth century, and in the course of time the Chinese community owned tin mines in all the states. It was in the late nineteenth century that the British recruited Indian coolies who came to work in the rubber plantations and factories owned by the British. The British preferred Indian coolies to the local population, because the Malays preferred fishing and cultivation to "regimented employment". The Indian coolies were also employed by the Chinese mine-owning community and sugar-barons. Thus, the ethnic groups of Malaya, namely, Malays, Chinese, and Indians could not be integrated easily because they remained educationally backward. The British were also responsible for this heterogeneity, because they felt it was better to keep them segregated for their own good. Thus their policy ultimately resulted in the general neglect of the country. It was in 1920, that the British tried to change this policy through the decentralization of administration.

Multi-racial Society Undergoing Strain

During the periods, 1921-22 and 1930-32, the Chinese and Indian workers in Malaya faced unemployment. The unemployment figure rose to 60,000 by 1921-22 and two-thirds of those affected were Indians. Similarly, during the time of worldwide economic depression (1929-32), rubber prices fell sharply throwing many people out of work. Those who remained employed, had to suffer a decrease in wages (up to 50 per cent). As a result of this economic recession, there were serious strains in Malay's multi-racial society. The Malays became apprehensive because they constituted only 44 per cent of the population of the country by 1931 as compared to 51 per cent in 1911. This imbalance in the proportion of the population led to their hatred of Indian coolies (mainly Tamilians from South India). Furthermore, the Malays became aware of their increasing dependence on Chinese traders and moneylenders.

Increasing Communist Influence

By 1920, the Chinese settlers in Malaya became politically conscious, more so with the visit of Sun Yat Sen on exile in Penang, and the establishment of the Kuomintang party. The Communist wing of this party led by Michael Borodin wielded considerable influence over their comrades in Malaya. Malaya in the 1930s witnessed strikes and boycotts in plantations, mines, transport system, and naval construction works by members of the Communist Party.

Japanese Occupation

Malay-Chinese began to extend support to the Communist Party when Japan conquered parts of China prior to and during the Second World War. Japan conquered Malaya after the surrender of British Governor-General, Percival in February 1942 at Singapore. The Japanese who occupied Malaya discovered that the Malay-Chinese were a tough nut to crack. Many of these Malay-Chinese had suffered immensely during the period of economic depression. The unemployed squatted on government land, thereafter went underground, and subsequently joined the communist-guerilla groups. In the meantime, the Malayan people's anti-Japanese force launched its resistance movement directed against the Japanese occupation of their country. The Japanese army set up a military regime after disturbing the British political arrangements. Malaya was divided into eight provinces, and subsequently the island of Sumatra was also added. The four British protectorates in Malaya taken from Thailand by the British earlier (1909) were returned to Thailand. At the end of the war, the Japanese became friendly and gave hints to the Malays, that they could have a new Malaya with some additional territories. However, their promises could not materialise because they were increasingly coming under the pressure of the Malay-Chinese communist guerilla groups who were helping the British with arms supplies in the jungle hideouts. Thus the British could increase the pressure on the Japanese by a proper understanding with the communist guerilla groups. The communist guerilla groups began to destroy Japanese establishments till they surrendered in 1945.

The Birth of United Malay National Organisation (UMNO) – 1946

After the Japanese surrender, the British forces in Malaya left for Singapore after thanking the Malay communists for their cooperation during the war. However, the British government did not take any decisive step on the future of Malaya. In 1945, a British officer, Herald McMicheal , proposed to his government to convert all the Malay states into a town colony with common citizenship to all the locals. This was to be after the surrender of sovereignty by the concerned Sultans. This proposal at once provoked Malays to protest loudly. A district officer in Johore by the name Omn bin Zafar founded a pan-Malayan party which was renamed United Malay National Organisation (UMNO) in 1946 with the objective of spreading political consciousness among the Malays which would ultimately lead to Malaya's independence. It was decided that all the residents would have equal citizenship rights in a new federal set-up after excluding Singapore.

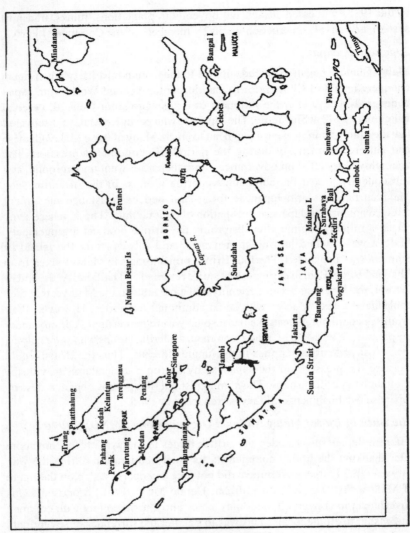

Indonesia and Malaysia

Malayan Insurgency (1948)

In the meantime, the Malayan Communist Party tried to deliver a last blow to British rule by destroying the European rubber plantations and tin mines. Their insurgency succeeded to some extent but the common people at large did not like violent activities. The British, unlike their counterparts, the French and the Americans in Indo-China, were quite successful in crushing the Malayan insurgency by 1951. The situation was defused at the political level by encouraging peaceful Chinese citizens to form their own political association called "The Malayan-Chinese Association" (MCA). The MCA eventually joined the UMNO for the common purpose of gaining Mardeka (independence for Malaya). The British Government took drastic steps to cut political activity by penalising 10,000 Chinese with deportation because they were not willing to co-operate with them in the counter-insurgency operation. At the same time, those who assisted the British were given benefits through the government's socio-economic programmes. They declared an emergency in Malaya to adequately deal with the insurgency of the communist guerillas. Their operations came to an end in 1960.

Malaya's Independence

The British sent Sir Gerald Templer to prepare a blueprint for the independence of the Malayans. General election was announced to the Federal Assembly in 1954. In the 1955 elections, the MCI Party (Malay, Chinese and Indians) won an absolute majority (52 out of 53 seats) in the 92- seat Federal Assembly and the majority leader, Tungku Abdul Rehman, started negotiations with the British for the total independence of Malaya. The British Government transferred its power and Malaya became independent and sovereign in 1957.

SINGAPORE

In the case of Singapore, the granting of independence was delayed due to communist activities of the Malayan communists who had captured the trade unions and attacked the school system in Singapore. This course of events compelled the left wing leader of the Labour Front, David Marshall, to submit his resignation as the leader of the interim government. Thereupon, his successor, Lim Yew Hock, a respected leader of the Chinese community, started negotiations with the British Government for the purpose of establishing an internal self-government for Singapore. It was to be led by a prime minister and cabinet. A security council composed of British and Malay-federal representatives was to be in charge of foreign affairs and defence.

Malaysia and Singapore

Elections to the Singapore Assembly took place in 1959, wherein the People's Action Party (PAP) led by a brilliant barrister, Lee Kuan Yew, won an absolute majority. This party secured independence of Singapore from the British in 1963. Sarawak and Sabah joined Singapore and they constituted a federation called Malaysia. It was in August 1965 that Singapore got herself separated from Malaysia to become an independent island state. This event took place partly due to the personal rivalry of the two great leaders, Tungku Abdul Rehman of Malaysia and Singapore's Prime Minister Lee Kuan Yew.

These statesmen differed on national ideology and identity. Malaysia emerged out of anti-colonial sentiments, struggle for self-rule, and finally national movement. This took place over a period of time. In Singapore, its Prime Minister, Lee Kuan Yew, took up nation-building activity with the infusion of Western system of education, Western capital, and Western type of governance. The learning of English was made compulsory in a Chinese-dominated city-state. Lee Kuan Yew turned Singapore into a model city-state with trade and business as the key component. What is Singapore today is mainly the work of this great statesman.

This chief architect of Singapore city-state relinquished his office in 1990. He was succeeded by Goh Chok-Tong. Goh continued the work of his predecessor – making Singapore an ideal city for promoting world trade, business and travel destination. Singapore maintained its close-links with the West and the East. Toady it is establishing commercial links with the emerging markets like China and India. The Asian Financial Crisis of 1997 affected Singapore.

Recently Goh was succeeded by Lee Hsien Loong, the eldest son of Lee Kuan Yew. He has included his father (Minister-Mentor) and his predecessor, Goh in the Cabinet. This third prime minister wants to make his city-state "a place that is hospitable to creative thinking".

Dr Mahathir Bin Mohamad

This favourite son of Kedah was born and brought up in the dusty capital of Alor Setar and eventually proved to be the miracle man of Malaysia. He is today described as the architect of Malaysia's booming prosperity. When he assumed the prime ministership way back in 1981, his countrymen were surviving on "what the rubber plantation offered them". This rickety economy of the country has been converted today into an engine of growth, thanks to the waving of the magic wand by Dr Mahathir. Leading the United Malay National Organisation (UMNO) with the coalition partners, he has been swept to power five times since 1981.

This long reigning prime minister has done his utmost to ensure ethnic peace "by bringing together the ethnic-Malay majority and the more affluent ethnic Chinese and Indian minorities." He was ruthless in suppressing all those elements which stood in the way of his socio-economic reforms. For example, he used the controversial Internal Security Act to suppress the Al-Arqam, an Islamic fundamentalist sect which tried to disturb the communal harmony of the country.

His main grievance against the opposition parties had been that they denied his government the required two-thirds majority in Parliament – the accusing finger pointing towards the Chinese living in his country. The adage of Lord Acton : "Power corrupts and absolute power corrupts absolutely" fits the description of Mahathir in recent times. During the late 1990s Malaysia was battered by financial crisis as a direct result of the recession. The poor farmers in the countryside are groaning, and the lower middle class has become concerned about the income disparity. To combat inflation Mahathir invited nearly 1.5 million unskilled foreign workers – a potential threat to maintaining ethnic peace. Malaysia's economic success depended heavily on importing foreign technology – notably the Japanese.

Role of the Opposition

In the midst of the recent economic crisis, the opposition parties became very critical, and Mahathir lashed out against them. He dismissed the Deputy Prime Minister, Anwar Ibrahim on September 2, 1998 on charges of sodomy. Anwar leading a crowd of 30,000 marched through the capital, accused Mahathir of corruption and asked him to step down. Mahathir sent him to prison on charges of sodomy and corruption which he denied. Anwar's wife, Wan Azizah Wan Ismail, carried on her husband's campaign against Mahathir by accusing him of "enriching and protecting business cronies" and spending more than $50 million on building his new palace. Leading the Justice Party (while her husband is languishing in jail) she joined the other opposition parties in demanding the "abolition of colonial era security laws and Special Branch Secret Police." Azizah and other opposition leaders were also demanding the reform of the judiciary, the electoral system, and of cronyism. On the eve of the 10th general elections (held on November 29, 1999), the opposition parties and Mahathir (leading 14 coalition partners) traded charges. Mahathir has described his ex-Deputy Anwar as a CIA agent, for he is colluding with foreign powers to dethrone him.

Election Results (November 1999)

The whole world watched the polling with great interest since the opposition parties led by the aggrieved Azizah took up the cudgels to fight the almighty Prime Minister, Mahathir. The election results were announced on November 30, and Mahathir won with two-thirds majority (148) in the 193-member Parliament. Azizah retained her seat. The opposition Islamist Party gained some ground in the Malay heartland. The Prime Minister defeated the opposition candidate, Subky Latif, with 65 per cent votes cast in his favour.

Mahathir led his coalition party to victory in the general elections held in March 2004 by obtaining 198 seats out of 219 in the Parliament. The members of the ruling coalition elected Abdullah Ahmed Badawi (formerly working as Deputy PM) as the new prime minister. The Parte Islam Se Malaysin (PAS) which stood for converting Malaysia into an Islamic state received its worst drubbing in the elections. It must be remembered that the Muslims constitute 55 per cent of the population followed by the ethnic Chinese (30 per cent).

Indians (8 per cent) and others. The latter two fully supported the BNP (Barisan National Party) in the recent general elections with the hope that its government would follow a moderate or secular policy. Recently, the new PM declared that he would adopt 'Islamic governance' instead of 'Islamic Laws'. This policy is in tune with the majority Malay-Muslim state as in the past.

In the Western world Mahathir has remained as the most controversial figure despite his most remarkable achievements. After his long reign (1981-2003), he welded the multi-racial society into a powerful nation. He made Malaysia a secular state despite a Muslim majority, and strove hard to maintain racial harmony. In recent years he castigated the West for its obsession with the 'war on terrorism'. While vacating his office he advocated "moderate and progressive Islam". He thinks that the West's war on terrorism is in fact a war on Islam. He blamed the US and Israel for practising "state terrorism" and hoped to see in future, Muslims using their clout (probably using oil as weapon) to overcome their "weakness in military terms".

Economy

In the proximity of Kuala Lumpur (present Malaysian capital), a new capital, Patrajaya, was built. Mahathir hopes to make Malaysia a fully industrialised nation by 2020. In the seventh five year plan, both public and private sectors have decided to spend $ 180 billion. The nation's privatisation programme is in full swing. The new government hopes to make Malaysia's manufactures world-competitive. Malaysia today specialises in producing technology products such as the Silicon-chips, disc-drives and air-conditioners. It has become a top trading nation. Rubber, palm-oil, pepper and technology products are exported. During the period 1998-97, Malaysia registered a high GDP growth, ie 9 per cent and enjoyed a per capital income of about $ 4000 by 2003. Services contribute around 43 per cent of the GDP. When Malaysia was hit by a recession in 1997, it lost nearly 5 per cent of its present growth. The affluent ethnic Chinese and Indians have contributed their mite to the economic growth. Malaysia is playing a significant role in ASEAN, APEC and the OIC.

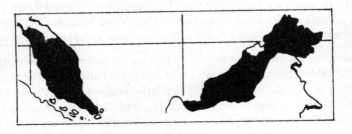

Malaysia

23

INDONESIA

HISTORICAL BACKGROUND

As mentioned earlier, South-East Asia includes countries of the mainland (Burma, Thailand, Kampuchea, Laos and Vietnam) and also the "insular" countries, namely, Malaysia, Singapore, Indonesia and the Philippines. Among the insular countries, the most prominent is Indonesia. Today, she has 13,000 islands of which about 6,000 are inhabited. Of these inhabited islands, the most prominent are Java, Sumatra, Kalimantan, Sulavesi and Irian Jaya. Since Indonesia is situated along the maritime trade route between China and India, her early kingdoms played a prominent role as an intermediary. They also enjoyed benefits of a brisk maritime trade and commerce. Secondly, the archipelago came under the influence of Hinduism and Buddhism until these religions were overshadowed after the advent of Islam. In the early centuries of the Christian era, Chinese scholars and pilgrims halted their journey for a couple of months, particularly in Sumatra or Borneo, and learnt Sanskrit and Pali before reaching India. It was in Indonesia that great Hindu kingdoms flourished, thanks to the services of enterprising Indian merchants.

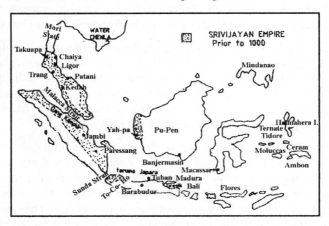

Java and Srivijaya up to AD 1025

Sri Vijaya Kingdom in Sumatra

It was during the last decades of the fourth century AD that the island of Sumatra witnessed the rise of a small Hindu kingdom called Sri Vijaya. During the next three centuries, it emerged as a powerful kingdom extending its control over a major part of Malaysia. Furthermore, it launched a number of maritime expeditions for the conquest of the neighbouring island of Java. The greatness of the Sri Vijaya kingdom was even recognised by China which established diplomatic and commercial relations.

The famous Chinese pilgrim named Itsing, stayed in Palembang for nearly six months to study the Buddhist text. Palembang turned into a great city and was known for its great Buddhist (Mahayana Buddhism with a large number of monasteries and monks) centre. The kings of Sri Vijaya maintained commercial and diplomatic relations with both India and China. The famous Chinese pilgrim sailed in one of the king's ships to Tamralipti. Another Chinese pilgrim by name Wu-Ling also set sail from the kingdom of Sri Vijaya to Nagapatam in India in a ship belonging to the king of Sri Vijaya.

The Sailendra Dynasty

The kingdom of Sri Vijaya came to be ruled by the Sailendra dynasty from the eighth century. The Sailendra kings took a leading role in converting the Sri Vijaya kingdom into what is called the Sailendra empire. The Sailendra empire took its birth in Central Java, and the early kings had great leanings towards Mahayana Buddhism. Many historians believe that the Sailendra empire was an extension of the Sri Vijaya kingdom. However, there are other scholars who believe that the Sailendra empire was founded by an exiled Funanese led by Bhanu who declared himself a Sailendra. There is yet another theory, which indicates that the Sailendra kings hailed originally from Kalinga (India).

After a century of its birth, the Sailendras lost Khambuja and Java but inherited all that was a part of the kingdom of Sri Vijaya. This was because their vassal, Prince Patapan of the Sanjaya dynasty, usurped the throne of Sailendra in Java after the death of the last king, Samaratunga. However, Samaratunga's son, Balaputra, ascended the Sri Vijaya throne without much difficulty because his mother was a princess of Sri Vijaya before her marriage.

It was from the island of Sumatra, that the Sailendras built a great empire. Arab writers called this empire Zabag or Zabaj, often making frequent references to the enormous power and wealth possessed by this empire. As regards the conquest of Sailendra kings, it must be noted that they invaded Tongking and Champa and also defeated the Chenla kingdom. Their idea was to bring the mainland of South-East Asia under their control. However, they lost Chenla to Jayavarm II, the great founder of the Khambuja kingdom in the early part of the ninth century. The Sailendras subsequently conquered Chenla again, and also ruled some parts of Angkor and Champa.

In contrast to their aggressive attitude towards their mainland neighbours, the Sailendra emperors maintained friendly relations with India (except the Chola empire) and China. For example, King Balaputra built a monastery at Nalanda in India and got five villages from Devapala, the Pala Emperor (Indian ruler), for its maintenance. The Chinese records mentioned that the Sailendras established diplomatic relations with China in the tenth century. These relations were renewed in the twelfth century with the exchanging of embassies in AD 1156 and 1178.

Cholas and Sailendra Empire

The Sailendra emperors could not maintain friendly relations with the Chola emperors with the result that there were frequent conflicts. It is likely that Chola Emperor Rajendra Chola became extremely jealous of the growing power and wealth of the Sailendra empire. He launched maritime expeditions against the Sailendras in AD 1017. It was not until a few years later, that these maritime expeditions succeeded in their mission. Again Virarajendra Chola also dispatched maritime expeditions for chastising the Sailendra empire and became successful in the conquest of Kadaram after seven years. The Sailendra emperor got it back after agreeing to pay annual tributes to the Chola emperor. After a couple of years, Kulottunga Chola fought against the Sailendra empire and destroyed Kadaram. Unfortunately, the Chola emperors found it difficult to maintain their control over the Sailendra empire for a considerable time and therefore, concluded peace treaties. There existed cordial relations between these two naval powers during the time of Rajaraja. He permitted the Sailendra Emperor to construct a Buddhist vihara in Nagapattinam.

The Sailendra empire declined from the twelfth century, and the Chola emperors may be held partly responsible. The empire shrunk into a small kingdom by the fourteenth century. It left a rich cultural legacy for posterity. The Sailendras upheld Mahayana Buddhism and spread it all over their empire. Hinduism also spread during the time of King Vishnu who started constructing Buddhist monuments of Chandi Kalasam, Chandi Mendut and the world famous Borobudur complex in Java (AD 778). The Borobudur complex has nine terraces carved out of a single hill representing nine lives of Gautama the Buddha before he attained Nirvana. The work was completed by Vishnu's grandson Samaratunga in AD 824. Indo-Javanese art and architecture witnessed its glorious days. Sailendra rulers introduced Indian alphabets. Mahayana Buddhism undoubtedly enjoyed great patronage.

Al-Beruni, a Muslim historian of the 11th century, described the Sailendra empire as a Gold country, and name given to the Malay Archipelago by the Indians in those days was Suvarnadvipa (Golden Island). It must be remembered that the empire became wealthy and powerful not only due to its maritime trade but also for extensive cultivation of foodgrains.

JAVA (MATARAM)

Four inscriptions, near Batavia, testify that by the fifth century AD, the island of Java had witnessed the spread of Hindu religion and culture. Among the many ancient Hindu colonies, which were founded in the Malay Archipelago, Java happens to be a prominent one. A legend says, that one of the colonies in Java was founded by Aji Saka, who was closely related to some of the heroes of the *Mahabharata*. Fa-hian, a famous Chinese chronicler mentions that Java was known as Yava. And he visited it in AD 414-415.

The Mataram kingdom was one of the small kingdoms in Central Java, which was founded by Sanjaya, a staunch worshipper of the Hindu god, Lord Shiva. He maintained cordial relations with the Sailendra empire. However, the last Sailendra King, Samaratunga, gave his daughter in marriage to Prince Pikatan, a scion of the Sanjaya dynasty, but this matrimonial relationship did not prevent a war between the two kingdoms. The Sailendras finally lost the kingdom of Central Java and shifted their activities to Sumatra. It was a century later that the Sanjaya line of kings shifted their capital from Central to East Java (probable reason might be the outbreak of a pestilence or an earthquake). Their new kingdom in Eastern Java was named Mataram.

While the Sailendra emperors, mainly patronised Mahayana Buddhism, the Mataram kings of Eastern Java championed the cause of Brahminical-Hinduism. To match the feat of the Sailendras in the construction of Buddhist viharas, the Mataram kings built three great temples or *Chandis* one each for Lord Brahma, Lord Vishnu and Lord Shiva in their capital city, Prambanam. Around these main temples, they also built small temples, the walls of which depict the events of the *Ramayana*. Buddhism also continued to flourish, King Sindhok (AD 929-948) patronised scholars who produced two great works, the Javanese-*Ramayana* and the Tantrik Buddhist work, *Sang Hyang kamahayanikan*.

By the late eighth century, the Mataram kings established full control over the whole of Central and Eastern Java. During the next century, the islands of Bali and Western Borneo also came under their fold. The Mataram kings maintained cordial relations with Moluccas for the purpose of trade. The Mataram kingdom enjoyed a flourishing trade in spices, which was in demand both in China and the Arab world. Unfortunately, the port facilities in the Straits of Moluccas were under the control of the Sailendra empire. Therefore, for using the port facilities taxes had to be paid, which sometimes created friction. Mataram challenged the supremacy of the Sailendras which resulted in war. Eventually, Mataram was defeated and its capital destroyed in 1006 AD.

However, with the decline of the Sailendra empire, mainly at the hands of the Chola emperor, the kingdom of Mataram emerged into the political scene once again. This was mainly due to the dynamic leadership of Prince Airlangga who married the Mataram princess. Airlangga exhibited great statesman-like qualities in foreign relations by following a policy of "forget and forgive". He established a cordial relationship with the declining Hindu kingdoms. He ended the religious rivalry between Hinduism and Buddhism and established communal harmony in his kingdom. He tried to make his kingdom truly secular by reducing the importance of Brahmin priests and Buddhist monks. He confiscated their land-estates and property. It was during his time that the Mataram kingdom witnessed political and social cohesion.

Since he did not leave behind a natural heir, he made arrangements for the division of his kingdom into two parts (Kediri and Jungala), each to be ruled by his foster sons. Unfortunately, this act of his proved most unwise. Both these kingdoms became rivals and consequently became weak. However, in the course of time the Kediri kingdom began to flourish from the 11th to the 13th century. The Chinese records mentioned that the Kediri kingdom became the greatest maritime power, even surpassing the Sailendra empire. It extended its control over many islands including Bali, Borneo and South-Celebes. Its ports attracted spice trade especially from the Moluccas. Many Gujarati merchants from India were eager to trade with the kingdom of Kediri instead of Sailendras for the simple reason that the former levied less taxes on imports and exports.

Singhasari Kingdom in East Java

The Kediri kingdom witnessed the overthrow of its last king, Kritajaya in 1222 by an adventurer named Ken Angrok, who shifted the capital to Singhasari. The dynasty of Sangrok was called Singhasari. With his new dynasty we see the decline of Hindu culture and civilisation in Java and the succession of Javanese culture. The greatest among Singhasari kings was Kritanagara. During his time, he not only eliminated all his rivals, including the Sailendra kingdom, but maintained his supremacy all over insular South-East Asia. In international trade, his kingdom dictated terms to the other partners to conform since it enjoyed mastery over the two important straits, namely, the Malacca and the Sunda.

The Mongol Menace

As for meeting the challenge of the Mongol menace, Kritanagara eagerly looked forward to cooperation between his kingdom and the Champa. The Mongol Emperor, Kublai Khan, took serious notice of this threat and ordered Kritanagara to see him in Peking. Kritanagara sent the Chinese ambassadors back to Peking with their faces mutilated indicating that he was prepared for war. The Mongol Emperor organised a naval expedition (20,000 men in 1000 ships) to lay siege to Singhasari. In the meantime, the Mongol threat led to the killing to Kritanagara by a rival prince. Kritanagara's son-in-law Prince Vijaya managed to escape with his loyal troops to a village named Majapahit (meaning bitter fruit).

The Majapahit Dynasty and Empire

He finally agreed to become the vassal of the Mongol Emperor on condition that the killer of his father-in-law be removed from the Singhasari throne. The Mongol Emperor accordingly removed the usurper and made Prince Vijaya the King of the Singhasari kingdom. However, there was a change in the situation. A large fleet which King Vijaya had sent on an expedition to Malaya returned and this emboldened him to declare his independence. King Vijaya built an empire in the course of time and made Majapahit the seat of his capital. The new dynasty came to be known as Majapahit dynasty. Eventually a major part of South-East Asia came under the control of the Majapahit dynasty (fourteenth century)

The Golden Age of Javanese History

The credit for the emergence of the Majapahit empire as the great political commercial and maritime power in South-East Asia goes to the Prime Minister, Gajah Mada. He served as a premier during the period of King Vijaya and his successor Rajasanagara. In Javanese history, Gajah Mada is regarded as the greatest statesman of the Majapahit dynasty.

Unlike Kritanagara of the Singhasari kingdom, Gajah Mada tried to build an empire covering the territories of the whole of South-East Asia by "direct conquest". His greatest ambition was to build a vast empire as big as that of China. It was not an impossible task for this dynamic premier. At the time of his death, he had very nearly accomplished this task. With the exception of the western Sunda, which remained most indomitable and independent, the entire region of South-East Asia from the Philippines to the tip of Sumatra was conquered by Gajah Mada. Centuries after his death, the people of Java continued to cherish his heroic exploits. They continued to inspire the nationalists of Indonesia who eventually came under Dutch colonial masters. The Dutch claimed that they were the first to unite the people of Indonesian archipelago, which is very doubtful. It was in the fourteenth century, that the Majapahit empire established a monopoly over international trade thereby replacing the Sailendra empire. The ports of the Majapahit empire in north-eastern Java acquired a monopoly over the goods of Molucca which were badly required by China and the West.

Reforms of Gajah Mada

This great premier introduced several reforms to bring about political stability and administrative efficiency. He introduced a code of laws for the good governance of the empire. He got the land of his kingdom surveyed before levying the land tax. This was followed by the other parts of his empire. He worked hard to improve the conditions of the poor, and he was regarded by many as a great saviour. He extended patronage to Hindu and Javanese art, literature and religion.

Causes for the Decline of Majapahit Empire

The Majapahit empire declined rapidly by the early fifteenth century and almost came to an end with the conquest of Mohammedans. Emperor Rajasanagara divided his empire into two parts, after the death of Gajah Mada. This was done to avert a succession dispute between his nephew and his niece's husband. Unfortunately this act of his, proved to be the beginning of the end of his empire. The rise of a new kingdom in Malacca at that time posed a serious threat to the Majapahit empire because the latter lost control over the two straits.

The rapid rise of Malacca as a Mohammedan kingdom posed a serious threat. The Muslim traders from India and elsewhere had matrimonial connections with the families of small rulers in Java and Sumatra. The socio-religious aspects of life in this region were fast-changing with the spread of Islam. Thus, the golden age of Majapahit declined, and so also the influence of the Hindu religion and culture. In the meantime, the Emperor Yung China started demanding tributes from several vassal States including the Majapahit empire. By the early sixteenth century, the empire shrunk into a petty kingdom.

Islamisation of South-East Asia

The accounts of the Chinese annals, and also those of Marco Polo who passed through the straits of Malacca in 1293 refer to the beginnings of Islam in the Malay archipelago. The first country to be Islamised was the north-eastern part of Sumatra. Further Islamisation became easy because many Hindu rulers in the coastal districts of India were getting themselves converted, and they tried to spread Islam to the countries with which they traded. For example, Gujarati traders from India frequently went to South-East Asia, and brought about conversion of the local rulers of South-East Asia. Although, the local rulers of South-East Asia embraced Islam voluntarily (unlike in India), they continued to follow the Hindu/Buddhist customs and traditions.

In the course of time, factors such as the fall of the Majapahit empire, the rise of Malacca as its rival as well as a centre of Islam, brought about the rapid spread of Islam in the Malay archipelago. The Sultans of Malacca spread Islam throughout the length and breadth of their empire. Like Gajah Mada of the Majapahit empire, Tun Perak, the Bendahara (Chief Minister), worked hard to expand the empire. He worked under four Sultans, who succeeded one after the other. Through patronage, matrimony, and sometimes by corrupt means, Tun Perak became the de facto Sultan of Malacca. After his death in 1498, his office was taken over by a rival family member. This rival was Tun Mutahir (1500-1510), whose corrupt practices finally resulted in his execution in 1510.

The Portuguese Rule

A year later the Portuguese took advantage of the chaotic situation in Malacca and captured it. The last Sultan escaped to Pahang, a nearby island. In the early 16th century, Bantam, Moluccas, Borneo, Brunei and the Philippines came under the influence of Islam. As regards the Hindu kingdom of Champa, Islam spread from the Chinese side during the Champa-Vietnamese war (1470-71). During the war the kingdom of Champa did not receive any assistance from China, and therefore sought assistance from the Muslim States of Malacca and Java. The Champas took shelter in the Muslim kingdoms of Malacca, Sumatra and Java.

It was the city-state of Aceh, the northern-most part of Sumatra, which after the fall of Malacca, tried to imitate the culture of the Mughal empire. It copied some of the court-manners, dress, titles, laying of the gardens, art and architecture from the Mughal empire. This city-state maintained contacts with the Middle-east countries, and extended all facilities to Muslim pilgrims going to Mecca.

The numerous Muslim kingdoms in the Malay archipelago regarded the Portuguese as most uncivilized enemies. The Muslim merchants came to know that they no longer enjoyed the monopoly of spice trade that was being transacted from Cairo to the Moluccas. They regarded the Portuguese as the usurper who had snatched away the spice trade from them. They boycotted the Portuguese business in Malacca and gave much importance to the newly developed port of Aceh (north-east of Sumatra). The nearby Brunei was ruled by a Sultan. It was an important port of the island of Borneo, which received goods from Java, Moluccas and the Champa. The Portuguese got major trading concessions from the Sultan of Ternate in the Moluccas. However, the

Portuguese monopoly over spice trade continued until 1641 when the Dutch captured Malacca. During their regime, the Portuguese had built a large number of trading stations at Ternate, Amboyna, Tidore, Borneo, Celebes, New Guinea and Timor. They also held trading posts in Ayudhya (Thailand), Burma and Khambuja.

The Dutch Monopoly

The rise of the Anglo-Dutch combination against the Portuguese in South-East Asia was the direct result of the attempt made by the Spanish King, Philip II (also ruling over Portugal) to stop the Dutch Protestants from trading with Lisbon. It must be remembered that the Dutch had been buying spices from the Portuguese ports and thereafter selling them to Europeans. The policy of King Philip II was aimed at compelling the Dutch Protestants to total submission to Spanish rule. Unfortunately, this attempt backfired. The Dutch thereafter decided to go after the main source, the East Indies, for procuring spices. Therefore, South-East Asia assumed great importance as a region for the development of spice-trade.

The British and the Dutch established trading posts in almost all the places in South-East Asia for the purpose of trade. Before a proper understanding could be reached, the Dutch governor-general of the United East India Company, signed treaties with the native rulers which ultimately resulted in the alienation of the British. To eliminate their trade rival, the Dutch brought about a horrendous massacre of the British at Amboyna (1619). Thereafter the British became more interested in developing their trade with India. It was this loss of interest on the part of the British and the Spanish which enabled the Dutch to establish a monopoly on the spice trade. Unfortunately, the Portuguese remained in the field and they had to be eliminated.

The Dutch Capture of Malacca (1641)

The Dutch company prospered under the able leadership of General Jann Pieterscoon Coen (1618, 1623, 1627-29), the Governor-General, and this was partly due to the fall of the Portuguese trading posts, one by one, into the hands of the Dutch. However, the climax came when in 1641 the Dutch succeeded in the capturing the Portuguese strategic and prosperous trading centre, Malacca. This victory of the Dutch enabled them to establish their control over the strategic straits of Malacca and Sunda. The Dutch followed a policy of non-intervention with regard to the culture and customs of the natives. However, they developed political ambitions whenever the native states experienced political instability. In the course of time, the Dutch conquered the principal Javanese states of Bantam and Mataram. Unlike the Portuguese the Dutch set up indirect rule over the conquered native states. Their primary interest in the beginning was expansion of trade and profit. Through their local agents they compelled the local peasants to grow more spices by extending cultivation. The peasants had to sell their produce to the agents at low price and in turn paid low wages to the landless labourers working in their fields.

The Dutch established their capital at Batavia (Jakarta) in 1619 and organised their administration to suit local conditions. It was mostly managed by Dutch administrators. The Governor-General established a Council of State which was composed of representatives of the government, namely the governors of provinces and numerous residents. This system of administration continued for a long time. However, when the profits of the Dutch company began to decline, the government resorted to employing the migrant Chinese labourers to work on land and in factories at incredibly low wages.

Direct Rule of Dutch Government

Dutch rule had a serious impact on the local natives whose life had become miserable due to exploitation. Piracy and smuggling became the order of the day and this was due to mismanagement during the rule of the Dutch company. In Europe, the French Revolution ran its course, and was followed by Napoleonic rule. These events had some effect on the Dutch company over the East Indies in 1798 on grounds of mismanagement. At that time the rule of the Dutch company had spread to the nearby island, such as the Banda islands, the Moluccas, the Celebes, Java and Sumatra in South-East Asia, besides Ceylon in South Asia.

The Napoleonic wars in Europe and the subsequent settlement of the Congress of Vienna forced the Dutch to cede the Dutch Indies to the British. It was also in accordance with the wishes of King William V of the Netherlands who had sought British protection at the time when Holland was overrun by the French forces. The British forces occupied the Dutch Indies for a short period. After the settlement of the Congress of Vienna, the territories were returned to the Dutch, but Britain retained Ceylon for herself.

During the years 1800-1820, the East Indies had gone through a series of reforms probably reflecting the liberal philosophy prevailing in Europe at that time. The reform of the Dutch Indies began during Napoleonic rule in the Netherlands. It was introduced by a Dutch lawyer, Herman Daendals (1808-1810) in Java. His services were not very much appreciated even though he reduced corruption in the bureaucracy, and established an administration of justice in tune with the *adat* (local customs). Daendals encouraged the production of cash crops. He also tried to improve the means of transport and communication in Batavia and Surabaya.

British Reforms

When the British took over the island of Java from the Dutch during the period 1811-1860, Thomas Stamford Raffles was appointed Lt.- Governor by Lord Minto, the then Governor-General of India. Raffles had earlier worked as a British agent in the Malay States, and therefore was well-versed with their language and culture. Raffles sincerely believed in improving the conditions of the people of Java. His radical reforms brought about all-round development. It included the reorganisation of administration, the abolition of the old forced delivery system, tax restructuring, and revenue reassessment of agricultural lands. One of his most important reforms was the introduction of the Ryotwari systems by which the actual cultivator became the land owner subject to the payment of land tax directly to the government. Raffles introduced courts of Justice on the model of the British which included trial by jury in three large ports, namely, Batavia, Semarang and Surabaya.

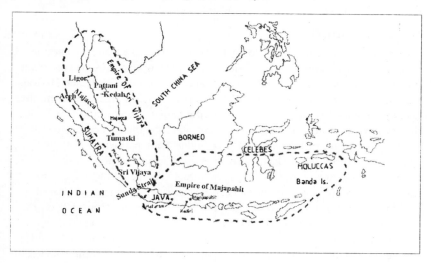

The Archipelago in AD 1400

Division of Malay Archipelago

The British transferred their power to the Dutch in 1816. In 1824, the British and the Dutch signed a treaty which provided for the division of the Malay archipelago into two regions. The British gained control over the Malay States whereas the Dutch exercised their sovereignty over the East Indies (Indonesia). Britain developed Tumasik, the strategic centre of trade situated at the southern tip of Malaya. Tumasik was renamed Singapore. The British also developed two other great centres, namely, Penang and Malacca. Penang was acquired in

1824 after giving compensation to Sultan Hussain and the Temenggong for their loss.

The Dutch Rule Continues

The restoration of Dutch reactionary rule in Indonesia soon after the liberal phase of British rule, was galling to the natives. Moreover, when the Dutch intervened in a dynastic dispute in the royal house of Jog-Jakarta, provoked deep resentment. This resentment turned into a war known as the Java war. The decision of the Dutch Government to construct a road across the Dipo-Negoro property, which was held sacred because of a sacred tomb, made conditions worse. The Muslim natives in this area declared a war against the Dutch government. Dipo was arrested and subsequently banished. Therefore, the war with the Dutch became inevitable with the result that the government lost 15,000 soldiers, mostly Europeans. A famine broke out in this region which resulted in the death of more that 200,000 people. This war with the natives had made the Dutch Government bankrupt.

'The Culture System'

To explore avenues for raising money from the natives, the Dutch Government introduced what is known as the 'culture system'. The man chosen to carry out this task was Johanes Van den Bosch, a perverted economic adviser. He was appointed Governor-General in 1830. Van den Bosch tried to complete the task by recourse to forced labour among the natives. According to his plan, the Javanese peasant was forced to raise cash crops for exports by working freely on one-fifth of his land in a year under the supervision of the native agents. As a result, the native cultivators were forced to neglect their own farm work so as to promote the Dutch venture. In the meantime, the Dutch set up a double government in Indonesia which separated power and responsibility. The responsibility for improving the production of cash crops fell on the shoulders of native supervisors and agents, while power was wielded by the Dutch Government. This government of Van den Bosch made Holland a prosperous country because of heavy exploitation of the natives and resources in Indonesia. He was rewarded with a baronetcy, and subsequently made a Count (1839). The Dutch economy showed great signs of progress because of the transfer of resources and wealth from Indonesia. The culture system of Van den Bosch resulted in widespread famines (1848-50) since land and labour were diverted from rice cultivation. The Dutch policy of exploiting the people of Indonesia engendered a sense of alienation. It was Eduard Douwes Dekker's *Max Havelar* which brought to light the outrageous evils of Dutch rule, and their atrocities perpetrated on the Javanese community under the culture system. This book was widely read in the Netherlands, and the government was forced to take necessary steps to mitigate the harsh conditions prevailing in Indonesia due to public outcry.

The new Constitution of 1848 of the Netherlands was liberal in character, and it assigned to Parliament the responsibility of looking after the Dutch colonies. Under the conservative rule, some major reforms were introduced which included the cancellation of the monopoly enjoyed by the Netherlands trading society, modifying the rigours of the repressive regime, and the removal of restraints on the production of rice (in order to prevent famines). Slavery was abolished in 1860. However, these reforms did not go far enough to improve the living condition of the people.

The Liberal Party came to power in the Netherlands in 1863 and continued the process of reforms. Van de Putte, the Minister of Colonies, abolished the culture programme in the cultivation of some cash crops in 1866, but sugar and coffee remained untouched until 1890 and 1917 respectively. The next dose of reforms tried to reduce the sufferings of the cultivators. It encouraged the process of privatisation, and gradually a large number of European entrepreneurs entered the production and marketing of commercial crops. As the Javanese population increased on a limited land, there was little prospect of further exploitation. Therefore, the European entrepreneurs ventured into the outer islands to increase the production of rubber, tobacco, oil and mining. They were allowed to exploit the lease lands and import capital and labour. The only relief felt by the Indonesian workers was that the wage contractors were afraid of breaking the new laws. The attempt of the Dutch to control the outer islands resulted in the outbreak of a war with a fanatical section of the Aceh. The war ended after 30 years (1873-1903) with disastrous results. Some powerful corporations in Indonesia gained huge profits but hardly cared for the welfare of the workers employed by them. Therefore, the government felt it necessary to intervene to remedy the situation.

The Ethical Programme

It tried to improve the conditions of the people through what is called the Ethical Programme which had been advocated by a large number of intellectuals in Indonesia. The Ethical Programme aimed at *mitigating* the hard conditions prevailing in the country due to the alien rule. But the European business community opposed this scheme because of the enormous expenditure involved in carrying it out. They regarded this as unnecessary and wasteful. Despite their opposition, the Dutch Government inaugurated this programme in 1901, of course, with a lot of misgivings. Under this programme, the government tried to promote agriculture and industry. It offered protection to the native industries. The Factory Act was passed in 1903 which tried to improve the condition of the labour. It tried to modify the control of labour recruitment policy of the government. A number of irrigation projects were undertaken to bring more areas under cultivation. Public-credit facilities were extended to the poor peasants to wean them away from moneylenders. The government also introduced a health programme and extended educational facilities to the native children. In spite of these efforts, the Ethical Programme of the government did not bring much relief to the people of Indonesia. The economy of the country began to slide. The Muslim-majority Indonesian population did not extend full support to the Ethical Programme of the government because they thought that it was based on Christian Ethics. When the Ethical Programme failed to achieve its objective, it led to the rise of political consciousness among the middle-class Indonesians.

The Sarekat Islam

The Sarekat Islam began as a political organisation of the Indonesian Muslims in 1911. Originally, its purpose was to chastise the Chinese rivals in the field of trade and commerce, particularly those engaged in the batik-cloth-trade. It tried to promote a sense of unity among the Indonesian Muslims in the face of the ever-growing influence of the Dutch Christian missionaries. The founder of this organisation was a charismatic leader named Umar Sayed Tjokroaminoto whose inspiring speeches cast a spell on the Indonesian Muslims living in rural and urban areas. By 1919, the Sarekat Islam claimed at least two million staunch supporters to its cause most of them being Javanese peasants. This organisation would not have been allowed to exist but for its professed loyalty to Dutch rule. In the course of time, this organisation received recognition from the Governor-General. Though split into a few factions, it had a common cause and a common approach to the crucial issues facing Indonesian society. These issues mainly related to the achievement of self-rule, socialism, and modernisation of the economy. It must be remembered that the First World War had its impact on the Indonesian economy. The people had to put up with inflation, levy of numerous taxes, and the erosion of the traditional authority wielded by native officials.

The Sarekat Islam appealed to the Dutch Government to concede several political concessions, and in response to it the Government granted what is known as the *Volksraad* (People's Councils) in 1918. However, these councils were composed of elected representatives to the extent of 50 per cent, the remaining being the nominees of the governor-general. All the nominees were Dutch nationals. The Volksraad unfortunately did not enjoy power of its own, but acted as an advisory body. To implement its proposed programme, it had to seek the permission of the Dutch Government at the Hague. Therefore, the Indonesian nationalists felt cheated and frustrated at these so-called concessions.

The Communist Party

In these circumstances, there arose a radical socialist group called the Indies Social Democratic Association. Unfortunately, a large number of communists infiltrated into this association. These communists began to use this association to promote vested interests. The communists hailed the formation of Comintern in 1919 and established contacts with it. This communist group subsequently identified itself as the PKI (Partai Kommunis Indonesia) and took into its fold a large number of radical members from the Sarekat Islam. Eventually, the communist party was established under the leadership of Henrik Sneevliet. It grew into a massive organisation and broke away from Sarekat Islam in the twenties. This was because the Sarekat Islam stood for Pan-Islamism and followed constitutional methods to attain its objectives. The communist party, on the other hand, prepared a revolutionary agenda and dreamed of establishing a communist state, even by means of violence, if necessary. The PKI condemned the economic exploitation of the country and stepped up its campaign against Dutch rule in Indonesia. It had a special appeal to the workers in all urban centres and tried to paralyze the Dutch regime by organising strikes. The PKI formed a large number of trade unions, and got them affiliated to the main centre at Canton.

The communists organised an uprising in November 1926 despite the reluctance from Moscow. But this revolt was crushed by the government. The government declared a ban on the communist party. A large number of communist leaders were imprisoned, and the others left the country. The communist movement in the country received a great setback and until 1941 it could not play any useful role in Indonesia. The main cause of the failure of the communist movement was that it could not establish a rapport with the other revolutionary movements, particularly the peasant movement. Secondly, the movement failed because the party was getting split into several factions each quarreling with the other. Thirdly, the communist party did not have a grass root level organization to enlist the support of millions of peasants suffering from the misrule of the Dutch. Even the urban workers did not show their enthusiasm in participating in a strike when the communist party called for it.

The New National Party (PNI)

The Dutch Government let loose its engine of oppression, and all political movements in the country were looked upon with great suspicion. In the meantime, the Sarekat Islam had lost its glamour and popularity. Therefore, the need of the hour was a new organisation which could be led by dynamic leaders. In these circumstances, a large number of student study centres became active and prepared the ground for the emergence of a new national party. The new national party happened to be the Indonesian nationalist party (PNI meaning Per Serikatan National Indonesia) which took its birth in 1927. It was led by two eminent leaders, Dr Sukarno and Djipro Mangun Kusuma. The former was an engineer by profession who became popular on account of his leadership qualities. He brought all the non-communist nationalists into his organisation, gave a flag to the party, and a national anthem (Indonesia Raya). Sukarno was inspired by the "example of India's Congress Party and its programme of mass pressure through non-cooperation", (*J F Cady*). The Dutch prevented Sukarno and his followers from spreading the national movement. They were arrested and sent to prison in the Flores Island in 1929. The great depression of 1929 worsened the economic conditions in Indonesia. To make matters worse a hundred thousand Javanese labourers returned home from abroad.

The Partindo

The post-depression period in Indonesia witnessed the rise of a new socialist party Partai Indonesia (in short *Partindo*) led by Sutan Sjaharir and Mohammed Hatta. Both of them had returned from Europe. Sukarno joined them after completing his prison term. However the Dutch government sensed trouble and quickly acted against all the three. Sukarno went into exile in 1933 to avoid arrest, and the two others were arrested and sent to New Guinea. Thus, the Indonesian nationalist movement was devoid of leadership, and could not make much progress until the Japanese occupation during the Second World War. During this period, the Dutch Government adopted the policy of extending political concessions to the people by piecemeal method. Unfortunately, this piecemeal method did not satisfy the people of Indonesia, since it was devoid of any move towards providing a responsible government with the cooperation of the people. Hence, political tensions prevailed. The Dutch government tried to suppress all legitimate movements of the people and therefore, became quite unpopular. Under these circumstances, the Indonesians were prepared to welcome the Japanese occupation of their country hoping to attain self-rule in future.

When the Second World War broke out, the Dutch refused to arm the Indonesians to defend themselves from the Japanese aggression, with the hope that they could hold on to its colony. In the end, the politically conscious Indonesians welcomed the arrival of the Japanese who released the Indonesian leaders, Sukarno, Sjaharir and Hatta from prison.

The Japanese Occupation

As early as 1933, Japan had been making attempts to gather enough support for her future rule in Indonesia by wooing the Muslim population. Some Japanese students were sent to West Asia to study Islam, and on their return founded the Islamic Association in Tokyo. This association held its World

Congress in 1938 and invited Indonesian delegates to attend. The Japanese Government sent delegates to the Islamic federation called MIAI held at Surabaya in 1937 for the purpose of wooing the conservative Muslim groups of Indonesia to its side. In fact, this was intended to create a feeling of revulsion to the Dutch rule of Indonesia. When the Japanese army occupied Indonesia in 1942, it included a large number of Muslim soldiers who were accompanied by Haji-robed Japanese.

What Japan planned to do was to encourage Indonesian religious groups to play an important role, and at the same time suppress political associations such as Sarekat Islam and PNI. In her opinion, the latter two should have no hold on the people. Subsequently, Japan tried to impose her rule on Indonesia with the support of the Islamic Federation (MIAI) which included groups such as reformist Muhammadijah and conservative Nahdatul Ulama. The scribes of the MIAI attended training camps held by the Japanese where they were indoctrinated. In these camps, the greatness of the Japanese culture and leadership was stressed. Afterwards they were sent to the villages to act as agents to urge the Indonesians to extend whole - hearted cooperation to Japanese rule. In the course of time, the MIAI realised the game of the Japanese army, and put forward several of its demands in 1943, which the latter was unable to concede. When the MIAI failed to extend full cooperation the Japanese Government took the next step, that is to sponsor a new political organisation called Putera. This organisation tried to attract the attention as well as cooperation of two great Indonesian leaders, namely Sukarno and Hatta. The Japanese asked these two leaders to take over the leadership of this organisation which was supposed to implement the Japanese policies and economic programmes in Indonesia. In return the Japanese promised political autonomy to the country, and the two leaders agreed to lead this organisation. Suspicious of the Japanese promise, these two leaders clandestinely encouraged underground Indonesian leaders to carry on with their activities against Japanese imperialism. Sukarno and Hatta agreed to help the Japanese in the recruitment of soldiers to the Japanese army, provide supply of materials, and mobilise enough resources to help the Japanese to achieve their goal of establishing "Greater East Asia Co-prosperity Sphere" all subject to the condition that the country would be granted political autonomy. This agreement remained valid until 1943, when Putera was abolished. In Java, the Japanese plan did not yield results. The Javanese hated the racial superiority and arrogance of the Japanese, and also their methods of exploiting the labour force. The Japanese army snatched away great quantities of foodgrains from them in order to feed its soldiers.

The last step of the Japanese to seek the cooperation of the Indonesians was taken by establishing a political party known as the Masjmi Party which was composed of native scribes and village teachers. This organisation was founded for the purpose of securing the cooperation of the natives for assisting their defense against the invading allied forces. From mid-1944 onwards, Japan began to suffer a series of reverses in the Second World War, and in September 1944 promised total independence to the Indonesians. On the eve of the Japanese surrender to the Allies, the people of Indonesia led by Sukarno declared independence and formed a republic in August 1945 with the moral support of the Japanese. However, the story of the Indonesian struggle against the Dutch colonial rule did not end as expected. The exiled Dutch Government decided to return to continue its rule over Indonesia from its headquarters in Batavia.

The Indonesian Revolution (1941-45)

The last phase of the Indonesian struggle for freedom may be termed a "revolution" since Indonesia had to challenge the return of Dutch on the one side, and forge a united front against the communist threat on the other. So it took another four years for her to achieve sovereignty and independence. The British forces came to Indonesia to accept the surrender of the Japanese. They were helped in this process by the nationalist government. Subsequently 200,000 Dutch prisoners held by the Japanese in the Indonesian prisons were released. The Dutch Government which was in exile sent Dr Van Mook after the Japanese surrender with the instruction to denounce the nationalist government led by Sukarno. He was appointed for the purpose of restoring Dutch rule in Indonesia. In the meantime the nationalists in Indonesia demanded that their republic be recognized by the government of the Netherlands before any negotiations could take place. Subsequently, Sukarno resigned in favour of Sutan Sjaharir. After rejecting the demand of the nationalists, the Dutch started capturing island after island and posed a serious challenge to the Indonesian nationalist government. Negotiations continued between the new Indonesian republic and the Dutch Government in the occupied territories. It finally ended in the signing of the agreement with the mediation of the British Government.

The Linggerdjati agreement envisaged not only the formation and control of the Indonesian Republic but also the inclusion for Borneo and the "Great East". This was to be called the United States of Indonesia (USI) and constitute a part of greater Netherlands-Indonesia. The USI was to seek admission as a member of the United Nations. The Union Government of the USI was to extend its control over important subjects like defence, foreign affairs and finance. However, the working arrangement between the government of the Netherlands and the Indonesian Federation did not bring about political unity of the country. In fact, the Indonesians hated indirect rule of the Dutch. Within three months of the signing of the agreement, there arose a quarrel between the Dutch Government and the Indonesian Republic. It resulted in the armed invasion of the Dutch which had serious international repercussions.

India and a host of non-aligned countries appealed to the UN to bring about a cease-fire between the two parties. This cease-fire came into force from August 1, 1947. A committee composed of the representatives of the US, Australia and Belgium was set up which worked for establishing durable peace. The committee proposed a plebiscite to ask the people whether they would like to remain with the Republic or under Dutch sovereignty. Before anything tangible could take place, the Netherlands Government shocked the world with another invasion of the Indonesian Republic terming it 'police action'. The non-aligned nations led by India in the United Nations were outraged. An Asian conference was convened by India's Prime Minister, Jawaharlal Nehru, which strongly condemned the Dutch aggression. The United Nations Security Council brought about a cease-fire in Indonesia. The Dutch Government finally agreed to transfer power and sovereignty to Indonesia after coming under the pressure of the newly independent countries of Asia and Africa. The formation of the United States of Indonesia took shape with six states (Indonesia being one). During its transitional phase, it was to be led by the Netherlands. The Dutch felt very awkward in the new political set-up and therefore, quit Indonesia. Thus Indonesia gained her freedom and sovereignty from Dutch colonial rule. In the course of time, the federal set-up was dismantled without any war. Dr Sukarno was elected president of Indonesia with absolute powers.

The Post-independence Era

After gaining sovereignty and independence from the Dutch, Indonesia witnessed a period of political instability due to the existence of the multi-party system, each party working at cross purposes with the other. These political parties vied with one another to form the government and among them the most important were the Nationalist Party (PNI), the Communist Party (PKI) the Nahdatul Ulama (Orthodox Muslim Party) and the Masjumi Party. The last mentioned adopted a pro-Western policy, while the Nationalist turned into anti-Western. The Communist Party and the Nahdatul Ulama also adopted an anti-Western stand. Unfortunately, political rivalries and bickering weakened the central government which forced President Sukarno to resort to drastic action. In the meantime, the Indonesian economy was faced with the problem of inflation (1945-55). Prices of commodities doubled, followed by the balance of payments crisis. Many evils such as corruption and smuggling brought about further worsening of the economic situation in the country. Foreign investors lost confidence in the Indonesian Government which was thinking of nationalising many industries.

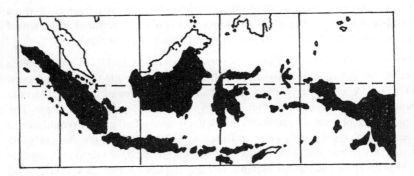

Indonesian Republic

Dr Sukarno's Guided Democracy (1957)

In the midst of deep crisis, President Sukarno realised that the time was not yet ripe for Indonesia to enjoy the luxuries of democracy. It had to be guided because no political party enjoyed a clear mandate of the people in Parliament. There was, therefore, no question of establishing a stable government. He assumed extraordinary powers after describing Indonesia's democracy as "chatter box democracy". His drastic step to assume powers which was not granted by the Constitution was resented by various political parties and some military units. They staged their protest. Some islands in Indonesia, like Borneo and Sumatra took steps in the direction of seceding from the Union. President Sukarno's response to this dangerous situation was swift and timely. He declared an emergency in the country, and appointed an emergency cabinet with Doctor Dwanda as its head. The country came under martial law since there was a threat of civil war. An attempt was made on the life of Sukarno, but it failed. Fortunately, Sukarno was able to overcome all these formidable difficulties because there was no foreign interference. He was able to restore the political unity of the country after suppressing all rebellious elements.

Foreign Policy

In foreign relations, President Sukarno followed the policy of strict neutrality at a time when the world was in the grip of Cold War. In consistence with the goals of non-alignment, Indonesia was able to organise the famous Bandung Conference in 1955 (Western Java). Many leading personalities belonging to non-aligned nations like Jawaharlal Nehru, President Tito, Nasser, Bandarnaike attended this conference, and discussed many problems facing the non-aligned countries. They endorsed the Panchasheel proposed by India (five principles of co-existence) as the basis for conducting foreign relations. The Panchasheel agreement was signed by India. Egypt, Burma, Indonesia, Vietnam, Yugoslavia, Poland and Austria. The agreement covered such aspects as respect for human rights, settlement of disputes by peaceful means, non-interference, and so on. In this conference, the member countries upheld Indonesia's claim to Western New Guinea. They denounced Western imperialism and colonialism in the strongest terms.

Unfortunately, the spirit of the Bandung Conference remained ephemeral, since China attacked Tibet (1955-59) and India (1962). President Sukarno of Indonesia supported China in the Sino-Soviet struggle over their borders.

A number of attempts were made on the life of Sukarno but all of them failed. There was an ongoing tussle between Sukarno on the one side and the communists on the other. The fight between the communists and non-communists brought the country to the brink of civil war, but President Sukarno was able to avert it. It was due to his harsh methods that he became unpopular. The Communist Party in Indonesia organised an attempt to overthrow his regime but failed. In the midst of this confusion the Indonesian army took advantage and brought about the arrest of Sukarno. The army gave an ultimatum to him to step down. Sukarno's dictatorship spanning over two decades in Indonesia ended in 1967. He died in June 1970 after a three-year house arrest. He was succeeded by General Suharto in 1968.

Suharto (1968-1998)

The military regime of General Raden Suharto had been in power in Indonesia for more than three decades. He was elected president in 1968 soon after the deposition of Sukarno, thanks to the military coup. His popularity soared high due to rapid economic strides. Indonesia, the fourth most populous country in the world and with the largest Muslim majority, had a facade of democracy, with the president adopting dubious means to keep himself in power. His Golkar Party won a majority of seats always as the opposition was in disarray. President Suharto, who received full backing of the army, became a past-master in the politics of manipulation. The opposition parties have accused him of 'rigging elections' nepotism and corruption. It was not until 1993, that the late Sukarno's daughter, Sukarnoputri, emerged as an important opposition leader. She became a rallying point of protest against Suharto's 'New Order' regime representative in character—fully backed by the military.

What were the contributory causes for Suharto's downfall in 1998? President Suharto's regime lacked legitimacy, since he got elected for nearly seven terms through the politics of manipulation. The Electoral College was filled with military and government servants, all owing allegiance to Suharto. Furthermore, the Constitution gave wide-ranging powers to the elected president so that he could instil fear in his opponents. Suharto proved that he was responsible for making Indonesia a strong and prosperous country and it was a fact. After three decades of his corrupt regime, the tide turned against him.

In July 1997, the woes of Indonesia began. The currency turmoil affected South-East Asia, and the economic collapse overtook many countries including Indonesia. In the midst of this crisis, Suharto managed to get re-elected president for the seventh term, with his party securing 75 per cent vote in March 1998. Coming as it did after the drought caused by El Nino in 1997, the economic crisis in 1998 with the tumbling rupiah, and corruption and nepotism of the repressive regime was too much for the masses to bear. Suharto was unable to halt the slide. His efforts to overcome these problems were directionless and half-hearted. He refused to accept the reforms advocated by the International Monetary Fund (IMF), and the latter refused to help his government.

During the last year of Suharto's repressive regime, the economy shrank by 6 per cent, and the rupiah lost 80 per cent of its value. The government was unable to contain the inflation which caused great suffering to the masses. The economy could not recover, and the veil covering Suharto's corruption' nepotism and favoritism was lifted. The Indonesians came to know that Suharto had amassed a personal fortune of $ 40 billion at a time when their poverty had increased by 100 per cent within one year (*World Bank estimate*).

Meghawati Sukarnoputri

The growing popularity of Meghawati Sukarnoputri among the discontented masses was too much for Suharto to bear, and he prevented her from running for office in 1996. When she was organising a sit-in demonstration in protest, the security forces unleashed their brutality against the demonstrators. Opposition to Suharto's repressive regime took a violent turn, and people burnt and looted Chinese-owned shops. As the situation was growing worse each day, Sukarnoputri (leader of the PDI party) joined hands with the other reformist parties like the National Awakening Party led by a secular-Islamist, Abdurrahman Wahid, and the National Mandate Party led by Amien Rais, a professor. The latter was leading the students' revolt.

Suharto's Exit

The immediate cause of Suharto's downfall was the outbreak of the student's revolt. Four students were killed by the security forces and it led to violent protest. The government was paralysed, and the capital, Jakarta, turned into an inferno with students fighting pitched battles against the security forces. The opposition parties lost no time in joining the student demonstrations, and demanded Suharto's resignation. Suharto realised that the situation was beyond his control and relinquished his office on May 21, 1998. He asked his life-long protege and Vice-President, the 63-year-old Bacharuddin Jusuf Habibie, to take over the presidency. The transfer of power brought to an end the month-long violence in the country which left nearly 500 dead. The economic collapse affected neighbouring countries like South Korea and Japan since their banks had given loans to many enterprises and individuals in Indonesia.

Return to Democracy

Amien Rais, the leading opposition leader and head of a large Muslim organisation, *Muhammadiya,* immediately urged the new president to hold fresh elections. He asked the president to appoint an enquiry commission to investigate the financial and business dealings of Suharto, and his family members who had amassed great wealth through corrupt practices. Habibie, unlike his predecessor, allowed freedom of expression, and prevented a situation that would have allowed the military to intervene. In a surprise move, this technocrat-turned-president promised to hold parliamentary elections. The People's consultative Assembly rejected the accountability reports presented by him (355-322 votes), thereby expressing its loss of confidence in his government. Habibie declared that he would not contest for the post of president after the general election.

The most historic election was held in all the 27 provinces of Indonesia on June 7, 1999, which was supervised by the International Election Observation Mission (consisting of election monitors of 23 countries including India) headed by ex-president of the US, Jimmy Carter. Meghawati's PDI, Wahid's National Awakening Party, and Rais's National Mandate Party formed a united front based on a common agenda—the return to democracy. After a long delay, results were announced . Meghawati's party got a lead followed by the two others. It was expected that the electoral college would choose Meghawati as the president in November. But the result went in favour of Abdurrahman Wahid. Being friendly rivals in the contest, President Wahid (a great Islamic scholar who advocates secularism) appealed to the electoral college to elect Meghawati as Vice-President. Since Wahid is handicapped by two paralytic strokes and impaired vision, it is expected that Meghawati would play the role as *de facto* president. Wahid consulted her before forming his new cabinet. The role of the army in civil administration is considerably reduced, and General Wiranto has been shifted to a less important job. A close aide of Sukarnoputri, Kwik Kian Gie was given the important portfolio of Economics Minister.

Succession of Meghawati

The physically-handicapped Indonesian President tried to create problems for Meghawati's succession in spite of his removal by the People's Consultative Assembly. To ward off danger to his position, he issued a decree declaring emergency in the country. However, the Supreme Court declared the decree illegal, and the army too was not in favour of the president's continuation. The dejected president was forced out of office paving the way for Meghawati Sukarnoputri to succeed. President Wahid's major failure may be traced to his inability to suppress the elements which supported ex-President Suharto. The government under Wahid was unable to arrest Tommy Suharto (son of ex-President Suharto) for his misdeeds.

After her succession, Meghawati began to face formidable challenges. The 'Free Aceh' movement had gained ground thereby threatening the territorial integrity and sovereignty of Indonesia.

Bali Bombing

After the 9/11 (2001) attacks by the terrorists in the US , the US government under President G W Bush declared a 'war on terror' and appealed all the nations to join in the efforts. The UN too supported this global war on terrorism through its Security Council Resolution. The Muslim countries were rather sceptical, and Indonesia being the largest Muslim-populated country remained unenthusiastic. Its government did not want to provoke the radical Muslim community. It was not until the bombing at the night club of Kuta in Bali Island on October 12, 2002, that the Indonesian government woke up from its slumber. The number of foreign tourists killed was 202 and many were injured. The government traced the culprits who belonged to the *Jemmah Islamia,* a fundamentalist outfit having its link with the Al-Qaeda. The Jemmah Islamia is led by a Muslim cleric named Abu Bakar Bashir, who is accused of masterminding the Bali bombing. The one who executed the bombing at Kuta was Amrozi (nick named 'Smiling Bomber'). He was executed after the court found him guilty.

Economy

The 1997 recession spread all over South-East Asia including Indonesia. Foreign direct investment came to a virtual halt. Many bankers caused a mess by misappropriating the financed loans to the extent of $ 16 billion. The deepening recession further caused a massive public debt. The tragedy at Bali resulted in the drop of foreign direct investment by nearly 35 per cent. A poor country with 215 million people, many of them below the poverty line, could barely cope with this economic debacle. President Meghawati's government is coaxing the errant bankers to return saying it would not persecute them. Indonesia's economy is showing signs of economic recovery these days.

Presidential Election

In the first ever direct election for the presidency held in Indonesia, the final round of vote-counting in September 2004 brought victory to Susilo Bambang

Yudhoyono, a former security minister of Meghawati's Cabinet. Meghawati lost due to the disaffection of people over her not coming to grips with the economic stagnation (Indonesia is the only country that has not yet fully recovered from the Asian financial crisis of 1997), the civil strife, the separatist movements, and of course terrorism. The newly elected president has to act decisively to repair the damage.

EAST TIMOR'S INDEPENDENCE

The Dutch and the Portuguese concluded an agreement in 1859 which split the island of Timor into two parts, the west held by the former, and the east by the Portuguese. When the Portuguese abandoned East Timor in 1975 the Indonesian security forces invaded it. It was annexed and thereafter turned into a 27th province in 1976 despite the protests from the local natives. President Suharto's Government treated the Christian East Timorese as second class citizens, and the United Nations had not recognised this annexation and colonisation. During the late 1970s, tens of thousands of East Timorese died fighting the Indonesian army during their struggle for freedom. As early as 1974, Fretlin (the Revolutionary Front of Independent Timor) was founded, and its guerilla groups known as *Falantil* were actively engaged in overthrowing Indonesian rule. Year after year, the East Timorese liberation movement gathered momentum, but Suharto's resolve to suppress this movement had no respite. Those who resisted Suharto's repressive regime were tortured or jailed or murdered. Many mourners attending the funeral of those killed were also shot by the Indonesian army in 1991, and the next year witnessed the capture and imprisonment of resistance leader Xanana Gusmao. The people's plight in East Timor received international attention in 1996 when the Nobel Peace Prize was awarded to two East Timorese, Bishop Rev Carlos Belo and human rights activist Jose Ramos Horta. Suharto's exit paved the way for the much talked about referendum to materialise, since his successor Habibie had to yield to so much international pressures as well as South African leader Nelson Mandela's appeal for mediation.

In the meantime, the pro-Jakarta militia started its wave of terror to subdue those who wanted to vote for independence. Not only did the people of East Timor vote on August 30, 1999, but also others who had fled the country. Soon after the voting, the pro-Jakarta militia slaughtered thousands of East Timorese, destroyed their houses, and attacked the UN staff and journalists — all in the presence of Indonesian troops. The UN gave an ultimatum to the Indonesian Government to stop acts of loot, arson and violence in East Timor within 48 hours and release jailed leader, Xanana Gusmao. The Timorese capital, Dili, looked like a ghost town with Timorese fleeing for their life. The UN mandated peace keeping force was sent to East Timor to help the Indonesian army and local authorities to restore law and order. President Habibie had earlier imposed martial law to restore order. The US president's threat to Indonesia served its purpose. Ninety per cent of the voters voted to break away from Indonesia. East Timor became free but the people there face hunger, lack of shelter, and total chaos. The UN has recently proposed to raise a $500 million package of assistance for East Timor.

REFERENDUM IN ACEH

The threat of Indonesia's disintegration looms large. In the 1950s President Sukarno had promised Aceh autonomy because this province played a prominent role in the independence movement of Indonesia. Unfortunately it was not given autonomy as promised but identified as Special Area. Subsequently President Suharto promised to raise the living standards and give religious freedom (a purely Muslim province) but nothing came out of it. Instead, his government exploited the region for its oil and gas, and sent the army to crush the rebels who demanded imposition of Islamic law. His successor, Habibie, felt sorry for this tragedy, and promised to grant autonomy. What made the people of this province angry was the west-Aceh incident in which the Indonesian soldiers killed a religious leader along with his 50 followers. The people there felt outraged, and the movement for independence gained momentum. The new Indonesian President, Abdurrahman Wahid, has agreed to hold a referendum in seven months time, fervently hoping the people to vote for autonomy and not independence. If Aceh secedes, there is a possibility that Indonesia would disintegrate soon. Many districts of Indonesia's west coast, particularly the Aceh with the Banda-Aceh city, was battered by the Tsunami (December 26, 2004) which killed more than 100,000 people. The rehabilitation work for those who survived this disaster may take several years. The new millennium has brought no respite from political crises. Christians and Muslims have been at each other's throats in Ambon and the Island of Malaku. 'Free Papua' movement in Irian Jaya province is causing unrest.

24
CAMBODIA (KAMPUCHEA OR KAMBUJA)

Before India's cultural influence spread to South-East Asia, there existed an indigenous civilisation — the Bronze Age civilisation, specifically named as Dong-Son civilisation. Several Neolithic Bronze Age sites were discovered which date back to 2000 BC. Around 1000 BC, there existed a more advanced Bronze-Age Dong-Son civilisation which was characterised by the use of bronze drums. The vestiges of this civilisation were discovered in a village called Dong-Son in the Tongking delta. The Dong-Son people were known to have irrigated their lands, domesticated animals, shown a fondness for sea faring and had some knowledge of astronomy. They developed contacts with the outside world after building and sailing on their canoes. They practised ancestor worship and built temples on elevated places like small hills or platforms. They kept the ashes of the dead in jars. It was in the early centuries of the Christian era that South-East Asia came under the increasing influence of Sino-Indian culture. The Dong-Son civilisation was Austronesian, and there is evidence that rice cultivation was in vogue since 6000 BC.

A majority of the people living in Kampuchea today claim Khmer ancestry which is identified with race and language. The original homeland of the Khmers is not clearly known. Scholars are divided in their opinion but they migrated along the Mekong River and settled in Kampuchea, after driving out the Malays.

It can be said that most of the early kingdoms in South-East Asia were founded by the Malays, leaving apart a few which were founded by Indian adventurers. Among them the most important are Langasuka (with Patani as capital) and Tamralinga. These two kingdoms flourished mainly due to maritime commerce, and subsequently they declined. More advanced and prosperous kingdoms flourished not in the Malay peninsula but in the Indo-Chinese peninsula and they were Funan and Champa, both Hindu kingdoms. The Hindus of South India established the Funanese kingdom and its first ruler was Kaundinya, a Brahmin, during the first century AD. Its capital was Vyadhapura which is situated near modern Phnom Penh.

The kingdom of Funan was further enlarged by Fan-Shih-Man in the third century AD with the acquisition of South Vietnam, Kampuchea, Central Thailand, North Malaya and Southern Burma. The Funanese empire played an important intermediary role in Sino-Indian trade. The Funanese King, Fan-Shih-Man, encouraged ship-building and maritime trade. He sent diplomatic missions to India and China. Two Chinese envoys stayed in Funan in the third century AD. They have left valuable information regarding the glorious days of Fan-Shih-Man. Sanskrit became the court language, and Hinduism was patronised. It was in the fourth century AD that another Kaundinya patronised Hinduism. In the fifth century Buddhism became a popular faith. The Funanese were highly cultured and civilised and not barbarians as may appear from the account of Kang Tai. The Funanese empire owed allegiance and paid tribute to China till its fall in the middle of the seventh century AD.

The Khmer Empire

The Funanese empire was replaced by the Khmers who were descendants of a mythical ancestor named Kambu Svayambhuva. This is how the land of the Khmers came to be known as Khamboja, or Cambodia or Kampuchea (from 1920). In fact, these Khmers or Khambujas had come from Chenla, a vassal state of the Funanese empire in which Hinduism had been established a few centuries ago. It was King Chitrasena, brother of Baravarman, who conquered Funan and thereafter extended his control over a vast area which included Lower Burma, Upper Malay peninsula, Central Thailand, Kampuchea and Southern Vietnam. Although the Chenla-Khmer kingdom became a great land power, it could not achieve the maritime supremacy of its predecessor. Therefore, it could not play a very effective intermediary role in the maritime

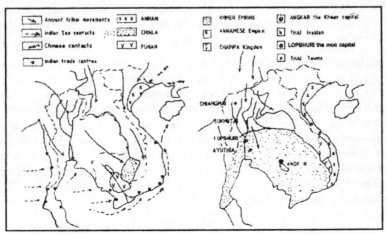

Khmer's Beginning   Khmer Empire

trade between China and India. In the course of time, the Chenla-Khmers suffered a split and lost a profitable maritime trade. Their weakness attracted the attention of aggressive and greedy neighbours such as Sri Vijaya's Sumatran kingdom and the Sailendra kingdom of Java.

The Khmer Empire under Siege

The Sailendra kings of Java desired to unite the whole of South-East Asia under their control and made bold attempts to conquer the mainland of South-East Asia which included the Chenla, Tongking and Champa kingdoms. Their continuous raids forced the divided Khmers to remain united. Fortunately, they found an able leader in the person of King Jayavarman II (AD 802-850), who had spent some years as hostage in the court of the Sailendra king. The threat of the Sailendra and Champa kings was warded off and in due course of time the Khmer empire was revived. It was he who 'shifted the focus of Khmer activity from the Mekong delta to the region around the Tonle Sap Lake in Western Kampuchea. The Khmer glory then spread westwards and northwards, and Angkor and its surroundings became the main focus of attention during the next five centuries (9th to 14th).

King Jayavarman II revived the Shaiva Tantrik cult of Devaraja (divine kingship) and its associated beliefs under which funeral sites of the kings were built inside the temples. The kings styled themselves *Chakravartin* (emperors), and the cult of Devaraja was continued by his successors. Temples of the Hindu god, Lord Shiva, were built with Hindu cosmology in view, that is at the exact centre of the capital city.

The great period of temple-building activity began with King Jayavarman III, who extended the boundaries of his kingdom to include Laos in the north. His son and grandson, namely Indravarman I and Yashovarman, built temples of Lord Shiva. King Yashovarman made the capital city attractive by building palaces. He was a great Sanskrit scholar who wrote a commentary on Patanjali's *Mahabhasya*. He patronised Sanskrit literature and built a new capital Yashodarapura, on the top of a hill, Phnon Baken.

King Rajendravarman of the tenth century became a great patron of Buddhism. Subsequently, King Suryavarman II, and his teacher Divakara pundit, were responsible for the construction of the greatest Hindu temple in South-East Asia, the Angkor Vat (temple for Lord Vishnu) which became one of the wonders of the world. It was built near the capital, Angkor Thom. This famous and long-lost temple was built in Dravidian style with sculptures depicting the important scenes of the *Ramayana*, the *Mahabharata* and *Harivamsha*. This temple consists of beautiful pyramids, towers and galleries.

The kingdom of Champa was subjected to several invasions by the Kambuja rulers, and King Suryavarman occupied it for nearly two decades. He was a great Sanskrit scholar and a Buddhist. His military expeditions against the kingdoms of Annam and Champa proved too costly. They led to the decline of the Khmer empire soon after his death. The king of Champa inflicted a naval defeat and destroyed the capital.

Revival and Fall of the Khmer Empire

Kambuja's decline was halted by the last great ruler, King Jayavarman VII (AD 1181 - 1280). His vast empire included the whole of Indo-China except southern Malaya, Tongking and upper Burma. He founded a new capital, the famous Angkor Thom, and surrounded it with a wall and a ditch. He built the famous temple of Bayon which is known for its architectural wonder. He built numerous temples, hospitals, and choultries which resulted in a heavy drain on the royal treasury. It eventually led to the fall of the Khmer empire.

The Chams and the Thais, particularly the latter, who were encouraged by the Mongols were responsible for the breakup of the Khmer empire. Secondly, the decline of the Khmer empire was attributed to the rise of Theravada Buddhism which denied the concept of the divine origin of kingship. The shrunken Khmer kingdoms which existed acknowledged the authority of the Thai kings. The little Kampuchea had to satisfy the whims of the two powerful neighbouring kingdoms—Thailand and Vietnam, by sending tributes to both from 1802 onwards. However, the succession dispute involving Kampuchea's throne in 1812 invited the wrath of these two powerful neighbours.

King Rama II of Thailand withdrew his troops from Kampuchea hoping that the King of Vietnam would do likewise. Unfortunately, this did not happen. The Thai King Rama III invaded Kampuchea in 1831 which forced the Khmer King to flee his country. He went to Vietnam for assistance. The Vietnamese army which supported the Khmer King defeated the Thai forces but made Kampuchea a province of Vietnam in 1834.

Kampuchea Turns into a French Protectorate

The woes of Kampuchea are a never ending saga. When the patriotic Kampucheans unofficially recognised a pro-Thai prince of their own, Prince Ang Duong, it caused a war between Thailand and Vietnam. This war was waged on Kampuchean soil and caused terrible misery. King Ang Duong wrote a letter to the French Emperor, Napoleon III (1852) seeking his assistance to liberate his country from the clutches of his powerful neighbours. Little did he know that the French Emperor himself was ambitious and wanted to build a French empire in Indo-China. After the King's death, the French forces conquered Vietnam in 1862 and claimed their right over the kingdom of

Kampuchea. Kampuchea became the French protectorate after King Norodom signed a treaty. After diplomatic melodrama between France and the Thai King, Mong Khut, during the next three years, the Thai Government gave up its claim of sovereignty over Kampuchea (1866) in return for the French recognition of Thailand's right over the Kampuchean provinces of Battambang and Siam Reap.

During the last decade of the 19th century, Britain and France were at loggerheads over Thailand's role of a buffer zone between them. Finally, there was a settlement in 1907, wherein it was decided that Thailand cede to France the two Cambodian provinces of Battambang and Siam Reap.

Roots of Kampuchean Nationalism

During the heydays of "religious nationalism" in the 1930s, the Thais demanded from France the return of Siam Reap and Battambang. This nationalism in Thailand was directed against Western imperialists. Thai nationalism became more pronounced and assertive with Japan's success in South-East Asia during World War II. The Japanese assistance to Thailand to secure the two provinces from the French was not without conditions. Thailand surrendered the two Cambodian provinces to the victorious Allies at the end of the war. Thai nationalism also affected Kampuchea in the sense that a national movement also began in Kampuchea. One common factor which affected most South-East Asian countries was Japanese victories and encouragement given to nationalist forces struggling against Western imperialism.

Struggle for Freedom in Cambodia

During the last months of World War II, King Norodom Sihanouk of Cambodia declared the independence of his country. Suspecting King Sihanouk's pro-French attitude, the Japanese encouraged the free Khmer movement which was led by a French-educated liberal named Son Ngoe Thanh. He was editing a Khmer language newspaper, *Nagaravatta* (the City News). Along with another celebrated Pali scholar, Pach-Chhoeun, Son organised a national movement with its centre at the Buddhist institute in Phnom Penh. While Pach was arrested by the French police, Son escaped to Japan in 1942.

The free Khmer movement led by Son took a new turn in March 1945 with the Japanese taking over direct control of the administration of Indo-China. Son was encouraged to oppose the return of French colonial rule in Cambodia as well as King Norodom Sihanouk (who had become known for his pro-French sympathy). However, the King pacified Son and appointed him as his premier. The King concentrated in himself all the powers of the land and did not give scope to Son to play a useful role. Therefore, Son staged a coup, with the result that the King had to give up his authority. But Son's success proved short-lived, since the Allied troops which landed in Kampuchea in 1945 deposed him. He was sentenced to 20 years of hard labour for plotting to overthrow a legitimate government. This sentence was commuted later, and Son went to Thailand after his release. With the permission of the Thai Government Son set up a provisional government of Cambodia on the soil of Thailand.

Hostility Towards French Rule

The French tried to grant an autonomous status to Cambodia in 1946 but King Norodom Sihanouk felt that French rule over his kingdom was unbearable. There was a change of attitude found in the King's behaviour during this time. He began to hate the French domination and began to sympathise with the liberation struggle. In the meantime, the Democrat Party in Cambodia opposed the continuation of French rule, and subsequently the King himself championed the cause of liberation. The people of Cambodia began to treat the King with great respect since he symbolised in his person the national aspirations. His immense popularity forced the members of the Khmer Issarak (free Khmer movement) to surrender and join the Democrat Party. They all expected that King Norodom would lead the nation towards achieving the goal of total independence. In spite of the best efforts of the King in this direction, the French continued to waver.

They were prepared to give autonomy, but not total independence to Cambodia. Therefore, the King had to face a number of difficulties since a large majority of the population and the National Assembly totally opposed the continuation of French rule. It was at this time that Son returned to the Cambodian capital to revive the freedom movement. The King was not prepared for this and therefore, did not tolerate Son's activities. The King continued to act like a dictator and dismissed the Cabinet with the hope that the National Assembly would grant him unlimited powers to govern the country.

Total Independence (1953)

In January 1953, Sihanouk surprised everyone by asking people to join him to fight for independence, and tried to secure international sympathy for his freedom movement. His whirlwind campaigning across France and the United States was for this purpose. It was in the month of November that his efforts were crowned with success. After protracted negotiations with the French Government, Kampuchea was granted total independence on November 9, 1953. The King returned to Kampuchea on the independence day which incidentally happened to be his birthday.

Foreign Relations

During the next few years, Kampuchea under Prince Sihanouk tried to achieve consolidation and integration. She followed the policy of neutrality in foreign affairs in spite of the Indo-China war. The Khmers of Kampuchea accorded him divine status and appreciated his efforts to free the nation from French control. Sihanouk carried out major electoral reforms and even abdicated his throne so as to enable the people to choose him as an undisputed constitutional monarch through a referendum in 1960. The people of Kampuchea confirmed his position by casting their votes in his favour. His political party, namely, the Popular Socialist Community, received a thumping majority and its opponent, the Democrat Party, lost heavily in the general election.

In foreign policy, Sihanouk had to face serious challenges. The most important aspect of his foreign policy was to see that the Indo-China war did not disturb his state. Unfortunately, Thailand and Vietnam had been aggressive neighbours casting their covetous eyes on Kampuchea. King Sihanouk tried in vain to secure an alliance with the Government of the United States in order to seek military protection. At the same time, he endorsed Jawaharlal Nehru's principles of Panchasheel (five principles of co-existence). Nehru helped Sihanouk in getting an assurance from Communist China and the Democratic Republic of Vietnam that they would not pose a threat to Kampuchea's sovereignty and independence.

In the midst of the Vietnam war, the US forces and the communist guerillas started violating the borders of Kampuchea. It was this situation which led Sihanouk to sever diplomatic ties with the United States in 1965. Sihanouk described the United States as the "number one enemy". He gave tacit consent to the Vietnamese communists to use the borders of his country as sanctuaries to save themselves from the heavy bombing raids of the US. He recognised the National Liberation Force (NLF) which maintained a legation in his capital, Phnom Penh. He leaned more and more towards Communist China, probably expecting the latter to restrain North Vietnam from arming and aiding the Khmer Rouge communist rebels operating on Kampuchea's borders in 1968. When this attempt failed, he normalised his country's relations with the United States.

The Khmer Rouge

It must be remembered that in 1954, the Vietminh (North Vietnamese soliders) stopped supporting the cause of the Khmer Resistance Force (KRF) which was fighting for the total independence of Kampuchea and also against Sihanouk. This was because Hanoi was under pressure from China, India and Russia. The "Hanoi Khmers" withdrew their forces to North Vietnam. This was considered a gross betrayal on the part of a band of young rebels known as the New Khmer Rouge in Kampuchea which included leaders like Pol Pot, Khieu Samphan, Leng Sary, Hou Yuon and so on. These leaders played on the sensitivities of those who were against Sihanouk (particularly the tribal people and urban youth) and made them plot for the overthrow of the Government of Sihanouk.

Kampuchea, a Pawn in International Power Politics

As mentioned earlier, Sihanouk restored normal relations with the United States Government in 1968. He appointed Lon Nol and Prince Serik (both known for their opposition to communism) to advise him on important matters. Unfortunately, when he went abroad for medical reasons, these two advisors brought about the end of his government in 1970. This happened at a time when Sihanouk was on his way back home from his trip abroad. It compelled King Sihanouk to take political asylum in Communist China. It was there that he set up a new government of Cambodia in exile. President Nixon began to interfere in the pro-US Lon Nol regime by sending assistance to crush the Khmer Rouge. The US policy under President Nixon spread the Vietnam war to Kampuchea also.

Poor Kampuchea became a pawn in national and international power politics. She was to witness a terrible civil war with the Khmer Rouge communist guerillas led by a Maoist, Pol Pot, capturing the capital of Phnom Penh (April 1975). Pol Pot succeeded in establishing what is known as the Kampuchean People's Republic. It was his regime which let loose a reign of terror in the country which cost nearly 1.7 million lives, and forced tens of thousands of Kampucheans to flee to the neighbouring country of Thailand.

By January 1979, the Vietnamese troops invaded Cambodia and captured Phnom Penh. They set up a new Government led by Heng Samrin. But this Government was not recognised by the United Nations. Several attempts to dislodge the Vietnamese troops from Cambodia failed miserably. Thus Vietnam controlled Cambodia during the next four years. It was in 1989 that the exiled King Sihanouk staged a comeback after becoming the leader of a coalition of anti-government forces. All the factions involved in the Cambodian conflict came together under the aegis of the United Nations to bury their hatchet and signed an agreement in October 1991.

Attempts at National Reconciliation

The Vietnamese-controlled Phnom Penh administration in Cambodia (1979-1993) finally came to an end. Under the supervision of the UN observers, a multi-party general election was held in May 1993 in Cambodia for setting up a Constituent Assembly. The Khmer Rouge boycotted the polls. The royalist Funcinpec party secured a large number of seats. An interim government was set up by three political parties. A new Constitution was drafted in September 1993, and it was approved by all. Prince Sihanouk was invited and subsequently made King of Cambodia. The new government declared the Khmer Rouge as outlaw in July 1994. The Khmer Rouge formed its own government under the leadership of Pol Pot, the cold-blooded murderer of millions of his countrymen. The new government did not want the Khmer Rouge guerillas to create problems. Hence, the two Premiers, Hun Sen and Prince Ranariddh decided to start negotiations with the Khmer Rouge to persuade it to join the mainstream of national politics. This was to end in a national reconciliation with the Khmer Rouge participating in the next elections to be held in 1998.

In June 1997 the rebels in the Khmer Rouge reported that Pol Pot was captured in the jungles. In the meantime, the military units loyal to the two premiers started fighting in Phnom Penh. Hun Sen, the second co-Premier, emerged supreme with his loyal troops taking control of Phnom Penh in July 1997. Prince Ranariddh (son of King Sihanouk) fled the country and sought the intervention of the United Nations. Cambodia's military court passed a 30-year sentence on Prince Ranariddh for colluding with the outlawed Khmer Rouge to overthrow the legitimate government of Hun Sen and bringing arms to the country illegally. Prince Ranariddh was stripped of his parliamentary immunity. The ASEAN appealed to the UN to "ensure Ranariddh's return to Cambodia." In April 1998, Pol Pot died in a jungle-hut close to the border of Thailand. With his death, a bloody chapter in Cambodian history ended. The United States Government is insisting on the trial of the other notorious Khmer Rouge leaders, namely, General Ta Mok ("the butcher"), Khieu Samphan, and Nuon Chea, for the war crimes. They have surrendered to the government after leaving the jungle hideout. Unfortunately, Hun Sen is not keen on the trial of these criminals by a UN appointed tribunal for crimes committed against humanity. In July 1998, elections were held in Cambodia, and Hun Sen emerged the winner. The opposition parties accused his party (Cambodian People's Party) of rigging the elections.

Recently King Norodom Sihanouk reappointed Hun Sen as the prime minister following one year political stalemate. In the last election held in July 2003, the Cambodian People's Party (CPP) won a majority of seats in the Parliament, but fell short of 2/3 majority required to govern the country alone. His rival Chea-Sim, acting head of the state and the president of the CCP, was forced to flee the country to avoid arrest.

25

VIETNAM (ANNAM+CHAMPA)

One of the Bronze Age sites of the Dong-Son culture was discovered a few decades ago in Vietnam. The people belonging to the Mongoloid race living on the borders of south China migrated to other parts of the South-East Asian peninsula long time ago. Those who came to the Vietnamese borders spoke a language akin to the Thai group of languages but mixed with some Mon-Khmer words. When there was an increase in the flow of emigrants from China in due course, the people living on the borders drifted towards the Red River delta. Vietnam is known by other names such as Namviet and Annam and the people came under the influence of the Chinese rather than the Indians in ancient times. Namviet was under the influence of a secessionist Chinese state in Canton for about two centuries. However, with the emergence of the Han empire of China these parts were annexed in 111 BC. Namviet adopted a Chinese type of state as well as government, and it was based on "rice culture" or "agrarian based civilisation". This Namviet kingdom under Chinese control continued to exist on the irrigated plains for more than a thousand years. It copied the cultural patterns of some neighbouring countries in general, but the major influence was Chinese. What is interesting is that it borrowed ideas on laws, politics, religion and administration from India. The Mahayana form of Buddhism spread to Namviet in the 5th century AD through Chinese scholars. In the meantime, the Indianised-Champa kingdom grew rapidly on the coast of South Vietnam.

The Rise and Growth of Champa Kingdom

The Chams, who inhabited the Champa kingdom, belonged to a Malaya-Polynesian group believing in the Devaraja cult. The Champa kingdom grew along the south coast of Vietnam and the people were known for sea-faring since agriculture could not flourish due to scarcity of cultivable lands. In the course of time, the Chams became quite prosperous because they acted as agents of maritime trade that was going on between China and India on the one side, and China and the West on the other. An early Chinese record informs us that a local official Kin-Lien (Sri Mara) overthrew the Chinese authority and declared its independence in AD 192. Ever since its birth, the kingdom of

Map of Indo-China

Champa expanded towards the north by taking advantage of the decline of the Han empire. The continuous raids of the Champa kingdom from the time of King Sri Mara and his successors resulted in the conquest of Tonkin. However, the imperial ambitions of the Champa kingdom were checked after the birth of the Tsin dynasty in China around the third century AD. The kingdom of Champa under Fan-Yi sent its ambassador to the court of the Chinese emperor in AD 284 indicating the end of its hostility towards China. But this was to be a temporary truce, and its wars with China resumed during the middle of the fourth century. The imperial policy of the Champa kingdom resulted in the acquisition of three districts in North Vietnam (Nhut-Nam) which were then under Chinese control.

The Indian rulers with Chinese names continued to rule the Champa kingdom for the next few centuries. The greatest among the Champa kings was Fan-Hu-Ta (AD 380-413) who is identified as Bhadravarman. He was a great Sanskrit scholar. He ruled over three provinces of the Champa kingdom, namely, Amaravati, Vijaya and Panduranga, and built the Bhadresvara (Lord Shiva) temple at Mi-Son. Sanskrit was patronised as the language of his court. A protracted war with China during his reign resulted in the recovery of Nhut-Nam.

After the death of Bhadravarman, the kingdom of Champa suffered defeat and destruction at the hands of Chinese forces. It was forced to acknowledge the suzerainty of the Chinese time and again. By AD 527, the dynasty founded by Sri Mara ended. There were several other Hindu dynasties which ruled Champa till the 13th century, and many sent tributes to China. These Hindu kings built temples for the Hindu gods, patronised Sanskrit, and administered their states on the basis of Hindu customs and traditions.

Annamite (Vietnamese) Invasions

It is from the tenth century that one observes the frequent invasions of the Annamites (Vietnamese). There was a continuous rivalry between the Champa kingdom and the Annamite kingdom situated in the north till the sixteenth century. This rivalry resulted in the loss of two northern provinces for the Champa kingdom. The Annamites had become bold by the sixteenth century and declared their independence. One of the last rulers of the Champa kingdom took refuge in Khambuja on account of the frequent raids of the Annamites. In the meantime, the Annamites established their control over the Mekong delta.

Who were these Annamites? They were the descendants of those who had long ago settled in the "Tongking rice-bowl" of the Red River delta, which had become a province of the Chinese empire. It was in AD 939, a time when the Tang empire in China was declining, that the Annamites, led by Ngo Quyen, declared their independence. They named their independent kingdom Dai-Co-Viet. However, since the forces of the Champa kingdom frequently raided their territories, the rulers of Dai-Co-Viet felt it necessary to acknowledge the suzerainty of the Chinese empire. They remained vassals of the Chinese, expecting that China should come to the rescue of their state, whenever the Cham forces invaded their territory. It was also expected by Dai-Co-Viet that China would adopt a policy of non-interference with regard to her internal matters. The tributary status of Dai-Co-Viet continued till 1885.

The Li Dynasty

The Li dynasty ruled over Vietnam for nearly two centuries (AD 1010-1225) and maintained a Chinese pattern of administration. The kings of this dynasty successfully overcame natural disasters such as floods and droughts which occurred in their state by organising a good irrigation system.

The Tram Dynasty

The next dynasty to assume power was the Tram dynasty which ruled Vietnam for more than 175 years. The kings of these dynasties were able to organise the defence-preparedness of the country in the face of Mongolian invasions in 1257, 1285 and 1287. The Mongols captured Hanoi three times, but after recovering a tribute each time the kingdom was set free.

The Conquest of Vietnam

The famous Ming Emperor, Yung Lo, made a determined attempt to make Vietnam a province of China. The imperial forces appeared on the borders of Vietnam in 1418 at a time when a war of independence had broken out. The Ming Emperor succeeded in his mission, but soon realised his mistake. By this time the people of Vietnam had decided not to come under Chinese rule. Therefore, the Chinese imperial forces were pulled out of Vietnam. The old tributary system was restored and Vietnam turned into a vassal state.

The Le Dynasty (1428-1788)

The leader of the independence movement in Vietnam was Le Loi, who after overthrowing the Chinese suzerainty assumed the title of an emperor. But he continued to send his tributes to the Chinese emperor to maintain cordial relations. His kingdom came to be called Dai-Viet (meaning great). In 1417, the Annamite Emperor, Le Thanh-Ton, marched his troops and also ordered his fleet for the capture of the Champa city, Vijaya. Thus ended the long established kingdom of Champa. In its place, there appeared a petty Champa kingdom which struggled hard to achieve independence in 1543 but failed.

Partition of Vietnam

Several factors such as population growth, political intrigues among Vietnamese generals and the inability of Vietnam to expand all contributed to the decline of the new Vietnamese kingdom. In the meantime, the Mac dynasty founded by Mac Dang Dung (a Vietnamese General) established its control over the Tongking region in 1527. China gave its recognition to this new kingdom. However, the new kingdom of Tongking was overthrown in 1592 by Trinh, a nobleman related to yet another new family called Ngu Yen. The Ngu Yen dynasty started ruling over the south central region of Vietnam. There was no love lost between the Trinh family based in Hanoi and the Ngu Yen family with its headquarters at Hue with the result that the country witnessed a civil war for about half a century (1620-74). Vietnam remained divided into North and South because of these two warring dynasties. The Ngu Yen dynasty closed the narrow coastal lane that connected the northern neighbour by erecting two great walls along the seventeenth parallel. The Ngu Yen dynasty began to conquer the southernmost territories which belonged to Kampuchea and annexed all the regions up to the Mekong delta.

The Advent of Europeans

The Vietnamese ports were visited by Japanese and Chinese merchants for the purpose of trade in the past. The Portuguese arrived here in the 16th century to buy raw silk. The Jesuits followed the Portuguese merchants in 1615 and attempted to start their missionary work. But, the Trinh rulers forbade the

Jesuits from entering their kingdom because they did not like their proselytising activity. The Jesuits thereafter went to the Ngu Yen kingdom in the south where they were tolerated, not because of their activities, but because of the prospects of trade and supply of arms. Now and then, the missionaries were persecuted for abusing the customs and traditions of the natives. In the course of time, the Jesuits gained the confidence of the courtiers with their practical knowledge of science and medicine. They gave the Vietnamese "the modern form of Vietnamese writing". A French Jesuit named Alexander Rhodes established a Christian mission in North Vietnam in 1627 and gained the full confidence of the people of the Ngu Yen kingdom in the South. In the meantime, the French East India company acquired the licence from the French Government to trade in Vietnam. Its rivals, the British and the Dutch, had been waiting in the queue for concessions from rulers of the kingdom. The French evinced keen interest in Vietnamese culture and civilisation.

The Tayson Rebellion

In the history of Vietnam, the last quarter of the 18th century proved to be a watershed because the country witnessed a revolution followed by unification. The authors of the revolution were the Tayson brothers, who were supported by the common peasants in bringing about the unification of the country. The Tayson brothers were disgusted with the corrupt administration of the Tongking and gathered the support of the common people and peasants and staged the revolt. They succeeded in their coup against the Trinh regime in the North and the Ngu Yen regime in the South (1778-1786). The Chinese invasion followed in 1788 for the ostensible purpose of restoring the old Le dynasty, but it failed miserably because of the heroic efforts of the Tayson brothers. The hero who successfully repulsed the Chinese attacks was one of the Tayson brothers and he was proclaimed the Emperor of united Vietnam with the name Quang-Trung. However, he had to send an envoy to the Chinese imperial court to secure recognition of his government for united Vietnam. His short rule of four years witnessed the rise of nationalism coupled with xenophobia.

The Revival of Ngu Yen Family

The surviving heir of the Ngu Yen family, named Ngu Yen Anh, enjoyed the sympathy of the people. He was living in the Ca Mau peninsula where he had taken refuge during the time of revolution. He was indeed lucky to secure the support of a French priest named Pigneau de Behaine. This French priest pleaded the cause of the unfortunate prince with the government at Versailles. Pigneau concluded an alliance with the French Government acting on behalf of the unlucky prince. It was not long before French volunteers led by Pigneau arrived in Vietnam with several shiploads of arms from Pondicherry. The French assistance proved to be very valuable to the prince in his fight against the usurpers, he captured Saigon in 1788 and followed it by the capture of Hue in 1801 and Hanoi in 1802. Unfortunately, Pigneau lost his life in 1799 fighting the battles. Prince Ngu Yen Anh was proclaimed the emperor of Annam in 1892 with the title of Gia Long—the title indicating the political unification of the Tongking and Mekong deltas. He secured the recognition of the Chinese court for his government after agreeing to pay tributes.

Achievements of Gia Long

Gia Long provided dynamic leadership to his country and took steps for the consolidation of Vietnam. Among his several reforms, the most noteworthy were the territorial reorganisation of the whole country and the shifting of the capital to Hue. The territories of his country were constituted into three divisions, namely, Tongking, Annam and Cochin-China, which were in turn sub-divided into 26 provinces. In each province, there were districts, sub-districts and hundreds of villages. Gia Long administered the country on the model of the Chinese and he was assisted by a large number of ministers who constituted the Supreme Council. Civil servants were appointed after passing the Civil Service examination and they were further trained to achieve mastery of the new code of laws, which "was based on the Chinese principles of jurisprudence". Gia Long is remembered in Vietnam for the yeoman service rendered to his subjects. It was he who took up the task of reconstructing national life following three decades of civil war. He is also remembered for having laid the Mandarin Road, which covers a distance of 1,300 miles connecting three important cities, namely, Hue, Hanoi and Saigon. The Marxist historians have been very critical about his achievements because he came to power with the help of the French Government.

The French Conquest of Indo-China

The persecution of French missionaries and converts in Vietnam began in the early 19th century by Emperor Minh Mang. It became the main reason for the intervention of the French Government in the internal affairs of Vietnam. The matter became worse when the Emperor prevented the entry of foreign missionaries, followed by the destruction of a few Catholic churches in Vietnam. The lives of the Christian missionaries were in danger. The Emperor closed Vietnamese ports to all foreign merchants. In 1846, French ships went on the offensive and blockaded the port of Da Nang for nearly two weeks following it up with continuous bombardment. This was done as a protest against the policy of the Vietnamese Government towards foreigners in general, and for passing the death sentence on a French priest in particular. The French Government expected the Vietnamese Government to grant pardon to the French priest. Unfortunately, the continuous bombardment resulted in the death of several hundred Vietnamese. In the meantime, the French Emperor, Napoleon

III, who was waiting for an opportunity to improve his sagging popularity at home intervened in Vietnam on behalf of the French Catholic priests.

The French-Vietnamese Treaty

The successors of Minh Mang named Thien-tri (1841-47) and Tu-duc got into serious trouble because of the diplomatic pressure from France. After signing a treaty in 1862, Tu-duc ceded to France the three provinces in Cochin-China, including Saigon. The treaty promised French merchants and missionaries commercial and religious freedoms respectively, and by another clause in the treaty, they promised a future French protectorate over Annam. The right to navigate on the Mekong River for trade purposes further strengthened the French political and commercial control over Vietnam. While the French historians have attributed the easy success of the French to the inefficiency of the administration of the Vietnamese rulers, the historians of Vietnam have discarded this theory and blamed the backward looking mandarins of their country for bringing about this debacle. The defeat of Vietnam enabled France to put forward her claim over the kingdom of Kampuchea by virtue of replacing Vietnamese overlordship. Eventually, the Franco-Khmer Treaty was signed.

It took another eleven years for France to extend her control over the whole of North Vietnam, thanks to the ambitious and adventurous activities of her explorers, namely, Admiral Duprei, Francis Garner, and Jean Dupuis. In the course of a perilous expedition aimed at discovering a new trade route to south China, Da Lagrec lost his life. His partner Garnier managed to return to Saigon safely via Hankow. He produced a voluminous report detailing how the Red River route (which he had explored) would be specially beneficial to France in the long run. It would secure commercial benefits and finally pave the way for acquiring the Tongking delta. In fact, the South Chinese trade in silk, tea and textiles passed through the Tongking delta and not through Canton as believed earlier.

The Occupation of Tongking Delta

After the fall of the second French empire there was a hue and cry in France that she should make a very bold attempt to build an empire in Indo-China. It was this ambition which compelled the French Government to explore the Mekong delta region under the leadership of Jean Dupuis. His efforts were supported by Garnier and blessed by the governor of Cochin-China, Admiral Duprei. The French explorations provoked Vietnamese Emperor Tu-duc, who lodged a serious protest. However, Admiral Duprei pretended as though he would punish the French explorers who were guilty of carrying out these expeditions into the Vietnamese territories. Whatever may be the case, the French ultimately occupied the Tongking delta. A few furious mandarins shot dead Garnier. The French Government continued to feign ignorance about the expedition and also incursions into the Vietnamese territories. The Vietnamese Emperor finally signed a treaty in 1873 with the French Government which provided three ports of Tonking for French commerce and also the stationing of French troops and consul.

North Vietnam Becomes a French Protectorate

Within another decade, the French Government under Jules Ferry got an opportunity to extend further control over North Vietnam. The Government blamed the Vietnamese Emperor for violating the treaty of 1873, in that the latter continued to send tribute to a Chinese emperor even though Vietnam had come under French control. Secondly, it was very annoyed when the Vietnamese mandarins obstructed the progress of the French expedition led by Henry Riviere at the Red River delta. The objective of the expedition was to get rid of the bandits operating there.

China recognised the French control over North Vietnam after signing the Treaty of Tientsin in 1885. This treaty provided for many commercial and railway concessions to the French by China in preference to other Western nations in the south Chinese provinces of Yunnan and Vietnam. "The Treaty marked the extinction of the nearly two millennia old subordinate relationship between Vietnam and China and completed the French domination over all of Vietnam."

ORIGINS OF VIETNAMESE NATIONAL MOVEMENT

The early traces of Vietnamese nationalism go back to the early centuries of the Christian era when the Vietnamese made bold attempts to oppose Chinese domination. Subsequently, the Vietnamese continued to revolt against the Chinese domination in the early fifteenth century. After the conquest of Vietnam by the French in 1885, the French imperialists started following a policy of assimilation with respect to the people of Vietnam. In their attempt to accomplish this, they destroyed the traditional village autonomy and imposed Central control. French rule was also opposed by the natives of Cochin-China in the 1860s and also in the early decades of the 20th century. The resistance movement in this region was led by the scholar-gentry which enjoyed the support of the peasants.

Nationalist Leaders

Two major events of the early 20th century that had a deep impact on the progress of the Vietnamese national movement, viz the defeat of Russia at the hands of Japan (1904-05) and the overthrow of the Manchu dynasty in China in 1911. These events inspired two Vietnamese leaders, Phan Boi Chan and Phan Chan Trinh, to organise a national movement for the liberation of Vietnam. The former was a popular writer and scholar in addition to heading an organisation called Duy Tan Hoi. He advocated enlightened monarchy as a panacea for all the ills of Vietnam. On the other hand, Phan Chan Trinh discarded it as obsolete and pleaded for the introduction of the Western type of democracy in Vietnam. Phan Chan Trinh was arrested and sent to languish in French prison for his audacity to organise a tax resistance movement in 1908. The Vietnamese participated in the First World War with the hope that their conditions would improve after its conclusion. However, their hopes were dashed to the ground, since the French Government was not prepared to concede their demands.

Birth of the Vietnamese Nationalist Party (VNQDD)

There emerged a number of political organisations, some Marxist and others non-Marxist which instigated uprisings against the continuation of French rule in Vietnam. Out of them, the Vietnamese Nationalist Party (VNQDD) founded in 1927 had a large following, mainly due to the adoption of the principles of nationalism, democracy and socialism (Sun Yat Sen's principles) as their objectives.

The Marxist group included communists and Trotskyites and these two groups merged in the course of time under the dynamic leadership of Ngu Yen Ali Quoc (known later as Ho Chi Minh).

Ho Chi Minh was born in a mandarin family in 1890. He joined the marine service and left his homeland as a cabin-boy. He spent some years in London and subsequently in Paris, where he wrote pamphlets for the leftists. Intensely patriotic, he waved placards outside the Versailles Conference demanding self-determination for his country. He joined the French Socialist Party. Thereafter, he visited Moscow as a Communist Party delegate in order to participate in the Peasant International. He went to Canton to work as an assistant and translator to Michael Borodin, who became the Russian advisor to the Kuomintang Party in China. In the meantime, Ho Chi Minh formed the Thanh Nien, ie, the Association of Vietnamese Revolutionary Youth. Inspired by the Comintern, Ho Chi Minh gave opportunities to many volunteers of his newly-founded organisations to take training in China and Russia. In 1930, Ho Chi Minh united the three communist groups under the banner, Indo-China Communist Party (ICP). It consisted of 1,500 members and enjoyed the general support of many peasant organisations in Vietnam.

The Revolt of 1930-31

A revolt against French rule in Vietnam was organised by VNQDD in 1930, which failed despite popular support. This was because of a leak by which the French authorities came to know of the impending event well in advance. The French authorities crushed this revolt mercilessly and got many leaders arrested, and some executed. The political void left by the decline of VNQDD was to be filled by the communists. The ICP organised a revolt of the peasants in May 1930, which failed leading to hundreds of communists getting arrested with some even being executed. Fortunately, the leader of the ICP, Ho Chi Minh, escaped to Hong Kong. In due course, Ho Chi Minh was arrested and jailed by the British during the period 1930-33.

Constitutional Monarchy

The frequent uprisings in Vietnam had the desired effect on the makers of French foreign policy. The French Government tried to secure public sympathy in Vietnam by asking Prince Bao Dai to become the constitutional monarch and introduced necessary reforms. A moderate and liberal leader named Ngo Dinh Diem, who headed the Interior Ministry went ahead with his plans to introduce reforms which his country so badly needed. Unfortunately, the reforms did not get underway because the King had to seek the consent of the French Government. The French withheld consent for no reason. Probably, the French Government felt that the reforms were too radical for its acceptance. Ngo Dinh Diem resigned as the Chief of the Reform Commission in 1933. The Popular Front Government in France ordered the political prisoners in Vietnam to be released and the ICP took advantage of this opportunity to reorganise itself into a political party, the Democratic National Front, attracting into its fold not only the leftists but also the patriotic rightists. The leaders of this party were Pham Van Dong and Vo Nguyen Giap, who subsequently worked hand in hand with Ho Chi Minh.

In the meantime, the Popular Front Government in France fell, with the result that the Communist Party was banned. When the Second World War broke out, the Japanese overran the whole of South-East Asia. In the case of Indo-China, Japan came to an understanding with the French Vichy Government in 1940 that it could continue its rule over Vietnam on condition that it permitted Japanese military activities in the Vietnamese ports. The French Government was also asked to make available the vast resources of Vietnam to the Japanese.

The Japanese act of permitting the French colonial government to continue functioning incurred the wrath of the Vietnamese. When Ho Chi Minh was released from prison, he convened a meeting of the Central Committee in south China (1941) where it was decided to change the political objective from "agrarian reforms and class revolution to the immediate goal of independence ...". It was in these circumstances that the League of Independence of Vietnam (Viet Minh) was established, and Ho Chi Minh chosen as its Secretary-General. The Viet Minh decided to start Salvation Associations everywhere to fight the enemies of Vietnam, namely, France and Japan. By 1944, the Viet Minh had a strength of 5,000 volunteers who controlled three border provinces. This force was commanded by the most redoubtable

Vietnamese General, namely, Vo Nguyen Giap. In 1945 he was also commanding guerilla forces known as the Viet Cong, and at the same time establishing bases in the Tongking region.

In March 1945, the Japanese who were playing second fiddle to the French in Vietnam, finally seized power after imprisoning the French rulers. They established a puppet regime of Emperor Bao Dai (this time to act as a Japanese agent after forsaking the French). In the meantime, the Viet Minh was successful in establishing what is called liberated zones on the Vietnamese-Chinese borders. It was from these liberated zones that the Viet Minh tried to penetrate into the Red River delta.

The Aftermath of Japanese Surrender

In the middle of August 1945, the Japanese forces surrendered to the Allies with the result that there was a political vacuum in Vietnam. Emperor Bao Dai abdicated in favour of the Viet Minh, the only power there to run an independent government in Vietnam. Ho Chi Minh declared Vietnam's independence to a milling crowd on September 2, 1945 after the capture of Hanoi. This event heralded the birth of the Democratic Republic of Vietnam.

Vietnam Partitioned

Following the conclusion of the war, the Allies decided that Vietnam should be governed by Nationalist China and Britain, the former to operate above the 16th parallel and the latter below it. The British released the French officials from prison in South Vietnam and asked them to administer the territory temporarily on her behalf. Ironically, France which had herself been occupied by the German army witnessed the liberation of her soil by the Allied troops. She lost no time now in asserting her imperial rights over the whole of Indo-China. The Chinese troops with VNQDD and the Dong Minh Hoi partitioned Hanoi, the capital of North Vietnam into several pockets giving authority to the Viet Minh to look after only a few pockets. The struggle of the Viet Minh in the south was to no avail. Her appeal for help from the USA and China became a cry in the wilderness.

It was at this time that Ho Chi Minh, as the leader of Viet Minh, found his job most difficult and challenging. He had to take up the task of liberating and uniting the divided country from formidable enemies. Undaunted by these adversities, he carefully planned to destroy the enemies so as to bring about freedom to his country. He was aware that it would mean a long struggle against the Western imperialists.

Ho Chi Minh suddenly announced the dissolution of the ICP on November 5, 1945, and agreed to cede 10 seats to VNQDD in the forthcoming elections for the National Assembly. He agreed to share power along with Dong Minh Hoi.

Forming a coalition ministry, he signed an agreement with France permitting the French troops to replace the Nationalist Chinese troops in Hanoi. What he desired in return was France's recognition to the Democratic Republic of Vietnam as a free state with its own government but under the control of the French Union. The modalities of the actual working of this new set-up were to be accomplished through negotiations between the concerned parties. Ho Chi Minh was in fact planning to eliminate foreign powers one by one from Vietnamese soil like Bismarck who accomplished this for Germany in the 19th century. He was quite successful in expelling the Nationalist Chinese troops who had been causing a lot of trouble in his country.

The Indo-China War (1946-54)

At the conference held in Fontainebleau the French made things difficult for the Democratic Republic of Vietnam by breaking the promises made earlier, and separating Cochin-China from Vietnam. In fact, the French wanted to rule Cochin-China through a puppet regime. What followed was hostile actions by both, but France exceeded its limit by launching aerial and naval bombardments at the Port of Haiphong in November 1946. These bombardments caused heavy casualties, killing nearly 6,000 Vietnamese civilians. The Viet Minh retaliated by attacking the French strategic posts everywhere, including Hanoi. A full scale Indo-China war broke out lasting eight years between the Viet Minh forces of North Vietnam and the French-American led South Vietnamese forces. The Viet Minh forces (including the Viet Cong) showed their devotion and dedication to the cause of Vietnamese independence which evoked popular sympathy.

The Recognition of DRV

Showing no desire to terminate her colonial rule, France declared in 1949 the emergence of the Republic of Vietnam as a part of the French Union, with Laos and Cambodia being treated as associated states. In the meantime, Britain and the United States declared their recognition to the French-controlled Vietnamese Republic which provoked the Soviet Union and Communist China to retaliate by declaring their recognition to the DRV led by Ho Chi Minh. The Cold War thus spread to Indo-China thanks to the rivalry between the two superpowers.

The Course of the War

The war which dragged on for nearly eight years tested the patience, courage and the strength of the Viet Minh. During this critical time, the redoubtable Viet Minh General, General Giap, employed the methods of guerilla warfare. The Viet Cong came to be dreaded by the French and subsequently by the American forces in the Vietnam war. France was at the end of its tether because the war took a heavy toll and also seriously disturbed the French political system, that is French ministries rising and falling frequently. The war ended disastrously for France, in spite of American assistance, with the capture of their strongest fortress, Dien Bien Phu (May 7, 1954), by the Viet Minh forces. The Viet Minh lost a staggering toll of nearly 50,000 soldiers, while the French forces lost 70,000 men. France lost its interest in holding on to this colony and sued for peace. At the Geneva Conference, which began the next day, the two parties to the Indo-China war agreed to the following terms:

1. Vietnam was to be temporarily divided into two parts, the North and the South with the dividing line being the Seventeenth parallel.

2. France to give up her control over North Vietnam and the Viet Minh to evacuate her troops from South Vietnam, as well as Laos and Cambodia.

3. General election would be held in July 1956 for the whole of Vietnam for the purpose of deciding reunification of the country.

4. France was to declare the total independence of her protectorates, namely, Cambodia and Laos. After achieving independence, these two states were to remain neutral.

Geneva Agreement Violated

Thus, North Vietnam came under the control of the Viet Minh with Hanoi as its headquarters, and the South with Saigon as its capital. The Geneva Accord was to be implemented under the aegis of the International Control Commission constituted by India (Chairman), Poland and Canada. The terms of the Geneva Accord agreed upon by both France and the Viet Minh were not in written form. Unfortunately, the accord was violated mainly by South Vietnam with the support of the United States and France.

In the meantime, the French appointed Ngo Dinh Diem as the prime minister of South Vietnam. He attracted the attention of the United States after he solved the Catholic refugee problem. It was then that the US assisted him to consolidate his position vis-a-vis the Chief of the State, Bao Dai. A referendum in October 1955 brought about the fall of Bao Dai and his replacement by Ngo Dinh Diem. The US-supported Ngo Dinh Diem refused to endorse the Geneva Accord which included the holding of the general election in July 1956 for the purpose of reunification of Vietnam. Thus, the US Government began to play a game aimed at containing communist expansion in South and South-East Asia. In their scheme of things, the South Vietnamese President perfectly fitted as a useful tool. After failing to save China from the jaws of communism in 1949, the United States was not prepared to give up her next opportunity of saving Vietnam from communism.

Ngo Dinh Diem's oppressive policies alienated the sympathies of the South Vietnamese. His land reforms were not radical enough to bring about a proper redistribution of lands among the landless. He was accused of favouring the people of his own community, the Catholics, who had come from North Vietnam. He was also accused of misusing the economic assistance provided by the United States Government.

The North Vietnamese leaders were also very unhappy at the turn of events which kept Vietnam a divided country. The international community did not make any serious attempt to pressurise the US-supported South Vietnamese Government to ratify the Geneva Accord and hold elections. It was at this critical juncture (May 1959) that the Ho Chi Minh-led North Vietnamese Government decided to liberate South Vietnam by overthrowing the Diem regime. It was for this avowed purpose that North Vietnam established the National Liberation Front (NLF) in South Vietnam in 1960, with the support of the disgruntled South Vietnamese. The brain behind this scheme of encouraging the South Vietnamese to revolt against their government was that of Ho Chi Minh. North Vietnam started giving secret assistance to the southerners in the form of arms supplies, military training and provision of manpower. In the 1960s South Vietnam witnessed several insurgencies against its government with the connivance of the North Vietnamese Government.

The Fall of Diem

In 1962 the Diem Government faced a serious crisis known as the Buddhist crisis. The president's brother and his wife were involved in the stopping of the celebration of the birthday of the Buddha. The Buddhist monks were provoked and thereafter revolted. The oppressive regime of Diem crushed this revolt mercilessly without giving any thought to the possible repercussions. A Buddhist monk felt so outraged by these merciless killings of his brethren that he committed self-immolation. The whole world came to know of this great tragedy, and the US took cognizance of Diem's unpopularity. In the end, the South Vietnamese generals brought about the overthrow of the Diem Government. The president and his brother were assassinated on November 1, 1963 with the tacit support of the American Government. What followed was a game of musical chairs played by the greedy army generals of South Vietnam. It was this situation that provided a good opportunity to the National Liberation Front to extend its control and influence over hundreds of villages in South Vietnam.

The US Involvement in the Vietnamese War

In August 1964, President Lyndon Johnson informed the Americans that an armed American vessel *Turner Joy* joining the *USS Maddox* had been attacked by the North Vietnamese torpedo boats outside the North Vietnamese territorial waters (the Gulf of Tongking). Subsequently, the President informed the Americans that he was retaliating to the war-like situation by ordering aerial bombardment of North Vietnamese military installations. Without knowing much about what was happening in the Gulf of Tongking, the Americans Senators and Representatives gave full authority to the president to take suitable action against North Vietnam.

Thus, the US administration was involved in an undeclared war with Vietnam and perpetrated horrible atrocities on the people of North Vietnam. The American blunder was exposed by Senator Fulbright who became a severe critic of the president's Vietnamese policy (*see* his book *Arrogance of Power.*) It became necessary for North Vietnam to give adequate assistance to the NLF in South Vietnam. For Johnson who dragged the US into the quagmire (dirty war), it cost him his chance of getting re-elected as president. He declined to contest for the second term, and his successor, Richard Nixon, got elected as US President on the promise of ending the Vietnam war, which had incidentally spread to Cambodia.

President Nixon regarded the Vietnam war as a no-win situation. His National Security Adviser, Henry Kissinger, played an important role in bringing about the end of the Vietnamese war. It had cost 45,627 American lives by 1971. About this time the United States Government had spent nearly $150 billion. South Vietnam had suffered the worst ravages of the war. North Vietnam had turned into a desert after heavy bombardments by the US Air Force. Despite these adversities, the people of North Vietnam showed their indomitable courage proving to the world that no superpower on earth could subdue them.

The Vietnam war forced US Defence Secretary McNamara to resign in 1967. He expressed his opinion freely and frankly by saying there was no use of continuing the war. Finally, the Paris Peace Accord was concluded in January 1973 which formally declared the end of the Vietnamese war. Ho Chi Minh symbolised in his person Vietnamese nationalism. It was his finest hour. The Paris Peace Accord was the culmination of the untiring efforts of great statesmen of North Vietnam and the US, namely, Le Duc Tho and Henry Kissinger. In recognition of their peace efforts, these two great statesmen were jointly awarded the Nobel Peace Prize. The three parties which signed the accord did not keep it. The Democratic Republic of Vietnam invaded the South at a time when the US was withdrawing her forces from Vietnam. President Thieu of South Vietnam ordered the retreat and final surrender of his troops to the invading North Vietnamese army. Saigon was captured by the North Vietnamese forces in April 1975. It was renamed as Ho Chi Minh city. Thus the two parts of Vietnam finally got united in 1976 under the leadership of Ho Chi Minh.

Post-Vietnam War Period

The United States Government learnt a bitter lesson after its fiasco in the Vietnam war, and that was not to poke its nose into the wars of liberation. The Americans lost 58,000 lives in this undeclared war, and McNamara, the then Defence Secretary, confessed in his memoirs, that it was a terrible mistake. On the 20th anniversary of their inglorious exit from Vietnam, the Americans did soul searching as to why they went to Vietnam in the first place. Initially, they thought that the struggle in Vietnam was about the spread of communism. Unfortunately, they did not know that it was a war of national liberation.

The Socialist Republic of Vietnam came into existence on July 2, 1976, and the government chose to remain friendly with China and the Soviet Union. But the People's Republic of China stabbed her in the back by going to war over the border dispute. It took some years for the two communist countries to bury the hatchet.

However, what came as a great surprise to all was the US Government's recognition of Vietnam. On July 11, 1995 the US formally recognised Vietnam and resumed diplomatic relations. But, before according her recognition, the US asked the Hanoi Government to render "fullest possible accounting" of the 1600 odd missing American service personnel lost in the Vietnam war. Hanoi was kind enough to comply with this request.

After the Vietnam war, the country went through a traumatic period. Vietnam had to rebuild her shattered economy. The war was over 25 years ago, but the economy is still in the doldrums. Some economic analysts believe that Vietnam became a poor nation, not because of the war, but because of communism. The present US policy is directed towards weaning Vietnam away from communism and helping it embrace a free market economy. President Bill Clinton has shown interest in normalising relations with Vietnam with a view to exploring its market, and targeting it as a possible destination for US investment. On July 28, 1995, Vietnam joined the Association of South East Asia Nations (ASEAN) as its seventh member. The ASEAN is struggling to remove the trade barriers being erected by the developed countries, and secure for its partners opportunities for economic development. It is encouraging trade among the member countries themselves on better terms. China is aware of US moves towards establishing closer economic ties with Vietnam, and perceives it as a step to keep her isolated.

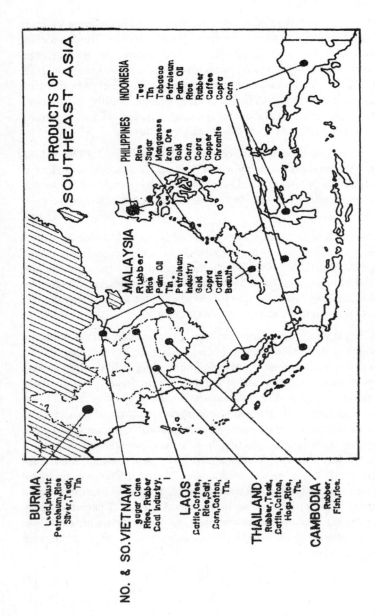

Products of Southeast Asia

PART III
SOUTH ASIA

Part III

SOUTH ASIA

26

INDUS VALLEY CIVILISATION

The discovery of Indus civilisation in 1922 was of great significance to the world in general and India in particular. To India, it added a new chapter to her history. As a result, she could rightly be proud of having produced a civilisation which is as old as that of ancient Egypt or Mesopotamia.

Excavation work mostly carried on in Punjab, Sind, and Baluchistan has revealed that Indus culture – known as Harappan culture – had spread over an area of 1200 x 700 miles. Of the more than 140 sites discovered so far, three are of great importance. They are Mohenjodaro on the banks of the Indus, Harappa on the banks of the Ravi and Lothal on the Kathiawar coast. The discoveries in these three important centres revealed the extent of urbanity achieved by its inhabitants. In the absence of written records (the script on the seals is yet to be deciphered) it would be premature to draw inferences or conclusions. However, noted archaeologists and historians have nevertheless been giving accounts about the culture of the people.

Date of Harappan Culture

The antiquity of this civilisation has been engaging the attention of great archaeologists and scholars for quite some time. A few have ventured to suggest tentative dates as to when this civilisation might have flourished. A few Harappan seals found in Mesopotamian sites dating back to King Sargon of Agade (Akkad) made scholars like Dr Wheeler fix the chronology of this civilisation to about 2500-1500 BC. Sir John Marshall has given a much earlier date, that is 3250-2750 BC, taking into consideration the striking similarities between Indus and Sumerian cultures. The radio-carbon dating test conducted at the Tata Institute of Harappan culture revealed that the civilisation was flourishing around 3000 BC.

Founders

Probably the most important issue that comes up every time relates to the founders. Were they foreigners? Or Aryans? Or Dravidians? After examining a few skulls at the sites, scholars are of the opinion that the Indus people belonged to a mixed stock – proto-Austroloid, Mediterranean, Alpine, and

Mongoloid. The present south Indian population belongs to the first two elements generally. Similarities have been found between Harappan religion and the Dravidian religion. All these indications have made some scholars take the view that Dravidians founded the Harappan culture. There are strong indications to show that Harappan culture was essentially native in character.

To have a glimpse of their achievements, one should observe their ruined cities and other relics.

A few scholars believe that Harappa and Mohenjodaro were once the twin capitals of Indus civilisation. These two cities, situated 400 miles from each other, show similar features. While Mohenjodaro appears to be well preserved, Harappa is in a state of utter ruin, and sometimes the features are beyond recognition.

MOHENJODARO

One of the conspicuous features of the city of Mohenjodaro is its town planning. Systematic town planning must have preceded the construction of the city. The city could boast of straight streets running due north and south and east and west, bisecting each other at right-angles. Some of the broad streets (34 feet in width) run for nearly half-a mile. The roads are not paved.

The Residental Complex

The houses were of varying sizes and built of burnt bricks with mud and mortar as binding materials. Stones were not used for construction purposes. In each house, there were rooms, a kitchen and a bathroom. The bathroom was constructed nearest to the street so that the waste water went directly to the main drainage system of the city. Each house was well supplied with water from a brick-lined well. Most of the houses had an upper storey connected by a narrow staircase.

Drainage System

One of the unique features of Mohenjodaro city is its elaborate drainage system. It is a fact that no other city in the world at that time had such an excellent drainage system. Each street and bylane had a well-paved drain on either side which collected waste water from each house adjacent to it. The drains were laid well below the street level and the waste water of the big city was flushed into the Indus River.

Public Buildings: The Great Bath

Towards the west of this city lay the citadel-mound and a few public buildings. One of the most prominent of these is the Great Bath (180"x108") which contains a swimming pool (39"x23"x8'). This swimming pool is surrounded by thick walls, wide verandahs and small bathrooms. On all sides of the pool there were steps. Provisions were made to drain all the dirty water from the pool regularly and fresh water filled in.

Granary and College

The other structures are the granary and a college. The former served as a warehouse for storing foodgrains and the latter was probably used as a meeting place of public officials. One may say that the whole city was well maintained by the municipal authorities by supplying water for constructing public wells, dustbins to throw garbage, providing street lights and an excellent drainage system.

Socio-economic Life

In many respects the Indus people living in the cities must have enjoyed quite a colourful life as can be surmised through some of their relics. Their daily food consisted of beef, mutton, pork, fish, corn-products, vegetables, fruits and milk. The discovery of a large number of spindle whorls testifies to the fact that they generally wore stitched cotton garments. Men used a *shawl* or *chadar* which was drawn over the left shoulder, and a *dhoti* to cover the lower part of the body. They kept short beards and whiskers and sometimes shaved the hair on the upper lip. They kept long hair and combed it backwards regularly. Sometimes they coiled it into a knot on the top of the head.

Women seem to have enjoyed freedom and status in society. Many of them were fond of fashions and luxuries as can be seen from the articles they used. They kept themselves beautiful by using a wide variety of toilet and cosmetic articles. Their toilet table contained bronze mirrors, ivory combs of different shapes, lipsticks (*chanhudaro finds*), collyrium, face-paint, powder, and hair-wash. They were familiar with hairstyles.

Along with cosmetics the women of Indus adorned themselves with a wide variety of ornaments. Wealthy women wore ornaments of gold, silver, ivory, faience and precious stones. Their ornaments consisted of necklaces, finger-rings, girdles, nose-studs, earrings, bangles and anklets. The poor were happy with ornaments made of shell, bone, copper and terracotta. Ornaments, like necklaces, were made of different types of beads and they were in great demand. The wearing of ornaments was not confined to womenfolk alone but the male members of the family also wore them. The toilet articles of male members, such as ivory combs and razors were also discovered. Dressing tables with bronze mirrors were found.

Amusements

A number of playthings such as a game-board with the dice pieces, marbles and balls and other kinds of toys belonging to children were discovered at the sites. So one can say that a crude game of chess was probably the most popular form of pastime. We may also say that the children were not neglected as can be surmised from a number of playthings and toys for children. Other forms of pastime for the elders were bull-fighting and hunting of wild animals.

Rural Economy

To feed the vast population residing in a number of cities, large-scale cultivation of foodgrains must have been undertaken. While the Indus population showed urban characteristics and bias, a considerable part of the rural population lived in the surrounding villages with agriculture as their main occupation. In addition, they kept livestock, raised poultry and looked after dairy. They sent cartloads of wheat, barley, cotton and date-palm to the cities for sale.

Urban Economy

In cities like Mohenjodaro several industries including the home-made spun cloth developed. There were professional classes like potters, carpenters, masons, jewellers, ivory-workers, goldsmiths, weavers, blacksmiths and dyers. The potters produced beautifully decorated pots. Most of the pots were wheel-turned. Polychrome pottery (painted in several colours) was also discovered at Amti, 70 miles south of Mohenjodaro. The potters also made big jars for storage of foodgrains and other things. Chanhudaro may have also been a great centre for pottery and terracotta toys for children.

Indus craftsmen showed their great skill by producing beautiful copper and bronze vessels, household utensils, objects and ornaments, and bronze figurines. A little bronze-figure of a dancing girl exhibits their remarkable craftsmanship. Indus craftsmen also achieved remarkable success in lapidary work. They produced artistically made stone-beads, especially of agate and carnelian.

Trade and Commerce

There is evidence to prove that many people in the cities were engaged in trade and commerce. They used bullock-driven carts as a means of transport to carry goods from one city to another. Inland trade flourished. Besides inland trade, the Indus traders had commerce with many countries of West Asia, Crete and Egypt. There is a good deal of evidence to show that the Indus people maintained commercial relations with the Sumerians. Lothal must have served as the most important port of the Indus people to carry on maritime trade. It also had a dockyard where ships were built for overseas trade. Some Indus seals were discovered in the ruined cities of Sumeria.

Seals

The connection between seals and trade has not yet been established clearly. The Indus seals are square in shape and made of steatite. More than 2,000 seals have been found. They must have been used by the consignors to seal the packed goods before sending them to the proper destination. It may have been used by the customs authorities also.

The carvings on the seals include human beings, divinities, animals, composite figures, and mythological figures. Some seals contain secular scenes such as a man attacking a buffalo.

Religion

As no temple has been found, ideas about their religion are mostly derived from the seals, stone-statuaries and some terracotta figurines. A large number of terracotta figurines of a female elaborately decorated with a crescent-shaped head dress have been found in many Indus cities. So it is assumed that these figurines represent the Mother Goddess. To substantiate this further, another seal from Harappa contains a scene depicting a human sacrifice being offered to the Earth-Goddess. Many historians believe that the Shakti cult was popular at that time, particularly during the pre-Aryan age. Numerous seals from Harappa and Mohenjodaro contain the representation of the Male-God. The most common among them was that of a god with three faces seated on a platform in a yogic pose with a trident and surrounded by a few animals. Scholars believe that he is the prototype of the later Indian Lord Shiva. Again, the discovery of many cylindrical and conical stone pieces which look like *Shivalinga*, have confirmed the view that Shiva worship was common. The Indus people must have worshipped a number of semi-human and semi-bovine gods. The worship of a number of mythical animals, snakes, and sacred trees like the *pipal* and *neem* was in vogue. The representation of *Swastika* and the wheel also suggest the worship of the Sun-God. The people offered animal sacrifices. The discovery of sacrificial altars of a square shape suggest offerings to the Fire God.

The disposal of their dead was done in three forms, namely, complete burial, fractional burial and post-cremation burial. The first involved the burial of the whole body with other articles such as pots and offerings in a pit, the second involved the burial of the bones and skull of the dead person, all placed in a big urn with other objects. The third refers to the collection of the ashes and bones of the dead and placing it in an urn along with other articles and burying it underneath the floor of a house. A few cemeteries were found in Harappa and Lothal.

Defence

Harappa which lies on the bed of the Ravi is known for its fortification and a citadel. It appears that the city was well fortified so as to prevent the invasions of foreigners. Mortimer Wheeler, after seeing the granaries, barracks, and working platforms of Harappa, observes that they constitute "an example of cantonment planning significantly within the shadow of the citadel." A large number of weapons such as axes, spears, daggers, stone-maces, slings, swords, bows and arrows indicate that they were acquainted with the art of warfare. It should be noted that the weapons of war were made of copper and bronze. Looking at the kinds of weapons used and the metals with which they were made, it appears that the Indus people were unwarlike in character.

Political Organisation

A noted archaeologist, S R Rao, is of the opinion that the Indus people "were pioneers in founding an empire even before the establishment of the Sargonid Empire in Mesopotamia," and in all probability it was "administered by a benevolent ruler with a secular outlook."

Due credit should be given to the rulers for introducing a uniform system of civic administration, town-planning, public sanitation, enforcement of regulations on trade, introduction of weights and measures and standardisation of all products suitable for internal and international trade.

Among the notable contributions made by them were the Indus script, tolerance of divergent religious practices in their empire; their art and craft as seen on the seals, clay-models and ornaments, and finally the science of yoga.

Decline of Indus Civilisation

Much speculation has been made on the decline and fall of this great civilisation. Of the many popular theories concerning this, one may accept that natural calamities such as widespread floods, shifting of the monsoons and soil-erosion are contributing factors for its decline.

27

VEDIC CIVILISATION

The founders of Vedic civilisation were the Indo-Aryans. It is generally agreed that the early Aryan tribes had originally lived somewhere in the western part of Asia. They left their original homeland due to many reasons such as the dearth of grassy lands for feeding their cattle, increase in their population, climatic changes and curiosity to visit new lands. Thus large scale migrations of Indo-Europeans (Aryans) took place around 2500 BC One of their branches moved towards Europe and the other towards Iran. Those Aryans who lived in Iran were called Indo-Iranians. However, another big batch of Aryans moved farther east and reached India. They are called the Indo-Aryans. The fact that the Indo-Aryans were in some way related to the other branch of the Aryan family ruling over some parts of Mesopotamia (Mittanis and Kassites) is revealed after an inscription was discovered in Boghzkoi (Asia Minor). The Mittanis of Upper Euphrates and the Kassites of Babylonia worshipped Aryan gods such as *Indra*, *Varuna*, *Mitra* and *Nasatyas*.

Aryan Wars and Settlements

Their early entry into India (around 2000 BC) was opposed by the native inhabitants (most probably Dravidians) resulting in wars. The *Rig Veda* mentions numerous battles fought between the early Aryans and the *Dasyus*. Furthermore, the *Rig Veda* describes how the Aryans destroyed the numerous towns and forts belonging to the Dasyus before making their settlements in the *Sapta-Sindhu* region (Punjab). The process of Aryanisation of the Sapta-Sindhu region was gradual because the wars with the local inhabitants continued for a long time. However, those who were defeated got absorbed into the Aryan population.

Vedic Literature

Much of our knowledge about the Aryans is derived from the four Vedas. The earliest and most important among them was the *Rig Veda*. The language in which it is written is commonly known as Sanskrit. According to a few reputed scholars, its composition must have been completed about 1500-1200 BC. The *Rig Veda* is considered by many scholars as a great "source-book" for the study and appreciation of the development of Hindu culture. The *Rig Veda Samhita* was followed by the *Yajur Veda Samhita, Sama* and *Atharva Vedas*. While the *Rig Veda Samhita* is a collection of 1017 hymns divided into ten *mandalas,* the *Sama Veda* happens to be a collection of melodies. The *Yajur Veda* is something like a `guide-book' for the rituals. A major part of this work contains a collection of magic spells which were chanted by priests at the time of sacrifices. From the point of view of a historian, the *Atharva Veda* is important in the sense that it describes the beliefs and superstitions of the early Aryans.

The Brahmanas are prose commentaries on the Vedas. The *Aranyakas* (forest-texts) were probably composed in seclusion at hermitages and include philosophical doctrines and mystic meanings of the text of the Vedas. The Upanishads deal with speculative thinking on the part of the sages. It contains spiritual thinking on such topics like the universal soul, the Absolute, the Individual self, the mysteries of nature and other things. To put it briefly, it contains the wisdom of our ancestors.

The next class of literature is known as the Vedangas. They are six in number, namely, *Siksha* (phonetics), *Kalpa* (ritual), *Vyakarana* (grammar), *Nirukta* (etymology), *Chhandas* (metrics), and *Jyotisha* (astronomy). These six Vedangas are meant to help one in the "proper understanding, recitation, and the sacrificial use of the Vedas."

The second Vedanga deals with the ritual part of the study. If one desires to acquaint oneself with this, he should begin with the oldest Sutra works known as *Kalpa-Sutras*. The *Kalpa-Sutras* are again classified into two categories – the *Srauta Sutras* (great rites performed by a number of priests) and *Grihya-Sutras* (a householder's domestic rites and sacrifices). The two other Sutra works are *Dharma-Sutras* (customary law and practice), and the *Sulva-Sutras* (rules laid down for constructing the fire-altars). The *Kalpa-Sutras* are of importance to us in "the correct understanding of the Vedic passages."

Area of Occupation

As mentioned earlier, the early Aryans occupied the land of the seven rivers (the Sapta-Sindhu) which extended from the Kabul Valley in the north to the river Ravi in the south. The Rig Vedic people were tribal in character and each tribe occupied a particular region. Sometimes they fought among themselves. The *Rig Veda* mentions the *Dasarajna*, that is the battle of Ten Kings which resulted in the victory of the Bharatas who gave their name to this country.

Political Organisation

To begin with, the early Aryans were led by their tribal leader both in times of war and peace. The dictates of the tribal leader were obeyed by all. However, after their settlements in the Sapta-Sindhu, they evolved monarchy as their form of government. The tribal leader came to be called Rajan. Kingship became hereditary in the course of time. Thus the Sapta-Sindhu area was divided into a number of small tribal kingdoms, each ruled by a king. His main function was to lead the people in times of war, and during peace time he was to protect his subjects from the attack of his enemies. Other kingly duties included punishing the wicked and upholding of the *Dharma*. The Aryan king lived at a royal palace in the capital with all pomp and majesty and received tributes from his subjects.

Next to the king in importance was the *Purohita* (the Chaplain) who invoked the blessings of the gods through his hymns to confer favours upon the king. The *Rig Veda* mentions great Purohitas like Visvamitra and Vasishtha and their great services to the state. Sometimes they acted as a check to the growing powers of the king. They commanded great respect both by the ruler and the subjects.

The *Senani* was appointed by the king to be in charge of armed forces of the kingdom. He recruited able bodied men and gave them training in the art of warfare. His other duties included providing the soldiers with necessary weapons and keeping the army alert and well-trained during peacetime.

The *Gramani* was the leader of the village. He was entrusted by the king with the task of collecting revenue from his village. The village was generally looked after by him.

The most popular representative bodies of the *Rig Vedic* age were the *Sabha* and the *Samiti*. A few lines in the *Rig Veda* indicate that the former was associated with men known for their wealth and position. When they assembled in a big hall they discussed not only social matters but also important political issues, if any. Collectively, the Sabha wielded great influence over the king and the administration. It might have also acted as a check on the arbitrary powers of the king. The Samiti was more political in its character than the Sabha. It included the representatives of the common people and a few influential Brahmans and heads of aristocratic families. It was in the Samiti that the political affairs of the kingdom were freely discussed. The debates in the Samiti were probably of a high order and the decisions arrived at by the king in his individual capacity were likely to be influenced by their wisdom.

Non-monarchical forms of government also existed among a few states. Oligarchy was in vogue in a few states where several members of the royal family exercised power jointly. References are also made, in the *Rig Veda*, to *Jana* (republics) where a *Jyeshtha* (elder) exercised his authority.

The idea of one world government under an enlightened ruler was also not unknown to the early Aryans for the *Rig Veda* mentions it in the phrase *Visvasya Bhuvanasya raja*. So it was natural that the early Aryan rulers strove hard to rise from a position of tribal chieftaincy to that of the status of an emperor through a continuous process of expansionism by means of wars. They received tributes and oath of loyalty from the defeated rulers.

Vedic Society

The main prop of Vedic society was the family. A healthy family-life based on love and affection among the family members was an important feature. Father was the head of the family and, therefore, commanded respect and obedience from the other members. All the members of the family or joint-family lived in the same house – a house made of wood and bamboo. Next to the father in importance was the mother. She looked after the management of household affairs and helped her husband in performing religious ceremonies and sacrifices. Marriage was considered sacred and binding. The marriage tie bound husband and wife for life till death separated them.

Children were educated. The education of girls was not neglected and is proved by the fact that Visvavara, Apala and Ghosha composed hymns and rose to the position of Rishis. It was the duty of the parents to get their daughters married when they attained the age of puberty. Girls and boys enjoyed the liberty of choosing their life partners.

Monogamy was common and polygamy was not altogether unknown. Only kings and nobles practised the latter. No reference to polyandry is made. So also there is no reference to child-marriage. The birth of a son was always preferred to the birth of a daughter. A number of families bound by kinship and living in a village formed a clan. A number of clans living in an area constituted a district. A number of these districts formed the tribe.

When the Aryans entered India and settled in the Sapta-Sindhu region, their *varna* (colour) and *Sajatya* (kinship) tightly knit them into a compact society. However, during the latter Vedic period, non-Aryans were taken into the fold of society as free men. The class distinctions must have begun at the fag end of the Rig Vedic period. The *Purusha sukta* appears in the tenth *mandal* (chapter) of the *Rig Veda* saying that the Brahmans, Kshatriyas, Vaisyas and Sudras appeared from the *Purusha* (the primeval creator) through His mouth, from His arms, from the thighs and from His feet respectively. None of the ugly features of the present caste system seemed to have been present as inter-marriages and change of occupations were quite common. Untouchability was almost unknown. Then when did the caste system develop? The answer to this question should be traced to the new environment the Aryans had to adjust with, when their tribes migrated further east. The genesis of the warrior class (Kshatriyas) was the result of systematic conquests undertaken by the Aryan rulers. They needed a permanent class of fighting men. Those who specialised in the Vedic studies and sacrifices constituted the priestly class (Brahmans). Many others who settled down and engaged in the pursuit of agriculture, trade and commerce were known as Vaisyas. Many aborigines living in the villages as well as those who belonged to the wild tribes came to be known as Sudras. The caste system in its rigid form must have taken place when the Aryans conquered the Middle country (*Madhya-Desa*).

Their food was mainly composed of animal flesh, vegetables, rice, barley, bean and sesame. They made bread and cakes out of flour. They liberally consumed milk and milk products such as *ghee*, butter and curds. They ate fruits. They were also addicted to the drinking of *sura*, a liquor made from barley and corn. *Soma* plant juice was also a popular alcoholic drink which they even offered to the gods.

Their dress (*vastra*) consisted mainly of *vasas* (lower garment) and the *adhivasa* (an over-garment). The wearing of an under-garment (*nivi*) came into vogue during the later Vedic Age. References are made to special type of garments, some embroidered, worn by dancers, brides and others. People living in hermitages made good use of the skin of animals (especially deer) for making garments.

Names of several ornaments worn by men and women are mentioned in the *Rig Veda*. The *Karnasobhana* was an ornament attached to the ear and mostly worn by men. The brides wore *Kurira*, a kind of head ornament. *Khadi* was something like a ring worn as armlet. *Nishka* was an ornament of gold gracing the neck. There were other ornaments like the *mani* and *rukma*.

Some of their amusements included gambling, chariot-racing, dancing with females to tunes of *dundubi*, playing dice and wrestling. Music was both vocal and instrumental. The Aryans were very fond of material pleasures of life and did not worry about disease or death.

They maintained a high standard of morality. People lived in contentment and did not take to crimes such as stealing, robbery and murder. Morality among women was also very high.

Economic Conditions

A large majority of the early Aryans were cattle-breeders. They loved pastoral life. They lived in villages. They owned land, houses, horses and cattle. They cultivated the lands and grew crops of wheat and barley. They considered the cow as a sacred animal (*aghnya*). A man's wealth was known by the size of his cattle.

Weaving in cotton and wool flourished as an industry. Textile and woollen garments were produced in various colours. Dyeing and embroidery were known. The services of a carpenter were found necessary for constructing houses, for household utensils and also household furniture. Carpenters supplied chariots, carts, boats, and ships. Village-blacksmiths supplied articles made of iron such as sickles, razors, and ploughshares. They also produced weapons such as spears and swords.

Goldsmiths produced excellent ornaments in gold and catered to the fanciful rich. The leather workers supplied a number of articles such as shoes, bow-strings, reins, water-casks, thongs and hand-guards. There were a number of other professionals like butchers, potters, barbers, boatmen, moneylenders and hunters. There were physicians and priests whose services were found to be invaluable.

Inland and river-trade seemed to have flourished. A few hymns of the *Rig Veda* refer to trading with distant lands for profit. The chief means of transport of goods was the cart driven by oxen. Boatmen helped traders to transport the goods across the river. Most of the trade was carried on by barter. A few traders accepted *nishka*, a small gold piece. The Aryan traders were also probably engaged in sea-borne trade.

The early Aryans were religious. They offered prayers and sacrifices to their beloved gods. They were known for "the punctilious observance of religious rituals" they did this in order to please the gods and expected many things in return such as birth of male children, good harvest and prosperity.

All the Vedic gods are manifestations of the forces of nature. They can be classified into three categories, namely, (1) the terrestrial gods like Prithvi, Agni, Soma and Brihaspathi; (2) the atmospheric gods like Indra, Maruts, Vayu, Parjanya and Rudra; and (3) the celestial gods such as Varuna, Dyas (the sky god), Ushas (dawn), and Asvins and all the gods associated with the Sun god like Mitra, Savitri and Vishnu. Almost all the gods are male gods. Temple and image-worship seemed to have been absent. Many early Aryans appear to have been fond of Indra (thunder-god associated with war) and Varuna (god of rain). Agni personified as fire-god was the beloved of all and through him the other gods received sacrifices of their devotees. The early Aryans believed that the gods "subdue the forces of evil," reward the righteous and punish the sinners. They were not particularly concerned about death or life after death. As a matter of fact they were more interested in earthly existence and therefore, offered sacrifices to various gods making them to bestow prosperity, longevity of life, health, male-children, power, and defeat of their rivals.

28

JAINISM

The sixth century BC is considered one of the important epochs in the history of India for the reason that it gave birth to two great religions – Jainism and Buddhism. This age was marked by religious turmoil since the Hindu religion had lost its pristine glory and simplicity and degenerated into an amorphous cult. The priestly class – the Brahmans – arrogated to itself a position of pre-eminence and interpreted the sacred lore only to a few. Performance of sacrifices and meaningless rituals was given more prominence than finding a path to attain salvation. The layman lost his sense of devotion and attachment to God thanks to the services rendered by Brahmans. In these circumstances, many felt disgusted and took to an ascetic way of life as advocated in the sacred scriptures like the *Aranyakas* and the Upanishads. There was also a terrible reaction to Brahminical Hinduism, especially coming from Kshatriyas.

In the meanwhile, a few religious orders were founded by the wandering ascetics or hermits. These wandering ascetics were known as *Shramanas* or *Parivrajakas*. Then came the *Samkya* school founded by Kapila. He did not believe in the existence of God and his philosophy wielded considerable influence on Mahavira and the Buddha. The new religious orders did not gain much popularity and they became defunct.

However, there emerged two new sects which gained immense popularity. They were Jainism and Buddhism. Both were founded by men who belonged to the Kshatriya class. They led the revolt against the imposition of Brahminical religion by the priestly class and also against the perpetuation of the caste system

Parsvanatha (8th Century BC)

Jain tradition says that its religion is as old as the human race. It also claims to have produced 24 *Tirthankaras* (saints). The first twenty *Tirthankaras* (Rishaba being the first) appear to be legendary characters. However, the last two, namely, Parsvanatha and Mahavira, are historical figures. Parsvanatha seems to have lived 250 years before the birth of Mahavira. He was the son of King Asvasena of Benares. He became an ascetic at the age of 30 and the sect he founded gathered a large number of followers called *Nigranthas*. Parsvanatha insisted that his followers practise four great virtues, namely (a) *Satya* (truth), (b) *Ahimsa* (non-injury to life), (c) *Aprigraha* (non-possession of property), and (d) *Asteya* (non-stealing).

Early Life of Vardhamana Mahavira

Vardhamana Mahavira was the 24th and the last *Tirthankara* according to Jain traditions. He was born around 540 BC in Kundagrama, a suburb of Vaishali (the capital of Videha). His parents were Siddharatha and Trishala. Trishala was the sister of Chetaka, a prominent Lichhavi prince of the time who ruled the Vajji confederation. Being noble by birth, Vardhamana was brought up in the midst of luxury. He married Yasoda and subsequently a daughter was born. She was named Anojja or Priyadarsana.

Soon after the death of his old parents, Vardhamana took the consent of his brother to renounce worldly life. He left home in his 32nd year and became a monk. He discarded his clothes (*Digambara*) and spent the next twelve years of his life in meditation and self-inflicted tortures with the object of achieving perfect knowledge (*keval-jnana*). At the end of this period, he succeeded in becoming a *kevalin* (omniscient). Vardhamana came to be known as *Jina* (conqueror) and Mahavira. Vardhamana Mahavira spent the rest of his life in preaching his doctrines to the people of Magadha, Anga, Mithila and Kosala. His religion attracted a large number of followers, and amongst them were kings, powerful nobles, wealthy merchants and house-holders. He lived till his 72nd year and passed away at Pawa near Patna. Mahavira was a contemporary of the Buddha but they never met.

His Teachings

The followers of Mahavira were called *Nigranthas*. Even today many of them consider him not a founder of a new religion but as a great reformer. Mahavira began his preaching career to reform the sect founded by his predecessor Parsvanatha. Besides the four vows prescribed by Parsvanatha for his followers, Mahavira added the fifth, ie, the observance of *Brahmacharya* (chastity).

One of the main facets of Jainism is the belief in the soul and *Karma*. Mahavira declared that every element is a combination of material and spiritual factors. The former perishes but the latter does not. An individual is subject to a cycle of birth and death. To liberate the soul from the bondage of *karma*, it is necessary to destroy the latter. This can be achieved by an individual by practising the five vows, namely, *Satya, Ahimsa, Aprigraha, Asteya* and *Brahmacharya*.

In addition to observing the above five vows, a true Jain should also follow the three-fold path (called *Ratnatreya*) to attain "the pure and blissful abode" (*Siddha Sila*). They are Right Belief, Right Knowledge, and Right Conduct.

By Right Belief he meant belief in Jainism, and by Right Knowledge the liberation of the soul. Right Conduct implied strict observance of the five vows in the day-to-day life of an individual.

The doctrine of non-injury is also one of the important tenets of Jainism. Mahavira emphasised that not only do human-beings, birds and beasts have souls but also plants, metals, water and wood. Therefore, an individual should avoid harming these things. An individual should conquer his senses and lead a life of austerity and self-mortification.

Mahavira did not believe that the Universe was created by God or make any reference to Him. Change is a natural phenomenon. Birth and death is natural and applicable to men and matter.

Mahavira also rejected the Vedic principles as unimportant and condemned the sacrificial rituals performed by Brahmanas. He believed in the freedom of women and allowed them to join his order as *Sarmini* and *Sravikas*.

Religious Literature

The teachings of Mahavira are contained in the fourteen old texts called *Purvas*. Towards the end of the 4th century BC, a great famine broke out in Bihar which led to thousands of Jains heading towards Mysore led by Bhadrabahu. Those Jains who stayed behind convened a council to compile the Jain texts. They are twelve in number and called *Angas*. About the sixth century AD another council was held in Valabhi to bring about the final collection of all Jain scriptures and put it in writing. They were written in the Prakrit language.

Svetambara and Digambara Jains

When Bhadrabahu returned to the north with his followers, he found his co-religionists clad in white (*Svetambaras*) despite the injunction. But Bhadrabahu and his followers strictly adhered to the old rule and remained nude (*Digambaras*). The Digambaras refused to acknowledge the canon drafted during their absence and adhered to the principles enunciated in the 14 Purvas. The schism in the Jain religion might have occurred sometime during the first century AD.

Spread of Jainism

Several classes of *Angadharas* spread the teachings of Mahavira after his death. As mentioned earlier, Jainism got the royal patronage and counts great kings like Chandragupta Maurya and Samprati as its chief patrons. Bimbisara showed great respect to Vardhamana Mahavira when the latter met him. After the decline of the Mauryan empire, Jainism spread to the western and southern parts of India. Jain monasteries were built during the rule of Sakas, Ksatraps, and Rajputs in western and northern India. King Kharavela of Kalinga was a great patron of Jainism. The Satavahanas, the Gangas, Chalukyas, Rashtrakutas and Hoysalas who ruled the South also patronised Jainism.

The impact of Jainism on Indian culture is profound and worthy of mention. It propounded a new philosophy called "Syatvad" which aims at achieving the welfare of the individual on the one hand and the community in which he lives on the other. Although the principle of *Ahimsa* was known to Hinduism, it was Jainism which brought about its universal acceptance. The idea that plants have life in them was proved beyond doubt in the early years of the 20th century.

Jainism rendered great service to humanity by not recognising the caste system and established the principle of equality. Even women were considered an important section and their freedom was advocated by no less a person than Mahavira.

The Jain religion gave stimulus to vernacular literature. The early Jain literature was in Prakrit. Mahavira had preached his doctrines in the language called Ardhamagadhi, a language known to many people in his days. It was in this language that the 12 Angas came to be written. But the unique contribution of Jainism to literature was giving birth to the Apabhramsa language. Jain works produced during subsequent centuries were all in vernacular languages including Sanskrit. Some of the most prominent scholars who produced Jain literature were Hemachandra, Hari Bhadra, Sidha Sena, Nagachandra and Pujyapad. In Karnataka, Jainism made considerable progress and under its influence many Jain works came to be written.

Jainism wielded profound influence on Indian art and architecture. The followers of Jainism built Jain temples, monasteries and hospitals. The most popular Jain temple at Mount Abu was constructed by Kumarapala, a king who was served by the most noted Jain author, Hemachandra. Jain stupas, statues, and carved pillars still exist in Mathura, Gwalior, Chittor, Abu and other places. At Udaigiri and Ellora one sees the cave temples with beautiful sculpture and architecture. One should not forget the Hathigumpa caves (in Orissa) and the colossal statue of Gomateswar in Sravanabelgola.

29

BUDDHISM

Scepticism and religious turmoil influenced the course of events during the sixth century BC in India. Brahminical Hinduism had lost its hold on the common people mainly due to its insistence on the performance of meaningless rituals and sacrifices, and with its vague spiritual speculations. What the common man needed was a simple pathway to attain salvation. The *chaturvarna* system became rigid and lacked rationale. The priestly class dominated the scene, and afraid of losing its position came in the way of the regeneration of Hindu society. The reaction to this priestly-dominated religion came not from the lower classes but from the Kshatriyas. Gautama Buddha and Vardhamana Mahavira both belonged to the Kshatriya clan and they led the revolt.

Early Life of the Buddha

Before attaining enlightenment, the Buddha was known as Siddhartha. He was born in the year 566 BC at Lumbini near Kapilavastu. He belonged to the Sakya clan and his parents were Raja Shuddhodhana and Mayadevi. Mayadevi died soon after child-birth and Siddhartha was looked after by his aunt and step-mother Prajapati Gautami. Several legends (the *Jataka* stories) have been woven around the childhood life of Siddhartha. Raja Shuddhodhana consulted court astrologers to predict the future life of his son and they prophesied the greatness of his son in the realm of thought. Worried about his son's monkish predictions, Raja Shudhodhana got his son married to Yesodhara at the age of sixteen. Prince Siddhartha led his life in luxurious surroundings and did not have much knowledge of the sufferings of life experienced by the common man. After the birth of his son, Rahula, he began to feel uneasy. The visions of sickness, old age and death had great impact on his life. It led to his Great Renunciation during the 29th year of his life.

During the next six years of his life, Siddhartha led the life of a wandering ascetic and received instructions from two teachers called Alara and Udraka. When the teachers could not satisfy his curiosity regarding life and its purpose, he left them and reached Uruvela (near Gaya). It was there that he practised the most severe penances. His thirst for truth remained unquenched and he was reduced to a skeleton. After taking bath in the river Nairanjana, he gave up fasting. He reached Gaya where he sat under a *pipal* tree in deep meditation. At last his meditation was rewarded with the attainment of supreme knowledge and insight. He was called the *Buddha* (The Enlightened One).

He spent the rest of his life preaching his doctrine. He died at the age of 80 at Kusinagara.

Teachings of the Buddha

The Buddha delivered his first sermon at the Deer Park near Benaras. This sermon is known as *Dharmachakra Parivartana* (the turning of the wheel of Dharma). His followers included the five ascetics who had parted his company earlier. He taught his followers to recognise the four "Noble Truths" (*Arya Satya*). The first truth is the existence of sorrow *(Dukkha)*. The second truth relates to the main cause of sorrow, that is, desire *(Trishna)*. The third refers to the elimination of sorrow *(Nirodha)*. The fourth truth reveals how sorrow or sufferings can be eliminated by following the eight-fold path (*Ashtanga - Marga*).

The Eight-fold Path

It is through the practice of *Ashtanga Marga* that one can attain salvation or eternal bliss. The noble eight-fold path includes (1) Right Views (2) Right Intention (3) Right Speech (4) Right Action (5) Right Living (6) Right Effort (7) Right Mindfulness and (8) Right Concentration.

The Buddha believed in the Hindu doctrines of Karma and rebirth. He explained that by following the eight-fold path the individual soul cuts the cycle of births and deaths and attains eternal bliss or salvation.

The Buddha did not ask his followers to practise penances or austerities on the one hand or advocate leading a life full of pleasures. He chose the Middle Path *(Madhyama Marga)* which avoids both the above extremes. Even a householder can follow the eight-fold path and attain salvation.

Buddhist Order of Monks (Sangha)

The Buddha rejected the principles of the Vedas and condemned the performance of bloody sacrifices. He denied the existence of God and asked his followers to lead a life of simplicity and purity. He established the Buddhist Sangha where his disciples received instructions and led a life of simplicity and morality. He did not make caste or class distinction before taking them into the fold of the Buddhist Sangha. During the early stages of Buddhism, he did not allow women to join the Sangha, but a little later they were also permitted. An organisation for the Buddhist nuns was also founded.

Spread of Buddhism

Several factors led to the popularity of Buddhism in northern India. The Buddha was known for his magnetic personality. He explained the doctrines of his religion in Pali, a language spoken by the people. He made his teachings popular by narrating them in the form of parables. He kept the doors of his religion open to all irrespective of caste or class. Princes and paupers vied with each other to embrace this Middle Path. There were no priests, no rituals to be observed, and no costly sacrifices to be performed. Even a householder could practise the eight-fold path and attain salvation. Finally, the Sangha, founded by the Buddha propagated the tenets of the Master after his passing away.

But the most important factor for the spread of Buddhism lay in the royal patronage it received. Buddhism enlisted the support of great rulers of early times like Bimbisara, Ajatasatru, Emperor Ashoka, Kanishka and Harshavardhana. Emperor Ashoka not only embraced Buddhism but made the religion popular throughout the world by sending his missionaries. He held the third Buddhist Council (the first two were held within a century after the death of the Buddha at Rajagriha and Vaishali) at Pataliputra under the leadership of Mogaliputta Tissa. It settled some outstanding disputes and finalised the compilation of Buddhist scriptures. Emperor Kanishka convened the fourth Buddhist Council at Kundalavana (in Kashmir) which prepared commentaries (*Upadesa* and *Vibhasha Sastras*) on the Sacred Scriptures. The Sacred Text came to be known as *Pali* which is divided into three *Pitakas* or baskets. They are the *Sutta Pitaka*, the *Vinaya Pitaka*, and the *Abhidhamma Pitaka*.

Rise of Mahayana Buddhism

The schism developed most probably during the time of Emperor Kanishka. A marked deviation from the practices of the old religion occurred. The simple and revered teacher or the Buddha came to be worshipped as a god. His images were made and prayers were offered to them. The images of the Buddha and the Bodhisattvas adorned the walls of *Viharas* and *Chaityas*. Sculptors of the Gandhara School of Art made the statues of the Buddha. The *Jataka* stories formed the theme of many of the carvings on the rock-cut halls and caves. This new Buddhism came to be known as Mahayana Buddhism (or the Great Vehicle) and it is associated with the name of Nagarjuna, a philosopher of the Satavahana period in Indian history.

Contribution of Buddhism to Indian Culture

Buddhism catered to the spiritual needs of the community through its insistence on chaste and ethical principles of life. The Buddha, like Christ, enjoined upon his followers to return good for evil, truth for a lie and non-enmity for enmity. It advocated restraint and urged its followers to overcome greed and anger. Mercy and kindness for men and animals found its place of honour in the realm of Buddhist thought. Buddhism laid emphasis on the principle of *Ahimsa* (non-injury). Its teachings had profound influence on great personalities like Emperor Ashoka and Mahatma Gandhi.

Buddhism broke the barriers of caste and class and promoted feelings of social and national unity. It paved the way for the political unity of the country under the Mauryan Emperors. Other contributions of Buddhism include the development of Pali language and literature and the establishment of centres of learning all over India. The Buddhist monasteries in India in those days served as centres of learning. In the course of time not only were religious texts taught but secular subjects were also introduced. It may not be entirely wrong to say that Buddhism served the educational needs of the community in ancient times.

By far the greatest contribution of Buddhism to Indian culture lay in the development of art and architecture. A large number of ruined monasteries stand today to point out the glory of Indian art and architecture. The Buddhist monks introduced rock-cut architecture. They built their *Viharas* by hewing the rocks. Their artists and architects did splendid work by building the *Chaityas*. Carvings of the Buddha are found on the Chaitya Halls at Karle. The Stupas of Sanchi and Bharhut exhibit their excellent carvings. It may not be an exaggeration to say that early Indian art was profoundly inspired by Buddhism.

30

HINDU IMPERIALISM

The post-Buddhist India witnessed the growth of Hindu empires. Magadha became a cradle of three great empires. The Haryanka dynasty produced great rulers like Bimbisara and Ajatasatru. They built a great empire in India and made Pataliputra the seat of their capital. They established a sound system of administration. Besides Hinduism, Jainism and Buddhism also found patronage of rulers and merchants and in due course became popular. Taxila became a great centre of learning. There was considerable progress made in the fields of agriculture and industry. Industrial guilds developed. Trade and commerce made headway with the growth of towns like Benaras, Saketa, Rajagriha, Champa, Kausambi, Sravasti and Vaishali. The rulers and nobles patronised art and architecture as revealed in the recent excavations at Rajgir. Pliny speaks of Rome's relations with India.

The Nanda Rule over Magadha

After the fall of the Haryanka dynasty in Magadha, the Nanda dynasty established its sway. Its founder was Mahapadmananda. He was a man of low origin. He retrieved his position and honour by destroying many ruling Kshatriya families which were out to destroy him. The Nanda empire extended from the borders of Avanti to Anga. The kingdom of Kalinga might have also come under Nanda control. The last ruler, Dhanananda, turned into a tyrant. The enemies of Dhanananda plotted to overthrow his rule and they turned to Chandragupta Maurya, a former commander of the Magadhan army, for help. With the help of Kautilya or Chanakya, a Brahmin, Chandragupta overthrew the Nanda rule and established his power.

Alexander's Invasion

When the last Nanda ruler was ruling Magadha, Alexander the Great invaded India (327 BC). King Ambhi of Taxila was frightened at the sight of the approaching Greek army led by Alexander. He surrendered without resistance and offered great hospitality to the invader. Ambhi helped Alexander to attack the kingdom of Porus which was situated between the Jhelum and the Chenab.

The battle of Hydapses witnessed a spirited fight offered by King Porus but it was in vain. After the defeat, Porus was taken captive and brought before Alexander. When asked by Alexander how he should be treated, Porus replied that he should be treated as one king treats another. Alexander was very much impressed by his personality and asked him to continue ruling his kingdom as his vassal. Alexander continued to march further with his army. He defeated a large number of small kingdoms. When he decided to fight the mighty Magadha kingdom, his soldiers revolted. They felt homesick and wanted to go home. So Alexander ended his career of conquest and began marching home. On his way back, he died at Susa (328 BC). Although Alexander's invasion did not produce direct results, it had its impact on Indian culture. The Indians realised the need for political unity and it enabled Chandragupta Maurya to achieve the same easily. Secondly, the contact with the Greeks opened avenues for Indian trade and commerce with Western countries. Thirdly, the Greek influence was felt on Indian astronomy and philosophy.

Chandragupta's Career of Conquest

After assuming power, Chandragupta Maurya embarked upon a career of conquest. During the 24 years of his reign he subdued a large number of states and became the master of northern India. He also overthrew the foreign yoke by inflicting a crushing defeat on Seleukos Nikator, one of the generals of Alexander who was in charge of Eastern Dominions. After marrying the daughter of Seleukos, Chandragupta Maurya received from him the provinces of Aria (Herat), Arachosia (Kandahar), Gedrosia (Baluchistan) and Paropanisadai (Kabul). Plutarch says that Chandragupta conquered the whole country with an army of 600,000 soldiers. Chandragupta's empire extended from Pataliputra in the east to the Hindukush mountains and Herat in the north-west and west and up to Mysore in the south. According to a Jain tradition, Chandragupta Maurya became a Jain monk and spent the last days of his life in Sravana Belgola in Mysore.

Bindusara (300 BC- 273 BC)

Chandragupta Maurya was succeeded by his son, Bindusara, around 300 BC. He might have ruled the empire for about 27 years. We have no detailed account of his reign. He was described as *Amitraghata* (slayer of foes). He continued to maintain diplomatic relations with Syrian King Antiochos I (son of Seleukos). Deimachus succeeded Megasthenes as ambassador to the court of Pataliputra. When there was a revolt at Taxila, Bindusara sent his son Ashoka to suppress it.

Emperor Ashoka (273 BC-236 BC)

Bindusara was succeeded by his son, Ashoka. According to the Ceylonese chronicles, there ensued a bloody struggle for the throne soon after the death of Bindusara. These works mention that Ashoka killed all of his 99 brothers and succeeded to the throne. Known for his extreme cruelty, he earned the nickname, *Chandashoka*. It was in the eleventh year of his reign that Emperor Ashoka fought one of the bloodiest battles in history. As the kingdom of Kalinga did not show its allegiance to the Mauryan Emperor, it was invaded. The thirteenth Rock-Edict of Ashoka describes the horrors of this war. Nearly 100,000 were killed and 1,50,000 were taken captives. The blood of the killed and the injured flowed like a river. This horrible scene left an indelible impression upon the Mauryan Emperor. Struck with deep remorse for causing the sufferings of thousands, the Emperor decided to turn over a new leaf in his life. Unable to bear the anguish, he declared that he would wage no more wars but would try to conquer the hearts of the people by following the policy of *Dharma* (love and compassion). He embraced Buddhism and worked day and night to improve the moral life and material welfare of the masses. The Emperor set a personal example of what he was preaching to the people. He gave up the pleasures of royal life and undertook journeys to meet the subjects living in his empire. He was assisted by the *Dharmamahamatras* in achieving the goal of moral and material uplift of the masses. The message of the Buddha was spread to the neighbouring countries. Emperor Ashoka sent missionaries to Egypt, Syria, Macedonia, Cyrene, Ceylon, Lower Burma and Sumatra. The Emperor's son, Mahendra, and daughter, Sanghamitra, were sent to Ceylon to spread the message of the Buddha and they were successful in converting the ruler of that country into a Buddhist. After the death of Emperor Ashoka, the Mauryan empire began to decline rapidly. The Mauryan rulers organised a sound system of administration.

Mauryan Administration

The empire was divided into five provinces, namely Prachya and Madhyadesa, Kalinga, Avanti Dakshinapatha, and Uttarapatha. Their respective capitals were Pataliputra, Tosali, Ujjain, Suvarnagiri, and Taxila. The first province was directly ruled by the Emperor from his headquarters at Pataliputra and the rest by his appointed Viceroys. The Emperor was assisted by a cabinet of ministers and other senior officials. Chandragupta Maurya employed spies and received reports from them about the condition of the people living in different regions of his empire. Kautilya's *Arthasastra* gives an idea about the Mauryan polity. The Mauryan rulers were enlightened despots who followed high ideals of kingship. They discharged their onerous duties like administering justice, giving protection of life and property to their citizens, maintaining age-old customs and traditions, promoting trade and commerce and helping people who were affected by floods and famines. They safeguarded the integrity and sovereignty of the country by maintaining a well-organised standing army of 600,000 foot soldiers, 30,000 cavalry, 9,000 elephants and thousands of chariots. The administration of the military machine was in the hands of the members of six boards, each looking after one wing of the above plus commissariat.

Similarly, the important capitals or cities enjoyed autonomy. Each city was governed by a commission of 30 members which was divided into six boards. Each board was in charge of one or two departments. The departments were industrial and mechanical arts, foreign residents, registration of births and deaths, sales, exchanges, supervision of manufactured articles and collection of taxes on sales. The Greek ambassador, Megasthenes, describes the administration and social life of Pataliputra in his work, *Indica*.

Social Conditions

The Mauryan emperors promoted religious and social harmony. They encouraged agriculture, industries, trade and commerce. Megasthenes divided Mauryan society into philosophers (Brahmins), farmers, herdsmen and hunters, traders and artisans, warriors and government officers. The joint family system was in vogue. The position of women began to deteriorate. The members of the royal family and nobles patronised singing, dancing, acrobatics and dramatics. The rulers and nobles were fond of hunting but Ashoka seems to have restrained them from these pastimes. The common people amused themselves with meat-eating, drinking, animal fights and hunting. Slavery prevailed.

Economic Conditions

Agriculture and cattle-rearing continued to be the major occupations of the rural masses. In cities and towns, several industries and crafts developed, most notably textiles, carpentry, mining and metallurgy, manufacture of drugs and scents and boat-building. India's premier products were silk-fabrics, linen-cloth, woollen blankets and gold-embroidered clothes.

Inland and foreign trade went on briskly. The contact with the West developed after Alexander's invasion enabled traders to send Indian goods to the West. The government built ships and gave it to merchants for hire for the transport of their merchandise. The inland river system also enabled merchants to transport their merchandise by boat.

Religious Conditions

Hinduism maintained its hold on the vast populace of the Mauryan empire although it had to compete with Buddhism, Jainism and several other heterodox creeds. Buddhism received royal patronage under Emperor Ashoka and its ascendancy as a world creed was in the offing. Jainism also made considerable progress in some parts of Bihar, Western India and the South. The Jain tradition mentions that Chandragupta Maurya became a Jain monk and retired to the South to spend the last days of his life.

Mauryan Art and Architecture

A number of Ashokan pillars on which his edicts are engraved are not only known for their "beauty and vigour" but also exhibit high engineering and technical skills of the artist. The Sarnath pillar with the figure of four lions exhibits the artistic excellence of the Mauryans at its best. Ashoka seems to have erected about 84,000 *stupas* all over India, the most prominent being the Sanchi Stupa according to tradition. With respect to Mauryan architecture, contemporary Greek writers make references to the most beautiful and splendidly built palaces at the capital, Pataliputra. Even Fa-Hien, the Chinese pilgrim who came to India 700 years later, extols the beauty of these palaces.

Learning and Literature

Learning and literature received great attention of the rulers and the ruled. Taxila, which served as the capital of the Uttarapatha (a Mauryan province) was fast becoming a great centre of learning. Kautilya, the author of *Arthasastra* and minister of Chandragupta hailed from that place. The Mauryan age produced three great works, namely, *Arthasastra* of Kautilya or Chanakya, *Kalpasutra* of Bhadrabahu, and the *Katha Vatthu* of the Buddhists.

POST-MAURYA PERIOD

The Sungas (187-75 BC)

A Brahmin *senapati* of the last Mauryan Emperor, Pushyamitra Sunga, killed his master on the parade ground at the sight of the army. His coup succeeded and he became the master of the central portion of the Mauryan empire, the rest having declared its independence. The important events of his reign include the defeat of King Yagnasena of Vidarbha by Pushyamitra's son, Agnimitra (hero of Kalidas's *Malavikagnimitra*), the Yavana invasions and their defeat, and the revival of Brahmanism. At the same time, there was the revival of art as can be seen at Barhut and Sanchi.

Kanva Rule (75 BC - 30 BC)

Vasudeva Kanva, a Brahman minister of the last Sunga ruler, Devabhut killed his master and succeeded to the Sunga throne. He and his successors ruled the shrunken empire for the next 45 years. It was during this time that the Greeks established their control over Punjab. About 30 BC, the Satavahanas or the Andhras overthrew the Kanva rule and established their power in the Deccan.

Satavahanas of the Deccan

The Puranas, inscriptions and coins enable us to record the history of the Satavahanas. According to the *Aitreya Brahmana*, the Satavahanas were of mixed blood of Aryan and non-Aryan origin – and who established a small kingdom in the Deccan and owed allegiance to the Mauryan emperors. The first ruler was Simukha. The next great ruler was Satakarni I and in his time the kingdom became an empire with the conquest of Malwa, Vidarbha and parts of the South. The Nanaghat inscription refers to him as Dakshinapathapati (Lord of the South) and he celebrated various religious sacrifices to mark his imperial status. On these occasions he gave gifts to the Brahmans generously. With the death of Satakarni I, Satavahana power in the Deccan suffered a setback due to the Scythian invasions. The fallen fortunes of the dynasty were retrieved by Gautamiputra Satakarni, the greatest of the Satavahana rulers. He ruled the kingdom from about the beginning of the second century AD. He built a large empire after destroying the powers of the Scythians (Sakas), Yavanas (Greeks) and Pahlavas (Parthians). His empire extended from the Malwa region in the North to the southern borders of Karnataka in the South. In commemoration of his victory over the Kshaharata ruler, Nahapana, he struck coins in his name and issued them. He protected and maintained the four social orders and did not allow matrimonial relations with the foreigners. He ruled the empire according to the best Hindu traditions. Gautamiputra Satakarni was succeeded by his son, Vasisthiputra Pulamayi who ruled the empire from his headquarters at Pratishthana or Paithan. His brother, Vasisthiputra Satakarni, married the daughter of Rudradaman I, a Saka Satrap (Viceroy). But, despite these matrimonial relations, Rudradaman inflicted a crushing defeat on his southern relative. The next great Satavahana ruler was Yajna Sri Satakarni who defeated the Western Satraps and conquered their southern territories. After his death the glory of the Satavahana began to fade rapidly. Satavahana power vanished about the middle of the third century AD.

Greek Rule in India

While the Sungas tried to stem the tide of the invasions of the Bactrian Greeks, the latter established their kingdoms in the north-western part of India. Demitrios established his sway over Afghanistan, Punjab and Sindh. One of his successors, Menander, began his glorious reign after his military conquest of northern India. Although a Greek, he became a great scholar and patron of Buddhism. After his discourse with Nagasena, a great contemporary scholar of Buddhism, he got himself converted to Buddhism. This discussion is covered in a Pali work called *Milinda Panha* (Questions of Menander). Menander ruled India with headquarters at Sakala (modern Sialkot). The next important Indo-Greek king was Antialkidas who ruled the north-western part of India with his headquarters at Takshashila (Taxila). He sent his ambassador, Heliodorus, to the court of the Sungas at Vidisa. Heliodorus became a follower of Bhagavata religion and erected a Garuda pillar in honour of Vasudeva. The Sakas invaded the Greek settlements and the power of the Greeks declined.

Parthians

The Parthians (Pahlavas) revolted against their Seleucid master and set up an independent kingdom. During the third century BC Mithradates, the Parthian king, invaded Sindh and his later successor, Maues, established a kingdom in western Punjab. The most famous king of the Parthians was Gondophernes. According to Christian traditions, he received Christ's apostle St. Thomas in his country. He and his family became Christians.

Sakas or Scythians

The Sakas were driven out of their homeland by a nomadic tribe called the Yueh-Chi. Subsequently, they invaded Bactria where they destroyed Greek power. Gradually they came to India and established three kingdoms in India, namely, the kingdoms of Mathura, Takshashila and Malwa-Kathiawar. The rulers governing the first two kingdoms were known as northern Satraps and the rulers of the third kingdom were known as western Satraps. The western Satraps belonged to the Kshaharata race and built a kingdom on the ruins of the early Satavahana empire. They attained glory during the time of Nahapana. But the Satavahana ruler, Gautamiputra Satakarni, defeated him and restored the fallen fortunes of his family.

Chashtana and Rudradaman

The next great western satrap was Chashtana who founded a new dynasty and recovered a large part of the lost territory from the Satavahanas. His grandson was Rudradaman who ruled from AD 130 to AD 150. He probably gave his daughter in marriage to Vasishitaputra Satakarni, brother of Vasishitaputra Pulamayi. It appears Rudradaman defeated the Satavahanas twice during his lifetime even though he had matrimonial relations with them.

Kushanas

About 165 BC the Yueh-Chi (Turkish) tribe was driven out of their original homeland on the Chinese frontier. They then settled in the Oxus Valley after expelling the Parthians. The Kushanas belonged to this tribe. They got divided and ruled five principalities. It was Kadphises I who welded all of them into a nation. Kadphises I belonged to the Kushan section of the Yue-chi tribe. After attacking and defeating the Parthians he occupied Ki-pin, Kabul and the Indian north-western borderland. He issued copper coins which look similar to those issued by Roman Emperor Claudius. The next ruler was Wema Kadphises or Kadphises II who is credited by the Chinese with having extended his empire into the interior parts of northern India. He embraced Saivism and styled himself as *Mahisvara* on his coins. The subjects in his empire must have enjoyed a prosperous life as can be seen by the gold coins issued by the Kushana Emperor.

Kanishka I (Founder of Saka Era)

Kanishka could be described as the greatest among the Kushanas. He was the successor of Wema Kadphises and scholars say that the Saka era of AD 78 began with his reign. According to Chinese historians a Kushan king had fought with the Chinese General, Pan-Chao, sometime during the last quarter of the first century AD and it is believed that the Kushan ruler may have been none other than Kanishka I. Again, Hiuen Tsang makes a specific reference to the Chinese hostages held in the court of Kanishka.

Kanishka built a large empire which extended from Gandhara to Oudh and Benares and included the regions of Kashmir, Punjab, and western UP Outside India, his empire included Afghanistan, borders of Sindh and Khotan and Kashgar. The seat of his capital was at Purushapura, or Peshawar. The people of India often remember this great ruler for having built beautiful monuments and the patronage rendered to Buddhism. He built a wonderful Chaitya (Buddhist abode of worship) at Peshawar which evoked great admiration of travellers in those days. The Kushan sculpture which includes a decapitated statue of himself has excited the wonder of many. Kanishka convened the fourth Buddhist Council at Kundalavana (in Kashmir) which was presided over by a great Buddhist, Vasumitra. Ashvaghosha, the learned biographer of the Buddha, was also invited to the council which was to collect all Buddhist manuscripts and prepare commentaries on them. About 500 monks from all parts of the world participated in the conference. It may be said that Mahayana Buddhism made its beginnings during the time of Kanishka.

Significance of Kanishka's Reign

Kanishka achieved the desired political unity of northern India. Although Kanishka showed a leaning towards Buddhism his coins indicate his eclectic nature. Trade flourished since Kanishka ruled both northern India and Central Asia. The age of Kanishka contributed much to the development of art, architecture and literature. The Gandhara school of art reached the pinnacle of glory during the time of Kanishka. The Gandhara sculptors made beautiful images of the Buddha and the Bodhisattvas.

THE GUPTA AGE

Early Rulers

After the fall of the Kushana empire, the political unity of the country was again achieved during the time of the Imperial Guptas. The Puranas mention the names of Sri Gupta and Ghatotkacha as the earliest Gupta rulers who ruled over the small kingdom of Magadha. The third ruler of the Gupta dynasty was Chandragupta I who assumed the high sounding and imperial title of

'Maharajadhiraja' and consolidated his position by marrying the princess of a powerful ruling family, Lichchavis. Kumaradevi, the Lichchavi princess, added to the prestige and power of the imperial Guptas. It is said that the Gupta era commenced with the accession of Chandragupta I to the throne in 320 AD. At the time of his death, Chandragupta might have built an empire whose territories extended from Allahabad to the southern parts of Bihar. Chandragupta nominated one of his sons, Samudragupta, to be his successor. The Allahabad pillar inscription speaks of the career and achievements of Samudragupta. The inscription is a Prasasthi (eulogy) of Harisana, a court-poet of Samudragupta. After assuming power, Samudragupta embarked on a career of conquest. The names of nine kings whom he defeated in northern India are given, and unfortunately it is difficult to identify the regions they ruled. Samudragupta's campaigns and annexations of the territories of the defeated rulers had profound effect upon the neighbours. The Malavas of Malwa, the Arjunayanas of Alwar and Jaipur, Yaudheyas of northern Rajasthan, Madrakas of Sialkot and Abhiras of Central India submitted to his authority voluntarily. Not satisfied with the conquest of North India, Samudragupta launched a great campaign to subdue the powerful rulers of South India. He defeated the confederacy of south Indian rulers whose names are Mahendra of Kosala, Vyghra-raja of Mahakantara, Mantaraja of Kurala, Mahendragiri of Pishtapura, Svamidatta of Kottura, Damana of Erandapalla, Pallavak king Vishnugopa of Kanchi, Nilarja of Avamukta, Hastivarman of Vengi, Ugrasena of Palakka, Kubera of Devarashtra and Dhananjaya of Kushtalapura. All of them acknowledged the supremacy of Samudragupta and they were asked to continue as feudatory rulers. After *digvijay* over the South, he celebrated the *asvamedha* sacrifice to indicate his imperial status. Samudragupta's fame not only rests on his great conquests but also on his statesmanship. He followed different policies towards the defeated states. He annexed the states of some rulers, exacted tributes from some, and maintained friendly relations with the others. The Emperor's personal accomplishments are many. Some of his coins show that he was an accomplished artist who played the lyre. His courtiers called him *Kaviraja*. The *Asvamedha* coins indicate his implicit faith in Vedic religion. He was a great lover of learning as can be seen from the Prasasthi of his court-poet Harisena.

Chandragupta II Vikramaditya (AD 380-413)

Soon after the death of Samudragupta, his son Chandragupta II ascended the throne. Before attacking the Sakas in the west, Chandragupta II consolidated his position by matrimonial alliances with the powerful rulers such as the Nagas and the Vakatakas. He married the Naga princess, Kuberanaga. He gave his daughter Prabhavati in marriage to a powerful prince of the Vakataka ruling family, Rudrasena II. The Sakas were foreigners who had settled on the western side of his empire. He considered their presence as a great menace to his empire. He launched a campaign against them with the result that the last Saka Satrap, Rudrasimha III, was defeated and killed. Thus, India was liberated from the occupation of foreigners on her sacred soil. After this conquest, western Malwa and Kathiawar were added to his dominions. The Gupta empire spread from the coast of the Bay of Bengal to the coast of the Arabian Sea. This conquest was of great significance since the ports of the west coast were engaged in commerce with the West. Chandragupta II assumed the title, *Vikramaditya* and *Sakari* and issued gold and silver coins in his name. The Gupta empire reached the acme of its glory during his time. Many have described his age as the golden age. Fa-Hien, a Chinese pilgrim who came at this time, has spoken highly of the efficient system of government and the acts of charity of moneyed classes. In the field of art, architecture and literature the Gupta age stands distinguished. Chandragupta was a liberal patron and his court was adorned by the *Navaratnas* (nine gems meaning nine great and learned men). The greatest among the nine was Kalidasa, the poet par excellence. Next came Dhanavantari, the great physician of the time. The third in line was Varahamihira, the great astronomer. The fourth was Amarasimha, the lexicographer; the fifth, Shanku, the architect; the sixth, Kshapanaka, the astrologer; the seventh, Vararuchi, the grammarian; the eighth, Vetalabhatta, the magician and the ninth, Ghatakharpara, probably a poet.

Kumaragupta and Skandagupta

Chandragupta's successor was Kumaragupta who ruled over the empire from AD 415 to 455. He seemed to have ruled well after observing his performance of the *Asvamedha* sacrifice. However, during the last years of his life, the Gupta empire was subjected to serious troubles by the Pushyamitras living near the Narmada Valley. It was Prince Skandagupta who saved the empire from these marauders. Prince Skandagupta next turned his attention to the Huns who were invading and conquering some provinces. His efforts to repel the aggression of the Huns succeeded and they were expelled from India. After his glorious victory over the Huns, Prince Skandagupta assumed the title, *Vikramaditya*. His rule ended about AD 467 and subsequently, we do not have enough records to trace Gupta history.

Inscriptions record that the Gupta empire continued to survive despite the troubles from the Huns. Its decline began rapidly from the early sixth century AD. The later Guptas did restore the glory, but only for a short time during the seventh century AD.

Religion

The Gupta age is known for the revival of Brahminical Hinduism. The emperors revived the Vedic sacrifices and protected the four castes. A new feature of the religious life of the people was the Bhakti (intense devotion to God) cult. Religious toleration was another feature worth noticing during that age.

Gupta Age, the 'Gilded Age'

The Gupta age is also known for its literary grandeur. It produced great men like Kalidasa and others. The Puranas were recast. In the field of science the Gupta age could boast of having produced great scientists like Aryabhata and Varahamihira. Narada and Brihaspati contributed to the legal system of the age.

POST-GUPTA PERIOD

The Vardhana Dynasty

The disintegration of the Gupta empire began in northern India due to the constant invasions of the Huns. It was not until the early seventh century, that an attempt was made to stem this tide of disunity and confusion. The Vardhana dynasty which ruled over the kingdom of Thaneswar succeeded in establishing the political unity of northern India. After a series of personal tragedies Harshavardhana came to power in Thaneswar in AD 606. The nobles of Kanauj offered the crown of the late Grahavarman, brother-in-law of Harsha, to Harshavardhana since Rajasri, the widowed queen, had no intention of ruling the kingdom. To what extent Harshavardhana took revenge upon the enemies of his brother-in-law is not clearly known. But he got the assistance of Bhaskaravarman, the ruler of Kamarupa (Assam). Harsha's attempt to conquer the South was foiled by the powerful Chalukya ruler, Pulakesin II. Harsha patronised scholars and Buddhism. Hiuen Tsang, the Chinese pilgrim, became his personal friend and guest. He assisted Harshavardhana in holding the Kanauj Assembly where he became the highly honoured guest of the Emperor. Harsha also held the Prayaga Assembly where the Chinese pilgrim was also present. It was here that Harshavardhana gave away everything to the poor and needy and received his ordinary garments from his widowed sister. Harsha was a great patron of learning and literature. He gave liberal donations to Nalanda University where scholars from home and abroad received special instructions on Mahayana Buddhism. Harsha was an accomplished writer whose works, *Nagananda*, *Ratnavali* and *Priyadarshika*, attained great status in literature.

Early Chalukyas of Badami

In the Deccan, the early Chalukyas played an important role in uniting the Deccan between the sixth and eighth century AD. The most distinguished ruler of the dynasty was Pulakesin II (AD 609-642). He won victories against his neighbours like the Kadambas and the Pallavas and built an empire which extended from the border of the Narmada to the Cauvery. One of his significant victories was against Harshavardhana who tried to conquer the South. However, the tragic end for himself and his empire came when his traditional foe, the Pallavas of Kanchi, invaded Badami under the leadership of King Narasimhavarman I. The Chalukyan empire witnessed confusion and chaos for the next 13 years. Its glory was revived by Vikramaditya in AD 654. Pulakesin II maintained diplomatic relations with the Persian empire under Khusru II. One of the paintings at Ajanta shows the reception accorded to the Persian embassy by the Chalukya king. The Chalukya rulers enriched the culture of ancient India with their patronage of art, architecture and literature. A few paintings at Ajanta and the temples built at Badami and Pattadakal stand as testimony to their encouragement.

Pallavas of Kanchi

In the far South, the Pallavas ruled from the fifth century AD to the ninth century AD. One of their earliest rulers was Vishnugopa to whom there is a reference in the Allahabad pillar inscription. From the sixth century onwards, the Pallava rulers became very powerful and blazed a trail of glory. The first ruler was Simhavishnu who may have inflicted crushing defeats on the Cholas, Pandyas and the Ceylonese rulers. The next ruler was Mahendravarman I and with him the Pallava-Chalukya struggle for the supremacy of the South began. Mahendravarman converted himself from Jainism to Saivism. The Chalukya ruler seemed to have gained an upper hand in the struggle for supremacy till it was halted by Narsimhavarman I, son of Mahendravarman I. His forces invaded the Chalukya capital, Badami, and it was seized. Pulakesin II lost his life in the battle. The Chalukyas took revenge during the time of Vikramaditya I and Vikramaditya II. In the course of time the Pandyas also attacked the Pallava kingdom and it declined rapidly from the ninth century AD onwards. Aditya Chola defeated Aparajita Pallava and established a new kingdom in its place during the ninth century AD.

The Pallavas contributed to art, architecture and literature. Their cities and towns including the famous Mamallapuram abound with temples, carvings and great works of sculpture. Rock architecture came to be patronised. The Pancha-pandava Rathas (Chariots of Pandavas) are hewn out of rock boulders. The kings also contributed to literature. Mahendravarman I was an artist and writer of great repute. He wrote a famous burlesque titled *Mattavilasa-Prahasana*.

It must be noted that Kanchi had been serving as a great centre of learning in the south. Many *Vaishnava* and *Saiva* saints imparted instructions and made Kanchi a great religious centre. Hiuen Tsang mentions that there were 100 monasteries and 10,000 priests at Kanchi. Scholars of various hues flourished.

They mainly included the Jain, Buddhist, the Vaishnava and Saiva scholars. Vatsyayana, a renowned logician of that time, lived in Kanchi. Even a great prince like the Mayurasarman of the Kadamba dynasty stayed here for completing his studies.

The Pratiharas

Turning our attention to the Deccan and the North between the eighth and the tenth centuries, we see the rise and rivalry of three great empires, namely, the Palas, the Pratiharas and the Rashtrakutas. Harsha's capital, Kanauj, attracted their attention as worth coveting as a symbol of prestige and pride. The Pratiharas held their sway over northern India for nearly a hundred years (middle of the ninth to the middle of the tenth centuries). The true founder of the Pratihara empire was Bhoja who made strenuous efforts to rebuild the empire after the disastrous defeat of his predecessor, Nagabhatta II. He was successful in capturing Kanauj, which remained with the Pratiharas till the last days. Bhoja fought his rivals, the Rashtrakutas and the Palas tried to recover Gujarat and Malwa. He died in AD 885 and his son, Mahendra Pala, extended his sway over the Magadha and northern Bengal. Al Masudi, a native of Baghdad, visited his kingdom and mentions the prestige enjoyed by the Pratihara rulers.

The Palas

The Pala kingdom was established in AD 750 by one Gopala. The greatest King was Dharmapala (AD 770-810). A triangular fight ensued for the possession of Kanauj among the Palas, the Pratiharas and the Rashtrakutas. In the first round Dharmapala was beaten by the Vatsaraja of the Pratiharas, but the latter was defeated by King Dhruva of the Rashtrakutas. King Dhruva did not occupy Kanauj thus leaving the issue to be settled between the Pala ruler and the Pratihara King. It was then that Dharmapala seized Kanauj, following his conquest of Malwa and Gujarat.

The Rashtrakutas

The Rashtrakutas produced great warriors and administrators, and they ruled the Deccan making Malkhed (Manyakheta) as their capital. The kingdom was founded by Dantidurga, who overthrew the early Chalukya dynasty in Badami in AD 752. To gain supremacy, the Rashtrakutas fought the Pratiharas for the control of Malwa and Gujarat. In the South, they carried on their wars with the Eastern Chalukyas of Vengi, the Pallavas of Kanchi and the Pandyas of Madurai. Dhruva (780-793) and Govinda III (793-814) conquered many parts of North and South India during their lifetime, thus proving they were invincible. Indra III and Krishna III (939-965) were undoubtedly great kings. Al Masudi mentions the name of Balhara as one of the greatest kings of India whose suzerainty was respected by all the Indian rulers. The Rashtrakuta history is incomplete if we do not mention the name of Amoghavarsha (814-880). His long reign witnessed peace and prosperity. This great King wrote a famous treatise in Kannada titled *Kaviraja marga* and patronised art and literature. His reign witnessed religious tolerance, and he came under the influence of a Jain preceptor, Jinasena (the author of *Adipurana*). The Rashtrakuta emperors, as mentioned earlier, were great patrons of art and architecture. For example, Krishna I (756-772) built the famous rock-cut monolithic shrine of Kailasa at Ellora, and Amoghavarsha made the capital, Manyakheta, beautiful with great buildings and gardens.

The Later Chalukyas of Kalyani (AD 973-1189)

The last Rashtrakuta ruler, Kakka II, was defeated in a battle by a scion of the early Chalukya dynasty named Taila II. He continued Chalukyan rule after recovering all the territories lost by his ancestors. He defeated King Munja of Malwa and claims to have defeated the Chola Emperor, Rajaraja the Great. His successor, Satyasraya, enlarged his kingdom by defeating the Silaharas of northern Konkan, but met stiff resistance from the Cholas. In fact, the Cholas invaded his kingdom and snatched away large chunks, but Satyasraya was able to recover them with great difficulty. The next important ruler was Somesvara I (AD 1042-68) who continued the traditional rivalry with the Cholas for the capture of Vengi, the Eastern Chalukyan capital. This ruler shifted his capital from Manyakheta to Kalyana. The next ruler was Somesvara II who struggled with his brother Vikramaditya VI because he was undermining his position with the assistance of some feudatories and neighbouring kings (Kadambas, Hoyasalas, Pandyas and Yadavas).

Vikramaditya VI (AD 1076-1126)

He conspired to bring about the deposition of his brother, and he was successful in this mission. He inaugurated a new era, the Chalukya-Vikrama year which remained in force for the next fifty years. After ascending the throne he congratulated the Ceylonese ruler for defeating the Chola Emperor. The reign of Vikramaditya VI was marked by a series of rebellions, some led by feudatories. The most important among them was Hoysala Vishnuvardhana. All of them were suppressed and Hoysala Vishnuvardhana too offered his submission after a struggle. The Chalukyan emperor was able to capture Vengi, and thus eliminated the influence of the Cholas there. He crushed the revolts of the Silharas and the Yadavas. He patronised art and literature. Bilhana, a famous writer, wrote the Emperor's biography, *Vikramankadevacharita*. Vignaneswara, another noted jurist, produced *Mitakshara*, a commentary on *Yagnavalkyasmriti*.

Somesvara III *(AD 1126-1138)*

The decline of the later Chalukyan empire began with Somesvara III since he was not able to defend his empire from the onslaughts of the Cholas and the Hoysalas. The latter declared their independence. King Somesvara III is remembered today for his great encyclopaedic work, *Mansollasa* (also known as *Abhilashitartha Chintamani*). After the fall, there emerged what is known as the Kalachuri interregnum which witnessed the rise of Basaveswara, the greatest social reformer of the twelfth century.

The Cholas of Tanjavur

After the eclipse of the Pallavas, there arose the Chola kingdom with its capital at Tanjavur in the South. It ruled South India from the ninth to the thirteenth century AD. Its great rulers established their sway over the Chola *mandalam*, meaning the Chola country which lay between the two rivers, the Pennar and the Vellar. The Cholas achieved remarkable progress under the leadership of one of their greatest rulers, Rajaraja I (985-1014). His great exploits are engraved on the walls of the Rajarajeswara temple at Tanjavur. He fought many battles and defeated the Cheras, the Pandyas, the rulers of Mysore, and the Eastern Chalukyas of Vengi and invaded Ceylon. His brilliant campaigns, both on land and sea, were highly successful. Under his leadership, the Chola empire became a great sea power. The maritime conquests included the islands of the Laccadives and Maldives and northern parts of Ceylon.

Rajaraja's Contribution

Besides being a great conqueror, Rajaraja the Great was also a great administrator and patron of art. He introduced many reforms in the administration to serve the cause of the poor and built splendid temples. Being a Saivite, he built the Rajarajesvara temple at Tanjavur in honour of God Shiva. His religious toleration is proved by the fact that he gave permission to the Sailendra king of Java to build a Buddhist vihara near Negapatam.

Rajendra Chola's Exploits

Rajendra Chola, son of Rajaraja the Great, succeeded to the Chola throne in 1014 and ruled for about 30 years. He may be described as an illustrious son of an illustrious father. His great exploits included the defeat of the Pandyas, the Cheras, and the Chalukyas of Kalyani. The Chola army led by him marched victoriously up to the banks of the Ganges in Bengal defeating a number of rulers of Kalinga, Orissa and south Kosala on the way. Mahipala, the Pala King of Bengal, was also defeated. On his return, he built a new capital, *Gangaikondacholapuram*. He also assumed the title, *Gangaikonda*. Not satisfied with the victories achieved on land, he sent several naval expeditions against the Sailendra kings of Java and succeeded in defeating them. Thus, the

Cholas built an overseas empire which included Java, Sumatra, Malaya Peninsula and Ceylon. Like his illustrious father, Rajendra Chola rendered great services to the people by introducing reforms in administration and patronising art and literature. His successors carried on his good work during the succeeding generations. With the invasion of South India by Malik Kafur the Chola power declined rapidly.

Chola Administration

The Chola emperors were enlightened despots. They divided their empire into *mandalas* (provinces). They sent members of the royal blood to serve as Viceroys. The emperor was assisted by ministers and a coterie of officials as in modern government. Similarly the Viceroys were also assisted by ministers and officials. One of the great features of Chola administration was the local administration of villages. It was in this field that we observe that Cholas followed the principles of democratic government. Their village assembly was democratic in character as it consisted of elected representatives. The Uttaramerur inscription gives an idea of how a village assembly of Uttaramerur consisted of elected members, each elected by the adult voters of one ward and also gives detailed description of the process of election. The village assembly divided itself into committees, each committee consisting of some experienced members looking after one aspect of village affairs. Maintenance of temples, agriculture, irrigation, collection of taxes, construction of roads, market regulations and the like were looked after by committees. Thus, democratic principles were very much operating in the affairs of village assemblies. It must be noted that even the Chola emperors respected the decisions of these assemblies.

Other Contributions

The Chola emperors encouraged learning, literature, art and architecture. The educational institutions imparted instructions on the Vedas, Puranas, *Dharmasastras*, astronomy, science and various *sastras*. The Chola artists have created beautiful stone as well as bronze statues of gods and goddesses.

The marvel of Chola architecture can be seen in Tanjavur and other important towns of South India. The Rajarajaesvara temple, the Brihadesvara temple, and Rajendra Chola's Shiva temples show the beautiful architecture of the Cholas. The Chola temples are famous for their *vimanas* (towers) and big courtyards.

The Chola empire prospered due to brisk trade and commerce. The Chola traders maintained commercial relations with China, Malaya, western Gulf countries, and the islands in South-East Asia.

The Chola emperors were the followers of either Saivism or Vaishnavism. They built temples in honour of Lord Shiva or Lord Vishnu. They also built temples for many goddesses. The Chola emperors allowed freedom of worship and offered necessary protection to practise one's own religion.

The Chola emperors encouraged Tamil literature. Kamban's *Ramayana* is regarded as a great classic in Tamil literature. Jayagondar wrote *Jiwaka Chintamani*. Some Buddhist scholars wrote a few works in Tamil. Sanskrit literature also made considerable progress. Thus, the Cholas made remarkable progress in many fields and thereby enriched Indian culture.

31

EARLY MEDIEVAL INDIA

The Sultanate Period

The Arab invasion of Sindh in AD 711 failed to consolidate Muslim power in India. The spread of Islam did not take place until the early eleventh century with the frequent invasions of India by Mohammed of Ghazni (AD 998-1030). His dozen or so invasions witnessed the plunder of many cities situated in northern and western India, the most noteworthy being that of Somnath. Mohammed of Ghazni had no intention of conquering and consolidating his hold over India. Therefore, it had to wait till the advent of Mohammed of Ghor (AD 1173-1206). Although his earlier attempts to defeat Indian rulers failed, he was finally successful in establishing his hegemony over much of North India after the defeat and execution of Prithviraj Chauhan in the second battle of Tarain (AD 1192). After the defeat of Jaichandra (rival of Prithviraj of Delhi), at Chandawar, we see the beginnings of Turkish rule in India. Qutbuddin Aibek, a trusted slave, was given charge of looking after the conquered territories in India. Subsequently, Bihar and northern Bengal came under the control of slave rulers (the Mameluk Sultans). Iltutmish (1210-36) protected and consolidated the Turkish empire in India. His successor was his daughter, Raziya Begum whose short reign (1236-39) witnessed the rise of the Turkish chiefs known as "the forty" or Chahalgani. They opposed her as they did not like to be ruled by a woman who was appointing non-Turks to high positions. They also resented her close relations with an Abyssinian noble. The struggle ended in the victory of one of the famous Turkish chiefs, known as Ulugh Khan (Balban). Balban became the Sultan in 1265 and made every effort to increase the power and prestige of the Turkish monarchy. He ruled his dominions with iron hand, and maintained law and order. He appointed spies for the purpose of informing him about the activities of the Turkish nobles and Hindu chieftains. His punishments were so severe that nobody, the high or the low, had the courage to oppose him. He protected the country from the menace of Mongols. After his death (1286), Delhi witnessed chaos for four years until the Khalji nobles led by Jalaluddin Khalji took over the leadership in 1290.

The Khalji Dynasty

Jalaluddin Khalji was treacherously murdered by his nephew, and son-in-law, Alauddin Khalji (1296-1314). Alauddin crushed all revolts of the rivals and disgruntled nobles, and adopted very harsh methods to keep himself in power. He established his sway over the Deccan and the South after the four successful military expeditions undertaken by one of his favourite commanders, Malik Kafur. The kingdoms of Yadavas of Devagiri, the Hoysalas of Dwarasamudra, the Kakatiyas of Warangal, and the Pandyas of Madurai were subjected to the raids and plunder of Malik Kafur, and he went as far as Rameswaram. Alauddin's internal reforms, particularly on market control and agrarian aspects, have been described as progressive since they aimed at removing rural and urban poverty. However, the market regulations applied to Delhi and its suburbs only. Barani, the historian of the time, describes his revenue reforms as aiming at "preventing the burden of the strong falling upon the weak". Alauddin protected the northern borders of his empire from the invasions of Mongols by undertaking various measures.

The Tughluq Dynasty

After the death of Alauddin, power passed on to the Tughluqs (1320-1412). Mohammed bin Tughluq (1324-51) made his mark as an "ill-starred idealist" and proved to be far ahead of his times. His controversial experiments, though well-intentioned, namely, the transfer of the capital and the introduction of token currency, landed him in serious trouble. His revenue experiments also failed leading to terrible loss to the exchequer and outbreak of famines. His hot temper coupled with very harsh measures alienated the sympathies of the common people. Rebellions broke out in many parts of his empire which were sometimes led by the ambitious nobles. In this process of disintegration we see the birth of Bahamani and Vijayanagar kingdoms in the Deccan. His successor, Firuz Tughluq, did his best to prevent the breakup of the Delhi Sultanate. He tried to build a theocratic state and ruled according to liberal principles. His revenue reforms included many concessions to feudal lords. The *jiziya* (poll tax) was imposed on Brahmans too, who were earlier exempt. Firuz is remembered today for his humanitarian measures, and the construction works undertaken by the Public Works Department. He built towns (Hissar and Firuzabad), dug canals, laid gardens, and built mosques and hospitals. After his death, Delhi was ruled by the Sayyids (1414-51) and the Lodis (1451-1526), following the invasion of Timur (1398-99).

The Vijayanagar Empire (1336-1565)

The Deccan witnessed the birth of the Vijayanagar kingdom in 1336 which was founded by the Sangama family, notably, Harihara and Bukka, on the advice of sage Vidyaranya. A decade later (1347), the Bahamani kingdom came into existence following a declaration of independence from the control of Tughluq rule. There was a clash of interests between the Hindu kingdom of Vijayanagar and the Muslim kingdom of Bahamani, which led to many wars, especially over the Tungabhadra Doab. As there was a check over northward expansion, the Vijayanagar kings concentrated on expanding the empire towards the South. It led to the defeat of the sultanate of Madurai. King Devaraya II made his mark as the greatest of Vijayanagar kings in the fifteenth century (1422-1448). He seems to have followed a secular policy, and Nuniz (a Portuguese writer who visited Vijayanagar in the 16th century) mentions that many South-East Asian kingdoms including Sri Lanka paid tributes to him. But the early 16th century witnessed the golden era of Vijayanagar under Krishnadevaraya (1509-30). He was undoubtedly the greatest among all the South Indian kings. It was he who brought glory to Vijayanagar by defeating all the kings, Hindus and Muslims, in the Deccan and the South, and took up the work of consolidation. He maintained friendly relations with the Portuguese who had captured Goa in 1510 from the Sultan of Bijapur. Besides being a great writer (author of *Amuktamalyada*), he patronised art and literature. It was a golden era of Telugu and Kannada literature. His magnificent court was adorned by the famous eight poets. Abdur Razzaq describes Vijayanagar as one of the greatest cities in the world, known for its fabulous riches. Krishnadevaraya thus shines as a great warrior, statesman, writer and administrator.

The Bahamani Kingdom

The Bahamani kingdom took its birth in AD 1347 after a revolt of *sadah amirs* against the misrule of Mohammed bin Tughluq. The rebels elected Ismail Mukh as their leader but he abdicated his power in favour of Alauddin Hasan Bahamn Shah (1347-58). Gulbarga became the seat of the capital of this rebel kingdom till 1425, and thereafter it was shifted to Bidar. Rivalry with the Vijayanagar kingdom over the possession of the Tungabhadra Doab marked the early history of Bahamani kingdom. Among the early rulers, the reign of Tajuddin Firuz Shah (1397-1422) was noteworthy because he defeated the Vijayanagar kings, Harihara II and Devaraya I; the latter gave his daughter in marriage to him along with Bankapur as his dowry. This sultan was a master of many subjects and languages. He was also a good calligraphist and poet.

The next great personality we come across in the Bahamani kingdom during the Bidar period is Mohammed Gawan (a Persian by birth) who served at least three sultans as minister. It was due to his political sagacity that the Bahamani kingdom reached the zenith of its glory. His kingdom expanded on all sides, particularly towards the west, that is the Konkan and Goa. The Godavari-Krishna Doab was also annexed. Mohammed Gawan is remembered today for his most noteworthy reforms — administrative, revenue, military and educational. His growing popularity made his rivals jealous, and they hatched a conspiracy for his execution. Their plan succeeded when Mohammed Shah, in a drunken state, ordered the execution of his great minister, little suspecting any conspiracy. With the death of this great minister in 1481 and also following the death of the Sultan a few years later, the Bahamani kingdom got split into five independent states (five sultanates), namely, the Imad-Shahi dynasty of Berar, the Adil-Shahi dynasty of Bijapur, the Qutb-Shahi dynasty of Golconda, the Nizam-Shahi dynasty of Ahmednagar and the Barid-Shahi dynasty of Bidar.

32

LATER MEDIEVAL INDIA

Zahiruddin Mohammed Babur (1526-30)

The early sixteenth century saw a chaotic situation prevailing in India. India was divided into several independent states, each at war with the other. Political disunity in northern India attracted the attention of Zahiruddin Mohammed Babur, a fugitive prince of Farghana. He became the undisputed master of Afghanistan after his attack and capture of Kabul and Ghazni in 1504. After having failed to recover Samarkhand, Babur turned his attention to the conquest of India. Conditions in the Lodi kingdom of Delhi had turned from bad to worse since the ruler, Ibrahim Lodi, faced innumerable revolts from his disaffected nobles. The Afghan rulers of Bengal, Malwa and Gujarat also hated the Lodi Sultan of Delhi. Alam Khan Lodi, the uncle of the Sultan, claimed the Delhi throne but after failing to secure the same, invited Babur to invade India. The ruler of the most powerful Rajput kingdom of Mewar by the name of Rana Sangram Singh (also known as Rana Sanga) also assured Babur of his assistance if he were to attack the Lodi kingdom. Babur marched at the head of an army of 12,000 disciplined soldiers and conquered Punjab. After its conquest he proceeded towards Delhi. He fought the most significant battle on the plains of Panipat in April 1526 against the numerically superior forces of Ibrahim Lodi. The Afghan army led by Ibrahim Lodi perished. Ibrahim Lodi lay dead on the battlefield and Babur became the ruler of Delhi. He occupied Agra and laid the foundation of Mughal rule in India.

Babur's occupation of Delhi and Agra, and his intention to stay in India permanently, enraged Rana Sanga of Mewar. Hostility and war between the two became inevitable when Rana Sanga gave refuge to Alam Khan Lodi and supported the cause of Mohammed Lodi for the Delhi throne. Babur fought Rana Sanga in the battle of Khanua (1527). The Rajput army was routed and its leader, Rana Sanga, who was badly wounded, was forced to retire. The Mughal victory over the Rajputs was total and Babur became the undisputed master of Delhi. In 1528, Babur attacked Chanderi and captured it. The Afghans, who felt thoroughly humiliated after their defeat by a foreigner, rallied round under the leadership of Mohammed Lodi and challenged Babur in 1529.

Babur fought them on the banks of the Ghagara and inflicted a crushing defeat. Thus all his enemies were subdued. Babur died in December 1530 after nominating his eldest son, Humayun, as his successor to the Mughal throne.

Humayun

The premature death of Babur created difficulties for his inexperienced son. Humayun had to consolidate the gains that his father had left for him. His brothers and relatives were extremely jealous, cruel and cunning. The Afghans waited for their opportunity to recover the throne of Delhi. In the end Humayun lost his throne to Sher Shah and went into exile in 1540. He stayed in Persia for nearly 15 years. After the death of Sher Shah the Afghan empire began to decline on account of internal feuds. Taking advantage of the dissensions, Humayun conquered all the territories from Peshawar to Lahore in May 1555. Then he occupied Punjab. He fought and defeated Sikander Shah in the battle of Sarhind. When Sikander Shah fled Humayun occupied Delhi in July 1555. Then he added Agra and Sambhal to his small kingdom. He died in January 1556. Bairam Khan, a close friend of Humayun, crowned Akbar as the successor at Kalanaur on 14th February 1556. Akbar, son and successor of Humayun, was then fourteen years old when he ascended the throne. During the lifetime of his father he had worked as the governor of Ghazni. He helped his father during his last days in consolidating Mughal rule in Punjab. As Akbar was too young, Humayun allowed his friend Bairam Khan, to act as his son's guardian. It may be remembered that just before Humayun captured Delhi, it was contested by all the Afghan rulers. A minister of Sultan Adil Shah by the name Hemu captured Agra and Sambhal and laid claim to the throne of Delhi soon after the death of Humayun. Hemu succeeded in capturing Delhi and assumed the title 'Maharaja Vikramaditya'. Akbar convened a council of war at Jalandhar where his nobles advised him to retreat towards Kabul. But Bairam Khan advised Akbar to reject their advice and urged his ward to attack Delhi. Akbar faced Hemu on the plains of Panipat in November 1556. When the battle started, an arrow struck one eye of Hemu and he fell down unconscious. Feeling the absence of their leader, Hemu's army lost courage and fled. Hemu was taken captive. While Akbar hesitated to kill the wounded Hemu, Bairam Khan felt no pity in cutting off his head with his sword. Bairam Khan wielded his power and influence as *wazir* of the empire for nearly four years. During this period Akbar began to expand and consolidate the territories of his kingdom. When Bairam Khan proved to be overbearing and his loyalty was in doubt, Akbar ordered for his voluntary exile.

AKBAR (1556-1605)

Akbar's great desire was to bring about the political unity of India under Mughal supremacy. Therefore, he sent messages to the independent rulers of northern

India to submit to his authority and pay tributes. When many of them refused to respect his authority, the Emperor declared war against them.

Knowing the nature and character of the Rajput rulers of his time, Akbar adopted a wise and conciliatory policy towards them. He was able to secure their loyalty and affection by employing many talented Rajputs into his army and diplomatic service. More than all he married a Rajput princess of Amber and respected her religious rights. But the chief of Mewar, Rana Pratap Singh, raised his banner of revolt. Akbar defeated him in the famous battle of Haldighat (sometimes compared to the Battle of Thermopylae) in 1576 but could not destroy Mewar's spirit of independence. The Sisodiyas continued to resist Mughal authority till the last days of Akbar.

Establishment of Mughal Paramountcy in India

Between 1558 and 1561, Akbar conquered Malwa, Gwalior, Ajmer and Jaunpur. He took Gondwana in 1564 after defeating Rani Durgawati. He conquered Bengal during the same year. He established his supremacy over Gujarat in 1569, Kabul in 1585, Kashmir in 1586, Sind in 1591, Orissa in 1592 and Baluchistan in 1595. By about 1600 Akbar extended his sway over a part of the Deccan which included Khandesh, Berar, part of Ahmednagar and the forts of Burhanpur, Daulatabad, Asirgarh and Ahmednagar. Realising that without the cooperation of the Hindus, it would be difficult to have political stability, he altered his religious policy from that followed by his predecessors.

Akbar's Religious Policy

He befriended the Hindus by abolishing the detested taxes such as the *Jaziya* and the poll tax and extended to them his policy of religious tolerance. Although he was illiterate he often summoned various theologians to hear about and discuss the principles of many religions. He finally founded a new religion which he believed would be acceptable to one and all in India. It was *Din Ilahi*. He took the first step towards achieving Hindu-Muslim unity in our country.

Administration

Akbar divided his empire into 12 provinces or *subas* and appointed *subadars* to rule over them. Each *suba* was divided into *sarkars* and each *sarkar* subdivided into *paraganas*. Every officer of the state held a civil and military rank and provided soldiers and supplies to the Mughal Emperor. The Centre was headed by the Emperor who enjoyed unlimited authority. The Emperor took the assistance of the prime minister (*vazir*), the Mir Bakhshi, the chief Sadar, the chief Qazi, the Muhtasib, the Khan-i-Saman, the Daroga-i-topkhana and Daroga-i-dak-chauki in carrying out the day-to-day administration.

Estimate of Akbar

Both the Hindus and the Muslims began to look upon Akbar as a truly national king. Akbar was also a social reformer who tried to do away with such social evils as the *sati*, infanticide and child marriage. In the words of Edwards and Garrett, "Akbar has proved his worth in different fields of *action*. He was an intrepid solider, a great general, a wise administrator, a benevolent ruler, and a sound judge of character. He was a born leader of men and can rightly claim to be one of the mightiest sovereigns known to history..."

Jehangir (1605-27)

Akbar's son, Jehangir, continued his father's policy of conquest and annexation. Mewar, Bengal, Kangra, Ahmednagar and Bijapur all submitted to his authority. Jehangir married Nurjehan, a most beautiful and highly intelligent lady who became a de facto ruler. She managed the affairs of the empire so efficiently that she caused jealousy among many of the emperor's opponents. It was during Jehangir's reign that Captain Hawkins, an English envoy, came with a letter from King James I of England seeking permission to trade. His visit was followed by the appointment of Sir Thomas Roe as ambassador to the Mughal court. Jehangir gave permission to the English company to establish their factory at Surat. Guru Arjundev (the sixth Guru of the Sikhs) was executed under the order of Jehangir.

Shah Jehan (1628-58)

Jehangir died in 1627 and Nurjehan attempted to place her son-in-law, Prince Shahriyar, on the Mughal throne, but her brother foiled her attempt and succeeded in placing his own son-in-law, Prince Khurram (Shahjehan), on the throne in 1628. Shah Jehan suppressed the revolts of the Bundelas and the subadars of the Deccan. He extended the Mughal authority to the Deccan by destroying the power of the Nizamshahis of Ahmednagar and compelling the rulers of Bijapur and Golconda to accept Mughal suzerainty. He drove the Portuguese out of Hughli for their nefarious acts concerning women belonging to his palace.

The age of Shah Jehan is considered by some historians as the golden age in Mughal history on account of new constructions. Mughal architecture reached the height of its glory during his time. He built Taj Mahal in Agra in the ever-loving memory of his deceased wife, Mumtaz Mahal. The other Mughal monuments which stand to his credit are Diwan-i-khas, Diwan-i-am, Moti Masjid, and Lal Qila (Red Fort). Shah Jehan's peacock throne was a cynosure of all eyes in those days. When Shah Jehan fell ill in 1658, all his four sons contested for the throne. Aurangzeb eliminated all his rivals, one by one, by a *coup de grace*, imprisoned his ailing father, and ascended the Mughal throne in 1658.

Aurangzeb (1658-1707)

Aurangzeb turned into a religious bigot and alienated the sympathies of many non-Muslim communities such as the Hindus and the Sikhs. Hindu temples were destroyed and the Sikh Guru, Tegh Bahadur, was executed on the orders of the Mughal Emperor. In 1679, Aurangzeb reimposed the *Jaziya*. Thus the Hindus could no longer look upon him as a national king but as a misguided fanatic. So his empire was shaken by a series of revolts staged by the Sikhs, the Satnamis, the Rajputs and subsequently by the Marathas under the leadership of Shivaji.

Shivaji (1627-80)

Aurangzeb expanded Mughal dominions by adding a part of Assam after the defeat of Ahoms. He also put an end to the rule of Shia rulers over Bijapur and Golconda. Since Maratha leader Shivaji proved to be elusive and dangerous to his empire in the Deccan, Aurangzeb came down to the Deccan to deal with him. Crowning himself as *Chhatrapati* (king of kings), Shivaji continued to pose a serious threat to Aurangzeb's empire despite the latter's several engagements with him. The result was that the Mughal Emperor lost many men. The endless war with the Marathas sapped the strength of his empire. The death of Shivaji and the weak rule of Sambhaji did not deter the will of the Marathas to carry on their struggle for freedom. Aurangzeb died in 1707 without achieving his goal. The decline and fall of the Mughal Empire followed soon after his death.

33
BRITISH RULE IN INDIA

The rise of modern imperialism began in the nineteenth century. The European powers extended their control over the countries of Asia and Africa after defeating the respective native powers. The outbreak of the industrial revolution in Britain, and its subsequent spread in Western Europe, resulted in the growing demand for raw materials and new markets. It was to meet these twin demands, and also to achieve political prestige, that the European powers eagerly looked forward to acquiring colonies in Asia and Africa. European merchants of the early centuries had come to Asiatic countries particularly for trade. The native powers allowed them to carry on trade on their soil. However, subsequent events provided ample opportunities to these foreigners to establish their sway over the natives. Political disunity of the country and internal rivalry among the native states attracted the attention of the foreign powers. Adept in political machinations and intrigues, the foreign merchants sought to take advantage of the political turmoil. They finally managed to subjugate the native powers and build empires.

Among the many Asian countries which came to be dominated by the European imperialists in general and the British in particular, mention must be made of India and China.

British East India Company's Wars

After the fall of the Mughal empire, there was a political vacuum and the Marathas struggled to fill this void. They did not succeed and so the country, consisting of big and small sovereign states, lacked political unity and a strong leader. The Mughal empire continued to exist as a shadow of its former self. While the Portuguese were satisfied with establishing small colonies in Goa, Diu and Daman, Dupleix, the Governor of the French East India Company, dreamt of establishing a French empire in India. The Anglo-French rivalry of the early 18th century resulted in the three Carnatic wars. Dupleix's dream vanished and the French in India were totally defeated by the British. The siege of Arcot by Robert Clive marked a turning point in the military fortunes of the British. The three Carnatic wars not only resulted in the defeat and ignominy of the French, but paved the way for the English to have sway over the Carnatic region. After his victory over the French, Robert Clive became a hero. He was sent to Bengal to deal with Nawab Siraj-ud-daula, who according to some English writers, had caused the so-called "Black Hole tragedy." Clive hatched a plot to dethrone him and finally forced him into a battle — the Battle of Plassey in 1757. Clive won the battle easily as Mir Jafar, the Comander-in-Chief of Siraj-ud-daula, betrayed his master by changing sides soon after the Battle began. Siraj-ud-daula fled the battlefield but he was subsequently caught and killed. Clive rewarded Mir Jafar with the nawabship of Bengal. The new Nawab learnt to his regret that the company officials were making too frequent a demand for money for him to satisfy. Finding Mir Jafar to be good for nothing, the company officials made his son-in-law, Mir Kasim, take over the nawabship. Mir Jafar was forced to retire. Mir Kasim, the new Nawab, discovered that the British company officials were secretly engaged in dubious trade practices by misusing the *dastaks* and causing heavy drain to his treasury. He desired to put a stop to it by catching the culprits. It became the main cause of another war — the Battle of Buxar. The Mughal Emperor and the Nawab of Oudh went to the rescue of Nawab Mir Kasim, but the British led by Major Munro inflicted a crushing defeat upon the allies at Buxar in October 1764. Mir Kasim became a fugitive, the Nawab of Oudh fled to the Rohilla country, and the Mughal Emperor came over to the side of the English. In the meanwhile, Clive was raised to the peership and sent to Bengal to deal with the political situation. According to the treaty of Allahabad, the Nawab of Oudh was restored to his position on condition that he cede Kora and Allahabad. These territories were given to the Mughal Emperor, Shah Alam, to maintain his royal dignity. In August 1765, the Mughal Emperor issued a *farman* granting to the company the *diwani* of Bengal, Bihar and Orissa. In return for this favour, the Mughal Emperor was promised an annual sum of rupees 26 lakhs. Thus the English Company became a virtual master of the largest province in India. Lord Clive established a double government which was later abolished and Warren Hastings set up a new system of administration in India. The Regulating Act of 1773 vested authority in the hands of the Governor-General and his Council and set up a Supreme Court at Calcutta. The new Governor-General made an attempt to codify the Hindu and Muslim laws. The Company thereafter stood forth as the Diwan and took charge of the responsibility of collecting land revenue through its own collectors.

Wars in the South

The governors of Bombay and Madras embroiled the company in wars with the Marathas and the Mysore ruler respectively. As things were not going in favour of the company, the Governor-General felt inclined to take the matter into his own hands. It was due to his effective intervention that the prestige of the company was saved. It may be remembered that Hyder Ali of Mysore had almost succeeded in expelling the English from the Carnatic but the English bought some more time by concluding a humiliating treaty with him.

Expansion of British Empire

Lord Cornwallis defeated Tipu Sultan of Mysore in the third Anglo-Mysore war and inflicted a humiliating treaty. He took the Sultan's sons hostage. Cornwallis entered into a new treaty with the ruler of Oudh. Lord Wellesley aimed at establishing British paramountcy over India and for this purpose prepared a plan – the subsidiary system of alliances – to coax native powers to get British protection. The Nizam followed by the Peshwa and the ruler of Tanjavur joined this alliance. Tipu refused to sign the treaty and so a war – the fourth Anglo-Mysore war – was forced on him. He fought the English bravely and perished in 1799. Thus, the company established its sway over Mysore, Malabar and the Canara districts. Wellesley's rule witnessed enormous expansion of British power. The Maratha leaders Holkar, and Sindhe, were forced to sign the subsidiary treaty after the second Anglo-Maratha war. Lord Hastings fought the Marathas, and put an end to their power. The Rajput rulers were forced to acknowledge the paramountcy of the British. The rulers of Malwa, Bhopal and Bundelkhand also became the allies of the British company by signing the subsidiary treaty.

William Bentinck

The 'Forward policy' of the British had its respite during the Governor-Generalship of Lord William Bentinck. Being a staunch liberal, he made British rule popular with his reforms.

The most radical change that he brought about was the introduction of the Western system of education. The Persian and Sanskrit languages lost their position of pre-eminence and that place was taken over by English. The other reform was the suppression of *sati* by law.

Lord Dalhousie (1848-56) and Annexations

The power of the British East India Company reached its pinnacle during the time of Lord Dalhousie. The second Anglo-Sikh war was fought (1848-49) and Punjab was annexed to the British territory in March 1849. The second Anglo-Burmese war was fought in 1852 and the British annexed Pegu. To bring Indian territories belonging to the native rulers under British control, Lord Dalhousie enforced a doctrine called the 'Doctrine of Lapse'. By the application of this doctrine, he annexed states like Satara, Udaipur, Jhansi, Nagpur and Sambalpur into the British dominions for the sole reason that the rulers of these states had no natural heirs to succeed to the respective thrones. He annexed others also but they were not approved by the company authorities. Peshwa Nanasaheb lost his pension and title soon after the death of his father, former Peshwa Baji Rao II. Even the Mughal Emperor would have lost his title had not the company authorities intervened. Dalhousie's treatment of the ruler of Oudh has no parallel. Oudh was taken over by the British on account of misgovernment even though it was not a dependent state like others. So in a moral sense, the use of the doctrine of Lapse was wrong and roused the indignation of many rulers like Rani Laxmibai of Jhansi and Nana Saheb who staged a revolt in 1857. One may say that the Great Uprising of 1857 was the direct outcome of Dalhousie's policy towards the native states. In 1885-86 the British waged the third Burmese war and annexed Upper Burma. Britain also got Malaya with its capital, Singapore. Britain fought the Afghan wars to safeguard her interests in India from a likely danger posed by Russia. Finally, Britain and Russia came to an agreement on their spheres of influence in South Asia before the First World War broke out.

34

INDIAN NATIONALISM

The origin of Indian nationalism is traced to the Great Uprising of 1857 — an episode derisively described by British historians as a mere 'Sepoy Mutiny.' Although it failed to achieve its objective, its consequences were far-reaching. This episode in the history of our struggle for independence shook the British Government and Queen Victoria admitted the omissions and commissions of the British East India Company. Her proclamation was followed by constitutional reforms. The Act of 1858 ended the company's rule in India and marked the transfer of all its powers to the British Crown. However, the brutal suppression of this uprising left too deep a scar on Indians to heal easily. It kept reminding them of their subjugation to the whims of alien rule.

The Legacy of British Rule

The benefits of British rule to Indians were many. Among them the most important was the western system of education. It transformed the very outlook of middle class Indians. The educated middle class was influenced by the philosophy of British liberals and they eagerly looked forward to the achievement of self-rule. The West's achievements in science and technology highly impressed the Indians. The spread of English language and literature was achieved through its adoption as a curriculum in schools and colleges. The learning of English not only enabled a person to get a job in the Civil Service but also provided a common platform for exchanging of ideas. The introduction of rail and road transport broke down the geographical barriers and enabled the Indians to travel to various parts of India. The introduction of the postal system during the time of Dalhousie was a great leap forward in the means of communication and was followed by the telegraph system. Another boon of the British to the Indians was the evolution of the administration of justice. The industrialisation of the country began slowly from the middle of the nineteenth century. Finally, the most splendid contribution of the British to the Indians was the organisation of an efficient system of administration. The rule of law brought all the Indians together on an equal footing and made them conscious of their identity.

Factors Responsible for the Rise of Nationalism

Despite these benefits the Indians were not happy on account of what one may call as the British acts of omission and commission. India became a helpless victim of British imperialism. Lord Lytton's Afghan war was expensive and without any justification. While famines ravaged this country taking a heavy toll, the Viceroy held a lavish Delhi Durbar for the native princes just to remind them of their subjection to the British Queen. He further caused deep humiliation to the Indians by gagging their press. The Indians were prohibited from carrying weapons for self - protection. The Indian economy had no chance to improve itself, particularly after the neglect of agriculture and the denial of protection to village industries. Unemployment of the educated increased and, to make matters worse there was the flow of gold to Britain. The free trade policy adopted by British administrators played havoc with the Indian economy.

Pioneering work in reforming the Hindu religion and its caste-ridden society was taken up by Raja Ram Mohun Roy. He founded the Brahmo Samaj with a view to cleanse Hindu society and religion of evils and for that purpose he advocated the abolition of the dreadful custom of "Sati" and the study of Western science and literature. His Brahmo Samaj infused a sense of nationalism among its followers. Swami Dayanand Saraswati founded the Arya Samaj with a view to bringing about a cultural, social and political homogeneity among the Indians. His motto was 'India for the Indians'. He exercised a "great nationalising influence upon his followers". Swami Vivekananda started the Ramakrishna Mission in memory of his master (Swami Ramakrishna Paramahansa). A large number of its branches all over the world spread the teachings of Swami Ramakrishna. The Ramakrishna Mission set up many schools, colleges, hospitals, orphanages and dispensaries. Swami Vivekananda rendered great service to the cause of the Hindu religion by explaining its subtleties to the Westerners. The Prarthana Samaj and the Theosophical Society also contributed much to the awakening of self-respect and nationalism among the Indians. They craved for emancipation.

The vernacular press in India played a dynamic role in awakening the masses and also identified the economic problems facing the country. It urged the British Government to find solutions. It donned the garb of an adversary with a penchant for criticism. It took up the cause of the poor and the downtrodden and demanded justice. It enlightened the public on many political and economic issues and drew attention to the existence of many social evils in the country. It exposed the many unfair practices of the British Government and enlightened the people on how they would be affected.

The Bill controversy at the time of Lord Ripon further alienated whatever sympathy the Indians had for the British. A chance to right the wrong and keep the Europeans on a footing of equality with Indians was foiled by British jingoists. To the educated Indians it appeared as though the goal of self-government was "not a luxury but a necessity". It did not take much time for the educated Indians to unite for the cause of self-government. A giant step in this direction was taken by Allen Octavian Hume, a former ICS officer, when he laid the foundation of the Indian National Congress in 1885. Its first session was held at Bombay under the presidentship of W C Bannerjee. The Indian National Congress represented the Indian masses, and in due course attracted the cream of intellectuals in India. It tried to safeguard the interests of the Indians, and in its annual sessions, demanded representative bodies, separation of the executive and judicial functions, trial by jury, pruning of military expenditure, reduction of taxes, and simultaneous conduct of ICS examinations both in England and India. Appropriate resolutions were passed for this purpose and submitted to the Government of India. During the formative years, the Congress received encouraging response from government officials, but later on the government became suspicious.

Lord Curzon's Regime (1899-1905)

The Indian Councils Act of 1892 was passed but it failed to satisfy the Indian National Congress for the simple reason that instead of giving representative bodies it provided for consultative councils. All further demands of the Congress to the British Government fell on deaf ears. The regime of Lord Curzon, despite its administrative efficiency, was detested by many Indians. Curzon believed in the 'Whiteman's burden theory' and hardly bothered to understand the national mood. His high-handed actions like the officialisation of Calcutta University, and reducing the autonomy of the Calcutta Corporation to a farce, evoked loud protests from Indians. His reactionary regime ended with the partition of Bengal which provoked the Indians as never before.

Rise of Extremism

The partition of Bengal had its impact on the Congress. It widened the rift between the Moderates and the Extremists which ultimately led the latter to leave the party itself at the annual session held at Surat. The extremists were led by Lokmanya Bal Gangadhar Tilak who called for a halt to the cringing attitude of the Congress in its dealing with the British Government, and recommended a militant approach to get the grievances of the Indians redressed. The movement against the partition of Bengal became strong, and in Bengal, it took the form of boycott of British goods. The *Swadeshi* movement received generous support from the Congress. In Maharashtra, Tilak whipped a propaganda against British misrule through his fiery speeches and writings. He published a paper, *Kesari*, which fanned national feelings. Tilak organised Ganesha festivals and trained the youth to prepare for great sacrifices. He was found guilty of sedition in the Rand murder case and sentenced to long imprisonment in Mandalay.

Further Developments

The Congress' demand for self-government was rejected by Lord Minto but constitutional changes were brought about by the Act of 1909. The worst feature of this Act was the introduction of the separate electorates and it was a deliberate attempt on the part of the British not only to drive a wedge between the Hindus and the Muslims but also to take the wind out of the sails of the national movement. The moderates in the Congress could not make much progress, and their stalwarts, Sir Pherozeshah Mehta and Gokhale died. There was a reconciliation between the extremists and the moderates in 1915. Tilak was released early on account of his ill-health. Shortly after his return from Mandalay prison, he joined Mrs Annie Besant in starting the Home Rule movement in 1915-16. The Home Rule movement was started on the model of the Irish movement and it gathered the support of the public. In the meanwhile, the Congress patched up its differences with the Muslim League (1913) and both demanded that the British grant self-government in 1916 (Lucknow Pact). It may be recalled that World War I was in its crucial stages, and in August 1917, Montagu, the Secretary of State for India, declared his offer of responsible government. He came to India and conferred with the Viceroy, Lord Chelmsford, about the necessity of ushering in another dose of political reforms. Their discussions ended with the publication of a report – Montagu-Chelmsford Report – which formed the basis of the Government of India Act of 1919. During these years political unrest took a violent form particularly in States like Bengal, UP and Punjab, and the British Government resorted to repressive measures.

Jallianwala Bagh

In April 1918, the Rowlatt Committee submitted its report on the nature of criminal conspiracies against the British Government . It suggested certain steps to stem the tide of violent activities by revolutionaries. On the basis of its recommendations, the British passed the Rowlatt Act which restricted the freedom of the people. The agitation against the enforcement of the Rowlatt Act by the Indians spread everywhere. One such peaceful agitation in the Jallianwala Bagh near Amritsar met with unusual and unexpected British brutality. General Dyer, the British Police Chief, ordered his constabulary to open fire on the innocent mob which had assembled to listen to their leaders. Hundreds were killed and the Punjab Governor continued to terrorise the people of that State with his wanton brutalities. The Jallianwala Bagh tragedy deeply shocked the people of the country, and in protest, Rabindranath Tagore renounced his knighthood. The anti-British feelings rose to a high pitch and

Gandhiji entered the political arena to take up the cudgels for the country against the British.

GANDHIAN ERA (1919-47)

Born at Porbandar (Gujarat) on October 2, 1869, Mohandas Karamchand Gandhi went to London to qualify for the Bar. He became a barrister-at-law and went to Natal (South Africa) to practise his profession. He was shocked at the racial discrimination practised by the White government. He fought against the South African Government to secure the civic rights for the Indians. He adopted a novel approach – the *satyagraha* – to ventilate the grievances of the native Indians. After his struggle in Africa, he returned to India in 1915. From the early years of his political career, he came under the influence of G K Gokhale whom he called his "political guru". He launched his satyagraha movement for the abolition of the indenture system for recruiting Indian labourers for other British colonies. The British yielded. He scored another victory against the British by means of the satyagraha movement at Champaran when they agreed to redress the grievances of Indigo cultivators. Another movement organised at Khaira also succeeded. So Gandhi took up the cause of the poor and the downtrodden and struggled for their emancipation. He "brought politics from the drawing rooms of the educated middle class to the humble homes and fields of the peasantry". He supported the British in their war efforts but warned them that their tyranny in India, referring to the Rowlatt Report, would be resisted at all costs. The Jallianwala Bagh tragedy shook his conviction regarding the British sense of justice and fair play. He prepared himself to launch an epic struggle against British misrule which he described as 'satan' urged (*Shaitan*). With the backing of the Congress, he launched the non-cooperation movement (1920-22). He awakened the masses with his call to boycott courts, legislatures, educational institutions, British goods and the like and the elite to discard British titles, if any. Gandhiji also extended his full support to the Khilafat movement organised by the Muslims in India in order to bring pressure upon England to change her policy towards the Turkish Sultan.

He went to Gujarat and launched the satyagraha (non-violent protest) at Bardoli in 1922. The constructive side of the non-cooperation movement included the adoption of *swadeshi*, removal of untouchability, and Hindu-Muslim amity. The non-cooperation movement spread all over the country and the British administration was paralysed. The British Government was in serious trouble and in its usual way resorted to repressive methods. The situation for the British worsened with the outbreak of a revolt of Moplahs in Malabar and the Akali movement in the Punjab. When the non-cooperation movement, which was *non-violent*, turned violent resulting in the deaths of some police personnel in Chauri-Chaura (UP), Gandhiji felt extremely sad and gave a call to halt this movement. He undertook a fast and later he was arrested and sent to prison. His followers, Motilal Nehru and C R Das, were disappointed with the cessation of the movement while it was in full swing. They formed a new party called the Swaraj Party. The 1919 Act came into force in 1921. In the ensuing elections, the Swaraj Party won some seats. Their motto was to wreck the constitution from within. The Congress was disappointed with the new Act since it neither provided a responsible government at the Centre nor was the working of the Dyarchy satisfactory in the provinces. Separate electorates were continued. Motilal recommended a revision of this Act and the British appointed the Muddiman Committee for this purpose.

All-white Simon Commission Boycotted

In 1927, the British Government appointed a committee under the chairmanship of Sir Simon to look into the working of the Constitution provided by the Act of 1919 and suggest measures for improvement, if any. Accordingly, Sir Simon arrived with his team but the Congress boycotted this commission since it did not include a single Indian. But the commission continued its work despite the boycott and submitted its report to the Government in 1930. In the meanwhile, the Congress took the initiative to convene an All-Parties Conference at Delhi in 1928 to discuss the question of a new constitution for India which would give a fully responsible government. The conference appointed Motilal Nehru as the chairman of a committee and asked him to submit a report. The Nehru Committee suggested that the nomination status should be the political objective. The Congress gave an ultimatum to the British Government to give a constitution based on the Nehru Report at a date not later than December 1929. As there was no serious response from the British side, the Congress declared that the Nehru Report had lapsed. In its annual session, it accepted Jawaharlal Nehru's resolution declaring that *Poorna Swarajya* (total independence) be the goal. Under the presidentship of Jawaharlal Nehru the Congress got ready to launch several movements — the boycott of Central and State legislatures and the launching of the Civil Disobedience Movement. Gandhiji again assumed the leadership of the freedom struggle.

Gandhiji's Dandi March

Gandhiji started his Civil Disobedience Movement with the famous 'Dandi March', a journey undertaken on foot from Sabarmati Ashram to the Dandi beach to break the salt law as a token of his protest. The Dandi March attracted nationwide attention and similar movements were started elsewhere also. Millions participated in this movement, and as usual, the British Government resorted to oppressive methods. Gandhiji and other national leaders were arrested and sentenced to jail. Thousands of their followers were also sent to prison. The Congress boycotted the First Round Table Conference held in

London in 1931. It was convened to discuss the future constitutional set-up in India.

The Gandhi-Irwin Pact (1931) and the Communal Award

The First Round Table Conference ended in failure mainly because the largest political party in India, the Indian National Congress, did not participate in it. So Lord Irwin , the Indian Viceroy, summoned Gandhiji who was at that time undergoing prison sentence and reached an agreement with him. As a part of the agreement, the British Government released all the prisoners and withdrew the ordinances, and on his part, Gandhiji withdrew the Civil Disobedience Movement. The Congress agreed to participate in the next Round Table Conference. It was a matter of pride for the Congress that the British Government recognised its "status and authority" to speak for political India. Gandhiji attended the Second Round Table Conference as the sole representative of the Congress but found that the British statesmen were suspicious and conservative. He failed to convince the British regarding the right method to solve the communal problem. The attitude of the British disappointed him and he returned to India very much disappointed. The British made matters worse by announcing the 'Communal Award.' Seats in the legislatures were distributed on the basis of caste and creed. The Congress boycotted the Third Round Table Conference. On the basis of the discussions held in all the three conferences the British Government prepared a White Paper which resulted in the legislation of the Government of India Act of 1935.

The Act of 1935 and the Origin of Pakistan Movement

The Government of India Act of 1935 provided autonomy to the British provinces and installed a dyarchy at the Centre. The Congress was not happy at the way the Act sought to establish a federal set-up. What it desired was a new constitution to be drafted by a truly representative Constituent Assembly. The Act came into force in 1937. The Congress formed ministries in seven provinces (UP, Bombay, Madras, Central Provinces, Bihar, Orissa and NWFP) and joined the coalition ministries in Sind and Assam. The Muslim League failed to secure a majority in any province. The Congress practically ruled the whole country with the exception of Punjab and Bengal. However, its rule was a short-lived one. It may be noted that the Muslim League secured 110 seats out of the 482 Muslim seats in the eleven provinces and so was peeved about it. As the Congress had Hindu members in majority, the Muslim League began to have its own apprehensions at the prospect of Muslim minority coming under Congress rule in many states. It issued statements regarding the atrocities committed by Hindus everywhere and about the bias of the Congress ministries.

Mohammed Ali Jinnah, the leader of the Muslim League, began to advocate the theory that the Muslims in India constitute a separate nation and he began to work towards achieving this end. The Muslim League held its session at Lahore in 1940, and under Jinnah's leadership, demanded a new homeland for the millions of Muslims living in Punjab, NWFP, Kashmir, Sindh and Baluchistan. It may be remembered that the idea of a new homeland for the Muslims in India was propagated by the famous Muslim poet, Mohammed Iqbal, in 1930.

When World War II broke out in 1930, the British Viceroy declared India's participation in it on the side of the British without even informing the Central Legislature or the Congress Party. The Congress Party executive immediately ordered the Congress ministries in all the states to resign as a mark of protest. Accordingly, Congress ministries resigned.

Failure of Cripps Mission

In 1942, pressure mounted on the British Government to bring about the end of the stalemate. President Franklin Roosevelt made a fervent appeal to the British Prime Minister, Winston Churchill, to find a political solution to India's struggle for independence. The British Prime Minister dispatched Sir Stafford Cripps on a mission to India in 1942 to consult Indian leaders on certain constitutional proposals. If accepted by the latter it would be implemented at a later date. As the Cripps proposal assumed the form of a promise from the British to be implemented after the war (incidentally, the fortunes of the British in the war were at its lowest ebb), Gandhiji aptly described the Cripps proposal as " a post-dated cheque", and somebody added "on a crashing bank." The Congress rejected Cripps proposal and it was followed by the rejection of the Muslim League. The Muslim League reiterated its demand for a separate Muslim State, 'Pakistan.' Soon after the failure of the Cripps mission, war clouds began to hang over India also. The British had suffered a severe drubbing at the hands of the Germans, and the Japanese had conquered by March 1942 most of South-East Asia and were knocking at the doors of India. Gandhiji quite rightly felt that while Britain could not save herself from her enemies, there was no point in holding on to India. Japanese submarines began to move menacingly in the Bay of Bengal.

'Quit India' Movement (May 1942)

So Gandhiji launched a movement to drive the British out of India. He appealed to the good sense of the British to 'Quit India' as their presence in our country was inviting Japanese invasion. Failing to get a satisfactory response, he launched the greatest movement in his life, the "Quit India" movement. The agitation spread all over the country and the British Government was paralysed. Thousands were arrested including the leaders of the Congress and houses had to be hired by the Government to turn them into jails as all their prisons were full. Large-scale violence followed after the arrest of Gandhiji and other leaders. Very much pained at the course of events, Gandhiji undertook a fast in February 1943. He was not released despite his illness. In the midst of this political turmoil, another great tragedy struck India. The devastating Bengal famine took a very heavy toll of lives. Gandhiji asked Jinnah to accept the formula put forward by Sri C Rajagopalachari on the issue of a separate state for Muslims. But Jinnah rejected this offer and it appeared that he wanted Pakistan on his own terms and conditions.

Wavell Plan and Shimla Conference (1945)

In 1945, Wavell, the British Viceroy in India, put forward his plan to end the deadlock between the Congress and the Muslim League. But even this plan did not bring about amity between the Congress and the Muslim League as the latter insisted on its right to nominate Muslim members to the Viceroy's Executive Council at the Shimla Conference.

Subhas Chandra Bose and the INA

The story of India's freedom struggle is not complete without a reference being made to the heroic saga of Subhas Chandra Bose. Subhas Bose left the ICS and joined the Congress. But his differences with the Congress made him leave it and form what is known as the Forward Bloc. As the British were watching his activities, he had to leave the country secretly. He reached Berlin and discussed the question of India's independence with the Nazis. Thereafter he went to the Japanese-occupied Malaya and Burma and organised the Indian National Army (INA) by recruiting the Indians there.

His aim was to invade India with his INA and liberate her. It may be noted that the INA conquered Manipur and Aishevpur thus covering an area of 10,000 square miles. The INA's attempt to liberate India failed and a number of INA soldiers were captured by the British. About this time Subhas Bose was supposed to have died in a plane crash. A few of the INA soldiers like Shah Nawaz, Dhillon and Sehgal, had earlier deserted the British army and joined the INA. They were tried by a court-martial and sentenced to death. Jawaharlal Nehru pleaded their case at the time of their trial. They were released.

Cabinet Mission (1946)

In 1945, the Labour Party came to power in England after the general elections. It was in favour of India's independence. Its government sent to India a Cabinet Mission to solve the political deadlock. The members of the Mission held meetings with the leaders of the political parties and thereafter held a conference in Shimla. In this Conference, the leaders of Congress and the League failed to arrive at a compromise. Despite the disagreement between two major political parties in India, the Mission submitted its own proposal or plan in May 1946. It rejected the demand for Pakistan for various reasons. It recommended a Union of India consisting of British and princely-ruled States. It provided full autonomy to all the States, and the Union was to deal with subjects like defence, foreign affairs, communications and revenue matters. It also provided for a Constituent Assembly to frame a new Constitution for India. After the promulgation of the new Constitution, the British Government was to give up its powers of paramountcy. The Cabinet Mission urged the necessity of forming an Interim Government. At the Meerut session of the Indian National Congress, a resolution was passed urging the British to convene the Constituent Assembly for drafting a new Constitution and declare India as an independent and sovereign republic.

Towards Independence

Jawaharlal Nehru was invited by the Viceroy to form the Interim Government and he did so in September 1946. Although the Muslim League was called upon to join the ministry, it did not do so. However, it changed its mind soon and agreed to join. The Muslim League was not happy at the turn of events, that is the rejection of Pakistan by the Cabinet Mission, and so the country was plunged into chaos and communal riots broke out. The Muslim League refused to join the Constituent Assembly. Prime Minister Atlee's statement on 20th February about the British Government's definite intention to transfer power not later than June 1948 undermined the Cabinet Mission's insistence on the necessity of maintaining the unity of India. It encouraged the Muslim League to cause large-scale disturbances in India. The Labour Party Government in Britain appointed Lord Mountbatten as the Viceroy and he came forward with his plan to solve India's political problem. He convinced the Congress leaders of the inevitability of the partition of the country after explaining Jinnah's adamant stand. Accordingly, India was divided. India, that is Bharat, became free on August 15, 1947. Pakistan was born on August 14, 1947. The leaders of the Congress requested Lord Mountbatten to continue to work in India as the first Governor-General of Independent India. India's Constitution came into force from January 26, 1950 and on that day she became a Sovereign Democratic Republic.

35
FIFTY YEARS OF INDIA'S INDEPENDENCE

Before the British left India, they partitioned the country which led to a plethora of problems. Nearly 562 princely states remained independent and had to be integrated into the Indian Union. They had to choose between India and Pakistan, and almost all of them chose to be incorporated into India, thanks to the yeoman service rendered by Sardar Vallabhbhai Patel. In the case of Hyderabad State, Sardar Patel had to take police action, since the Nizam refused to incorporate his state into India.

Raja Hari Singh, ruler of Jammu and Kashmir, took his own time to decide about merging his state with India with the result that Pakistani mercenaries invaded his kingdom. Sheikh Abdullah, the Chief Minister, and Hari Singh sought India's help to expel the Pakistani intruders. They signed the Instrument of Accession with India, and Prime Minister Jawaharlal Nehru sent Indian forces to Kashmir to expel the foreign intruders. He appealed to the United Nations about Pakistani aggression in Kashmir. Unfortunately, the United Nations did not take adequate steps, and the issue became very complicated in the course of time.

When India became free from British rule, what attracted the attention of the world was the appalling poverty in the country. The Constituent Assembly was formed with Jawaharlal Nehru as its Chairman to draft India's new Constitution. After wide-ranging discussions with the other members of the Constituent Assembly, the draft of India's Constitution was ready. Among those who contributed their expertise to the framing of the Indian Constitution were great men like Ambedkar, B N Rao, Tej Bahadur Sapru and Krishna Swamy Iyer. These legal luminaries and social thinkers tried to incorporate certain provisions in the Constitution to fulfil certain goals, namely, democracy, republicanism, secularism, removal of illiteracy and untouchability, fundamental rights, independence of the judiciary, introduction of a uniform civil code in due course, employment opportunities to all and finally safeguarding the interests of the members of the Scheduled Caste, Scheduled Tribe and backward communities. Social development and economic progress had to go hand in hand within the framework of our Constitution. The Constitution envisaged decentralisation of power by including the Panchayati Raj system (*see the 73rd and 74th amendments*).

The Nehru Era

With the advent of independence, and the ushering in of the new Republic, Rajendra Prasad became the first President and Jawaharlal Nehru, the first Prime Minister. Under Nehru's charismatic leadership India made rapid strides of progress in the political, economic and social spheres. India launched its Five-year Plans so as to transform the poverty-stricken country into a modern industrial nation. Nehru was inspired by the progress achieved by the Soviet Union under the five-year plans, and equally by the efforts of Sir M Visveswaraiah to transform Mysore into a modern princely state through ten-year plans. During the initial stages of the second Five-year Plan, he sought the assistance of a famous statistician, Professor Mahalanobis.

The first Five-year Plan (1951-56) laid stress on the development of agriculture, on which nearly three-fourths of India's population depended in those days. Furthermore, the aim of this plan was to rehabilitate the Indian economy which was adversely affected by the Second World War, the Bengal famine and the partition of the country. This plan achieved many of its short-term objectives such as an increase in agricultural production and the rise of national income (by about 11 per cent). The second plan (1956-61) aimed at "rapid increase in national income so as to raise the standard of living in the country" and laid stress on rapid industrialisation. There was much emphasis on the development of basic and heavy industries. The other objectives included were provision of employment opportunities and the reduction of inequalities of income. Unfortunately, the increase in population during this period adversely affected the prospect of the increase in the per capita income. It appeared as though the framers of the plan were overambitious. At the same time, the success of the plan was plagued by adverse internal and external situations (China's invasion of India, 1962).

The third Five-year Plan (1961-66) aimed at increasing the national income by about five per cent per annum, self-sufficiency in foodgrains, expansion of basic industries, and providing equality of opportunity to one and all. It also aimed at bringing about reduction in the disparities of income and wealth. The plan targets could not be achieved due to Chinese invasion (1962), hostilities with Pakistan (1965), and bad weather conditions (1965-66). The Nehru Era ended following the death of India's greatest prime minister. During the Nehru Era, there were no doubts that India emerged as one of the industrialised nations with a powerful state capitalism. The economy was modernised to a great extent and Nehru's dream of making India a modern nation turned into reality.

However, the country continued to face poverty, illiteracy, inflation, unemployment and so on.

After the completion of the third Five-year Plan, there came what is known as a Plan-Holiday. The annual plans came into vogue from 1966-67 to 1968-69. 1966-67 was a year of drought but the year 1967-68 witnessed the country's economic recovery, thanks to the 'Green Revolution' in Punjab, Haryana and Western UP. The fourth Five-year Plan (1969-74) aimed at "growth with stability" and "progressive achievement of self-reliance". The PL 480 import of foodgrains from the United States was given up. Unfortunately, the plan did not succeed, and so also the spread of the Green Revolution. Industrial production lagged far behind (3.9 per cent instead of the expected 8 per cent).

The fifth Five-year Plan (1974-79) set forth two objectives : removal of poverty (*garibi hatao*) and achievement of self-reliance. This plan also did not succeed, since the "real income of the poor has not shown an increase, neither has unemployment declined". The Janata government assumed power in 1977, which decided to terminate the fifth Five-year Plan (1978). The Janata government formulated its own plan for 1980 with "Growth for Social Justice" as its motto.

However, it collapsed, and the Congress (I) government won the general election in 1980. It shelved the Janata government plan, and launched the sixth Five-year Plan (1980-85). This plan tried to assess the achievements and failures of three decades of planning so as to evolve a new strategy to eradicate poverty in the country. It also aimed at strengthening the infrastructures of agriculture and industry. The sixth Five-year Plan was able to achieve the annual growth rate of 5.2 per cent.

The seventh plan (1986-1991) was launched in 1986. The year 1987-88 witnessed drought. But the next year 1988-89 witnessed India's highest growth rate of 10 per cent thanks to the bounty of good monsoons. During this year, the manufacturing sector showed an increase of 9 per cent. However, the rate of inflation touched 8.4 per cent. By 1989-90 India was facing the depletion of foreign exchange reserves, that is facing the balance of payments problem. This was due to the lack of confidence among NRIs about India's economic growth. By early 1991, India faced the greatest economic crisis, vide, her foreign exchange reserves that were found to be sufficient for importing goods for the next twenty days only.

The New Industrial Policy

The Congress government led by P V Narasimha Rao with Finance Minister Manmohan Singh began to tackle this issue on emergency lines. The World Bank and the IMF came to the rescue of the Indian Government to tide over the balance of payments crisis by advancing huge amounts. At the same time, the World Bank and the IMF put pressure on the Congress regime to introduce a structural adjustment programme followed by liberalisation. Thus, Narasimha Rao's government was forced to discard the Nehruvian strategy of achieving economic growth through state capitalism. The new industrial policy was announced by the then Finance Minister, Manmohan Singh, which laid emphasis on the role of the private sector in the growth of the Indian economy.

The public sector which had attained commanding heights during the last four decades did not receive much importance, since it could not deliver the goods/ or bring about the expected growth of the Indian economy. After two years of Plan Holiday (1990-92), the eighth Five-year Plan was launched on April 1, 1992. The plan aimed to promote human resources (human capital), agriculture, and physical infrastructure. Due to liberalization policy of the new government, India's growth rate reached 5-6 per cent. During this liberal era, the industrial sector registered high growth. The balance of payments position in recent years has remained very satisfactory, but the yawning fiscal deficit remains alarming.

Social Scenario

India has been lagging behind in tackling several social issues such as population, illiteracy, female infanticide, unemployment and women's health, when compared to her neighbour, China. The Constitution had prescribed a uniform civil code for the country which has not been taken up so far. Since these problems were not tackled effectively, poverty and ignorance have reigned supreme. Furthermore, there are regional and sectarian conflicts which have checked the progress of the country. Another alarming feature is the brain-drain (India has the world's third largest scientific personnel), which has become a matter of great shame to the Indian community. Unfortunately, India ranks far below in the human development index. The UN human development index has assigned India the 135th rank out of 174 countries in 1996.

In recent years, two other issues have also raised their ugly heads, namely, corruption and criminalisation of politics. The government and the people of India have to meet these challenges in the coming years so as to ensure a free democratic system and society in the country. A note of consolation about India is that it is a vibrant democracy and has developed a capacity to weather many storms. She has held free and fair elections regularly and is enjoying the freedom of the press. India has proudly joined the nuclear club as a member with peaceful intentions.

India's Foreign Relations

India is situated in the most strategic part of South Asia and is flanked by neighbours like Pakistan, China, Nepal, Bangladesh and Burma. It is but natural that she is destined to play a major role in world affairs. It may be remembered that she is the world's second largest democracy, the first being the United States. India has produced a great culture and civilization. While in other newly independent countries of Asia, democracy remained only in name, India in contrast has had a vibrant democracy. Therefore, as a mature democracy, she developed the ability to play a very important role in international affairs ever since she became independent. Under the charismatic leadership of Jawaharlal Nehru, India pursued a policy of neutrality at a time when the two superpowers were in the midst of Cold War. It was this Cold War which created a tense situation in Asia.

India's Non-alignment

These two superpowers frequently came into conflict over extending their spheres of influence, and looked upon the Third World countries as pawns in the game of international chess. They formed military alliances and created international tensions in many regions. Nehru opposed the formation of all military alliances. He, along with other great statesmen like Nasser and Tito, tried to build a third bloc of non-aligned countries. The non-aligned countries eschewed military alliances and declared their peaceful intentions with the neighbouring countries. Nehru formulated the Panchasheel namely, the five principles of co-existence. During the Nehru era, it became a bedrock of India's foreign policy. The non-aligned countries under the leadership of Nehru, Tito and Nasser attracted almost all the Third World countries which had shaken off the shackles of colonial rule of the Western masters. They played a very important role in the maintenance of peace and order under the auspices of the United Nations.

Very early in her career, India as an independent nation, happened to defend her territorial integrity and sovereignty with regard to the issue of Kashmir (1947-48). Taking advantage of the fluid political situation in Kashmir, Pakistan launched aggression. Raja Hari Singh and his Chief Minister Sheikh Abdulla decided to integrate their state with the Union of India. These statesmen signed the Instrument of Accession and became a part of India. It was then that Prime Minister Nehru sent Indian forces to expel the Pakistani-supported intruders in Kashmir. Unfortunately, this issue got out of hand while being debated in the UN. Pakistan took full advantage of every opportunity to blame India for the conflict of Kashmir.

The People's Republic of China maintained friendly relations with India during the early years of India's independence. India even took up the issue of the admission of the People's Republic of China into the United Nations in spite of the US veto. This 'friendly' country stabbed India in the back in 1962 by allowing her forces to occupy Indian territories along the McMahon line. Communist China did not recognize the McMahon line, and therefore, there ensued war between India and China in which the former was defeated. It caused great humiliation to India. The Panchasheel agreement existing between these two countries was grossly violated. It took a long time for India to restore normal relations with China. Pakistan invaded India again in 1965 over the issue of the Rann of Kutch. The then Prime Minister, Lal Bahadur Shastri, took this issue to the World Court. The World Court decided in favour of India. Peace was restored after signing the Tashkent agreement on January 4, 1966.

The third conflict with Pakistan arose over the issue of Bangladesh. Bangladesh declared her independence from Pakistan in 1971. The Pakistani army tried to quell the revolt. Hundreds of thousands of Bangladeshi refugees crossed the borders and entered Indian territories. India gave shelter to all these refugees hoping that there would be an end to this situation. Unfortunately, the Pakistani army continued to harass the people of Bangladesh. The Mukti Bahini (as the liberation army of East Bengal, presently Bangladesh, was called) tried its best to defend the freedom. The international bodies remained mute spectators to this grim situation. The Mukti Bahini sought the help of the Indian government to intervene. It was then that India under the leadership of Indira Gandhi sent Indian forces to rescue Bangladesh from the clutches of Pakistan. The war ended in the defeat and surrender of Pakistani forces to the Indian army.

During the next few decades, India was surrounded by two hostile neighbours, namely, Pakistan and China. China continued to give military and moral support to Pakistan to fight India. Even the United States showed a tilt towards Pakistan because the latter happened to be a member of US-sponsored military alliances.

Relations with Nepal

Relations with Nepal remained friendly until the Hindu kingdom decided not to depend too much on India. It may be remembered that Nepal is a land-locked country and therefore received substantial trade concessions from India. Despite these trade concessions, and economic assistance, Nepal did not feel like meeting her obligations. She began to hobnob with China which was not liked by India. Nepal mischievously proposed to India (at the instance of China) to recognize her region as a zone of peace to which India countered with another proposal declaring the nearby countries as a region of peace. However, after the restoration of democracy in Nepal, and the frequent visits of Indian leaders, Nepal emerged as a friendly country to India.

India's Relations with Sri Lanka

India faced another problem with regard to her relations with Sri Lanka. This issue was related to the repatriation of Tamil workers in central Sri Lanka who were denied citizenship despite being born and working there. This issue was amicably settled. However, the indigenous Tamils in south Sri Lanka created a problem with their open revolt. This was because the government discriminated against them and treated them vindictively. It may be remembered that the Government of Sri Lanka enjoys the support of the Sinhalese majority which has remained hostile to the Tamil minority section.

The Sri Lankan Tamils in the north-east started demanding autonomy for their province which was denied. The extremist sections happened to be the LTTE which declared the north-eastern part as independent and has been waging a war against the Sri Lankan Government. Unfortunately, India was involved in this struggle because the Tamils in Sri Lanka received lot of sympathy from the Tamils of Tamil Nadu. In other words, the domestic politics of Sri Lanka and the subsequent violence which broke out transcended the borders of Sri Lanka. At the request of the Sri Lankan Government, Prime Minister Rajiv Gandhi sent Indian forces to restore peace in the northern region in July-August 1987. The IPKF (Indian Peace Keeping Force) tried its best to restore peace in Sri Lanka. However, the Lankan Government soon decided not to allow the IPKF to play its useful role due to domestic compulsions. The LTTE carried out the assassination of India's Prime Minister, Rajiv Gandhi, at Perambudur (Tamil Nadu).

Peace-keeping Role

India has been lauded by the international community several times for her peace-keeping role in many parts of the world which witnessed great conflicts. For example, the Indian forces maintained peace under the aegis of the United Nations after peace was concluded in Korea. These forces played a dynamic role in carrying out the repatriation of war prisoners. Similarly, the Indian Peace Keeping Force was sent to Cyprus where the Greeks and the Turks were engaged in war. This force was able to maintain peace in trying circumstances. Again the Indian forces were sent to Congo for peace keeping operations. So also Ethiopia in recent times. India always offered necessary medical assistance to countries affected by floods, famines, epidemics and earthquakes. One should note that India's foreign policy contains certain basic principles. Among them the most important are a) anti-colonialism, b) anti-racialism, c) peaceful co-existence and d) non-alignment.

Diplomatic Achievements

India could boast of several diplomatic achievements. The first was in Korea, where she solved the issue of prisoners of war in 1953. Again India used her diplomatic tact to bring about the first Geneva agreement on Indo-China in 1954. India scored another diplomatic victory when the People's Republic of China was admitted into the United Nations in October 1971. It may be remembered that it was due to her pressure on the US that China was admitted into the UN. India flexed its muscles to bring about total disarmament in the world from the time of her independence.

World Nuclear Disarmament

In 1988, India's Prime Minister, Rajiv Gandhi, put forward a plan for comprehensive nuclear disarmament within a time-frame. Unfortunately, some major powers rejected this, and the US got the Comprehensive Test Ban Treaty (CTBT) approved by the General Assembly of the United Nations, which unfortunately remains discriminatory. India has remained at the forefront in all peace-keeping efforts under the aegis of the United Nations. She happens to be one of the founders of the SAARC (December 1985) which is playing a very important role in maintaining peace in South Asia. India maintained continuing and close relations with the Soviet Union, which was viewed with suspicion by the United States. During the Nehru Era the United States always took the side of Pakistan, because Nehru opposed all military alliances. In fact, the Soviet Union rendered great help to India during critical times, particularly over the issues raised in the United Nations.

POST-RAJIV PERIOD

During the 9th Lok Sabha poll, an anti-Congress wave, in the wake of the Bofors scandal, swept all over North India. Although the Congress Party got a simple majority, it allowed the Opposition Janata Dal leader, V P Singh, to become the seventh prime minister of India (December 1989). The new government told the Swedish company, Bofors, that no further contracts would be signed until it came clean regarding the bribes paid. The government's acceptance of the Mandal Commission Report (on reservation of jobs) caused a controversy. The Bharatiya Janata Party (BJP) and others termed the government's acceptance of the report as politically motivated. In the meantime, BJP leader L K Advani led a *Rath Yatra* to build a temple at Ayodhya. The Ayodhya tragedy spread communal violence. Thus, the National Front Government led by V P Singh made its exit, due to loss of confidence in the Lok Sabha. The Congress Party extended support to the breakaway group of the Janata Dal led by Chandrasekhar to form the government, since the BJP and the Left parties refused to form the government.

Chandrasekhar was sworn in as the prime minister of a minority government in November 1991. His tenure was short (five months), because the Congress withdrew its support on the issue of police surveillance of Rajiv Gandhi's residence. In the next general election, the Congress Party won a majority, largely due to the sympathy wave (Rajiv was assassinated), and the 10th Lok Sabha witnessed on June 21,1991, the assumption of power by the Congress government under the leadership of P V Narasimha Rao. This government completed its five-year term in 1996 and ushered in economic reforms as prompted by the IMF and the World Bank. A paradigm shift in the government's economic policy took place with Manmohan Singh taking over the finance portfolio.

In the next Lok Sabha elections, the BJP emerged as the single largest party in the Lok Sabha (161 seats), and therefore its leader, A B Vajpayee, was invited by the president to form the government. It had the shortest tenure, that is 12 days only. H D Devegowda, the Janata Dal leader, became the next prime minister. He continued in office for eleven months and was replaced by the United Democratic Government of I K Gujral on April 22, 1997 (another coalition government).

After the next general election, the 12th Lok Sabha was constituted in March 1998, and being in majority, the BJP led by Vajpayee formed another coalition government with the support of 18 political parties. Though the coalition partners remained united, the AIADMK leader, Mrs Jayalalitha, pulled it down after 13 months by withdrawing her party's support. Surprisingly the Vajpayee government lost the confidence of the Lok Sabha by only one vote! The vote tally was 269-270 on April 17, 1999. In the fall of all coalition governments, the Congress Party played a decisive role. Vajpayee resigned, and President K R Narayanan asked Sonia Gandhi, leader of the Congress, to form the government if she could muster enough support. As she failed to do so, the president had to order a general election.

The BJP and its allies formed a National Democratic Alliance with a common agenda and fought the elections. They won 303 seats in the Lok Sabha, a clear majority. Vajpayee was sworn in as the prime minister on October 13, 1999. Vajpayee's election victory at Lucknow, where he was pitted against the Congress nominee, Karan Singh, was no surprise since he had to his credit the Kargil victory and a buoyant economy. A seasoned politician, an excellent orator, a mature thinker, and a moderator are some of the virtues Vajpayee is known to have. The Congress received its worst drubbing in election history (Congress and its allies got 134 seats.) In contrast to India's reaffirmation to have democratic governance – the NDA led by Vajpayee promised good governance – Pakistan came under military rule after General Pervez Musharraf overthrew Nawaz Sharif's government in a *coup*.

Foreign Relations

India's foreign policy is based on the pursuit of national interest. India's history and geography have compelled her to play a meaningful role in the establishment of peace and stability in South Asia. Jawaharlal Nehru's Panchasheel doctrine guided the external relations of India since the days of independence. However, India's peaceful disposition and non-aligned policy have been misunderstood as a sign of weakness by some of India's neighbours. Hence, Pakistan's three wars with India over Kashmir (1947, 1965 and 1971). Despite the Tashkent agreement (1965) and the Shimla Accord (1972), Pakistan has been carrying on a proxy war with India by sending mercenaries and trained militants across the border. In every international forum she has raised the issue of Kashmir hoping to gain diplomatic victory, and also pressurises the West to compel India to agree to hold a plebiscite. She has been appealing to the US Government for mediation by giving a grim picture of Kashmir.

The Kargil War

Pakistan's proxy war with India since 1989 reached its climax in May-June 1999 with the outbreak of the Kargil war. For India, it was a betrayal of trust, since the two Prime Ministers, Vajpayee and Nawaz Sharif, had declared in Lahore a few months earlier that they would settle the dispute in a peaceful manner. Even before allowing the peace accord a chance to succeed, Pakistan sent armed intruders, supported by her army, into the Indian-side of the Line of Control (LoC) along an 80 km stretch north of Kargil. The armed intruders dug in at heights of 16,000 ft of Kargil mountains and started pounding the strategic highway linking Srinagar and Leh. To Prime Minister Vajpayee, it was a stab in the back because the plan to send armed intruders and terrorists by Pakistan into the Indian side of the LoC must have taken place during his peace mission to Lahore.

The whole world was aghast at this betrayal, and India's military (*Operation Vijay*) and diplomatic offensive yielded results. The close allies of Pakistan, namely the US, China and Japan, were convinced that Pakistan had committed aggression. India proved that Pakistani soldiers too were involved in the conflict since some of their dead bodies were found with identifications. Pakistan was caught red-handed, and heeding the advice of President Clinton, she withdrew the intruders and regulars. In the meantime, the Indian army and Air Force carved out a niche for themselves in their heroic efforts to throw out the invaders entrenched at a height of 16000-18000 ft. The UN and the US have not heeded India's appeal that Pakistan be declared as a terrorist state as the latter exports terrorism to India, Central Asia and Afghanistan.

Indo-Soviet Relations

P V Narasimha Rao was the first PM to visit Russia in June 1994 (after the collapse of the erstwhile USSR) and sign eleven agreements. Russian President Boris Yeltsin and India's PM vowed to jointly fight terrorism. The political agreement reaffirms bilateral relations and defence agreements. Russia supported India's sovereign right to defend herself through *Operation Vijay* against Pakistani intruders when they violated her border (Kargil Sector).

Indo-US Relations

When President Clinton assumed office, India's relations with the US were cautious at first. This was because the US had carried its 'human rights' dogma to the extreme as a means of interfering in the internal affairs of other countries. When India conducted five underground nuclear tests at the Pokhran range in Rajasthan in 1998, the US imposed economic sanctions. It was followed by the European Union, and by Japan. The West was reluctant to recognise India as a nuclear power. India impressed upon the US of her urgent need to have nuclear deterrence in view of the repeated wars with Pakistan, and Sino-Pak collusion (China and North Korea have supplied missiles to Pakistan). It was this logic that prevented India from signing the Nuclear Non-Proliferation Treaty (NPT) and the Comprehensive Test Ban Treaty (CTBT). India found that both are clearly discriminatory. Time and again, India declared a first No-Use as its nuclear doctrine. When the US stopped supplying cryogenic engines, India proved to the world that it can invent its own; and no arm-twisting by any superpower would work.

Pakistan's support to terrorist outfits in India, Afghanistan and other Central Asian countries, and the clear violation of the LoC by Pakistan regulars which resulted in the Kargil War, have made the US rethink her tilt towards Pakistan. The recent successful military coup in Pakistan leading to military rule has shaken the faith of the US. At the time of writing, the US withdrew its economic sanctions against India, and expressed its desire to renew her relations on a sound footing. Indo-US cooperation with regard to fighting terrorism in the world, and the US ban on terrorist outfits such as the Taliban and the groups following the dictates of Osama bin Laden, the exiled Saudi billionaire, are some of the moves bringing India and the US closer.

Sino-India Relations

The People's Republic of China (PRC) is emerging as another great superpower. After Rajiv Gandhi's visit to China, relations have improved. In September 1993, India and China signed a peace accord during P V Narasimha Rao's visit to China. The two Asian giants signed a trade protocol in Delhi in June 1994 for establishing direct trade and economic ties. The two leaders,

Narasimha Rao and Premier Li Peng, renewed their faith as the basis of establishing the New World Order on two different occasions marking the 40th anniversary of Panchasheel. On a historic visit to India, the Chinese President, Mr Jiang Zemin (first visit by a Chinese President) signed an agreement with India on November 29, 1996 committing both countries to a decision not to use military force to attack each other, or cross the line of control along the Indo-China border. Furthermore, both the countries committed themselves to reducing the troops manning the border.

Relations with Other Countries

India has maintained good relations with other countries. She has championed the cause of Palestinians who are struggling for their homeland. India has also maintained good relations with Israel since the time of Prime Minister Morarji Desai. It has taken active part in the SAARC summits and also the NAM (Non-Aligned Movement). The SAARC (South Asian Association for Regional Cooperation) Council of Ministers met in Nuwara Eliya (Sri Lanka) during the third week of March and discussed common problems affecting them all. They discussed the setting up of SAFTA (South Asian Free Trade Agreement), a single Economic Union by 2001. In the NAM summit held in Durban on September 2, 1998 India made it "loud and clear" that there is no place for any third party involvement in resolving the Kashmir issue as Jammu and Kashmir will remain an integral part of India. Vajpayee said that the "real problem is one of cross-border terrorism". The NAM summit approved India's stand to call for an international summit to plan a "joint global response to terrorism of all forms and manifestations". In the Association of South East Asian Nations Regional Forum Ministerial Meeting held in Singapore on July 28, 1999, India's External Affairs Minister, Jaswant Singh offered to sign a protocol to make South-East Asia a nuclear-free zone. India also offered her cooperation to ASEAN in the field of space research.

India's Progress in Science and Technology

India has made rapid strides of progress in science and technology. India has gate-crashed into the exclusive Nuclear Club - whether the other members liked it or not. It was in May 1998 that India carried out Pokhran II — five underground nuclear tests. The Buddha smiled only once in 1974 (Pokhran I). The Prime Minister, Vajpayee, congratulated our brilliant scientists on this rare feat — incidentally on Buddha Poornima Day (May 13). A country, wedded to peace and non-violence, had to take this step looking to India's security-threat perception. India's Intermediate Range Ballistic Missile, named Agni II, was successfully test-fired on April 11, 1999 and it has a range of 2,500 kms. It may be used as a weapons system. The US, China and Pakistan have not liked the Agni project, but India achieved this capability for the sake of national security. Russia was the only big power to support India, while others were extremely critical.

Scientists of the Indian Space Research Organisation (ISRO) have made India proud by sending many communications and weather satellites since the inception of the organisation. Latest in the INSAT series is INSAT-2E. It was successfully launched on April 13, 1999. It cost 220 crore rupees to build and it has 17 C-band transponders which can be used for telecommunications, TV broadcasting and meteorological services. Thus, India has joined the club of advanced nations with this space venture which has the potential of earning precious foreign exchange if put to commercial use for the benefit of developing and developed nations. In information technology, India is acknowledged as a superpower. India invented the super computer—PARAM.

Indian Economy

The size of the Indian economy was GNP $421 billion in 1998. The ninth Five-year Plan (1997-2002) is underway. The objective is to achieve a common minimum programme, namely, priority to agriculture and rural development, accelerating the growth rate of the economy, ensuring food availability to the poor, providing basic minimum services including universal primary education, checking population growth, empowering women and so on. During the period 1996-98, there was a decline of 2 per cent (from 7 to 5) due to slowdown in agriculture and industrial production.

The volume of India's share in world trade is less than one per cent. The World Bank has warned that the fiscal deficit should be brought down, and it was estimated to be 5.1 per cent in 1998-99. India's total foreign exchange reserves are around $31 billion. India attracts around $4 billion of foreign direct investment.

Epilogue

The Bharatiya Janata Party (BJP) formed the government after the general elections with an alliance of 22 parties (called National Democratic Alliance) since no party received a clear majority in Parliament. It was led by the BJP stalwart and statesman, Atal Bihari Vajpayee. With the alliance partners, the BJP formulated a common agenda on the basis of which programmes and policies were implemented. Despite many initial hiccups, the National Democratic Alliance (NDA) somehow achieved commendable success in its policies and programmes. The Congress, the leftists and other political parties (calling themselves as secular front) were unable to defeat the NDA in power, despite many scandals surfacing.

The NDA gave a big boost to the economy through its programme of liberalisation. A separate ministry was set up known as the disinvestment ministry to carry out privatisation in banking and insurance sectors (except Defence). Foreign Direct Investment (FDI) was encouraged, and India received much attention from global investors as a good destination for investment. India's progress in liberalising telecom and IT sectors gave much fillip to the economy. India's exports received much boost, and many Indian products could compete successfully in world markets. India's GDP (8.2 per cent) in recent months has been considered spectacular and therefore India is considered as the fastest growing economy next only to China. But manufacture and agriculture still lagged behind. Successive droughts led many farmers to commit suicide, as they were unable to repay the loan.

The war on Iraq had adverse impact on Indian economy with contracts worth $1.5 billion lost. Again, the US companies cancelled software contracts with Indian companies and many engineers lost their jobs.

The Kargil war and the military stand-off with Pakistan, reduced the much needed resources for carrying out other welfare works. The second generation of economic reforms were also carried out with much caution in view of world economy reeling in recession. The Foreign Exchange reserves reached a new high of more than a $100 billion, indicating investor's confidence in India's vibrant democracy and economic boom. India played an important role in the WTO Conference held in Cancun by demanding better terms of trade (removal of restrictions by Western nations on their imports and stopping of subsidies given to farmers) for developing countries. This conference, consisting of 148 member countries, failed to achieve its objectives because the rich countries opposed the demands of the developing countries.

The new government carried forward the look east policy to its logical end by establishing close links with Far-Eastern and South-East Asian countries. Japan had serious reservation about its cooperation when the nuclear test at Pokhran was carried out. After the resumption of dialogue with Pakistan, the Japanese assistance resumed. The US lifted economic sanctions on India and Pakistan when both these countries joined her in the war on terror. The US further strengthened her relation with India by its cooperation and modernisation of defence. The US put pressure on both India and Pakistan to give up their hostility for one another and peacefully resolve their outstanding disputes. She always extended her cooperation as a 'facilitator' rather than as a mediator, since India insisted on no third party interference in Kashmir dispute. Although the US depended on Pakistan's cooperation to tackle the Taliban and Al-Qaeda militants on Afghan-Pakistan border, she however maintained the right balance with regard to India, since the latter had been victim of cross-border terrorism. It was the intense pressure from the US that led the Pakistani president to ban the militant outfits (encouraging violence in Jammu and Kashmir) in its country.

On its part, the US also put all these terrorist organisations in its banned list. In a way, the US recognised that what is going on in Jammu and Kashmir was not a local insurgency (as argued by Pakistan) but acts of terror organised by terrorists across the border. The US put pressure on Pakistan to dismantle the training camps within its border and also in Pakistan-occupied Kashmir. The US also has viewed Pakistani blackmail (Musharraf threatened the use of nuclear weapons to settle Kashmir dispute) with serious concern.

The visits of Chinese leaders, Li Peng and Jiang Zemin, to India paved the way for friendly relations – particularly considering bilateral trade and border disputes. Vajpayee's visit to China in June 2003 promoted friendly cooperation, particularly after China came to be ruled by the fourth generation of new leaders. China has accorded its approval to the merger of Sikkim (a Himalayan Kingdom) with India. Vajpayee's visits to several countries in the East and West further strengthened the bond with those countries. Neighbouring Myanmar extended its hand of cooperation and promised that it would not tolerate anti-India activities on its soil. The Sri Lankan government, with the new Prime Minister Rajakapse, desires good relationship with India, and wants the latter to play the role of mediator to settle the ethnic conflict. India played an important role in the ASEAN as a partner and many countries in South-East Asia recognise India's stable democracy with its vibrant economy as a model to be emulated. India established friendly relationship with Israel in spite of some misgivings in the Arab countries. India signed extradition treaty with the UAE, Britain, South Africa, and other countries so that criminals taking shelter there could be brought to face a fair trial for the crimes committed in India. Pakistan and Bangladesh have not been cooperative in this respect.

The recently held general election in India resulted in the Congress-led coalition forming the government under the leadership of Dr Manmohan Singh, a renowned economist. The coalition government of the United Progressive Alliance is ruling the country with a common minimum programme. The Communist Party of India and the Communist Party of India (Marxists) are lending support from outside. Their support is vital for the stability of the government, which otherwise implies that the economic reforms process may not have smooth sailing.

36

PAKISTAN

At the stroke of midnight on August 14, 1947, Pakistan became a sovereign and independent country. She was carved out of United India. The founder of this new nation was Mohammed Ali Jinnah (*Quaid-e-Azam*), who earlier advanced what was known as the two-nation theory to the British Viceroy. He threatened the British that if Pakistan was not constituted, the country would face dire consequences. The riots took place in Bengal. Jinnah played the communal card and asked his people to observe Pakistan Day. It was a day of great tragedy, as Muslims and Hindus indulged in mutual bloodbath, looted shops, and set fire to everything they came across. The British Viceroy, Lord Mountbatten, was convinced that Pakistan must be created to appease the Muslims.

The Idea of Pakistan

The idea of Pakistan was promoted by the Muslim League which was founded in 1906. Its great leader was Mohammed Ali Jinnah. Jinnah and his colleagues began to make the Muslims in India conscious that when India became free, they would be ruled by the Hindus. Therefore, their future would be in danger. The idea of Pakistan was also promoted by a great Urdu poet, Mohammed Iqbal. The League passed the Pakistan resolution at its Lahore session in 1940 demanding a separate and independent nation for the Muslims within the territories constituting British India. In fact, the Muslim League did not carry on any struggle for freedom as such to bring about the new State of Pakistan. It tried to oppose the Indian National Congress at every stage doing the necessary spadework for the British to create Pakistan. Jinnah was quite successful in his mission and Pakistan became a reality to the utter disappointment of the leaders of the Indian National Congress which included a large number of Muslim leaders like Maulana Azad and so on.

East Bengal and Sylhet formed the eastern wing of Pakistan, while the western wing consisted of four provinces, namely, Sindh, Baluchistan, Punjab and NWFP. East Pakistan lay separated from the West by over a thousand miles of India's territory. Moreover, the majority of Pakistan's population lived in the Eastern wing consisting of 15 per cent of the territory, whereas the Western wing had 85 per cent. In a nutshell, it may be said that the British pressurised by the Muslim League, created Pakistan knowing fully its geographical incongruity, and cultural, linguistic and racial disparities. Furthermore, the Bengalis, the Sindhis, the Pathans and the Baluchs formed a sizeable minority section in East and West Pakistan. Therefore, they were compelled to fight for a fair share of power and autonomy against the ruling Punjabis in Pakistan. Mohammed Ali Jinnah, the founder of Pakistan, hardly realised the potential inner conflicts that the new nation would face in the future. He tried to stress the unity of the new country in the name of religion, that is Islam. He died in September 1948 leaving his country with a Muslim League party which was bereft of great leaders like him and with a fragile foundation. Hence this country had to depend upon the civil servants to play a major role. In the course of time, the Pakistani army began to dominate the political scene because of the continuing threat to political stability.

Constitutional Framework

The first Constitutional Assembly consisting of members elected from the provincial assemblies was convened in 1947 (soon after the independence) for the purpose of drafting a permanent constitution for the country. Unfortunately, the liberal principles with which Jinnah had created Pakistan had to be diluted, and subsequently, religious influence began to pervade the drafting of the constitution. Pakistan was to be an Islamic state guided by the teachings and principles of Islam. However, there was no clear-cut idea as to how Islam was to play a role in serving or guiding the new State. Several controversies arose in the course of time. The constitution was finally completed and adopted after a decade in 1956.

Political Instability

During this decade, Pakistan faced several crises, such as war with India over Kashmir, the assassination of Liaquat Ali Khan (1951) and communal disturbances in Punjab. The Pakistani army and bureaucracy led by the Punjabi elite played a dominant role. In the midst of this political turmoil, the federal court of Pakistan tried to keep reminding politicians about running the country and the government on constitutional norms by a duly elected civil government.

Since the first constitution could not function smoothly, there was to be a second one. It came into effect in March 1958. Pakistan was declared a Republic with a president as its head. The constitution provided that no law could be passed by the National Assembly which contravened Islamic injunctions. In spite of this second constitution, Pakistan was plagued by internal troubles, since no party enjoyed clear majority in the Central Legislative Assembly. Soon after, the President (Iskander Mirza) and the Prime Minister quarrelled over their jurisdictions which forced the President to declare martial law in the country (October 1958). The second constitution was also abrogated with Central and provincial assemblies getting dissolved and political parties being banned.

Pakistan had no less than six prime ministers during the period 1951-58 but curiously had only one army General, namely, General Ayub Khan. The point to be stressed here is that the country always depended upon the army for restoring political stability in the country. President Iskander Mirza had to resign in the wake of the paramount role played by the army. The army superseded him and Pakistan came under the regime of General Ayub Khan (subsequently promoted as Field Marshal). Field Marshal Ayub Khan took over the charge of running the government and declared martial law administration in the country. He introduced what is known as the System of Basic Democracies to make the administration more accessible to the representatives of the people.

The 1962 Constitution

This constitution of 1962 introduced the presidential system of government envisaging a dual role for the president, that is to act as president and prime minister at the same time. He was to be indirectly elected by an electoral college. Since political parties were banned, the National Assembly included various groups which owed loyalty either to their leaders or regions. Ayub Khan was re-elected the country's president in 1964. Unfortunately, the regime of Ayub Khan in Pakistan also did not bring peace. It was plagued by popular agitations. Students in Pakistani universities rose in revolt against Ayub's regime. Similarly, regional leaders also revolted over wide-ranging issues. Popular agitations against his regime forced him to resign in March 1969. Ayub Khan transferred his power to the commander-in-chief of the Pakistani army, General Yahya Khan. General Yahya Khan abrogated the constitution of 1962 and imposed martial law throughout the country.

East Pakistan Secedes

The regime of Yahya Khan witnessed the independence of Bangladesh (the eastern wing of Pakistan) following a civil war from March 1971. There were many reasons for the emergence of Bangladesh as an independent and sovereign country. The major role for this was provided by the Awami League which was led by Sheikh Mujib-ur-Rahman. It must be remembered that the eastern wing of Pakistan which became Bangladesh had several grievances. The people here felt that they were neglected on many counts by the Pakistani Government which was dominated by the Punjabi elite.

They were not properly represented in the National Assembly by the administration, or in the armed forces of the country. The Awami League led by Sheikh Mujib-ur-Rahman proposed autonomy for East Pakistan. When his party swept the polls in the first free election held in December 1970, winning 160 out of 162 seats in the Provincial Assembly, and 160 seats in the National Assembly, trailed by the Pakistani People's Party (PPP) led by Zulfikar Ali Bhutto with 80 seats, he put forward a six point formula envisaging a loose federation for the country. This did not find favour with the president. President Yahya did not invite Sheikh Mujib-ur-Rahman to form the government and tried to postpone the convening of the National Assembly. He proposed to Sheikh Mujib-ur-Rahman to form a coalition government with the cooperation of the PPP led by Zulfikar Ali Bhutto.

Eventually, East Pakistan was not happy with this proposition, and the Sheikh's Awami League declared independence and sovereignty in the name of the Republic of Bangladesh. What followed was the civil war, in which India participated. The Pakistani army which tried to quell the revolt of its eastern counterpart got defeated by the Indian armed forces. It led to the resignation of President Yahya Khan. He was succeeded by Zulfikar Ali Bhutto of the PPP who declared martial law administration. During his regime, Pakistan faced many troubles. He was deposed by General Mohammed Zia-ul-Haq after a bloodless coup on July 5, 1977.

General Zia's Military Regime (1977-88)

The next eleven years witnessed the iron rule of General Zia. He assumed power in July 1977 after a bloodless coup (Bhutto was deposed) ostensibly to bring about normalcy in Pakistan, hold elections, and transfer his power to a civilian government. He established a martial law regime with himself acting as Chief Martial Law Administrator, and set up a Military Council consisting of four members to advise and assist him. President Choudhuri remained as *dejure* head of state. In September he lifted the seven-year-old emergency on the pretext of holding general election. He postponed the intended elections on the ground of political instability, and imprisoned Zulfikar Ali Bhutto on charges of ordering the murder of the father of his (Bhutto) opponent. The Lahore High Court sentenced Bhutto to death in March 1978, and he was hanged on April 4, 1979 despite appeals for pardon from several heads of state. To legitimise his dictatorship Zia introduced a Council of Advisers which remained subordinated to the Military Council. He replaced it with a cabinet of 22 civilian and military members, and again replaced this with a new civilian cabinet in April 1978. When President Choudhuri resigned his office, General Zia took over his office and powers. In October 1979, he banned all political activities. His martial law orders severely restricted personal freedom and gagged the press, and the independence of the judiciary. Despite his restrictions, nine opposition political parties came together in March 1981 and formed an alliance for the purpose of restoring democracy in the country. Their movement was called Movement for the Restoration of Democracy (MRD).

Islamisation

Zia declared an interim constitution and set up *Majlis-i-Shura,* a 300-member Federal Advisory Council. This council's main function was to evolve a democratic system in tune with Islamic tenets, give its advice on suitable legislation to be passed, and discuss economic development. The power of the civilian courts had earlier been curtailed and the military court had been made supreme.

Zia realised that his regime was becoming unpopular, and therefore, declared that he would lift martial law, but would continue as President to complete the 'Islamisation' of Pakistan. He sought to know through a referendum whether the people liked his 'Islamisation' or not.

The MRD realised the trick Zia was playing to keep himself in power and therefore, boycotted the December 1984 referendum. Zia received the desired popular mandate to continue as president to complete the Islamisation, *Nizam-e-Mustafa* (the Prophet's ordained system). Zia then gave orders for holding the third general election for the National Assembly on February 25, 1985 and for the provincial assemblies on February 28. These elections were boycotted by the MRD. He revived the Constitution of 1973 – which he had suspended after declaring Martial Law – in order to remain supreme. The new assemblies at the Centre and in the provinces exhibited their feudal character since these were composed of landed families. Zia-ul-Haq appointed Muhammad Khan Junejo, a member of the Muslim League, as the civilian prime minister. He withdrew the martial law and military courts to show that democracy had been restored (December 1985).

Benazir Bhutto

The Movement for the Restoration of Democracy organised public demonstrations throughout the country to resist Zia's dictatorship and non-party assemblies. It was at this time that Benazir Bhutto, daughter of the executed Zulfikar Ali Bhutto and co-chairman of the Pakistan People's Party, arrived from London (after her self-exile). Her return intensified the struggle against Zia's regime. Noted for her charm, charisma and oratorial skills (ex-president of the Oxford Union), she drew a large and sympathetic crowd everywhere in the country. When she demanded fresh elections in Pakistan on the basis of the original constitution (1973), Zia banned the holding of political rallies which were scheduled to be held on Independence Day celebrations (August 14, 1986). As the political parties remained adamant, many members of opposition parties were arrested.

President Zia and his PM were at loggerheads over several issues, notably on Afghanistan, Islamisation, partyless democracy and so on. This friction led to the dismissal of the Junejo Ministry on May 29, 1988. Zia promised to hold elections within three months. However, the polls would be on a partyless basis. Benazir Bhutto appealed to the Supreme Court to turn down Zia's order, and the latter, after reviewing the petition (July 1988) declared Zia's stipulations as unconstitutional. In other words, political parties have a right to participate in the elections. Before Zia could wriggle out of this situation, he was killed in a plane crash with military officials on August 17, 1988 near Bahawalpur. Zia's death profoundly altered the situation in the sense that political parties now had a chance to restore a full-fledged democracy in the country. Ghulam Ishaq Khan, a close friend of Zia, and incidentally the Chairman of the Senate, assumed the office of president. The acting president set up an interim government and agreed to hold elections in November on a party basis.

Led by Benazir Bhutto, the Pakistan People's Party (PPP) secured 92 seats, which enabled it to form the government at the Centre. Benazir was sworn in PM on December 2, 1988, and Ghulam Ishaq Khan was elected President. Benazir's woes were many. She did not have a comfortable majority in the National Assembly, and the Senate was dominated by the Islami Jamhoori Ittehad (IJI). Being the main opposition party, it remained hostile. The IJI's prominent leader was Nawaz Sharif who virtually controlled the Punjab province. In the meantime, differences cropped up between the prime minister and the president, and the former appealed to the Supreme Court as to whether the president enjoyed discretionary powers to make judicial appointments. A no-confidence motion was brought against her government by the opposition parties, but it was defeated on November 1, 1989 since it fell short of 12 votes. In the byelections, the PPP suffered several reverses and the IJI succeeded in persuading members of the Mohajir Quami Movement (MQM) to withdraw support to Bhutto's coalition government. In the meanwhile, the government had to control the terrible ethnic conflicts in Sindh on the one side, and maintain good relations with the provinces which were ruled by opposition parties. Fortunately, the Pakistani army remained a mute spectator, and the drama ended with the President dismissing Bhutto's government on August 6, 1990, dissolving the National Assembly, and ordering fresh elections on August 8, 1990. Ghulam Mustafa Jatoi was named as the caretaker PM.

Nawaz Sharif

After the announcement of results of the general election, the leader of the IJI, Nawaz Sharif, was elected PM on November 6, 1990. This eleventh prime minister of Pakistan was soon at loggerheads with the president, and was, therefore, sacked on April 18, 1993. Sharif petitioned the Supreme Court against wrongful dismissal, and the latter annulled his dismissal thus creating a constitutional impasse. Looking at the worsening situation, the Pakistani army intervened as the arbitrator and set up a provisional government with Moeen Qureshi (a former Vice-President of the World Bank) as caretaker prime minister until the next general election to be held in October.

Benazir Again

In the general election held in October, Benazir Bhutto's PPP won a comfortable majority. Benazir became the PM (for the second time) on October 19, 1993. Mrs Bhutto got Farooq Ahmed Leghari elected as the new president. However, the two did not get along well. The style of Benazir's functioning became controversial and the president warned her repeatedly to mend her ways or face dismissal. But she never seemed to care. In the meantime, talks with India over the issue of Kashmir failed. There were strong rumours that Benazir and her husband (appointed as Overseas Investment Minister), Asif Ali Zardari, had amassed great wealth through corrupt means and practices. The president dismissed her government on November 5, 1996, and dissolved the National Assembly. He called for fresh elections. Benazir Bhutto was subsequently charged with corruption and misdemeanour.

Nawaz Sharif As PM

Benazir Bhutto's PPP was trounced by Nawaz Sharif's Pakistan Muslim League by a landslide margin in the election held on February 3, 1997. Nawaz Sharif became the PM for the second time on February 17. As anticipated, the president and the PM soon quarrelled when the former permitted an inquiry to be held into Nawaz Sharif's misuse of power during his first stint as PM. In the legal battle that ensued the president lost, and therefore resigned. It looked as though the prime minister had become all too powerful for the first time in Pakistan's history. Pakistan's polity still remains feudal and absolutist in character, and Nawaz Sharif showed his penchant for making money. He believed in one-upmanship, and prepared plans to make the country rich. His 'India Smear' campaign and proxy war yielded rich dividends. Following in the footsteps of his mentor, General Zia, he proposed a Bill which sought to implement the Objectives Resolution as an integral part of the Constitution (Zia had not completed this). He tried to quicken the process of Islamisation of Pakistan by proposing the 15th Amendment Bill which sought to make the *Quran* and the *Sunnah* "the Supreme Law of Pakistan".

To get even with India, when the latter carried out five underground nuclear tests (Pokhran II) in May 1998, Pakistan went ahead by conducting five nuclear tests despite the warning from the US. The US, followed by others, imposed economic sanctions as they had earlier done on India. India's PM Vajpayee realised that there should not be any confrontation between the two countries which could lead to a nuclear war. Hence he took the olive branch to Lahore on February 20, 1999. Sharif signed the Lahore Declaration ostensibly to keep India off guard as proved by the Kargil war (*see Chapter on India*). Humiliated by the setbacks suffered in bringing the Kashmir issue to the focus of world attention in several international fora, Pakistan made the final gambit. The Pakistani army and the Inter-Services Intelligence (ISI) could not succeed in Kashmir because of international pressure. Pakistan was diplomatically isolated during the Kargil war, and Nawaz Sharif had to eat humble pie. President Clinton categorically told him to withdraw the militants and Pakistani regulars from India's side of the line of control. After Nawaz agreed to this and returned home from Washington, he had to face protests from the opposition, not excluding the Pakistani generals.

Role of the Army

It must be remembered that in Pakistan the buck stops at the army headquarters. It has always remained the final arbiter, and no politician dares to challenge its interference. In fact, Pakistan was ruled by army generals during half of its existence. The state has been scarred by no less than four "full-fledged military coups since 1947". Sharif appeared to hint that the army was to be blamed for the Kargil fiasco and hence tried to split it. However, the army was terribly annoyed at Sharif's meek submission to the dictates of Washington and Delhi – and he was even prepared to sign the CTBT treaty. Nawaz's sacking of General Pervez Musharraf, the army chief (while returning from Colombo by air) on October 12 was the last straw on the camel's back. It led to a military counter-coup followed by military rule in Pakistan. General Musharraf is in no hurry to restore civilian rule in Pakistan. He has kept Nawaz Sharif under house-arrest. Sharif has been charged with treason and corruption. The military regime is busy these days launching its offensive against bank defaulters.

Pakistan's Economy

The most important question to be asked is: what ails Pakistan's economy? The reasons for Pakistan's ailing economy are innumerable. The most important are defence expenditure ($2.8M), debt servicing ($5.6M), and meeting the pay hikes of a bloated bureaucracy. Pakistan's poverty ratio is 34 per cent and savings, a paltry 12 per cent. It attracts an average of $500 million as foreign direct investment. The inflation rate is around 8 per cent. The economic survival of Pakistan depends upon the assistance of international financial institutions, like the World Bank, the IMF, and other financial agencies, and has foreign exchange reserves of nearly $1.8 million. Corruption being rampant, many people thrive on blackmarketing and smuggling. Many analysts believe that a full-fledged war with India would certainly bring disaster.

Pakistan's Domestic Conditions

Pakistan's domestic scene looks appalling. Ethnic and commercial conflicts have taken a heavy toll, particularly in the Sindh and Karachi areas. The Urdu-speaking Muhajirs have been treated like second class citizens. They are demanding equal rights and autonomy. The Shia-Sunni violence is frequent. The poor people have little hope of getting their grievances redressed from the feudal type of politicians who are keen on enriching themselves at the cost of the former. It was in these circumstances that Imran Khan, the famous cricketer, started a political party, Movement for Social Justice, in April 1996.

Religious Fundamentalism

Religious fundamentalism has taken deep roots since the time of Zia-ul-Haq. He mixed religion with politics; Pakistan always declares that it gives moral support to militant outfits — such as the Taliban and Harkat-ul-Ansar to wage holy wars against the Russians in Afghanistan, and Indians in Kashmir respectively. The whole world knows where the money for these wars comes from and who supplies these weapons. It is estimated that 2,000 to 5,000 students from *madrasas* in Pakistan have joined the Taliban which now control 90 per cent area of Afghanistan after fighting bloody battles with the enemy. Its deep involvement in several secessionist movements in Central Asia is posing a serious threat to the territorial integrity of Russia, China and India.

Nuclear Weapons

No country should be denied the right to self-defence, but Pakistan's nuclear strategy is aimed only against India — the enemy No. 1. Several European nations and China have supplied nuclear material with which Pakistan was able to make nuclear bombs. The US which showed great concern with regard to nuclear proliferation allowed her ally to make these bombs. She did not show any concern when China and North Korea assisted Pakistan in carrying out her missile programme. The *Ghauri* missile that Pakistan has produced has a range of 1,500 kms, and is designed to carry nuclear weapons. The Chinese-made M-11 missiles with a range of 300 kms have moved close to the side of the Punjab border. Pakistan, like India, has refused to sign the Comprehensive Test Ban Treaty (CTBT) saying that India is posing a serious threat, even though India has come out with its no-first use doctrine. It is a pity that Pakistan has not agreed to sign a no-war treaty with India. In olden days the US supplied F-16 Jets to Pakistan. Pakistan's latest F-series can be fitted with *Ghauri* missiles.

Musharraf's Military Regime

After becoming the Chief Executive, General Musharraf set up the National Security Council and Cabinet, The members were mostly handpicked and known to toe the line of the dictator. His crackdown on bank defaulters (which included the brothers of jailed Nawaz Sharif and a few ministers) brought him some adulation. However, the critics were quick to point out the corruption rampant in the army (some Corps Commanders came to be humorously called Crore Commanders for amassing huge wealth) for which the dictator had no answer. The CHOGM (The Commonwealth Heads of Government Meeting) expelled Pakistan from the Commonwealth, and the US government became a harsh critic. The latter imposed economic sanctions, and feeling a bit disappointed, the Pakistani Chief Executive visited Islamic countries like Saudi Arabia, the UAE, Qatar and Turkey for acquiring legitimacy for his regime. Bowing to the international pressure, and also the harsh judgement delivered by Pakistan's Supreme Court recently, General Musharraf, announced local elections be held in January, elections to the provincial assemblies in August and parliamentary elections in October 2002). He announced executive pardon to the jailed PM, and permitted him, his family members, and relatives to leave Pakistan. Saudi Arabia provided shelter to this group.

Although the general would like the country to adopt a secular outlook, despite being an Islamic country, the religious Right (clerics and militant groups), which wields power in the army circle, may not allow this. With a battered economy, Pakistan led by this military general, would have to take tough decisions. If he has to acquire legitimacy for his regime, he has to restore democracy and rein in the militant and fundamentalist groups. The latter is hell bent on declaring *jehad* on India over the Kashmir issue. As far as India is concerned, they would like the general to stop cross-border terrorism so that peace talks can begin.

Absence of US Tilt

Following the cessation of the Cold War, and the disintegration of the Soviet Union, the US did not deem it fit to depend on Pakistan. With the advent of Clinton administration, the so called US tilt towards Pakistan was absent. Human rights became the main issue in the US foreign policy matters, and Pakistan stood discredited due to General Musharraf's *coup* in Pakistan. Pakistan's support to the tyrannical rule of Taliban in Afghanistan, and its helping hand extended towards what India called 'cross-border terrorism' in Jammu and Kashmir further alienated the sympathy of the US towards that country.

War on Terror

The terrorist attack on the World Trade Center on September 11, 2001, turned the situation for Pakistan from bad to worse. The US declaration of war on terror by the Bush administration, with its appeal to the civilised countries to aid its efforts to destroy terrorism, had a telling effect on Pakistan. Pakistan's support to Taliban regime in Afghanistan, particularly the latter giving shelter to Al-Qaeda terrorists, focused the attention of the US. Al-Qaeda terrorists who masterminded the attack on the US brought Pakistan in the line of fire. Bush's clarion call to countries with 'you are either with us or against' left no choice for Pakistan but to rein in the fundamentalist elements, both within Pakistan and outside. The Taliban regime (recognised by only three countries – vide, Pakistan, Saudi Arabia and the UAE) in Afghanistan had to go since it refused to hand over Al-Qaeda terrorists, including the world's most dreaded mastermind Osama bin Laden.

The US's war on Afghanistan, with the assistance of friendly countries and the Northern Alliance (those who were ousted by Taliban) had all the attributes of the Gulf War. The high-tech war (US warships launching precision-guided-missiles followed by heavy bombings from the US and British Air Squadrons all against specific targets) led to the defeat of Taliban forces. The Taliban fled to the mountains, leaving one city or the other, to the invading forces of Northern Alliance. Pakistan today is playing a dominant role in the US's efforts for apprehending militants and the Al-Qaeda terrorists hiding in the border regions (Afghanistan-Pakistan border). Thus Pakistan sconced itself as the front-rank ally of the US, although the Sunni clerics and Islamic fundamentalist are so much agitated. In fact these elements have made serious attempts to assassinate the president who is also the chief of the army staff.

Realising the plight of the Pakistani president who is sticking his neck out to assist the war efforts of US, the latter waived economic sanctions, provided military-hardware, and arranged liberal economic assistance despite India's reservations. The US government also turned a blind eye when its intelligence sources exposed Pakistan's transfer of nuclear technology to countries considered by the US President as 'axes of evil', namely North Korea, Iran and Libya. Pakistan is designated by the US administration today as a non-NATO ally, reminiscent of the Cold War era. The Commonwealth re-admitted Pakistan into its fold.

Many political analysts believe that Pakistan's foreign policy is India-centred, and mainly about the Kashmir issue. Musharaff, like his predecessors, believe that success in Pakistan's foreign policy mainly rests on resolving the dispute of Kashmir in his favour, and therefore raising the issue in every international fora has been the annual feature. Pakistan's paranoia is shared by many Western nations along with China and Japan, since they are of the view that two nuclear neighbours may launch a nuclear war any time.

But the US's pressure on both Pakistan and India to resume dialogue on Kashmir – it was abruptly ended with the Kargil war – did work to a certain extent. But the militant's attack on Indian Parliament was too much for India to stomach since she insisted Pakistan to stop cross-border terrorism as a precondition before talks could resume. India, in an aggressive mood, mobilised its troops on the western border. The world eagerly waited with bated breath as to whether it would all end in a nuclear war in South Asia. The US diplomacy began in a feverish pitch to bring the two nuclear neighbours to end their hostile moves. Both countries responded, but India insisted that Pakistan's cross-border terrorism should end. The Agra summit where President Musharaff and his and Indian counterpart Prime Minister Vajpayee met did not meet with success. But peace parleys continued. People to people contact started. Both countries resumed diplomatic relations, which had ceased earlier. On the eve of Jammu and Kashmir general election, Vajpayee agreed to resume talks with Pakistan. The SAARC summit held recently, with other factors, such as Cricket Test Series, created congenial atmosphere. As of now, the secretary-level talks are continuing for taking steps to improve relations, and of course the Kashmir issue being the core issue.

2002 Election

The political parties at home and international pressure from outside forced the Pakistan president to hold general elections in October 2002. But before that he held a referendum which favoured his continuation as president and army chief. As a first step towards restoring democracy, he ordered elections for the local bodies in all the provinces. The next step was taken towards restoring the Parliament itself. The general elections of 2002 produced a hung parliament with no political party gaining majority of seats. Political analyst believe that the president desired this kind of situation, so that he can remain the arbiter of things in Pakistan. It must be remembered that Benazir Bhutto (PPP) and Nawaz Sharif were not allowed to contest. The 30 member EU team expressed its displeasure over the election process by saying that it suffered from serious flaws.

Dummy Democracy

Thus the Pakistan Muslim League (Quaed-e-Azam) which won the largest number of seats in the 272 member Parliament, formed the government with the support of like-minded parties. This coalition chose Mr Zafarullah Khan Jamali as the prime minister. In the mean time, the president armed himself with extraordinary powers, both civilian and military, as to make the Parliament a tool in his hands. He achieved this by getting the 1973 Constitution amended. He created the National Security Council which is dominated by military advisors. Opposition parties have been vociferous in demanding that Musharaff should not occupy two posts (presidency and chief of army staff). After two years in office, Prime Minister Jamali resigned – reaffirming the perception that the president is the real ruler. The army rules the roost in Pakistan, as the saying goes.

37

BANGLADESH

Bangladesh is surrounded not only by Indian territories but also by Myanmar (Burma) in the east, and the Bay of Bengal in the south. At the time of the partition of India, East Bengal was composed of Muslim majority population. When Pakistan became a reality, East Bengal along with Sylhet constituted East Pakistan. Strangely, East and West Pakistan were separated by 1600 kms of Indian territory. When Pakistan took its birth it had five provinces, East Pakistan being one of them (1955).

In the course of time, East Pakistan felt unhappy at the way West Pakistan dominated over it. This bitter feeling eventually led to a struggle for freedom. East Pakistan became Bangladesh after achieving independence on December 16, 1971. What factors led to the demand for independence?

Language and Emotional Integration

The main difference between East and West Pakistan lay in the language and emotional integration. Pakistan thrust Urdu as her official language even on its eastern counterpart where the majority of the population was emotionally attached to the Bengali language (even though they happened to be Muslims). On February 21, 1952, the people of East Pakistan went on a strike as a protest against the domination of the Urdu language which was thrust on them. This strike resulted in violence, and a large majority of students in East Pakistan held a rally. The police tried to break the strike which resulted in the killing of a number of East Pakistani students.

The 'language day' was also observed by the East Pakistanis to protest against the domination of Urdu. Due to these ugly and unhappy incidents, the Pakistan government finally adopted Bengali as the joint official language of the country. However, the people of East Pakistan were not happy. They found that their region was not represented on par with the western counterpart in the central legislature. Similarly there was a feeling that they were not adequately represented in the administrative set-up and the armed forces in the country. Furthermore, Western Pakistan received more development expenditure while the eastern wing was neglected, although it was densely populated.

These east-west differences, and the subsequent resentment expressed in the East culminated in the formation of a political party, the Awami League, which was led by Sheikh Mujib-ur-Rahman. The Awami League started demanding autonomy for the East. It won an overwhelming victory in the national general election held in December 1970, and secured a majority of seats in the Pakistan National Assembly. It was hoped that the President of Pakistan, Yahya Khan, would invite Mujib-ur-Rahman to be the prime minister of the country. However, the Pakistani President tried to ignore Sheikh Mujib's claim for the prime minister's post.

The president, instead, tried to bring about a possible compromise and started negotiating with a number of other parties, including the Awami League. Unfortunately, these talks failed. Yahya Khan adopted dilatory tactics and postponed the convening of the new National Assembly. His action provoked violent agitations in East Pakistan. It was then that the Awami League led by Sheikh Mujib-ur-Rahman decided that East Pakistan should unilaterally secede from the Union. The Sheikh declared independence of the People's Republic of Bangladesh on March 26, 1971.

Civil War

With the declaration of independence, a civil war broke out in Bangladesh. President Yahya Khan outlawed the Awami League and got all the leaders arrested. The Pakistani army was mobilised to crush the rebellion of Bangladesh. Sheikh Mujib-ur-Rahman was arrested and put on a secret trial in Pakistan. But the people of Bangladesh continued to resist the onslaughts of the Pakistani army which was occupying their country. The resistance movement of the people was led by the "Mukti Bahini", an irregular freedom-fighting group. They carried on a relentless fight against the brute force of the Pakistani army.

The civil war in Bangladesh cast deep shadows across the border, ie, India. Innocent people of Bangladesh were being persecuted by the Pakistani army. This forced millions of Bangladeshis to flee, and cross the border to reach India. India went on receiving millions of Bangladeshi refugees who were escaping the onslaughts of the Pakistani army. The strength of the refugees touched nearly 10 million, and India's Prime Minister, Indira Gandhi, started appealing to Pakistan and the international community to do something immediately. In the meantime, the Mukti Bahini of Bangladesh was losing its battle. It made a fervent appeal to the Indian Government to come to the rescue of their country.

When India failed to get proper response from the international community and the Pakistani Government failed to restore normalcy in Bangladesh, she decided to take unilateral action. In the meantime, Pakistan attacked India in the west on December 3. Prime Minister Indira Gandhi declared war on Pakistan on December 4, 1971. Pakistan complained to the UN about India's aggression, and tried to secure the military support of the United States Government. President Nixon at that time ordered the US Seventh Fleet to move towards the coast of Bangladesh to intervene on behalf of Pakistan. However, at the last minute, wisdom prevailed on the US Government. Finally Pakistan was defeated, and her armed forces surrendered to the Indian army on December 16, 1971. Thus, the independence of Bangladesh became a reality, thanks to the help rendered by the Indian army. Sheikh Mujib was released by the new Pakistani President, Zulfiqar Ali Bhutto (Yahya Khan's government fell after the Pakistani defeat) in January 1972.

Sheikh Mujib returned to Bangladesh and became the first prime minister. The new government of Bangladesh was recognised by the international community, and it secured a seat in the United Nations. A provisional constitution was set up and it declared Bangladesh as a secular State and provided for parliamentary democracy. The birth of Bangladesh left Pakistan angry. In a fit of anger, Pakistan left the Commonwealth. Eventually, Pakistan gave its recognition to Bangladesh in February 1974. Earlier, Bangladesh had a new constitution (December 1972).

Unfortunately, Bangladesh was frequently plagued by political turmoil, military rule and floods ever since its inception. The opposition groups in the Bangladesh National Assembly resorted to terrorism in 1974 to browbeat the government led by Mujib. The violence in the country led to the imposition of emergency and subsequent withdrawal of constitutional rights for the citizens. The political system in Bangladesh changed from parliamentary democracy to a presidential form of government, with Mujib-ur-Rahman as its first president. In the new political set-up the president was to enjoy absolute power. President Mujib-ur-Rahman created the Peasants and Workers party, the only party allowed to function in the country. His action alienated the sympathies of a number of Islamic groups and also a number of army Majors. Subsequently, a group of Islamic Majors staged a coup in August 1975. Sheikh Mujib and his family members were assassinated.

Bangladesh: A Troubled Country

Since then, Bangladesh has experienced frequent political disturbances due to coup and counter-coup by army Generals. A national referendum held in June 1978 recognised General Zia (Major General Zia-ur-Rahman and his policies) as the ruler. Zia secured his victory and set up a council of ministers to advise him. In February 1979, parliamentary elections were held, and Zia's Bangladesh Nationalist Party (BNP) won by a thumping majority. Since General Zia became very popular among his subjects, the martial law in the country was lifted. General Zia did not live long since he was assassinated following a coup in May 1981.

Ninety five per cent of the people of Bangladesh speak Bengali even though 85 per cent of the total population is Muslim. The rest include Hindus, Christians and Buddhists. They constitute the minority sections. Dhaka is the main capital and Chittagong and Khulna are the chief ports. Bangladesh is undoubtedly one of the poorest countries in the world.

The man who led the attempted coup, Major General Muhammad Abdul Manzur, was himself killed throwing the country into utter confusion. Justice Abdus Sattar, the Vice-President, assumed the reins of administration as the acting president of Bangladesh. But, this acting president found the country ungovernable as strikes and demonstrations, held against the culprits involved in the coup, became the order of the day. The opposition parties also moved in to demand presidential elections. The Bangladesh Nationalist Party, divided into few groups, finally nominated Abdus Sattar as their candidate for the presidency. In the November 1982 election, he secured overwhelming support and was elected president. Coming to the conclusion that the country was ungovernable, he formed a National Security Council in January 1982. Sattar had made it known that he would like to implement Zia's policies before things could take shape, Lieutenant General Hossain Mohammed Ershad, the Chief of Army Staff and member of the National Security Council, staged a successful bloodless military coup on March 23, 1982. General Ershad eventually became the Chief Martial Law Administrator of the country. The Constitution was suspended and Parliament dissolved. After a short tenure of Asanuddin Choudhury as temporary civilian president, General Ershad replaced him on December 11, 1983.

President Ershad's economic policies succeeded to some extent and he could gain popular support. However, numerous political groups led by Shaikh Hasina Wazed and Begum Khaleda Zia (daughter of Shaikh Mujib and widow of General Zia respectively) demanded the early restoration of democracy in the country. It was only on November 10, 1986 that the Martial Law was lifted. By the Seventh Amendment, the Constitution was restored, but it ensured the continuance of President Ershad's Martial Law Decree.

A large number of government supporters launched a new political party called the National Party. General Ershad was re-elected president in October 1986. The National Party won a majority of seats in Parliament in the general election held in March 1988. General Ershad's corrupt rule was brought to an end after a popular revolt in December 1990. This was because the victory of the National Party in the 1988 election was in dispute. Ershad was deposed and arrested, and Shahbuddin Ahmad assumed office as the acting president. The general election was held in February 1991 in Bangladesh.

Bangladesh Politics

The Bangladesh National Party (BNP) led by Begum Khaleda Zia swept the polls with 140 seats in the Jatiya Sansad (one-House Parliament with 300 seats), followed by 95 seats secured by the Awami League led by Shaikh Hasina, and 35 seats won by the Jatiya Party led by Hossain Ershad. Ex-President Ershad was serving a jail term for six years. He was released on parole, as his party extended unconditional support to Shaikh Hasina in the formation of the new coalition government following her victory in the general elections held in June 1996. Her party, the Awami League, had won 146 seats, the BNP 116, and the Jatiya Party 32.

Political Ideologies

The Bangladesh Nationalist Party led by Khaleda Zia and the Awami League led by Shaikh Hasina traded charges. The former accused the latter of serving the interests of India, and turning Bangladesh into an "Indian Market". The Awami League accused the BNP of being a "protector of Pakistani interests". It is a fact that the BNP supported Pakistani fundamentalists. To prove its allegation the Awami League showed how the seven-party alliance under the BNP has lent its support to the separatist movements in the north-eastern states of India.

The BNP and its allies are supporting "Bangladeshi nationalism" based on Islamic tenets. In contrast, the Awami League advocated "Bengali nationalism" under the rubric of secularism. Shaikh Hasina's government is at present trying to reverse the trends set in the country after 1975 (military rule and so on) but has not shied away from taking the support of Ershad. The "self-confessed killers" of Sheikh Mujib-ur-Rahman (the founding father of Bangladesh and father of Shaikh Hasina) have been arrested. In the meanwhile, Ershad withdrew his support to the government saying that his party would maintain its "distance". However, the Awami League continues to have a majority – though not substantial. Thus, Bangladesh politics has seen "three bloody coups, 19 botched coup attempts, and the assassination of two heads of government after the exit of Mujib-ur-Rahman."

Bangladesh signed the Ganga Water Sharing Treaty with India which has benefited her. She signed another treaty known as Chittagong Hill Tract (CHT) peace accord by which thousands of Chakma refugees (Bangladeshi nationals in exile) were sent back by India. The BNP has not liked this. But, Shaikh Hasina Wajed is bent upon establishing good relations with India. Recently, India and Bangladesh signed an agreement establishing rail-link between the two countries (Jessore-Benapol). Similarly, India and Bangladesh agreed to introduce Calcutta-Dhaka shuttle bus service to enable friends and relatives to visit each other's country.

Khaleda Zia's Government

In the bitterly fought general elections held on October 1, 2001 the Bangladeshi Nationalist Party (a four party alliance namely, Jamaat-e-Islam, the Islamic Oikya Jote, the Bangladesh Jatiya Party and Bangladesh Nationalist Party) led by Begum Khaleda Zia defeated its rival, the Awami League (led by Shaikh Hasina), and wrested control of the government. While Shaikh Hasina appealed to the electorate to return her to power on the track record of her achievements, Begum Khaleda Zia accused the Awami League government of "misrule, terrorism and subservient policy" during its five year term in office.

Within a year, the administration of Begum Khaleda Zia began to face growing criticism for the way it handled several issues. Some of the charges levelled against the administration include large-scale persecution of minority community, the all pervasive corruption, deteriorating law and order situation, nexus between criminals and politicians, repression of political opponents, and violation of human rights. A number of political scandals has rocked the government. The government is under pressure for its cover-up regarding gold smuggling involving a cabinet minister. Then there are the textbook scandal and the fuel controversy. The wheat-scam too put the government in a fix.

The international image of Bangladesh has been tarnished with the Danish Government withdrawing $45 million assistance to the Ministry of Shipping. Amnesty international has cited numerous cases of illegal detentions, torture and violation of human rights; and the United Nations Development Programme (UNDP) has sharply criticised the country's criminal justice system.

The BNP government has been drawing flak for undoing the good work done by the previous government, for unleashing police repression, torture of journalist, and the closure of Ekusha TV. Furthermore, the government is accused of giving shelter to the fleeing Al-Qaeda terrorists of Afghanistan and the banned members of United Liberation Front of Assam (ULFA).

The US authorities black-listed Bangladesh (along with 23 other countries) as part of its immigration policy since January 2003. Neighbouring India has been urging Bangladesh Government to rein in the Indian militants who have fled, and taken shelter in Bangladesh.

The BNP government's proposal to amend the Constitution (14th amendment bill) introduced in May 2004 has been severely criticised by the Opposition Awami League. The latter says that the proposed amendment run "contrary to the original spirit of the Constitution" for it does not involve issues such as governance, corruption or deteriorating law and order situation in the country. Some political analysts say that the government is going soft on a militant Islamic outfit called the 'Jagrate Muslim Janta Bangladesh' (JMJB), which has a large following. This militant outfit has chosen Taliban as role model. There is no need to remind that Bangladesh is one of the poorest countries in the world. The foreign direct investment (FDI) has dropped from $280 to $70 million in 2000-2001.

Bangladesh Economy

Today Bangladesh is undoubtedly one of the poorest countries in the world. Political instability, coupled with recurring natural calamities, have been mainly responsible for this state of affairs. Her per capita income GDP is hardly $240 and GNP is $1,380. The literacy is hardly 37 per cent. The country's economy is sustained by agriculture and fishing. The main agricultural crops are rice, sugarcane and cotton. The jute industry is famous. In recent years, both the political parties have adopted an agenda for introducing "market reforms".

38

NEPAL (NEPAL ADHIRAJYA)

Nepal today is an independent and sovereign Hindu kingdom – in fact, the only Hindu kingdom in the world. It is a land-locked country lying on the lap of the highest Himalayan ranges (including Mount Everest). This country is surrounded by China's Tibet in the north, and the Indian territories on all other sides. Majority of the people in this Hindu kingdom speak Nepalese, and Kathmandu is the capital. Though the Nepalese were descendants of the Mongol tribes, there is much admixture of Indian blood.

Thousands of years ago, the hardy Nepalese were divided into a number of hill clans, each clan ruling over a petty principality. Of these hill clans, the Gurkhas became prominent in 1559. Ranjit Malla of Bhatgaon and his successors ruled a major part of Nepal till 1769. The hardy Gurkhas succeeded them after overthrowing their dynasty. These Gurkhas were led by King Prithvi-Narayan Shah (1769-75).

Absolute monarchy became the order of the day. The country achieved unification by 1846. During this period, successive kings appointed Mukhtiars (prime ministers) to seek advice pertaining to the administration of the state. However, there was a political change soon after the so-called incident known as "Kot Massacre". This massacre paved the way for the emergence of a strong man, Jung Rana Bahadur, who happened to supersede the monarchy in Nepal. He forced the reigning queen to appoint him as the prime minister, and subsequently, usurped the absolute power of the state. Since then, the post of the prime minister became hereditary in the family of the Ranas. After this coup, the Ranas became the real masters of the kingdom, and monarchy became titular. The Ranas appointed other members of their family and relatives to all the high posts in the military and administrative services. In fact, the Ranas and their relatives "lived like medieval princes".

Anglo-Nepalese War

The Gurkhas tried to extend their control over all the other clans and desired to expand their dominions – especially the ill-defined frontiers of Bengal. In their attempt to do so they encroached on the borders of the British East India

Company. The latter had by then occupied the district of Gorakhpur in 1801. By 1814, the Gurkhas had become a menace to the British East India Company, and Lord Hastings launched a British offensive against them. The Anglo-Nepalese War (1814-16) resulted in the defeat of the Gurkhas by the British. They signed the treaty of Sagauli by which they surrendered their districts of Kumaon and Garhwal. They agreed to accept a British Resident at Kathmandu. Subsequently, they withdrew from Sikkim also. They remained very friendly towards the British. And the British company recognised their bravery and martial talents and recruited them into its army. Nepal remained friendly towards the British ever since the treaty of Sagauli.

When India became a free and sovereign country in August 1947, Jawaharlal Nehru hoped that the Nepali National Congress Party supported by Jayaprakash Narayan would put an end to the Rana's rule in Nepal. Thereafter, he expected close relations to exist between India and Nepal. Unfortunately, this did not take place. The Nepali National Congress turned into Nepali Congress after the merger with the Nepali Democratic Congress in 1948. Its president was M.P. Koirala. His brother, B P Koirala, played an important role in Nepali politics.

The regime of the Rana was overthrown by the Nepali Congress in 1951 with the support of King Tribuvan Bir Bikram Shah Deva. Nepal once again came under absolute monarchy. During the decade 1951-60, Kings Tribuvan and Mahendra permitted the rise of political parties and the establishment of a representative government. In 1959, a new constitution was drafted and came into force. In accordance with the constitution, general election was held to choose representatives for Parliament. However, within a year (December 1960), the King dissolved Parliament, arrested Prime Minister B P Koirala of the Nepali Congress, and scrapped many provisions of the constitution. All political parties were banned.

Thus Nepal once again came under the iron rule of the Nepalese king. In April 1961, the king was able to achieve the unification of the kingdom with the integration of 15 feudal chieftainships. The king changed his mind and introduced a new constitution in December 1962, which re-asserted absolute royal authority. This constitution provided for a "partyless" system of government. It was to be on the basis of village panchayats (village councils). The king enjoyed the power to appoint and dismiss prime ministers. This kind of constitution established a titular democracy which remained in force until 1990.

In December 1962, Nepal was declared a Hindu state, probably to give her a distinct identity. In January 1972, King Mahendra died. He was succeeded by

Prince Birendra. In 1980, the king appointed the Constitutional Reforms Commission which recommended a few changes in the constitution. These were accepted and the king issued a decree (the king alone enjoyed the authority to introduce amendments) to give effect to this. Direct elections were allowed on a non-party basis. Accordingly elections were held in May 1981 and Thapa of the Rashtriya Panchayat was re-elected prime minister of the country. It must be remembered that political parties were not recognised, and, therefore, caste politics began to play a major role in the elections.

Foreign Relations

Nepal, being a land-locked country, maintained good relations with her big neighbours, namely, India and China. She signed a few agreements with both of them. In 1950, India and Nepal signed a treaty of Peace and Friendship. In a way, India was instrumental in restoring absolute monarchy in the kingdom of Nepal. King Tribuvan remained very grateful to India. But after his death (1955), his son, King Mahendra, deviated from this norm, and moved close to China. He wrote that "China would be more useful in making Nepal more assertive in international affairs".

Nepal and China signed a treaty of peace and friendship in 1960. This was because King Mahendra felt that India might support the cause of the rebellious Nepali Congress. A few members of this party had taken shelter in India. King Birendra, who succeeded King Mahendra, followed his father's policy. At the instance of China, and to the embarrassment of India, Nepal proposed a Zone of Peace in 1972. In response to Nepal's proposed Zone of Peace, India's Prime Minister, Morarji Desai, put forward a counter-proposal stating that South Asia be declared as a Region of Peace in 1977, taking the example of Indo-Nepalese relations as a model.

Nepal's Economy

Nepal is an underdeveloped country. Ninety per cent of the labour force is engaged in agriculture, forestry and fishery. Much of her foreign exchange earnings come from tourism (tourism attractions include the Buddha's birthplace and Mount Everest). Hinduism, Buddhism and Islam are the main religions. There is much illiteracy in Nepal.

Nepali Politics

The king ousted Thapa and set up a new council of ministers led by Lokendra Bahadur Chand, a former Chairman of the Rashtriya Panchayat. In May 1986, the general election was held and Marich Man Singh Shrestha, a former Chairman of the Rashtriya Panchayat, was elected prime minister. Unfortunately bitter rivalry between the Nepali Congress and the Communists made things worse and political instability became the order of the day.

Dissatisfied with the political situation, the people held pro-democracy demonstrations in April 1990, and the king was forced to accept what is known as " political pluralism". He dismissed the government and declared that the panchayat system of nominated councils stood abolished henceforth. He proclaimed a new constitution in November which curtailed his absolute powers. Thus, Nepal has a constitutional monarchy "based on a multi-party democracy". A two-chamber Parliament came into existence, with a lower chamber (Pratinidhi-Sabha) consisting of 205 members (10 members being nominated by the king).

Coalition Governments

Within a period of five years (1994-1999) there were as many as six governments in Nepal. Under a new system in 1994, the Communist Party of Nepal and the United Marxist-Leninist Party (CPN-UML) gained 88 seats in the general election held in November and formed the government. In September 1995 a five-party coalition government led by Sher Bahadur Deuba of the Nepali Congress assumed power. Yet another coalition government led by the Rashtriya Prajatantra Party came to power in March 1997. "Changing partners midstream" and pulling down the government on flimsy reasons became the order of the day. In December 1998, Girija Prasad Koirala formed a three-party coalition with CPN-UML and the Nepal Sadbhavana Party. When the Marxists pulled out of the coalition over non-implementation of a 25-point agreement, Koirala's government was in trouble. The king rejected his advice to dissolve the Lower House. However, at the last minute, one faction of the Communist Party agreed to support him. Koirala was sworn in as PM again on December 24,1998. The present Nepali Government is led by the patriarch of the Nepali Congress, Krishna Prasad Bhattarai. He is credited with having risen in revolt against the century-old Rana family in the 1950s. He also actively worked to bring about multi-party democracy in the country.

On June 1, 2001, King Birendra, Queen Aishwarya and their eight relatives were shot dead by inebriated crown prince Dipendra. The motive for the murder remains a mystery though there may be a family quarrel. The crown prince committed suicide or was killed. These deaths caused a pall of gloom in the Kingdom, and there was the danger of political chaos, what with the Maoist insurgency raising its ugly head. However, this danger was averted when Gyanendra, brother of the late king, was crowned king according to Hindu tradition.

Maoist Insurgency

With their main target being to uproot the monarchy and set up a communist republic, the Maoists had made great impact on the rural poor. Gradually they spread their ideas to the poor and also to students in the Nepali capital,

Kathmandu. Political instability coupled with frequent changes in governments encouraged the Maoists further. Finally the police was unable to control the Maoist violence. What was needed was military intervention, and the army was under the direct control of the king. In 2000 Bhattarai resigned as prime minister and he was replaced by G P Koirala. He was the prime minister for a short term, and his place was taken by Sher Singh Deuba. Deuba's Government agreed to the demand of land reforms. It was unable to stem the tide of the Maoist influence, and therefore announced cease-fire. It offered a wonderful opportunity to the Maoist to liberate many districts (out of 75) from government control. The weakness of the government became evident.

The new king then wisely decided to act in view of the worsening situation since the Maoists were attacking government offices, police stations, and the army barracks.

Emergency Declared

A state of emergency was declared. The fundamental rights of the people were revoked. The Communist Party was banned and the Maoists were declared insurgents. In the ensuing violence created by the Maoists nearly 2000 people lost their lives. The Communist Party of Nepal was declared as a terrorist organisation and the Royal Nepal Army (RNA) was given powers to deal with the volatile situation.

The King's Coup

Not satisfied with these measures, the king dismissed the prime minister and his cabinet on October 4, 2002, and himself exercised all executive powers as per article 27 of the Constitution of 1991. Five ministers of the dismissed cabinet were kept under house arrest. Parliamentary elections which were due to be held were postponed. The king formed an interim government and appointed Lokendra Bahadur Chand as the new prime minister. The new government was to administer the country through ordinances. Thus multi-party democracy was kept on hold by the new king.

Foreign Assistance

Neighbouring India and China were alarmed at the growing political instability in Nepal. The US and India supplied military hardware to enable the king to cope with the increasing violence. Disgruntled political parties, the violent Maoists and the pro-active king contributed to virtual anarchy in this Himalayan Kingdom. The political parties carried on their opposition to dictatorial attitude of the constitutional monarch. The political parties desired the restoration of multi-party democracy with a constitutional monarch.

Jana Andolan

In recent months, five political parties came together to form an alliance called Jana Andolan (people's agitation) in contrast to the Maoists campaign of 'People's War'. The Jana Andolan meetings demanded the end of the king's *coup,* and restoration of constitutional government, that is multi-party democracy. Thus, Nepal has gone through a political turmoil – with the three forces, namely the king, the political parties, and the violent Maoists pulling in different directions – making the lives of the common people miserable. The students joined the protest movement organised by the political parties.

The international community represented by friendly countries like India, China and the US desire an end to this political instability, which is being taken advantage by the Maoists. They have appealed to the king to work in the direction of bringing about constitutional monarchy in a multi-party democracy. An attempt is made by the king to create a congenial atmosphere. He has asked Sher Singh Deuba to head the government.

Whatever may be the case, the king's coup followed by rule through ordinances, especially the ordinance of Terrorist and Disruptive activities, has brought agonising reprisals including the student's agitation. The human rights watch has pointed out violation of human rights in large number of cases. The neighbouring countries of Nepal hope that political instability would end soon. The Maoists need to be persuaded to join the mainstream of national life by giving up violence, and work with others in establishing multi-party democracy.

39

BHUTAN
(DRUK-YUL – THE LAND OF THE THUNDER DRAGON)

Bhutan lies in the eastern Himalayas and is surrounded by China in the North and Indian territories on all other sides. A hereditary monarchy has been ruling over this kingdom since 1907. Monarchy was sustained by the British when they found conflicting authority, powers and jurisdictions in Bhutan all wielded by different persons and institutions. The British wanted someone, preferably a king (Druk Gyalpo) to command habitual obedience from the majority of the Bhutanese. They found such a person in Ugyen Wangchuk, the Tongsa Penlop (Governor of Tongsa). He proved to be loyal to the British interests. The British helped to get him unanimously elected as king on December 17, 1907, by an assembly composed of the representatives of the people, the government and the clergy. Thus, started the hereditary monarchy in Bhutan. Subsequently, the king was conferred the title of the Knight Commander of the Indian Empire by the British Indian Government "in recognition of the services rendered by him."

The Anglo-Bhutanese treaty was signed in 1910 by the then British Indian Government by which the Bhutanese foreign relations were supervised by the British Indian Government. This treaty remained in force until India's independence (August 1947), and was subsequently replaced by the Indo-Bhutan Treaty of Friendship. By this treaty, Bhutan agreed to seek the advice of the newly independent Government of India with regard to her foreign relations. But the king retained the right to decide whether to accept or reject the advice rendered by the Government of India. It should be remembered that Bhutan does not have a written constitution. Its role has been fulfilled by the ruling monarch.

The absolute monarchy in Bhutan gradually paved the way for a liberalised monarchy since October 1969. Some minor changes were observed in the political system as well as in the process of modernisation. The National Assembly (*Tshogdu*) was "reinstituted in 1953". The Bhutanese monarchs have played an important role in the process of modernisation of the kingdom. "King Jigme Sungye Wangchuk is a democrat not only in theory but also in practice". He ascended the throne in July 1972. The people found him to be very responsive to their aspirations, and the king made it a point to hear the grievances of people always. He was found to be very accessible to the villagers who came to submit their petition of grievances.

The Tshogdu, that is the National Assembly in Bhutan, consists of ten monastic representatives who are elected by the central and regional ecclesiastical bodies, and the rest are nominated by the king himself. The latter include the members of the council of ministers, commonly known as *Lhengye Shungtsog*. These members of the National Assembly serve the country for a term of five years. In 1965, the Royal Advisory Council (*Todol Tsokde*) was introduced with ten members. Bhutan today has twenty districts, and there is a Nepalese minority which constitutes 35 per cent of the population. Thimpu is the state capital and the official languages are Dzongkha, Lhotsam (Nepali) and English. By and large, the people of Bhutan belong to a sect of Mahayana Buddhism, and the religious community is quite powerful.

There are about 5000 Lamas who affect the religious life of the people. The Bhutanese Government contributes a substantial sum of money for the maintenance of numerous monasteries. Religion undoubtedly dominates the politics of Bhutan today. The Bhutanese kingdom remained almost in seclusion until the government inaugurated tourism in 1974. The Bhutanese economy is largely a subsistence one, subsistence farming being the backbone. And by world standards, this small kingdom happens to be one of the poorest countries in the world. It has also a low literacy rate, ie, ten per cent of the total population. Bhutan became a member of the United Nations in September 1971. Since then it has received monetary assistance for several of its projects from both India and the United Nations Development Programme (UNDP). The king set up a planning commission in 1972, and since then, several five-year plans were launched for the economic development of the country. Bhutan became a member of the South Asian Association for Regional Co-operation (SAARC) in 1985.

Political Modernisation

The political system of this small country is undergoing radical changes in recent years. It is transforming from authoritarian rule into a constitutional monarchy, with the king surrendering most of his powers. For a country and political system bound by age-old tradition, this is a welcome change. King Jigme Singye Wangchuk issued a royal edict (Kasho) during the sixteenth session of the National Assembly stating that the Assembly should make itself more responsive to the aspirations of the common people. In other words, the

Assembly should pass laws for the welfare of the people, and provide for clean and transparent administration.

The king initiated a more democratic system of governance by proposing: 1) that all cabinet ministers be *elected* by the National Assembly, 2) the Assembly should introduce a mechanism for moving a no-confidence motion against the king himself and 3) that the Assembly should assign specific role for the cabinet to discharge its responsibilities.

Progressive Reforms

Furthermore, the king proposed that he would not chair the meetings of the cabinet henceforth. The draft of the new constitution is getting ready. A national judicial commission is to be set up to frame laws for the purpose of holding a fair trial and prosecuting the guilty. A Royal Civil Service is also being set up for the recruitment of eligible persons for the administration. The king has surrendered his veto power for blocking the passed legislative bills. A High Court is also set up. It may take many years for the people to adjust themselves to changing situation, since they had followed traditions for many centuries. Political analysts believe that the king may be doing all this so as to gain international recognition for the country as being progressive.

40

SRI LANKA (CEYLON)

Ceylon is a big island situated below the tip of South India. It is known as Sri Lanka today. In the early ages it was called by the Sanskrit name *Simhaladweepa,* and Tambapanni and Sihaladipa in the Pali language. The Tamilians called Ceylon *Ilam.* The Greeks and the Arabs named her Taprovane and Serendip respectively. The first king (according to Mahavamsha chronicle) was Vijaya who must have ruled Ceylon during the sixth century BC. He hailed from the Gangetic plains of India. This was how the process of Aryanisation began over the Sinhalese language. The Sinhalese language is associated with Pali, and its origin is traced to the Brahmi.

While King Vijaya appears to be a legendary character, the first historical king of Sri Lanka was Devanampiya Tissa of the first half of the third century BC. Emperor Ashoka was his contemporary. It was at the instance of this great Mauryan emperor that the Devanampiya Tissa and his followers became Buddhists. Emperor Ashoka's son, Prince Mahendra, played an important role in the conversion of the Sinhalese king and his followers to Buddhism. Subsequently, the daughter of Emperor Ashoka, Sanghamitra, carried the branch of the sacred Bodhi tree to be planted at the Ceylonese capital, Anuradhapura. Buddhism has enjoyed great patronage in Sri Lanka since then.

Tamil Conquest

In the second century BC, a citizen of the Chola kingdom named Elara conquered Ceylon. It was King Dattagamani of the second century BC who liberated Ceylon from the successive Tamil invaders. His era witnessed the revival of Buddhism. But the Tamil kings invaded Ceylon every now and then during the reign of Vattagamani. They succeeded in capturing the Ceylonese capital, Anuradhapura. In the end Vattangamani succeeded in expelling the invaders.

It was King Gajabahu of Ceylon who took revenge upon the Cholas during the second century AD. He wreaked his revenge upon the Cholas because their King, Karikala, had caused the great destruction of Ceylon during his conquest. During the next four centuries Ceylon witnessed peace and prosperity. This age is described as a "Great Tank Building age", and King Mahasena played a conspicuous role. Mahasena's son was Meghavarna who was a contemporary of the Gupta Emperor Samudra Gupta. Meghavarna sent a mission to the Gupta emperor with gifts, and sought permission to build a monastery at Bodh Gaya for the sake of Saratha Sangraha. Fa-hien, the famous Chinese pilgrim, visited Ceylon on his way back to China in AD 414. The next important Ceylonese king was Buddhadasa who provided medical relief to many villagers by appointing one physician for every ten villages. He wrote a famous treatise in Sanskrit. It must be remembered that many foreigners and merchants visited Anuradhapura.

The discovery of gold coins belonging to the Roman empire in Ceylon testifies to this fact. Ceylon was deeply disturbed by civil wars from the sixth to the eighth century, and the Pallavas of south India took full advantage of this situation. During the last quarter of the sixth century AD, Simhavishnu Pallava appears to have defeated the Ceylonese rulers a number of times. King Narasimhavarman Pallava was responsible for restoring the exiled King Manavarma to the Ceylonese throne after sending two naval expeditions. The Chola supremacy of South India began in the tenth century AD with King Parantaka. He invaded Ceylon and brought about her subjugation. The exploits of Parantaka were repeated by the successive Chola emperors like Rajaraja I, Rajendra I, and Rajadiraja. The northern part of Ceylon including Polonnaruva was annexed by Rajaraja I. Emperor Rajendra I continued to rule over northern parts of Ceylon. Ultimately, the Chola emperors had to give up their authority over Ceylon because of successive attempts of the Ceylonese rulers to liberate their country.

The people of Ceylon, under the leadership of Vijayabahu, took advantage of the civil war which had broken out in the Chola empire, and declared their independence. Fortunately, King Vijayabahu (AD 1056-1111) received assistance from the King of Burma, Aniruddha. In 1073 Vijayabadu declared himself King of Ceylon and maintained good relations with the Chola emperors. The Chola emperor Kulottunga maintained cordial relations with Ceylon and gave his daughter in marriage to the Ceylonese prince. Vijayabahu revived Buddhism, and the Burmese King Aniruddha sent a large number of Buddhist monks to Ceylon for this purpose. In exchange for rendering help to him against the Cholas, Vijayabahu gave a tooth relic of the Buddha to King Aniruddha which was housed in Shwezigon pagoda.

Parakramabahu, the Great (AD 1153-1186)

After overcoming many internal troubles following the death of Vijayabahu, King Parakramabahu I ascended the Sinhalese throne. He waged war against the king of Pegu over issues connected with the elephant trade and the detention of a Ceylonese princess. The new Burmese king established cordial relations with Ceylon in AD 1174. Parakramabahu intervened in the succession dispute of the Pandyan kingdom by supporting a rival party pitted against a candidate supported by the Chola emperor. This was how the traditional enmity between the Cholas and the Ceylonese continued. These wars caused great havoc on both the sides and resulted in rapid economic decline. Thus, the intervention of the Ceylonese king did not bring any benefit.

Parakramabahu took steps to impose heavy taxes upon his subjects so as to make good the losses suffered during the wars. He had undertaken several important projects including the beautification of Polonnaruva and irrigation projects, for which he required money. Hence, the people of Ceylon suffered a heavy dose of taxation during his rule. The greatness of Ceylon reached its peak during his reign. His famous statue measuring eleven and a half feet in height represents "one of the finest sculptures in Ceylon". Even during the time of King Nissankamalla, the traditional enmity with the Cholas continued. This ruler rendered yeoman service to his subjects by carrying out many public works. After his death, the kingdom of Ceylon witnessed chaotic conditions. In 1263, the famous Pandya King, Jathivarman Sundarapandya, conquered Ceylon.

Cultural Influence

Hence the early history of Ceylon shows that she was more or less a dependency of South Indian rulers, except during the eleventh century AD. India's cultural influence over Ceylon goes back to the days of the Indian prince, Vijaya, who is regarded as the first king of Ceylon (fifth century BC). The second great feature of India's cultural influence on Ceylon was the introduction and spread of Buddhism from the time of Emperor Ashoka. Thirdly, the art and architecture of Ceylon was greatly inspired by the Dravidian art of the Cholas.

Trade and Commerce

Trade between the Roman empire and India during the period of Emperors Augustus and Vespasian was flourishing, thanks to the commercial entrepot situated on the southern coast of Ceylon. Merchants of China, South-East Asia, India and the Roman empire gathered there to exchange their commodities. Several Indian ships were found plying at the Gulf of Mannar, and Anuradhapura, and attracted the attention of several foreign merchants even though it was not a port city. The Ceylonese ports were made use of by Indian merchants to import spices, forest-resin, scented woods and silk from South-East Asia and China. These imported goods were subsequently sold in the markets spread all over India.

Advent of Portuguese

The Portuguese entered Ceylon in 1505 for the purpose of establishing their trade. At the end of the century they acquired the south-western districts of Ceylon. They captured Jaffna in 1619. But they met with stiff resistance while attempting to conquer the central kingdom of Kandy. The Sinhalese kings sought the support of the Dutch to expel the Portuguese. In the meantime, the Portuguese established their main settlements in southern and western parts of Ceylon. They remained there for nearly 150 years till the Dutch drove them out.

The Dutch Conquest of Ceylon

The decline of Portuguese power in South-East Asia during the last decade of the fifteenth century paved the way for the other European powers to enter the arena. The most notable among them were the Dutch who captured the monopoly over spice and pepper trade. They were able to accomplish this task after eliminating the Portuguese control over Malacca and Ceylon. After losing their foothold in India, the Dutch began to establish their commercial empire in South-East Asia, particularly Ceylon. The Dutch established their monopoly over spice trade and made huge profits by selling it to European countries.

The Dutch traveller, Lin Schoten, has given a graphic account of his voyages in South-East Asia. He visited many ports of South-East Asia and India. The Dutch merchants were able to prosper mainly because of the pepper trade. It was during one of their visits to South-East Asia that they established contacts with Ceylon. Prospects for trade appeared very bright in this region, and, therefore, they formed the East India Company in 1602 on the model of the British. The Dutch ships passed through Portuguese Goa, Ceylon and Malacca to reach the ports of South-East Asia. The natives of these regions hated the Portuguese so much so that they welcomed the entry of the Dutch. The Dutch were prepared to meet any threat posed by the Portuguese, whose main centres happened to be Malacca and Colombo. It must be remembered that Ceylon offered to the Europeans some of its valuable products like spices, tea, rubber and cinnamon. The Portuguese made their impact upon the Ceylonese in many respects. For example, the Ceylonese capital, Colombo, is a Portuguese name. Similarly, many Christians living in Ceylon have Portuguese names.

King Raja Sinha II of Kandy sought Dutch support in 1638 to overthrow the Portuguese domination. The Dutch resorted to deceit and dubious diplomacy and occupied the Ceylonese ports of Galle and Negombo. In the meantime, the Portuguese lost Malacca to the Dutch, and in the hope of recovering the territories they had lost, signed a treaty with the Dutch in June 1641 regarding acquisitions in Ceylon. But, the treaty became infructuous, since its ratification was delayed by the Dutch Government. Consequently, the Portuguese strongholds were blockaded by the Dutch. The Dutch fought the Portuguese off the coast of Nagapatnam in 1644. Though the Portuguese recovered from these setbacks, they were unable to hold on to their settlements in Ceylon due to the resistance of King Raja Sinha II of Kandy.

The Dutch rule in Ceylon could not continue for a long time. The central kingdom of Kandy established its contact with the British East India Company through an agreement made for the purpose of driving out the Dutch (1795). Rajdi Rajasinha (1780-1798) offered friendly terms to the British. During the Napoleonic era, France conquered Holland, and the British took advantage of this situation and expelled the Dutch. In 1796, the Dutch had to transfer their power and possessions in Ceylon to the British East India Company.

Ceylon was constituted as a part of the Madras Presidency in 1796. Accordingly, many districts taken over from the Dutch were administered by the British East India Company. However, a revolt of the natives against the British in late 1796 resulted in the establishment of a dual government in 1798. Since this system did not work well, the British Crown took over the maritime provinces under its direct control in January 1802.

The British Government tried to take over the central kingdom of Kandy by launching military expeditions. The first expedition failed. However, the second succeeded mainly because the subordinate chiefs of the Raja of Kandy helped the British. It must be remembered that they had nursed their grievances against their Malabari King, Sri Vikrama Raja Sinha. The chiefs of the central kingdom of Kandy signed a convention in 1815 by which the British guaranteed their "Right, Privileges and Power" – and also agreed to respect the ancient laws and customs – and protect the religion of the Buddha.

Towards Self-government

The British Government appointed Cole Brooke-Cameron Royal Commission of Enquiry in 1831 to recommend reforms necessary for an efficient administration of Ceylon. This commission recommended unified administration for all the British-held territories in Ceylon. Accordingly legislative measures were passed to implement the recommendations. Legislative and executive councils were set up in 1833. A few Ceylonese were nominated to these councils. The British Government also set up the required Civil Service for the purpose of administration. The central kingdom of Kandy which had existed for more than 2000 years, was integrated with the rest of the territories.

Rise of Political Consciousness

In the early years of British rule, the Ceylonese did not entertain the thought of liberation. This was mainly because the new administration provided a number of jobs to the educated middle class. The Ceylonese began to enjoy the benefits of the British rule and the British Government gave wide publicity to the welfare measures they were implementing. There were also the Sinhala-Tamil differences which came in the way of political consciousness. However, the above statements need not rule out resistance to the continuation of the British rule. Sporadic rebellions or revolts marked the early era of the British rule in Ceylon. For example, a great rebellion broke out in Kandy in 1817-1818 which was directed against the British rule. The British Government suppressed this rebellion mercilessly. There was another revolt in 1848, but this was also crushed.

The Role of the Middle Class

One of the great benefits of the British administration was the introduction of the Western system of education. A large number of Ceylonese took advantage of this opportunity and in the course of time, developed political consciousness. They constituted what is known as the educated middle class. They became fully aware of the exploitative nature of the British rule by the end of the 19th century. They formed many associations, political and professional, and began to represent their grievances to the British. As in India, the British did not bother to redress their grievances.

One of the foremost organisations that tried to mitigate the sufferings of the Ceylonese was the Ceylonese National Congress. It was founded in December 1919. Unfortunately, this organisation became sectarian and championed the cause of Sinhalese nationalism, treating the Tamil minority with derision. It advocated the promotion of Buddhist interests to the exclusion of others. Thus, this communal organisation could not achieve its objectives. The Sinhala Maha Sabha was formed in 1937 and it was founded by S. W. R. D. Bandaranaike. By 1944, the All-Ceylon Tamil Congress was founded, naturally by the Tamilians. There were other associations, but all of them had a sectarian outlook.

Communal Politics

In fact, communal tensions blocked the progress of many of these associations in the first half of the twentieth century. The communal tensions rose to a high pitch "during the period of Donoughmore constitution." This was a new constitution established to provide self-government to the Ceylonese. Ultimately it was D S Senanayake's secular United National Party (UNP) which secured the largest number of seats in the House of Representatives in the August-September 1947 general election. The British Parliament passed the

Ceylonese Independence Act in December 1947. The war-weary British Government granted independence to Ceylon on February 4, 1948.

D S Senanayake became the first prime minister in 1948 leading the UNP, which included Ceylonese Tamils and Muslims (minorities). Under his leadership Ceylon began moving towards a real emotional integration—all ethnic and minority groups joined hands to work for the progress of the country. Unfortunately, he died in 1952. His son, Dudley Senanayake succeeded him. Dudley continued his father's policy till he was removed from office over the rice subsidy issue in 1953. The next prime minister was Sir John Kotelawala who was a good administrator.

In the 1956 general election, the UNP suffered a humiliating defeat from a coalition formed by S.W.R.D Bandaranaike which included Sinhala nationalists and the left wing groups. It must be noted that Bandaranaike represented the Sri Lanka Freedom Party (SLFP) which was established in 1951. Except for a brief interruption of three months, this SLFP-led coalition remained in power till 1965. This coalition also included the Lanka Sama Samaja Party (LSSP). When Solomon, who founded the SLFP, was assassinated in 1959 by a Buddhist monk, his widow, Sirimavo Bandaranaike, took over the mantle of leadership. Sirimavo took advantage of the anti-Western feelings and also anti-Tamil feelings among the majority Sinhalese to project herself and her party as the patron of Sinhalese culture and language. Her government gave importance to Buddhism and promised to the people the nationalisation of foreign-owned plantations, and also cancellation of military agreements with Britain. Unfortunately, these promises could not be fulfilled. Ceylon had to face communal riots in 1956 and 1958. Religious fanaticism grew in the country.

Ethnic Strife

In the 1960 general election, the UNP returned as the single largest party to Parliament, but without a working majority. Hence after its short life, the SLFP returned to power in July 1960 under the leadership of Mrs Bandaranaike. The policies of the SLFP, which aimed at the revival of Sinhala culture, language and Buddhism, alienated the sympathies of the Tamils in Sri Lanka. The economic policies of the SLFP were not sound since the government faced an increase in budget deficits, a balance of payments problem, and lacked foreign capital. Subsequently, the Tamils in northern parts of Sri Lanka felt very disappointed and disgusted at the way the government was tackling economic problems facing the country. Mrs Bandaranaike's government declared emergency, and curbed the unrest of the people with illegal detentions of citizens, and suppression of strikes. There was growing opposition to her government which ultimately got defeated.

The general election of 1965 brought the UNP back to office under the leadership of Dudley Senanayake. Unfortunately, the country continued to face serious problems, not only economic. The Tamils formed a separate party. In the 1970 general election the SLFP with LSSP and the Communist Party formed a United Front coalition Government and ruthlessly suppressed the revolt of the left-wing Janatha Vimukthi Peramuna (JVP – People's Liberation Front).

It declared an emergency in the country. Subsequently the JVP was banned in 1972. Ceylon was renamed Sri Lanka. In 1976, the Federal Party (Tamil Party) with the other Tamil groups in Sri Lanka, formed the Tamil United Liberation Front (TULF) and gave a clarion call for Eelam (a separate Tamil State in northern and eastern parts of Sri Lanka). Since the 1977 general election, Sri Lanka has been facing widespread violence caused by frequent conflicts between the Sinhalese majority and the Tamil minority, with the latter demanding a separate state.

In September 1978, a new constitution was drafted and declared. Sri Lanka came to be known as the Democratic Socialist Republic of Sri Lanka. It came into force in September 1978, and Jayewardene became the first executive president. The ethnic conflict in Sri Lanka continues with the two Tamil militant groups vying with each other, the most violent and extremist group being the Liberation Tigers of Tamil Eelam (LTTE) led by Prabhakaran.

After the completion of his first term, Jayewardene was re-elected in 1982 for a second term running for six years. In a referendum, he received the mandate of the people to extend the life of Parliament up to 1989. Those who cast their votes against the extension of the life of Parliament were mainly from Jaffna (3.1 million : 2.6 million). In May 1983 the government of Jayewardene promulgated an emergency to deal effectively with the worst terrorism Sri Lanka had seen. The Sri Lankan army was let loose to suppress terrorism, and there were frequent outbreaks of violence in Jaffna and Colombo resulting in more than 400 deaths. The three left-wing parties were banned (including the JVP). Curfew and press censorship followed. The month of July, 1983 witnessed the resignation of 16 TULF MPs in protest against the prolongation of Parliament, and in August 1983 the 'no-separation' amendment to the Constitution was passed which denied civic rights to those advocating separatism. The boycott of Parliament by the 16 TULF members resulted in forfeiting their seats. The All-Party Conference was convened in January 1984 to discuss the most crucial issue – granting regional autonomy – and failed to arrive at any agreement. The northern part of the country witnessed violent outbursts during the months of November and December 1984, and the government proclaimed another state of emergency.

In June 1985 Jayewardene met the Indian PM Rajiv Gandhi in New Delhi to mediate in the dispute with the Sri Lankan Tamil separatists. Rajiv's government tried to persuade the Sri Lankan Tamils to agree to a devolution of power instead of demanding full independence. The Tamil violence in the northern region in February 1986 compelled the Sri Lankan government to increase the defence budget and launch military offensives. These offensives did not yield the desired results despite the internecine fighting between the Tamil Eelam Liberation Organisation and the LTTE. The latter emerged as the most dominant among the Tamil groups in Sri Lanka.

Rajiv-Jayewardene Accord (1987)

The island's ethnic crisis appeared to have come to a point settlement when Rajiv Gandhi and Jayewardene signed an accord. The LTTE appeared eager to adhere to the accord, which included the arrival of Indian Peace Keeping Force (IPKF) to help the two parties to end/and cease hostilities. It would further see to it that the LTTE and other militant groups surrendered their arms to the government. The Indian Peace Keeping Force would supervise the Sri Lankan Government's work at amalgamating the Northern and Eastern provinces (where the Tamils are in majority) into one administrative unit. The IPKF consisting of 7,000 troops arrived in Sri Lanka in July-August 1987. Initially the IPKF succeeded in its mission. However, in September it was finding the task of disarming the Tamil militant groups very difficult. The two factors which complicated the situation for the Peace Keeping Force were the fighting which broke out among the Tamil militant groups themselves and the domestic politics in Sri Lanka. The mission failed and the Sri Lankan Government welcomed the withdrawal of the Indian Peace Keeping Force. The LTTE did not like the direct intervention of the IPKF in the internecine fighting among the Tamil militant groups. The LTTE supremo, Prabhakaran, took revenge by bringing about the assassination of Rajiv Gandhi in Sriperembudur (Tamil Nadu, India).

President Premadasa

The Sri Lankan Government set up provincial councils according to the peace plan, and Varadaraja Perumal of EPRLF was elected the chief minister of the North-eastern Province in November. The prime minister of Sri Lanka, Ranasinghe Premadasa, of the UNP, get elected as president on December 20, 1988 after defeating his rival, Sirimavo Bandaranaike of the Sri Lanka Freedom Party. Parliament was dissolved, and on January 11, 1989 emergency was lifted. The country's general election was held in February and the UNP won by a majority. D B Wijetunge, former finance minister, was appointed as the prime minister. After the assassination of President Premadasa by a suicide-bomber on May 1, 1993, PM Wijetunge was elected president, and his place was taken by Ranil Wickremasinghe.

Chandrika Kumaratunga

The Sri Lankan president sprang a surprise by dissolving Parliament on June 26, 1994 and ordered general election to be held in August. Political analysts were of the opinion that the president had taken this course – a less risky course – to ensure the continuation of his presidency, and the electoral victory of his party. However, the electorate rejected the UNP and voted in favour of Chandrika Kumaratunga's (daughter of Sirimavo Bandaranaike) People's Alliance with a big margin. The Tamil groups were in disarray. Since Chandrika promised that she would solve the ethnic strife in the country, a majority of the Tamils voted in favour of her party. She formed the government, and in the subsequent presidential election held on November 9, 1994, she was elected president by a big margin, 62.2 per cent of votes. She formed a new government after appointing her mother, Sirimavo Bandaranike, as the PM.

LTTE Renews Fighting

The Sri Lankan army and the Tamil Tigers stopped fighting, and made peace which held for nearly 14 weeks in early 1995. President Chandrika hoped against hope that the peace would continue. But the LTTE did not give her army any respite, as they mined two naval patrol boats in the eastern port of Trincomalee in April killing 12 sailors. She was convinced that the LTTE was not keen to negotiate for peace, and hence launched 'Operation Leap Forward' by the Sri Lankan army, with air and naval support on July 9, 1995. The purpose of this large scale military exercise (the first was in 1987) was to enable the government to deal with the Tamil Tigers from a position of strength. In the meanwhile, the LTTE virtually 'eclipsed' other political organisations which represented the Tamils. The LTTE has set up office in some parts of the world, and speaks for Tamils of Sri Lanka. In July 1996, the Sri Lankan forces recaptured the Mullaitivu military base from the Tamil Tigers. The government finally banned the LTTE in January 1998. In another onslaught, the Sri Lankan security forces captured the town of Kilinochchi, after taking control of Northern Jaffna peninsula. But this victory proved temporary since the town was recaptured by the Tamil Tigers in September after fierce fighting. The Sri Lankan army lost 700 soldiers in this battle. The government, however, took pride in the capture of Mankulan, a strategic town linking all routes. Thus, the see-saw battles are going on, with a no-win situation either for the government or the Tamil Tigers.

The 15-year-old civil war has not come to an end in spite of several peace offers made by President Chandrika Kumaratunga. Recently the LTTE supremo, Velupillai Prabhakaran, said that the Sinhala leadership lacked the political will, but was prepared to negotiate peace with the government preferably through third party mediation. The UNP and the moderate Tamil Parties (TULF) have appealed to the government to seize this opportunity and bring peace to the trouble-torn island.

The LTTE has launched major offensives in November 1999 constituting the third phase of the campaign which has yielded spectacular results in regaining the lost territories. While the Wanni war was going on with Vavuniya town being threatened, the election to the presidency was announced. Pollsters predicted a tough presidential race, since Chandrika Kumaratunga has not fulfilled her promises of the last elections—that is to bring ethnic strife to an end. The Tamils, who hold the key to her election victory may not vote for her. While the TULF asked the Tamils to reject both the candidates, Chandrika Kumaratunga (of People's Alliance) and Ranil Wickremesinghe (the Eelam People's Democratic Party, EPDP) asked the Tamil voters to repose faith in Chandrika and vote for her.

Presidential Election (1999)

The Presidential election was fixed for December 21, 1999. Chandrika's election rally was held at the Town Hall in Colombo on December 18. It was marred by a loud explosion. The suicide bomb which exploded in the suburb killed the former army chief, Major General Lucky Alagama who was campaigning for the UNP candidate, Ranil Wickremasinghe. Wounded Chandrika took oath as president for the second term of December 22. Her People's Alliance obtained more than 51 per cent of the votes polled, and defeated the UNP by a margin of 7 lakh votes. The polls proved that Chandrika no longer enjoyed the support of Tamil minority in the country.

Elusive Peace (2000-04)

The economic outlook for Sri Lanka appeared bleak in 2000 since the fighting with the LTTE started two decades ago. The defence budget was close to 6 per cent of the GDP. Donor countries were keen to see the end of the civil war and political solution had to be found to this trouble-torn country. As India sulked to mediate between the two belligerents – Sri Lankan forces and Tamil Tigers – it was Norway, which took up the initiative. With the peace talks in the offing the LTTE considered it wise to declare a unilateral cease-fire. However, the peace talks did not go far enough for the LTTE's satisfaction, so it struck. This time it was the Sri Lanka's Air Force base at Kotunayake (near Colombo) in July 2001, incidentally coinciding with the date of Tamil Riots of July 1983. This attack on the Air Force base became an issue causing much acrimony between the People's Alliance and the United National Party. Then there was the acrimonious debate on the making of the new constitution.

In December 2001, Ranil Wickremesinghe of the United National Party was elected the new prime minister. Being a robust optimist, he had none of the reservations or notion of President Kumaratunga about engaging the LTTE in peace talks and finding a solution to the ethnic conflict that is destroying Sri Lanka. There was a second-round of peace talks held at Nakhon Pathom (Thailand) in October-November 2002. The LTTE surprised everyone by agreeing to the peace process and promised that it would enter the main stream of national life. It would allow all political parties in the northern and eastern Sri Lanka, the areas administered by it, to participate in the same. What was the reason which made the die-hard LTTE to agree for the peace talks? For one thing, it is because of the changing situation in the world, specifically the war on terror waged by the US with international support. Secondly, the LTTE had not received any encouragement from any quarter to carry on war – of all from India. The rank and file of the Tamil Tigers too felt that it is useless to wage war, with a government led by President Chandrika Kamaratunga. The Sri Lankan president (whose husband was assassinated by the LTTE) could hardly take a soft stand with regard to the LTTE, the latter too often found wanting in resolving the dispute.

The Government-LTTE peace talks was generally welcomed, despite the reservation of the Sri Lankan president. However, the president was too wary about the prime minister yielding too many concessions, thus jeopardising the sovereignties and territorial integrity of the country. There was another problem that had to be dealt with, namely, the treatment meted out to the minority communities in eastern Sri Lanka (Trincomalee, Batticaloa and Amparai) which had come under LTTE control. In these areas the Muslims, Sinhalese and the Tamils are in equal number.

The LTTE demanded that the ban imposed on its functioning by the Sri Lankan Government be lifted so as to enable it to continue the peace-process. Then there was the other demand, that the High Security Zone (including Jaffna which the Sri Lankan Forces captured from the LTTE way back in 1995) be removed. The LTTE too conceded the demands of the Sri Lankan Government and extended cease-fire. This was a clever move on its part to gain international recognition or legitimacy. Ultimately the LTTE came forward with another proposal—the recognition of its interim government in the northern and eastern Sri Lanka within the framework of Sri Lankan Constitution. When there was stalemate, the peace talks was suspended.

In July 2003 the government offered LTTE a Provisional Administration Structure to the areas under its control. But the LTTE wanted an interim governing authority which should remain beyond the pale of the constitution.

In the meantime, the international donors promised more than $2 billion in aid-assistance, if a settlement is reached. While the Wickremesinghe government was studying the LTTE's final demand, came the next political crisis in November 2003.

While the prime minister was away, the president, in her constitutional capacity, took over the three ministries (defence, interior and mass communication) under her direct control. The president's rivalry with the prime minister – her party is in the opposition – came to the fore. The PM's return from abroad did not ease the internal conflict in the government. The peace process thus came to a halt with Norway declaring that it would no longer continue as mediator. The LTTE threatened that it would not lay down its arms (one of the most unfortunate preconditions of peace process) till a final settlement is reached. Wickremasinghe's parleys with the president to restore the *status-quo ante* has not borne fruit. However, the president made it clear that she would not stand in the way of peace process but would closely watch the moves of the LTTE which is demanding things which are beyond the framework of the Constitution. The new constitution is in the making. Earlier, the Sri Lankan president dismissed 39 junior ministers, when the prime minister criticised her conduct. The president dissolved the Parliament in February 2004. She asked Wickremesinghe to remain as caretaker prime minister.

In the snap polls (held in April 2004) the president's political party (a combine of Sri Lanka Freedom Party and Janatha Vimukthi Perumana) secured 105 seats, eight seats short of majority in the 225 member parliament. She appointed Raja Pakse, leader of her political party, as the new prime minister. His task is cut out, to continue the peace process with the LTTE and bring to an end the ethnic conflict which has taken more than 60,000 lives during the last two decades. In the recently-held provincial elections, the ruling party got majority of the seats in Provincial Assemblies. The Tsunami catastrophy has made his task more ardous. The Tsunami, which destroyed the coasts of south and Southeast Asia on December 26, 2004 killed more than 30,000 people and left one million families homeless.

Part IV

CENTRAL ASIA

41

AFGHANISTAN

In ancient times, Afghanistan was known by the name Aryana and subsequently as Khurasan (the land of the rising sun). Afghanistan, a mountainous and land-locked country, is situated in the heart of Central Asia. It connects East Asia with the West on the one hand and the Indian subcontinent on the other. The country is a "vast stony plateau" with broad plains and "well watered streams". A long time ago, Afghanistan served as a bridge between China and Europe. The famous "silk road" passed through Afghanistan. In the early stages of history, Afghanistan became a stronghold of Buddhism and Zoroastrianism.

The word "Afghan" has a legend behind it. Ibrahim was a descendant of Adam. One of Ibrahim's descendants was Talat, whose son's name was Afghan. It was this Afghan who gave his country the name Afghanistan. There is a story which says that his pregnant mother, while experiencing great pains before his birth, heaved a sigh of relief after the delivery saying "Afghan" (meaning 'I am free').

Origin of Afghans

During the period of 900 years (550 BC-AD 490), Afghanistan was subjected to frequent invasions by the Iranians, Macedonians, Mauryans, Shakas, Indo-Parthians, Kushan and Sassanian kings. To a great extent Afghanistan was influenced by Iranian culture. Ibn Batuta says that "Kabul is inhabited by people from Persia called Afghans". Afghan society was composed of a "mixture of many peoples including the Jewish as their tradition avers, but more particularly from the Iranian, Ephthalite or Turkish and Indian stocks". The Ghalgis and the Lodis who lived in most parts of Afghanistan represented these groups. The Pathans lived in eastern Afghanistan, and also in the country of Roli.

Arab Invasions

The Arabs invaded Afghanistan in the seventh century and also in the ninth century. As a result, some conversions took place. Probably in those days, Kabul was inhabited by Buddhist, Jews and Muslims. Alberuni, a historian of the twelfth century, refers to the succession of the Indian kings in Afghanistan who made Wai-Hind the seat of their capital. From the accounts of other historians, it may be concluded that eastern Afghanistan did not witness the spread of Islam until the tenth century AD.

Afghan Emigration

The Afghans came to India as soldiers during the time of Mohammed of Ghazni. Similarly, Mohammed of Gaur brought 12,000 Afghans with him to India to fight Prithvi Raj Chauhan in the Second Battle of Tarain (1192). Some Afghans who were serving Sultan Qutb-ub-din Aibek were raised to the rank of nobles. During the time of sultans Iltutmish and Balban, the Afghan soldiers were most sought after as they excelled in horsemanship and bravery. The Mohammedan and Hindu kings welcomed Afghans and appointed them to guard the frontier posts of their kingdom in recognition of their war-like qualities. They were best suited to deal with the Mongol invaders and robbers.

Timur led Afghan contingents to conquer India. In the course of time, the Afghan rulers controlled extensive regions, from Punjab to Bengal. It should not be forgotten that many Afghan merchants came to India for the purpose of trade. They prospered mainly because of their business shrewdness. They brought well-bred horses from Persia and Afghanistan to India and sold them to the Muslim and Hindu kings. They were known for their honesty and sincerity. The seventy-five years of Lodi rule (1451-1526) in India was "singularly free from religious intolerance except for a few acts of Sikandar Lodi". Subsequently, Sher-Shah, who hailed from the Sur tribe of the Afghans during the middle of the 16th century, proved to be the most illustrious king of Hindustan.

Afghanistan and Mughal Empire

During the heyday of the Mughal empire, the Kandahar and Kabul regions of Afghanistan became a bone of contention. A serious rivalry took place for the control of Kandahar between the Mughal emperors on the one side and the Persian emperors on the other. Mughal Emperor Akbar sent his half-brother, Mirza Hakim, to govern Kabul. The Afghan tribes such as the Yousufzais, the Afridis and the Khokhars proved very dangerous to the security of the north-western parts of the Mughal Empire. Prince Murad and minister Todarmal were sent to crush the revolts of Yousufzais. Kabul subsequently became a province of the "Mughal Empire", and Kandahar was attacked frequently by the Persians. But Jehangir lost Kandahar to the Persians. Mughal Emperor Shah Jehan subsequently conquered it only to lose it again to the Persians. The stakes on Kandahar between the two went up forcing the Mughals to use all the resources and ingenuity for its occupation. In the course of time, the loss of Kandahar to the Mughals delivered a serious blow to the flourishing trade between Afghanistan and India. Mughal Emperor Aurangazeb faced serious problems in dealing with the rebellious tribes of Afghanistan.

Towards Modern History of Afghanistan

The credit for making Afghanistan into an independent state in 1747 goes to an Afghan general named Ahmed Shah Durrani. After the assassination of his master, Nadir Shah of Persia, the Afghan soldiers elected Ahmed Shah, one of the able commanders, to rule over Afghanistan. On his succession, Ahmed Shah declared Afghanistan as an independent state, free from Persian control. At the time of his accession, the country had disintegrated, and some parts were ruled by foreigners. Afghans were divided into groups and clans and lacked a sense of unity. Ahmed Shah's greatest achievement lay in welding these different groups of people into a nation. Afghans today remember him as the father of the nation. He governed the kingdom wisely for nearly twenty-six years and died in 1773.

His son Timur (1773-1793) shifted the seat of his capital from Kandahar to Kabul. He organised a sound administration and improved the efficiency of the government. Unfortunately, he did not prove to be as wise as his father, and therefore, a civil war broke out. His son, Zaman Shah, made things worse by his misrule thereby plunging the country into political turmoil. Revolts and internecine wars sapped the energy of the country making it a "pawn in the international game played by Russia and Great Britain in Central Asia". In Afghan politics of those days two Sardars, namely, Fateh Khan and Dost Mohammed, played an important role as the king-makers.

In the course of time, the Afghan chiefs chose Dost Mohammed as Amirul Muminin (commander of the faithful) in an open assembly. This was in recognition of his political sagacity and effective leadership. One of his rivals was Shah Shuja, who ran away to Ludhiana in 1816 on knowing that Dost Mohammed had become the Amir of Afghanistan. Shah Shuja came into contact with the senior officials of the British East India Company, and started seeking favours from them. The company granted him pension and recognised him as the Afghan king-in-exile. In the meantime, Dost Mohammed occupied Ghazni and Kabul, but was unable to recover Peshawar, which had been conquered by the Sikhs in 1834.

Russia's Forward Policy

Russia's southward expansion in the direction of Central Asia perturbed the Indian Governor-General, Lord Auckland. When the border town Herat was threatened by the Shah of Persia at the instigation of Russia, the British Government realised that for strategic reasons Afghanistan should be made subject to its control or influence. The Court of Directors was of the opinion that Auckland should intervene in the affairs of Afghanistan so that the Russian/ Persian threat to Herat may be checked. Diplomatic moves were set afoot, and the Afghan Amir, Dost Mohammed, was ready to oblige the company. However, he laid down a condition that the British should persuade the Sikhs to return Peshawar to Afghanistan.

Anglo-Afghan Relations

When his request was turned down by the British, he turned to Russia/Persia for help. Auckland's further diplomatic missions to influence Afghanistan failed. The company got ready to fight. Just before the outbreak of the First Anglo-Afghan War (1839-42), the Persians released the siege of Herat. Therefore, the company had no reason to go to war with Afghanistan. But Lord Auckland felt that Dost Mohammed should be taken to task, and the exiled Prince, Shah Shuja, should be made the Amir of Afghanistan.

The First Ango-Afghan War proved to be quite disastrous to the British, despite their victories. Shah Shuja was not popular among the Afghans, and therefore they did not want the British to crown this undesirable prince as the king of Afghanistan. While the British were successful in enthroning Shah Shuja, their troops faced great danger while retreating from Kabul. Once the British troops started leaving Afghanistan, Shah Shuja remained helpless in the midst of his rebellious subjects. In 1842, he was assassinated. His assassination exposed the weakness of Auckland's forward policy.

Lord Ellenborough, who replaced him began to follow altogether a new policy towards Afghanistan. Dost Mohammed was restored to the Afghan throne when Sir John Lawrence became the Governor-General. Sir John Lawrence was not swayed by the wars of disputed succession in Afghanistan. He followed what is known as the policy of "masterly inactivity towards Afghanistan". Lord Lytton reversed the policy of Lawrence and precipitated the outbreak of the Second Afghan War (1878-80).

The Russians started posing a new threat to the British interests in Central Asia in general and India in particular by sending General Stolietoff to conclude an agreement with Afghanistan so as to enable them to extend influence. But the Afghan Amir, Sher Ali, decided to remain neutral in the face of British pressure. He did not make any special efforts to welcome the new Russian mission. The Russian General threatened Amir Sher Ali (son of the late Dost Mohammed), with dire consequences. In fact, the Russians stated that they would overthrow his government, and make his rival, Abdur Rehman, the Amir of Afghanistan. Naturally, the Afghan Amir was forced to yield to Russian political pressure.

Before the Russians could conclude an agreement with Afghanistan, General Stolietoff was ordered to withdraw his mission from Afghanistan. This sudden about-turn was caused by the Treaty of Berlin which was concluded in 1878. By this treaty, Britain and Russia reached a broad agreement regarding Central Asia. But the British Viceroy Lytton tried to force the Afghan Amir to accept a British mission in Kabul. When the latter refused, the situation led to the outbreak of the Second Afghan War.

The Afghans were defeated by the British troops, and Amir Sher Ali fled to Turkestan. The new government in Afghanistan headed by Yakub Khan (eldest son of Amir Sher Ali) signed the Treaty of Gandamak by which Afghanistan came under British control. The British attempt to disintegrate Afghanistan was foiled when Lord Lytton resigned his office and left for England. The Gladstone Ministry in Britain began to view the Afghan situation in a new light.

The new government recognised Abdur Rehman as the Amir of Afghanistan following the abdication of Yakub Khan in the midst of the war. Abdur Rehman contributed much to bring about national unity among his listless subjects. He provided an efficient administration and took several measures to bring about the modernisation of his country. His government was successful in maintaining law and order. He tried to bring about secularisation by discarding religious influence. The pensions granted to the mullahs by the previous government were withdrawn. Afghanistan witnessed rapid economic progress with the development of modern means of transport and communications, banking and industries.

After Abdur Rehman's death, his son Habibullah succeeded to the Afghan throne in 1901. He followed in the footsteps of his father by hastening the process of modernisation. It was during his time, that Afghanistan witnessed the inauguration of many modern education institutions, hospitals, hydro-electric schemes and so on. He patronised trade and commerce. Amir Habibullah refused to ratify the Anglo-Russian Treaty on Afghanistan which was signed without his consent. He felt that this treaty compromised the independence of Afghanistan. As a result, Anglo-Afghan relations were strained to such an extent that a conflict became inevitable. The Amir sent his forces to invade India under the instigation of German agents. The Afghan incursions were repulsed by the British forces in India. Subsequently, Afghanistan signed a peace treaty with India in 1921, by which Britain conceded the right of Amir to conduct his foreign policy without British interference. In 1922, the two parties established full diplomatic relations.

King Amanullah

It was after the assassination of Habibullah in 1919, that his son Amanullah succeeded to the Afghan throne. In tune with the changing political situation the great king realised the need for political reforms in his country so as to give his subjects their legitimate share in running the government. The first Afghan Parliament was convened with 150 representatives, each elected by voters from their constituency. Amanullah undertook a seven-month tour of Europe in 1927. After his return, the pace of reforms in his country accelerated.

The new era witnessed the modernisation of the educational system, upgradation of the national economy, a modern legal system and so on. In his bid to Westernise his country on the model of Kemal Pasha's Turkey, King Amanullah invited experts from many advanced countries, particularly Germany to help him to industrialise his country. The air services in Afghanistan came to be established, and there was an air-link between Germany and Afghanistan. Britain recognised the independence of Afghanistan in 1921. Both these countries established diplomatic relations. The Afghan educational system witnessed radical reforms which provoked the orthodox sections of society.

After his return from abroad, King Amanullah introduced further reforms particularly in the fields of education and the status of women. In all his public speeches, he laid stress on the need for making his country secular. He wanted women to be free from the constraints of orthodoxy. He desired that they should participate in all walks of life. The reforms of Amanullah provoked a tribal revolt which led to the fall of his government. He fled the country after abdicating his throne in favour of his elder brother Inayatullah. To complicate the situation further, the Afghan Ambassador in Moscow organised a force with Russian assistance for the purpose of invading Afghanistan to lend support to the king. But it was too late and it had no popular backing. Therefore, the envoy had to retreat with his forces.

Afghanistan witnessed further inroads into political stability on account of the rule of bandits in some regions. She was subjected to a reign of terror unleashed by a great dacoit, Bacha-I-Saqaw, who subsequently became the Afghan king for nearly nine months. During this time many political leaders in Afghanistan came to be assassinated one by one. Fortunately, Bacha's tyranny was short-lived and he was replaced by Mohammed Nadir Khan. Nadir Khan played a very important role in promoting the welfare of the Afghans and earned respect. The Afghans proclaimed him as their King.

His ten-point policy-declaration put the nation on the rails of progress once again. He planned to introduce some more reforms, which covered areas like education, industries, defence, commercial relations and the infrastructure of his country. The Afghan Parliament introduced necessary measures for the implementation of these reforms. It was during his time that constitutional monarchy was established on the principles of Islam. In 1931, the Constitution was revised. The Grand National Assembly, besides the two other Houses, ushered in democratic institutions. Unfortunately, this Afghan King was assassinated in 1933. He was succeeded by his son, Mohammed Zahir Shah, who completed the work started by his father.

Contemporary Afghanistan

Afghanistan registered commendable progress under the leadership of King Mohammed Zahir Shah who ruled form 1936 to 1958. In 1937, Afghanistan signed a pact with Iran and Iraq, and thereafter remained neutral during the Second World War. However, her neutrality caused great anxiety to the Allies who were bent upon defeating the Axis powers in the Second World War. They put pressure upon the Afghan Amir to accept their demands. The Afghan economy came under severe strain due to the long war. Her export trade suffered immensely. Her dependence on India for the import of goods increased and as a consequence her policies came to be influenced by the British Government. It was this increasing dependence upon India by Afghanistan which led to closer diplomatic ties with Britain. The two countries upgraded their diplomatic missions to the rank of full-fledged embassies by 1948.

The administration of the country was in charge of the prime minister who was in close touch with his colleagues in the cabinet. It was in 1958 that Afghanistan witnessed a sudden increase in the establishment of educational institutions (658 schools) and newspapers (50). The University of Kabul was founded in 1956 which afforded an opportunity to students to pursue higher education. It had 168 professors and 1,295 students with various faculties. Forty-eight faculty members happened to be foreigners. The country launched its First Five Year Plan in September 1956 so as to bring about rapid economic development. Agriculture was given prime importance. The plan included the establishment of community development centres which carried out several programmes in villages for the people's welfare. The emphasis was on education, health and employment opportunities for all.

During the height of the Cold War, Afghanistan remained neutral and "pursued a policy of non-alignment under the leadership of Prime Minister Sardar Mohammed Daoud (1953-63)". He was the King's cousin and also brother-in-law. Prime Minister Daoud brought about the overthrow of the Afghan monarchy in 1973. After the king fled the country, he proclaimed himself president and prime minister of the new Afghan Republic. Daoud promised to introduce necessary reforms for the progress of the country.

Daoud urged Afghan women to discard old traditions and customs. He carried out many other social reforms so as to make his country modern. Unfortunately, his land reforms did not meet with success. In the course of time, he gave important jobs to his relatives and friends. His administration became inefficient and corrupt. It was this situation that brought about the overthrow of his government in April 1978. In the second revolution, the Communists seized power and established the People's Republic under the leadership of President Taraki with the support of Soviet Union. When his government became unstable because of rebellions, the Soviet forces invaded and occupied Afghanistan in 1978-79 to protect the Afghan Communists in power.

The Soviet occupation of Afghanistan, and its support to the Communist Government was galling to many Afghan groups. The Afghan Mujahideen (holy warriors) started resisting the Soviet occupation, but were unable to make much progress. Najibullah became the President of Afghanistan in 1989. With several countries, prominent among them being the US and Pakistan, supporting several groups of Mujahideens to fight against the Soviet-controlled regime he could not make headway. In the meantime, the UN proposed a peace plan that intended to end the Soviet support to the Najibullah government in Afghanistan, and invited the old Afghan King Zahir Shah to take charge. The Soviet leader, Mikhail Gorbachev, and the US President gave their consent. However, the Mujahideen groups were not happy. As the Soviet troops in Afghanistan found it difficult to control the rebel Mujahideen groups, the Soviet leader decided to withdraw in 1989. President Najibullah announced the formation of a military council in order to rule the country, but the rebel Mujahideen groups set up an interim government in exile led by Sighbatullah Majaddidi. He transferred his power to a Mujahideen leadership council. After launching major offensives against the Soviet-backed regime of Najibullah, the Mujahideen factions reached the outskirts of the Afghan capital, Kabul. Najibullah's regime was overthrown in 1992, and he took shelter in the UN office in April.

The Civil War

After ousting Najibullah's government in Kabul, the warlords of the rebel Mujahideen groups started fighting among themselves over power sharing. Hekmatyar's forces which controlled the outskirts of Kabul and the town of Jalalabad, fought forces of the new President, Burhanuddin Rabbani. The latter had the support of General Abdul Rashid Dostum. After some time General Dostum deserted the president and supported Hekmatyar. The fighting reduced the capital, Kabul, into a rubble. The civil war took nearly 10,000 lives, mostly civilians. Half the population of the city fled. The control of the capital became a very important issue between the rival guerilla warlords.

The Rise of Taliban

Taliban is a fanatical Islamic movement, which originated in the Kandahar district of Afghanistan. The founder father was Mullah Mohammed Omar who lost an eye while fighting the Soviet troops which had occupied Afghanistan. After the Soviet troops left the country in 1989, he found that the warlords had turned the country into rubble with their internecine fights, and innocent people were put to severe hardships like looting, bribery and rape of women. He started a school with about 30 members —mostly young students (Taliban means 'Students of religion'). This movement showballed into a big organisation with moral, material and financial support of countries like Pakistan and Saudi Arabia. In the course of time, the Afghan refugee students who had fled the country due to civil war joined hundreds of *madrasas* (started by Pakistan on its side of the border), run by Jamiat-e-Ulema Islami, a traditionalist Sunni party. By 1994-95 the Taliban established its military outfits in order to unite the country under its banner.

Talibanisation of Afghanistan

Gulbuddin Hekmatyar who had "parted ways' with President Rabbani in 1994 returned to the fold, and the latter was made the prime minister in June 1996. However, Rabbani's government was suddenly overthrown by the Taliban militia in September 1996 after capturing Kabul. The Taliban militia took Najibullah, the former Communist President, captive and hanged him in the heart of the city. In the meanwhile, both Rabbani and Hekmatyar fled the city. The students Taliban militia took complete control of Kabul and set up a six-member interim government. The government employees and the people were ordered to strictly follow Islamic customs, manners and dress. The Afghan women were put to severe hardship. The ousted government which was dominated by the Tajiks like Rabbani, Ahmad Shah Masood retreated to the Tajik traditional strongholds in the north. The theatre of the Afghan civil war shifted to the north after 1996, with Pakistan fully backing the Taliban militia. Countries neighbouring Afghanistan, mainly Iran, Russia and India, have taken serious note of the spillovers of the civil war, especially with outside interference. The Teheran Conference took up this matter. The year 1997 did not go well with the Taliban as the northern-based opposition coalition made some headway in its effort to push back the Taliban militia towards Kabul.

Role of the UN

The civil war in Afghanistan left thousands of Afghan families homeless, more than 20,000 civilians dead, and 100,000 wounded. The UN was deeply concerned about the situation and offered its mediation in 1998 to end this conflict.

Although both the parties to the civil war agreed to work for peace, exchange prisoners, and restore normalcy, they violated the UN brokered-deal. Fighting between the two erupted on May 2, 1998. In addition to the tragedy caused by the civil war, Afghanistan was rocked by two earthquakes, the first one in February, and the second in April, with 4,000 and 5,000 dead respectively. In August the Taliban captured Mazar-e-sharif and other towns in the north, and claimed to be in control of ninety per cent of Afghanistan.

Support to Militants

The Taliban, having the moral and material support from Pakistan and Saudi Arabia, has unleashed its terror by organising and training terrorists. The Al Badr recruits Pakistani militants who are let loose in Kashmir to foment trouble. Then, there is the Harkat-ul-Ansar which also operates in Kashmir, with the Al Badr's support. The Al Badr II recruits foreigners (Arabs and Sudanese) to lend support to the rebels operating in Chechnya, Bosnia and Dagestan. In recent times, the Taliban has given shelter to the exiled Saudi billionaire, Osama bin Laden, who is said to be running terrorist camps in Afghanistan. The US has offered reward for his capture, since she believes that he matermimded the bombing of her embassies in Africa. The UN has not recognised the Taliban Government yet, but its representative is allowed in the UN. It is said that there are ten million landmines scattered around in Afghanistan posing serious problems to its citizens. Nearly two million Afghans have taken shelter in Pakistan and Iran. Afghanistan is the least developed country in the world.

UN Sanctions

The UN Security Council imposed sanctions on the Taliban's tyrannical regime in December 2000 for its human rights abuses, giving refuge to Osama bin Laden (the Al-Qaeda leader) and other atrocities (not forgetting the destruction of the monolithic statue of the Buddha at Bamian). Taking shelter in Afghanistan, the Al-Qaeda was involved in the bombings of the US embassies in Kenya, Tanzania and fomenting rebellion in Russian controlled Chechnya. India welcomed the move because the Taliban in the past had hijacked an Indian Airline's passenger plane and held passengers as hostages. Moreover, Pakistan was in the dock for having patronised the Taliban regime along with Saudi Arabia.

US Strikes

The Taliban's support to Al-Qaeda's terrorist activities even after the 9/11 attack on the WTC in New York and Pentagon (the US Defence Establishment) in 2001 forced the US administration to act swiftly. When the Taliban regime refused to handover the leader of Al-Qaeda and his gang to the US, the US forces started aerial strikes and bombardments to dislodge the

Taliban regime. Ground support to the US came from the Northern Alliance led by Ahmed Shah Masood and Rabbani (all Tajiks). The high-tech war (missiles from warships and precision guided bomb attacks) carried on by the US and allied forces flattened Kabul and other strongholds of the Taliban. The Taliban forces led by Mullah Omar fled to the mountains bordering Pakistan, and hoped to retrieve its position with the help of the Pushtun warlords. It must be remembered that it was the US which had supported the Taliban in its efforts to oust the Soviet forces in Afghanistan years earlier. In the meantime the US and its allies put pressure on Pakistan to force the Taliban to surrender. In spite of its best efforts, Pakistan failed to achieve this goal. Unfortunately, Pakistan was caught in the web of its own making, that is, supporting and recognising the Taliban Government.

Afghan War

During the months of October and November the US started its intensive bombings while the ground troops of Northern Alliance (which received military hardware from the US) made headway towards Kabul. The civilian population of Afghanistan suffered heavy casualties when bombs missed the military targets. Finally, the Taliban militia fled to the mountains leaving Kabul to be occupied by the forces of Northern Alliance. The common people rejoiced at the defeat of the Taliban. Except for a few pockets of resistance, Afghanistan, by and large, remained peaceful. This situation enabled the leaders to form an interim government with the blessings of the exiled king. Hamid Karzai became the president, and many of the Afghan warlords agreed to recognise the new government and promised to support it. The NATO troops are stationed in Kabul and other cities as a protection force to help the government. The new government immediately restored civil rights to the people and promised to give a democratic constitution. In January 2, 2004, the new constitution was approved (after protracted negotiations with the warlords) by the lower *jirga*. The new constitution provides for a democratic set-up under a presidential system. Amidst tight security never seen before, the presidential election took place on October 9, 2004. Mr Hamid Karzai won, after defeating 15 rivals; most notably his greatest rival Mr Yunus Qanooni. The Taliban made many efforts to trigger violence during the election period, but none of them succeeded. Mr Karzai received 41,05,122 votes, that is more than the fity per cent of the votes cast and he was officially declared the winner on November 3, 2004.

The new president has an arduous task ahead of him. He has to maintain law and order in the country in the face of several threats coming from the Taliban which is regrouping its forces in the mountainous areas. He has to win over all the warlords to his side. He needs financial and military supports from the

Western allies and India. He has to secure the support of the common people Pushtuns, Tajiks, Hazaras, Bahichis and Ugbeks owing allegiance to their respective warlords to carry out several development projects. It is hoped that this war-torn country would have a bright future under the leadership of the new president. It is also hoped that the Taliban and the Al Qaeda would be brought to justice in the new democratic framework of Afghanistan.

42

IRAN (PERSIA)

Modern Iran was earlier known as Persia, the name given to it by the ancient Aryans. The Indo-Aryans, who conquered Persia around 2500 BC influenced the culture of her native people. It was in the sixth century BC that Persia attained great heights of glory under Emperor Cyrus (550-29 BC). He defeated the king of Medea and incorporated this kingdom into his empire. It comprised Assyria, Lydia and Asia Minor. In the course of time, the Greek cities of Asia-Minor also came under the control of Emperor Cyrus. The eastern borders of his empire touched the Hindu-Kush mountains and the western borders remained adjacent to Asia Minor. Emperor Cyrus was known for his religious tolerance.

His son Cambyses II was known for his wild temper, cruelty, and religious intolerance. He conquered Egypt but could not retain it for a long time. His successor, Emperor Darius I (521-486 BC) may be regarded as the greatest Archamenid emperor in world history. His reign witnessed all-round progress. The Ionian Greeks in Asia Minor revolted after getting encouragement from their compatriots living in the other Greek city states. Emperor Darius crushed this revolt mercilessly. He tried to teach a lesson to the people of Greek city states by launching a war. However, the Persian army suffered humiliation at the hands of the Greeks at the famous battle of Marathon. This was probably the only setback that Emperor Darius suffered in his lifetime. He divided his empire into 20 *satrapies* (provinces) which included Gandhara and the Indus Valley.

His son, Xerxes, decided to take revenge upon the Greeks who had defeated his father. He launched several military expositions both on land and sea to bring about the defeat of the Greeks. The Persians defeated the heroic Greeks at the famous battle of Thermopylae. However, his success in this battle proved to be short-lived. The Greeks of all city states joined to resist his onslaught. In the end the Persian army led by Emperor Xerxes was defeated in successive battles. Unable to bear further humiliation, Xerxes decided not to wage war against the Greeks.

His successor was Darius II, who was in turn succeeded by Darius III. It was during the time of Emperor Darius III that Persia was invaded by the Macedonian forces commanded by Alexander the Great. Alexander defeated the Persian army (which included Indian soldiers also) in three successive battles, namely, Granicus, Issus, and Arabela (334-31 BC). Subsequently, the Palace of Darius III was destroyed, and the emperor was assassinated. However, the revival of the Persian empire began after the decline of Alexander's empire – this time by the Parthians and the Sassanids. In the sixth century BC, Persia witnessed the birth of the great religious leader, Zarathustra, who encouraged his followers (Zoroastrians) to worship the almighty god, Ahura Mazda.

Persia was conquered by the Seleucids, and subsequently by the Parthians. Thereafter, came the rule of the Sassanids (AD 242-642). The founder of the Sassanid dynasty was Ardashir who overthrew his Parthian overlord in AD 224 north of Isfahan. He was mainly responsible for the revival of Zoroastrianism which had declined in Persia due to suppression. The peak of the Sassanid power was achieved under the leadership of King Khosran Anolisirvan (531-79) after the conquest of Syria. But his son, Khosran Parveez, was defeated by the Byzantine Emperor, Heraclius. With the Arab conquest of Persia (AD 637-42), the Sassanid dynasty came to an end.

The rulers of the Abbasid dynasty ruled over the Muslim world, including Persia, as Caliphs with Iraq as the centre. As a province of Iraq, Persia was divided into two provinces, one ruled by the Buyids and the other by the Seljuk Turks. The Buyids ruled Persia for nearly 130 years. Thereafter, occurred the invasions of the Mongols during the first half of the thirteenth century. Subsequently, Persia was ruled by Likharids (1256-1353). It was a century and a half later that the Safavids ruled Persia (from 1501 to 1732). They made Shiism their official religion.

The Safavid Dynasty

The founder of the Safavid dynasty was Shah Ismail I, who did his utmost to extend the frontiers of Persia in order to conform to the ancient borders. He warded off all the threats to his empire from the Ottomans and Uzbegs. His was "the first truly Iranian dynasty since the Arab conquest". His successor tried to emulate his example.

The next great ruler was Shah Abbas I. He is described by many historians as one of the great statesmen who "reorganised and centralised the Safavid State". His glorious reign was marked by the extension of Persia's frontiers and "cultural efflorescence". After crushing the revolts of the Uzbegs, he turned his attention towards the Ottomans who were invading western Iran. He was successful in expelling them from the western borders of Iran. He shifted his capital to Isfahan. It was during his time that Persia witnessed the golden age in the realm of art, architecture and learning. The Persians enjoyed great prosperity due to brisk trade and commerce. There was a continuing clash between the Sunni Turkey and the Shiite Iran, each helping the enemy to fight the other.

The Rise of the Kajar Dynasty (1779-1925)

After the fall of the Safavids, Persia was invaded by Afghans. The Russians and the Turks also invaded Persia. However, the Afghan threat to Persia was warded off by the Kajar dynasty. It was founded by Nadir Shah (1736-47) who did his utmost to recover all the lost provinces, and conform to the boundaries of Persia as existed during the time of the Safavid dynasty. Persia under the Kajar dynasty was bent upon recovering her territories which had been snatched away by her neighbours, namely, Turkey, Afghanistan and Russia. Her attempts to recover these territories resulted in the border disputes with Turkey, Afghanistan, Russia and Britain.

Persia waged wars against them to recover her territories. Since Persia is situated in the heart of Asia and occupies a strategic geo-political region, its control was most sought after by European powers. It was in the early nineteenth century (during the reign of Fath Ali Shah) that we see an intense rivalry among the European powers to secure control over Persia. The city of Herat which lay across the borders between Persia and Afghanistan became a bone of contention between the two. Britain and Russia vied to gain control over Persia in the middle of the nineteenth century.

Russian and British Interests in Persia

In the middle of the nineteenth century Russia tried to expand her empire at the cost of her Central Asian neighbours. Persia became her obvious choice. Britain also tried to contain Russian expansionism by gaining a foothold over the southern parts of Persia. These two big powers used Persia as a stepping stone for carving out spheres of influence in Central Asia. Russia followed a forward policy which threatened the British interests in Afghanistan and India. Britain did her best to prevent Russia's influence in these regions by persuading the governments of Persia and Afghanistan to support the British policy. Britain desired that these two states should act as a buffer, thereby protecting her interests in India. In fact, Britain offered to guarantee the independence of these two countries provided they supported the British Government. Unfortunately, the Persian Government proved to be too weak to withstand the political pressures of these two big powers.

In the early twentieth century, Persian merchants closed their shops and gathered at the gates of the British Embassy in Teheran to pressurise the British Government to persuade their king to grant a constitution which provided for the parliamentary form of government with universal franchise. In other words, the people at large desired that the royal authority should be limited. Their attempt succeeded, but in 1907, Russia and Britain signed an agreement which established mutual understanding with regard to facing the menace of Germany. This agreement outlined their respective spheres of influence in Asia in general and Persia in particular.

The Shah of Persia was encouraged by these powers to deny the constitution which he had earlier granted to the people. The opposition parties in the Persian Parliament attempted a *coup* in 1902 which succeeded in dethroning their king. Shah Mohammed Ali fled the country after abdicating his throne. The new Sultan, Ahmed Mirza Shah, restored law and order in the country. Unfortunately, Persia was subjected to frequent interference by the big powers which plagued her politics in the early twentieth century. It resulted in the construction of Persia's independence, particularly during the course of the Great War (1914-18). During the course of the war, Russian and British forces occupied her soil, and the then Sultan, Shah Ahmed, was too weak to resist the pressures of these two countries. However, Persia maintained her neutrality during the course of the war for namesake.

In the meantime, Russia withdrew her troops from northern parts of Persia due to the outbreak of the Russian Revolution (1917). Britain got a wonderful opportunity to force her way. The idea of the British was to gain control over the countries in the eastern part of the Turkish empire and also in Persia. It was in the interest of the British to prevent Persia from being represented as a sovereign country in the Paris Peace Conference. Therefore, Persia, ie Iran, was not represented in the said conference, and Britain acted as her spokesman.

Oil Imperialism

What made Iran so important in the eyes of Britain, besides her geographical importance, was the availability of vast oil reserves which remained untapped. The first person to obtain oil concession from Iran was an Australian, Knox D'Arcy. In 1972, Baron de Reuter, a British citizen, secured a similar concession from the reigning Shah of Iran. D'Arcy founded the first oil company for further exploitation. After some time, the Shah of Iran and the other local chieftains, were offered partnership in a company for tapping oil reserves and sharing profits. Ultimately, D'Arcy founded a full-fledged Anglo-Persian oil company.

The British conspired with the tribal chieftains in Iran and attempted a *coup* which forced the Shah of Iran to abdicate his throne. Subsequently, the British oil enterprise known as Burma Oil purchased the oil company of D'Arcy by paying compensation. In 1912, a pipeline was laid to connect the oil wells to Abadan, 145 miles away, for the purpose of refining the oil. It was through these oil companies that Britain virtually controlled Iran. It enabled her to win the First World War against Germany. Britain began to play an increasing role in protecting her oil interests in Iran from foreign intruders. The Anglo-Persian oil company was managed by the British directors, and the British Government enjoyed the power of veto. Britain ensured a majority of votes in her favour in the general body meetings held by the company. The Anglo-Iranian Treaty of 1919 turned Iran into a British protectorate. Russia was not in a position to pose a threat to the British interests in Iran owing to a civil war following the Russian Revolution.

Rise of Iranian Nationalism

Iran's status was relegated to that of a British protectorate which implied the occupation of the British troops. The British Government also extended its control over the army and the treasury. Britain offered a loan of two million pounds at 7 per cent interest for the purpose of introducing necessary reforms. The humiliating terms meted out to Iran by this treaty roused the nationalist Iranians, and the Iranian Majlis (Parliament) refused to ratify the treaty. There was widespread protest against Britain which forced her to withdraw her troops from Iran and close its military and finance missions in Teheran. The strength of the British forces was greatly reduced and were eventually withdrawn.

Iran's relations with the Soviet Union improved considerably since the latter readily gave up her privileges and concessions. So the Soviet Union sympathised with the cause of Iranian nationalism. In fact, she was trying to expose the British duplicity regarding a loan offered by Britain to Iran earlier. But the Russian help had a cutting edge. The Soviet Union tried to establish a new Soviet Republic at Gilan, a town in Iran. The Soviet Government tried to help Iran's rebel leader, pro-Communist Kuchik Khan, to set up a republic. However, Iran lodged a serious protest against the military moves of Russia which eventually led to friendly negotiations. It ended in a treaty of friendship between the two countries. Subsequently, the Soviet troops at Gilan were withdrawn. The Iranian forces occupied Gilan, thanks to the Soviet Union's preoccupation with her domestic problems. Britain's reluctance to take any hasty step with regard to Iran's domestic affairs augured well for that country.

Riza Khan's Relations with Afghanistan (1925-41)

Riza Khan was a commander of the Iranian Cossack division who staged a successful *coup* in February 21, 1925 and subsequently became the prime minister. He succeeded in dethroning Shah Ahmed, the last king of the Kajar dynasty. Riza Khan became the king of Iran in 1925, and the dynasty which he founded was called the Pehlavi dynasty. He took bold steps in settling many frontier and river water disputes with the neighbouring country of Afghanistan. The two countries concluded agreements which created a climate for mutual trust and confidence. In June 1921, Iran and Afghanistan signed a comprehensive treaty of friendship on the basis of mutual respect, equality and trust, and agreed that their future relationship should be governed by the prevailing international laws. Iran and Afghanistan further agreed to maintain neutrality, if any one of them was involved in a war with a third party. In 1927, another treaty was signed committing both the countries to non-aggression, and settlement of outstanding disputes by arbitration—preferably employing a mutually agreed neutral country as arbitrator. The visit of the Afghan King and Queen, Amanullah and Souraiya, to Iran in 1927 contributed substantially to the friendly ties existing between the two countries. In March 1934, both of them again agreed to settle their border and water disputes through the arbitration of Turkey.

In July 1937, the foreign ministers of Iran, Turkey, Iraq and Afghanistan signed a treaty of friendship in Sa'dabad Palace (near Teheran). Iran and Afghanistan settled their water disputes (the division of the waters of the Helmand River) on the basis of Goldsmid award in 1938. However, this award did not come into force due to the intransigence of the Afghan Government. In 1939, the two countries concluded agreements for improving their communication links.

Riza Khan's Domestic Reforms

Riza Khan was inspired by the work of Kemal Ataturk for modernising Turkey. He also desired to modernise his country, and therefore, introduced several reforms. He restored political stability in the country by crushing all revolts. For example, the pro-Communist Kuchik Khan's revolt against the Pehlavi dynasty was crushed. Other provincial rebellions in Azerbaizan and Khorasan were put down. The rebellions of the powerful Khurdish tribes in the north were also subdued. Thus, law and order was restored in the country. Riza Khan was able to accomplish these tasks with the help of his highly disciplined army.

He reorganised the army into a highly efficient and disciplined force. He improved the means of transport and communications in the country by undertaking the construction of roads, bridges, railways and so on. It was during his time that the Trans-Iranian railway line was built to connect the Persian Gulf with the Caspian Sea.

Introduction of Secular Education

Iran's educational system was in the hands of the clerics. It had become obsolete and therefore, required revamping. Riza Khan took steps to emancipate the educational system from the control of the clerics. He encouraged the opening of new schools by foreigners who introduced the modern educational system. Under the new educational system, the French influence predominated. Riza

Khan enabled a large number of students to get education by starting more schools and colleges.

Another important feature of the new educational system was the introduction of vocational schools. In the course of time, this monarch tried to introduce free and compulsory education for all children. In 1935, the University of Teheran was founded with six faculties, and the government encouraged brilliant students to go abroad for higher studies by offering scholarships. But in 1932, he banned the establishment of foreign schools in his country. Compulsory religious education was discontinued in 1930. The new syllabi encouraged students to develop patriotism and civic sense of duties.

Legal Reforms

Prior to 1925, all disputes in Iran were settled by religious courts on the basis of the *Shariat*. The religious leaders, therefore, assumed great importance and commanded respect from the people. Earlier attempts to improve the judicial system were foiled by the clerics. Riza Khan did not like these developments. After he established his authority firmly over the whole country, he introduced civil and criminal courts modelled after the French. He introduced a code of laws similar to that of Code Napoleon. The religious leaders resisted all these changes but he overruled all their objections. In 1939, Riza Khan introduced a new Penal Code akin to the Italian model.

Secularism and Emancipation of Women

It must be remembered that religion played a great role in the public life of Iran and religious leaders wielded great influence over the people. Therefore, Riza Khan took necessary steps to reduce the importance of the clergy by introducing several changes. For example he banned religious processions like the *Muharram* and the infliction of self-torture by the processionists. The government took over the ecclesiastical lands and established boards for better management at places like Mashhad and Qum.

Women were considered inferior and played absolutely no role in public life. However, Riza Khan introduced necessary social reforms to emancipate the womenfolk. The veil (*burkha*) was abolished in 1936. Women were free to work. Their movements were not restricted. Polygamy was discouraged. A man marrying for the second time would have to get the consent of his first wife. Women were encouraged to hold public office. Girls enjoyed equal educational opportunities on a par with boys. They were encouraged to wear Western dresses, and the royal family set an example in this respect. These social changes caused widespread unrest all over Iran. However, the opposition to the social changes was curbed. The Persian language received much attention from scholars. They made attempts to purify and simplify it further. In 1935, the government established an Iranian academy for literature.

Economic Development

Iran witnessed the beginnings of modern industrialisation during the regime of Riza Khan. He strengthened the infrastructure of the country further by improving and modernising the means of transport and communication as mentioned earlier. His country attracted foreign investments, particularly in the field of oil exploration and refining.

In the early phases of economic development, Riza Khan sought the advice of an American expert, Dr Arthur Chester Millspagh. It was Millspagh who tried to reorganise the Iranian public finance. It was again due to his efforts that Iran made substantial progress in modern industrialisation. Iran attracted investment from foreign engineering firms, specially the European countries. They started their enterprises in Iran and contributed much for the development of Iran's infrastructure.

It must be remembered that the economic development of the country was mainly in the hands of the State Government. When Dr Millspagh resigned, he was replaced by a German economist. During this second phase of economic reforms, the Iranian Government established the Bank of Iran in 1928 which exercised the sole authority of issuing the country's currency. The Iranian Government made serious efforts to establish new industries and encourage foreign trade. Steps were taken in the direction of overcoming the dubious business tactics of the Soviet Union. The Iranian Foreign Trade Monopoly Act came into force in 1931. Riza Khan invested his personal funds in some industrial ventures particularly the hotel industry. It must be remembered that Iran's main source of wealth lay in its oil reserves and oil supply.

Foreign Relations in the 1930s

The Anglo-Iranian relations in the 1930s were at odds and evens. Britain played her trump card by declaring that she alone could save Iran from Soviet interference. She made a few attempts to weaken the regime of Riza Khan, but they were foiled. He allowed the Americans to start their oil explorations and compete with the British. In fact, Riza Khan symbolised Iranian nationalism by acting firmly while dealing with foreign powers. He safeguarded the interests of Iran despite the brow-beating tactics of Britain. Concessions offered to the Anglo-Persian company were extended up to 1993 but on certain conditions. These conditions proved to be very beneficial to the interests of Iran.

One of the great powers which did not gain in the oil politics of Iran was the Soviet Union. Iran started giving oil concessions to foreign companies in the north, much against the provisions of the 1921 treaty, which she had signed with the Soviet Union. When the Second World War broke out, Iran declared her neutrality, and therefore did not expel the Germans. In fact, before the outbreak of the Second World War the ruling classes of Iran sympathised with the rise of Nazism in Germany and Iran signed a few agreements of trade with Germany. During the course of the war, the British and the Soviet forces occupied Iran in August 1941. It led to Riza Khan's abdication of the throne in favour of his son, Mohammed Riza.

The Germans, who wielded great influence in Iran for a short while (ie during the early years of the war), began to flee the country. The Soviet Union reiterated her demand for oil concessions. Iran appealed to her to wait till the war was over. After the Second World War, Iran was deeply disturbed due to anti-Western feelings, and the Majlis (the Iranian Parliament) rejected all proposals offering concessions to foreign firms. In fact, some of the political parties were seriously thinking of nationalising all foreign oil companies, and Dr Mossadegh advocated this policy.

While under occupation, Britain and Russia signed a treaty with Iran thereby promising to withdraw their forces soon after the war was over. Dr Millspagh returned to Iran to offer his advice on many important matters. He enjoyed wide executive powers. Unfortunately, he resigned his post in a huff after the Iranian press commented adversely upon his style of functioning. The American Government was indeed sympathetic towards Iran during the period of occupation. Roosevelt, Churchill and Stalin expressed their desire for the maintenance of "independence, sovereignty and territorial integrity of Iran" at the Teheran Conference held in December 1943.

The Post-War Oil Politics

In 1945, Iran faced a serious crisis because the Tudat members acting in the name of democracy, and abetted by thousands of Soviet agents, deposed the Iranian governor of Tabriz, and declared the province of Azerbaizan as an autonomous republic. It was headed by a Comintern agent, Jafar Pishavari, who acknowledged publicly the assistance of the Soviet Union. Iran appealed to the United Nations against the Soviet Union's "aggressive interference". The Soviet Union did not fulfil the pledge made in the Tripartite treaty of 1942—viz the withdrawal of Soviet troops from Iran.

The motive behind the Azerbaizan crisis was that the Soviet desired to exploit the oil resources from the conquered Iranian territory. However, this crisis was resolved when the two countries negotiated and arrived at an agreement regarding the oil concessions. The draft agreement provided for the setting up of a joint Soviet-Iranian oil company each sharing the profits. Nevertheless, anti-foreign feelings were running high in Iran. The oil politics continued to obsess the minds of the British and the American policy makers in the background of Iranian moves for nationalising foreign oil companies.

The Last Phase of Iranian Nationalism

Oil politics had made the people of Iran wary of foreign interference, and the Iranian Majlis refused to ratify the agreement signed with Russia. There was a secret understanding between the governments of the United States and Iran over oil concessions to be offered to foreign powers, which complicated the relations with the Soviet Union. It was in this situation that Dr Mohammed Mossadegh made his debut in politics and represented popular revulsion to foreign interference. Dr Mossadegh became the Prime Minister of the country and advocated the nationalisation of foreign enterprises. He nationalised the Anglo-Iranian oil company since he felt that the British were sharing too much of the profit.

However, Dr Mossadegh's tenure of office was cut short since he was deposed in a military *coup*. The Shah of Iran himself organised this *coup* so as to bring about the fall of Dr Mossadegh. The Iranian Majlis was dissolved and Iran was not bailed out even though she had preferred to sell oil to the communist countries and Japan at cheaper rates. General Zahedi who succeeded Dr Mossadegh after a bloody *coup* enjoyed the secret support of the Shah of Iran. This event is known as the White Revolution in the history of Iran. However, even General Zahedi's government was short-lived. In the meantime, Dr Mossadegh was put on trial and jailed. The new government signed a few oil agreements with the major foreign powers and created a consortium of eight oil companies. Iran cancelled the fisheries contract with the Soviet Union.

In the next two decades the Shah of Iran ruled the country like a dictator because there was practically no opposition from the Majlis. He introduced and encouraged the western ways of life with the help of his cronies. He received ample funds from the United States Government under the Point Four programme. Iran signed the Baghdad Pact in 1955 which was mooted by the United States to contain communism. The Shah set up a secret police department called Savak to exterminate his enemies. He felt quite secure on his throne in 1961 and ordered the dissolution of the Majlis. The old constitution became invalid after the establishment of the Shah's despotism.

Popular Resistance

The Shah initiated what is known as the "White Revolution" in Iran to bring about a radical socio-economic change, which was in tune with Western culture. Scores of night clubs, restaurants, cinema-theatres, and casinos were soon seen in major cities. While the rich could whet their appetite with food and entertainment, the poor remained largely neglected. The Western press described the Shah's regime as enlightened, progressive and constitutional. But it hardly noticed what a vice-like grip the Shah had over the Majlis, the press and so on. In fact, the Shah had banned all political parties except his own, that is the National Resurrection Party. All of them went underground, namely, the Islamic Republican Party, the Hizbullah, the National Front, the Muslim People's Party and the Tudeh. The Kurds had their own political party. Resistance to his regime began with the student disturbances in 1961. The Muslim clergy also opposed him, and it resulted in the expulsion of Ayatollah Khomeini in 1963. He had to take shelter in Iraq.

Popular discontent found its expression in the form of strikes, demonstrations and violence in many cities of Iran in 1977. When the Revolution broke out, the Shah tried to pacify the people by dismissing the prime minister and the Savak officials. But what the people desired was not cosmetic changes in the administration but radical transformation of the socio-economic system.

On September 8, 1978, the Shah declared martial law to control the chaotic situation. But the Iranian army was divided, and a section openly supported the Shia spiritual leader, Ayatollah Khomeini. The long resistance succeeded when the Shah left Iran during the middle of January 1979. Khomeini, who had threatened the Shah's regime with "jehad' (holy war), returned to Iran after 15 years' exile. The people of Iran received him with great joy.

The Revolution

Khomeini declared the Shah's regime illegal and held a nation-wide referendum in March 1979. The Iranians approved the transformation of Iran into an 'Islamic Republic" on April 1, 1979. Khomeini ordered public trial of the ardent supporters of the Shah's regime, and the guilty (about 600 men) were executed. The Savak (Secret Police) was abolished, and a revolutionary council was set up. Western imports and customs were banned. Egypt and the Soviet Union recognised the new revolutionary regime.

Theocratic State

A Constituent Council composed of 73 experts drafted the new Constitution which was published in June. The Constitution recognised the Shia form of Islam as state religion. As for the administration, there was to be a popularly elected president, a unicameral legislature, and a Supreme Court. Above all, the supreme authority of the state was vested in *Wali Faqih* (a Saint or Guardian). The *Wali Faqih* was to be assisted by a small council for the purpose of carrying out the administrative function of Islamic state as laid down in the Koran. Iran's relations with the United States deteriorated since the ailing Shah was welcomed as a guest and his ill-gotten wealth was locked up in American banks. Iran's oil-money was also locked up in US banks, and therefore Iran demanded the return of the disgraced dictator and also the money.

Hostage Crisis

On November 4, 1979 the Iranian revolutionaries (mostly students) besieged the American Embassy in Teheran (the Iranian capital) and took 66 Americans as hostages. They were released only after 444 gruelling days. The Soviet Union vetoed the US proposal in the Security Council to apply economic sanctions against Iran. Kurt Waldheim's mission (the Secretary-General of the UN) also failed to get the hostages released. The UN condemned the Iranian action.

In the meantime, Bani Sadr was elected president of the Islamic Republic, but he found it difficult to work with the all-powerful Khomeini and therefore, had to go. His successor was assassinated. Iran's foreign policy was "marked by antagonism with the West especially with the United States". President Carter's secret mission to rescue the hostages in Iran failed due to a technical snag developing in the American helicopter. Eight American servicemen lost their lives in this incident. The West did not accept the Iranian revolution although the Soviet Union welcomed it. The Shah died in July 1980 in Egypt. Iran demanded the return of her frozen assets along with Shah's ill-gotten wealth from the US Government. The American hostages were released on January 21, 1981 through the mediation of the Algerian Government. The US released the Iranian assets as a part of the bargain. In the last week of June, the counter-revolutionaries struck at the Islamic Party headquarters by exploding a bomb which killed more than 60 people including Iran's main functionaries. Prime Minister Mohammed Ali Rajai, and the Speaker of the Majlis, Rafsanjani, had a narrow escape. There were demonstrations by the pro-clergy and it was followed by summary trials and executions of suspected counter revolutionaries. Ayatollah Khomeini imposed a *fatwa* on Indian-born British writer Salman Rushdie in 1989 for his allegedly blasphemous novel, *The Satanic Verses*.

Iran-Iraq War

Iran left the CENTO and joined the non-aligned countries. In the meanwhile, Iraq invaded Khuzistan, the south-western province of Iran known for its rich resources—petrol and gas. The war between the two may be described as the longest one (1980-88) in Iran's history. Iran recovered some territories from the enemy in 1982, and the war eventually spread to the Persian-Gulf region in 1984. The West opposed Iran's threat to close the Straits of Hormuz, and Iraq's use of chemical weapons to gain an upper hand. The Arab world and the non-aligned countries failed to bring about peace between these belligerents. Khomeini died in 1985. By 1988, both the countries agreed for a cease-fire. In June 1990, a major earthquake in Iran killed 40,000, injured 100,000 and made 400,000 homeless.

Post-Khomeini Era

Ayatollah Khomeini was succeeded by Ali Akbar Hashemi Rafsanjani. During his period, the Iranian clergy were gradually losing their hold on the government because the people had suffered enough. They desired a change from extreme rigidity to moderate governance. Owing to this desire of the people a moderate cleric, Mohammed Khatami, was sworn in as president in August 1997. He defeated Ali Akbar Netaq Nuri in May. He was born in Ardakan and subsequently became a clergyman. He held the post of Minister for Islamic Culture and Guidance in 1982, but had to resign after 10 years because President Rafsanjani yielded to the pressure from the conservatives. He remained in the background for about four years, and suddenly showed himself up as a joint candidate "of the Pro-Rafsanjani moderate and the country's neo-leftist wing to challenge for the presidency". Over 70 per cent of the voters in the presidential election desired a change for the better, that their society should be pluralistic and multi-sectoral. Khatami stood for "greater freedom of expression and the rule of law". In recent years Khatami has been struggling to speed up reforms, while his powerful rivals have carried on intrigues against him. Recently, the Managing Editor of the *Khordad* newspaper, Nouri has been sentenced to five years imprisonment by a special clerical court for carrying out anti-Islamic propaganda. Pro-Khatami followers have not liked it. The *fatwa* imposed on Salman Rushdie has been lifted.

Reformists Disappointed

The pro-reform government of Mohammed Khatami received serious setback in carrying forward its reform programme mainly due to the conservative elements that dominated the Council of Guardian (upper house). It caused great disappointment to the followers of Khatami as well as college and university students. The conservative elements of the Council of Guardian is led by Khamenei (The Supreme Leader) who vetoed all reformist measures. In fact, the conservative elements were responsible for contriving jail terms for the followers of Khatami through conservative court judges. It was left to Khatami to appeal to the people that these convictions are unconstitutional. What is happening in Iran is that liberals are facing continuous opposition from the conservative elements. President Khatami is feeling helpless since he is restrained from implementing the much needed reforms to make Iranian society more democratic.

Khamenei Posing Problems

On the twenty-fifth anniversary of Iranian revolution, many parliamentarians resigned in protest against the ban imposed on 3,500 candidates from contesting the elections. In fact ten reformist political parties decided to boycott the February elections (2004). The Islamic Iran Participation Front has become desperate at the slow pace of reforms and are wondering why President Khatami remains as a 'figurehead'. The reformists in Iran accuse Khamenei for suppressing the pro-democracy movement by exercising his legal powers, even though he is supposed to remain 'neutral' and also keep himself above party politics in his capacity as the 'supreme leader'.

Relations with the US

In the eyes of the US Government, Iran has remained as one of the 'axes of evil' (the others are North Korea and Libya), as a country sponsoring terrorism. This charge is being denied by the Iranian Government several times. Relations between the two countries had strained ever since the 'hostage crisis'. But in the aftermath of 9/11 in the US, Iran is becoming a focus of attention for other reasons. Iran has denied links with the Al-Qaeda, and some of Al-Qaeda operatives in its country were arrested and handed over to Saudi authorities.

However, the US Government is still suspicious and would like to know about its clandestine nuclear programme. The International Atomic Energy Agency (IAEA) has been putting pressure on Iranian government (Iran has signed earlier the non-proliferation treaty) to be more transparent about its nuclear programme and made several demands on openings its Uranium-enrichment plants. Iran's reply that she is carrying out her nuclear programme for peaceful purposes has not satisfied the IAEA. While Russia has helped Iran in building its nuclear facilities, Britain, France and Germany have joined the US in asking Iran to open up its nuclear facilities for inspection.

The US believes that Iran, a Shiite country, might have been involved in the growing resistance to the occupation forces in Iraq. Another matter of concern to the US is the support given by Iran to the Hizbullah (a terrorist organisation) in Lebanon. It must be remembered that the US Government has imposed sanctions on Iran.

Iran's Economy

Iran's oil reserves is the fourth largest in the world, while the gas reserves is the second largest. Unfortunately, Iran is unable to exploit these resources to the full extent due to shortage of capital, paucity of technical personnel, antiquated technology, and absence of partnership with Western companies. Due to the US sanction, oil production has slumped by about 20 per cent.

President Khatami's two term of presidency has come to an end, and Iran's reforms have been stifled by the conservative elements. The earthquake that hit Bam, a historic town in December 2003, had taken heavy toll of lives. Iran's historic legacy, namely, the 2000-year-old-citadel built by the Safavids, is now in ruins.

43

IRAQ

Early History

Iraq was known as Mesopotamia in ancient times. The Mesopotamian civilisation took its birth in between the two rivers, the Tigris and the Euphrates, around 4000 BC. Mesopotamian civilisation left a rich legacy for posterity, such as the script, calender, weights and measures, mathematics, astronomy, code of laws and so on. Present day Iraq has inherited this rich legacy. Iraq became a part of an Arab empire after the spread of Islam.

The Caliphate established its headquarters in Baghdad, an old town, which turned into a great city in medieval days. Baghdad became a great centre of Islamic culture. In those medieval days, Baghdad could boast of the rule of Caliph Haroun-Al-Rashid, who had become a legend as a famous and wise king. The stories of the Arabian Nights were mostly connected with the city of Baghdad. Islam spread to Western India during the Abbasid Caliphate of Baghdad in the eighth century. The Arab scholars of Baghdad translated most of the ancient Greek classics, and also the Hindu book of Mathematics into Arabic. In the course of time, Baghdad, where the merchant of all countries met became Iraq's capital. It was also known for its fabulous wealth. The great Mosque of Baghdad became a typical example of Islamic architecture. The Abbasid Caliphate was overthrown by the Seljuk Turks in the 11th century. In the course of time, the Ottoman Turks established there empire which included Iraq. However, at the end of the First World War, the Ottoman empire disintegrated.

The British and the French hastened the process of the disintegration of the Ottoman empire by encouraging the Arab kings to declare their independence at the end of the war. According to the Treaty of Sevres, the Ottoman empire lost Palestine, Mesopotamia (Iraq) and Trans-Jordan to Britain. The revised Treaty of Lousanne compelled Turkey to give up her claim to Hejaz, Trans-Jordan, Palestine, Iraq and Syria. The British Government set up the Hashemite kingdoms in both Iraq and Jordan during the period of mandate. Unfortunately, the people of these two countries did not like their monarchs. The British interest in holding on to Iraq lay in the oil-fields of Mosul, and also to keep open the transport and communication link with the rest of the Middle East. It was in 1930, that Britain granted independence to Iraq. Britain, however, kept her military garrisons. She also retained the right to control Iraq's oil companies.

Subsequently, the territories governed by Britain were in a state of anarchy. The situation became worse with the outbreak of the Second World War in 1939. Britain created the Arab legion (16 divisions stationed in Egypt) so as to crush all opposition to her influence and control. Iraq broke off diplomatic relations with Germany at the instance of Britain. The Iraqis generally supported Germany and expected her to win the Second World War.

In 1940, Nuri-es-Said resigned as prime-minister and Rashid Ali succeeded him. Unfortunately, Rashid Ali turned hostile to the British because he did not like British control and influence over Iraq. He refused to cut off diplomatic relations with Italy, when the latter joined the Axis powers against the Allies during the Second World War. In fact, Rashid Ali hoped to take the assistance of Nazi Germany to oust Britain from Iraq. The supporters of Rashid Ali (the Syrian nationalists and Muftis) planned to bring about the end of British presence in Iraq.

Unfortunately, this *coup* failed because of General Taha-el-Hashimi. Rashid Ali subsequently regained his authority as prime minister. After a short interval, he forced the Regent, the infant king, and Nuri-es-Said to go into exile. He even refused to grant permission to Britain for the landing of Anglo-Indian troops in Basra. He tried to surround the British-controlled airport at Habbaniya. He was able to secure meagre assistance after much effort from Germany, which was of no avail.

Britain responded to his hostile moves by ordering the Royal Air Force to bomb Baghdad. The British attack of Baghdad resulted in the overthrow of Rashid Ali's Government in Iraq. Subsequently, he fled to Iran, and Nuri-es-Said returned to Baghdad and formed his ministry (1941-44). Subsequently, the royal family also returned to Baghdad. During his period, the Kurds in Iraq revolted.

Iraqi-British Relations

During the post-war era, Iraq demanded that Britain revise the old treaty, which provided for the stationing of British garrisons in Iraq. Britain agreed to revise the treaty and accordingly evacuated her troops in October 1947. What angered Iraq was that Britain continued to retain the strategic airports at Habbaniya and Haiba. Britain needed these airports in order to promote her own interests in the Middle East region — the Mosul oil field and communications with the East. After Britain signed another treaty at Portsmouth, the Iraqi Government failed to ratify it. During the succeeding years, Britain was too pre-occupied with the issue of Palestine.

Iraqi-Israeli War

Iraq joined Syria, Jordan and Lebanon and struck at Israel soon after Britain ended its mandate over Palestine. In this first Arab-Israeli war (also known as Israel's war of independence), Iraq and her allies suffered humiliating defeat. In the aftermath of Iraq's defeat, the political situation turned volatile. The political parties took advantage of the weakness of the government and staged a number of coups. The constitutional party was led by Nuri-es-Said who was supported by the feudal lords, Sunnis and the conservatives. Its main rival was *Umma* or the National Party of Shias. Another important party was Istiqlal (independence party). There were others like the Baathists and Communists. The government tried to suppress the Communists for fear that it would spread communism in the country.

Britain established friendly relations with Iraq so that the latter would join the Baghdad Pact which included Turkey, Pakistan and Iran. Iraq was admitted into this Baghdad Pact for the purpose of containing the spread of communism in the Middle East. Unfortunately, the other Arab countries led by President Nasser of Egypt did not take a sympathetic view of Iraq joining the Baghdad Pact. In the course of time, the Nuri government in Iraq became unpopular because of its inefficiency. The monarchy in Iraq was also in danger. As anticipated, Iraq was rocked by a revolution led by Brigadier General Abdul Karim Kassem who was supported by the Istiqlal Party. Iraq's monarchy was overthrown on July 14, 1958, and it was followed by the massacre of King Feisal II, Nuri-es-Said and others.

For the next five years, Kassem ruled Iraq with the support of a Revolutionary Command Council. His government received a liberal supply of arms from the Soviet Union. During these five years, Iraq did not make much progress. The government faced a number of problems. The Kurds, who constituted 18 per cent of the Iraqi population, were mostly concentrated in the Mosul area. They were treated badly by the government. Kassem subsequently put forward Iraq's claim to Kuwait in 1961. Mustafa Barzana, the leader of the Kurds, appealed to his compatriots living in other countries (Iran, Syria and Turkey) to establish a homeland for the Kurds. His revolt against the Iraqi Government was crushed.

The Coups of 1963 and 1967

Kassem's government was overthrown after a successful coup organised by Colonel Abdul Salam Areef in 1963. Subsequently, Kassem was executed. In the meantime, the Iraqi-Arab Socialist Union became a popular political party which dominated the political scene in Iraq. This party envisaged a union of three countries, namely, Iraq, Syria and Egypt. Colonel Areef began to face a tough problem while dealing with the Kurds in Iraq. Unfortunately, he met with an accident and died in 1966.

His brother, Abdul Rehman, carried on the administration. It was during his time that the Arab States fought another war with Israel in 1967. Iraq remained neutral, and subsequently, Rehman's government proved to be incompetent and inefficient. The Baathist military leader, General Ahmed Hassan Al Bakar, and his young colleague, Saddam Hussein, staged a successful coup. The first named became the president and prime minister, and the second became the vice president of the country. Both these leaders worked very hard to "transform Iraq into a modern state". It was surprising to note that instead of rivalry and jealousy, as was in vogue in most Middle-Eastern countries, both worked with great understanding. They provided an efficient government which the people of Iraq badly needed.

These two leaders along with a revolutionary council of 22 members established a new government. In the course of time the Soviet Union became an ally of Iraq, and in 1973, the Revolutionary Council accorded recognition to the Communist Party in Iraq. Iraq did not participate in the 1973 Suez war, nor in the Camp David Accord. Although Iraq did not fight Israel, she still continues to be in a state of war in the absence of any peace treaty. The idea of Pan-Arabism gained ground, and its ideology included the destruction of Israel, and the strategic control of the whole of Persian Gulf (as opposed to the partial control of it by Iran). This was because of the potentiality of abundant supply of oil.

Iran-Iraq War (1980-88)

Navigation on the Shatt-al-Arab had remained disputed between Iraq and Iran and defied solution. Furthermore, Iran occupied the islands of Abu Musa, Tunbi and Straits of Hormuz. The Pan-Arab movement led by Iraq prevailed and subsequently led to Iran-Iraq clashes. In July 1979, Al-Bakar resigned and paved the way for Saddam Hussein to succeed him. There was a peaceful transfer of power. President Saddam Hussein faced two important problems on assuming the office of presidency – the rebellious Kurds in the north and a hostile Iran in the east.

Iran and Iraq traded charges; Iraq blamed Iran for training and arming the Kurds in her territory, and also annexing the three islands (Arabistan). Iran accused Iraq of suppressing the Shia population in her territory. Iraq was also afraid that Iran under Ayatollah Khomeini (spiritual leader of the Shia community) may export the Islamic revolution to her territory.

Border clashes between the two countries brought about the war which was officially declared in September 1980. The immediate cause of the war was that Iraq charged Iran with attacking a number of Iraqi villages. The Iraqi army made strategic moves to capture the Abadan oil fields in Iran. When the war began, Syria supported Iran. She accused Iraq of supporting religious fundamentalists in her country. The Security Council of the United Nations then called upon both the countries to observe truce. The long war between Iraq and Iran brought about exhaustion, and finally they agreed to observe the truce.

The Gulf War (1991)

Hardly had the war ended between Iraq and Iran, there came another war – the Gulf War – between Iraq and the US led coalition. The main cause of the war was Iraq's invasion of Kuwait in August 1990. Kuwait became a British protectorate in 1914. Iraq considered Kuwait as a part of its kingdom. Soon after the independence of Kuwait (1961), Iraq claimed it as its own. But she did not pursue the matter. However, in 1990 Iraq and Kuwait had a dispute over oil prices. This matter precipitated Iraq's invasion and occupation of Kuwait. The Arab nations were taken by surprise, and all of them condemned this action. When Saddam Hussein refused to vacate his troops from Kuwait, the UN had to intervene. When the efforts of the UN also failed to get Iraq to vacate by January 15, 1991, the US and her allies (29 nations in all) started their military attacks on Iraq —*code word: the Desert Fox.* Saddam Hussein urged his compatriots to fight this powerful coalition, and called it 'mother of all battles'. This high-tech war carried on by the US and her allies (with laser-guided missiles and stealth bombers) destroyed Iraq's main installations. The oil wells of Kuwait were set ablaze which caused ecological damage to the Gulf region. Unable to fight, the Iraqi soldiers surrendered without a fight on the ground. Saddam's forces suffered massive defeats, and Iraq agreed for peace after withdrawing from Kuwait.

Cease-fire Agreement (1991)

Saddam survived the holocaust, and his representative to the UN, agreed to obey the UN terms of peace. The UN imposed economic sanctions, and this was to continue till Iraq's nuclear arsenals, armaments and chemical weapons were totally destroyed. For achieving these objectives the UN sent its inspectors to Iraq's factories and laboratories. The economic embargo on Iraq by the UN caused great hardships to the people, but they still adore their hero, Saddam. Iraq's oil-revenues from exports came to a dead-halt and she was not allowed to purchase anything from other countries.

Plight of Iraq

The US and its allies tried to eliminate Saddam Hussein but they did not succeed, for the Iraqis admire him. Thereafter the US and the allies made serious efforts to cause severe hardships to the Iraqis by imposing economic sanctions.

Oil for Food Programme

Following repeated appeals from Iraq to the UN to lift the sanctions and the cooperation extended by her to the UN inspectors, the Security Council agreed finally to start what is known as "the Oil-for-Food" programme in 1996. Iraq was allowed to import basic necessities such as food and medicines for her 22 million subjects. The UN set up what is known as the Weapons Inspection team (UNSCOM) for Iraq's compliance with the Security Council's resolution to destroy its lethal and chemical weapons. But in recent years this UNSCOM has been working like the agent of the US often complaining of non-cooperation from the Iraqi Government. While Saddam holds on in spite of terrible hardships inflicted on his people, the US and her allies have plans to attack his country.

The Threat of War

Iraq took on a collision course when Saddam Hussein called on his compatriots to wage a holy war against his oppressors in January 1998. In February, the US threatened to strike when the weapons inspection team reported non-cooperation from Iraq. However, the war was averted when Kofi Annan, the UN Secretary-General, brokered a peace deal between the two. In July, 1998 Saddam declared he would take action if the UN embargo was not lifted. Pictures of innocent and ailing children suffering due to various maladies and malnutrition had no effect on the oppressors. The US and her allies had been maintaining a large military presence in the Gulf, and in December 1998 the US and UK began air strikes on Iraq (December 28, 1998 – January 4, 1999). This was done in retaliation to Iraq's alleged non-cooperation to the inspection team. Iraq suffered heavy damage as in the 1991 war. (In 1995, Saddam had been re-elected president indicating his popularity.)

The Second Gulf War

Exercising its sovereign right, Iraq forced the UN weapons inspectors (who were investigating Iraq for Weapons of Mass Destruction) to quit the country in 1998. Since then the US and its allies were waiting for an opportunity to strike at Iraq for they desired a 'regime change'. After the defeat of Taliban in Afghanistan President George W Bush and Tony Blair put intense pressure on the UN Security Council for approval to strike at Iraq. The Iraqi Government finally yielded to the UN Security Council's desire that the weapons inspectors be once again permitted to investigate about Iraq's WMD. Before the inspection was over, the US and its allies decided on a pre-emptive strike at Iraq. But France, Germany and Russia opposed this move in the UN Security Council. These three powers wanted a report from the Chairman of the weapons inspectors who had inspected Iraqi weapons establishments.

Despite the disagreement in the Security Council, the US-led coalition attacked Iraq. The reason for the war being that Saddam was making weapons of mass destruction, has used chemical weapons against Iran and his own people (at Halabja) and had violated human rights of his subjects. Moreover, the US-led coalition led by President Bush presumed that Saddam Hussein of Iraq was in touch with Al-Qaeda terrorists. But many members of the UN including the Gulf States believed that the US-led coalition is more interested in acquiring the vast oil resources of Iraq after the removal of the Iraqi president. Iraq's oil resources are vast, next only to Saudi Arabia.

The UN became a mute spectator when the US-led coalition served a 48 hours ultimatum to President Saddam Hussein and his sons to leave the country. When there was no response, the war began on March 20, 2003, despite warnings from Iraqi president that he would take the war anywhere in the world. He appealed to his people to 'draw your sword' against the invaders. The world watched the high-tech war (through TV channels) conducted against Iraqi political and military establishments, and the large scale destructions of cities and towns including the capital, Baghdad. It was in Baghdad that the coalition faced fierce attack by Iraqi ground forces. By May 1, the war officially ended in the defeat of Saddam Hussein, and on December 13, he was captured after months of search. His sons were killed earlier in his home town Tikrit. Iraq was occupied by the coalition forces, and Mr Paul Bremer was appointed administrator of Iraq. The Iraqi resistance against occupation forces after the capture of Saddam Hussein has remained unabated. This happens so even after the transfer of sovereignty by the occupation forces to the new Iraqi Government on June 28, 2004 (two days ahead of the supposed transfer). The US troops numbering 135,000 is still protecting the new government. The interim Prime Minister of Iraq, Mr Iyad Allawi had declared amnesty to resistance fighters involved in minor crimes. The new government is going to arrange elections in January 2005.

Financial Aspects of the War

During the war, the US president appealed to the Congress to sanction $75 billion for waging the war. Among the coalition partners, the most important were Britain, Spain, Italy, Australia and subsequently Japan. Most of the Iraqi towns, including the capital, were heavily bombed which caused heavy civilian casualties besides immense damage to buildings, bridges, civilian and military installations. The defeated army set fire to oil installations during the period of resistance. With the advent of the war, Russia, India, and several other countries suffered heavy financial losses (due to Iraq's inability to meet its contractual obligations). India suffered because Iraq could not supply oil under 'food-for-oil' programme. Russia lost $3 billion. Iraq's civilian population are suffering the most today, as their life is seriously disrupted. Hospitals, schools, colleges and other establishments have been closed. Tens and thousands of Iraqis have lost their jobs.

Iraq Today

The new government with the support of the coalition forces are facing violent resistance from the Shia population in the south, especially from those fighters led by the Shia cleric leader Muqtada-al-Sadr. This leader wants the coalition forces to leave the country. Fighting between the two erupted once again after a short truce in the holy city of Najaf. In the north, the Sunni Muslims, loyal to Saddam Hussein, have been resisting the occupation forces in Tikrit, Mosul and other towns. Attacks on Allied forces, police stations, offices and other public buildings along with car-bomb explosions (in Baghdad, the UN had to close its office when its Chief died) have become the order of the day.

Report of the Commission

An enquiry commission in the US recently reported that former Iraqi President Saddam Hussein was not involved with Al-Qaeda terrorists and that Iraq did not possess any weapons of mass destruction (the main reason for launching the war by the US president). The US Government has come under fire for abusing human rights of the Iraqi prisoners held at Abu Graib prison. With the re-election of President Bush in the 2004 election, the future of Iraq is still in a shroud of uncertainty. More than six hundred American soldiers have lost their lives in the continuing violence in Iraq.

Iraq's Economy

The mainstay of Iraq's economy is oil. Nearly one-third of the population depends upon agriculture. There is a large minority of Kurds in the north-east which creates problems for Saddam. The value of the Iraqi dinar has depreciated since the Gulf War. The second war has caused total chaos. Oil exports (1.8 million barrels a day) has come to standstill since the pipelines are destroyed by insurgents. Iraq's reconstruction may take decades, since political instability continues.

PART V

WEST ASIA

44

THE RISE OF MODERN TURKEY

The rise of Arab nationalism had its earliest origin in the Napoleonic conquest of Egypt (1799) and the defeat and humiliation of Turkey at the hands of the West soon after the World War I. It was also an outcome of Western impact on the Arab countries. Many of these Arab countries had been subjected to great hardship due to Western exploitation. In the first instance, it began in Egypt under Mohammed Ali who was acting as a governor of the Ottoman empire. Mohammed Ali defied the authority of his master, the Ottoman Emperor, and gave Egypt a semblance of Western democracy. He introduced Western political institutions for which he was called "Father of Modern Egypt". He opened his country to Western influence and introduced several reforms.

The defeat of Turkey during the First World War, and the humiliating treatment meted out to the Ottoman emperor by the Western powers engendered patriotic feelings among the Turks. In fact, Mahatma Gandhi in India organised the Khilafat movement to champion the cause of the Turks against the West.

One of the modern elements of Arab nationalism is Arabism which spread all over the Arab lands. Its origin is traced to the rise and spread of Islam. The Caliphate encouraged Arabism to develop, but in the end it resulted in the struggle for independence by those Arab countries which were subjected to the control of the Ottoman empire. The disintegration of the Ottoman empire after its defeat in the First World War, and the abolition of the Caliphate gave a big boost to Arab nationalism.

However, this temporary upsurge of Arab nationalism did not succeed as expected. France and Britain received their mandates from the League of Nations to rule over those lands which were under the control of the Ottoman Emperor earlier. For instance, France acquired Syria and Lebanon, and Britain acquired Palestine, Mesopotamia (Iraq) and Trans-Jordan. Egypt came under the British control since the successors of Mohammed Ali proved to be incompetent to rule over the country. When Turkey joined Germany during the First World War, Egypt became free and Britain established her control over her.

Nationalism Succeeds in Turkey

The first country where nationalism experienced its victory was Turkey. It came under the control of Mustafa Kemal Pasha. The defeat of the Ottoman empire (Turkey with its far-flung empire) at the hands of the Allies resulted in the imposition of a humiliating treaty—the Treaty of Sevres. The Ottoman Emperor meekly submitted himself to the Allies. This abject surrender of their Sultan made his subjects furious. They were unable to bear this humiliation any longer. It encouraged the Young Turks—a band of young and patriotic Turks—to revolt. In fact, the Young Turks had been demanding a new constitution enshrining basic rights to all citizens, and restrictions on monarchical despotism.

Mustafa Kemal Pasha, the leader of the Young Turks, joined the Turkish army, and in the course of time, decided to strike at the crumbling monarchy. He was born in Selonica in 1880. He joined the military staff college in Constantinople where he showed his skill and proficiency in all subjects including mathematics. His favourite teacher used to call him Kemal (meaning perfect). Kemal Pasha was influenced by the revolutionary literature of France, and hence his senior colleagues in the army felt that he was too dangerous to stay in the capital. Therefore, they managed to get him posted at Damascus. Kemal Pasha was disgusted at the way in which his country was being managed by the incompetent Sultan. He was unhappy to note the inefficiency and corruption prevailing in all the departments of the administration. He took part in the 1908 revolt by the Young Turks against the Sultan. The Young Turks demanded a new constitution based upon democratic principles.

It was Kemal Pasha who forced the Sultan to grant the new constitution in 1908. During the course of the Great War, Turkey joined on the side of Germany. Kemal Pasha proved himself a worthy commander with his daring exploits. Unfortunately Turkey was defeated in the war, and the Sultan had to sign the Treaty of Sevres. Kemal Pasha condemned the terms of the treaty as extremely insulting and humiliating. With the backing of the army he staged a revolt. He organised the Nationalist Party, which opposed the despotic monarchy. The Sultan made several attempts to crush these revolts but failed.

The Allies intended to bring about the disintegration of the Ottoman empire, and imposed a crushing burden of compensation. They proposed that the finances of the Ottoman empire should be managed by them. After the Treaty of Sevres was signed by the Sultan, Turkey lost Thrace and Smyrna. The Greek troops plundered Smyrna, a commercial and religious centre. The Young Turks were enraged and Kemal Pasha pledged to avenge this insult. He set up a parallel government with its headquarters at Ankara in 1919. It was republican in character. In the meantime, the common people of Turkey no longer regarded the Sultan as their leader, and changed their allegiance to the Ankara Government. The parallel government set up by Kemal Pasha signed agreements with Russia and Italy, and the latter vacated her troops from Turkish soil.

The Graeco-Turkish war began when the Greeks from Smyrna were expelled by the Turks. Thereupon the Greeks invaded Anatolia (Asia Minor), and the Turkish forces led by Kemal Pasha delivered quick blows and drove them away. Turkey recovered the Dardenelles and Constantinople, and Kemal Pasha was hailed as the hero of the nation. The British did not come to the rescue of the Greeks as hoped. When Kemal Pasha threatened Constantinople itself which was under the control of the British, the British Government faced a serious crisis. The British Prime Minister, Lloyd George, declared that he would defend the freedom of the Straits under any circumstances. Ultimately, the French Government mediated and brought about an armistice in October 1922. The Allies realised the strength of Turkish nationalism and the capacity of the new leader.

They offered to replace the Treaty of Sevres. All the contending parties met at Lausanne (Switzerland) and signed the treaty in 1923. The Treaty of Lausanne brought about an amicable settlement between Turkey on the one side, and the Allies on the other. As per its terms, Greece surrendered Smyrna, eastern Thrace, Gallipoli and the Dodacanese islands to Turkey. An exchange of their population on each other's territory was agreed upon. It was a great diplomatic victory for Kemal Pasha for which he was called Ghazi.

Kemal Pasha announced the abolition of the Turkish Sultanate, and subsequently, Sultan Mohammed VI fled the country. He declared Turkey as a republic on October 29, 1923. Even the last link with the past, the Caliphate was abolished on March 3, 1924. Caliph Abdul Mejid II was driven out of the country. A new constitution was proclaimed and Kemal Pasha and his friend Ismet Pasha were declared president and prime minister respectively in 1924. Turkey enjoyed democratic institutions with an elected parliament based on universal franchise of male citizens. The country's capital was shifted from Constantinople (renamed Istanbul) to Ankara, to mark the inauguration of a modern era in Turkish history.

Benevolent Dictatorship (1924-38)

According to the new constitution, Kemal Pasha exercised absolute authority. However, he did not misuse his powers. His dictatorship was tempered with three important elements: 1) his liberal inclinations, 2) his benevolence and 3) sharing of power, partnership with the people's party. During his fourteen years of office, Turkey witnessed a total transformation. It turned from a medieval country into a most progressive modern country. This transformation was achieved through the introduction of several reforms. He divided the much shrunken territories of Turkey into 62 *Viloyets* (provinces), which were sub-divided into 430 *Kazas* (districts). Each Kaza was further divided into *Nahiyas*. The purpose of bringing about territorial reorganisation was to increase the efficiency of administration and at the same time hasten the process of centralisation. By 1937, Kemal's ideas and philosophy (titled as six principles of Kemalism) were incorporated into the constitution. These six principles of Kemalism were as follows: 1) Republicanism, 2) Nationalism, 3) Populism, 4) Etatism (constructive intervention of the State in the national economy), 5) Secularism (separation of religion from the State) and 6) Revolutionism (radical departure from the old traditions or precedents).

Work of Consolidation

The national pact of Ankara, the constitution and the six principles of Kemalism gave a new legal and ideological basis to the birth of a new nation. Muslim clergymen who opposed Kemal's far-reaching reforms were persecuted. But some fanatics who came in the way of reforms by fomenting disturbances in the country were summarily executed. The revolts of the Kurdish tribes were crushed, and their leaders executed or banished. The reforms of Kemal Pasha were introduced in two stages: a) those of the 1920s and b) the 1930s. Kemal Pasha realised that the process of modernisation of Turkey was going to be difficult unless he dealt severe blows against the fanatics or the fundamentalists.

Secularisation

Kemal Pasha took radical steps to separate religion from politics. He persuaded the National Assembly to delete Islam as a state religion from the constitution. In response to his desire, the National Assembly unanimously voted for it. He abolished the Sultanate and the Caliphate. He ordered the closure of all Muslim monasteries and institutions. It was followed by the confiscation of their properties. The religious courts, the *Shariat,* were disbanded. The Ministry of Pious Foundation was dissolved. All secret religious sects were outlawed. The mullahs were forbidden from wearing religious robes outside there mosques. In the place of governing the religious matters, he established the Board of Religious Affairs and Pious Foundation as a part of the State Government. The State allowed freedom to practise any religion in 1937 by bringing about an amendment to the constitution.

Westernisation

In tune with a new secularisation policy, the government of Kemal Pasha changed certain rules regarding dress, manners and code of conduct for the citizens. The wearing of fez cap and *kurta pyjama* by the people was

.discouraged, and in its place the government encouraged people to wear Western dresses like trousers, shirts and hats. The government also encouraged European manners and habits among the people. The weekly holiday was changed from Friday to Sunday. The European calendar came into vogue. The Greek names in many places were changed to Turkish names, for example, Constantinople came to be called Istanbul.

New Code of Laws

In accordance with the basic policy of State secularism, Kemal Pasha replaced the old Ottoman code of laws—religious and civil. Along with it went the Millet system. In their place, the government introduced a new code of laws, which was based on the European model. The government adopted the Swiss type of civil code, the Italian model of penal code and the German pattern of criminal code. These codes of laws based on the European pattern, established the equality of all the citizens before the law. Of special importance was the emancipation of women—a very bold step taken by Kemal Pasha in those days. Polygamy, which was in vogue and sanctioned by the *Shariat* was discarded in 1925, and women were eligible to hold public office. The citizens had to take the permission of the government for remarriage. Women could exercise their franchise after an amendment to the constitution passed in 1934. In fact, 13 women deputies were elected to the grand National Assembly in 1935. The state government discouraged the purdah system.

After a visit of a Turkish delegation to a congress in 1926, it was resolved that the Latin alphabet be introduced in the country, since the Arabic script had become outdated. The Turkish Government also explored ways to make the Turkish language more pure, popular and scientific. The Arabic language was replaced by the Turkish language in due course of time. The Turks were encouraged to adopt surnames like the Europeans. The Gregorian calendar which had been in vogue for centuries came to be replaced by the Muslim lunar calendar. The government also introduced the metric system of weights and measures.

Educational Reforms

It is said that the "secret of Kemal's success can be attributed to the strict enforcement of educational reforms". He introduced a modern system of education, which was in tune with the basic policy of secularisation. He eliminated the influence of religion in the educational system. He introduced a liberal and modern educational system so as to make the people understand and appreciate what parliamentary democracy was. He made education compulsory for children aged between 7 and 16. He was eager to ensure that the vocational schools and institutes produced enough graduates to make trade, agriculture, forestry and commerce prosper in the country. With regard to reforming the university system that is higher education, the State had the benefit of the advice of a Swiss professor, Dr Mokhe. A medical college was established in Istanbul which made rapid progress after the induction of a new faculty consisting of twenty foreign professors. The university system produced graduates some of whom became civil servants, diplomats and scientists in the course of time. The secular character of education proved to be very successful. School and college teachers gave moral support to the new educational system introduced by Kemal Pasha. Some of the meritorious teachers received salaries which were better than what was offered to the Europeans. The state also encouraged extra-curricular activities such as sports, games, boy scout movements, gliding and parachuting. Illiteracy in the country was reduced from 95 per cent to 50 per cent during the period of Kemal Pasha.

Planned Economic Development

Kemal Pasha inaugurated planned economic development in the country on modern lines. The State budget was presented to the Assembly, and the balancing of the budget was to be carried out through a progressive system of taxation. The State assumed direct control over several industries in tune with the policy of Etatism. Turkey experienced economic development through plans. The Soviet influence may be seen in the formulation and implementation of economic policies. Naturally, this process called for sacrifices of the Turkish citizens for achieving the long term goals. There was a four-year plan for agriculture, a five-year plan for industry, a three-year plan for mining and a ten-year plan for building infrastructure. The Turkish Government invited foreign experts (Austrian, German, Hungarian and British) for consultation and also to guide the young civil servants in managing various industrial enterprises. During the tenure of Kemal's presidency, agricultural production rose by 57 per cent and industrialisation by 70 per cent.

Financial Reforms

The banking industry – mainly government owned – played an important role in the financial management of the country such as the issue of currency, regulation of credits, promotion of State-owned industrial enterprises, mining and farm production. The Turkish Government sought foreign assistance to support her economic plans and bring about rapid economic development. The modern banks of Turkey provided credit facilities to agriculture, trade, industry, mining and other core sectors of the economy. The Turkish Parliament passed social legislations to mitigate the sufferings of the people caused by rapid industrialisation. The Central Labour Office opened its branches in all towns and cities for the administration of labour laws which were passed in 1935.

Foreign Policy

After the Great War, the Ottoman empire lost its far-flung provinces. She was greatly reduced in size. However, the reduction in her territories did not bring about demoralisation. It was believed that the reduction in the size of the empire was a blessing in disguise. In fact, the Young Turks believed that the nation was going through a process of rejuvenation. They believed that their state would emerge as closely knit, homogeneous and strong. Kemal's foreign policy was tempered with pragmatism and sobriety. These two virtues helped him deal with the problems facing the country, particularly in relation to foreign countries. He was able to build a strong and prosperous nation in due course. The military victories he scored over his enemies gave him confidence particularly while negotiating with foreign countries regarding disputes and problems.

Anglo-Turkish Relations

As for Britain, Turkish relations could not be very smooth and happy. There was growing resentment against the British, because they remained an imperialist power. The Treaty of Lausanne left the issue of oil-rich Mosul open, and Mosul was temporarily occupied by the British troops. Turkish claim over Mosul, a town situated on the south-eastern border with Iraq, forced Britain (the mandate power) to refer the dispute to the League of Nations in 1924. The League of Nations appointed an international commission to go into this dispute. The commission pronounced its verdict in favour of Turkey. But the Council's verdict had no important effect, and finally Britain compromised by ceding a part of oil-rich Mosul to Turkey in return for a promise to let her have 10 per cent of the oil production in Mosul.

The British occupation of Constantinople or Istanbul, her pro-Arab-cum-pro-Greek attitude, the assistance given to the Turkish minorities, and the help rendered to the Kurds in Mosul alienated the sympathies of the Turks for the British Government. In fact, Turkish suspicions about a sinister British plot to undermine her sovereignty and territorial integrity was getting confirmed. Naturally, these factors drove Turkey into the embracing arms of the Soviet Union.

The Turkish-Soviet Agreement

As early as 1921, Kemal's foreign minister Bekir Saini Bey went to Moscow to negotiate a treaty of friendship with the Soviet Union. Both the nations considered themselves revisionist and anti-entente, and therefore, despite differences in political ideology, signed the said agreement. The Soviet Union also sympathised with Turkey's modern aspirations and her anti-imperialist and anti-entente attitude. It helped Moscow to prove that she was on the side of the exploited nations and colonies of Asia.

Relations with Other Countries

Turkey joined the League of Nations on July 18, 1932, and thereby indicated her peaceful intentions. A treaty with Greece, her well-known enemy, marked her desire to thrown in her lot with the Balkan nations. In 1934, she signed the Balkan entente pact, which ensured the independence and sovereignty of Balkan nations. With regard to relations with Italy, Turkey had her own reservations. Italy had always been imperialistic in her ambitions. When Mussolini invaded Abyssinia, Turkey supported the League's economic sanctions against Italy. The stalemate over the straits finally ended in a settlement in favour of Turkey. In 1936, the Montreaux convention modified the provisions of the Lausanne Treaty so as to enable Turkey to fortify the straits regions. In other words, Turkey was able to exercise her military control over this strategic waterway, even though Russia exhibited her anxiety.

As for Turko-German relations, they remained unaffected. Turkey sought the help of German exports and specialists in building her infrastructure. When Hitler came to power in Germany, Turkey's economic ties with that country got further strengthened. In fact, Turkey's foreign trade with Germany showed marked signs of progress, and 50 per cent of Turkish exports went to Germany. The favourable trade with Germany provided great relief to Turkey, which was suffering from the worst effects of economic depression in the early 1930s. Unfortunately, this relationship did not continue when Hitler's Germany and Mussolini's Italy concluded an agreement known as the Rome-Berlin axis. This was because Germany promised to support Italian claims in Northern Africa and ignored the Turkish interests in that region. When Italy invaded Albania, Turkey got ready to join the camp of Britain and France. Hitler sent Franc Von Papen, his ambassador, to Ankara, to strengthen the existing Turko-German relations. He desired to prevent Turkey joining the Anglo-French alliance against Germany. This German ambassador tried his best to persuade Turkey to remain neutral, but failed (1939-41). Kemal Ataturk (Father of the Turks) died in November 1938 at the age of 58. Before his death, he realised his great ambition—to build a strong and prosperous Turkey. He was succeeded by Ismet Inonu, formerly the first prime minister of the Turkish Republic. He was re-elected president twice. When the Second World War broke out in 1939, Turkey declared her neutrality. However, she changed her mind and became an ally of France and Britain. She did not declare war on Germany till February 1945.

Turkish Politics

The Republican People's Party founded by the Ataturk followed the ideals and principles for nearly three decades. However, this party got defeated in the 1950 general election by the newly-formed Democrat Party. This Democrat

Party was formed by the dissidents of the Republican People's Party, namely, Celal Bayir and Adnan Menderes and so on. The Soviet Union under Stalin demanded modification of the Montreaux Straits Convention. This was opposed by Turkey. Turkey became a staunch ally of the United States of America, and joined the NATO as an associate member in 1950. She turned into an anti-Communist country at the instance of the allies, particularly the United States.

Political instability marked the next couple of years in Turkey with the Democrat Party getting split. In the meantime, Turkey witnessed the emergence of a large number of political parties, the most important being the Justice Party. The Justice Party was founded by General Ragip Gumspala. The Democrat Party held the reigns of power by foul and crooked means and added to the political instability of the country. It must be remembered that since the time of Ataturk, the Turkish army had been specially assigned the role of protecting the democracy. Taking advantage of political instability in the country, General Gursel staged a *coup* in May 1960 and executed his former enemies—mostly from the Democrat Party. General Gursel's Government remained a caretaker government till the drafting of a new constitution. The Justice Party came to power in 1965 after two successive coalition governments. After the coalition government fell in 1965, the country came under the leadership of Suleiman Demirel.

Since the time of President Inonu, Turkey received large amounts of military and economic aid from the United States Government. There was great deal of progress in industry and agriculture. However, during the period of political instability the country had suffered much.

Foreign Relations

The relations between Turkey and Arab States were not good since the latter were mainly responsible for the breakup of the Turkish empire. In the meantime, Turkey's alliance with the capitalist countries of the West annoyed many Arab governments. However, it must be said on behalf of Turkey, that she joined the NATO in 1952 to protect her own interests. In 1955, Turkey signed a treaty of friendship with Iraq, which eventually turned into the Baghdad Pact with some more members joining it. After the end of the Baghdad Pact, Turkey joined the CENTO (Central Treaty Organisation) proposed by the United States. Turkey was included among the countries to receive economic aid under the Marshall Plan. Under the influence of the United States, the Turkish Government had to outlaw the Communist Party (*the Truman doctrine*).

However, the relations with the United States were ruffled due to her invasion of Cyprus in 1974. It must be remembered that the island of Cyprus was divided between Greece and Turkey. Both these countries had joined the NATO. In the Greek-held Cyprus, there was a strong nationalist movement known as the Enosis founded by Archbishop Makarios. Greece wanted the whole of Cyprus to come under her control but Turkey was against it. When there were serious disturbances in Cyprus, the NATO had to intervene to prevent a war between the two countries. A temporary truce was concluded between the two, known as the "Davos Spirit," but this did not last long. Since then, Greece adopted a very hostile attitude towards Turkey's entry into the European Union by saying that "unless the Cyprus issue is resolved" Greece will not cast its veto. Turkish relations with Iran, Iraq and Syria were not cordial. Iraq's invasion of Kuwait led to the Gulf War in 1990. Turkey supported the UN sanctions against Iraq. She was angry with Iran because the latter was spreading religious fundamentalism in her educational institutions. Turkey maintained friendly relations with the Arab States in general, and those who were close to the US in particular.

The Last Three Decades

Suleiman Demirel was re-elected in 1969, and within two years political conditions began to worsen. The army kept watch while Demirel resigned. Coalition governments became the order of the day, and Demirel and Bulent Ecevit played musical chairs for power till 1979. Following an economic crisis the Turkish army had to issue a stern warning to politicians to pay attention to national matters instead of squabbling. In November 1982, the draft constitution was ready. Early in 1983, the army lifted the ban on political parties, but it debarred 160 politicians including Ecevit and Demirel from participating in elections. General election was held in 1983, and the Motherland Party won 212 seats, Populists 117, and the Nationalist Democracy Party 71. Thus, the Turkish army maintained law and order, conducted the elections under its supervision, and ensured smooth functioning of democracy. It preserved the values of the Kemalist revolution by keeping at bay "irresponsible politicians, Muslim fundamentalists and political adventurers." The martial law, which was imposed in 1978, was withdrawn in 1984. In November 1983, the Turkish Cypriots residing in the northern part of the Cyprus island, declared their independence, and their Republican State was recognised by Turkey. In February 1991, a limited use of the Kurdish language was permitted by the government. In July 1993, Turkey had elected the first woman Prime Minister, Tansu Ciller. In 1996, the Islamic Party formed a coalition government which tried to give a distinct identity to Turkey as a Muslim State. But the Islamist leader, Erbakan, was replaced by conservative Yilmaz. The Islamist Party was banned in January 1998. Similarly, another important political party, the Welfare Party, was also banned for being anti-secular. A rail link called the 'silk route' became operational in May 1996, and it connected Turkey and China through Central Asia. When the Greek part of Cyprus applied for membership of the

European Union (EU), Turkey prepared a plan to integrate the northern part (Muslim dominated) into its fold. Turkey's application for membership of the EU was rejected in December 1997.

Kurdish Problem

Turkey, Iraq and Iran have Kurds living on their borders, and they have been demanding a separate and independent state. Their movement for a separate state gained ground with the activities of PKK (Kurdish Liberation army), which is funded by overseas Kurds. In February 1999, Turkey apprehended Abdulla Ocalan, the fugitive leader of the Kurdish Workers Party, after an undercover operation. The trial of Ocalan, and the death sentence passed on him, provoked widespread protests against the Turkish Government. The Kurdish rebels in Europe, who consider Abdulla Ocalan as their icon, let loose violence in many European cities. Turkey appealed to the European Union to condemn Greece for its complicity in Ocalan's affair since Greece is its member. In 1998, Turkey's relations with Syria worsened further over the latter's alleged support to Kurdistan's Workers Party for carrying out terrorist strikes inside her territory. Turkey and Syria have quarrelled over the sharing of river waters. Turkey and Israel have established close military ties in recent years, and Jordan is likely to join them. The subtle influence of the US could be seen in this enterprise, and Syria is wary of it.

AKP Government

In November 2002, the Islamic Party of Justice and Development (AKP) led by Recep Tayyip Erdogan (a former Mayor of Istanbul) won an absolute majority of seats in the Parliament and formed the government. It is considered as a unique event since no religious party came to power in Turkey – a secular country – since the rule of Kemal Pasha. More so, as the Turkish army has been assigned the responsibility of keeping the country that way. Turkey's secular credentials has not been affected so far—a factor turning favourable for Turkey's entry into the European Union which though in principle has been accepted yet would take a few more years to be implemented. The second factor that is favouring Turkey's entry into the EU is its 'strategic ties' with Israel.

However, the EU has laid down a few conditions for compliance by the new Turkish Government. They relate to the role of the Turkish army, recognition of the Kurdish language and relations with Greece on Cyprus (Turkey has retained its troops there). More importantly, the EU has asked Turkey to carry out many reforms in the country. If after all this, Turkey succeeds in joining the EU it will be a unique event—a Muslim country in the predominantly Christian populated European Union.

45

THE RISE OF ISRAEL AND THE PALESTINIAN PROBLEM

The modern Israelites claim to be descendants of Hebrews or Jews, who once upon a time led a nomadic life. The ancient Hebrews lived in the Tigris-Euphrates Valley before they left for the "promised land" led by Patriarch Abraham. They settled in Palestine (named after Philistine) around 2200 BC. When a famine broke out in this region, Abraham's grandson, Jacob (also known as Israel), asked his followers to move towards the plains of Ancient Egypt. The Pharaohs of Ancient Egypt treated the Jews like slaves, and employed them to build great pyramids.

The Jews suffered great hardships for a few hundred years at the hands of their Egyptian masters until their Prophet Moses rescued them. Moses led the Jews to the Promised Land, the Palestine, and asked them to abide by the Ten Commandments. The kingdom of Palestine was ruled by wise kings like David and Solomon. Judaism could boast of great Prophets like Amos, Isaiah, Jeremiah, Ezekiel and Isaiah II. Judaism (religion of the Jews) was the first religion advocating the worship of one God. Unfortunately, fate ordained the Jews to suffer throughout history. This was because their land, the kingdom of Palestine, was overrun by the ancient Egyptians, the Chaldeans, the Romans, the Byzantines, the Arabs and the Turks.

The main exodus of the Jews began after the Roman conquest of their homeland. Titus, the Roman emperor, put down their revolt mercilessly and destroyed their temple of Jehovah in Jerusalem. He expelled them from their homeland in AD 70. Most of them fled to many parts of Europe and settled there. Wherever they went they were hated and ill-treated (anti-Semitism) by the natives. This was because the Christians of Europe held the Jews mainly responsible for the crucifixion of Christ and his followers. In fact, Jesus Christ and his Apostles were Jews earlier before they started Christianity. The Jews suffered terrible hardships due to this prejudice in all the Christian countries for hundreds of years. Despite their sufferings, they did not lose the hope that one day they would be united and go back to their homeland.

They contributed substantially to the growth of religion and philosophy. In fact, the Old Testament in the Holy Bible was the creation of the ancient Jews which the Christians revere. There was one more reason why anti-Semitism grew by leaps and bounds in Europe, and this was because the Jews took to the money-lending business. They amassed wealth. The Jewish community in Europe produced great scholars, scientists, financiers, bankers, businessmen, politicians and even movie-makers. Their rise everywhere was due to their intelligence and hard work. The rise of Jews in all walks of life caused extreme jealousy, and subsequently Hitler began to persecute them and ordered their massacre. During the Second World War, millions of Jews were sent to the gas chambers by Nazi Germany. The rest fled to the other parts of Europe to escape persecution, the main exodus being to Palestine. During the days of great distress, they did not lose their faith in God and believed they were God's chosen people.

Rise of Zionism

After the First World War, there was a growing feeling among the Jews that they should go back to their ancient land of Palestine, where they could live with respect and dignity. This feeling was transformed into a movement in Europe called Zionism. During the last decade of the 19th century, and the first two decades of the 20th century, Zionism made rapid strides of progress, thanks to the support of European politicians. The first conference of this movement was held in 1897 in Europe under the dynamic leadership of Theodore Herzl where he proposed to establish an independent Jewish state in Palestine. Subsequently, the Palestine Colonial Trust and the Jewish National Fund were created by Herzl in 1900 to financially assist the homeless Jewish settlers to settle in Palestine. Baron Edmund de Rothschild of Paris helped the Jewish community to purchase lands in Palestine where 50,000 Jewish settlers could be settled.

During the course of the First World War, the British Government encouraged the Arab kings to revolt against their master, the Ottoman Emperor, who was on the side of Germany, by holding out the promise of independence. Accordingly, many Arab kingdoms declared their independence from the Turkish master hoping to secure freedom at the end of the war. But before the war was concluded, Britain and France had come to an understanding (Sykes-Picot agreement) how they should share the spoils after the disintegration of the Ottoman empire. In other words, Britain and France did not cherish the idea of Arab States becoming independent.

The Balfour Declaration (1917)

Coming under the influence of the powerful Jewish lobby, the British Foreign Secretary, Sir Arthur Balfour, declared on November 2, 1917, his support to the cause of creating a Jewish national home in Palestine. One of the most powerful members of the Jewish lobby in Britain was Dr Chaim Weizmann, a Jewish biochemist, who subsequently held an important post in the British Admiralty during the war. As a mark of appreciation for his meritorious services to the British during the war, the British government declared its support to Zionism. The Balfour Declaration was a great step in this direction. The British Government and the politicians were well aware of the fact that they were opening the Pandora's box — the rise of Palestinian problems in West Asia.

Arab Opposition

The Arabs felt betrayed by the Balfour Declaration. They felt that the Jewish home state in the midst of Arab lands had no locus standi. They were of the opinion that this supposed new home of the Jews would create endless feuds with the Arabs and may lead to continuous wars as such. The Arabs strongly protested against British attempts to please the Jews by creating a new homeland for them in Palestine. It amounted to denying freedom to the local Palestinian-Arabs promised during the war.

The Jewish Homeland

In pursuance of the Balfour Declaration, Britain took the following steps to create a homeland for the Jews. Firstly, the establishment of a civil administration under Sir Herbert Samuel, who was appointed the High Commissioner (incidentally he was one of the framers of the Balfour Declaration). All active Zionist members in Britain were appointed as senior officers to create and administer the new state. Secondly, Britain introduced necessary legislation for facilitating the Jewish emigration, and Jewish ownership of land in Palestine.

The British Mandate

During the last year of the war (1917-1918), a Jewish legion under Vladimir Jabotinsky defeated the Turks and occupied the whole of Palestine. The Allied forces' Supreme Council led by Britain declared that Palestine would not be restored to the Ottoman Emperor. The Ottoman empire was broken up after the war and the Arab lands came to be shared by the victors, ie, Britain and France, according to the Sykes-Picot agreement. Instead of granting independence to the Arabs, who had become free from the control of the Ottoman master at the instance of Britain, the Ottoman territories (with the exception of mainland Turkey) came under the Mandate system of the League of Nations. Thus the Arab aspirations of national independence were shattered, and Palestine came under a mandate system in 1920. Under this system Britain was given charge of looking after Palestine.

There was continuous emigration of Jews from Europe to Palestine, and its population increased from roughly 84,000 to 159,000 during a period of five years (1922-27). At the time of the San-Remo Conference (1920), Palestine witnessed the first violent riots when the Jewish immigrants tried to prevent the celebration of a Palestinian religious festival. Riots broke out once again in May 1921. In 1929, the Palestinian resentment against the British was expressed by a riot in front of Al Buraq (the Wailing Wall) in Jerusalem. This revolt caused further violent clashes between the Jewish immigrants and the Arab Palestinians all over Palestine.

Although the Jews suffered much, they put up a brave resistance, thanks to the moral support given by the United States. During the period 1933-39, there were further violent clashes between the Jewish emigrants and the local Arab-Palestinians, specially in the wake of the Nazi persecutions and the fleeing of the Jews. In 1935, the Arab-Palestinian resistance turned into an armed rebellion under the leadership of Izzuddin A-Qassam, and the British military installations became their main target of attack. The Palestinians got united and constituted the Arab Higher Committee to lead the resistance movement against British colonisation.

After the death of Al-Qassam, the Palestinians declared a strike which spread all over the country in April 1936. They demanded total independence. The British Government resorted to repressive methods to control the Palestinian uprisings. Unfortunately, its attempt failed, and Britain appealed to the Arab kings to curb insurgency in Palestine. In the meantime, the British Government appointed a Royal Commission to inquire into the causes of "disturbances". The commission concluded that the Palestinian reaction was the result of British creation of the Jewish homeland in Palestine. It was a logical sequence. Therefore, the commission recommended partition of Palestine between the Arabs and the Jews as a solution to the problem. The British Government accepted the recommendations in July 1937 even though the Arab-Palestinians rejected it. Another revolt broke out against the British, and a clarion call was given for full independence. Thus Britain failed to solve the problem and resorted to repressive methods.

The Jews

The Jews had their own grievances against the British Government. This was related to the restrictions imposed on the availability of lands for occupation, employment opportunities, and checks introduced for further emigration. In 1930, the World Zionist Organisation criticised the British Government for cancelling the emigration permits given to 2000 Jews.

The Arab States formed the Arab League to support the cause of the Palestinian Arabs, and Britain felt that her mandate over Palestine may cause further troubles. Hence she surrendered the mandate to the UN in May 1948 without solving the Palestinian question. Thus "Palestine became a sore spot for conflicting interests of Arab nationalism, Zionism and British Imperialism". After the Second World War, the US emerged as a global power and started interfering in the Palestinian issue. The Palestinian problem became more complicated. The Jewish agency pleaded for a separate state before the United Nations under the leadership of Ben Gurion. The United Nations appointed a special commission on the Palestinian issue.

The Birth of Israel

The UN General Assembly backed the partition of Palestine between the Arabs and the Jews with the moral backing of the Big Powers. Incidentally, there was a call for the creation of the Zionist State of Israel in Palestine. The Jewish leaders in Tel-Aviv proclaimed the birth of Israel on May 15, 1948, and elected Dr Chaim Weizmann as the firs president, and Ben Gurion as the first prime minister. The US and the Soviet Union gave their recognition to this newborn state. The Arab States refused to recognise the birth of Israel and prepared for war. They broadcast to the Arab-Palestinians to leave their homes temporarily so that they could return to their homeland after the defeat of Israel. This resulted in the mass exodus of Arab-Palestinians from their native land, thus creating refugee problem for the neighbours.

The Arab-Israeli Wars

Flouting the will of the United Nations (which created Israel) Egypt, Syria, Lebanon, Trans-Jordan and Iraq launched their attacks on Israel. Israel purchased arms from France and Czechoslovakia and put up a very brave resistance. The Arab States were defeated, and the Palestinians lost their homes and property. So in 1948, Israel was said to have been reborn after a fight with her Arab neighbours. The war ended in armistice agreements between the two belligerents which were arranged by the United Nations. As a result of the war, Israel by virtue of her victory gained 77. 4 per cent of the total land in Palestine instead of 56.4 per cent allotted to the Jewish State by the UN partition-plan.

The agreements established four zones along the armistice line between Israel and the Arab States. The General Assembly of the UN accepted the report of Count Bernadotte, which provided for the return of the refugees who were expelled from their homes, and for compensation to be given to them. Israel rejected the settlement of the refugee problem, and the demarcation of the boundaries created by the partition resolution. Despite her defiance, Israel was admitted to the UN as a member in May 1949 (her first attempt failed in 1948), thanks to the support of the Big Powers.

The Suez War of 1956

Surrounded by the hostile Arab States, Israel adopted an aggressive attitude (as the best form of self-defense), and took advantage of every opportunity to attack her Arab neighbours. When President Gemal Abdel Nasser of Egypt nationalised the Suez Canal Company, the British and the French prepared for war. Israel joined these two States in attacking Egypt—the Suez War of 1956. In this Suez War, Egypt received heavy blows from Britain, France and Israel. Israel occupied the West Bank of Gaza and snatched away some neighbouring territories. In the meantime, the United States Government intervened (she was not consulted earlier by Britain and France) and brought about a truce between the belligerents under the auspices of the United Nations. Had not Israel agreed to sign this truce, the Soviet Union would have intervened on behalf of Egypt. Egyptain President Nasser was deeply humiliated.

The Six Days War (1967)

The hostility between the Arab neighbours and Israel continued for a long time. There broke out another war known as the Six Days War in 1967. Israel shot down more than 500 enemy planes, and roughly 15,000 Arabs were killed in the war. Israel lost only 777 men but conquered 26,476 sq kms of Arab land on the Golan Heights, in Samaria and Judea (West Bank of the river Jordan), in Gaza Strip and in Sinai. Israel snatched away the old city of Jerusalem from Arab control. The Straits of Tiran were opened.

President Nasser's hopes of destroying Israel were dashed to the ground. For the Arabs, the result was horrendous. Thousands of Palestinian refugees lost their homes and properties, and moved towards the neighbouring Arab States. The Arabs suffered a most humiliating defeat, and Israeli Prime Minister Levi Ishkol felt highly elated because his dream came true. Unfortunately, his moderate stand did not please the orthodox Jews. He was succeeded by a school teacher, Mrs Golda Meir, who proved to be a most remarkable statesman. The Mapan (the Labour Party) which controlled the government was fast losing ground by 1969. Subsequently, the coalition cabinets in Israel became the order of the day. Nasser of Egypt died in 1970. He was succeeded by President Anwar Sadat. Israel cut the lifeline of Egypt by blocking the Suez Canal. The loss of income from the Suez Canal seriously undermined the economy of Egypt. However, Egypt was getting ready to fight another war with Israel, with massive assistance from the Soviet Union.

The Yom Kippur War (1973)

The Yom Kippur War broke out between Egypt and Syria on the one side and Israel on the other in October 1973. Both these parties fought fiercely with very grave consequences. There were heavy casualties on both sides, and it looked as though Israel would be defeated. It was at this critical juncture that the United States Government came forward to help Israel with massive support of arms. Instead of facing defeat Israel somehow retrieved her position. The United Nations brought about a cease-fire. On the Syrian front, Israel was highly successful and was about to occupy its capital Damascus. However, the United States Government realised that there would be a threat to Israel from the Soviet Union, and hence arranged for cease-fire immediately. Israel could not repeat her success story this time and therefore Golda Meir had to resign.

Israeli Occupations

The first general election in Israel took place for the Knesset (Parliament) on January 25, 1949, and David Ben Gurion of the Mapai (the Socialist Party) assumed office as prime minister. He was supported by the orthodox Jewish community. Subsequently, Israel passed what is known as the Law of Return, which made every Jew who went to Israel a citizen. On March 10, 1953, Parliament passed what is known as the Land Acquisition Law by which all the lands vacated by the Arabs in Israel became the property of the new occupants. Israel did not pay any compensation to the fleeing Palestinian Arabs who left their homeland. In fact, Israel became the property of the new occupants. Israel did not pay any compensation to the fleeing Palestinian Arabs who left their homeland. In fact, Israel began to advocate a theory by which she claimed that what she conquered from the Arab States belonged to her by right. Therefore, she encouraged the Jewish immigrants from all over Europe and Russia to settle in all the occupied lands such as the Golan Heights, Samaria, the Gaza Strip and so on. She kept Jerusalem under her control, after the defeat of Jordan. She encouraged all the Jews from the United States and the Soviet Union to emigrate and settle in Israel. However, there was poor response from the Jews of these two countries. The Soviet Union did not encourage the Jews in her territory to emigrate for her own reasons.

Progress of Israel

Israel was patronised by the powerful Western nations. They encouraged her to fight the Arab neighbours so as to develop a will to survive. However, when they found it inconvenient because of the Soviet threat, they encouraged Israel to adopt a moderate stand. This was what happened after 1973 Yom Kippur war. The population of Israel increased from 6,50,000 to more than one and a half million by 1958. Through her conquests she added an extra 26,000 sq miles. Israel made rapid strides of progress in agriculture, industry and commerce. She transformed the desert lands into green fields by encouraging Kibbutz (collective cultivation). The Jews who occupied the Arab lands were encouraged to cultivate the lands and produce more food. Israel completed a large number of irrigation projects. Her will to survive in the midst of very hostile neighbours has surprised the whole world. Israel has become a nuclear power in modern times.

The Palestine Liberation Organisation (PLO)

In 1964, the Arab Summit took place at Alexandria, and the outcome was the creation of the Palestine Liberation Organisation (PLO) and the Palestine Liberation Army (PLA). The Arab States attending this summit agreed to finance these organisations. The homeless Palestinian Arabs in the meantime developed a strong feeling called *Fida* (a cause worth dying for) for the redemption of their homeland from Israeli control, and this was to be God's will. The PLO claims to represent and assist the millions of Palestinian Arabs, wherever they are. It is a large body consisting of representatives of many Palestinian groups, the most important being the Al-Fatah. The PLO resembles a government-in-exile. After the 1967 defeat, the PLO was led by Yasser Arafat. The Palestinian Arab refugees and the PLO began to make Jordan their temporary home. But its guerillas annoyed King Hussain of Jordan who expelled them. One of those who was thus expelled was Yasser Arafat, who bore a grudge against the King of Jordan.

Israel's role in the 1973 Yom Kippur war was not impressive, and Prime Minister Golda Meir had to resign in 1974. Yitzhak Rabin succeeded her. The Sinai agreement was reached between Israel and Egypt on September 4, 1975 by which the former ceded lands having some passes and oil-fields in return for oil from Egypt. Israel, however, was bent upon shifting the Israeli settlers in the occupied lands elsewhere. Egypt's treaty with Israel was not liked by the Arab neighbours. Israel started founding Israeli settlements in the West Bank and Gaza, and the Palestinians were treated as second class citizens. Israel refused to accept the establishment of a Palestinian state. The Arab States were equally adamant – they wanted a Palestinian state. In the meantime, Prime Minister Rabin resigned after a no-confidence motion against his government, and in the 1977 general election the Likud Party gained power. The ex-guerilla leader, Menachem Gein formed a coalition cabinet. In contrast to this tough leader, President Sadat of Egypt personified peace and goodwill. In a shocking move for the Arabs, he went to Israel and spoke to the Israeli Parliament about the peace needed in the Middle East and solution to the Palestinian problem.

President Carter's Initiative

While Israel did not respond to Sadat's appeal, it was the turn of President Carter of the US. He went to Israel and addressed the Knesset (Parliament) about the need to come to an agreement. He went to Cairo where he received his secret formula. Then he made both the presidents agree to hold talks. The result was the Camp David Accord.

Camp David Accord (March 26, 1979)

It was signed in Washington. Under the agreement, Israel agreed to withdraw its forces from Sinai and demolish its settlements in phases. On its part Egypt agreed to end its economic boycott of Israel and allowed Israel to purchase oil from Sinai. The question of granting autonomy to the people residing in the West Bank and the Gaza Strip had to be negotiated, and it had to be decided by Israel, Jordan and the Palestinians over a five-year period. Although, the peace accord was not satisfactory from the point of view of the Arabs and the Palestinians, the Camp David Accord may perhaps be described as the first step in the direction of forming the Palestinian state. However, it had to be realised after protracted negotiations spanning a period of over a decade. Israel withdrew from Sinai in April 1982.

President Reagan in his televised address to the nation in September 1982 spoke of the US foreign policy, and as for the Middle East he ruled out the creation of a Palestinian state. In 1983, Israeli Prime Minister Begin stepped down from office, and his place was taken by Shamir. In the July 1984 general election, the Labour and the Likud polled 35.4 and 31.9 per cent votes respectively, and hence a peculiar arrangement in administration followed. Shimon Peres of the Labour was to be the PM for the first half of the term, followed by Shamir of the Likud Party for the next.

Long Peace Process

In August 1993, Israel and the PLO finalised an agreement that would grant limited autonomy for the Palestinians in the Gaza Strip and the West Bank town of Jericho. In September, Israel and the PLO signed a peace treaty regarding the plan for Palestinian self-rule in Washington. The long-drawn peace process was rudely disturbed by the Hebron massacre on February 25, 1994, and the PLO recalled its negotiators in protest. (A Jewish settler killed more than 50 worshippers in a Hebron mosque). It must be remembered that a fortnight earlier both had signed a partial agreement on the details of Palestinian self-rule and Israeli withdrawal from Gaza and Jericho. In March the two parties continued peace negotiations. In early April Israel agreed to the stationing of a 10,000-strong Palestinian police force in Gaza and Jericho. In October, Israel and Jordan signed a peace treaty ending the state of their war for over 46 years. During the next month Israel and the PLO signed an agreement which extended Palestinian self-rule to the West Bank. The Palestinian self-government was set up in Jericho, and Yasser Arafat was sworn in as the Head of State, following the May accord between Arafat and Rabin. In 1995, the Israeli troops evacuated the West Bank town of Bethlehem for Palestinian control. In November, Yitzhak Rabin was assassinated. In January 1996 Arafat became the first elected president of Palestine.

Benjamin Netanyahu

In the June 1996 Israeli elections, the Labour Party was defeated by the rightwing Likud Party led by Benjamin Netanyahu who categorically rejected the proposal for a separate state for the Palestinians, as was done by Shimon Peres earlier on 23rd February. On July 30, 1997, Israel withdrew its delegation which was conducting negotiations with the Palestinian representatives in Washington, following suicide bombings in a Jerusalem market. A long stalemate followed.

Ending of Stalemate

The negotiations between Israel and the PLO continued in Oslo (Norwegian capital). It was there that a time-table was set (deadline) for early settlement of the dispute. It was there that Arafat decided to declare the birth of the independent State of Palestine on May 4, 1999.

The Wye-River Accord

After nine days of haggling, the Peace Accord was signed by the leaders of Israel and the PLO at Wye River Plantation in the State of Maryland (USA) on October 23, 1998. President Clinton, whose popularity declined due to the Monica Lewinsky affair, sought to revive his prestige by getting this accord signed. This was at a time when Netanyahu was "caught between the hawks and doves at home," and Arafat was "eager to retain his popularity". The Peace Accord provided for Israeli troop withdrawal by a further 13 per cent from the West Bank. Under the accord, the Palestinians were to reduce their forces from 40,000 to 20,000 in this region (Oslo accord) and the PLO and other militant organisations were to delete from their charter the demand relating to the elimination of Israel. The Palestinians were also to set up an airport and a seaport at Gaza and so on. Additional troop withdrawal from both sides was to take place when the talks reached a "final status". Benjamin Netanyahu, the right wing politician, had no intention of fulfilling all these terms—all in the direction of creating a new Palestinian State. During his tenure, he scuttled all the peace initiatives. This issue of implementing the accord was pushed to the backburner when Parliament voted for holding new elections.

The people of Israel desired a change in the leadership—as they were fed up with Netanyahu's lacklustre leadership. They favoured Ehud Barak of the Labour Party whose fame rested on the laurels he had won in the army. He was the most decorated army-Chief who had earlier worked as foreign minister during the tenure of Shimon Peres. People talk of his exploits which include a daredevil capture of a Belgian airline plane from the hijackers at the Tel Aviv airport and freeing of the hostages.

West Asia Peace Talks Revive

Yasser Arafat of the PLO and Ehud Barak restarted the peace process (May 4th deadline given by Arafat had been invalidated by the Wye Accord) by signing an agreement on September 5, 1999 at Sharm-El-Sheikh in Egypt which gave a new life to the dead Wye Accord. The signing ceremony was attended by Madeleine Albright (US Secretary of State), Hosni Mubarak (Egyptian President) and King Abdullah of Jordan. On this occasion Ehud Barak, the Israeli PM, said that the Israelis and Palestinians should seize this historic opportunity "to shape a better future". He appealed to the Syrian President to join them to establish peace. The new agreement provides land for security and gives the concerned parties a full year to conclude a peaceful settlement. The new Israeli Parliament approved the agreement, and the understanding is that Palestinians will not declare their state as independent until September 2000. However, the new Israeli president has expressed his wish to implement the agreement in a piecemeal fashion so as to protect the Jewish settlements on the West Bank from being attacked. Israel desires to retain Jerusalem as Israel's capital.

Unfortunately the 1999 peace accord was disrupted with continuing cycle of violence (second Intifada). In the prime ministerial election of 2001 Ehud Barak was defeated by the Likud Party's military leader, Ariel Sharon (bull dozer). Sharon had gained popularity earlier as a hawkish defence minister who carried out the massacres of the Palestinians at the Sabra and Shatila Camps. Today he dreams of 'Greater Israel'. On his assumption to the new office he rejected the earlier decision of ceding territorial concessions to the Palestinians in Jerusalem. He promised his people that he would achieve total security within 'hundred days'.

Ariel Sharon hardened his attitude towards the Palestinians after the commencement of the second intifada, characterised by militant and terrorist attacks inside Israel. The US President Clinton's peace plan was rejected. The Arab League was dejected. The peace accords at Oslo, Wye and Taba were set aside.

However, a new peace plan was floated by the US, Russia and the EU in 2002 with the hope that a final settlement could be achieved in bringing peace to West Asia by 2005. The road map envisages step-by-step building of Palestinian institutions side by side with bringing peace and security to Israel. Israel's list of reservations regarding this peace plan was attended by US. Israel has rejected the idea that Palestinians should have the right to return to their old homes located in Israel.

Israel's Aggressive Moves

With continuing violence, the US considered Yasser Arafat as useless, since he is unable to rein the extremist and militant elements. Israel attacked Arafat's headquarters at Ramallah, but he survived the siege. Hamas, the militant arm of PLO, declared unilateral cease-fire. When Sharon's Likud Party won victory in the Israeli general election after defeating the Labour Party in January 2003, Sharon turned more aggressive.

In August 2003, Israel attacked the strong holds of Hamas in Palestinian territory and killed its leader. The Islamic militant of Jihad quickly declared that the cease-fire ended. Suicide bomb attacks were carried out in Jerusalem and Israel responded by stopping all peace talks and put on hold the "transfer of security responsibility for two West Bank towns to the Palestinians". It ceased all moves to withdraw from Qalquilya and Tericho as proposed by the Peace Plan. The West Bank and the Gaza Strip were sealed off to prevent border-crossing. Israel attacked the militant camps near the Syrian capital Damascus.

This was followed by Israel building a wall (stretching about 350 kms) along the West Bank despite the strong objection of the US. The building of the wall on the Palestinian side of the West Bank will cause great misery to the Palestinians (they lose their farmlands and jobs). Today the Palestinians feel that the construction of the wall would come in the way of establishing their independent state. Recently the World Court ordered the breaking down of the wall, which is approved by the General Assembly of the UN. But Israel is defiant and says that wall would serve the purpose of checking the militants and terrorists from entering Israel.

In Geneva, an unofficial peace accord was approved but Israel is not yet ready to implement it so long as the PLO and other militant organisations perpetrate their atrocities in the Israeli towns and cities. Recently President Bush made it clear to the Palestinians that their suicide attacks and bombings in Israeli territory should stop so as to make the unofficial accord meaningful. In fact the militant Palestinian factions had agreed to this in Cairo earlier in the presence of the Palestinian Prime Minister, Ahmed Qureia. But they were not prepared to stop their attacks on the Jewish settlers and soldiers in Gaza and the West Bank.

In the meanwhile, Syria announced that it was ready for talks with Israel, in response to the latter's invitation. Israel expects Syria to give up its claim on the Golan Heights. Israel carried out the assassination of the Hamas spiritual leader, Sheikh Ahmed Yassin on March 22, 2004 in Gaza City. Hamas, the militant organisation of the Palestinians, elected a new leader, Dr Rantisi, (one of the founders of the Hamas with Gaza City as its base) a die-hard. Dr Rantisi was killed by Israeli missile attack. Who will be the next victim of Israeli attack? Ariel Sharon had declared earlier that Yasser Arafat has to go if a solution has to be found to the Palestinian problem. But now the death of Yasser Arafat leaves the West Asian problem at large with no solution in view. All eyes are on Israel and Palestine to see what turn the West Asian crisis takes.

46

SYRIA AND LEBANON

Syria is a Muslim kingdom situated in the eastern part of the Mediterranean and surrounded by Lebanon and Israel in the west, Iraq in the east, Jordan in the south and Turkey in the north. Long time ago, Syria was the home of a great civilisation. She has a long history originating from the days of the Phoenicians and the Assyrians. The Hyksos originating from Syria were most war like and moved in horse-drawn chariots towards ancient Egypt and conquered it. They ruled Egypt for nearly 200 years. The Assyrians, another warlike community, conquered Syria after the fall of its capital Damascus. The Chaldeans who succeeded the Assyrians extended their authority over Syria under their great King Nobopolassar. Subsequently, Syria was included in the Macedonian empire of Alexander the Great.

Ashoka, the great Mauryan Emperor, sent his missionaries to Syria to propagate Buddhism. In the course of time, Chinese merchants travelled across Syria in order to reach the Roman empire to sell their goods. Mohammed, the Prophet spent most of his time in Syria during his early days. Islam spread to Syria during the time of the first Caliph Abu Bekr (632-634). Muawiyah, who belonged to the Omayyad tribe, became the governor of Syria, and subsequently declared himself Caliph after the death of Ali. He transferred the capital of the Arab empire to Damascus (the present capital of Syria). Syria became a part of the Roman empire during the second century AD. Emperor Justinian lost the kingdom of Syria to Persian Emperor Khusru-I. In the course of time, Damascus became one of the greatest centres of learning under the Arabs.

The Abbasid Caliphate was overthrown by the Seljuk Turks in the 11th century AD. In the course of time, Emperor Saladin, the great crusader, conquered Syria during the twelfth century AD. Eventually, the Ottoman-Turks captured Constantinople in 1453, and overran much of the Arab empire. Thus Syria became a part of the Ottoman empire which disintegrated after the First World War.

Syria Comes under the French Mandate

Soon after the defeat of Turkey in the First World War, Syria came under the mandate system introduced by the League of Nations. France was given charge of both Syria and Lebanon. France carried on the administration of these two countries and tried to improve the welfare of the peoples there. She submitted annual reports to the League of Nations about the progress achieved in these two territories. Unfortunately, the great principles underlying the mandate system came to be flouted by France, and the peoples in these two territories were subjected to much exploitation. But the League of Nations was helpless and the sufferings of the people continued. There broke out a few rebellions and these were suppressed easily.

The Second World War

During the Second World War, France collapsed early in 1940, after the German onslaughts. The victorious Germans set up a friendly Vichy Government in France which co-operated with the Germans in opposing Britain and the United States. The Vichy government allowed Italo-German commissions to operate in Syria. But this was opposed by Britain. In the meantime, Britain supported the Anglo-Free French force which occupied Syria in 1941. General De Gaulle sent his representative, General Catroux, to Syria with a promise that Syria and Lebanon would be made independent after the war. Britain supported this offer with her own guarantee. Before full independence could be granted to these countries, they had to sign the necessary treaties.

Unfortunately, the Free-French Force was unable to fulfil her terms and suspended the constitutions in Syria and Lebanon. However, due to British pressure, the suspended constitutions were restored in 1943. General election was held in Syria and the national government was formed by the National Black led by President Shukri Kuwatly. But the Free-French insisted that the mandate system continue. The newly elected government under Kuwatly opposed the French stand, with the result that there was a tense situation in Syria. It was again the British and the Americans who intervened, and the Free-French declared the end of its mandate over Syria and Lebanon. These two countries became independent in 1944, and the two big powers recognised their independence. In early 1945, Syria declared war on Germany, and after the war became a member of the Arab League. She was admitted as a member of the United Nations, but the French troops continued to occupy her soil. Britain, as a guarantor of the Syrian and Lebanese independence, threatened to take action against the French. In the meantime, Syria and Lebanon appealed to the United Nations for the withdrawal of French troops from their countries. Ultimately, France had to withdraw her troops from these two countries.

The Syrian Army

After Syria's independence, the Baath Party played a major role. It had been in existence during the war and its ideology included the restoration of unity, freedom and socialism. This party's influence transcended the boundaries of

Syria. In spite of the multiplicity of parties playing a major role in Syrian politics, the ultimate authority was that of the army. In other words, the Syrian politics was dominated by the Syrian army.

In fact, many coups were staged by the army to topple the elected governments. In the course of time, Syria was confronted with the problem of the Palestinians created by the birth of Israel. In the wake of Israeli threats to her security, the Syrian President Kuwatly proposed to merge his country with Egypt and form what is known as the United Arab Republic (UAR). Egypt agreed, and the UAR came into existence on November 1, 1958 under President Nasser. Its headquarters was located at Cairo, the Egyptain capital. Unfortunately, serious differences between Syria and Egypt in September 1961 led to their separation.

Arab-Israeli Wars

From 1948, Syria and Lebanon talked about the liquidation of Israel, and started importing arms from the Soviet Union. In the 1948 war, Syria suffered defeat at the hands of Israel, and the Palestinian problem became acute. In the 1967 war, Israel captured the Golan Heights, and the Syrian capital, Damascus, was in danger. The defeat of the Arab States in this war resulted in the large scale exodus of Palestinian Arab refugees. They took shelter in Syria and created problems. In 1969, the Syrian Government led by General Hafiz-al-Assad, brought about a reconstruction of the country after the defeat in the 1967 war. Even though the refugees came in large numbers to Syria, the Syrian Government was able to maintain law and order.

Syria under General Assad made progress in agriculture. Industries came under government control. The government carried out the work on the Tabqa dam across the river Euphrates.

In 1973, Syria adopted a new constitution which introduced a presidential form of government similar to the one in the USA. General Assad became the first president and he ensured the country internal political stability (coups had become the order of the day before 1973). In the 1973 Arab-Israeli war, Egypt was the first to strike at Israel after crossing the Suez Canal. Egypt and the other Arab States could boast of victory. After the Sinai agreement in January 1974, the UN troops came to be stationed at the canal zone. However, tank and artillery duels continued between Syria and Israel even after the truce.

President Nixon of the US visited Damascus in June 1974, but he did not get a warm reception. In the meantime, the Soviet Union offered massive arms assistance to Syria which included the sending of Soviet advisors. With President Sadat coming to power in Egypt, Egypt did not show the same enthusiasm, like the other Arab states, to continue the war with Israel. But Syria did not adopt this attitude. Egypt concluded the Camp David Accord with Israel which was rejected by the Arab States including Syria, and Yasser Arafat of the PLO. In 1981, the SAM missile crisis broke out which brought Israel and Syria on to the verge of war. In the meantime, Israel invaded Lebanon in 1982 with the result that all the Arab States moved their forces into Lebanon. Lebanon with her Christian government faced the worst crisis in her history.

The tragedy of Lebanon was that she was a divided country with warring religious communities (each subdivided into sects), namely, the Christians, the Muslims and the Druzes (hybrid of Muslim-Christian community). These communities started living in separate enclaves for fear of reprisals from the others. The French regarded Lebanon as a non-Arab country in the early days because the non-Arab population, that is the Christians, were in majority. These Christians were Westernised and progressive in the 19th century, and the European powers in those days compelled the Ottoman Emperor to appoint a Christian governor to Lebanon. This Christian governor was to be advised by an administrative council representing different religious communities. The French founded a number of education institutions which co-existed with the age-old Muslim institutions.

Unfortunately, communal harmony did not last long because the Muslims and the Christians had their own quarrels. The Muslims bore a grudge that the Christians had "monopolised economic and political power". The Christians tried to belittle the Arab achievements. The Muslims on the other hand developed hatred towards the Christians because they were more progressive and Westernised. They did not like the Christians to adopt a condescending attitude. Lebanon maintained strict neutrality during the Israeli war of independence in 1948.

Attitude of Israel and Syria

Israel and Syria regarded Lebanon as part of the Biblical Palestine and therefore vied with each other for its occupation. Syria in fact coveted the territories of both Israel and Lebanon so as to build a greater Syria. Lebanon was afraid that her territories may be taken over by the United Arab Republic (Union of Egypt and Syria). However, this Union broke up within a few years and the Lebanese-Christians heaved a sigh of relief. Even in the Suez war of 1957, Lebanon remained neutral. The Christians were afraid of the influx of Palestinian refugees after the war, because it would upset their numerical superiority in the country. After the presidency of Chamoun ended, the next two presidents were Chares Hilu (1964-70), and Suleiman Franjieh (1970-76), who succeeded one after the other. The Palestinian problem continued to tax their energies and there was no quick solution to this problem.

The Palestinians who were settled in Lebanon began to attack Israeli positions from their bases in Southern Lebanon. Naturally, Israel was indignant and retaliated aggressively. The status of the Palestinian refugees in Lebanon had been decided by the Cairo agreement in 1969, and some of the terms were kept secret by President Nasser and the Chairman of the PLO, Yasser Arafat. Thus, these secret terms compromised the state sovereignty of Lebanon. The Christians were unhappy when Israel attacked the Palestinian secret bases in her territory.

In the course of time, Lebanon faced a civil war, with numerous factions including the Arab Palestinians carrying on their war of attrition in her territory. Because of the prospect of a civil war looming large in the seventies, the Lebanese community split up into Christian, Muslim, Druze and pro-Syrian fronts, each with its own factions. The Lebanese front was a coalition of Christian factions headed by Kata'ib, a party of Maronite-Phalangists led by Gemayel family. As against this, there was a national movement (also known as FPPNP) formed by the various Muslim and Druze groups in Lebanon. There was a pro-Syrian faction which was aligned with the national movement. Among the Palestinian Arabs settled in Lebanon, there were two main groups, namely, the PLO led by Yasser Arafat and the Popular Front for the Liberation of Palestine (PFLP) led by George Habash.

In the old constitutional set-up (1926), the president was given unlimited powers, and by 1976 President Franjieh had to slightly amend the constitution so as to provide equal representation to the Muslims, that is 6:6 (instead of 6:5). Israel took full advantage of the factional fights going on in Lebanon and the subsequent weakening of the Lebanese Government under President Franjieh and Prime Minister Rashid Karami. Israel encouraged and supported the Right Phalangists (Christians) to fight the Palestinians and the Muslims who were supported by Syria and other Muslim powers. The situation became complicated in the on-going civil war in Lebanon because of other Muslim countries joining the fray. The whole country suffered immensely due to terrorism, violence and bloodshed. The situation reached a climax when Syria occupied the Bekar Valley, and thereafter occupied the whole of Lebanon except the border areas with Israel in 1976. Unfortunately, Syria could not control the factious fights in Lebanon in spite of her best efforts. In the meantime, the leader of the Progressive Socialist Party, Kemal Jumblatt, a stout opponent of Syria, was assassinated in 1977. The Muslims and Christians in Lebanon attacked each other and the Syrian troops could not contain the resultant bloodshed.

Taking advantage of this situation, Israel which was sympathetic towards the Christians in Lebanon raided the southern borders of Lebanon from where the Palestinian guerillas had been operating. The internal conflicts in Lebanon plus the war with Israel continued. Unfortunately, the Arab League had no plan to settle the Palestinian refugees who had taken shelter in Lebanon. The Israeli-Syrian war gradually extended to Iraq. In June 1981, the Israeli planes destroyed Iraq's nuclear plant which was capable of producing atomic weapons. This extension of war with Iraq was undoubtedly a violation of Iraq's sovereignty. However, Israel defended her position saying that she had not signed any peace treaty with Iraq earlier. The situation got further complicated when the Israeli ambassador in London was shot dead by a Palestinian terrorist. Israel retaliated immediately by invading Lebanon, and the UN condemned this invasion. The United States and the Soviet Union who had remained helpless for long intervened to contain the situation. Israeli forces were asked to withdraw by the United Nations.

In 1985, President Assad was re-elected for another seven-year term. There was a tussle between President Assad and Iraqi leader Saddam Hussein for the control of the Baath Socialist Party. Syria helped the rebel faction of the Palestinian organisation to overthrow Yasser Arafat from the leadership of the PLO. It must be remembered that Syria was assured of oil supply from Iran at a low price for her support in the Iran-Iraq war (1980-88). Rivalry with Saddam Hussein forced Assad to shut down Iraq's oil pipeline running through his country. Syria took active part in the on-going Arab-Israeli conflict and allegedly encouraged terrorism. This situation led to Britain breaking off diplomatic relations with Syria. Syria was further found to be training and equipping Palestinian guerilla groups to continue their subversive activities in some parts of Europe (example, West Berlin incident).

Peace in Lebanon?

In 1982, Israel invaded Lebanon, and the United Nations intervened in the dispute. In May 1983, Lebanon agreed to remove all foreign troops from her soil, but Syria opposed this move. Kidnapping of foreign nationals and terrorist bombings by Islamic militants became common. In October 1990, Elias Hrawi, a consensus candidate of all the Arab powers, became president of Lebanon with the support of the Syrian-backed militia. This was after the defeat of the Christian army led by General Michel Aoun. In the continuing civil war in Lebanon, nearly 1,25,000 persons were killed. It was in 1991 that Syria signed a treaty with Lebanon thereby recognising it as a separate and independent State. It is time that Maronite Christians and the Sunni Muslims in Lebanon (42 and 57 per cent of the population) buried the hatchet and shared power in an amicable manner to run the administration.

Israeli-Syria Peace Talks (2000)

Both Syria and Israel should stop interfering in the affairs of Lebanon (both claim Lebanon as a part of their kingdom). It is heartening to note that Israel and Syria are burying the hatchet through the efforts of President Clinton, with the former agreeing to give up a part of the Golan Heights.

When the war was launched against Iraq by the US-led coalition forces in 2003, Syria was in an awkward position, since it was ruled by the Baathist Party – the same party that was ruling Iraq. Though there was no love lost between Syria and Iraq ever since Saddam Hussein came to power. In fact, Syria broke off her relations with Iraq, and in the aftermath of 9/11, she provided information to the US Government regarding the terrorist outfits and their activities in its region.

Syria-US Relations

However, the US was not at all satisfied on two counts. Firstly the US during the Iraqi war, believed that Syria was helping the Saddam-loyalists in their resistance against the occupation of US-led coalition forces and also giving shelter to those who fled Iraq. Secondly, Syria was patronising the militant outfits like the Hamas who have been seriously threatening Israel's security. The US had applied sanctions on Syria since the ruling Baathist Party championed the cause of 'Pan Arab' nationalism and anti-imperialism. Syria looked upon the US as ungrateful country as she had backed the US-led forces in the first Gulf War against Saddam Hussein. Syria expects the US to remain aloof from Israel and ensure that the latter return to her the Golan Heights (land captured in 1967 war by Israel). Israel had agreed to this four years ago (2000) but is yet to keep its word. Moreover, Israel's airforce attacked certain Syrian targets near Damascus saying that there were training camps being run by the Palestinian militants. Syria has not responded to this attack militarily (Syria and Israel had signed cease-fire agreement twenty years ago), but expects friendly nations like Britain and India to persuade Israel to remain peaceful and return the Golan Heights to her.

Militant Sunni groups in Syria have vowed vengeance against Israel. They want Israel to be destroyed. The Israeli-occupied Golan Heights consists mainly of Druze who are loyal to Syria.

Syria cannot afford to have confrontationist approach towards Israel, since its economy is ailing with high unemployment rate, inflation and paucity of foreign capital. The US imposed sanctions recently and accused Syria of supporting the Palestinian militants, and secretly obtaining nuclear, biological and chemical weapons.

47

HASHEMITE KINGDOM OF JORDAN

After the disintegration of the Ottoman empire following the Great War, many Arab States came under the mandate system. One of them was Trans-Jordan. The League of Nations created three categories of mandates (A, B, C) and Trans-Jordan was placed in A category and brought under the control of Britain. The Kingdom of Jordan was founded by Ameer Abdulla in 1920 after liberating its capital Damascus from the French. The British Government allowed him to occupy Trans-Jordan (part of Palestine), and in 1923, got it separated from Palestine under Article 25 of the League of Nations. Britain created Jordan out of the area which was situated on the east of the river Jordan. It included territories taken from the northern half of Turkey and the kingdom of Hejaz.

The British established their rapport with Ameer Abdulla and saw to it that he provided a stable government. In 1929, Ameer Abdulla introduced consultative government. The British signed a treaty in 1938 assuring their friendship and participated in bringing about the efficiency of his administration. It must be noted that Trans-Jordan provided a strategic link which enabled the British to move their troops from the east to the west (from Iraqi ports to the Suez Canal) during the Second World War. Jordan was the only country where the British were always welcome. Britain revised her treaty with Trans-Jordan in 1946 after ending her mandate.

Thereafter, Trans-Jordan came to be called Hashemite Kingdom of Jordan. In 1948, Britain started giving large subsidy to her as a mark of friendship. King Abdulla dreamed of uniting the Arab States and hoped to find a solution to the burning problem created by the Palestinian Arabs. He was a very wise king. His proposal for the future of Palestine was rejected by Israel and also by the Arab States. So when the Arab-Israeli was broke out Jordan occupied the West Bank and the old city of Jerusalem. He concluded an armistice with Israel after the war, and the Jordanian Parliament declared him king of Palestinians. His position was recognized by a number of nations except the Arab States. The Arab States were not happy about his new designation and instead, they recognised all Palestine governments established at Gaza.

Unfortunately, Abdulla became unpopular in the Arab States, and in July 1951 was assassinated by a fanatic.

His son Hussein succeeded to the throne. The new Parliament in Jordan approved of the annexation of Arab Palestine, the West Bank and the old city of Jerusalem into Jordan. The new king tried to make his country a modern state. As he was English-educated, he was exposed to liberal reforms. He refused to let his country join the Baghdad Pact, which was mooted by the United States Government. Britain refused the annual subsidy to Jordan to show her resentment. He opposed Parliament when it urged the unification of Jordan with Egypt and Syria. Instead he formed the Hashemite federation by joining hands with Iraq which unfortunately proved to be short-lived (note that King Feisal I of Iraq was the brother of King Ameer Abdulla).

Jordan made considerable progress, despite a major part of the country being a desert. The first state university was founded in 1962. The Jordanian king and the PLO leader Yasser Arafat were not on good terms because the latter was expelled. Since Yasser Arafat considered the monarchical government of Jordan reactionary he tried to overthrow it. During the 1967 war with Israel, Jordan lost the West Bank and a part of Jerusalem. This terrible war left many Palestinians homeless, and they poured into Jordan. The king was gracious enough to grant citizenship rights to many of them.

In the 1973 war with Israel, Jordan could not recover the West Bank and a part of Jerusalem. Subsequently, Jordan gave up its claim to the West Bank, and recognised Yasser Arafat as the true representative of the PLO. In 1977, the king's third wife met with an accident, and he remarried an American citizen in May 1978. The United States Government studied the grave situation prevailing in the Middle East in 1982, and revised its policy of giving unlimited support to Israel. The US Government began to talk of Palestinian autonomy in the West Bank and Gaza with undivided Jerusalem under Israel's control. King Hussein in the meantime recalled Parliament (1983-1984) and suggested a review of Jordan's relations with Egypt. He also invited Gasser Alright for negotiations regarding the future of Palestinian refugees.

King Hussein of Jordan lent his support to Iraq during the Iran-Iraq wars (1980-88). However, when the Gulf War broke out in 1991, Jordan remained neutral. Tens and thousands of Palestinian refugees started arriving in Jordan after Iraq occupied Kuwait. Jordan's economy was in peril. In 1994 Jordan and Israel signed a peace treaty and the Israeli troops withdrew from the Arava Valley in 1995. In a joint declaration at Washington, both the countries ended their 46 years of hostility. King Hussein wanted the Arabs and the Jews to live in peace and good neighbourliness. The West and Israeli leaders regarded him as a great statesman and visionary. He died of cancer in 1999. His funeral was attended by great world leaders, a testimony to his greatness.

King Abdullah

Before his accession to the Jordanian throne, many considered Abdullah as a playboy. However, after his accession he took the job seriously. He is at present trying to establish cordial relations with Syria and Saudi Arabia on the one hand and with London and Washington on the other. In recent years the Jordanian economy has worsened with the unemployment figure touching 27 per cent. The Arab States do not want Amman (Jordanian capital) to lean heavily on the West for aid, but help to promote Arab solidarity in the face of Israeli threats. The United States Government is doing its best to provide security and well-being of Jordan, through military and financial assistance. King Abdullah has made it clear to the West that he would not compromise on the rights of the Jordanians. But he has spurned the offer of the Palestinian leader, Yasser Arafat, for forging a confederation between Jordan and the would-be Palestinian state. One should note that two-thirds of the Jordanian population comprises Palestinians. They created problems for the late King Hussein. One should note that the bread-riots in 1996 shook the country. Jordan is heavily dependent on foreign loans since its economy has been ailing due to recession for the past few years.

Hamas

Ever since the day of his accession, King Abdullah has laid stress on maintaining "national unity and equality: code words for fairer treatment of Jordan's Palestinian majority". It was Hamas (an extremist faction of the PLO) which played a very troublesome role in Jordanian politics, and the new king went hammer and tongs to suppress it. Hamas also played its politics to prevent peace process with Israel. The king closed its offices in Amman. This may be considered the boldest and a new factor in Jordanian politics. The biggest political party in Jordan is the Islamic Action Front which acts as the political arm of the Muslim Brotherhood. King Abdullah's wife is Rania who is a Palestinian, and the Palestinian party has gained a few seats in the Jordanian Parliament.

In 2000, the new Jordanian king expressed his wish, that Jerusalem – a bone of contention between the Palestinians and Israelis – be declared the capital of both Israel and Palestine, in view of the formation of the new state of Palestine in 2005. There are others who believe that Jerusalem be declared as the world's capital.

Jordan maintained friendly relations with Iraq (during Saddam's rule) for the latter supplied oil. The Jordanian king encouraged partnership between

Jordanian and Iraqi businessmen. Again Jordan maintained friendly relations with the US since exports to that country touched nearly $231 million recently from $7 million in 1996. The Jordanian monarchy enjoys good reputation in the US, and after the deposition of Saddam Hussein of Iraq, it expects US patronage in terms of trade and influence in that country.

48

SAUDI ARABIA

The original inhabitants of Arabia were the camel breeding Bedouins. They moved across the sandy deserts on camels, and a majority of them carried on trade. Arabia produced date-palm in plenty and contained a number of oases in the deserts which provided water. The Bedouins spoke Arabic. Therefore, they were known as Arabs. They belonged to several tribes, each worshipping an idol. They carried these idols to the temple of Kaaba at Mecca during the annual festival. These warring tribes observed truce during this holy month. After observing the religious festivities, they carried back their idols to their villages.

Into this world of warring tribes was born Mohammed. He founded Islam which became a popular religion in Arabia. He built an Islamic kingdom during his lifetime. His successors were known as the Caliphs who turned the Arab kingdom into an empire for the purpose of spreading Islam. The Arab empire under the Caliphs conquered some parts of Europe, northern parts of Africa, and a major part of Asia. In the course of time, the Ottoman Turks inherited this vast empire after the capture of Constantinople in 1453. During the course of the Great War, Britain encouraged the Arabs to revolt against their Turkish master. Britain agreed to support the cause of their unity and independence with monetary incentives (subsidies) and chose Lawrence as their agent to support the Arabs.

The British pledge of support was contained in the famous correspondence (October 1915) between Sheriff Hussein of Mecca and Hedjaz and the British High Commissioner, Sir Henry McMahon. The former was planning to drive the Turks out of Arabia in 1916 and free the "Arab Race from the Persian Gulf to Mosul, from the Red Sea to Beirut and Damascus". The British appointed the two sons of Sheriff Hussein, Prince Abdullah and Prince Feisal as the rulers of Trans-Jordan and Iraq respectively.

Sheriff Hussein was a descendant of the Prophet who eagerly hoped to revive the Caliphate centering in Mecca with himself as the Caliph in 1924 (ie after Mustafa Kemal Pasha had abolished the Caliphate in the modern State of Turkey). Unfortunately, the British pledge to the cause of Arab independence was totally modified by the Sykes-Picot agreement of 1916 which provided for the establishment of the spheres of British and French influence over the supposed independent Arab States. This agreement came as a great setback to the Arab rulers. However, what made them angry was the declaration of Lord Balfour in November 1917 about the creation of "A National home for the Jewish people" in Palestine. The British sensed the anger of the Arab States and tried to pacify them after the statement at the San Remo Conference in 1920. This statement mentioned that the Straits in the Arabian peninsula would be granted independence, but those adjacent to the Mediterranean would become mandated territories.

Ibn Saud of Saudi Arabia

The dream of Sheriff Hussein to succeed to the Caliphate was shattered by the rise of Ibn Saud, the head of the ultra-conservative and puritanical Wahabis of Nazd. This king helped the Allies against Turkey during the war. He captured Hasa from the Turks thereby extending the border of his small kingdom to the Persian Gulf. Unfortunately, he was not given due recognition by the Allies at the time of the Paris Peace settlement (1919). However, Ibn Saud started expanding his dominions by encroaching upon the territories of his neighbours. He defeated and expelled Sheriff Hussein and declared himself King of Hedjaz and Nedj.

Ibn Saud's next move was to drive out Ibn Rashid of Jebl Shemmar and he was quite successful in this mission. Another important task which was carried out was the suppression of the rebellion of puritanical extremists led by one Faysal Ud Dawish. The country of Ibn Saud was surrounded by the British and French military bases in the Middle East, and he had no strength to challenge these two countries. It must be admitted that Britain also realised that she should remain friendly with this powerful ruler to promote her own interests in the Middle East.

Foreign Relations

King Ibn Saud continued to consolidate his power by suppressing the rebellions of many tribesmen living in the north. Subsequently, Saudi Arabia was at war with Yemen which was under the control of an Imam. It resulted in the defeat of the Imam and the conclusion of a peace treaty called "A treaty of Islamic Friendship and Arab Brotherhood". After this war, Ibn Saud of Saudi Arabia entered into a commercial agreement with the State of Bahrain. It was followed by his visit to Kuwait to improve Saudi-Kuwaiti relationships which had been strained due to trade conflicts. Saudi Arabia signed a treaty with Iraq known as Arab Brotherhood and alliance. Subsequently, Egypt also signed a friendship treaty with Saudi Arabia.

However, Ibn Saud's leadership of all the Arabs remained unacknowledged by Amir Abdullah of Trans-Jordan, son of Sheriff Hussein of Mecca. It must be remembered that Ibn Saud had driven the family of Sheriff Hussein out of Hejaz in 1925. The strained relations between the two ceased after the conclusion of a treaty of friendship in 1933. Thus Ibn Saud of Saudi Arabia had made his country the leader of Arab nationalism and brotherhood. A couple of years later, the Second World War began and the Arab countries did not show any enthusiasm in participating in it on the side of the Allies.

Of the many great achievements Ibn Saud had to his credit, the most important was his ability to bring about the unity of his country and the people. He infused the discipline of Wahabism upon his subjects and maintained law and order in the country. He has been described as the maker of modern Saudi Arabia. As oil was discovered in his country in 1938, the imperialist powers including the United States were eager to have good relations with Ibn Saud. At the time of his death (1953), Saudi Arabia was recognised by the Western nations as the most powerful country in the Middle East. During the Second World World War, the whole of the Arab world was occupied by the Allies except Saudi Arabia.

Oil Exploration and Refining

The main source of revenue of the Saudi Government came form oil exports to the United States and other Western countries. It was estimated that half of the total revenue of Saudi Arabia came from oil revenues, and it must be remembered that Saudi Arabia is the largest exporter of oil in the world today. The other sources of revenue of Saudi Arabia was derived from the pilgrim tax. This tax is imposed on foreign Muslim pilgrims arriving at Mecca every year during the time of *Haj*. Saudi Arabia's petro-dollars began to increase after the 1973 oil crisis. The OPEC countries increased the price of oil in 1973 as a bargaining point with the Western nations mainly because the latter were supporting Israel in her aggressive attitude. As a result almost all the countries of the world were very seriously affected. Saudi Arabia has been investing these petro-dollars in many banks and companies in the US and European countries. It is a pity that with such vast resources to her credit, the common people in Saudi Arabia are unable to make both ends meet.

Saud Ibn Abdul Aziz (1962-69)

After the death of King Ibn Saud, the second son named Saud Ibn Abdul Aziz succeeded to the Saudi kingdom. He governed his kingdom from 1953-64. Unfortunately, this king proved to be easy-going and did not show his ability to govern the country wisely. He was guided by a council composed of the members of the royal family. Taking advantage of the weakness of the administration, financial speculators began to play havoc. Although there was no love lost between the king and, his brother, Prince Feisal, the latter was able to become the prime minister of the country with the support of many members of the royal family. It must be remembered that Saudi Arabia has no constitution as such, and is guided by Koranic principles and the Shariat. Prince Feisal was able to reorganise the government on the basis of monarchical powers and prerogatives. His administrative reforms included a check on corruption and abuse which had crept into the administration. Unfortunately, the king did not agree with this radical step, and therefore ordered for the reversion of the reform process. He tried to get rid of Prince Feisal but failed. The royal advisory council backed the prince in his fight against the king. After a palace coup King Saud Ibn Abdul Aziz was deposed in 1964.

King Feisal (1964-75)

After assuming power, King Feisal was confronted with many challenging problems. It was a time when in the Middle East, countries looked upon President Nasser in Egypt as the hero who would redeem his pledge to exterminate Israel and free the Arab World. King Feisal was not an admirer of President Nasser, although his predecessor was. It was this situation that brought about a conflict between him and President Nasser of Egypt. In the Yemeni civil war (1962), Saudi Arabia and Egypt took opposite sides.

During the 1967 Arab-Israeli war, Egypt and her allies faced humiliating defeat. Saudi Arabia had remained neutral and therefore was not affected. Looking at this gloomy situation the Arab world was facing, Saudi Arabia extended liberal financial assistance to Egypt to make up for the losses suffered as a result of closing the Suez Canal. The hostility which had existed between Egypt and Saudi Arabia over the Yemeni civil war also subsided. The oil producing Arab countries threatened Israel's Western supporters with oil embargo if they continued to support Israel in her aggressive activities. Saudi Arabia gave liberal aid to Jordan, which had given shelter to a large number of Palestinian-Arabs during the 1967 war.

The OPEC and Trucial Sheikhdoms

The Organisation of Petroleum Exporting Countries (OPEC) was established with 13 members, out of which seven were Arab States. The OPEC has played an important role with Saudi Arabia as its leader in fixing the oil prices meant for export to other countries. As mentioned earlier, the oil producing countries of the Middle East used oil as a weapon to improve their bargaining power with the rest of the world. Unfortunately, the hike in the oil prices in 1973 affected the developing and the underdeveloped countries to a large extent. Saudi Arabia had minor disputes with the Trucial Sheikhdoms, particularly Oman, Bahrain and the UAE which became free in the 60s and 70s. Iran and Saudi Arabia did not remain on friendly terms because the former desired to control the passage between the Persian Gulf. Saudi Arabia was angry when Iran annexed a few islands in the Persian Gulf. King Feisal was a "conservative, cautious and colourful ruler." He was assassinated by his nephew (who was mentally depressed) on March 30, 1975. The assassin was executed, and King Khaled succeeded to the throne. Since Saudi Arabia is powerful and rich, she has been able to influence to some extent the foreign policy of the United States Government. King Khaled died in 1982, and was succeeded to the throne by his half-brother, Crown Prince Fahd, who had earlier acted as the country's foreign minister.

Britain dominated the entire Persian Gulf between the two seas after the Soviet withdrawal from Iran. When she withdrew from Iran, she kept her control over the oil fields. Again, small principalities like Kuwait, Qatar, the Trucial States and Bahrain had come under direct and indirect control during the time of the British. These kingdoms had become important because of the discovery cf oil. Bahrain became a very important centre because it had a British naval base. Oil was discovered in Kuwait in 1938. She had become a British protectorate by the 1899 treaty. She achieved independence in 1961. Bahrain became independent in August 1971, so also Qatar. The Trucial States included Abu Dhabi, Sharjah Dubai, all of which produced oil. In the course of time, seven of these oil producing principalities formed an autonomous union called the United Arab Emirates with its capital at Abu Dhabi. Dubai became the main port with a busy international airport. The economy of the Emirates depends mainly on oil. However, during recent years trade and international banking have assumed great importance.

After hiking the oil prices, Saudi Arabia (the major oil producer) became one of the wealthiest countries in the world. This country with 6,000 princes was known for lavish spending, notwithstanding the import of modern weapons and air force jets from the number one arms producer — the US. All the petro-dollars were deposited in American banks. Saudi Arabia has spent huge sums of money for building mosques all over the world, and stood as a great champion for the cause of Islam. The holy places of Mecca and Medina attract millions of pilgrims from all over the world every year.

King Fahd

King Fahd's worries grew with the Gulf War. Saudi Arabia had to take the lead in saving Kuwait from the clutches of Iraq's Saddam Hussein, and this involved allowing the troops of the US and her allies to occupy her soil till the war was over. The war was won but it sullied the image of the king to a great extent. He was accused of dividing the Muslim world by setting one Muslim nation against the other.

Another anxiety is about Iran's *mullahs* (Iran follows the Shia faith) who are found to be exporting their revolution to other countries. Thus, the danger to Saudi Arabia is lurking closeby. Old family quarrels kept Jordan away from

Saudi Arabia's influence. A border dispute with Yemen has caused some moments of anxiety, and riots of angry Muslims in Bahrain have sent "shivers down royal spines." Dissidence is growing among the Islamic countries (Algeria, Morocco, Egypt, and Bahrain) because of increasing poverty and growing religious fundamentalism. Saudi Arabia is no exception. The wealth has not percolated to the masses. It is common knowledge that the king's American friends are preaching the necessity of pruning lavish expenditure (budget cuts and reduction of fiscal deficits) on the one hand and encouraging him to buy expensive goods and weapons from them on the other. The Saudi kings never tolerated dissidence or public criticism. The Shias in the country feel estranged in a Sunni majority country. The Saudi Government has imposed strict censorship on radio, press and TV. Foreigners have to conform to certain Islamic injunctions regarding dress and manners. There are at present more than 5 million foreign workers in Saudi Arabia. In April 1997 and April 1998 there was a fire at Mecca (350 killed) and a stampede at Medina (118 died) respectively.

Saudi-US Relations

The holy land of the Muslims has been in the eye of the storm since the September 11 attacks on the World Trade Centre and the Pentagon (New York and Washington DC respectively). The reason being that fifteen of the nineteen terrorists involved in the heinous crime were Saudis. The mastermind behind this attack (as in the earlier attacks on the US embassies in Kenya and Dar-e-Salam) is the Saudi millionaire, Osama bin Laden, the leader of Al-Qaeda. Osama hated the Americans for he believed that their forces used the sacred land to fight another Muslim country (Iraq), and supported the Saudi royal family in its authoritarian rule. He considers America as a devil, out to destroy Islam with its crass materialism, corruption, and moral degradation. America's support to Israel against Palestinians is another reason. Many militant jihadi outfits all over the world have been inspired by the Al-Qaeda, and some of them are affiliated to it.

The US-Saudi relations, since the 9/11 attacks, have undergone dramatic change. The US believes that the members of the Saudi royal family is involved in funding dubious charitable organisations which have promoted Al-Qaeda's interests. The withdrawal of the US troops from Saudi Arabia was the direct outcome of the worsening relations. However, the Saudi royal family is doing its best to allay the apprehensions of the US by its vigorous crackdown of terrorist outfits in recent years. The destruction of the oil installations at Al Khobar by the terrorists has caused much concern among the countries importing crude oil from Saudi Arabia. Today Saudi Arabia is concerned about the security of its oil installations and pipelines.

SELECT BIBLIOGRAPHY

Cressey, G B

Asia's Lands and Peoples, New York: McGraw Hill, 1963

Edwards, Michael

Asia in the European Age, Bombay: Asia Publishing House, 1961

Kennedy, J

Asian Nationalism in the Twentieth Century, London: Macmillan, 1968

Panikkar, K M

Asia and Western Dominance. London: George Allen and Unwin, 1967

Thomson, Ian

The Rise of Modern Asia, London: John Murray Ltd., 1957

EAST ASIA

Clyde, PH and B F Beers

The Far East, New York: Prentice Hall, 1966

Fairbank, Reischauer and Craig

East Asia Transition and Transformation, Boston: Houghton Mifflin, 1973

Gupta, R. S

History of Modern China, New Delhi: Sterling Publishers Pvt. Ltd., 1981

Latourette, K S

A Short History of the Far East, Rev. Edn. New York: Macmillan, 1964

Michael, F H and G T Taylor

The Far East in the Modern World, New York: Holt Rainehart and Winston, 1956

Vinacke, Harold M

The History of the Far East in Modern Times, New York: Alfed A Knopf, 1987

SOUTHEAST ASIA

Bastin, J and H J Benda	*A History of Modern Southeast Asia. Colonialism, Nationalism and Decolonisation,* New Jersey: Prentice Hall, 1968
Beri, K K	*History and Culture of South East Asia: (Ancient and Medieval),* New Delhi: Sterling Publishers, 1994
Beri, K K	*History and Culture of South East Asia (Modern),* New Delhi: Sterling Publishers, 1994
Buchanan, Keith	*The Southeast Asian World: An Introductory Essay,* London: George Black and Sons, 1967
Buss, Claud A	*Southeast Asia and World Today,* Princeton, NJ: Van Nostrand, 1958
Cady, Joh F	*Southeast Asia. Its Historical Development,* New York: McGraw Hill TMH. Edn, 1976
Hall, D G E	*A History of Southeast Asia,* London: Macmillan, 1986
Harrison, Brian	*Southeast Asia: A Short History,* London: Macmillan, 1960
Tarling, Nicholas (Edited by)	*The Cambridge Histroy of South East Asia. Vol I & II,* Cambridge: Cambridge Unviersity Press, 1993

SOUTH ASIA (INCLUDING CENTRAL)

Avery, Peter	*Modern Iran,* New York: Frederick A Praegar, 1965
Bernard, Lewis	*Arabs in History,* New York: Hutchinson's Universal Library, 1966

Bernard, Lewis   The Emergence of Modern Turkey, New
                                  York: Oxford University Press, 1961

Bernard, Lewis   The Middle East and the West, London:
                                  Weidenfield & Nicholson, 1964

Bose, Sugata and Ayesha Jala   Modern South Asia: History, Culture and
                                  Political Economy, Delhi: Oxford
                                  University Press, 1998

Chandra Richard de Silva   Sri Lanka, A History, New Delhi: Vikas
                                  Publishing House (P) Ltd., 1992

Dharmakumar (Edited by)   The Cambridge Economic History of
                                  India, Vol. 2. Delhi: Orient Longman,
                                  1984.

Dodd C H and M E Sales   Israel and the Arab World, London:
                                  Routledge, 1970

Fiddur, Robin   Syria and Lebanon, London: John Murray,
                                  1965

Frazer-Tydler, W. K.   Afghanistan. A Study of Political
                                  Development in Central and South Asia,
                                  3rd edn revised by M C Gillett. London:
                                  Weidenfield and Nicholson, 1968

Khan M M and J P Thorp (Eds.)   Bangladesh: Society, Politics and
                                  Bureaucracy, Dhaka: Center for
                                  Administrative Studies, 1984

Kirk, G E   A Short History of the Middle East, 7th edn,
                                  London: Methuen, 1964

Laquer, Walter   The Road to War. 1967: The Origins of
                                  the Arab Israel Conflict, London:
                                  Weidenfield and Nicholson, 1968

Longrigg Stephen H   Iraq, London: Oxford University Press,
                                  1958

Low, D A (Edited by)   Soundings in Modern South Asian
                                  History, London: Weidenfield and
                                  Nicholson, 1968

Majumdar R C and Pusalkar   History and Culture of the Indian People,
                                  Bharatiya Vidya Bhavan Published Vols.

Misra, K P (Edited by)   *Afghanistan in Crisis,* New Delhi: Vikas Publishing House, 1981

Morroe, Berger   *The Arab World Today,* New York: Doubleday, 1964

Muni S D (Edited by)   *Nepal: An Assertive Monarchy,* New Delhi: Chetna Publication, 1977

Nehru, Jawaharlal   *Discovery of India,* London: Meridian Books, 1951

Paramanand   *Political Developments in South Asia,* New Delhi: Sterling Publishers, 1988

Ram, Rahul   *Royal Bhutan,* Delhi: Motilal Banarsidass, 1983

Raychoudhuri Tapan, and Irfan Habib (Eds)   *The Cambridge Economic History of India,* Delhi: Orient Longman, (reprint), 1984, Vol.1.

Rodinson, Maxime   *Israel and the Arabs,* London: Penguin Books, 1968

Talbot, Ian   *Pakistan, A Modern History,* Delhi: Oxford University Press, 1999

INDEX